MODERN IRISH LIVES
Dictionary of 20th-century Irish Biography

Modern Irish Lives

Dictionary of 20th-century Irish Biography

GENERAL EDITOR

Louis McRedmond

GILL & MACMILLAN

Gill & Macmillan Ltd
Goldenbridge
Dublin 8
with associated companies throughout the world
© Gill & Macmillan Ltd 1996
0 7171 2198 4
Print origination by
Carrigboy Typesetting Services, Co. Cork
Printed by ColourBooks Ltd, Dublin

A catalogue record for this book is available from the British Library.

1 3 5 4 2

Contents

Introduction   vii

List of Contributors   xi

Glossary   xiii

Dictionary   1

Introduction

It was not easy. For an underpopulated country in a relatively limited historical epoch, 20th-century Ireland has been home to more persons of distinction, notoriety, achievement or plain human interest than anyone can imagine who has not taken on the chore of compiling a biographical dictionary. Add to that the certainty that no two citizens of Ireland will agree on who merits entry in such a book or on what should be said about those who eventually appear there, and the multi-horned nature of the compiler's dilemma becomes painfully obvious.

The bravely self-confident compiler persists regardless, makes his own selection of names and biographical information, his own assessment of the people chosen. He offers the result to the public with equanimity for what it is, the view from one man's vantage point. By contrast, the timorous compiler seeks help, persuades others to share the task with him. He hopes virtuously thereby to produce a comprehensive and authoritative work of a standard he could never attain on his own. Perhaps he hopes also, subliminally, venally, that the blame for what goes wrong will be diverted from himself to his advisers.

I am timorous. I sought help. What is of value in this book – and there is much of value – is more likely to be the contribution of others than of the general editor. I say this without false modesty. The simple fact is that others put forward more names, assembled more data and wrote more of the content than I did. The second expectation of the timorous, however, failed to transpire. The blame for whatever deficiencies are found here must rest with me and the publishers, since between us we bear the responsibility for what and whom in the end it was decided to include or exclude, for the editing which shortened or added to contributed text, for stylistic changes.

But who were these others who contributed so much to the enterprise? They fell into two categories, consulting editors and researchers. Specialists over a range of professional, cultural and social activities accepted the publishers' invitation to be consulting editors. Their names are printed on another page. Most were requested to draw up lists of people within their sphere of expertise who they felt should appear in the encyclopedia; some were provided with lists already drawn up. The general editor imposed a draconian limit on the number of names on every list. Consulting editors wrote entries for as many or as few names on their lists as they chose.

Recent or comparatively recent graduates formed the greater number of researchers, whose task was to take the names left over by the consulting editors, together with further lists of names drafted by the general editor, and prepare short factual entries on these. In a few cases researchers wrote longer entries on names within their own fields of study. Sometimes additional specialists were engaged to advise on specific entries. The general editor did not resist the temptation to participate at this stage and contributed many entries of varying lengths himself.

Because of the extensive changes made in the course of editing each of the submitted texts as well as the volume as a whole, it would be invidious to attribute individual entries as they are now published to named consulting editors or researchers. It should be noted, too, that a number of entries were inserted and some deleted by decision of the general editor rather than of any contributor.

In considering names for inclusion certain basic criteria were applied. 'Irish lives' was taken to mean the lives of people who had spent their formative years in Ireland, south or north, or who carried out the greater part of their lives' work there, or who associated themselves in a special way with the country – for example, by adopting Irish citizenship: this let in the famous scientist, Erwin Schrödinger. Emigrants who made their careers in foreign countries qualified, but not the descendants of emigrants unless they met one of the other criteria: this excluded John F. Kennedy.

'Twentieth century' was defined as a reference to the years in which a person was active in his or her calling. So a 19th-century politician like John Dillon, who remained prominent in politics after 1900, was eligible for inclusion but not Justin McCarthy, who lived into the 20th century but had ceased to be an active politician by 1900. Living persons were to be considered as well as the dead: a decision of manifest benefit to users of the book as a work of reference, although it will doubtless prove to be an ongoing embarrassment to the general editor! Let me hasten to say at this point that all recommendations to the publishers for inclusion or alteration in later editions will be carefully considered.

The introduction of the living created a practical problem which I was unable to circumvent. Many names in every aspect of national life sprang to mind. They could not be sifted on the basis of their significance as easily as the dead, whose achievements were completed and could be weighed in the balance. A living lawyer or businesswoman or sportsman might in 10 or 20 years be forgotten, having fallen from temporary eminence, or might have succeeded beyond the imagining of 1996 and become a personality of world renown. As a consequence, the book may appear to be loaded in favour of the living with people featuring in its pages who, their present status notwithstanding, seem scarcely to belong to the company of the great names from the past which appear in earlier or later entries. The timorous compiler hesitates to predict, to choose, so the balance tilts to the present.

Inconsistencies of style and presentation have been deliberately retained, despite the extensive editing already mentioned. The book should make pleasant reading for the browser as well as the digger for facts. It would, I believe, have been boringly monotonous if all entries were composed to a similar formula; it would have been artificial to use the same approach in recording the career of a medical consultant and that of a rock musician. It is hard enough to hint at the flavour of any life within the narrow bounds of a biographical note. If the tone of the telling helps, let it.

A few other points. The book is not a *Who's Who* or *Who was Who*. It therefore often omits significant items of personal information – e.g. parentage, names of spouses, numbers of children – when these do not manifestly relate to the matters being recorded. Then again, comparisons are invidious. The comparative length of entries does not imply an editorial judgment on the comparative importance of persons. Sometimes, it arises from differences of approach between different contributors, as already mentioned. In other cases it represents a balance between contributors' judgments and those of the general editor. Or it may have to do with the space required to summarise a variety of achievements in a long and varied life by contrast with perhaps equally important achievements within a single field of activity or over a shorter number of years.

Sources were myriad. Contributors resorted to a variety of methods to get their information, including a variety of reference books. The most widely used authors must be acknowledged with gratitude. Prominent among them were those stalwarts of Irish biographical assemblage, each a model of the brave and self-confident compiler: Harry Boylan, the third edition of whose *Dictionary of Irish Biography* is nearing completion; Maureen Cairnduff, whose second edition of *Who's Who in Ireland – The Influential 1,000* sold out virtually overnight; and Ted Nealon, who has recast his invaluable *Guide to the Dáil and Seanad* on the heels of every general election during the past 20 years.

Also very useful were *A Biographical Dictionary of Irish Writers* by Anne M. Brady and Brian Cleeve, *Northern Ireland: A Political Directory 1968–93* by W.D. Flackes and Sidney Elliott, *1882–1982 Beathaisnéis a hAon – a Dó – a Trí* by Diarmuid Breathnach and Máire Ní Mhurchú, Robert Hogan's *Dictionary of Irish Literature*, the *Who's Who, What's What and Where in Ireland* published by Geoffrey Chapman in association with *The Irish Times* in 1973, *Fyffe's Dictionary of Irish Sporting Greats* by John Gleeson, and *The Guinness Book of Irish Facts and Feats* by Ciaran Deane. The biographical information in the *Centenary History of the Literary and Historical Society of University College, Dublin, 1855–1955*, edited by James Meenan, the *Field Day Anthology of Irish Writing*, under the general editorship of Seamus Deane, and *Modern Ireland 1600–1972* by R.F. Foster helped to complete numerous entries as well.

To all these books, their authors and editors, the general editor and publishers are most grateful for smoothing the path of compilation. Others merit our thanks too. Those who offered advice and assisted in various ways included Brian Farrell, Raymond Byrne, Seán Mac Réamoinn, Colm Tóibín and the Irish Architectural Archive through its Director, David Griffin. Many gaps would have remained unfilled but for the diligent retrieval of information by my wife Maeve. And I must especially say that the work could not have been begun, progressed or completed without the support, commitment, friendship and professional competence of Fergal Tobin and his colleagues at Gill & Macmillan.

While I have the floor, let me make one more comment in the form of a question. Is it not extraordinary that Ireland lacks a definitive dictionary of national biography, with every entry a signed and extended essay on the model of the great English *DNB*? We have the scholars, we have the information and, heaven knows, we have subjects in abundance. I understand that the Royal Irish Academy has such a project in hand. This is good news and merits every assistance from state and institutional sources.

Louis McRedmond
Dublin, September 1996

Contributors

GENERAL EDITOR

Louis McRedmond

CONSULTING EDITORS

Gregory Allen	*John Horgan*
Gerald Barry	*Karl Johnston*
Marcus Bourke	*Mary Jones*
Terence Brown	*J.B. Lyons*
Art Byrne	*Sean McMahon*
Jane Carty	*Bill Meek*
Frank D'Arcy	*Kenneth Milne*
Marian Deane	*Donal O'Donovan*
Sean Dooney	*Sean O'Reilly*
Dave Fanning	*Cathal O'Shannon*
Gordon Gillespie	*Neil A. Porter*
David Guiney	*Hilary Pyle*
Maurice Hartigan	*Anthony Roche*

Peter Young

ADVISERS ON SPECIFIC ENTRIES

John Costello (W.J. Leech)
Declan Kiberd (G.B. Shaw)
The late Augustine Martin (James Joyce and W.B. Yeats)
Joseph J. Ryan (Fritz Brase)

RESEARCHERS AND OTHER CONTRIBUTORS

Rowan Conroy	*Ciara Higgins*
Maria Ní Dhochartaigh	*David M. Kiely*
Laurence Flanagan	*Deirdre O'Flynn*
Paul Gallagher	*Paul Power*
Brian Galvin	*Cormac Sheridan*
Sinead Grennan	*Fergal Tobin*

Jonathan Williams

Glossary of Terms, Abbreviations, Acronyms and Contractions

The more familiar university degrees, professional qualifications and British honours noted in the entries are omitted from this list.

AAA	*Amateur Athletic Association*
AAI	*Association of Artists in Ireland, Association of Advertisers in Ireland Limited or Architectural Association of Ireland, depending on context*
Aer Lingus	*The Irish national airline*
Aer Rianta	*The Irish national airports authority*
AIB	*Allied Irish Banks*
Alexandra	*Alexandra College, Dublin*
Ampleforth	*Ampleforth Abbey, York, England*
Aosdána	*An affiliation of artists engaged in literature, music and the visual arts, established by the Arts Council and akin to an academy, acceptance into membership of which is recognition of the artist's distinction in his/her field*
Ard-fheis	*The annual conference of a political party*
B. or b.	*born*
BBC	*British Broadcasting Corporation*
Belvedere	*Belvedere College, Dublin*
Blackrock	*Blackrock College, Blackrock, Co. Dublin*
Bord Fáilte Éireann	*The Irish Tourist Board*
Bord na Móna	*The turf (peat) development board*
Cambridge	*Cambridge University, England (preceded in more extended entries by name of college)*
Castleknock	*St Vincent's College, Castleknock, Dublin*
Catholic Action	*A movement to co-ordinate lay activity in the Roman Catholic Church, founded in 1930 by Pope Pius XI*
CBC	*Christian Brothers' College*
CBS	*Christian Brothers' School*
Ceann Comhairle	*Speaker in Dáil Éireann*
CIE	*Córas Iompair Éireann (the Irish transport authority)*
Clongowes	*Clongowes Wood College, Naas, Co. Kildare*
Clonliffe	*Holy Cross College, Clonliffe, Dublin*

C. na nG.	*Cumann na nGaedheal, a political party now defunct*
C. na P.	*Clann na Poblachta, a political party now defunct*
C. na T.	*Clann na Talmhan, a political party now defunct*
CND	*Campaign for Nuclear Disarmament*
Coláiste Mhuire	*Gaelscoil Choláiste Mhuire (Christian Brothers' College, Parnell Square, Dublin)*
Concern Worldwide	*An Irish voluntary relief agency providing assistance to the people of underdeveloped countries*
Council of State	*Advisory body to the President of Ireland*
CUS	*Catholic University School, Dublin*
CYMS	*Catholic Young Men's Society*
D. or d.	*Died or daughter, depending on context*
Dáil Éireann (popularly, the Dáil)	*The chamber of deputies or lower house of the Oireachtas*
DCU	*Dublin City University*
DIAS	*Dublin Institute for Advanced Studies*
district justice	*A judge of the lowest division in the judicial system of the Irish Free State and the Republic of Ireland; now district judge*
DIT	*Dublin Institute of Technology*
DL	*Democratic Left, a political party*
DMP	*Dublin Metropolitan Police, the police force for Dublin city and county and Co. Wicklow until 1925 when it was amalgamated with the Garda Síochána*
Downside	*Downside Abbey, Bath, England*
DU	*University of Dublin (see below)*
DUP	*Democratic Unionist Party*
EBU	*European Broadcasting Union or European Boxing Union, depending on context*
EC	*European Community*
ed.	*educated or edited, depending on context*
EEC	*European Economic Community*
Emergency	*Popular name in neutral Ireland for the years of World War II (from the state of emergency declared by the Dáil upon the outbreak of war)*
ENSA	*Entertainments National Service Association (entertainers of British forces during World War II)*
ESB	*Electricity Supply Board*
ESRI	*Economic and Social Research Institute, Dublin*
Eton	*Eton College, Berkshire, England*
EU	*European Union*
Executive Council	*The government of the Irish Free State*

F	*Fellow of (preceding the acronym of a professional, educational or cultural body)*
f.	*father*
FAI	*Football Association of Ireland*
FÁS	*Foras Áiseanna Saothair (The Training and Employment Authority)*
FF	*Fianna Fáil, a political party*
FG	*Fine Gael, a political party*
FRS	*Fellow of the Royal Society*
FWUI	*Federated Workers' Union of Ireland*
GAA	*Gaelic Athletic Association*
Gaeltacht	*One of those parts of Ireland where Irish is the vernacular language (plural: Gaeltachtaí).*
Garbally Park	*St Joseph's College, Garbally Park, Ballinasloe, Co. Galway*
garda	*A member of the Garda Síochána*
Garda Síochána	*'Protector of the peace', the police force (at first called Civic Guard) which replaced the Royal Irish Constabulary in the Irish Free State in 1922 and absorbed the Dublin Metropolitan Police in 1925*
GATT	*General Agreement on Tariffs and Trade*
Glenstal	*Glenstal Abbey, Murroe, Co. Limerick*
GOAL	*An Irish voluntary agency for Third World relief*
Gonzaga	*Gonzaga College, Dublin*
GORTA	*'Famine', a development-aid agency for the eradication of hunger in the Third World, the Irish National Committee of the United Nations Freedom from Hunger Campaign*
GPO	*The General Post Office in Dublin, which was the headquarters of the Irish Volunteers and the Citizen Army during the Easter Rising, 1916*
Green	*The Green Party*
guard	*A garda*
Harrow	*Harrow School, Harrow-on-the-Hill, London*
Harvard	*Harvard University, Massachusetts, USA*
IAL	*Irish Academy of Letters*
IBEC	*Irish Business and Employers' Confederation*
ICTU	*Irish Congress of Trade Unions*
IFA	*Irish Farmers' Association*
IFS	*Irish Free State, the name of the Irish state as a Commonwealth dominion from 1922 to 1937, after which it was constitutionally named Ireland or Éire. When it withdrew from the Commonwealth in 1949 its description was declared by statute to be the Republic of Ireland.*
ILO	*International Labour Organisation*
IP	*Irish Parliamentary Party (at Westminster prior to 1922)*

IRA	*Irish Republican Army*
IRB	*Irish Republican Brotherhood*
IRTC	*Independent Radio and Television Commission*
ITGWU	*Irish Transport and General Workers' Union*
IWWU	*Irish Women Workers' Union*
King's Inns	*The Honorable Society of King's Inns, Dublin (specifically, the Society's law school)*
KSG	*Knight of St Gregory (papal honour)*
Labour	*The Labour Party*
Leas	*Vice/Deputy*
M	*Member of (preceding the acronym of a professional, educational or cultural body)*
M. or m.	*married*
Maynooth	*St Patrick's College, Maynooth*
NCAA	*National Colleges' Athletic Association*
NCEA	*National Council for Educational Awards*
NESC	*National Economic and Social Council*
Newbridge	*Newbridge College, Newbridge, Co. Kildare*
NI	*Northern Ireland*
NICRA	*Northern Ireland Civil Rights Association*
NICS	*Northern Ireland Civil Service*
NIHE	*National Institute of Higher Education, the name given to third-level colleges established in Limerick and Dublin which in 1989 became respectively the University of Limerick and Dublin City University*
North Mon.	*North Monastery Christian Brothers' School, Cork*
now/current(ly)	*as of mid-1996*
NS	*National School (preceded by place name)*
NUI	*National University of Ireland, the university established in 1908 with University College, Dublin, University College, Cork and University College, Galway as its constituent colleges. St Patrick's College, Maynooth became a recognised college of the NUI in 1910.*
NUU	*New University of Ulster (now University of Ulster)*
O'Connell School	*O'Connell Christian Brothers' School (primary and secondary), Dublin*
OECD	*Organisation for Economic Co-operation and Development*
Oireachtas	*Parliament, consisting of Dáil and Seanad. Also an annual festival of Irish culture.*
OPW	*Office of Public Works*
Oxford	*Oxford University, England (preceded in more extended entries by name of college)*
PD	*Progressive Democrats, a political party*

Portora	*Portora Royal School, Enniskillen, Co. Fermanagh*
(An) Post	*(The) national postal service*
present tense (used in an entry)	*normally, as of mid-1996*
PRHA	*President of the Royal Hibernian Academy*
PRIA	*President of the Royal Irish Academy*
QUB	*Queen's University, Belfast, the name under which the former Queen's College in Belfast, which had been affiliated to the Royal University of Ireland, became a separate university in 1908*
Radio Éireann	*The national radio service prior to its combination with Telefís Éireann under the name Radio Telefís Éireann*
RAM	*Royal Academy of Music*
RAMC	*Royal Army Medical Corps*
RCPI	*Royal College of Physicians of Ireland*
RCSI	*Royal College of Surgeons in Ireland*
RDS	*Royal Dublin Society*
RHA	*Royal Hibernian Academy of Arts*
RIA	*Royal Irish Academy*
RIAI	*Royal Institute of the Architects of Ireland*
RIAM	*Royal Irish Academy of Music*
RIBA	*Royal Institute of British Architects*
RIC	*Royal Irish Constabulary, the police force throughout Ireland prior to 1922, except in Dublin and Wicklow where the police force was the Dublin Metropolitan Police*
RNLI	*Royal National Lifeboat Institution (Ireland)*
Rockwell	*Rockwell College, Cashel, Co. Tipperary*
Royal Academical Institution	*Royal Academical Institution, Belfast*
RTÉ	*Radio Telefís Éireann (the Irish national broadcasting service)*
RUC	*Royal Ulster Constabulary, the police force in Northern Ireland from 1922*
Rugby	*Rugby School, Warwickshire, England*
RUI	*Royal University of Ireland, a board established in 1879 to conduct examinations at university level, grant degrees and appoint to fellowships. A number of existing third-level colleges, including University College, Dublin (as the college of the Catholic University was soon to rename itself) and the Queen's Colleges in Belfast, Cork and Galway, were affiliated to the RUI, which ceased to function in 1909 following the establishment of the National University of Ireland and Queen's University, Belfast.*
s.	*son*

St Columba's	*St Columba's College, Rathfarnham, Dublin*
Sandhurst	*Royal Military Academy, Sandhurst, England*
Saoi	*'Learned person'. Highest rank in the membership of Aosdána.*
SDLP	*Social Democratic and Labour Party*
Seanad	*Seanad Éireann, the Senate or upper house of the Oireachtas*
Senator	*A member of the Seanad*
SF	*Sinn Féin, a political party*
SIPTU	*Services Industrial Professional Technical Union*
Stonyhurst	*Stonyhurst College, Lancashire, England*
Stormont	*Location near Belfast of the Northern Ireland Parliament building. Popularly, the former parliament of Northern Ireland.*
Synge Street	*Synge Street Christian Brothers' School, Dublin*
(An) Taisce	*'Treasure', a voluntary body which promotes protection of the Irish environmental and architectural heritage*
Tánaiste	*Deputy Prime Minister*
Taoiseach	*Prime Minister*
TCD	*Trinity College, Dublin, the sole constituent college of the University of Dublin*
TD	*Teachta Dála, a Dáil deputy (i.e. a member of parliament)*
Telecom Éireann	*The state company responsible for operating the national telecommunication services*
Telefís Éireann	*The national television service prior to its combination with Radio Éireann under the name Radio Telefís Éireann*
Trócaire	*'Mercy', an Irish Roman Catholic agency for Third World development*
UCC	*University College, Cork, the name under which the former Queen's College in Cork, which had been affiliated to the Royal University of Ireland, became a constituent college of the National University of Ireland in 1908*
UCD	*University College, Dublin, the name eventually adopted by the college of the Catholic University of Ireland after its affiliation to the Royal University of Ireland in 1879 and under which it became a constituent college of the National University of Ireland in 1908*
UCG	*University College, Galway, the name under which the former Queen's College in Galway, which had been affiliated to the Royal University of Ireland, became a constituent college of the National University of Ireland in 1908*
UCLA	*University of California at Los Angeles*
UDA	*Ulster Defence Association*
UEFA	*Union of European Football Associations*
UL	*University of Limerick*

UN	*United Nations*
UNESCO	*United Nations Educational, Scientific and Cultural Organisation*
University of Dublin	*The university founded in 1592 of which Trinity College, Dublin is the sole constituent college*
UNPROFOR	*United Nations Protection Force (in former Yugoslavia)*
UU	*University of Ulster (formerly New University of Ulster)*
UUP	*Ulster Unionist Party*
UVF	*Ulster Volunteer Force*
VHI	*Voluntary Health Insurance Board*
Volunteers	*The Irish National Volunteers, founded in 1913, or, depending on context, either of the two bodies into which they split in 1914, the National Volunteers (who continued to accept the leadership of John Redmond) and the Irish Volunteers (who opposed service in the British army and from whom were drawn most of the insurgents in the Easter Rising, 1916)*
Waterpark	*Waterpark Christian Brothers' College, Waterford*
WBA	*World Boxing Association*
WBC	*World Boxing Council*
Wesley	*Wesley College, Dublin*
Yale	*Yale University, Connecticut, USA*

A

ABERCORN (James Albert Edward Hamilton), third Duke of (1869–1953), first Governor of Northern Ireland, b. 30 Nov. 1869, s. of second Duke and Lady Mary Anna Curzon, ed. Eton, d. 23 May 1953. Commissioned into 1st Life Guards 1892. Appointed to the largely ceremonial position of NI governor in 1922. He had been active in politics for a number of years and had served as MP for Derry 1900–13 and Lord Lieutenant of Tyrone 1917–22.

A BRÚN, Garech (1939–), founder of Claddagh Records, b. Glenmaroon, Chapelizod, Dublin, 25 June 1939, grandson of Ernest Guinness, ed. Le Rosey, Switzerland, m. Princess Purna Harshad of Morvi 1982. Established Claddagh Records 1959 to record traditional Irish art and music. SAMUEL BECKETT, Robert Graves, PATRICK KAVANAGH and THE CHIEFTAINS, which he founded, feature among Claddagh's diverse recordings. Recorded the music of Irish composer John Field, creator of the nocturne, and the harper-composer Carolan. He also published the music of FREDERICK MAY and SEÁN Ó RIADA.

British subject. His Irish houses, Luggala, Blessington, Co. Wicklow and Woodtown Manor, Rathfarnham, Co. Dublin, are let, the latter to the folk group Clannad. A world traveller, he spends two months every year in Luggala, three in India. He was a major figure in the campaign to prevent the OPW from building an interpretative centre near Luggala, which won a notable victory in the Supreme Court in 1993.

ACTON, Charles (1914–), music critic, b. Iron Acton, Bristol, ed. Rugby and Trinity College, Cambridge. Undertook a variety of occupations both before and after 1939, when he came to Ireland, where his family had an estate at Kilmacurragh, Co. Wicklow. He was later to recall how, as a schoolboy, he had attended performances conducted by Sir Adrian Boult and Elgar, while as a student he had heard Richard Strauss conduct *Salome* and *Elektra* in Munich. Acton played the bassoon

with the Dublin Orchestral Players. He was music critic of *The Irish Times* 1955–86, as which he established a formidable reputation for sternly demanding high standards of performers but also for generously praising them when, in his opinion, they attained excellence. He campaigned tirelessly for better funding for music, a proper concert hall in Dublin and related objectives, some at least of which he was to see achieved. Governor of the RIAM from 1955, fellow 1990. A selection of his reviews, *Acton's Music*, edited by Gareth Cox, was published in 1996. In 1951 he married Carol Little, who, as Carol Acton, was also to become a distinguished music critic.

ADAMS, Gerry (1949–), politician, b. Belfast. The dominant figure in the republican movement since the early 1980s, he has played a central role in the gradual assertion of the importance of a political, as opposed to a military, strategy. He was interned in 1971, and took part in the secret talks between the IRA and the British government the following year. In 1983 he secured the leadership of Sinn Féin and won the seat for West Belfast in the Westminster elections. He caused a split in SF when his proposal for an end to the policy of abstention from the Dáil was carried at the 1986 Ard-fheis. Between 1988 and 1994 he was involved in intermittent talks with JOHN HUME. The consensus at which they eventually arrived was a significant step in the process which led to the IRA ceasefire announced in Aug. 1994. He subsequently established a rapport with the governments of ALBERT REYNOLDS and JOHN BRUTON, and made a number of promotional visits to the USA on behalf of SF, which were initially facilitated by President Bill Clinton in spite of vehement opposition from the British government. He blamed the British Prime Minister, John Major, for the delay in the initiation of all-party talks on the future of Northern Ireland, as envisaged in the Downing Street Declaration of 1993 issued by Reynolds and Major, but the British authorities in turn charged Adams and SF with causing the delay by their refusal to seek a prior gesture from the IRA towards the decommissioning of arms and explosives. The ending of the IRA cease-fire in Feb. 1996, the subsequent bombings in England and the shooting dead of a garda detective in Adare, Co. Limerick had severely undermined the relations of the Irish, British and American governments with Adams by mid-1996. Although elected to the NI Forum in May 1996 (which SF then refused to attend) he and his party's representatives were debarred from attending the all-party talks on NI, which began in June 1996, until such time as the IRA renewed its ceasefire.

AE. See under Russell, George.

AHERN, Bertie (1951–), politician, b. Dublin, ed. St Aidan's CBS, Whitehall and Rathmines College of Commerce, Dublin and UCD. Worked as an accountant before entering the Dáil in the Fianna Fáil landslide of 1977. He was appointed assistant govern-ment whip in 1980 and chief whip in Mar. 1982, in which position he served until the fall of the HAUGHEY government in Nov. of that year. He held various opposition front bench appointments in the mid-1980s before enter-ing cabinet as Minister for Labour on the return of FF to government in 1987. In his four years at Labour he established a reputation as a con-ciliator. He was promoted Minister for Finance in Nov. 1991. A strong supporter of Haughey, his position in the party was so secure that he survived the fall of his patron and under ALBERT REYNOLDS retained this position.

He succeeded Reynolds as leader of FF in Nov. 1994 when the government collapsed in the débâcle over the appointment of Harry Whelehan as President of the High Court. He was widely seen as the ideal person to bridge the antagonisms within FF which were the legacy of the leadership contests over the preceding 15 years, an assessment borne out by his judicious front bench appointments as leader of the opposition. However, FF's failure during the greater part of 1995 to exploit potential divisions between Fine Gael, Labour and the Democratic Left, the parties making up the coalition government, and his support for divorce in the referendum campaign of that year, brought murmurings of disapproval and intimations of incipient revolt among the more traditionally minded members of his own party in the Oireachtas and the country. His support in Feb. 1996 for the government's refusal to have further contacts with Sinn Féin, except through civil servants, until the IRA restored the ceasefire which it had called off was generally seen as a statesmanlike assess-ment of the national interest.

AIKEN, Frank (1898–1983), politician and revolutionary, b. south Armagh, 13 Feb. 1898, ed. St Colman's College, Newry, d. 18 May 1983. His family were farmers in Armagh. He became a Sinn Féin organiser in the coun-ty in 1917 and was jailed the following year for running the Irish Volunteers. An active IRA officer during the War of Independence, he took the republican side in the Civil War after some initial hesitation. Became chief of staff of the IRA, a post he held until 1925, and as such ordered the ceasefire by the defeated republi-cans in 1923. His ousting as IRA leader was a result of the manoeuvrings which culminated in the formation of the Fianna Fáil party, which he joined on its inception in 1926. Elected for the Louth constituency in 1927 and at each succeeding election until his retirement in 1973.

One of EAMON DE VALERA's closest col-leagues, he held cabinet positions including Defence 1932–45 and External Affairs 1951–4 and again from 1957 until he left ministerial life in 1969. He was supportive of JACK LYNCH during the 1970 Arms Crisis. Aiken is prob-ably best remembered for his contributions to the UN, where he carved out an independent Irish stance.

ALANBROOKE (Alan Francis Brooke), first Viscount (1883–1963), British field marshal, b. Bagnères-de-Bigorre, France, 23 July 1883, ninth child of Sir Victor Brooke of Colebrook, Co. Fermanagh, and Alice Bellingham; childhood spent in Pau in the south of France; ed. Royal Military Academy at Woolwich; d. Hampshire, 17 June 1963. Joined Royal Horse Artillery and served in several senior artillery appointments during World War I. Chief of Imperial General Staff 1941. Brooke worked very well with the naval and air force commanders, Sir Alan Cunningham and Charles Portal, and was instrumental in the promotion of HAROLD ALEXANDER and Bernard Montgomery. Often described as Churchill's most trusted military adviser, he accompanied the British Prime Minister to the Allied conferences at Casablanca, Quebec and Moscow in 1943.

ALDERDICE, John Thomas (1955–), politician, b. Ballymena, 28 Mar. 1955, ed. Ballymena Academy and QUB. Psychiatrist by occupation. Leader of the Alliance Party since 1987. In the general election of that year he received over 10,000 votes in East Belfast, Alliance's best showing at a Westminster election, but did not win the seat. In 1989 he was elected to Belfast City Council, having failed to win a seat on Lisburn Council in 1981. He was also unsuccessful in the 1989 elections to the European Parliament. Alderdice has been consistent in his criticism of political intransigence, whether on the part of unionists or of nationalists. Asked on the announcement of the IRA ceasefire in 1994 whether he believed it was permanent, he commented: 'I have experience of working with people who have drink problems and I have seen many an alcoholic who has had "a complete cessation" of drinking and then returned to it at a later stage . . . We will judge them by their actions.'

ALEXANDER, Harold Rupert, Earl Alexander of Tunis (1891–1969), British field marshal, b. Caledon, Co. Tyrone, 10 Dec. 1891, spent most of his childhood at the family estate in Caledon, ed. Harrow and Sandhurst, d. Slough, England, 16 June 1969. Commissioned into the Irish Guards in 1911. He was one of the most brilliant Allied commanders of World War II, playing a crucial role in the expulsion of Axis forces from north Africa in 1943, and in the taking of Rome in Aug. 1944. In 1944 he became field marshal and was made supreme Allied commander in the Mediterranean theatre, which he remained until the end of the war. Governor-General of Canada 1946–52; Minister of Defence 1952–4.

ALLEN, Dave (1936–), comedian, b. David Tynan O'Mahoney in Dublin, 6 July 1936, s. of *Irish Times* managing editor Cully Tynan O'Mahoney. An early 'alternative' comedian, Allen reflects on life rather than telling jokes, with a stool, a cigarette and a drink as his props. He left school at 16, joined the *Drogheda Argus* as copy-boy, and went to London aged 19. After a succession of odd jobs, he compèred on the pop show circuit, including early Beatles shows. Changed his name because people couldn't pronounce it. Went to Australia, where he did his first one-man television show in Sydney 1963, then presented Channel 9's offbeat *Tonight*.

He married English actress Judith Stott in 1964. They returned to England, where he produced comedy series for the BBC and theatre shows. Toured America, Canada and Australia. Allen is an anarchic wit, whose television shows attract millions of viewers; he was one of the first TV performers regularly to use in his act words then considered obscene or taboo. Divorced in 1983, he now lives in Kensington with one of his four children.

ALLGOOD, Molly (1887–1952), actress, b. Dublin, 12 Jan. 1887, d. 2 Nov. 1952. Allgood, who used the stage name Máire O'Neill, joined the Abbey Theatre Company in 1905, and in 1907 played Pegeen Mike in the controversial production of J.M. SYNGE's *The Playboy of the Western World*, which was roundly abused by Dublin audiences but hailed as a masterpiece in London later that year. She was engaged to Synge at the time of his death in 1909 and played in his *Deirdre of the Sorrows* the following year. In 1911 she married George Herbert Mair, drama critic of the *Manchester Guardian*, and moved to England, working with the Liverpool Repertory Company. Following the death of her husband in 1926, she returned to Ireland and to the Abbey. She married the actor Arthur Sinclair, with whom she appeared many times in the plays of SEAN O'CASEY, both at home and on successful American tours. She was a sister of SARA ALLGOOD.

ALLGOOD, Sara (1883–1950), actress, b. Dublin, 31 Oct. 1883, d. Hollywood, 13 Sept. 1950. Allgood played Mrs Fallon in Lady GREGORY's *Spreading the News* on the opening night of the Abbey Theatre, 27 Dec. 1904, and became a full-time actress the following year, appearing in W.B. YEATS's *Cathleen ni Houlihan* and J.M. SYNGE's *Riders to the Sea*. In 1915 she played the lead in *Peg o' my Heart*, a slight but hugely popular comedy which subsequently toured Australia and New Zealand. She worked for a number of years in London but returned to the Abbey, where in 1924 she gave a memorable opening night performance as Juno in SEAN O'CASEY's *Juno and the Paycock*; she also took part in many successful American tours with the company. Allgood spent the last ten years of her life in Hollywood but was never offered film parts of any substance. She was a sister of MOLLY ALLGOOD.

ANDREWS, C.S. (Todd) (1901–1985), revolutionary, executive public servant, b. Dublin, ed. St Enda's, Synge Street and UCD. Joined Irish Volunteers 1917 and took part in the War of Independence and Civil War, in which he was adjutant to Liam Lynch, chief of staff of the anti-Treaty IRA. Early member of Fianna Fáil. Worked for the Irish Tourist Association and the ESB. Managing director and secretary Turf Development Board 1934. A visit to Germany and the USSR confirmed his view that the future of the bogs lay in production of macerated turf as fuel for electric power. Managing director Bord na Móna 1946. Andrews in 1958 left a thriving peat industry to become executive chairman of CIE. A Transport Act of that year gave him powers to close down uneconomic rail lines if alternative road services were offered. In all over a dozen lines were closed. The company's management and finances were restructured. But Andrews encountered severe industrial relations problems (CIE had 32 unions), and regarded his inability to cope with the bus workers as 'the biggest disappointment of my public service career'. At sixty-five he retired and in June 1966 he became part-time chairman of the RTÉ Authority; he shared SEÁN LEMASS's view of RTÉ as 'an instrument of public policy'. His reign, marked by a number of controversies, ended in 1970. Published two volumes of autobiography, *Dublin Made Me* (1979) and *Man of No Property* (1982).

ANDREWS, Eamonn (1922–1987), broadcaster, b. Dublin, 19 Dec. 1922, ed. Synge Street, d. London, 5 Nov. 1987. Was an insurance clerk and Irish amateur junior middleweight boxing champion (1944), occasional sports commentator on Radio Éireann (as which he covered live the boxing bout immediately following that in which he had won his title), full-time freelance broadcaster (1946) and newspaper columnist. Joined BBC, London in 1950 as a presenter of sports programmes, went on to achieve wide popularity as the presenter of major light entertainment programmes such as *What's My Line?* and the

long-running *This is Your Life*. Was said to be highest-earning performer on British television at this time. Founded Broadcasting and Theatrical Productions Ltd (later Eamonn Andrews Studios) to produce 'packaged' programmes and commercials for radio and television. Chairman of the advisory committee set up by the Irish government in 1959 to prepare for the introduction of television. It was reported that he turned down an offer to become director-general of the new Irish service, but he served as first part-time chairman of the Broadcasting Authority (later to become the RTÉ Authority) 1960–66, seeing Telefís Éireann (later RTÉ) launched on 31 Dec. 1961. At the same time he continued his broadcasting work at the BBC and involvement in a number of mainly Irish-based interests in the entertainment business.

ANDREWS, Sir James (1877–1951), lawyer, b. Co. Down, ed. Royal Academical Institution, St Stephen's Green School, Dublin, TCD and King's Inns, d. 18 Feb. 1951. BA 1899, called to Bar 1900, practised on NE circuit, KC 1918. Appointed Lord Justice of Appeal on new Supreme Court of Northern Ireland created under the Government of Ireland Act 1920; appointed to Privy Council of NI 1924; Pro-Chancellor of QUB 1929. Lord Chief Justice of NI from 1937 until his death, when he was the last of the original NI judiciary. Created a baron 1942.

ANDREWS, John Miller (1871–1956), politician, b. 17 July 1871, d. 6 Aug. 1956. A company director by occupation, Andrews was MP for Down at Stormont 1921–9 and for Mid-Down 1929–53. Chairman of the Ulster Unionist Labour Association and NI Minister of Labour 1921–37. He was Minister of Finance from 1937 until 1940, when he succeeded JAMES CRAIG as Prime Minister, a position he held for three years. Grand Master of Co. Down Orange Order from 1941, Grand Master of Ireland 1948–54 and of the Imperial Grand Council of the World 1949–54. In Sept. 1935 he said, 'Civil and religious liberty for all includes our opponents as well as ourselves, provided they act constitutionally and keep within the laws of the land.' However, in a letter to General Hugh Montgomery he added, 'The great difficulty in Ulster is, of course, that so many Roman Catholics are disloyal and determined to continue to work to put us in the Free State.'

ANNESLEY, Sir Hugh Norman (1939–), chief constable RUC, b. 22 June 1939, ed. Avoca School for Boys, Blackrock, Co. Dublin. Hugh Annesley joined the Metropolitan Police in 1958 and was promoted chief superintendent in 1974. Assistant chief constable Sussex Police from 1976. Deputy assistant commissioner Metropolitan Police 1981. Director of the Force Reorganisation Team in 1984 and assistant commissioner of the Metropolitan Police from 1985 until his appointment as chief constable of the RUC in 1989. He was awarded the Queen's Police Medal in 1986 and knighted in 1992. British representative on the executive committee of Interpol 1987–90 and 1993–4. During his tenure as chief constable the RUC has seen renewed allegations of collusion between police officers and loyalists (the force was cleared by the Stevens inquiry) and allegations of ill-treatment of suspects at Castlereagh holding centre. Relations between Annesley and the NI Police Authority have also been occasionally problematical. In Feb. 1996, shortly before the end of the IRA ceasefire, he predicted that if the IRA resumed its campaign, 'it would be across Northern Ireland and unquestionably in Britain'. In May 1996 he announced his intention to retire in the following Nov. but July found him in the eye of a new storm when he was accused by nationalists of yielding to pressure by permitting an Orange march along a Catholic road at Drumcree, Portadown, which he had previously banned and which had brought about a serious confrontation between the Orangemen and the RUC. It was afterwards widely believed that the chief constable had become a scapegoat in the affair through lack of direction from the British government.

ANTRIM, (Angela Christina McDonnell), Lady (1911–1974), sculptor and cartoonist, b. Eddlethorpe, Yorkshire, 6 Sept. 1911, m. eighth Earl of Antrim 1939. Was educated privately and received her artistic training under the sculptor D'Havelosse in Belgium and in the British School in Rome. Public commissions included a bronze sculpture and stained glass for Moyle Hospital in Larne and stone sculptures for St Joseph's Church, Ballygally, Co. Antrim and the parliament buildings in Newfoundland. Director of Ulster Television and for some years governor of the Ulster College of Art.

ARCHER, William (Liam) (1892–1969), lieutenant-general, b. Dublin. Joined the army in Mar. 1922 as a lieutenant-commandant. Was immediately appointed director of communications and later officer commanding, Signals Corps. Director of military intelligence 1932–41, he played a vital role in the negotiations with the British in 1938 regarding intelligence matters, and initiated many developments that were to prove vital during the Emergency. Assistant chief of staff in 1941, succeeded Lt.-Gen. DANIEL MCKENNA as chief of staff in 1949. He retired in Jan. 1952.

ARMOUR, James Brown (1841–1928), Presbyterian minister, b. Lisboy, Ballymoney, Co. Antrim, 20 Jan. 1841, ed. Queen's Colleges, Belfast and Cork, where he studied classics, m. Jenny Hamilton 1883, d. 25 Jan. 1928. He was called to minister to the Second Ballymoney congregation, a charge he held until his retirement in 1925. In 1885 he joined the staff of Magee College, Derry. He remained a liberal, arguing that his Church would fare better under Home Rule than it had since the Union. He disapproved of the growth of Carsonite unionism (and of physical force republicanism) and warned in a speech in 1893 that Presbyterians were 'sacrificing the power and progress of true Presbyterianism in Ireland for generations'.

ARMSTRONG, Arthur (1924–1995), artist, b. Carrickfergus, Co. Antrim, ed. QUB. Although he studied for a short time in Belfast College of Art, he was largely self-taught. He had his first solo exhibition at the CEMA in Belfast in 1961. The following year he moved to Dublin and exhibited in the RHA. His major prizes include the international art exhibition prize in Gibraltar in 1967 and the DOUGLAS HYDE gold medal at the 1968 Oireachtas. MRHA 1972. He exhibited widely in Ireland and in Spain, and a retrospective exhibition of his work was held in Belfast in 1981. In his landscape paintings Armstrong skilfully used colour and a richly layered surface texture to convey a sense of depth and mystery.

ARMSTRONG, John Ward (1915–1987), Church of Ireland bishop and archbishop, ed. Belfast and TCD, d. 21 July 1987. Ordained deacon 1938, priest 1939. Dean of

St Patrick's Cathedral 1958–68. Lecturer in liturgies Church of Ireland Divinity Hostel (now Church of Ireland Theological College) 1964–8. Bishop of Cashel 1968, Archbishop of Armagh 1980–86. Hon. DD (TCD) 1981. Played a leading part in *Prayer Book* revision as a member of the Liturgical Advisory Committee of the Church of Ireland, culminating in the publication of the *Alternative Prayer Book* in 1984. A committed ecumenist, member of the British Council of Churches and of the Irish Council of Churches, of which he was chairman in 1979. Did much to further the work of the Glenstal and Greenhills ecumenical conferences, and was for several years co-chairman of the Ballymascanlon Inter-Church Conference.

ARMSTRONG, Reg (1926–1979), motorcycle racer, b. Liverpool. In a career spanning 13 years (starting when he was 17) he rode AJS, Norton, Gilera and NSU machines. He was runner-up five times in the World Road Racing Championships, twice in 500 cc class (1953 and 1955, and never out of top six 1951–6), twice in 350 cc class (1949, 1952) and once in 250 cc class (1953). He won seven World Championship Grand Prix races between 1952 and 1956, and the Isle of Man Senior 500 cc TT in 1952; other TT results include two seconds and two thirds, and fourth and fifth in the Manx Grand Prix. His other 500 cc victories were the West German (1952, 1956) and the English (1953) Grands Prix. His 126.88 m.p.h., set in Berlin in his final racing year in 1956, stands as one of the fastest ever 500 cc averages. Taking up car racing, he became the first Irish driver to finish (fourth at an average of 102.40 m.p.h.) in the International Formula Junior Scratch event in the Phoenix Park. He also represented Ireland in clay pigeon shooting at the 1978 World Championship in Korea. Armstrong, who ran a motor assembly business at Ringsend in Dublin, died in a car accident near Avoca, Co. Wicklow, 24 Nov. 1979.

ARNOTT, Sir John Alexander, second baronet (1853–1940), newspaper proprietor, m. Caroline Sydney, DBE (d. 1933), three s. three d. Arnott's father, founder of the department store, bought *The Irish Times* in 1873 from the widow of the founder, Major Lawrence Knox. In 1900 Sir John became chairman and managing director, positions which he held until his death. He presided over the appointments as editor of John E. Healy and R.M. SMYLLIE. In 1902 the Arnotts inaugurated the Phoenix Park racecourse, which stayed in the family for most of the century. Their charitable interests included a dining hall on High Street, Dublin, where the indigent could get a three-course dinner for fourpence. Arnott's grandson, Sir John, was London editor of *The Irish Times* in the 1960s after the Arnott family lost control of the paper. Lived at Shearwater, Baily and 12 Merrion Square, Dublin. Hon. Lt.-Col. 4th Battalion Cheshire Regiment; DL, JP, Co. Cork and JP Co. Dublin.

ASHE, Thomas (1885–1917), revolutionary, b. Lispole, Co. Kerry, ed. De La Salle College, Waterford, d. 25 Sept. 1917. Became principal of a school in Lusk, Co. Dublin. An Irish-language enthusiast, poet and musician, he joined the Irish Volunteers and during the Easter Rising fought at Ashbourne in Meath. The death sentence passed on him afterwards was commuted to penal servitude for life. Released in the summer of 1917 but rearrested for a seditious speech made in Granard, Co. Longford. Died while on hunger strike in Mountjoy Jail.

ATTLEY, William J. (Bill) (1938–), trade unionist, b. Rathcoole, Co. Dublin, 5 Apr. 1938, ed. Rathcoole NS and National College of Industrial Relations, Dublin. Employed by the Workers' Union of Ireland (later the Federated Workers' Union of Ireland) as a branch secretary in 1968. In 1977 he became deputy general secretary of the union and in 1982 general secretary. Joint general president of SIPTU since 1990. Active in discussions with the social partners in connection with successive national pay agreements; closely involved with the Labour Party, not least through his association with FRANK CLUSKEY, also an FWUI member. Associated with JOHN CARROLL in the negotiations leading to the merger of the FWUI with the ITGWU as SIPTU in 1990. Member of the executive council of ICTU, the EU Social Committee and the European Trade Union Economic Committee; board member of a number of semi-state and voluntary organisations.

B

BALLAGH, Robert (1943–), artist, b. Dublin, 22 Sept. 1943, ed. St Michael's College, Blackrock and College of Technology, Bolton Street, Dublin. He is an outspoken commentator on issues of art and culture, and has earned a reputation for political astuteness and organisational ability in his dealings with Ireland's art bureaucracy. Before becoming a full-time painter he qualified as an architect and played with a showband for a number of years. His work has appeared in several exhibitions both in Ireland and abroad, including the Lunds exhibition of Irish artists in Sweden 1971. During the 1980s he designed the sets for several productions in the Gate Theatre in Dublin. His work on a number of commissions with a high public profile, including designs for stamps and book covers, and his involvement in various political causes have helped to maintain his position as one of Ireland's best-known artists.

BANVILLE, John (1945–), novelist, b. Wexford, ed. CBS and St Peter's College, Wexford. He had a regular column in *Hibernia*, worked as sub-editor on the *Irish Press*, and has been literary editor of *The Irish Times* since 1989. Member of the Arts Council 1984–8. Banville is closer to, say, Umberto Eco than to other Irish novelists; his historical fiction in particular reveals an understanding of the lives and times of great European thinkers – Copernicus, Kepler and Newton – through writing that is as elegant as it is informed. He has also published a number of short stories in literary magazines. Banville's fiction has an imaginative and intellectual sweep, allied to an almost poetic precision of language, that sets him apart from all his Irish contemporaries. Novels: *Long Lankin* (1970, revised 1984), *Nightspawn* (1973), *Birchwood* (1973), *Doctor Copernicus* (1976), *Kepler* (1981), *The Newton Letter: An Interlude,* novella (1982), *Mefisto* (1986), *The Book of Evidence* (1989), *Ghosts* (1993), *Athena* (1995). Translation: *The Broken Jug* (1994), a play by Heinrich von Kleist.

BARCROFT, Joseph (1872–1947), physiologist, b. Newry into a Quaker family, s. of Henry Barcroft, a company manager with interests in natural science, ed. Leys School and King's College, Cambridge. Elected to a fellowship at King's in 1889. His seniors in the Cambridge physiological laboratory were Michael Foster and John Newport Langley, and in 1925 he succeeded the latter in the chair of physiology. Research interests centred on the exchange of oxygen and carbonic acid in blood and tissues. He devised methods of making accurate measurements of gases in minute blood samples, and his investigations were extended to high altitudes in Tenerife and the Peruvian Andes. Publications include *The Respiratory Function of the Blood* (1912) and *Features in the Architecture of Physiological Function* (1934). He also investigated foetal respiration.

BARDWELL, Leland (1928–), née Hone, poet, novelist and dramatist, b. India of Irish parents and grew up in Co. Kildare, ed. Dublin and London. She worked for a time as a teacher in Scotland, before returning to Ireland. Has written stage plays, as well as drama for RTÉ radio and BBC radio, including *No Regrets*, a work based on the life and songs of Edith Piaf. Poetry: *The Mad Cyclist* (1970), *The Fly and the Bedbug* (1984), *Borderlines*, children's poems (1989), *Dostoevsky's Grave: New and Selected Poems* (1991). Stage productions include *Thursday* (1975) and *The Edith Piaf Story* (1983), a musical. Novels: *Girl on a Bicycle* (1977), *That London Winter* (1981), *The House* (1984) and *There We Have Been* (1989). Short stories: *Different Kinds of Love* (1987). She is joint editor of *Cyphers*, the literary magazine.

BARNES, Eamon (1934–), lawyer and public servant, ed. Multyfarnham College, Co. Westmeath, UCD and King's Inns. Practising barrister until he joined office of Attorney-General. Appointed first Director of Public Prosecutions in the history of the state upon the creation of this post under the Prosecution of Offences Act 1974.

BARRINGTON, Jonah (1941–), international squash player, b. Stratton, Cornwall, 29 Apr. 1941, ed. Cheltenham College and TCD, where he studied law for two years. He was capped 18 times for Ireland between 1966 and 1981, and his success and near-obsessive dedication to fitness had a huge influence on the game. He won the Irish Open in 1966, 1967, 1969 and 1979, and was runner-up (to his great rival, Geoff Hunt) in 1972 and 1976. He won the British Open (then the unofficial world title) in 1967, 1968, 1970, 1971, 1972 and 1973, having previously won the British Amateur title three times in succession, between 1966 and 1968. Other major victories included the Egyptian Open, the Australian and South African Amateurs in 1968, and the Australian and Pakistani Opens in 1970. He won the British Close in 1980 and 1981, and later the 1984 British Open Over-35 title. In 1994 he was president of the Squash Rackets Association. His brother Nick also played twice for Ireland.

BARRINGTON, Thomas J. (1917–), public servant, b. Dublin, ed. Belvedere and UCD, m., four s. two d. After some years in business, he entered the civil service in 1941 as an administrative officer in the Department of Finance, from which he was subsequently transferred to the Department of Local Government and Public Health. An early advocate of the need to enhance the quality of civil service thinking and management, he organised discussion groups of higher civil servants and edited a new journal, *Administration*. Influential in the establishment of the Institute of Public Administration in 1957, and three years later was appointed its first full-time director, an office he held until his retirement in 1977. Wrote extensively on issues surrounding the machinery of government in *Administration* and elsewhere, including *From Big Government to Local Government* (1980). Involved in introducing management skills to Third World developing countries, which led in time to the setting up of the Agency for Personal Service Overseas. His association with the public service, especially local government, prompted him to look critically at the concentration of decision-making in central government. Argued that the state should undo excessive centralisation in favour of autonomous powers of local

authorities. Chairman of the government-appointed Committee on Local Government Reorganisation and Reform 1990. Wrote *Discovering Kerry* (1976). Involved in running the annual Daniel O'Connell workshop in Derrynane, a forum for discussing varied issues of public policy in contemporary Ireland. Hon. LL D (NUI).

BARRY, Gerald (1952–), composer, b. Co. Clare. Studied in Dublin, Amsterdam, Cologne and Vienna. Principal composition teachers were Karlheinz Stockhausen and Mauricio Kagel. Lecturer UCC 1982–6. Member of Aosdána. Has written orchestral, chamber, instrumental, vocal and choral works, which include two operas, *The Intelligence Park* (1981–90), commissioned by the Institute of Contemporary Arts, London, and *The Triumph of Beauty and Deceit* (1991–2), commissioned by Channel 4; *Chevaux de frise* for orchestra (1987–8), *Hard D* for chamber ensemble (1992) and *The Conquest of Ireland* for bass and orchestra (1995), all commissioned by the BBC; piano works, *Swinging Tripes and Trillibubkins* (1986) and *Triorchic Blues* (1990), the latter commissioned by the GPA Dublin International Piano Competition; *Flamboys*, for orchestra (1992), commissioned by TCD; and Piano Quartet (1992). Awards include scholarships from Ireland, the Netherlands, Austria and Germany, the Marten Toonder award and the Macaulay fellowship. His works have been performed throughout Europe and in North America, and a commercial recording of piano and chamber music was released in 1994.

BARRY, John Joseph (John Joe, 'The Ballincurry Hare') (1924–), athlete, b. Joliet, Illinois, 5 Oct. 1924. His family moved to Ballincurry, Co. Tipperary when he was aged two. He was the first Irish athlete to earn a US sports scholarship, when he attended Villanova University. He set new Irish records at three miles, two miles and one mile, and his time of 4:16.2 for the last distance in 1949 bettered the previous best by more than two seconds. Also in 1949 he won the British AAA three-mile title, as well as the US One Mile Championship. He broke the world two-mile record, and represented Ireland in the 1,500 m and 5,000 m events in the 1948 London Olympic Games. He published an autobiography, *The Ballincurry Hare*.

BARRY, Kevin (1902–1920), revolutionary, b. Dublin, 20 Jan. 1902, ed. St Mary's College, Rathmines, Belvedere and UCD, where he studied medicine. He joined the Irish Volunteers in Oct. 1917, while still in Belvedere. Captured on 20 Sept. 1920 after an ambush in Dublin, in which a British soldier was killed; he was tried a month later and hanged on 1 Nov. His execution caused widespread resentment.

BARRY, Oliver (1940–), impresario, b. Banteer, Co. Cork, ed. St Colman's College, Fermoy. Worked successively in family wholesale fruit and vegetable business and as a laboratory technician with the Agricultural Institute before becoming a showband manager. Managed Earl Gill and the Hoedowners, the Freshmen, Stockton's Wing and, most famously, the Wolfe Tones. Launched Siamsa Cois Laoi in Páirc Uí Chaoimh, Cork, to raise funds for the debt-ridden GAA. Member of the RTÉ Authority 1982–5. Won franchise for first independent national radio service in Ireland, Century Radio, which, however, collapsed in 1991. World-famous performers he has brought to appear at Irish venues include James Last, Prince, Michael Jackson and Frank Sinatra. His biggest venture to date has been the Voices of the World concert at the Lansdowne Road rugby stadium, Dublin, in Sept. 1995, which involved choirs from many countries, totalling some 6,000 singers.

BARRY, Peter (1928–), politician and businessman, b. Cork, 10 Aug. 1928, s. of Anthony Barry, Fine Gael TD for Cork 1954–7 and 1961–5, ed. Model School and CBS, Cork. The leading shareholder in the family business, Barry's Tea. Elected to the Dáil in 1969 and at all subsequent elections; has held senior positions in FG since 1973 and was deputy leader of the party 1979–87. Contested the party leadership in 1987. Minister for Transport and Power 1973–6; Education 1976–7; the Environment 1981–2; Foreign Affairs 1982–7. Tánaiste for a brief period in 1987 following the resignation of Labour ministers in the then government.

Along with Taoiseach GARRET FITZGERALD he was heavily involved in the negotiations which concluded in the Anglo-Irish Agreement of 1985, and subsequently became the Republic's first co-chair of the Anglo-Irish Inter-Governmental Conference, established by the two governments. He comes from the wing of FG which retains the strong nationalism of the party's founders, whose first political allegiance had been to Sinn Féin.

BARRY, Sebastian (1955–), poet, playwright, novelist and children's author, b. Dublin, s. of actress Joan O'Hara, nephew of singer Mary O'Hara, ed. TCD. He has lived mainly in England and on the Continent since 1977. Awarded Arts Council bursary in 1982. Novels: *Macker's Garden* (1982) and *The Engine of Owllight* (1988). Novellas: *Time out of Mind* and *Strappado Square* (1983). Poetry: *The Watercolourist* (1983), *The Rhetorical Town* (1985) and *Fanny Hawke Goes to the Mainland Forever* (1989). Plays: *Boss Grady's Boys* (1989), *Prayers of Sherkin* (1991), *The Only True History of Lizzie Finn*, *The Steward of Christendom* and *White Woman Street* (1995). Children's fiction: *Elsewhere: The Adventures of Belemus* (1985). Edited *The Inherited Boundaries: Younger Poets of the Republic of Ireland* (1986). Barry's verse is as deliciously original as his drama, shunning rhetoric in favour of understatement, while his drama – *Boss Grady's Boys* and *The Steward of Christendom* in particular – has enjoyed much critical success.

BARRY, Tom (1897–1980), revolutionary, b. Rosscarbery, Co. Cork, 1 July 1897, m. LESLIE DE BARRA, d. Cork, 2 July 1980. One of the best-known and most effective of the 'flying column' leaders active in the southwest during the War of Independence. He helped to establish the West Cork Flying Column in 1919, shortly after being demobbed from the British army with which he had served in Mesopotamia. Under his command the Column took part in two of the major engagements of the war, at Kilmichael in Nov. 1920 and at Crossbarry in Mar. 1921. He rejected the Treaty and fought on the republican side during the Civil War, following which he was interned for a time in the Curragh. He held the position of superintendent with the Cork Harbour Commissioners 1927–65. Barry disapproved of the IRA's bombing campaign in England in the late 1930s and broke his association with the movement. During the Emergency he was an operations officer in the Southern Command. His account of the War of Independence, *Guerrilla Days in Ireland*, was published in 1949.

BARRY, Vincent (1908–1975), organic chemist, b. Cork, 17 May 1908, ed. North Mon. and UCD, d. Dublin, 4 Sept. 1975. Graduated in 1928, gaining first class honours and first place, and obtained his M.Sc. the following year. He became assistant to Thomas Dillon, Professor of Chemistry at UCG, with whom he worked on the chemistry of marine algae. In 1944 Barry was awarded a fellowship from the Medical Research Council of Ireland to investigate the chemotherapy of tuberculosis. He and his associates synthesised and tested a vast range of compounds, some of which were effective against the causative agent, mycobacterium, but none was ever fully developed to the drug stage. One compound, however, phenazine B663, became one of the front-line treatments against leprosy. Barry received a D.Sc. for his published work in 1939 and the Boyle medal in 1969. PRIA 1970–73.

BARRY-MURPHY, Jimmy (1954–), hurler and Gaelic footballer, b. Cork, 22 Aug. 1954. He ranks among Gaelic sport's greatest all-rounders. With St Finbarr's he won All-Ireland hurling club and football club medals, in 1975 and 1978, and 1980 and 1981, respectively, as well as five county football and six county hurling medals between 1974 and 1985. With Cork he won All-Ireland minor medals at hurling in 1971, at football in 1972, followed by an All-Ireland under-21 hurling medal the following year. In all, he helped Cork to win one All-Ireland Senior Football Championship (1973) and five All-Ireland Senior Hurling Championships (1976, 1977, 1978, 1984 and 1986), and he captained the losing All-Ireland hurling final teams in 1982 and 1983. He won two National Hurling League medals (1980, 1981) and one National Football League medal (1980), as well as four Railway Cup medals. He won two All-Star awards at football (1973, 1974) and five All-Star awards at hurling (1976, 1977, 1978, 1983 and 1986), being nominated in four different positions.

BARTON, Robert (1881–1975), signatory of the Anglo-Irish Treaty and cousin of ROBERT ERSKINE CHILDERS, b. Annamoe, Co. Wicklow, ed. Rugby and Oxford, d. Annamoe, 10 Aug. 1975. Elected Sinn Féin MP for West Wicklow 1918. Minister for Agriculture in the First Dáil. Founded the National Land Bank in 1920 and became

Minister for Economic Affairs the following year. As a delegate at the Treaty negotiations in London in 1921 he signed the Articles of Agreement, but later he supported EAMON DE VALERA. He left politics in the 1920s and went on to serve for many years as chairman of the Agricultural Credit Corporation and Bord na Móna.

BATES, Sir David Robert (1916–), D.Sc., FRS, theoretical physicist, b. Omagh, 18 Nov. 1916, s. of W.V. and Mary Bates, ed. Royal Academical Institution, QUB and University College London. From 1939 to 1945 he did war work with the Admiralty: 1939–41 at the Admiralty Research Laboratory, Teddington; 1941–5 at the Mine Laboratory, HMS *Vernon*. Lecturer in mathematics University College London 1945–50, promoted to reader 1951. Professor of Applied Mathematics QUB 1951–68 and of Theoretical Physics 1968–74. He held a special research chair from 1968 to 1982 and was then emeritus. Bates has held numerous visiting professorships and consultancies. His research has centred on the physics of planetary atmospheres, including that of the earth at high altitudes. This involves complex quantum mechanical calculations. His group has also done observational work. It has produced a number of distinguished physicists and has a high international reputation.

BATES, Sir Richard Dawson (1876–1949), politician, b. Belfast, 23 Nov. 1876, ed. Coleraine Academical Institution, d. 9 June 1949. Solicitor by occupation. Secretary of the Ulster Unionist Council 1906–21, during which time he was responsible for the organisation of the 1912 Ulster Covenant. Knighted in 1921, received a baronetcy in 1937. MP for East Belfast at Stormont 1921–9 and for Victoria 1929–43. A hardline unionist who was Minister for Home Affairs from 1921 to 1943, he was described by historian J.F. Harbinson (in *The Ulster Unionist Party 1882–1973*) as: 'A small man, physically and intellectually . . . His great strength was his meticulous attention to detail . . . he was the grey eminence of Ulster Unionism who remained in the shadow of Carson and Craig.'

BÉASLAÍ, Piaras (1881–1965), revolutionary, Gaelic scholar and writer, b. Liverpool, d. Dublin, 22 June 1965. He became active in the Gaelic League after moving to Dublin in 1904 but his belief that the cultural revival could make a significant contribution to the separatist cause was at odds with the League's apolitical official position. In the Easter Rising he commanded the 1st Battalion Volunteers at North King Street. He was editor of *An tÓglach* and, after twice escaping from prison, became director of publicity for the IRA in Feb. 1921. He was TD for East Kerry 1918–21 and voted in favour of the Treaty; later served as a commandant-general in the Free State army. From 1924 he concentrated on writing and scholarship. He translated works from English, German and French into Irish and wrote several plays, including *Fear na Milliún Punt* (1915) and *An Danar* (1929), as well as *Michael Collins and the Making of the New Ireland* (1925).

BEATTIE, John (Jack) (1886–1960), politician, b. Belfast, 14 Apr. 1886, d. 9 Mar. 1960. Jack Beattie was a Presbyterian and a Connollyite socialist. Stormont MP for East Belfast 1925–9 and the Pottinger ward of Belfast 1929–49, he was also Westminster MP for West Belfast 1943–50 and 1951–5 – the first Labour MP to sit at Stormont and the first from Ireland to sit at Westminster. He worked in a weaving company, Belfast Ropeworks and the Harland and Wolff shipyard before joining the army at the age of 17. After three years' service in South Africa, he returned and again went to work in the shipyard. He became assistant secretary to the Associated Blacksmiths' and Ironworkers' Society and in 1918 was appointed its full-time organiser for Ireland, resigning the post in 1925. At Stormont he was a bitter critic of the Unionist government and in 1932 threw the mace at the feet of JAMES CRAIG. Beattie succeeded HARRY MIDGLEY as leader of the NI Parliamentary Labour Party but later resigned and sat as an Independent Labour member and later as Irish Labour. In an address to the Ulster Union Club in Belfast he once stated: 'No Irishman worthy of the name, whether he be Catholic or Protestant, wants to see the historic North remain a kind of moth-eaten tail to John Bull's British lion . . . Partition, that insult to all Irishmen, must end.'

BEATTY, Sir Alfred Chester (1875–1968), mining engineer and philanthropist, b. New York (two grandparents were Irish), ed. Westminster School, Dobbs Ferry, New York, the Columbia School of Mines and Princeton University. His mining career, which started in Denver, Colorado, saw him in places as distant as the Rockies and Egypt. Developed a new way of extracting copper from low-grade ore. His interest in oriental manuscripts was sparked off by a visit to Egypt in 1913 and he eventually accumulated a priceless collection of 13,000 printed books and manuscripts, the most extensive ever held by a private citizen. It was housed in a library he built in Dublin in 1953, which on his death he left in trust to the Irish people. Awarded honorary doctorates by TCD and NUI; made a freeman of Dublin and an honorary citizen of Ireland. He died in Monte Carlo on 20 Jan. 1968, received a state funeral and is buried in Glasnevin, Dublin.

BECKETT, James Camlin (1912–1996), historian, b. 8 Feb. 1912, ed. Royal Academical Institution and QUB (MA), d. Belfast, 12 Feb. 1996. Began his academic career as history master in Belfast Royal Academy in 1934. Appointed lecturer in modern history in QUB in 1952; Professor of Irish History 1958–75. Other academic positions include Cummings lecturer McGill University, Montreal 1976, Mellon professor Tulane University, New Orleans 1977. Publications include: *Protestant Dissent in Ireland 1687–1780* (1948), *The Making of Modern Ireland 1603–1923* (1966), *Belfast: The Origin and Growth of an Industrial City*, ed. with R.E. Glasscock (1967), and *The Anglo-Irish Tradition* (1976). Has also served as editor of *Historical Studies*.

BECKETT, Mary (1926–), short story writer and novelist, b. Belfast, ed. locally. Trained as a teacher and taught in Ardoyne until 1956, when she moved to Dublin. Beckett published her first collection of fiction, *A Belfast Woman and Other Stories*, in 1980 to great critical acclaim, her emotionally charged and sombre work evoking comparison with the stark and moving storytelling of FRANK O'CONNOR and SEÁN O'FAOLAIN. Her following collection, *Give them Stones* (1987), was also well received, as was her début novel, *A Literary Woman* (1990), though it was seen as a considerable departure from her earlier work. Of late she has concentrated on fiction for children, in the wake of *Orla was Six* (1989). Her next novel, *Orla at School*, appeared in 1991, followed by *A Family Tree* (1992) and *Hannah or Pink Balloons* (1995).

BECKETT, Samuel Barclay (1906–1989), prose writer and playwright, b. Foxrock, Co. Dublin, 13 Apr. 1906 (Good Friday), s. of quantity surveyor William Frank Beckett, jnr, and Mary Jones Roe, ed. Portora and TCD. Nobel prize for literature 1969. Beckett's writings combined the obligation to express with the desire to achieve absolute silence and generated an endlessly resourceful tragicomedy of minimalism: in the prose fiction, where no statement could be left unqualified, and in the drama, where his characters improvised a mode of survival out of the most meagre of human resources. Beckett received a first class honours BA in modern languages and, after a spell at the École Normale Supérieure, returned to TCD as a lecturer in French. He resigned his position and spent the 1930s between Dublin, London and Paris, where he got to know JAMES JOYCE.

His earliest publication was an essay defending *Work in Progress* (*Finnegans Wake*), followed in 1931 by the appearance of a book on Proust; during the decade he continued to write criticism and also produced an impressive body of poetry. Like Joyce, Beckett began in fiction with a book of interrelated short stories set in Dublin, *More Pricks than Kicks* (1934), subsequently banned there. He increasingly took his own eccentric direction in his novel of an Irish Everyman, *Murphy* (1938), pursued into London exile and seeking refuge in an asylum from his body, the demands of the workaday world, his girlfriend, Celia, and a motley crew of Irish characters. Having had his fun with subverting and exploding Irish pieties, Beckett's subsequent prose shed as much of his inherited cultural baggage as possible in favour of a growing abstraction of language, character and setting. With the outbreak of World War II, he returned definitively to France and began to work for the Resistance when, as he put it, the Nazis started coming after his Jewish friends. Over a period of three years, while he and his wife, Suzanne, moved from place to place, he wrote the novel *Watt* (not published until 1953) to keep his hand in. From this point on, almost all familiar landmarks are obliterated from Beckett's writing, replaced by an open countryside through which his solitary figures tramp or a neutral room in which they hole up to write. In an intense period from 1947 to 1949, Beckett wrote all the novels of his famous trilogy, *Molloy, Malone meurt/Malone Dies, L'Innommable/The Unnamable*, in which the metaphysics of identity came under interrogation and the limits of self-expression were repeatedly tested. Beckett also took a late and unexpected turn to drama by composing his first and most famous play, *En attendant Godot/Waiting for Godot*, in 1948, as a move from the abstractions of his prose into a world of physical objects and tangible space, a tragicomic zone of human suffering and comic pratfalls. Things were never to be as mobile or relaxed again in Beckett's dramatic world.

In the later plays his characters undergo a process of increasing paralysis and confinement: Hamm in his wheelchair in *Fin de partie/Endgame* (1956), tyrannical in his treatment of servant and parents but still dependent on them to keep him going; Winnie in *Happy Days* (1961), buried first up to her waist, then to her neck, in sand, but verbally unstoppable. If his paired male characters still vie for dominance, many of his later plays concentrate on a female at stage centre, sometimes no more than Mouth in *Not I* (1973) – drawn, as he said himself, from women he knew in Ireland 'stumbling down the lanes, in the ditches, beside the hedgerows'. In his later prose writings, especially *Company* (1980), Beckett also tuned in more specifically to childhood scenes from the past in Ireland, juxtaposed with a figure lying alone in the dark listening to the voices that come to him. For all of his lifelong Paris exile, Beckett never stopped listening to Irish voices or translating them in a variety of formal and linguistic ways which gave them worldwide resonance. He died in Paris on 22 Dec. 1989 of respiratory problems and is buried in Montparnasse Cemetery alongside his wife, who predeceased him by less than a year.

BEDDY, James (1900–1976), public servant, b. Cobh, Co. Cork, ed. O'Connell School and UCD (D.Econ.Sc., LL D). MRIA. Inspector of taxes 1927–33. Secretary Industrial Credit Company 1933–49, subsequently chairman and managing director until 1969. First chairman of the Industrial Development Authority 1950, and also first chairman of the grant-giving authority An Foras Tionscal 1952. Lecturer in UCD 1952–69. Chairman Commission on Emigration and Other

Population Problems 1948–54, chairman Committee of Inquiry into Internal Transport 1956–7. Board member ESRI.

BEERE, Thekla (1902–1991), executive public servant, b. Kells, Co. Meath, ed. Alexandra and TCD (BA Mod., LL B, LL D 1960 *jure dignitatis*). Travelling student in the USA on a scholarship from the Rockefeller Foundation. Joined the civil service in the statistics section of the Department of Industry and Commerce and was transferred to the transport section, where she was closely involved with problems of supply during the years of World War II. Chairwoman of the finance committee of the International Labour Office in Geneva. In 1959 appointed secretary of the newly established Department of Transport and Power – the first woman secretary. Member Public Services Organisation Review Group, which recommended (in the Devlin Report) fundamental changes in the organisation and work of the public service. Chairwoman of the newly established Commission on the Status of Women 1970. Founder member (in 1931) and subsequently president of An Óige, the Irish Youth Hostel Association. At various times she was president of the council of the Statistical and Social Inquiry Society of Ireland and of the Irish Film Society and a governor of the Rotunda Hospital. When the *Irish Times* Trust was established in 1974 she was one of its first governors; she was also a director of the newspaper.

BEHAN, Brendan Francis (1923–1964), author, poet and playwright, b. Dublin, 9 Feb. 1923, ed. Daughters of Charity, North William Street and CBS, Brunswick Street, Dublin, m. Beatrice Salkeld, d. Dublin, 20 Mar. 1964. Left school aged 14 to be a house painter like his father, by whom he was also introduced to history, literature and the republican tradition. Joined the IRA, was charged in Liverpool with possessing explosives and sent to a juvenile detention centre. Shortly after release in 1941 he was arrested in Dublin and sentenced to jail for 14 years for shooting at a policeman; released under an amnesty in 1946. Began writing for radio and the *Irish Press* and in 1954 had a notable success with his play *The Quare Fellow*, produced in Dublin's Pike Theatre that year and in London by Joan Littlewood in 1956. In 1958 an autobiography,

Borstal Boy, was published, as well as a play in Irish, *An Giall*, staged some months later in an expanded English version as *The Hostage*. Behan was now established internationally and much admired for the hard-edged, softhearted, tragicomic quality of his writing, the best of it influenced by his republican background and prison experiences. His works were published and performed on the Continent and in the USA. He gave numerous television interviews, distinguished by his expressive turn of phrase, love of balladry, Dublin accent and ready wit. Several later books, however, fell short of expectations. Alcoholism and diabetes set in, leading to his premature death.

BEHAN, Dominic (1928–), writer, composer and broadcaster, b. Dublin. He left Ireland in 1947 to work in Britain and became actively involved in the labour movement, in both London and Dublin. Like his brother BRENDAN BEHAN, Dominic had inherited his parents' musical ability and gained a reputation as a balladeer, recording the album *Streets of Song* with Ewan MacColl in 1959. His most memorable composition was the hauntingly bitter 'The Patriot Game', which quickly entered the canon of Irish 'rebel' songs. He has achieved success as a journalist for numerous Irish and British papers, in addition to writing TV documentaries and hosting shows for RTE and British television. His publications include songbooks; *Teems of Times and Happy Returns*, an autobiography (1961); *My Brother Brendan* (1965); plays including *The Patriot Game, Posterity Bedamned* and *The Folksinger;* a novel, *The Public World of Parable Jones* (1989); and the official biography of Spike Milligan (1988).

BEHAN, John (1938–), artist, b. Dublin, ed. National College of Art, Dublin and Ealing Art College, London. A very influential figure in Irish art, both through his work as a sculptor and through the important organisational role he has played in the development of contemporary Irish painting and sculpture. He helped to establish the Project Arts Centre in 1967 and the Dublin Art Foundry in 1970. Best known for his sculpture in bronze of bulls, mythical figures and birds, he also works in aluminium, steel and brass. A retrospective of his work was held in Galway in 1994 and in the RHA in 1995. Several of his sculptures are in the collections of the Hugh Lane

Municipal Gallery and the National Gallery of Ireland. Behan is a member of Aosdána and currently lives and works in Galway.

BEIT, Sir Alfred (1903–1994), politician and art collector, ed. Eton and Oxford, m. Hon. Clementine Freeman-Mitford. Elected as Conservative MP in 1931 and sat in the House of Commons until he lost his seat in the post-World War II general election. During the war he was parliamentary private secretary to the financial secretary at the War Office and later moved to the Colonial Office. After losing his seat, he gave his time to the Beit Trust, which had been set up to finance and encourage scientific and medical research. Bought Russborough House, Co. Wicklow in 1952 to display the art collection started by an uncle in the late 19th century. Also had houses in London and Cape Province, South Africa. Many of his priceless paintings were stolen from Russborough House in 1974 but were later recovered. Loaned the bulk of his collection to the National Gallery of Ireland for the winter months, and later donated the 17 most famous paintings. In May 1986 18 masterpieces were stolen, including a Goya and one of only two privately owned Vermeers; they were recovered years later in Turkey and Belgium. Made honorary citizen of Ireland together with Lady Beit 1993.

BELL, Sam Hanna (1909–1990), writer and radio producer, b. Glasgow, 23 Oct. 1909, d. 9 Feb. 1990. Lived near Strangford Lough – the scene of his novel *December Bride* (1951) – and later in Belfast. Before 1945, when he joined BBC Northern Ireland (from which he retired as senior features producer in 1969), he held a variety of posts, including being responsible for Belfast's emergency food supply during the war. He was also active in left-wing politics and used his experience of urban poverty in *The Hollow Ball* (1961). His four novels portray the Ulster Protestant frankly and lovingly, and his work with SEÁN O'BOYLE and Michael J. Murphy in recording the songs and folkways of the province created a rich archive of Ulster life.

BENNETT, Louie (1870–1956), trade unionist, b. Temple Hill, Dublin, ed. Alexandra and in London and Bonn, d. Killiney, Co. Dublin, Nov. 1956. Born into a prosperous Anglo-Irish family, Bennett was active through-out her life in the cause of Irish women and labour. She helped to found the Irish Women's Suffrage Federation in 1911, serving as its first secretary, and was also involved in the formation of the Irish Women's Reform League, which highlighted the social and economic plight of women workers. She worked in a soup kitchen during the 1913 Lock-out and with FRANCIS SHEEHY SKEFFINGTON on the *Irish Citizen*. In 1916, along with her lifelong friend and colleague HELEN CHEVENIX, she was charged with the task of reorganising the Irish Women Workers' Union, marking the beginning of a 38-year commitment. At the time of her retirement as general secretary in 1955, the union (which amalgamated with the Federated Workers' Union of Ireland in 1984) had 10,000 members. First woman president of the Irish Trades Union Congress 1932. She wrote two novels in the early 1900s, *The Proving of Priscilla* and *A Prisoner of his Word*.

BERGIN, Liam (1913–1994), journalist and editor, b. Newbridge, Co. Kildare, 15 Aug. 1913, ed. Dominican College, Newbridge, d. Cabinteely, Co. Dublin, 6 Jan. 1994. Editor and managing director of the *Nationalist and Leinster Times*, Bergin was one of the most distinguished figures in Irish provincial journalism. He had a keen interest in international affairs, having travelled in Spain in the 1930s, just before the Civil War broke out, and throughout Europe in the years preceding World War II, interviewing many of the leading statesmen and literary figures of the time. As well as maintaining high journalistic standards, he had a strong interest in graphic design. The *Nationalist* won two major British newspaper design awards under his stewardship. Bergin was a visiting lecturer at Southern Illinois University School of Journalism in 1965 and 1971, a member of PEN and a correspondent for RIAS radio, Berlin.

BERGIN, Osborn Joseph (1873–1950), Celtic scholar, b. Cork, 26 Nov. 1873, ed. Cork Grammar and Queen's College, Cork, d. Dublin, 6 Oct. 1950. Having taken a classics degree, his interest in Irish drew him towards the Gaelic League and he gradually established himself as a Celtic scholar, taking up a teaching post at Queen's College, Cork in the subject in 1897. After further study in Berlin and Freiburg, where he took his doctorate in 1906, he became a professor in the School of Irish Learning. Professor of Early and Medieval Irish at UCD 1909–40, and first director of the School of Celtic Studies in the DIAS 1940. He was general editor of the RIA's *Dictionary of the Irish Language* and the author of many books, learned articles and scholarly editions.

BERKELEY, Sara (1967–), poet and short story writer, b. Dublin, ed. TCD and the University of California, Berkeley. Her first collection of poems, *Penn*, was shortlisted for the *Irish Times* award for poetry in 1986. Since then she has published two further volumes of verse, *Home Movie Nights* (1989) and *Facts about Water* (1995), in Ireland and in Saskatchewan, Canada. She is also the author of a book of short stories, *The Swimmer in the Deep Blue Dream* (1991). Her poetry is slightly uneven, yet holds promise of exciting things to come. It ' has been likened to eastern European verse written after World War II. As a delver into shadow areas of human consciousness, Berkeley has few equals among Irish poets of her generation. Since graduating from TCD she has divided her time between London and the USA, where she is engaged on a project for a computer company in San Francisco.

BERMINGHAM, Willie (1947–1990), fireman and founder of ALONE, d. Dublin, Apr. 1990. Found a dead old man in a pensioners' settlement in Charlemont Street, Dublin, which shocked him into forming ALONE ('A Little Offering Never Ends'), a voluntary organisation which helps old people living alone in poverty, 1977. Heightened public awareness with extensive poster campaign, 'Old People Die Alone', and urged people to check on elderly neighbours. Visited over 3,500 old people. Returned £5,000 allotted by Mary Flaherty, Minister of State at Social Welfare, and another £5,000 also granted from state funds in 1982, saying it was the government's job to deal with the poor, not his. Kept public concern alive with widely reviewed booklets *Alone* (1978), *Alone Again* (1982) and *Alone Once More* (1989), which he compiled jointly with photojournalist Liam Ó Cuanaigh. In 1986 built first customised privately owned old people's complex, in Artane in Dublin, with each house named after an elderly victim.

BERNAL, John Desmond (1901–1971), scientist, b. Nenagh, ed. Hodder School, Stonyhurst, Bedford School and Emmanuel College, Cambridge, d. 15 Sept. 1971. One of the most distinguished crystallographers of the century, he was also deeply interested in social problems and their interaction with science. A lifelong Marxist, he joined the Communist Party with his wife, Eileen, in 1923. His first appointment was at the Royal Institution 1923–7. In 1927 he was made a lecturer, and later assistant director of research, in crystallography at Cambridge. In 1937 he was appointed Professor of Physics at Birkbeck College in the University of London, a position he held until his retirement, when he was elected FRS.

His scientific work was marked by its breadth and ingenuity. While crystallography is a branch of physics, its applications are mainly in chemistry, biochemistry and, in his case, geophysics, elucidating the structure of complex molecules. Probably Bernal's best-known work was on the structure of viruses, but he worked also on metals and chemical compounds. His invention, independently of Paul Ewald, of the reciprocal lattice was of great practical importance.

During World War II he became closely involved in aspects of MULBERRY, the floating harbour so vital immediately after D-Day. He was awarded the Lenin peace prize in 1953. The Royal Society gave him its royal medal in 1945. He was, however, excluded from several conferences in the USA.

He wrote many papers and also – unusually for a scientist – several books, mainly on the social aspects of science and on the history of science. The most celebrated of these were perhaps *The Social Function of Science*, *The Physical Basis of Life* and *The Origin of Life*.

BERNARD, John Henry (1860–1927), Church of Ireland archbishop and academic, b. 27 July 1860, ed. Bray, Co. Wicklow, Newport, Co. Tipperary and TCD (which he entered shortly after his 15th birthday), d. 29 Aug. 1927. First scholar in mathematics. Ordained deacon 1886, priest 1887. Archbishop King's Professor of Divinity 1888–1911. Dean of St Patrick's Cathedral 1902–11. Elected Bishop of Ossory, Ferns and Leighlin 1911. Archbishop of Dublin 1915, Provost of TCD

1919–27, a translation that occasioned some unfavourable criticism of him in certain Church circles.

Though a scientist by early training, he wrote and edited many theological works, the most enduring being his two-volume *Commentary on the Gospel According to St John* (published posthumously in 1928). He received honorary degrees from Durham, Aberdeen and Oxford, was an honorary fellow of the RCPI, a commissioner of national education 1897–1903 and PRIA 1916–21. A politically alert man who called for stern punishment of the leaders of the Easter Rising, Bernard was an energetic member of the Irish Convention 1917, the body convened by British Prime Minister Lloyd George to attempt to find a solution to Irish political problems, which was described by R.B. McDowell as 'one of the most striking failures in Irish history'.

BEST, George (Georgie) (1946–), international footballer, b. Belfast, 22 May 1946. After joining Manchester United as a junior in 1961, he enjoyed a magnificent decade in the club's first team from 1964 onwards. He won two English Championship medals in seasons 1964–5 and 1966–7, a Fairs Cup medal in 1965 and a European Cup medal in 1968. In 361 games for United he scored 137 League goals, and he was Division One joint top scorer in 1968; other scoring feats include six goals in an FA Cup tie against Northampton Town in 1970 (a joint record). He played 37 times for Northern Ireland between 1964 and 1977, and scored nine international goals, as well as 11 in European competitions. Among his awards when at his peak was his nomination as European Player of the Year in 1968. His well-publicised raffish lifestyle brought his career to a premature end, and he later played for a variety of lesser clubs in England and the USA, as well as appearing for Cork Hibernians. His biography, *The Good, the Bad and the Bubbly*, was published in 1991. Best's innate genius has ensured him his place among soccer's true greats.

BEST, Richard Irvine (1872–1959), Celtic scholar, b. Ulster, d. Dublin, 25 Sept. 1959. He studied Old Irish in Paris under H. D'Arbois de Jubainville before returning to Ireland in 1904 as assistant director of the National Library; director 1924–40. Senior Professor of Celtic Studies DIAS 1940–47;

chairman of the Irish Manuscripts Commission 1948–56. PRIA 1943–6. His major work was the *Bibliography of Irish Philology and Manuscript Literature, Publications 1913–1941* (two vols. 1942).

BEWICK, Pauline (1935–), artist, b. Northumbria, 4 Sept. 1935, raised in Kenmare, Co. Kerry, ed. St Catherine's School, Bristol and National College of Art, Dublin. She is best known for her paintings but has also contributed to numerous publications both as a writer and as an illustrator. These include a book based on her experiences of two years travelling and working in Polynesia 1989–91. She also worked on stage set designs for a number of years before moving to Kerry from Dublin in 1973 with her husband and two children. She is a prolific artist and has had several solo exhibitions, including a major retrospective at the Guinness Hop Store in 1986. In 1981 she was selected to represent Ireland at the European Graphic Art Biennial in Baden Baden. She is a member of the RHA and Aosdána.

BEWLEY, Charles (1890–1969), diplomat, b. Dublin into a well-known family of Quaker merchants, ed. Winchester and New College, Oxford, where he became a Roman Catholic. Called to the Bar 1914 and practised on the western circuit. Sinn Féin agent Berlin 1921–3. Called to Inner Bar 1926. Appointed Irish Minister to the Vatican when diplomatic relations were established in 1929. Minister to Germany 1933–8. As an apologist for Fascism and Nazism, he caused embarrassment to the Department of External Affairs and was effectively dismissed in 1939. He settled in Italy, where he worked as a journalist, becoming involved in German propaganda activities during World War II, after which he was briefly interned. Lived in Rome until his death.

BEWLEY, Victor E.H. (1912–), founder of travelling people's organisation, b. Dublin, grew up on family farm in Rathgar, ed. Quaker boarding school then worked in family business, Bewley's Oriental Cafés Ltd. Retired as chairman 1977. Received honorary degree from TCD 1976. Became concerned about the conditions facing Ireland's travelling community after publication of Government Commission on Itinerancy 1964. Along with Fr Tom Fehily and Lady Wicklow, he founded the Dublin Committee for Travelling People and was its secretary for over 20 years. He was also secretary and later chairman of the National Council for Travelling People. Advised successive Ministers for the Environment about issues relating to travellers.

BHREATHNACH, Niamh (1945–), politician, b. Dublin, June 1945, ed. Sion Hill and Froebel College, Blackrock, Co. Dublin. Remedial teacher. Chairwoman Labour Party 1990–93. TD (Labour Dún Laoghaire) 1992. Minister for Education 1993–4 and since 1994.

BIGGART, Sir John (1906–1973), pathologist and educationalist, b. Templepatrick, Co. Antrim, ed. Royal Academical Institution and QUB, where his abilities were such that he won the Symington medal in anatomy and the university billiards championship in the same year. Having graduated in medicine in 1928, he held resident posts at the Royal Victoria Hospital before specialising in pathology. A fellowship at Johns Hopkins Medical School was followed by four years as lecturer in neuropathy at the University of Edinburgh and the publication in 1936 of his *Textbook of Neuropathology*. The following year he returned to Queen's as Musgrave Professor of Pathology.

A talented administrator, he was elected dean of the medical faculty in 1943, holding the post until his retirement in 1971, and for four years was also Pro-Chancellor of the university. During the war, he created a blood transfusion service for Northern Ireland.

BIGGER, Joseph Warwick (1891–1951), bacteriologist, b. Belfast, s. of Dr (later Sir) Edward Coey Bigger and Maude Coulter Warwick, ed. St Andrew's College, Dublin and TCD, as the family moved to Dublin in 1900 when Dr Bigger became medical inspector to the Local Government Board. Joe Bigger won a medical scholarship and the Purser medal for physiology. He graduated MB in 1916 and for three years was demonstrator in pathology and bacteriology at the University of Sheffield. Prior to his appointments as Professor of Bacteriology in TCD in 1924 and dean of the School of Physics in 1936, he had worked for the Local Government Board and held a chair in preventive and forensic medicine at the RCSI. His *Handbook of Bacteriology* (1925) went into four editions in his lifetime.

As lieutenant-colonel, Bigger served in the RAMC during World War II. Later he represented TCD in the Senate. His greatly desired research centre (the Moyne Institute) opened shortly after his death.

BINCHY, Daniel A. (1900–1989), jurist and diplomat, ed. Clongowes, UCD and Munich. Professor of Roman Law and Jurisprudence UCD 1924–46. Because of his knowledge of German he was appointed first Irish Minister to Berlin 1929–32, where, drawing on his linguistic and scholarly abilities, he made a remarkable impression for the representative of a new and small state. The German Foreign Office sought his comments on relations between the member countries of the Commonwealth, while his reports back to Dublin on German politics and politicians were unusually perceptive, not least on the menace represented by Hitler. In 1932 he returned to his university post. Together with MICHAEL TIERNEY and Frank McDermot, who had links with Fine Gael, he drew up suggestions for the composition of the Seanad under the proposed new constitution which surprisingly were adopted in large measure by EAMON DE VALERA. His study of *Church and State in Fascist Italy* appeared in 1941 but his principal interest was always in the field of legal history and in particular early Irish law. Editor of the six-volume *Corpus Iuris Hibernici* (1979).

BINCHY, Maeve (1940–), journalist and author, ed. Holy Child School, Killiney, Co. Dublin and UCD, m. author Gordon Snell. After some years as a secondary teacher, moved into journalism in 1968, when she joined *The Irish Times*. Wrote mainly colour stories, such as eyewitness accounts of British royal weddings. Her eye for detail, her ear for dialogue and her never-failing sense of humour made her hugely popular with the paper's readership. She went on to write many successful novels, including *Light a Penny Candle*, *Firefly Summer* and *The Lilac Bus*, several of which were adapted for television; a film of *Circle of Friends* was directed by PAT O'CONNOR. She continues to contribute a weekly column to *The Irish Times*. Hon. D.Litt. (NUI) 1990.

BING, Geoffrey Henry Cecil (1909–1977), lawyer and politician, b. China, 24 July 1909, the son of an Anglican clergyman from Co. Down, ed. Tonbridge School and Lincoln

College, Oxford, d. 24 Apr. 1977. Visiting fellow at Princeton University 1932–3. Called to the Bar in 1934, QC 1950. He joined the Royal Signals Regiment in 1941, was commissioned in 1943, a major 1944–5 and mentioned in dispatches. Labour MP for Hornchurch 1945–55. A prominent member of the Friends of Ireland group formed by Labour MPs in 1945, he attempted to introduce legislation to provide safeguards against discrimination and gerrymandering in Northern Ireland. Attorney-General of Ghana 1957–61 and adviser to President Nkrumah 1961–6. Legal adviser to Association of Scientific, Technical and Managerial Staffs after 1971. His publications include the strongly anti-unionist pamphlet *John Bull's Other Island* (1950).

BINGHAM, William L. (Billy) (1931–), international footballer and manager, b. Belfast, 5 Aug. 1931. He left Glentoran for Sunderland when aged 19, scoring 45 League goals for the English club between 1950 and 1957. In two seasons with Luton Town he scored a further 27 League goals, and won an FA Cup runners-up medal in 1959, before moving to Everton for two seasons, winning a League Championship medal in 1962–3. He later played for Port Vale. In 419 English League matches he scored 102 goals. He played 56 times for Northern Ireland between 1951 and 1964, scored ten international goals, and played in the team which reached the World Cup quarter-finals in 1958. Subsequently, he managed Southport, Plymouth, Linfield, Everton and Mansfield, as well as Greece from 1971 to 1973. He managed Northern Ireland in 118 matches up to 1993, guiding them to the World Cup finals in 1982 and 1986. He was awarded the MBE in 1981.

BLACK, Mary (1955–), singer, b. Dublin, 22 May 1955, ed. St Louis High School, Rathmines, Dublin. After a short period as a solo performer she joined De Danann in 1983 and recorded two albums with them. While her musical background is strongly traditional, her first solo album, *Without the Fanfare*, comprised mainly contemporary songs. A subsequent album, *No Frontiers*, was one of the bestselling albums in Ireland in 1989 and also enjoyed considerable success in the USA and Japan. Her third solo album, *Babes in the Wood*, spent five weeks at number one in the Irish charts. In 1987 and 1988 she was voted Best Female Artist in the Irish Rock Music Awards.

BLACKSHAW, Basil (1932–), artist, b. Glengormley, Co. Antrim, ed. Belfast College of Art. Studied in Paris for a number of years before returning to live and work in Antrim in the mid-1950s. He is a prolific painter and has had two major retrospective exhibitions of his work: in 1974 at the Arts Council Gallery and in 1995 at the Ormeau Baths Gallery, both in Belfast. He was chosen to represent Ireland in Rosc '88. Much of Blackshaw's work is figurative but he is not particularly concerned with producing precise representations of the subject. His use of light and his vigorous painting, which combine to create a lively, active surface texture, economically convey an impression of energy and movement.

BLADES, The, rock band. Led by singer-guitarist Paul Cleary, the Blades were an energetic Dublin three-piece in the tradition of the Jam, playing a stripped-down early 1960s sound and singing about Dublin working-class life. After releasing a number of well-received singles, including 'Ghost of a Chance' and 'The Bride Wore White', the band were signed to Elektra in 1984, but were dropped by the label soon after completing their first album, *The Last Man in Europe*. The album was finally released on an independent label in 1986, by which time Cleary had formed a new band, the Partisans. The Blades will go down in Irish rock history as the success story that should have been.

BLANCHFLOWER, Robert Dennis (Danny) (1926–1993), international footballer, manager and sports writer, b. Belfast, 10 Feb. 1926, d. London, 9 Dec. 1993. His career started with Glentoran, and he went on to play for Barnsley and Aston Villa before joining Tottenham Hotspur in 1954, remaining with that club for ten years. He played 337 League matches with Spurs (553 English League appearances in all), captained the club to its famous FA Cup and League double in 1961 and to retention of the Cup in 1962, and was in the Spurs team which won the European Cup Winners' Cup in 1963. He played 56 times for Northern Ireland, and captained the team which reached the 1958 World Cup quarter-finals, as well as playing for the Irish League and the Football League. He was manager of the Northern Ireland squad from 1976 to 1979, and also had a career as a sports writer, chiefly with the *Sunday Express*. His younger brother Jackie (b. 1933), of Manchester United, who was injured in the 1958 Munich air disaster, played 12 times for Northern Ireland.

BLANEY, Neil (1922–1995), politician, b. Donegal, 29 Oct. 1922, ed. Tamney NS and St Eunan's College, Letterkenny, d. Dublin, 8 Nov. 1995. He won the by-election caused by the death of his father, a Fianna Fáil TD 1927–48, and by the time of his own death was the longest-serving TD. Member of Donegal County Council from 1948 until 1957, when he received his first ministerial appointment, Posts and Telegraphs. Later in 1957 he became Minister for Local Government, an office he held until 1966. He was Minister for Agriculture and Fisheries 1966–70, when, along with CHARLES HAUGHEY, he was dismissed by the Taoiseach, JACK LYNCH, for allegedly not subscribing fully to government policy on Northern Ireland. He was arrested and charged with involvement in the illegal importation of arms but the charges were dismissed at a preliminary hearing. In 1971 he abstained on a vote of confidence in former defence minister Jim Gibbons and thereafter was regarded by Fianna Fáil as being no longer a member of the party. He fought subsequent elections on an Independent Fianna Fáil ticket. MEP for Connacht–Ulster 1979–84, 1989–94; following an illness, he did not contest the 1994 election. President of the FAI 1968–73 and subsequently a patron.

Regarded as one of Fianna Fáil's outstanding electoral strategists. Helped to organise TACA, a sometimes controversial fund-raising organisation for the party which featured prominent figures in Irish business life. The most forthrightly republican voice in Dáil Éireann. Campaigned for BOBBY SANDS and Owen Carron in the 'hunger strike' by-elections in Fermanagh–South Tyrone in the early 1980s.

BLEAKLEY, David Wylie (1925–), writer and politician, b. 11 Jan. 1925, ed. Ruskin College, Oxford and QUB. Worked in Harland and Wolff shipyard between 1940 and 1946. MP for the Victoria ward of Belfast at Stormont 1958–65. Lecturer in industrial relations in Dar es Salaam 1967–9 and subsequently a teacher at Methodist College,

Belfast 1969–79. As Minister of Community Relations (Mar.–Sept. 1971) he was the only Northern Ireland Labour Party member to serve in the NI government. Member of the NI Assembly 1973–4 and of the Convention 1975–6. He unsuccessfully contested Westminster elections in 1970 and 1974 and the 1979 elections to the European Parliament, and joined the Alliance Party in 1992. Chairman of the NI Standing Advisory Commission on Human Rights 1980–84. Chief executive of the Irish Council of Churches 1980–92 and president of the Church Mission Society since 1983. He has produced numerous publications on NI politics and community relations as well as on industrial studies.

BLOOMFIELD, Sir Kenneth Percy (1931–), public servant, b. 15 Apr. 1931, ed. Royal Academical Institution and St Peter's College, Oxford. Head of the Northern Ireland civil service from 1984 to 1991. Ken Bloomfield had a long and distinguished career in the civil service, serving as deputy secretary to the NI cabinet 1963–72, when he was one of TERENCE O'NEILL's chief advisers. Under-secretary at the Northern Ireland Office after the introduction of direct rule, he was also permanent secretary to the NI Executive in 1974. Permanent secretary at Housing, Local Government and Planning 1975–6, the Department of the Environment 1976–81, Commerce 1981–2 and Economic Development 1982–4. Appointed head of the NICS in 1984, he considered resigning in protest at the Anglo-Irish Agreement the following year. He was knighted in 1987, and in 1988 escaped unharmed when an IRA bomb exploded at his home. In 1991, after retirement from the civil service, he was appointed BBC governor for NI. A memoir, *Stormont in Crisis*, was published in 1994.

BLOWICK, John (1888–1972), Roman Catholic priest, co-founder of St Columban's Foreign Mission Society (Maynooth Mission to China), b. Belcarra, Co. Mayo, ed. CBS, Westport, St Jarlath's College, Tuam and Maynooth, d. 19 June 1972.

Ordained 1913 and appointed Professor of Theology at Maynooth in 1914. In 1916 he co-founded the Maynooth Mission to China with EDWARD GALVIN. Their intention was to recruit secular priests from Ireland for service in China. In 1918 they opened a seminary for the training of missionaries and adopted the name St Columban's Foreign Mission Society, with Fr Blowick as superior-general. In 1920 he accompanied the first group of Columbans to China before returning to Ireland to oversee the further development of the Society, with houses in the USA and Australia in the decade that followed. At Dalgan Park he pioneered a move away from the strict supervision characteristic of seminary life until the changes brought about by the Second Vatican Council. His *Priestly Vocation* (1932) set out his views on the formation of priests. In 1922, together with Lady Frances Maloney, he formed the missionary Sisters of St Columban and in 1924 the Columban Brothers, both of which were intended to serve alongside the Columban Fathers in China. In 1954 the work of the Columbans in China ended when their last member was finally expelled by the communist government. However, by that stage Blowick had seen them establish themselves in the Philippines and Korea, and by 1960 they were in South America.

BLOWICK, Joseph (1903–1970), politician, b. Belcarra, Co. Mayo, ed. local primary school. Farmer. TD (C. na T. Mayo South) 1943–65. Party leader 1944. Minister for Lands and Fisheries 1948–51 and 1954–7. Supervised major national programmes for reafforestation.

BLYTHE, Ernest (Earnán de Blaghd) (1889–1975), revolutionary, politician and promoter of the theatre, b. Magheragall, Lisburn, Co. Antrim, ed. local primary school, d. Dublin, 23 Feb. 1975. Clerk in Department of Agriculture, Dublin, 1904. Joined the IRB. Studied Irish at Gaelic League classes and, after working for some years as a journalist in Co. Down, in the Kerry Gaeltacht, where he came to know DESMOND FITZGERALD, with whom he collaborated in organising the Irish Volunteers. Imprisoned several times, and thereby unable to take part in the Easter Rising. Elected MP (SF Monaghan North) 1918, Minister for Trade and Commerce, First and Second Dáil, 1919–22. Supported the Anglo-Irish Treaty. Minister for Local Government 1922–3, for Finance 1923–32; Vice-President Executive Council 1927–32. Introduced annual subsidy for the Abbey Theatre but had to bear brunt of criticism for government decision to cut old-age pensions by a shilling and reduce the pay of teachers and police to cope with the depression of the early 1930s. Senator 1933–6, when he retired from politics. Managing director Abbey Theatre 1939–67. Gave special encouragement to plays in Irish. In his book *Briseadh na Teorann* he argued for reconciliation between the traditions as the prerequisite for ending partition. Also wrote several volumes of autobiography.

BODKIN, Thomas Patrick (1887–1961), lawyer and connoisseur of European painting, b. Dublin, 21 July 1887, ed. Belvedere, Clongowes, Paris, UCD and King's Inns, d. Birmingham, 24 Apr. 1961. Called to Bar 1911. Director National Gallery of Ireland 1927–35. Barber Professor of Fine Arts and first director Barber Institute, Birmingham, 1935–52. On the initiative of the Taoiseach, JOHN A. COSTELLO, he was commissioned by the government to write a report on the arts in Ireland 1951, which resulted in the establishment of the Arts Council. Dedicated himself to securing a settlement in Dublin's favour of the dispute over the disposition of his uncle Sir HUGH LANE's art collection. Served on a number of government committees, was a papal Knight of St Gregory and an Officier of the Légion d'honneur. Publications include *Hugh Lane and his Pictures* and *The Paintings of Jan Vermeer.*

BODLEY, Seoirse (1933–), composer, conductor and pianist, b. Dublin, ed. Dublin and Germany. Awarded D.Mus. from UCD. Associate Professor of Music UCD. Member of Aosdána. Works include five symphonies, two chamber symphonies and chamber, orchestral, choral, instrumental, vocal, liturgical and electro-acoustic music. His song cycles, *A Girl* and *The Naked Flame* (settings of poems by BRENDAN KENNELLY and MÍCHEÁL Ó SIADHAIL respectively), were commissioned by RTÉ, as was his String Quartet No. 2 and numerous other compositions. He is a lover of the Irish language and culture and much of his work has been inspired by traditional music; pieces bear evocative and original titles such as *The Tight-rope Walker Presents a Rose* (piano), *A Small White Cloud Drifts over Ireland* (chamber orchestra) and *The Narrow Road to the Deep North* (two pianos/piano solo). Awards include the Macaulay fellowship and the Marten Toonder award. Among his commercial recordings are *Music for Strings* (Decca), *Chamber Symphony No. 1* and *String Quartet No. 1* (NIRC) and *A Girl* (Gael-Linn).

BOLAND, Eavan (1944–), poet, b. Dublin, ed. London and New York, where her father, FREDERICK BOLAND, was Irish ambassador successively to the United Kingdom and the United Nations. Later attended the Holy Child School in Killiney, Co. Dublin and TCD. Has written, lectured and broadcast on literary subjects. Her collections of poetry include *New Territory* (1967), *The War Horse* (1975), *In Her Own Image* (1980) and *Night Feed* (1982). With MICHEÁL MACLIAMMÓIR she co-wrote *W.B. Yeats and his World* (1971). In 1968 she won a Macaulay fellowship for poetry. Her later work includes *The Journey* (1986), *Selected Poems* (1989) and *Outside History* (1990). Sharp observation of day-to-day life in modern Ireland and shafts of wry humour soften the edge of her intellectual style, making her one of the most popular Irish poets of the day.

BOLAND, Frederick Henry (1904–1988), public servant, b. Dublin, ed. Clongowes, TCD and King's Inns, m., one s. four d. Department of External Affairs 1929–36; principal officer Department of Industry and Commerce 1936–8; assistant secretary and then secretary Department of External Affairs 1938–50; ambassador to the United Kingdom 1950–56; permanent representative to the United Nations 1956–64. Boland played a major part in the formulation of post-war foreign policy at a time when Ireland was none too popular among the then dominant Western allies, who for long neither forgot nor forgave Irish wartime neutrality. At the UN he succeeded in establishing a delicate balance between providing broad Irish support for the anti-communist ethos of the time while ensuring that the country avoided any close association with power blocs or special interest groups. Throughout his career he showed a special talent for discreet diplomacy – in which he was sometimes frustrated by strong-willed Ministers for External Affairs like SEÁN MACBRIDE and FRANK AIKEN – but ironically the most dramatic impact he made in international relations was when, as president of the UN General Assembly (1960–61), he broke his gavel in a determined effort to call the flamboyant Soviet

leader, Nikita Khrushchev, to order. Following his retirement in 1964, he became Chancellor of DU and a director of a number of companies, including Investment Bank of Ireland, Arthur Guinness, Son & Co., Irish Distillers Group Ltd and IBM. He received honorary degrees from NUI (LL D) and San Francisco (D.Litt.), was a KSG and holder of the Swedish Grand Cross of the Northern Star. His wife was the artist Frances Kelly, and the poet EAVAN BOLAND is one of their daughters.

BOLAND, Gerald (1885–1973), politician, b. Manchester, ed. O'Brien Institute, Fairview, Dublin. Railway worker. Irish Volunteer, served under THOMAS MACDONAGH in Jacob's factory during the Easter Rising. Founder member Fianna Fáil 1926. TD (Anti-Treaty, later FF, Roscommon) 1923–61. Parliamentary secretary to President of Executive Council and to Minister for Defence 1932–3. Minister for Posts and Telegraphs 1933–6, for Lands and Fisheries 1936–7 and for Lands 1937–9. Minister for Justice 1939–48, as which he had to implement the stringent terms of the Offences against the State Act. These involved the establishment of military tribunals, special criminal courts and internment, and led to hunger strikes and executions, but assured the security of the state during the critical years of World War II. Boland was a senator 1961–9. His brother was HARRY BOLAND and his son was KEVIN BOLAND.

BOLAND, Harry (1887–1922), republican, b. Dublin, ed. Synge Street and De La Salle College, Castletown, Co. Laois. He was one of the central figures in the reorganisation of the Irish Volunteers after the release of those who took part in the Easter Rising, and was elected secretary of Sinn Féin in 1917. A close friend of MICHAEL COLLINS, he combined his underground IRB work with political activity and was TD for South Roscommon in the First Dáil. In 1919 he went to the USA as a representative of the Dáil, but failed in his efforts to heal the rift among American supporters of the Irish cause. He took the anti-Treaty side during the Civil War and was killed in July 1922. Brother of GERALD BOLAND.

BOLAND, John Mary Pius (1870–1958), tennis player, b. Dublin, 16 Sept. 1870, d. London, 17 Mar. 1958. A member of the prominent Dublin milling family, he was the father of the playwright Bridget Boland, and was the first Irishman to win an Olympic gold medal. As a student at Christ Church, Oxford he was a spectator at the first modern Olympic Games, in Athens in 1896, when a friend entered him in the tennis men's singles, in which there were only four contestants. On 30 Mar. 1896 he defeated the Greek Demis Kasdaglis to win the medal. Partnered by a German, Fritz Traun, he went on to win the doubles title also, insisting that an Irish flag replace the Union Jack at the subsequent presentation ceremony. In later life he was a barrister, writer and from 1900 to 1918 a Nationalist MP for South Kerry.

BOLAND, Kevin (1917–), politician, b. Dublin, s. of GERALD BOLAND. TD (FF Dublin South) 1957–70. Minister for Defence 1957–61, for Social Welfare 1961–6, for Local Government 1966–70. Resigned from government May 1970 in sympathy with dismissed ministers NEIL BLANEY and CHARLES HAUGHEY. Later that year he was expelled from the Fianna Fáil parliamentary party and resigned his party membership rather than support the government in a confidence debate. Founded his own party, Aontacht Éireann, which failed to win electoral support. Unsuccessfully challenged in the Supreme Court the constitutionality of the 1973 Sunningdale Agreement on Northern Ireland.

BOLGER, Dermot (1959–), novelist and publisher, b. Dublin, ed. Beneavin College, Dublin. A bright and gifted youngster with a fondness for literature, he co-founded Raven Arts Press at age 18, of which he became director, and later New Island Books. Bolger is a fecund talent, whose first novels, *Night Shift* (1985) and *The Woman's Daughter* (1987), with their far from flattering portrayal of contemporary urban Ireland, hit hard. Three more followed: *The Journey Home* (1990), *Emily's Shoes* (1992) and *A Second Life* (1994), earning him international acclaim and commercial success. He is also an accomplished poet, with six collections to date – *Never a Dull Moment* (1978), *The Habit of Flesh* (1980), *Finglas Lilies* (1981), *No Waiting America* (1982), *A New Primer for Irish Schools*, with Michael O'Loughlin (1985), *Internal Exiles* (1986) – and has written two plays: *A Dublin Quartet* (1992) and the Joycean *A Dublin Bloom* (1995).

His numerous editorial successes include poetry and fiction anthologies.

BOLGER, James (Jim) (1941–), horse trainer, flat and national hunt, b. Wexford, 25 Dec. 1941. He saddled his first winner in 1976, and from 1977 has been consistently in the top six of winners from Irish stables. His 100th winner for the year came in Sept. 1990, when he became the third Irish trainer to achieve this. He later set a new Irish flat season record with 134 winners. Other successes include winning the Epsom Oaks (Jet Sky Lady), the Italian 1,000 Guineas (Treasure Hope) and the Oaks (Ivyanna), and by June 1992 he had saddled his 1,000th winner. In that year his St Jovite was second in the Epsom Derby and won the Irish Derby, while in 1993 Blue Judge also finished second at Epsom. In terms of winnings he was top Irish trainer in 1990, 1991 and 1992, and also trained the most winners in the same period, with 119. Among his other winners have been Give Thanks (Irish Oaks 1983), Flame of Tara (Coronation Stakes), Polonia (Prix de l'Abbaye), Park Appeal and Park Express.

BONAPARTE-WYSE, Andrew Nicholas (1870–1940), public servant, b. Limerick, ed. Downside and the University of London, d. 1 June 1940. A descendant of Lucien Bonaparte (brother of Napoleon I) and of Thomas Wyse, 19th-century advocate of mixed education. Bonaparte-Wyse became inspector of national schools in 1895 in Cork and later in Ballymena. In 1915 he was appointed secretary to the National Board of Education. After partition he chose to work in the Northern Ireland civil service and in 1927 he became permanent secretary at the Ministry of Education in NI, as which he was frequently denounced by the *Catholic Bulletin*. Awarded the CBE in 1925, CB in 1939, in which year he retired to Dublin as a result of ill health.

BONNER, Packie (1960–), international footballer, b. Burtonport, Co. Donegal, 25 May 1960. He played Gaelic football for the county at all levels, including the senior team at age 18. Having left Keadie Rovers, he moved to Glasgow Celtic in 1978, with which club he rose to prominence through a distinguished career, and was first capped for the Republic of Ireland against Poland in 1981, being previously capped at under-21 level. He was the

Republic's first-choice goalkeeper from 1987, and was outstanding in the 1988 European Championship. His save (from Daniel Timofte) in the penalty shoot-out with Romania during the 1990 World Cup finals in Italy made him a sporting folk hero, and he was one of the most popular and admired players during what has become known as the (JACK) CHARLTON era. He passed LIAM BRADY's record of 72 caps in 1994, and in Oct. the same year he was given the captaincy of the Republic to mark his 78th international appearance. With Celtic he won five Scottish Cup medals, four Championship medals and one League Cup.

BOOMTOWN RATS, The, rock band, Ireland's punk pioneers. Led by BOB GELDOF, featured Pete Briquette on bass and pyjama-wearing Johnny Fingers on keyboards. The Rats hit the UK top 20 in Sept. 1977 with the punk anthem 'Looking after No. 1', making them one of the first acts of the genre to reach the pop charts. After their initial success they developed a more melodic musical style which, combined with Geldof's acerbic and witty songwriting and his natural storytelling ability, made them one of the most popular rock bands in the UK during this period. 'Rat Trap' (1978) and 'I Don't Like Mondays' (1980) both made number one in the singles charts, and they also released three highly successful albums. Subsequent Rats records stalled in the lower reaches of the charts.

BOUCHER, James Chrysostom (Jimmy) (1910–1995), international cricketer, b. Dublin, 22 Dec. 1910, ed. Belvedere, d. Spain, 25 Dec. 1995. Among the finest bowlers produced in this country – off-break – his long-standing record of 307 wickets in a total of 60 matches for Ireland between 1929 and 1954 was surpassed only by DERMOT MONTEITH. Played scrum-half for Old Belvedere and cricket for Phoenix. An off-break bowler of real quality, he headed the British first-class averages in 1937 and 1948 (the then Gentlemen of Ireland enjoyed first-class status at the time). Among his many exceptional performances were his six for 30 against India in 1936 and seven for 13 against New Zealand in 1937. He was honorary secretary of the Irish Cricket Union 1954–73.

BOURKE, Angela (1952–), writer and scholar, b. Dublin, ed. UCD (MA and Ph.D.

in Celtic studies) and Université de Bretagne Occidentale, Brest, France. She won several distinguished prizes and scholarships, including an NUI three-year travelling studentship in 1974, and has been published widely in learned journals and literary magazines in both English and Irish. Has held academic posts in North America and in Italy. Her short stories have appeared in English and Irish and she has made an extensive study of the social structure of rural Ireland during the past 200 years, as reflected in songs, stories, proverbs and riddles. She works in UCD and is a panel editor for vol. 4 of the *Field Day Anthology of Irish Writing*. Publications include: *Caoineadh na dTrí Muire: Téama na Páise i bhFilíocht Bhéil na Gaeilge* (1983), *Iníon Rí na Cathrach Deirge* (1989), *Iníon Rí an Oileáin Dhorcha* (1991), *Caoineadh na Marbh: Síceoilfhilíocht* (1992), and a collection of short stories, *By Salt Water* (1996).

BOURKE, Brian (1936–), artist, b. Dublin, ed. National College of Art, Dublin and St Martin's School of Art, London. After living abroad for a number of years he moved to Galway in the mid-1970s and continues to live and work there. Much of his early work from this period comprises expressionist studies of the Connemara landscape, noted for their rugged, lyrical qualities. He later concentrated on figurative painting and produced a series of portraits, including a number of humorous self-portraits. Bourke is a member of Aosdána and was chosen to represent Ireland in the Biennale de Paris of 1965 and in Rosc '88. A major retrospective exhibition of his work was held in Galway in 1988 and at the Royal Hospital, Kilmainham in Dublin 1989. He has also exhibited in Germany and Switzerland.

BOWEN, Elizabeth (1899–1973), novelist, b. Dublin, ed. Downes House School, Kent, TCD and Oxford, d. London, 22 Feb. 1973. Grew up partly in Dublin and partly in Bowen's Court, the family home near Mitchelstown, Co. Cork, which she inherited in 1930. Her adult years were spent between Ireland, England and the USA. During World War II she provided reports on Irish attitudes to the Ministry of Information in London. While her prodigious output reflected the lifestyles, mentalities and atmospheres of the various places and countries she knew, she retained a deep affection for Ireland as she perceived it from the 'Big House' of an Ascendancy family: she can be ranked among the last of the outstanding writers in the Anglo-Irish literary tradition. Her books include *The Last September* (1929), *The Death of the Heart* (1938), *Bowen's Court* and *Seven Winters: Memories of a Dublin Childhood* (1943) and *A World of Love* (1955). Her history of Dublin's Shelbourne Hotel was published in 1951.

BOWMAN, John (1942–), historian and broadcaster, b. Dublin, ed. Belvedere, UCD and TCD (Ph.D.). Joined Telefís Éireann (later RTÉ) 1962. Presenter and commentator on numerous current affairs programmes, on both radio and television; analyst of political developments and interviewer of politicians. Has chaired for a number of years the audience-participation political programme *Questions and Answers* on RTÉ television, and presented *Bowman's Saturday* on radio, a compilation of material from broadcasting archives at home and abroad. Author of *De Valera and the Ulster Question 1917–1973* (1982). President of the Irish Association for Cultural, Economic and Social Relations 1993.

BOWYER, Brendan (1938–), singer, b. Waterford, 12 Oct. 1938. He began his career with the Royal Showband in 1957. His ability to tailor American rock 'n' roll music to the tastes of Irish audiences, and his athletic and spirited on-stage performances, made him by far the most popular vocalist of the showband era of the 1960s. The Royal had several number one hits in Ireland, including 'Kiss Me Quick', 'No More' and the enormously successful 'The Hucklebuck'. In 1971 Bowyer left the Royal and joined the Las Vegas circuit with his new band, the Big 8. He has been based in Las Vegas since then. In 1977 he made a brief return to the Irish charts with his tribute 'Thank You, Elvis'.

BOYD, John (1912–), playwright, b. Belfast, ed. Royal Academical Institution, QUB and TCD. Boyd spent most of his career working as a producer with BBC Northern Ireland, during which time he also wrote several radio plays. He turned to the theatre relatively late in life – his first play to receive a stage performance was *The Blood of Colonel Lamb* (1967), originally written for radio but turned down as 'too controversial'. After his retirement, he took up writing full-time. *The Assassin* was produced at the Dublin Theatre Festival in 1969. *The Flats* (1971), *The Farm* (1972) and *The Street* (1977) were all produced at the Lyric Theatre, Belfast.

BOYDELL, Brian (1917–), composer and conductor, b. Dublin, ed. Dublin, London, Cambridge and Heidelberg. Awarded the Mus.D. degree of TCD in 1959, was Professor of Music there 1962–82 and subsequently became a fellow emeritus. Founder member of the Music Association of Ireland. Founder and director of the Dowland Consort. Conductor for over 20 years of the Dublin Orchestral Players. Member of the Arts Council and of Aosdána. Awards include honorary doctorate in music from the NUI; Commendatore of the Italian Republic; fellow of the RIAM. His compositions, which cover a wide range of orchestral, chamber, choral, vocal and instrumental music, include *In Memoriam Mahatma Gandhi* (1948) and *Megalithic Ritual Dances* (1956), for orchestra; *A Terrible Beauty is Born*, for soloists, choir and orchestra (1965); and three string quartets. Commercial recordings include *String Quartet No. 1* and *Symphonic Inscapes*.

BOYLAN, Clare (1948–), writer, b. Dublin, ed. St Louis High School, Rathmines, Dublin. Upon leaving school she worked as a sales assistant in Eason's, Dublin, before joining the *Irish Press* as a reporter in 1966. Between 1967 and 1984 she edited a succession of papers and magazines, including *Image*, and won a Benson & Hedges journalism award 1974. Her short stories have been published at home and abroad; one was filmed as *Making Waves*, nominated for an Oscar in 1988. Yet Boylan is primarily a novelist, with a wryness and elegance of style that is highly individual. Her novels are: *Holy Pictures* and *A Nail in the Head* (1983), *Last Resorts* (1984), *Black Baby* (1988) and *Home Rule* (1993). Short stories: *Concerning Virgins* (1990), *That Bad Woman* (1995). Other: *The Agony and the Ego: The Art and Strategy of Fiction* (1993) and *The Literary Companion to Cats: An Anthology of Prose and Poetry* (1994).

BOYLE, Dermot (1904–), air marshal RAF, b. 2 Oct. 1904, s. of A.F. Boyle, Belmont House, King's County (now Co. Laois), ed. St Columba's, RAF College and Cranwell. Commissioned into the RAF 1924. During

World War II served as air ADC to King George VI 1943 and as air commodore. He was promoted air vice-marshal in 1949 and air marshal in 1954. Chief of air staff 1956–9.

BOYLE, Leonard Eugene (1923–), Dominican friar, palaeographer and librarian, b. Donegal, 13 Nov. 1923. Entered Dominican order 1943, ordained priest 1949. D.Phil. (Oxford) 1956. Professor of History of Theology, University of St Thomas, Rome, 1956–61; Professor of Palaeography and Diplomatics, Pontifical Institute of Medieval Studies, Toronto, 1961–84. General editor *Calendar of Papal Registers relative to Great Britain and Ireland* (1970). Publications include *A Survey of the Vatican Archives* (1972) and *Medieval Latin Palaeography: A Bibliographical Introduction* (1984). Appointed prefect of the Vatican Library 1984.

BOYLE, Patrick (1905–1982), short story writer and novelist, b. Ballymoney, Co. Antrim, ed. Coleraine Academical Institution. Worked for 20 years at a Donegal branch of the Ulster Bank, later relocating to the bank's Wexford office, to retire as manager 25 years later. Started writing fiction at the age of 58, and took first, second, fourth and fifth prizes in a short story competition organised by *The Irish Times* in 1965. His winning entries were included in his first volume of stories, *At Night All Cats are Grey* (1966). This proved enormously popular and was followed by *All Looks Yellow to the Jaundiced Eye* (1969) and *A View from Calvary* (1976). Boyle's particular genius lies in his ability to delineate, with honesty and compassion, life in small-town Ireland, as seen through the eyes of the middle-aged bachelor. He wrote one novel, *Like Any Other Man* (1966), and his selected stories were gathered as *The Port Stain* (1983). MIAL.

BOYZONE, pop group: Keith Duffy, Steven Gately, Michael Graham, Ronan Keating and Shane Lynch. The band was formed in Nov. 1993 by Louis Walsh, an enterprising music promoter. A carefully planned marketing strategy, aimed specifically at pre-teen and teenage girls, has helped to make Boyzone the most popular music group among such young people in the UK and Ireland following the demise of their rivals Take That. In 1994 they were voted Best New Act by the teen magazine *Smash Hits*. They have had hits with cover versions of two 1970s songs, 'Working my Way Back to You' and 'Love me for a Reason', and their own song, 'Key to my Life', which made number one in the UK charts in 1995.

BRACKEN, Brendan Rendall, Viscount Bracken (1901–1958), politician and publisher, b. Templemore, Co. Tipperary, 15 Feb. 1901; ed. Mungret College, Co. Limerick and, after a spell in Australia, Sedbergh School, England; d. London, 8 Aug. 1958. Became close associate of Winston Churchill following introduction from J.L. Garvin, editor of the *Observer*. MP (Conservative North Paddington) 1929. Parliamentary private secretary to Churchill, and later Minister of Information, during World War II. Before the war he had enjoyed a successful career in publishing, founding the *Banker* and acquiring the *Financial News*, the *Investors Chronicle* and the *Practitioner* for his company, Eyre & Spottiswoode. After the war he became chairman of the *Financial Times* and founded *History Today*.

BRADFORD, Roy Hamilton (1921–), politician and writer, b. Belfast, 7 July 1921, ed. Royal Academical Institution and TCD. Bradford served in army intelligence 1943–7. A company director, he has also been a producer and writer for television since 1950. Unionist MP for the Belfast ward of Victoria at Stormont 1965–72, during which time he held the posts of assistant whip (1966), parliamentary secretary to the Northern Ireland Minister of Education (1967), chief whip (1968–9), Minister of Commerce (1969–71) and Minister of Development (1971–2). He was criticised by some members of the NI Executive for publicly expressing reservations about the Sunningdale deal while head of the Department of the Environment in the Executive in 1974. His offer of resignation was rejected by BRIAN FAULKNER. Bradford was the only Unionist member of the Executive to stand in the Feb. 1974 general election, when he was unsuccessful in North Down; he was again unsuccessful in the 1975 Convention election. Elected to North Down Borough Council in 1989 as an Ulster Unionist; mayor North Down 1995. His novels include *The Last Ditch* and (with Martin Dillon) *Rogue Warrior of the SAS*, a biography of BLAIR MAYNE.

BRADLEY, Daniel Joseph (1928–), Ph.D., FIEEE, F.Inst.P., MRIA, RFS, physicist, b. 18 Jan. 1928, ed. St Columb's College, Derry, St Mary's Training College, Belfast, Birkbeck and Royal Holloway Colleges, London, m. Winefriede M.T. O'Connor 1958, four s. one d. Primary school teacher Derry 1947–53; secondary school teacher London area 1953–7; assistant lecturer Royal Holloway College, London 1957–60; lecturer Imperial College, London 1960–64; reader Royal Holloway 1964–6. Professor and head of department QUB 1966–73; Professor of Optics Imperial College 1973–80. Emeritus professor University of London since 1980. Professor of Optical Electronics TCD 1980. Royal medal Royal Society 1983. Young medal Institute of Physics 1975. Many committees, visiting professorships and consultancies. Principal research interest: high-power fast lasers.

BRADSHAW, Harry ('The Brad') (1913–1990), professional golfer, b. Delgany, Co. Wicklow, 9 Oct. 1913, d. 22 Dec. 1990. He became a professional in 1934, was club professional at Kilcroney and at Portmarnock, where he was a legend for some 40 years. He won the Irish professional title ten times between 1941 and 1957. His achievements included winning two Irish Opens (1947, 1949), the Irish Dunlop (1950), two British Dunlop Masters (1953, 1955), the PGA Close and the Penfold Swallow, the last a tie (1958). He lost the 1949 British Open to Bobby Locke in a play-off, after his drive had lodged in a broken bottle in the second round at Sandwich. He played in the Ryder Cup in 1953, 1955 and on the winning side at Lindrick in 1957. He was on Ireland's first six Canada (World) Cup teams 1954–9, including the win with CHRISTY O'CONNOR in Mexico in 1958, when he lost the individual title only in a play-off. His 13 Moran Cup wins between 1940 and 1959 is a record.

BRADSHAW, Harry (1947–), broadcaster, b. Bray, Co. Wicklow. In the course of a long career with RTÉ radio he has worked as producer, collector and engineer on numerous series related to traditional music and folklore. He has employed his technical skills to remaster old recordings originally made on acetate discs, cylinders and 78s for subsequent reissue on his own Viva Voce label or through other agencies. He thus played an important role in making readily available the music of instrumentalists such as MICHAEL COLEMAN, JOHN MCKENNA, JOHNNY DORAN and MICKEY DOHERTY, a crucial element in the preservation of the historical tradition. In 1992 he won the folk music award of the American Association for Recorded Sound Collections, and in 1993 his publication on Coleman was included on the selected list of 'American Folk Music and Folklore Recordings' compiled by the American Folklife Centre at the Library of Congress.

BRADY, Charles (1926–), artist, b. New York, ed. Art Students' League, New York. After participating in a number of group shows he had his first solo exhibition in the Urban Gallery, New York in 1955. He travelled to Ireland soon afterwards and, after returning briefly to live in the USA, moved to Ireland permanently in 1960. He participated in a number of group shows over the next few years, including the Irish Exhibition of Living Art. He was awarded the DOUGLAS HYDE gold medal in the 1974 Oireachtas and the landscape award in 1979. Much of his later work comprises small-scale studies of everyday household objects, which, despite the familiarity of the subject and the simplicity of the composition, examine tone and colour with the same intensity revealed in his landscape paintings.

BRADY, Conor (1949–), journalist, b. Tullamore, Co. Offaly, ed. Cistercian College, Roscrea and UCD. Joined The Irish Times in 1969, leaving in 1974 to edit the Garda Review. Radio journalist with RTÉ 1975–6, features editor of The Irish Times 1977–9. Guardians of the Peace, a general history of the Garda Síochána, was published in 1974. He was founder editor of the Sunday Tribune 1981–2 before returning again to The Irish Times as deputy editor in 1985. In the following year he became editor of the paper.

BRADY, Liam ('Chippy') (1956–), international footballer, b. Dublin, 13 Feb. 1956. One of the Republic's greatest players, he was unlucky not to participate in any international competition finals, including the World Cup. He joined Arsenal in 1973 and played in three successive FA Cup finals, but was on the winning side only once, in 1979; he was also in the Arsenal team defeated (on penalties) by

Valencia in the 1980 European Cup Winners' Cup final. He won a record 72 international caps between 1974 and 1990, scoring nine goals, and also scored 43 goals in his 225 matches for Arsenal. He went to Italy in 1980, spending seven years there with Juventus – helping the club to win two League Championships – Sampdoria, Internazionale Milan and Ascoli, before returning to England to play with West Ham. He managed Glasgow Celtic for two years, resigning in 1993, and in Dec. of that year took over as manager of Brighton.

BRADY, Paul (1947–), musician and songwriter, b. Strabane, Co. Tyrone, ed. Sion Hill Primary, St Columb's College, Derry and UCD. He was part of the beat group scene in the 1960s, playing with the Inmates and the Kult, before forming his own band, Rockhouse. He surprised everyone in 1967 by joining the folk group the Johnsons – but with great success. He went on to play with Planxty, as well as collaborating with several pillars of the traditional music establishment. During this period he recorded the enormously successful solo album *Welcome Here Kind Stranger* (1978). The release of *Hard Station* in 1981 marked his return to rock; he toured with Dire Straits and Eric Clapton, and went on to become a highly respected international performer. His songs have been recorded by top artists such as Roger Chapman and Tina Turner and he is much in demand for film scores.

BRANAGH, Kenneth (1960–), actor and director, b. Belfast, 10 Dec. 1960, ed. Meadway Comprehensive School, Reading and RADA. He has been one of the best-known young actors in Britain for several years, and has also enjoyed a highly successful career as a dramatist and a director of plays and films. He took the leading role in several major productions with the Royal Shakespeare Company and with the Renaissance Theatre Company, which he formed in 1987. He also directed *Romeo and Juliet*, *King Lear* and *Coriolanus*. He has both acted in and directed several films, including *Henry V* (1987), *Dead Again* (1991), *Peter's Friends* (1992), *Much Ado about Nothing* (1993) and *Othello* (1995).

BRANDT, Muriel (1909–1981), artist, b. Belfast, ed. Royal College of Art, London, d. Dublin, 10 June 1981. After completing her studies, she moved to Dublin. Although the subject matter of her paintings was very diverse, she made her name as a formal portrait artist. Her first major commission was to paint a series of decorative murals in the Franciscan church of Adam and Eve on Merchants Quay. She painted the group portrait of directors of the Gate Theatre, including Micheál MacLiammóir and Hilton Edwards, which hangs in the foyer of the theatre. She also completed portraits of Sir Alfred Chester Beatty, George O'Brien and other famous personalities of the day. She was a member of the board of governors of the National Gallery and the RHA. Mother of Ruth Brandt.

BRANDT, Ruth (1936–1989), artist, b. Dublin, d. of Muriel Brandt, ed. National College of Art, Dublin, d. Dublin, Aug. 1989. After graduation she worked for a number of years as an illustrator and also took part in several group exhibitions, including the Irish Exhibition of Living Art and the RHA. In 1976 the Graphic Studio in Dublin held a retrospective exhibition of her work. She also undertook a number of architectural lettering commissions, which included work on the new Meteorological Offices in Glasnevin and stained-glass windows at Artane Oratory, in Dublin. In 1973 she began to concentrate on print work and had solo exhibitions in the Setanta Gallery in 1978 and the Lincoln Gallery in 1982. She became a full-time lecturer in the NCAD in 1976 but retired in 1988 due to ill health.

BRASE, Wilhelm *Fritz* (1875–1940), founder and first director of the Irish Army School of Music, b. Egestorf in the Deister, near Hanover, Germany, 4 May 1875, d. 2 Dec. 1940. His formal musical training commenced at the age of four with the study of piano, and he later attended the reputable Hochschule in Leipzig. In 1893 Brase enlisted in the Imperial German Army and in 1911 he was appointed conductor of the Kaiser Alexander Garde Grenadier Regiment 1 in Berlin, one of the most eagerly sought-after positions in German military music. His progress was interrupted by World War I, and the subsequent massive retrenchment in German forces led to his resignation from the army 1919. Accepted invitation from General Richard Mulcahy to move to Ireland and establish a music corps within the defence establishment. Among its objectives were the formation of bands of quality and the fostering of wind-playing in the country. Commissioned with the rank of colonel, Brase set up four military bands in the period 1923–8. He personally conducted the Army No. 1 Band and early recordings attest to the remarkably high standard achieved in a short time. He continued as an energetic director, arranger and composer until ill health forced his resignation in 1940. He is buried in Mount Jerome Cemetery.

BREATHNACH, Breandán (1912–1985), collector, uilleann piper and author, b. Hamilton Street, Dublin, s. of Padraic Breathnach, the last Dublin silk weaver, ed. Convent of Mercy, Weaver Square and Synge Street. He joined the civil service. Transferred from the Department of Agriculture to that of Education (of which his daughter NIAMH BHREATHNACH was to become minister in 1993), he was charged with amassing a collection of Irish folk music, a task later assumed by the Department of Irish Folklore at UCD.

An accomplished musician, he founded Na Píobairí Uilleann in 1968. His published work includes *Folk Music and Dances of Ireland*, co-editing the *Folk Music Journal*, the historical and analytical treatise *Dancing in Ireland* and the three-volume collection *Ceol Rince na hÉireann – The Dance Music of Ireland*. He also edited *An Píobaire* and contributed to *The New Grove Dictionary of Music and Musicians*.

In 1970 he founded the Folk Music Society of Ireland (Cumann Cheol Tíre Éireann) along with Dr Hugh Shields, TOM MUNNELLY and SEOIRSE BODLEY. On retirement he was engaged to lecture on traditional music at TCD and elected chairman of the Arts Council National Archive Advisory Council.

BREATHNACH, Páraic (1956–), arts administrator, b. Castlebar, ed. Coláiste Eanna, Galway and UCG. He is best known for his role as general manager/artistic director of Galway's MACNAS theatre group. Before helping to set up MACNAS he worked for a number of years as production manager for the Druid Theatre Company and the Galway Arts Festival. In his work for the festival he was instrumental in bringing to Galway a number of foreign groups, in particular Els Comediants from Spain, which were to have a major influence on the development of

MACNAS's brand of carefully choreographed but exuberant and highly colourful street theatre. He also established a number of subsidiary companies to control MACNAS's myriad activities and its commissioned work, including U2's 'Zooropa' tour in 1992 and the ICTU centenary celebrations in Dublin in 1994. Breathnach left MACNAS in 1995 to pursue a freelance career. He was appointed to the Arts Council in 1994.

BREEN, Dan (1894–1969), revolutionary, b. Soloheadbeg, Co. Tipperary, son of a small farmer, d. Dublin, 27 Dec. 1969. He led the attack on a party of RIC men at Soloheadbeg in Jan. 1919; this ambush, in which two policemen were killed, marked the beginning of the War of Independence. He was a formidable guerrilla commander and his exploits, both in Dublin and in Munster, are graphically described in his book *My Fight for Irish Freedom* (1924). Having voted against the Treaty, he was elected TD for Tipperary in 1923. He was the first opponent of the Treaty to take his seat in the Dáil (Jan. 1927). Went to the USA for some years and following his return served as TD (FF South Tipperary) 1932–65.

BREEN, John Joseph (1896–1964), air marshal RAF, b. Co. Cork, 8 Mar. 1896, s. of T.J. Breen, inspector-general of hospitals and fleets, ed. Beaumont College, Windsor and Sandhurst, d. Co. Wicklow, 8 Nov. 1964. Commissioned into the Royal Irish Regiment 1915. Seconded into the Royal Flying Corps in 1915 and transferred to the RAF in 1918. After a series of squadron commands during the inter-war period, appointed air officer commanding, No. 1 Bomber Group, 1940; director-general of the Air Ministry 1941–5.

BRENNAN, Garrett (1894–1974), deputy commissioner Garda Síochána, b. Castlecomer, Co. Kilkenny, d. 18 Feb. 1974. Wireless operator mercantile marine; brigade quartermaster Irish Volunteers; National Army. Superintendent Garda Síochána 1922. As chief superintendent Crime Branch, organised the new Garda Technical Bureau initiated in 1934 by Deputy Commissioner W.R.E. MURPHY. Under Brennan's direction forensic science was introduced in crime investigation in Ireland, later advanced by a close-knit team under Supt. George Lawlor (1897–1961) and Supt. Daniel John Stapleton (1886–1968), former commandant Army Ordnance Corps. Brennan was chairman of the Joint Representative Body; president Garda branch and national president St Joseph's Young Priests Society.

BRENNAN, Joseph (1887–1963), public servant, b. Bandon, Co. Cork, ed. Clongowes, UCD and Christ's College, Cambridge, of which he became a scholar and where he obtained firsts in Latin and Greek, m., one s. two d. Entered the first division of the civil service in 1911, being assigned to the Board of Customs and Excise. Transferred in 1912 to Chief Secretary's Office, Dublin Castle (the finance division). There he became familiar with all aspects of British rule in Ireland, being at different times private secretary to the under-secretary and the deputy secretary of the Privy Council. Had a part in the formulation of the financial clauses of the Government of Ireland Act 1920. During the truce with Britain he was introduced to MICHAEL COLLINS and later became adviser on financial matters to the team negotiating the Anglo-Irish Treaty. In Feb. 1922 he was invited by Collins to organise a financial system for the new state. He became the Irish Free State's first Comptroller and Auditor-General in Apr. of that year and in Apr. 1923 became secretary of the Department of Finance. There, with the concurrence of ministers, he laid down strict procedures to govern financial orthodoxy. Gradually, however, differences of opinion arose between Brennan and the ministers (and in particular his own minister, ERNEST BLYTHE) over departures from these procedures.

In 1927 he retired from the civil service and in Sept. of that year was appointed chairman of the Currency Commission, established to deal with banking and note issues. He was a member of the Irish delegation to the Imperial Economic Conference in Ottawa in 1932. Chairman of the Commission of Inquiry into the Civil Service 1932–5. In 1934 he became chairman of the Commission of Inquiry into Banking, Currency and Credit, which sat until 1938.

In 1942, on the dissolution of the Currency Commission, he became first governor of the Central Bank, to which were transferred the Commission's powers and duties, with additional authority. He resigned in 1953. Hon. LL D (NUI) 1938.

BRENNAN, Robert (1881–1964), revolutionary, author and diplomat, b. Wexford, d. Dublin, 12 Nov. 1964. Commanded 600 Volunteers in Wexford during the Easter Rising, received a death sentence, later commuted to penal servitude for life. His bureaucratic and diplomatic talents were drawn on by the government of the First Dáil, and he was responsible for establishing the Department of External Affairs. He opposed the Treaty and later became one of the first directors of the *Irish Press*. He resumed his diplomatic career in the late 1930s and undertook the delicate post of Minister to Washington during World War II. On his return to Ireland he devoted himself to broadcasting and writing.

BRENON, Alexander Herbert Reginald St John (1880–1958), film director, b. Kingstown (Dún Laoghaire), Co. Dublin, 13 Jan. 1880, ed. London, d. Los Angeles, 21 June 1958. He emigrated to the USA while only 16 and eventually found his way to Hollywood in the infancy of the movie business. Directed his first movie in 1910 and over the next 30 years made some 300 more, continuing to work long after the end of the silent era. Among his better-known films were *Neptune's Daughter* (1914), *Passion Flower* (1917) and the first ever version of *Beau Geste* (1926), starring Ronald Colman.

BRETT, Sir Charles Edward Bainbridge (1928–), architectural historian, b. 30 Oct. 1928, ed. Rugby and New College, Oxford. Sir Charles Brett was a journalist in the late 1940s before qualifying as a solicitor in 1953. A former chairman of the Northern Ireland Labour Party, he has also served on the Arts Council of NI 1970–76 and since 1994. Member of the NI committee of the National Trust 1956–83 and 1985–93. Chairman of the NI Housing Executive 1979–84. Brett served on the International Fund for Ireland 1986–9 and has been president of the Ulster Architectural Heritage Society since 1979. He was awarded a CBE in 1981 and knighted in 1990. His numerous publications on housing and planning include *Buildings of Belfast 1700–1914* (1967) and *Housing a Divided Society* (1986).

BRISCOE, Robert (1894–1969), politician, b. Dublin. Joined Fianna Éireann, sent on missions to Germany and the USA by

MICHAEL COLLINS, opposed Treaty, founder member of Fianna Fáil. TD (FF Dublin City South) 1927–65. Lord Mayor of Dublin 1956 and 1961. Prominent member of Irish Jewish community, led delegation of World Zionist Organisation in search of international support for settlement of Jews in Palestine 1939.

BROOKE, Basil (1888–1973), politician, b. Colebrook, Co. Fermanagh, 9 June 1888, a member of a family which had held land in Ulster since the plantation; ed. École St George in Pau, where his grandparents lived, Winchester and, following the family's military tradition, Sandhurst; d. 18 Aug. 1973. He served in India from 1908. Returning home on leave in 1912 he signed the Ulster Covenant, met EDWARD CARSON and helped train the UVF. During World War I he fought in the trenches and was awarded the Military Cross and the Croix de Guerre before joining the general staff as interpreter between General Byng and Marshal Foch.

After the war he went back to farming in Fermanagh, where he also became county commandant of the Special Constabulary and was active in the Orange Order. When he turned to politics, election from safe unionist constituencies was assured. He was a member of Fermanagh County Council from 1924 and of Stormont from 1929. He became a protégé of JAMES CRAIG, who soon made him Minister of Agriculture. The outbreak of World War II came as a shock to an elderly cabinet but Brooke, in charge of production, showed some adaptability. After the death in office of Craig and the ousting of JOHN ANDREWS, Brooke became Prime Minister in 1943.

For the 20 years that he presided over Northern Ireland Brooke depended upon his own charm and the luck of events. The war and its aftermath brought a measure of prosperity and as a result the Catholic minority became more resigned to its lot and rejected the IRA campaign of 1956. Brooke had difficulty getting his own supporters to accept postwar socialistic health and education legislation, and unionists were so upset by the declaration of the Republic of Ireland in 1949 that Brooke was forced to get the British government to reaffirm Northern Ireland's position within the UK to set their minds at rest.

Lord Brookeborough – he was ennobled in 1952 – presided over Northern Ireland during a peaceful period in its history. Later observers felt that if he had tried to understand and reconcile the minority, the North might have been saved from the troubles that followed. He resigned from office in 1963 and from parliament in 1967. He was married to Cynthia Mary Surgison. Two of their children were killed in World War II.

BROSNAN, Denis (1944–), managing director Kerry Group plc, b. Tralee, 19 Nov. 1944, ed. St Brendan's College, Killarney and UCC. He was appointed production manager of Golden Vale at the age of 23, shortly after completing his M.Sc. in dairy science. By joining the co-operative at a time when its major processing plant was just being built, Brosnan gained invaluable grounding in all aspects of the dairy industry. He later became principal founding partner of Kerry Co-operative. His experience and managerial skills have helped to develop Kerry into the largest food processing company in Ireland, employing over 3,000 people in Ireland and another 4,000 in Britain, the USA and Europe. He also has interests in the leisure and bloodstock industries.

BROSNAN, Paddy Bawn (1917–), Gaelic footballer, b. Dingle, 16 Nov. 1917. He played for the Dingle club and won six County Championship medals. He made his senior inter-county début with Kerry in 1936 and won three All-Ireland senior football medals – in 1940 (when he came on as a substitute in the final), 1941 and 1946. He was also on three losing Kerry teams, in the finals of 1938, 1944 – when he was the captain – and in the New York Polo Grounds match of 1947, when Cavan won. By his retirement in 1952 he had won 12 Munster SFC medals and three Railway Cup medals.

BROSNAN, Pierce (1952–), film actor, b. Co. Meath. His first major film role was opposite Bob Hoskins in the London gangster thriller *The Long Good Friday* (1980). In 1987 he was offered the leading role in a new James Bond film but was forced to turn it down when the producers of the American television series *Remington Steele*, in which he had starred since 1982, refused to release him from his contract. He continued to do some film work, including *Lawnmower Man* (1992) and *Live Wire* (1992). He finally got the chance to play Bond in 1995, when he took the lead role in *Goldeneye*.

BROWN, Christy (1932–1981), poet and novelist, b. Crumlin, Dublin, one of 13 children of a bricklayer, died at his home in Parbrook, Somerset, 6 Sept. 1981. Paralysed from birth by cerebral palsy. Taught to read by his mother and to co-ordinate movements and speech by Dr ROBERT COLLIS. Wrote and typed using the toes of his left foot, whence the title of his account of his childhood, *My Left Foot* (1954), a poignant evocation of Dublin working-class life and later the subject of an Oscar-winning film by JIM SHERIDAN. His autobiographical novel, *Down All the Days*, was translated into 14 languages. Other publications include several volumes of poetry, among them *Come Softly to my Wake* (1971) and *Inmates* (1981).

BROWNE, Anthony (1940–1960), MMG, soldier, b. Dublin. Joined the defence forces 1957. Member of 2nd Motor Squadron in Cathal Brugha Barracks. Served with the UN in the Congo (now Zaïre) 1960 as a member of 33rd Battalion. He was killed in an ambush along with eight other Irish soldiers; two managed to escape. First recipient of the Military Medal for Gallantry, the highest military honour in the defence forces. The citation reads: 'In recognition of his exceptional bravery involving risk to life and limb at Niemba, Republic of the Congo, on the 8th of November, 1960, in that he endeavoured to create an opportunity to allow an injured comrade to escape by firing his Gustav, thereby drawing attention to his own position which he must have been aware would endanger his own life. He had a reasonable opportunity of escaping because he was not wounded but chose to remain with an injured comrade.'

BROWNE, Deborah (1927–), artist, ed. Belfast College of Art 1946, National College of Art, Dublin 1947–50, Paris 1966–9. Began as a painter, moved to fibreglass in 1965. Initially made fibreglass shapes mounted on a monochrome printed background; later produced full three-dimensional free-standing sculptures.

BROWNE, Francis (1880–1960), SJ, photographer, b. Co. Cork, 3 Jan. 1880, ed. CBS, Cork, Belvedere, Castleknock and UCD, d. Dublin, 7 July 1960. Ordained a Jesuit priest 1915. From an early age he displayed an interest in photography. In 1912 he sailed on the maiden voyage of the *Titanic* from Southampton to Queenstown (Cobh), taking the last photographs of the ship before her loss. During World War I he was an army chaplain, winning both the Military Cross and the Belgian Croix de Guerre. In the course of a long lifetime he became one of the most important documentary photographers in Ireland. By the time of his death his collection numbered over 42,000 negatives. Three books of his photographs were published posthumously.

BROWNE, Michael (1887–1971), Dominican friar and cardinal, b. Grangemockler, Co. Tipperary, 6 May 1887, ed. Rockwell, d. Rome, 31 Mar. 1971. Entered Dominican order 1903. Further studies Rome, Fribourg. Ordained priest 1910. Novice-master at St Mary's, Tallaght, Co. Dublin, 1914. Lecturer in philosophy at the Angelicum University, Rome from 1919. Rector Magnificus, Angelicum, 1932–41. Elected master-general of Dominican order 1955. Appointed cardinal and ordained bishop 1962. Much involved in the preparations for, and proceedings of, the Second Vatican Council, especially the drafting of the document *On Revelation*. Appointed by Pope Paul VI to the first Synod of Bishops 1967, to which he presented a report on doctrine. He was brother of PÁDRAIG DE BRÚN.

BROWNE, Michael J. (1896–1980), bishop, b. Westport, ed. St Jarlath's College, Tuam and Maynooth, d. Galway, 23 Feb. 1980. Professor of Theology in Maynooth 1921–37 before being appointed Bishop of Galway. Represented Irish bishops, along with Cardinal WILLIAM CONWAY, at World Synod of Bishops in Rome in 1967, 1969 and 1971. During his time in Galway he was responsible for the building of many schools and churches. He commissioned Galway's new cathedral, which was opened in 1966.

BROWNE, Noel (1915–), politician and medical doctor, b. Waterford, 20 Dec. 1915, ed. Marist College, Athlone, CBS, Ballinrobe, Co. Mayo, Beaumont College, Windsor and TCD. Browne was a campaigner in the 1940s for the eradication of the then widespread disease of tuberculosis, from which he himself suffered. Persuaded to join the new Clann na Poblachta party, he was elected to the Dáil in 1948 on its ticket. In the inter-party government formed after that election, he was appointed Minister for Health. He became embroiled with elements in the medical profession and prominent members of the Roman Catholic hierarchy over the so-called 'Mother and Child' scheme for free pre- and post-natal services. His cabinet colleagues recoiled from the repercussions and his party leader, SEÁN MACBRIDE, demanded his resignation. As a result he became an arch-critic of Catholic Church conservatism and a hero to the radical left, but potential allies were antagonised by his inability to work easily within party structures. He was re-elected to the Dáil in 1951 as an Independent and in 1954 as a Fianna Fáil TD. Rejected by that party three years later, he again stood successfully as an Independent. A year later he co-founded the National Progressive Democrats and was elected to the Dáil for them. He joined the Labour Party in 1963, an idol to some, an ill-disciplined maverick to others. He broke with it in 1977 and subsequently helped to form the Socialist Labour Party. TD for the Labour Party 1969–73, Independent 1977–82. While with Labour he introduced the first family planning bill in Dáil Éireann. In 1990 he was backed by left-wing elements of that party for its nomination to contest the presidency but the effort quickly petered out. Author of a hugely successful autobiography, *Against the Tide* (1986).

BROWNE, Vincent (1944–), journalist and publisher, b. Co. Limerick, ed. Broadford NS, Ring College, Co. Waterford, St Mary's, Drumcollogher, Co. Limerick, Castleknock and UCD. In his role as editor/manager of various publications, he has consistently championed a comprehensive and incisive brand of investigative journalism. He worked as a journalist for RTÉ, the *Irish Press* and Independent Newspapers before founding *Magill* magazine in 1977. Although *Magill* went through several changes of editor in a short period of time, its exhaustively researched and lengthy articles were powerful critiques of every aspect of Irish public life. Browne was editor of the *Sunday Tribune* from 1983 until 1993. He went on to write columns for *The Irish Times* and *The Sunday Times* and to present an entertainingly provocative current affairs programme on a Dublin radio service, 98 FM.

BROY, Edward (Eamonn) (1887–1972), commissioner Garda Síochána, b. Rathangan,

Co. Kildare, son of a farmer, d. 21 Jan. 1972. DMP 1911; sergeant-clerk Detective Division. Agent for MICHAEL COLLINS in War of Independence. Arrested 1920 when carbon copies of confidential documents emanating from his desk were discovered in a raid; released after the Truce and as a trusted friend accompanied Collins to London for the Treaty negotiations. Member Police Organising Committee 1922; colonel National Army; adjutant Army Air Services 1922–3. Civilian secretary DMP 1923; on amalgamation with the Garda Síochána 1925 he was appointed chief superintendent Dublin Metropolitan Division; depot commandant; replaced Chief Supt. DAVID NELIGAN as head of Detective Division 1932. Succeeded EOIN O'DUFFY as Garda commissioner 1933 and served until 1938, presiding over recruitment of the Fianna Fáil nominees, the 'Broy Harriers'. Promoted sports in the Garda Síochána; president National Cycling and Athletic Association; president Olympic Council of Ireland 1935.

BRUEN, James (Jimmy) (1920–1972), golfer, b. Belfast. Despite his Ulster birth his clubs were Muskerry and Cork. Aged 16 he won the 1936 British Boys title at Royal Birkdale; he then won the Irish Close Championship in 1937 and 1938, when he was also Irish Amateur Open champion. The same year, at St Andrews, he became the youngest player to compete in the Walker Cup, aged 18 years and 25 days, when the home team won the trophy for the first time; this record was beaten by Ronan Rafferty in 1981. In 1946 he won the British Amateur Championship for his only time, at Royal Birkdale, though he continued to compete in the event until 1960. Other achievements include two Walker Cup places (1949, 1951), three times leading amateur in the Irish Open (1937–9), 24 Home International matches in four series for Ireland (1937–50) – winning 12 and halving five. He was an international selector 1959–62 and was captain and president of Cork Golf Club.

BRUGHA, Cathal (1874–1922), revolutionary, b. Dublin, 18 July 1874, ed. Belvedere. Lieutenant Irish Volunteers 1913, second in command to EAMONN CEANNT at the South Dublin Union in the Easter Rising. Although partially disabled as a result of wounds received during the fighting, he served as chief of staff of the IRA 1917–18. TD (Waterford) 1918. In the absence of EAMON DE VALERA and ARTHUR GRIFFITH, both of whom were in prison at the time, he was appointed acting President and presided at the meeting of the First Dáil in Jan. 1919. Minister for Defence 1919–22. Implacably opposed to the Treaty, he fought on the republican side in the Civil War and was killed in July 1922 during the fighting in O'Connell Street, Dublin.

BRUTON, John (1947–), politician, b. 18 May 1947, ed. Clongowes, UCD and King's Inns, m. Finola Gill, one s. three d. Lawyer, farmer, economist. On his election for Fine Gael in Meath at the 1969 general election, he became the youngest member of the Dáil. He was parliamentary secretary to the Minister for Education 1973–7 and to the Minister for Industry and Commerce 1975–7. He was Minister for Finance from June 1981 to Mar. 1982, when the government went out of office after losing a general election brought about because the budget agreed by the cabinet had been defeated in the Dáil. The FG–Labour coalition returned to power in Nov. 1982 and he became Minister for Industry and Energy. In Feb. 1986 he returned to Finance but the withdrawal of Labour from the coalition within a year meant that before he could introduce a budget in 1987 the Dáil was dissolved and a general election called: failure to agree on budgetary strategy had caused the break-up of the government. On Labour's withdrawal he also became Minister for the Public Service until the formation of the incoming Fianna Fáil administration.

When GARRET FITZGERALD resigned after the 1987 general election, Bruton contested the leadership but was defeated by ALAN DUKES. FG had lost 19 seats in that election, and after further poll disaster in the 1990 presidential election (its candidate, AUSTIN CURRIE, came third in the contest) Dukes resigned as party leader. Bruton was unanimously chosen as his successor.

In the general election of 1992 FG lost ten seats. During the campaign, Bruton had suggested the idea of a coalition comprising FG, Labour and the Progressive Democrats, with himself, as leader of the largest party, as Taoiseach. But he had not discussed the idea in advance with the other parties and this provoked resentment, especially in Labour, which eventually decided to form the country's first Fianna Fáil–Labour coalition. Continuing poor performance by FG in the opinion polls led to dissatisfaction with Bruton's leadership and he was challenged in Feb. 1994 but decisively defeated his party critics. His position was further boosted by a comparatively good party showing in the 1994 elections to the European Parliament.

His, and his party's, fortunes finally took a turn for the better with the collapse of the FF–Labour coalition in Nov. 1994. A new coalition was formed between Labour, FG and Democratic Left – the first change of government without an election in Ireland – and, 25 years after he entered the Dáil, John Bruton became Taoiseach. Widely respected for his hard work, although criticised for lack of personal charisma, he received a standing ovation from all sides in the Dáil when he assumed office.

The first 18 months of Bruton's term as Taoiseach were marked by sustained growth in the Irish economy and in the same period his government promoted and achieved, by a narrow margin at referendum, the abolition of the constitutional prohibition against the enactment of divorce legislation. In Feb. 1995, with British Prime Minister John Major, he launched the Anglo-Irish 'Framework Document', outlining new proposed relations between Northern Ireland and the Republic. Some of his opponents considered him to be excessively understanding towards unionist attitudes, yet he took a strongly critical position on British prevarication during the IRA ceasefire (Aug. 1994 to Feb. 1996) over all-party talks on the future of the North. He established a practical working relationship with GERRY ADAMS which all but foundered in the aftermath of the London bombings in Feb. 1996 and worsened further in June when a garda detective was shot dead at Adare, Co. Limerick and the IRA bombed a shopping centre in Manchester. The Taoiseach, however, resisted demands that government contacts with SF at officials-level should be totally severed. At the same time, he required an unequivocal condemnation of violence by SF and insisted that the IRA ceasefire would have to be renewed before SF could be admitted to the all-party talks which had begun in Belfast on 10 June. A new factor arose in the following month. The manifest sense of outrage with which the Taoiseach condemned the British authorities for yielding to force at Drumcree by permitting the withdrawal of a ban on an Orange march through a Catholic district, and for being neither impartial nor consistent in applying the law on that occasion, met with virtually universal approval in the Republic in spite of the frigid atmosphere which followed for a time in relations between London and Dublin. His ability thus to take a principled stand, whether against republican extremism or what he considered a British dereliction of duty, was seen to illustrate the strength of character which John Bruton brought to his office as head of government.

BRYAN, Daniel (1900–1985), colonel, b. Kilkenny. Studied medicine in UCD for two years. In Nov. 1917 he joined the Irish Volunteers and served in C and D Companies, 4th Battalion, Dublin Brigade. Joining the new National Army on 20 June 1922, he was immediately appointed to the rank of captain and posted to Portobello (later Cathal Brugha) Barracks as a staff officer on the general staff. Involved mainly with intelligence matters, an area on which he was to concentrate for most of his military career. During the Civil War his knowledge of anti-Treaty activities, particularly in the Dublin area, led to many arrests. He also played a prominent role in monitoring the activities of those involved in the 1924 'Army Mutiny'.

Following the Civil War he was an important figure in the development of the defence forces, especially regarding the Defence Plans Division set up on the return of the military mission from the USA 1926–7. He went back to military intelligence in 1934 and in 1941 succeeded Lt.-Gen. WILLIAM ARCHER as director of military intelligence, a post he held until 1952, when he was appointed commandant of the Military College. During his period as director he established an excellent intelligence system in conjunction with the Special Branch, which in later years drew favourable comment from such sources as MI5 and the Office of Strategic Services (precursor of the CIA). He retired from the defence forces in 1955. A founder member of the Military

History Society of Ireland, he did much to promote the cause of historical research.

BUCKLEY, John (1951–), composer and teacher, b. Co. Limerick, studied in Ireland and Wales. Member of Aosdána. His compositions have been performed and broadcast in over 30 countries worldwide. They include *Taller than Roman Spears* for orchestra (1977), *Pulvis et Umbra*, choir and orchestra (1979), Concerto for Chamber Orchestra (1981) and Symphony No. 1 (1988), as well as music for solo instruments, chamber ensembles, choirs and bands. His chamber opera, *The Words upon the Windowpane*, was first performed in 1991 and his Concerto for Organ in 1992. He has also composed ballet music (*Fornacht do Chonac Thú*, 1980) and film music (*The Woman who Married Clark Gable*). Awards include the Varming prize, the Macaulay fellowship and the Marten Toonder award.

BUDD, Frederick *Gardner* **Orford** (1904–1976), lawyer, b. Co. Clare, ed. Felsted, Essex, TCD and King's Inns, d. 9 Feb. 1976. BA (1925), LL D (1927). Called to Bar 1927, practised on Leinster circuit, Senior Counsel 1943. Elected senator for TCD constituency Aug. 1951, but never took his seat because he was appointed a High Court judge in Oct. of that year. Supreme Court judge 1966–75. Among the more notable cases he was involved in while on the bench were Educational Co. v. Fitzpatrick (1961), on the constitutional right to refuse to join a trade union, and McGee v. A.-G. (1974), which established a constitutional right to marital privacy.

BULFIN, Michael (1939–), artist, b. Devinlough, Birr, Co. Offaly, ed. UCD and Yale. He is a largely self-taught artist, beginning his career as a painter but from the early 1970s concentrating mainly on sculpture. He had his first one-man exhibition at the Project Gallery in Dublin in 1970. He exhibited in the 1969 Oireachtas and represented Ireland at the 1971 Paris Biennale. In 1968 he won the adjudicators' special award at the Irish Exhibition of Living Art. Former chairman of the Project Arts Centre. His abstract, formalist sculptures have a hard-edged simplicity and are often very large in scale. He has completed a number of major commissions, including one for the courtyard of the Bank of Ireland headquarters on Baggot Street in Dublin.

Bulfin is a professional forester and works with Teagasc.

BULL, Lucien (1876–1972), inventor, b. Dublin, 8 Jan. 1876, d. Paris, Aug. 1972. He was a pioneer of early cinematography and in 1908 invented the first electrocardiograph. Director Institut Marey, Paris 1914. He moved to England in the 1930s, becoming director of higher studies at the National Office of Research and Invention in 1937. President Institute of Scientific Cinematography 1948.

BUNWORTH, Richard (1918–1992), colonel, b. Cork, ed. Rockwell. Joined the defence forces in 1937 and was commissioned as a second lieutenant in Sept. 1939. He served for many years in the Military College and in Army Headquarters, and was serving as assistant chief of staff when he retired in 1978. He also had a distinguished career with the UN. He was officer commanding in the Congo (now Zaïre) when an Irish patrol was ambushed at Niemba in Nov. 1960 and nine of its members killed. He was also chairman of the Israel/Syria Mixed Armstice Commission when the Six Day War broke out in 1967, and his impartial reporting of events drew public praise from the then secretary-general of the UN, U Thant. In 1973 he was recalled as chief of staff of the UN Truce Supervisory Organisation at the onset of the Yom Kippur War.

BURKE, John (1946–), artist, b. Clonmel, ed. Crawford Municipal School of Art, Cork. Shortly after his graduation in 1967 he exhibited at the Irish Exhibition of Living Art and at the Oireachtas. In 1970 he received a Macaulay fellowship and spent a year working and travelling with the British sculptor Brian Kneale. In 1973 he had his first solo exhibition at Jury's Hotel in Cork, and a selection of his work was shown by the Arts Council in the grounds of Trinity College. He participated in 18 European Sculptors in Munich, 1978, and in Europenne at Malou Park in Brussels, 1979. He has completed several commissions and his work is in a number of collections in Ireland and abroad. The fine, delicate quality of his early work, which used thin painted pieces of metal, has been replaced by a more solid style in recent years.

BURKE, Richard (1932–), politician and EC commissioner, b. New York, 28 Mar. 1932, raised in Tipperary, ed. CBS, Thurles, UCD

and King's Inns. Prior to entering public life he was a teacher. TD (FG County Dublin) 1969; immediately appointed chief whip by party leader LIAM COSGRAVE. Minister for Education 1973; EC commissioner 1976.

On the completion of his four-year term he was invited back into Fine Gael by GARRET FITZGERALD and successfully contested the 1981 election for the party. Expecting a senior post in the subsequent coalition cabinet, he was shocked when he found himself excluded. He retained his Dublin West seat in the Feb. 1982 election, which led to the formation of a minority Fianna Fáil administration. The new Taoiseach, CHARLES HAUGHEY, offered to reappoint Dick Burke to the EC Commission, and after some heart-searching he availed himself of the offer, to the horror of many in FG. The stratagem by Haughey backfired when Fianna Fáil failed to win in the by-election created by Burke's resignation from the Dáil.

BURKITT, Denis Parsons (1911–1993), surgeon in Africa and discoverer of a form of childhood cancer known as 'Burkitt's lymphoma'; b. Lawnakilla near Enniskillen, Co. Fermanagh, ed. Portora (where an accident led to the loss of an eye), Dean Close in Cheltenham and TCD, where he moved from the School of Engineering to study medicine. He graduated MB in 1935, taking the FRCS Edinburgh in 1938 and proceeding MD in 1946. He married Olive Rogers, a nurse who shared his evangelical beliefs. Rejected in the early 1940s by the colonial medical service because of the ocular defect, Burkitt was accepted after serving with the RAMC in east Africa and Ceylon, and posted to Uganda. Noticing the high incidence of hydrocele in Lira, where he was first stationed, he embarked on a geographical study and found insect-borne filariasis to be the cause. At Kampala he had a large surgical practice and soon was aware that amputees became dependent on relatives because of the lack of artificial limbs. On his next furlough he studied orthopaedics and he returned to Kampala able to provide inexpensive plastic limbs.

Burkitt was a propagandist for increased fibre in the Western diet and his book *Don't Forget Fibre in your Diet* (1979) was a bestseller. *Epidemiology of Cancer of the Colon and Rectum* was published in 1971 and he was elected FRS the following year. His campaign for dietary change flourished, and being an attractive speaker he was given endless opportunities to ventilate his theories.

BURROWES, Wesley (1930–), writer, b. Belfast, ed. Royal Academical Institution and QUB. One of the most gifted and popular writers for theatre and television. He is particularly celebrated in the latter medium, being the originator of *The Riordans, Bracken* and *Glenroe*, consistently among the most popular RTÉ television programmes since the early 1970s.

BUTCHER, Eddie (1900–1980), traditional singer, b. Magilligan, Co. Derry. By occupation a labourer and road worker, he is recognised as an important source of classic ballads and other songs. His songs provided valuable research material for Dr Hugh Shields, author of, *inter alia, Shamrock, Rose and Thistle*. From the mid-1960s Butcher made numerous broadcasts, and records of his singing were issued on the Outlet and Leader labels and by the Ulster Folk Museum.

BUTLER, Hubert Marshall (1900–1991), translator and essayist, b. Bennetsbridge, Co. Kilkenny, ed. Charterhouse and Oxford. He taught English in Alexandria and Leningrad, and studied for three years in Yugoslavia. He was active in Vienna in obtaining visas for Jews fleeing Nazi persecution, 1938–9. Founded Kilkenny Archaeological Society in 1944 but resigned under pressure in 1952, a consequence of an imagined insult to the papal nuncio by Butler, who had condemned the forcible conversions and genocide of Serb Orthodox Christians by Croatians in 1941. He foresaw with chilling clarity the retribution exacted by the Serbs in the 1990s. Translated Leonid Leonov's *The Thief* (1931) and Anton Chekhov's *The Cherry Orchard* (1934), edited the review section of the *Bell* and self-published the scholarly if controversial *Ten Thousand Saints: A Study in Irish and European Origins* (1972). Collected essays: *Escape from the Anthill* (1985), *The Children of Drancy* (1988), *Grandmother and Wolfe Tone* (1990), *The Sub-Prefect Should Have Held His Tongue*, selected (1992), and *In the Land of Nod* (1996). Butler will be remembered as a liberal, compassionate voice, crying in the wilderness.

BUTLER, Rudolf Maximilian (1872–1943), dominant figure in the architectural establishment in the early decades of this century, b. Dublin, s. of John Butler, a barrister, and his German wife. About 1891, after a brief encounter with the wine trade, R.M. Butler joined the offices of W.G. Doolin and was taken into partnership with James G. Donnelly. Though comparatively new to the profession, he was active in its promotion, in 1896 joining the RIAI and assisting in reviving the AAI. In 1899 he took on responsibility for the country's architectural magazine, the *Irish Builder*, even acting as its proprietor for a few months, and he held the post of editor until 1935. In 1902 he was elected an associate member of the Institution of Civil Engineers of Ireland, in 1906 becoming an associate of the RHA. His first professional triumph was success in the competition for the new UCD building at Earlsfort Terrace in 1912; its dry classicism epitomised the values he brought to Irish architecture. With his appointment as Professor of Architecture at UCD in 1924, and through the pages of the *Irish Builder*, he exerted an influence on Irish architecture out of proportion to his particular talents.

BYRNE, Alfie (1882–1956), Lord Mayor of Dublin, son of a docker, who died when Byrne was 13, d. Mar. 1956. Worked as a theatre programme seller and barman before buying his own pub in Talbot Street. Entered politics at 27; elected to Dublin Corporation for North Dock ward with a large majority; elected member of House of Commons in 1915 by-election but lost his seat in 1918 general election. In the 1922 general election (the first after the Treaty) he was elected to the Dáil. From then until his death he was an Independent TD, except for three years when he was a member of the Seanad. Lord Mayor of Dublin for a record nine successive years 1930–39 and again 1954–5.

BYRNE, Damian Louis (1929–1996), Dominican friar, b. Galway, ed. St Mary's College, Galway and St Mary's, Tallaght, Co. Dublin. Ordained 1955. Spent most of his pastorate in Latin America, where his thinking was strongly influenced by the philosopher Ivan Illich. Helped to establish an Irish Dominican mission in Argentina. Became successively vicar provincial of the Dominicans in Argentina and then in Trinidad, provincial of Mexico and (1977) of Ireland. In 1983 he was elected master, the 84th successor to St Dominic as head of the order and the second Irishman, the first having been MICHAEL BROWNE. As master he wrote a long-remembered series of letters for the spiritual and practical guidance of Dominicans throughout the world (published in 1991 under the title *A Pilgrimage of Faith*). When his term ended he returned home from Rome and, in 1993, became secretary-general of the Conference of Religious of Ireland at a time of major crisis in the Irish Church. He organised a number of seminars for religious and bishops on the question of child sexual abuse by priests and was appointed to the bishops' advisory committee on the subject. The strain of dealing with this contentious matter was thought to have hastened his unexpected death.

BYRNE, Donn (1889–1928), novelist and short story writer, b. New York, grew up in south Armagh, ed. UCD, Sorbonne and Leipzig. Won prizes for fluency in Irish from an early age; was later commended by DOUGLAS HYDE, one of his teachers in UCD. Returned to New York *c.* 1911 and had short stories taken by *Harper's, Smart Set, Ladies' Home Journal* and *Scribner's*. Published first collection, *Stories without Women*, in 1915, and first novel, *The Stranger's Banquet*, in 1919. He came back to Ireland in 1922, lived for a time in Dublin, then bought Coolmain Castle, Kilbrittain, Co. Cork. Never a major writer, he nonetheless brought pleasure to a wide readership and enjoyed a lucrative career, cut short in 1928 when he drowned in Courtmacsherry Bay, Cork, after his car left the road. *Messer Marco Polo* and *The Wind Bloweth* (1922), *Hangman's House* (1925), *Brother Saul* (1927) and *The Golden Goat* (1930) are perhaps his best-known novels.

BYRNE, Edward (1872–1940), Roman Catholic archbishop, b. Dublin, 10 May 1872, ed. Belvedere, Clonliffe and Irish College, Rome. Ordained 1895. Held curacies at Rush, Kilsallaghan and Rolestown, Howth and Blackrock. Vice-rector Irish College, Rome 1901–4. Curate Pro-Cathedral, Dublin 1904–20. In 1920 appointed titular Bishop of Spigaz as auxiliary to Archbishop WILLIAM WALSH, following whose death in 1921 he was appointed Archbishop of Dublin. In 1922 he attempted to intervene in the Civil War but his peace proposals were rejected by the Provisional Government. Despite this he later enjoyed cordial relations with the governments of both W.T. COSGRAVE and EAMON DE VALERA. Throughout his episcopate he adopted a mainly pastoral role. He oversaw the establishment of parish structures in the new suburbs around Dublin during the 1920s and 1930s and the building of 19 new churches. He also attempted to build a cathedral to replace the Pro-Cathedral in Marlborough Street, which to him symbolised the pre-Emancipation Church in Dublin. In 1930 he purchased Merrion Square as a prospective site but he was forced to cancel the scheme due to the poor state of diocesan finances. He was a generous supporter of the work carried on in Dublin by the Society of St Vincent de Paul and the CYMS but adopted a hostile attitude towards the Legion of Mary. Quick to respond to the growing devotion to MATT TALBOT, in 1931 he initiated an inquiry into his life. Despite serious ill health throughout his episcopate, he successfully presided over the celebrations which marked the centenary of Catholic Emancipation in 1929 and the Eucharistic Congress in 1932. In 1931 Monsignor Francis Wall was chosen as his auxiliary but when he died on 9 Feb. 1940 he was succeeded as archbishop by Fr JOHN CHARLES MCQUAID.

BYRNE, Gabriel (1950–), actor, b. Dublin, ed. UCD. His acting career began at the Focus Theatre, from where he moved quickly to the RTÉ drama series *Bracken*. Thaddeus O'Sullivan gave him his first film role in *On a Paving Stone Mounted* (1978), and John Boorman set him on the road to stardom when he cast him as Uther Pendragon in *Excalibur* (1981). Some lesser and largely forgettable parts followed, but Byrne's big breakthrough came with his stunning interpretation of an Irish-American gangster in the atmospheric *Miller's Crossing* (1989). The part was seminal for his greatest achievement to date: the role of the supercool villain in *The Usual Suspects* (1995). He has also been involved in film production, with the highly successful *In the Name of the Father* and *Into the West* (1993). He published an autobiography, *Pictures in my Head*, in 1994.

BYRNE, Gay (1934–), broadcaster and columnist, b. Gabriel Mary Byrne, Dublin, 5 Aug. 1934, ed. Synge Street. The most familiar name, face and voice in Ireland for more than 30 years. Started in insurance, then moved into broadcasting when he became a presenter on Radio Éireann in 1958. Also worked with Granada TV, Manchester and with the BBC. After the establishment of Telefís Éireann (later RTÉ) in 1961 he concentrated on working increasingly, and finally exclusively, for the Irish service, on which he introduced many successful and popular shows, such as *Jackpot*, *Pick of the Pops*, *Film Night*, *The Rose of Tralee* and *Housewife of the Year*.

He produced and presented the first *Late Late Show* on 6 July 1962, which at the time of writing is the world's longest-running live television talk show, setting a duration record for Byrne both as producer and as host. Its consistent top audience ratings are evidence of its enduring appeal. In the 1960s and 1970s the programme was regarded as a pace-setter for Irish public opinion, promoting discussion of topics hitherto unmentionable in the media. It was a taboo-breaking, anti-traditional forum for controversial ideas, mirroring and shaping the modernisation of Ireland and strongly influencing the development of RTÉ itself.

An outstanding, even iconic, presenter and a dynamic producer, Gay Byrne staged the drama of Irish life. Few topics were off limits, nobody was too controversial to interview. Ironically, he himself was a moderniser with conventional middle-class conservative views. He was not a social radical – but his programmes had a radical effect on the introspective Ireland to which they were first broadcast. *The Late Late Show* started out as an eight-week summer filler. For years broadcast on a Saturday night, it returned to its original Friday night slot on 13 Sept. 1985. Since Nov. 1984 an edited one-hour version of the show has been broadcast on Channel 4.

On radio he presented *Jazz Corner* and *Music on the Move*, but he is best known for the hugely popular daily two-hour morning show, *The Gay Byrne Show* (1972–). He has written articles for various newspapers and magazines, and a regular column in the *Sunday World* 1977–95. Presented the television programme *People are Talking* (summers of 1986, 1987) on WBZ TV, Boston. There was something approaching a national crisis when he announced (1985) that he was considering

moving to the USA. Variously dubbed the 'Everyman' or 'Uncrowned King' of Ireland, or 'Uncle Gaybo', he occupies a unique status in public life.

In the 1990s he has cut down his enormous workload. Took on Joe Duffy as co-presenter of *The Gay Byrne Show* (1994). Retired as host of the Rose of Tralee festival after 17 years. He is married to Kathleen Watkins, the well-known harpist, singer and broadcaster, who was the first continuity presentation announcer on RTÉ television. Received six Jacob's awards, three for TV (1963, 1970, 1978), one for radio (1976), a special broadcasting award (1981) and a Golden Award (1991). Honorary doctorate in letters (TCD) 1988. Author of *To Whom it Concerns* and the autobiography *The Time of my Life* (1989).

Set up his own production company, GABBRO Ltd (1985). Fund-raising chairman for the Irish Cancer Society. Board member RTÉ Authority 1992–5. On the executive fund-raising committee and member of Board Research Foundation, Our Lady's Hospital for Sick Children, Crumlin, Dublin.

BYRNE, Sir Joseph Aloysius, KBE, CB, brigadier-general, inspector-general RIC 1916–20, ed. St George's College, Weybridge and in Belgium. Royal Inniskilling Fusiliers; deputy adjutant-general Irish Command 27 Apr. 1916. Inspector-general RIC 1916. Was among a number of senior police officers, Catholics with suspected nationalist sympathies – including Assistant Commissioner Fergus Quinn and Inspector Daniel Barrett DMP – eased into early retirement in 1920.

BYRNE, Ralph Henry (1877–1946), architect, b. Dublin, 25 Apr. 1877, s. of William H. Byrne, one of the leading Catholic architects in late 19th-century Ireland, ed. St George's College, Weybridge, m. Mary Josephine Mangan 1905. Took his articles with his father in 1896 and entered partnership with him in William H. Byrne & Son in 1902, the year in which he was elected to the RIAI. Joined the AAI in 1906, was elected a fellow of the RIAI in 1920 and its vice-president in 1938. Byrne's major works, notably the cathedrals at Mullingar, Co. Westmeath (1930) and Cavan (1937), like those of his contemporary R.M. BUTLER, reject European modernism for a conservative classicism.

C

CALDWELL, Johnny (1938–), boxer, b. Belfast, 7 May 1938. As an amateur he won the Irish National Senior Championship at bantamweight in 1956 and 1957. He won a bronze medal for Ireland at the 1956 Olympic Games in Melbourne at flyweight, turned professional in 1958 and won the British title at the same weight with a third-round KO over Frankie Jones in 1960. This was his last flyweight fight, and when he moved up to bantamweight he relinquished the title. In 1961 he outpointed the Algerian Alphonse Halimi to take the EBU version of the world bantamweight title, subsequently defending it successfully against the same opponent. Attempting to become the undisputed world champion, however, he lost in the tenth round to Eder Jofre of Brazil at São Paulo in Jan. 1962. Later that year he lost to Freddie Gilroy in a challenge for the British and Commonwealth titles, claimed them when defeating George Bowes, before losing them to Alan Rudkin in 1964. He retired in 1965 with a career record of 35 bouts, 29 wins (one KO), one draw and five defeats (three resulting from cuts).

CALLAGHAN, Mary Rose (1944–), writer, b. Dublin, ed. Dublin in Sacred Heart convents at Mount Anville and Monkstown, Loreto Abbey, Rathfarnham and UCD. She has travelled much abroad and taught part-time in the USA. She has produced three acclaimed and ground-breaking novels: *Mothers* (1982), concerning the lives of three unmarried mothers, *Confessions of a Prodigal Daughter* (1985), an exploration of mental illness, and *The Awkward Girl* (1990). She has written a play, *A House for Fools* (1983), a biography, *Kitty O'Shea: A Life of Katharine Parnell* (1989), and a novel for young adults, *Has Anyone Seen Heather?* (1990). Callaghan also writes short stories, book reviews and articles, and has contributed entries to the *Dictionary of Irish Literature* (1979). She divides her time between Bray, Co. Wicklow and the USA.

CALLAGHAN, William (1921–), DSM, lieutenant-general, b. Buttevant, Co. Cork. He joined the defence forces in 1939 and was commissioned in 1940. Serving in the Southern Command during his early years, he was later stationed in the Western and Eastern Commands. Appointed assistant chief of staff in 1979 and adjutant-general in 1980. He had considerable experience with the UN, serving one tour of duty in the Congo (now Zaïre) and three in Cyprus 1971–2. Senior staff officer United Nations Truce Supervisory Organisation (UNTSO) in the Middle East 1976–8 and acting chief of staff 1978–9. Force commander United Nations Interim Force in Lebanon from 1981 to 1986, when he was again appointed chief of staff UNTSO. He retired in June 1987. Awarded the DSM for his service in Lebanon. Hon. LL D (NUI) 1986.

CALLAGHAN, William Sydney (1928–), Methodist clergyman, b. Dublin, 20 Mar. 1928, third child of William Thomas and Emily Callaghan; ed. High School, Dublin, TCD (BA), Edgehill Theological College, Belfast and QUB (Dip.Ed.), m. Brenda Leesley 1968. Has been active for many years in community relations in Northern Ireland and has served as director of the Samaritans. He entered the ministry in 1947 and was superintendent of evangelism of the Methodist Church in Ireland 1955–62. He served as minister in Agnes Street and Donegall Square Methodist churches.

CAMPBELL, George (1917–1979), painter and stained-glass artist, b. Arklow, Co. Wicklow, d. Dublin, 18 May 1979. Worked first in Belfast, later in Dublin. Helped to found Irish Exhibition of Living Art 1943. Painted west of Ireland landscapes but will probably be best remembered for the powerful images of his paintings and drawings executed in Spain. MRHA.

CAMPBELL, Patrick, third Baron Glenavy (1913–1980), journalist, author and broadcaster, b. Dublin, 6 June 1913, ed. Rossall, Oxford, Germany and Sorbonne, d. Cannes, 10 Nov. 1980. Campbell started his career with *The Irish Times*, contributing 'An Irishman's

Diary' under the pen-name 'Quidnunc'. He worked in London on the *Sunday Dispatch* 1947–59 and as assistant editor of *Lilliput* magazine 1947–53, before joining *The Sunday Times* in 1961. He later went to live in the south of France and worked as a freelance writer and broadcaster, turning his famous stutter into a personal trade mark. He is perhaps best remembered for his appearances on the BBC television programme *Call My Bluff*. He wrote 16 books in all, including *The P-p-penguin Patrick Campbell* (1965) and *My Life and Easy Times* (1967).

CAMPBELL, Seamus Oliver (Ollie) (1954–), international rugby player, b. Dublin, 3 Mar. 1954. He won 22 Ireland caps (18 at out-half and four at centre) between 1976 and 1984, and played six Lions Tests (two v. South Africa in 1980 and four v. New Zealand in 1983). His 217 international points was an Irish record until Michael Kiernan surpassed it in 1988. A brilliant place-kicker, he was a superb all-round player and was the key man in 1982 when Ireland won the Triple Crown after a 33-year gap. He still holds the following Irish scoring records: most points in Five Nations Championship season (52, in four matches, 1982–3); most penalty goals in Five Nations Championship season (14, in four matches, 1982–3); most penalty goals in an international (six, v. Scotland in Dublin, 1982); most points for Ireland on overseas tour (60, in five matches, Australia, 1979). With Tony Ward he is the joint top scorer in an overseas tour match with 19 (Australia, 1979), and he shares with Dickie Lloyd the Irish record for most dropped goals in internationals with seven. His 21 points – six penalty goals, one dropped goal – against Scotland in 1982 was a record until Ralph Keyes scored 23 against Zimbabwe in the 1991 World Cup in Dublin. He was top scorer on both his Lions tours, with 60 in South Africa in 1980 and 124 in New Zealand in 1983.

CAMPBELL-SHARP, Noelle (1943–), publisher, ed. St John of God Convent, Wexford. After an early career in advertising and public relations, she bought the *Irish Tatler*. Relaunched as *IT* magazine, its success laid the foundations for the development of her publishing interests. She sold her interest in the company in 1989 but stayed on as chief executive.

CANNON, Moya (1956–), poet, b. Dunfanaghy, Co. Donegal, ed. UCD, where she took history and politics, and Corpus Christi College, Cambridge. Her book of poems, *Oar* (1990), centred on the landscapes of the Burren and Co. Galway, won the BRENDAN BEHAN award for a first collection. A second volume, *Murdering the Language*, is forthcoming. Cannon has given many poetry readings in Ireland, Britain, Germany and Austria, and has published poems in international journals and anthologies. She has broadcast on RTÉ radio and TV and on BBC Radio 4, and some of her verse has been successfully set to music. The current editor of *Poetry Ireland*, she lives in Galway, where she teaches at a special school for the children of travellers.

CARBERY, Ethna (1866–1902), pseud. of Anna Isabel MacManus, née Johnston, poet, editor and short story writer, b. Ballycastle, Co. Antrim. She spent most of her life in Belfast, where between 1896 and 1899 she edited, jointly with ALICE MILLIGAN, the *Shan Van Vocht*, a literary magazine with strong nationalist sympathies. She also contributed a great number of poems and short stories to other periodicals dedicated to Irish home rule, such as the *Nation* and *United Ireland*. She married the Donegal writer Seumas MacManus in 1901 but died the following year. Carbery was a committed patriot, and wrote several stridently nationalist ballads, of which 'Roddy MacCorley' is the best-known. Her poems, highly orthodox in style but considered 'charming' in their day, were collected as *The Four Winds of Eirinn* (1902) and enjoyed many reprints. There are two published volumes of short stories: *The Passionate Hearts* (1903) and *In the Celtic Past* (1904).

CAREY, John (Jackie) (1919–1996), international footballer, b. Dublin, 23 Feb. 1919. Won 29 Ireland and nine Northern Ireland caps, including two Victory Internationals, in six different positions. Carey joined Manchester United from St James's Gate in 1936, as a 17-year-old, and remained with them until 1953, scoring 17 goals in 306 matches. He was in the team that defeated Blackpool 4–2 to win the 1948 FA Cup, and also featured in the club's winning League Championship side of 1951–2. In 1947 he captained the Rest of Europe against Great Britain and he was named

Footballer of the Year in 1949. After his retirement in 1953 he managed Blackburn Rovers, guiding them back into Division One in 1958. He went on to manage Everton, Leyton Orient and Nottingham Forest before returning to Blackburn in 1969; when in 1971 they were relegated to Division Three for the first time he was replaced.

CARNEY, James (1914–1989), Celtic scholar, b. Maryborough (now Portlaoise), ed. Synge Street, UCD and Bonn. Professor DIAS. Authority on medieval Irish poetry and a participant in the disputes over the identity and dating of St Patrick.

CARR, Joseph Boynton (Joe, 'JB') (1922–), amateur golfer, b. Dublin, 18 Feb. 1922. Ireland's greatest amateur, he helped Sutton Golf Club to win three Barton Shields and six Senior Cups, won the Irish Amateur Open six times (1954, 1957, 1963, 1964, 1965 and 1967), won the British Amateur Open three times (1953, 1958 and 1960) and was runner-up in 1968. He was the leading amateur in the British Open twice (1958 and 1963) and in 1961 was a semi-finalist in the US Amateur Championship. He played a record ten times in the Walker Cup between 1947 and 1967 (captain in 1963); he was non-playing captain in 1965. He played in the Home Internationals every year from 1947 to 1969, also in the Eisenhower Trophy, the World Amateur Team Championship, in 1958 and 1960. In domestic competitions he won the East and the West of Ireland Championships a record 12 times each, and the South three times. He was a Walker Cup selector 1979–86 and captain of the Royal and Ancient 1991–2. His sons Roddy and John also played for Ireland, Roddy competing in the Walker Cup in 1971.

CARR, Marina (1964–), playwright, b. Dublin, brought up in Offaly, ed. locally and UCD. Plays: *Low in the Dark*, given first at the Project Theatre in Dublin 1989; *The Deer's Surrender* (1990); *This Love Thing* and *Ullaloo*, both staged first at the Peacock Theatre in 1991; *The Mai* (1994); *Portia Coughlan* (1996).

CARR, Tom (1909–), artist, b. Belfast, 21 Sept. 1909, ed. Slade School of Art, London. He is one of Northern Ireland's most respected painters and has produced a large body of landscape and figurative work. After finishing his studies he remained in London for a number of years and exhibited at several galleries, including the Royal Academy. In 1939 he returned to live in NI and spent much time painting in Newcastle, Co. Down. He has had several one-man shows in Belfast and Dublin, and his work has also been included in Oireachtas and RHA exhibitions. His paintings have been shown abroad in exhibitions organised by the Royal Society of Watercolour Painters, of which he is a member. He won the Royal Ulster Academy gold medal 1973 and the Oireachtas landscape award 1976. Retrospective exhibitions of his work were held at the Ulster Museum in 1983 and at the RHA in 1989.

CARROLL, John (1925–), trade union leader, b. Dublin, 8 Jan. 1925, ed. St Canice's CBS and O'Connell School. A musician in his early years, he joined the ITGWU in Apr. 1944, moving to the union's head office in Jan. 1947. He was appointed chief industrial officer in 1964, and elected vice-president in 1969 and general president in 1981. Vice-president of ICTU 1985–6, president 1986–7. He has served on the board of many semi-state companies, and was a member of NESC 1971–90. Member of the EC's Economic and Social Committee since 1973. Having joined the Labour Party at the age of 18, he was instrumental in maintaining strong links between his union and the party, notably during the early 1970s when there were several attempts to persuade the ITGWU to disaffiliate. He was also a key figure in the lengthy negotiations aimed at healing the split in the Irish trade union movement embodied in the rivalry of the ITGWU and the FWUI; when that split was finally ended by the creation of SIPTU he became the joint general president (with WILLIAM J. ATTLEY of the FWUI) in Jan. 1990 for the initial period of its existence.

CARROLL, Mella (1934–), High Court judge, b. Dublin, ed. Sacred Heart Convent, Leeson Street, UCD and King's Inns. A successful career at the Bar included chairing the Bar Council 1979, the first time a woman had done so. She was also the first woman to be appointed to the bench of the High Court (1980).

CARROLL, Patrick (1903–1975), commissioner Garda Síochána, b. Stradbally, Co. Laois, d. 6 Dec. 1975. Clerk; battalion staff officer National Army. Joined the police force as a guard and rose through the ranks. Police instructor; in collaboration with Superintendent, formerly District Inspector, Michael Horgan, adapted the *Royal Irish Constabulary Guide* (Andrew Reed) for use in the Garda Síochána (1934); chief superintendent Crime Branch: head of Special Branch. First headquarters officer to take charge in the new Dublin metropolitan area 1962. Garda commissioner 1967–8. Closely identified with representative bodies and the first commissioner to address the rank-and-file elected assemblies. His portrait in the Garda Museum is personally inscribed 'With abiding affection to the Garda Síochána'. President Irish Amateur Boxing Association; secretary/ treasurer Olympic Council of Ireland. Garda Golfing Society; for many years president.

CARROLL, Patrick Joseph (1897– 1982), deputy commissioner Garda Síochána, b. Clones, Co. Monaghan, son of an RIC constable, ed. St Patrick's College, Dublin, d. 17 Feb. 1982. Senior cadet in the class of Garda cadets recruited in 1923. Administrator with a meticulous eye for detail; vast knowledge of police duties and procedures. During the closing years of his service in the 1950s, breaking new ground, he researched Irish police history in the State Paper Office, Dublin Castle; his 'Notes for a History of Police in Ireland' (*Garda Review*, 1961–2) awakened an interest in police history which found expression in the creation of the Garda museum and archives in the 1970s.

CARROLL, Paul *Vincent* (1900–1968), playwright, b. Blackrock, Co. Louth, 10 July 1900, ed. St Mary's College, Dundalk and St Patrick's College, Dublin, d. Bromley, Kent, 20 Oct. 1968. Carroll moved to Glasgow in 1921, where he spent 16 years working as a schoolteacher and writing in his spare time. *The Watched Pot* was performed in the Peacock Theatre in 1930, followed by *Things that are Caesar's* at the Abbey in 1932. Carroll twice won the New York Drama Critics' Circle award for best foreign play – for *Shadow and Substance* in 1937–8 and *The White Steed* a year later. He retired from teaching around this time to pursue a full-time career as a dramatist and he moved to Kent in 1945, writing for the cinema and, later, television. Further plays included *The Wise Have Not Spoken* (1944) and *The Wayward Saint* (1955).

CARROLL, Peter Kevin (1926–), optical physicist, b. 13 Apr. 1926, s. of Bartholomew and Frances Carroll, ed. Synge Street and UCD (B.Sc. 1948, M.Sc. 1949, Ph.D. 1953, D.Sc. 1976), m. M. Raftery. Assistant lecturer QUB 1951–3. Postdoctoral fellowship National Research Council of Canada, Ottawa 1953–5 (with G. Herzberg). Lecturer UCD 1955–60. Research associate at University of Chicago 1960–64 (with R.S. Mulliken). Associate Professor of Optical Physics at UCD 1965–78. Professor of Optical Physics 1978–91. Director of spectroscopy laboratory UCD 1965–91. Published some 80 papers on spectroscopy in two areas, viz. high-resolution studies of diatomic molecules, particularly nitrogen, and emission and absorption studies of laser-produced plasmas in the soft X-ray region. Developed dual laser plasma technique for study of ionic and refractory species. Chairman of Irish branch of Institute of Physics 1970–72; council member IOP 1978–81. Vice-president RIA 1983. Chairman National Committee for Physics 1988–92. Council European Physical Society 1991–4. Boyle medallist of RDS 1988.

CARRUTH, Michael (1967–), boxer, b. Dublin, 9 July 1967. A product of the Drimnagh club, at the 1992 Barcelona Olympics he beat the reigning world champion Juan Hernandez of Cuba (13–10) in the welterweight final to become Ireland's first boxing gold medallist and its first Olympic gold winner since RONNIE DELANY. Previously, he had won four Irish national senior titles, in 1987 and 1988 (lightweight), 1990 (light-welterweight) and 1992 (welterweight). He represented Ireland at two European Championships, in 1987 and 1989, and at the 1988 Seoul Olympics. In 1989 he won a bronze by beating the American Skipper Kelp in the World Championship in Moscow, and in 1990 was selected on a European team for a match against the USA. He turned professional in 1993.

CARSON, Ciaran (1948–), poet, b. Belfast, ed. QUB. Civil servant, teacher and musician before becoming traditional arts officer with the Northern Ireland Arts Council. His collection of poems *The New Estate* (1976) illustrates his minimalist approach to language and imagery. Other work includes *The Insular Celts* (1973), *The Irish for No* (1987), *Belfast Confetti* (1989) and translations of modern Irish-language poetry. The dichotomy of rival cultures in Northern Ireland infuses much of his poetry, and a number of his writings have appeared in the USA as well as Ireland. He has also produced a guide to Irish traditional music (1986) and a book on the same subject, *Last Night's Fun* (1996).

CARSON, Edward (1854–1935), lawyer and politician, b. Dublin, 9 Feb. 1854, ed. Portarlington School, Co. Laois and TCD, d. Kent, 22 Oct. 1935. Called to Bar 1877 (and to English Bar 1893), Solicitor-General for Ireland 1892, MP (Lib. Unionist DU) 1892–1918. A brilliant advocate (who, it was said, never lost his Dublin accent), he was a crown prosecutor during the Plan of Campaign and later so successfully defended the Marquess of Queensberry in the libel proceedings brought by Oscar Wilde that Wilde himself was put on trial and convicted of homosexual offences. Became Solicitor-General in the Conservative government 1900 and was knighted the same year. On the Irish university question he supported the nationalist demand for a Catholic university.

In 1910 Carson became leader of the Irish Unionists in parliament. His passionate commitment to the union of Ireland and Great Britain overcame his discomfort with the narrower aspects of Ulster unionism, and in collaboration with JAMES CRAIG he threw himself into the rallying of Northern resistance to Home Rule once it became clear that the Liberal government was about to concede the measure. He did not hesitate to recommend illegal repudiation of the Home Rule bill if it were enacted and he won the support of such major British political figures as Andrew Bonar Law, leader of the Conservative Party, and F.E. Smith (later Lord Birkenhead). Carson's theatrical oratory helped to rouse loyalist and Orange enthusiasm to fever pitch in Ulster; the Solemn League and Covenant followed in Sept. 1912 with its pledge to refuse recognition to a Home Rule parliament. Carson also approved the formation of a military body, the Ulster Volunteer Force, in 1913. The invocation of loyalty to the king as the ground for threatening to refuse obedience to lawful decisions of the king's government found further reflection in the so-called 'Curragh Mutiny' by army officers in 1914.

In negotiations out of the public eye, however, Carson proved more pliable. Although a quadripartite conference at Buckingham Palace between the Unionists, Nationalists, British government and opposition broke down, the principle survived that part of Ulster might be exempted from Home Rule, at least for some time, and Carson eventually agreed to Home Rule for the rest of Ireland on this basis – to the chagrin of Southern unionists. World War I, the Easter Rising, the conversion of nationalists to Sinn Féin policies and the Anglo-Irish Treaty of 1921 rendered nugatory much of what Carson would have wished to see happen, but his compromise on the exclusion of a number of Ulster constituencies was to be implemented in the establishment of Northern Ireland as a partially self-governing entity within the UK, a development he supported. Minister in the wartime coalition governments, he received a peerage in 1921 (as Lord Carson of Duncairn) and served as Lord of Appeal (a senior judgeship) 1921–9. He was buried in St Anne's Cathedral, Belfast.

CARTY, Francis (1899–1972), journalist and editor, b. Wexford, ed. CBS, Wexford, d. Dublin, 8 Apr. 1972. Carty served with the South Wexford IRA during the War of Independence and sided with the anti-Treaty forces in the Civil War. He joined Fianna Fáil at the party's foundation in 1926 and worked as a sub-editor on the *Irish Press* 1932–44. With C.J. Fallon Publishers 1944–57 he became involved in the production of books for the emerging African countries, travelling extensively in west Africa 1950–53. Appointed editor of the *Irish Press* in 1957 and of the *Sunday Press* in 1962, a position he held until his retirement in 1968. He wrote two novels, *The Irish Volunteer* (1932) and *Legion of the Rearguard* (1934), and several volumes of the lives of the Irish saints.

CARY, Arthur *Joyce* Lunel (1888–1957), writer, b. Derry, ed. Tunbridge Wells, Bristol, Edinburgh, Paris and Oxford. In 1912 he served with the Red Cross during the Balkan War, he later joined the Nigerian Regiment and saw active service in the Cameroons campaign 1915–16. Invalided out of the army in 1920, he settled in Oxford and began writing, publishing his first novel, *Aissa Saved*, in 1932. He became a major novelist, and a respected race relations officer for the British government, working in this capacity in east Africa 1943 and in India 1946, where he helped make didactic films. Cary was in essence an English writer, though recollections of Donegal, which he often visited as a child, are found in his work, especially in *A House of Children* (1941), a semi-autobiographical novel that won the James Tait Black memorial prize. His finest works are *Mister Johnson* (1939), *Herself Surprised* (1941), *To Be a Pilgrim* (1942) and *The Horse's Mouth* (1944).

CASEMENT, Sir Roger (1864–1916), nationalist and civil servant, b. Sandycove, Co. Dublin, 1 Sept. 1864, raised in Ballycastle, Co. Antrim, ed. Ballymena Academy. He joined the British colonial service in 1892, and gained an international reputation as an investigator of human rights abuses through his reports on the treatment of rubber plantation workers in the Belgian Congo and Peru. He had strong nationalist sympathies and joined the Irish Volunteers in 1913, soon after his retirement from the civil service. He saw Britain's involvement in World War I as an opportunity for the revolutionary separatist movement. While his attempts to recruit Irish prisoners of war in Germany were unsuccessful, the Germans did provide a small supply of weapons to be used in the planned rebellion in Ireland. However, the vessel carrying the arms, the *Aud*, was intercepted off the Kerry coast on Good Friday 1916 and Casement was himself captured shortly afterwards. He was tried for treason after the Easter Rising and hanged on 3 Aug. 1916. An international campaign to have him reprieved lost momentum when the British government circulated a number of diaries, supposedly Casement's, containing details of homosexual activity. His remains were interred in Glasnevin Cemetery, Dublin in 1965.

CASEY, Bobby (1926–), fiddler, b. Annagh, Co. Clare. His father, John 'Scully' Casey, was an instrumentalist of great talent; those who testify to this include the famous fiddler Junior Crehan. His inherited skills established Bobby as one of the finest Irish fiddlers of the century. In 1952 he emigrated to London, where he associated with Michael Gorman, Roger Sherlock and other eminent expatriate musicians, who created what was a golden age of Irish music in exile, in time contributing to the revitalisation of the tradition in Ireland.

CASEY, Eamonn (1927–), Roman Catholic bishop, b. Co. Kerry, ed. St Munchin's College, Limerick and Maynooth. Ordained priest 1951; curate Limerick 1951–60; chaplain to Irish emigrants in Slough, England 1960–69. As the dynamic national director of the Catholic Housing Aid Society from 1963, he helped many emigrant and other families to buy their own homes in Britain, and in 1966 he founded the non-denominational organisation Shelter, to focus attention on the problems of homelessness and to work towards overcoming it. Bishop of Kerry 1969–76, Bishop of Galway 1976–92. Chairman Trócaire, the Irish bishops' relief and development agency for the Third World, 1973–92, as which he was highly critical of Western, especially US, political and economic involvement in developing countries. When it became known in 1992 that he had had a liaison with an American woman while he was Bishop of Kerry and that they had had a son, he resigned as Bishop of Galway. He went to Ecuador and devoted himself to pastoral work.

CATHERWOOD, Sir Henry *Frederick Ross* (1925–), industrialist and politician, b. 30 Jan. 1925, ed. Shrewsbury School and Clare College, Cambridge. Sir Fred Catherwood became a chartered accountant in 1951. He has held numerous posts in industry, including director-general of Britain's National Economic Development Council 1966–71 and chairman of the British Overseas Trade Board 1975–8. He was knighted in 1971. In 1972 he suggested that minority grievances at Stormont might be addressed through the use of a two-thirds majority voting system and the appointment of members of opposition parties to government posts. In 1985 Catherwood assisted the NI Assembly in producing a report on devolution. Conservative member in the European Parliament for Cambridge 1979–84 and Cambridge and North Bedfordshire 1984–94. President of the Evangelical Alliance since 1992. His memoirs, *At the Cutting Edge*, were published in 1995.

CEANNT, Eamonn (1881–1916), revolutionary, b. Glenamaddy, Co. Galway, 21 Sept. 1881, son of an RIC man, ed. CBS,

North Richmond Street, Dublin and UCD. An accomplished piper and athlete. Worked as a clerk in Dublin Corporation, joined the Gaelic League in 1900 and soon afterwards the IRB. A signatory of the 1916 Proclamation, he was executed in Kilmainham on 8 May 1916.

CHAMBERLAIN, Sir Neville Francis Fitzgerald (1856–1944), KCB, KCVO, lieutenant-colonel, inspector-general RIC, ed. abroad and at Brentwood School, Essex. Military career, 11th (Devon) Regiment, Central India Horse; India, Afghanistan, Burma, South Africa. Inspector-general of the RIC 1900–16. Inherited from his distinguished immediate predecessor, Inspector-General Sir Andrew Reed, the professional police force breaking with its paramilitary past, an ambition that was shattered by the re-emergence of physical force in Irish politics. At the outbreak of World War I he defended the status of the RIC as a civil police force against the ambitions of the British army to employ it as primarily a paramilitary organisation. Gave evidence before the Royal Commission on the 1916 Rising; he was succeeded as inspector-general by Sir JOSEPH ALOYSIUS BYRNE.

CHAMBERS, Anne (1950–), historian and biographer, b. Mayo, ed. Castlebar and UCC. Senior executive officer in the Central Bank. Works: *Granuaile: The Life and Times of Grace O'Malley* (1979), *Chieftain to Knight: Tibbott-ne-Long Bourke, First Viscount of Mayo* (1983), *Eleanor, Countess of Desmond* (1986), *La Sheridan, Adorable Diva*, a biography of MARGARET BURKE SHERIDAN (1989), and a novel, *The Geraldine Conspiracy* (1995). Chambers has also written a number of documentaries for RTÉ and is co-author of two film scripts.

CHARLTON, John (Jack) (1935–), international footballer and manager, b. Ashington, Northumberland, 8 May 1935. So far he is one of only six individuals to be awarded honorary citizenship of the Republic of Ireland. This was in recognition of his achievements with the national football team over a period of almost ten years, during which he guided the Republic to the World Cup finals of 1990 in Italy and 1994 in the USA, as well as the 1988 European Championship finals in Germany. The Republic won a famous 1–0 victory over England in Stuttgart in 1988, then drew 1–1 with the Soviet Union, before failing by 1–0 against Holland. The swell of public interest in football was phenomenal, and the thousands of Irish supporters who followed their team throughout its campaigns became an integral part of what was to be recorded as the Charlton era. In the 1990 World Cup finals in Italy Ireland drew 1–1 with England, were held to a scoreless draw by Egypt and then won a place in the quarter-finals in a historic penalty shootout with Romania, when PACKIE BONNER's save and DAVID O'LEARY's goal became an indelible part of the Republic's sporting history, before the side eventually lost to Italy.

The 1994 World Cup finals in the USA started with a dramatic first ever victory over Italy by 1–0, which was to be the highlight of an otherwise indifferent campaign, and subsequent failure to qualify for the 1996 European Championship in England brought Charlton's reign to an end. But his record had been remarkable – under him the Republic played 93 matches, won 46, drew 30, lost 17, scored 127 goals and conceded 63. In his earlier career Charlton had signed for Leeds United in 1952, but was not capped for England until 1965; he won the last of 35 caps in 1970 and retired three years later, having shared in England's World Cup win in 1966. In his lifelong career with Leeds he scored 95 goals in 772 games, won League Division Two in 1964, League Cup in 1968, the Inter-Cities Fairs Cup in 1968 and 1971, Division One in 1969 and the FA Cup in 1972. He was Footballer of the Year in 1967. Later he managed Middlesbrough, Sheffield Wednesday and Newcastle United. Awarded the OBE in 1974.

CHEVENIX, Helen (*c.* 1890–1963), trade unionist and pacifist, b. Dublin, daughter of a Church of Ireland bishop, ed. Alexandra and TCD, d. Dublin, 4 Mar. 1963. With friend and colleague LOUIE BENNETT she became involved in the formation of the Irish Women's Suffrage Federation and the Irish Women's Reform League in the early years of the century. Their names are synonymous with the Irish Women Workers' Union, with which they were involved for four decades. President of the Irish Trades Union Congress 1951. Prominent member of the Labour Party and, in the 1950s, an authority on nuclear disarmament and a committed pacifist – when such a stance was by no means the norm in the labour movement. At an annual meeting of Congress around that time, her motion on world peace caused uproar and was attacked as communist. Chevenix, a frail grey-haired figure at this stage, did not demur, however, and her calm argument gradually subdued the house to rapt attention. The resolution was passed unanimously.

CHICHESTER-CLARK, James (1923–), politician, b. 12 Feb. 1923, ed. Eton. Joined Irish Guards 1942, retired as major 1960. He entered Stormont as Unionist MP for South Derry in 1960, and became Minister for Agriculture in 1967. He objected to the pace of TERENCE O'NEILL's reforms and, having resigned from the cabinet in Apr. 1969, succeeded him as Prime Minister of Northern Ireland the following month. In Aug. 1969 the Chichester-Clark government was forced to ask for British troops to deal with the worsening situation in NI. The passing of responsibility for security to the army GOC and the disbandment of the Ulster Special Constabulary (B Specials) greatly undermined his position and he resigned as PM in Mar. 1971. Later created Lord Moyola.

CHIEFTAINS, The, traditional music group. In 1963 Paddy Moloney was asked by GARECH A BRÚN to form an ensemble for an album. He recruited a number of colleagues from Ceoltóirí Cualann, including flute player Michael Tubridy, whistle master Seán Potts, violinist Martin Fay, and in addition Davy Fallon on bodhrán. Moloney, a well-known piper, had collaborated with SEÁN Ó RIADA in arranging for Ceoltóirí Cualann, and as a result of rehearsal sessions the new group was established. In the years since, the Chieftains have become a major force in the domestic and international presentation of Irish music. Moloney has remained musical director, but personnel have changed over a period of more than three decades. Peadar Mercier was bodhrán player for some years, being succeeded by Kevin Conneff, who also introduced traditional singing as a regular feature. The gifted fiddler Sean Keane joined the group, and at a relatively late stage the flute spot was passed on to Matt Molloy, formerly of the Bothy Band and to many an unequalled exponent of his instru-

ment. Eventually, Derek Bell left his position with the Northern Ireland BBC Symphony Orchestra to add the harp to the line-up. The band has toured most parts of the world, including China during a historic visit in 1983. Moloney has encouraged the group corporatively and as individuals to work with artists from a wide musical spectrum. These include VAN MORRISON, Art Garfunkel, Paul McCartney, Mike Oldfield, JAMES GALWAY, Dolly Parton, Emmylou Harris and Linda Ronstadt. Moloney became experienced in arranging music for full orchestra, especially for the theatre and cinema. Music in this genre includes compositions for *The Playboy of the Western World* (ballet), *The Grey Fox*, *Barry Lyndon*, *The Ballad of an Irish Horse*, *The Year of the French* and *Tristan and Isolde*.

CHILDERS, Erskine Hamilton (1905–1974), politician, b. London, 11 Dec. 1905, s. of ROBERT ERSKINE CHILDERS, ed. Gresham School, Norfolk and Cambridge, d. 19 Dec. 1974. After graduating from Cambridge with an honours degree in politics and history, he spent a few years working in France for a travel agency. In 1931 he returned to Ireland and became advertising manager of the *Irish Press* on its foundation that year. He stood for Fianna Fáil in the Longford–Athlone constituency in 1938 and was elected to the Dáil. In 1961 he transferred to Cavan–Monaghan, which he represented until his election as President of Ireland in 1973. In 1944 he was appointed a parliamentary secretary and he joined the cabinet in 1951 as Minister for Posts and Telegraphs. Other positions he held were Minister for Lands and Fisheries 1957–9, Minister for Transport and Power 1959–66, Minister for Posts and Telegraphs again 1966–9, and Minister for Health and Tánaiste 1969–73. During the Arms Crisis of 1970 he strongly supported Taoiseach JACK LYNCH and publicly attacked CHARLES HAUGHEY and NEIL BLANEY. During his campaign for the presidency he promised a more open and relevant office. He toured the country by bus – the first time anyone had run such a campaign in that way in Ireland. The second member of the minority Protestant community to be elected to the post, he was a popular president until his death in office from a heart attack.

CHILDERS, Robert *Erskine* (1870–1922), nationalist and writer, b. London, 25 June 1870, raised in Co. Wicklow, ed. Haileybury College, Hertfordshire and Cambridge. Veteran of the Boer War. Despite his background he became a convinced Irish nationalist. In July 1914 he brought a shipment of arms for the Irish Volunteers from Germany on board his yacht, the *Asgard*. He served in the Royal Navy during World War I, but developed strong republican sympathies and was elected to Dáil Éireann for Kildare–Wicklow in 1921. Later that year he was appointed secretary to the Irish delegation which negotiated the Anglo-Irish Treaty. He opposed the Treaty, and in Nov. 1922 he was court-martialled for possession of a revolver and executed. His most famous book is *The Riddle of the Sands* (1903), a novel which foresaw the possibility of a German invasion of England.

CLANCY BROTHERS & TOMMY MAKEM, folk group, and a potent force in introducing to Ireland the folk wave predominant in the USA in the late 1950s. Their style, while international, was largely based on Irish material and their popularity encouraged many enthusiasts to explore their musical roots. The Clancys, Paddy, Tom (deceased) and Liam, from Carrick-on-Suir, Co. Tipperary, were introduced to Tommy Makem by the American collector Diane Hamilton. He was the son of Sarah Makem (b. 1900) of Keady, Co. Armagh, who possessed a huge repository of folk songs. After many spectacular concerts and tours the main group disbanded in 1969, with Liam Clancy and Makem continuing international careers as a duo and later as soloists.

CLANCY, Willie (1918–1975), multi-instrumentalist, b. Miltown Malbay, Co. Clare. His father played the flute and his mother concertina; he himself mastered whistle, flute and fiddle and was noted for his ability and humour as a storyteller and singer. In particular he is remembered as a magnificent piper, studying as a young man with JOHNNY DORAN, who influenced other prominent musicians associated with Clare such as Seán Reid and Martin Talty. Working for some years in Britain and the USA, he returned to Ireland in 1950 on the death of his father to carry on his carpentry business. Clancy's example was crucial in encouraging young people to play traditional music, and his premature death was mourned by the entire musical community, his friend SEAMUS ENNIS writing, 'He died of a big heart.' Since then he has been commemorated by Scoil Samhraidh Willie Clancy, an international summer school attracting students, enthusiasts and noted musicians.

CLANDILLON, Seamus (1878–1944), broadcaster, b. Gort, Co. Galway, ed. St Flannan's College, Ennis and UCD (RUI). Irish-language scholar and promoter of traditional music. Joined civil service, had reached rank of health insurance inspector when appointed first station director (later director of broadcasting) of the national broadcasting service, 2RN (later Radio Éireann), 1925. Launched the service in 1926 from a primitive studio in Little Denmark Street, Dublin. A brilliant innovator, with the minimum resources he was soon providing musical programmes, talks, drama, live sports coverage (then a rarity in Europe), embryonic news bulletins and weather forecasts; in the early days of the station he often sang a selection of songs on the air himself if he could not afford to engage sufficient performers. He oversaw the move to more commodious studios in the GPO (1928) and the establishment of a high-power transmitting station at Athlone (1932). With his wife, the singer Maighréad Ní Annagáin, he published *Songs of the Irish Gaels* (1927). Returned to the civil service 1934.

CLARE, Anthony Ward (1942–), psychiatrist, b. Dublin, 24 Dec. 1942, ed. Gonzaga and UCD. He has had a highly successful career as a psychiatrist and medical scholar, but is probably better known to the general public through his broadcasting work. He received his psychiatric training in St Patrick's Hospital, Dublin, and worked as head of department and Professor of Psychological Medicine at St Bartholomew's Hospital Medical College in London 1983–8. Clinical Professor of Psychiatry at TCD, and medical director of St Patrick's since 1989. His broadcasting work includes the radio programmes *In the Psychiatrist's Chair* and *All in the Mind*. He has also written and edited several popular books on psychiatry.

CLARKE, Austin (1896–1974), poet, playwright and novelist, b. Dublin, 9 May 1896, ed. Belvedere and UCD, d. Templeogue, Co. Dublin, Mar. 1974. Lectured in English at UCD

1917–21. In 1923 left for London, where he contributed book reviews to *The Times, Observer* and *Times Literary Supplement*. *The Bright Temptation* (1932), his first novel, remained banned in Ireland until 1954. Nonetheless, he returned in 1937 to work as a freelance broadcaster and reviewer. He founded the Dublin Verse-speaking Society in 1941, which, as the Lyric Theatre Company, produced verse plays at the Peacock and Abbey Theatres, including his own *The Viscount of Blarney, As the Crow Flies* and *The Son of Learning*. Presented a weekly poetry programme on Radio Éireann 1942–55, all the while maintaining a vast literary output – he produced over 30 volumes of poetry, fiction, drama and autobiography. Poetry titles include *Flight to Africa* (1963), *Mnemosyne Lay in Dust* (1966) and *Collected Poems* (1974). His two autobiographical volumes are *Twice round the Black Church* (1960) and *A Penny in the Clouds* (1968). He was a founder member of the Irish Academy of Letters, its president in 1952, and in 1968 recipient of its highest distinction, the Gregory medal. President Irish PEN 1939–42 and 1946–8; received first literary award of American-Irish Foundation 1972.

CLARKE, Harry (1889–1931), illustrator and stained-glass artist, b. Dublin, 17 Mar. 1889, s. of Joshua Clarke, a church decorator, ed. Belvedere and Metropolitan School of Art, Dublin, d. Coire, Switzerland, 6 Jan. 1931. Won a number of prizes as a student, including a travelling scholarship to France. His drawings for works by J.M. SYNGE, Poe, Elroy Flecker, Swinburne and others recalled the style of Aubrey Beardsley – asymmetrical construction, swirling, curving lines, exaggerated postures and physical features, all eye-catching and brilliantly executed. Other influences detectable in his output include the Celtic mysticism then popular in Ireland as well as the international art nouveau movement.

Translated to stained glass, mainly on religious themes with more formalised figures and rich colours, his imaginative approach reached levels of greatness which made him, with MICHAEL HEALY and EVIE HONE, one of the world's outstanding artists in the medium. Among the many fine examples of his stained-glass windows are those in the Honan College Chapel, Cork; St Patrick's Basilica, Lough Derg; the Catholic parish churches of Carrick-

macross and Ballinrobe; and the parish church (C. of E.) of Sturminster Newton, Dorset. Sadly, his 'Geneva window', commissioned as Ireland's gift to the International Labour Office in that city, was not acceptable to the government and eventually came to rest in the Wolfsonian Foundation in Miami.

Clarke was elected an academician of the RHA 1925, joined two years later by his wife, Margaret (née Crilly), a distinguished artist in her own right. With his brother Walter he restructured the family business under the name Harry Clarke Stained Glass Ltd (better known as Harry Clarke Studios) in 1930. Requiring treatment for persistent tuberculosis, he spent many months in a Swiss sanatorium prior to his death.

CLARKE, Kathleen (1879–1972), née Daly, revolutionary and politician, b. Co. Limerick, wife of THOMAS CLARKE. Interned in 1918. Vice-president of Cumann na mBan 1921. Elected TD 1918 and 1927, a Fianna Fáil senator in the 1930s, first woman Lord Mayor of Dublin 1939.

CLARKE, Thomas James (1857–1916), revolutionary, b. Isle of Wight, 11 Mar. 1857, son of an Irish soldier in the British army. He joined the IRB in 1878 in Dublin. In 1880 he emigrated to New York, where he joined Clan na Gael. Sent on a mission to England, he was arrested on arrival and sentenced to penal servitude. He served 15 years under a harsh prison regime. Upon his release in 1898 he was made a freeman of Limerick city. Emigrated again to America, where he married KATHLEEN CLARKE. He returned to Ireland in 1907 and the following year opened a tobacconist's and newspaper shop in Parnell Street. In July 1911 he organised the first ever pilgrimage to Wolfe Tone's grave in Bodenstown. He fought in the Easter Rising, and as the eldest member of the Provisional Government was given the privilege of being the first signatory of the 1916 Proclamation. He was executed on 3 May 1916.

CLIFFORD, Jeremiah Thomas (Tom, 'Musty') (1923–1990), international rugby player, b. Ballyporeen, Co. Tipperary, 15 Nov. 1923, d. 27 Sept. 1990. Also a soccer player of note. His 14 international caps was a club record for Young Munster RFC in Limerick, until it was surpassed by Peter Clohessy – a prop forward, like Clifford – against Scotland in 1996. Clifford was in the Ireland team captained by KARL MULLEN which won the Triple Crown for the second successive year in 1949, the only time the country has achieved this to date. He scored an international try against France at Lansdowne Road in 1951, when Ireland won the Five Nations Championship, and was deprived of another Triple Crown and Grand Slam only by the 3–3 draw with Wales in Cardiff. He had the distinction of being the first Limerick player to be selected for the Lions, and toured Australia and New Zealand with the 1950 side, also captained by Mullen; he won five Test caps, playing in 19 tour matches in all. Young Munster RFC's ground in Limerick is called Tom Clifford Park in his honour.

CLIFTON, Harry (1952–), poet, b. Dublin, ed. UCD. Taught English in west Africa for two years, later aid worker for Indo-Chinese refugees in Thailand, and journalist. He won the PATRICK KAVANAGH memorial award in 1981, and Arts Council bursaries for literature in 1982 and 1987. He was the Irish representative at the Iowa International Writers' Program, and writer in residence at the Robert Frost Place, New Hampshire 1986. His poetry is intelligent and lyrical; when not in continental mode Clifton can often be found railing at a Roman Catholic Ireland that has not been kind to her farrow. Collections: *The Walls of Carthage* (1977), *Office of the Salt Merchant* (1979), *Comparative Lives* (1982), *The Liberal Cage* (1988), *Selected Poems, 1973–1988* and *The Desert Route* (1992), *At the Grave of Silone* (1993) and *Night Train through the Brenner* (1994). Married to writer Deirdre Madden, he lives in Chatillon, France.

CLINCH, Phyllis E.M. (1901–1984), botanist, ed. UCD (B.Sc. 1923, M.Sc. 1924) and Imperial College of Science, London (Ph.D. 1928). During the 1930s, while at the Albert Agricultural College, Glasnevin, Dublin, she established a worldwide reputation for her investigation of potato viruses, work which was hugely beneficial to the Irish potato industry. She also carried out research into the viruses of tomatoes and demonstrated the transmission of Virus Yellow via sugar beet seed, a highly original result which attracted much attention from abroad. Received a D.Sc. in 1943

for her published work, appointed lecturer in botany in UCD in 1950, and in 1961 became the first woman to receive the Boyle medal.

CLUSKEY, Frank (1930–1988), politician, b. Dublin, 8 Apr. 1930, son of a butcher and trade unionist, ed. locally until the age of 12. Apprenticed in the meat trade. Branch secretary of the Meat Federation until he entered politics full-time as a Labour TD after the 1965 election. He excelled in the political rough-and-tumble at close quarters, and was particularly gifted as a parliamentary performer and strategist. He served for eight years as a member of the Dublin City Council, and briefly as Lord Mayor in 1968 (a year in which the council was dissolved by the Minister for Local Government for failing to strike a rate). Appointed parliamentary secretary for social welfare in the 1973–7 coalition government, as which he undertook important initiatives such as setting up the Combat Poverty Campaign. When he became Labour leader on 1 July 1977 he inherited a party that was substantially demoralised and ready to turn its back on government; much of his activity in the ensuing four years was aimed at ensuring that the door to political power would not be irrevocably shut by strong internal anti-coalition forces. It was a difficult task, which on the whole he accomplished, but he lost his seat, and de facto the party leadership, at the 1981 election. He was nominated to the European Parliament and served there briefly, winning his Dáil seat back at the following election. He became Minister for Trade, Commerce and Tourism in 1982, as which he successfully handled the PMPA insurance crisis, but he eventually resigned on 8 Dec. 1983 in the wake of the government's decision to rescue the Dublin Gas Company, a move which, in his opinion, failed adequately to protect taxpayers' interests. Serious illness cut short his parliamentary and political career.

COAD, Paddy (1920–1992), international footballer, b. Waterford. Having played for Glenavon and then Waterford, he moved to Shamrock Rovers in 1941. He scored 126 League of Ireland goals, and played in Rovers' three League Championship victories in 1954, 1957 and 1959. He scored 41 FAI Cup goals for Rovers, and won four cup-winners' medals, in 1944, 1945, 1948 and 1956, four runners-up medals and six Shield medals, including four in succession between 1955 and 1958. He won 11 international caps between 1947 and 1951, scoring three goals, and made many appearances for the League of Ireland. Later he managed and coached Waterford, guiding the club to its first League title in 1966.

COFFEY, Brian (1905–1995), poet, translator and editor, b. Dublin, son of the first President of UCD, ed. UCD and Paris. Was part of JAMES JOYCE's Parisian circle and a lifelong friend of DENIS DEVLIN. Also befriended THOMAS MACGREEVY and SAMUEL BECKETT. Later taught English at the University of Missouri and mathematics at London schools. Much influenced by Paul Claudel, Coffey was associated with the European avant-garde movement, and produced – alongside his own verse – very fine translations of the early French moderns, Stéphane Mallarmé in particular. He was consistently daring throughout his career and his later work identifies him as one of the first visual poets. Devlin's executor and editor. His collections include: *Poems*, with Denis Devlin (1930), *Three Poems* (1933), *Third Person* (1938), *Selected Poems* (1971), *The Big Laugh* (1976), *Death of Hektor* (1984), *Chanterelles: Short Poems* (1985), *Advent* (1986) and *Poems and Versions* (1991). Edited *The Collected Poems of Denis Devlin* (1964) and Devlin's *The Heavenly Foreigner* (1967).

COGHILL, Rhoda (1903–), composer, pianist and poet, ed. Leinster School of Music, TCD and in Berlin with Artur Schnabel. Official accompanist Radio Éireann 1939–69 while also maintaining a career as a soloist. Recipient of a Jacob's broadcasting award. Compositions include *Out of the Cradle Endlessly Rocking*, for tenor, chorus and orchestra.

COGHLAN, Eamonn Christopher (1952–), athlete, b. Dublin, 21 Nov. 1952. A schoolboy champion with the Celtic Athletic and Metro clubs, he went to Villanova University, Pennsylvania, where he was trained by Jumbo Elliott, and duly became 'The Chairman of the Boards' – the top middle-distance runner. He won 52 of 70 races between 1974 and 1987, including successive winning streaks of 15 and 14 in 1978–80 and 1983–5, respectively. Record seven times winner of Wannamaker Mile at Millrose. He also set six world indoor records at 1,500 m, the mile and 2,000 m, including the first sub-3:50 time indoors with 3:49.78 in 1983. Between 1974 and 1983 he won 11 Irish National titles, at 800 m (five), 1,500 m (five) and 5,000 m (one). After a 1,500 m Olympic fourth in 1976 and a 5,000 m fourth in 1980, he won the World Cup 5,000 m in 1981, and achieved true greatness when winning the inaugural World Championship 5,000 m in 1983 at Helsinki. Among his other achievements are the AAA 1,500 m (1979), four NCAA 1,500 m/mile indoors and out (1975–6), 15 Irish outdoor records (1975–6) and a run on Ireland's 4 x 1 Mile world best (1985). In 1994 he became the first person over 40 to run a sub-four-minute mile, with a time of 3:58.15 at Boston.

COGLEY, Mitchel V. (1910–1991), sports journalist, b. Chile to Irish parents, d. Dublin, 10 Nov. 1991. Joined the staff of the *Irish Press* at its launch in 1931 and moved to the *Sunday Independent* in 1939. Sports editor of the *Irish Independent* 1943, a position he held until his retirement in 1975. He contributed a weekly column for several years afterwards. Cogley was particularly associated with boxing and hurling, but his versatility embraced all codes – he covered five Olympic Games, starting with London in 1948, and was the only Irish newspaper reporter to cover the 1947 All-Ireland football final between Cavan and Kerry in New York.

COLBERT, Con (1893–1916), revolutionary, b. Limerick, 19 Oct. 1893, ed. CBS, North Richmond Street, Dublin. Became an officer in the Irish Volunteers. During the Easter Rising, he commanded the garrison in Watkins's brewery and the Jameson distillery. Executed in Kilmainham 8 May 1916.

COLE, John Morrison (1927–), journalist and political correspondent, b. 23 Nov. 1927, ed. Belfast Royal Academy. A journalist at the *Belfast Telegraph* 1945–56 and at the *Manchester Guardian* 1956–75, becoming deputy editor in 1969. From 1975 to 1981 he worked at the *Observer*, deputy editor from 1976. Cole is, however, best known as political editor of the BBC 1981–92. He described Harold Wilson as his first political friend at Westminster. In his political memoirs, *As It Seems to Me* (1995), he noted, 'Lady Thatcher's "conviction politics" have transformed the tone of British public life, and not for the better.' David McKie of the *Guardian* noted: 'With his endearing grin, his brogue and his old-fashioned overcoat, John Cole, over his 11 years as the BBC's political editor, undoubtedly established himself as the most famous political broadcaster ever. What is scarcely more disputable is that he was the best ever, too.'

COLEMAN, Michael (1891–1945), fiddler and to many the dominant figure in Irish traditional music in the 20th century, b. Knockgrania, in the Killavil district of Sligo. He was brought up in a musical family living on a smallholding in an area celebrated for its instrumental richness. His elder brother Jim enjoyed a considerable reputation as a fiddler; important as this was, it is generally accepted that Michael Coleman was also influenced in his formative years by techniques associated with the pipes.

In 1914 he emigrated to New York, marrying Marie Fanning, originally from Monaghan, in 1917. His musicianship being widely acclaimed, he was able to make a living teaching and performing. Between 1921 and 1936 Coleman recorded extensively (initially by means of the pre-electric acoustic system) on the Shannon, Vocalion, Columbia, Okeh, New Republic, Pathé, O'Beirne de Witt, Victor, Brunswick and Decca labels, with reissues on the Intrepid, Coral and Ace of Hearts labels and HARRY BRADSHAW's (b. 1947) Viva Voce double cassette.

Early in his career in the USA his association with the Keith Theatres vaudeville circuit brought him to many concert venues. His recordings on 78s were to prove a fundamental influence on the development of traditional music in Ireland, not only for fiddlers. The legacy of Coleman is apparent in the work of other instrumentalists such as flute player Seamus Tansey and ace accordionist Joe Burke (who issued a tribute album). In 1974 he was commemorated by the unveiling of a monument at Mount Irwin, Co. Sligo, erected by the Traditional Society formed in his honour.

COLLERAN, Emer Mary (1945–), academic, b. Castlebar, 12 Oct. 1945, ed. St Louis Convent, Kiltimagh, Co. Mayo, UCG (B.Sc., Ph.D.), DCU and TCD. Associate Professor of Microbiology UCG. As a chairwoman and subsequently council member of An Taisce,

she has been actively involved with environmental issues for many years and is a member of the European Environmental Bureau working groups on agriculture and the environment. Her extensive research background, notably in the application of anaerobic digestion technology for both biogas production and pollution control, testifies to her conviction that scientists must take account of the human and environmental implications of work in the natural sciences. In 1991 she was appointed to the Council of State by President MARY ROBINSON. Since 1992 she has been involved in the Trieste University initiative in the preparing of a Magna Charta of Human Duties, an initiative promoted by a group of Nobel prize-winning scientists in recognition of the need to define obligations logically implied by the Declaration of Human Rights.

COLLEY, George (1925–1983), politician, b. Dublin, 18 Oct. 1925, ed. Scoil Mhuire, St Joseph's CBS and UCD. Solicitor. His father, Harry, had been a Fianna Fáil TD for Dublin North-East 1947–57 and George Colley was elected there for the same party in 1961, when he joined sitting FF TD CHARLES HAUGHEY. They subsequently developed an intense and bitter rivalry. Colley was parliamentary secretary to the Minister for Lands in 1965 before joining the cabinet later that year as Minister for Education. In 1966 when his party leader and Taoiseach, SEÁN LEMASS, decided to step down, Colley declared himself a candidate for both offices. When it looked like becoming a divisive contest between Colley and Haughey, Lemass persuaded JACK LYNCH to stand as a compromise candidate. Haughey and the other contenders stood aside but Colley went ahead and was defeated by Lynch 52 votes to 19. Later the two became firm allies and friends. Minister for Industry and Commerce 1966–70, for the Gaeltacht 1969–73 and for Finance from 1970 (on Haughey's dismissal from government) to 1973 and again 1977–9.

He was a forceful advocate of stoic principles in public life, which he memorably underscored in a speech about 'low standards in high places' – taken to be coded criticism of others in FF who had forged links with business and property interests. When Lynch retired as Taoiseach late in 1979, Colley once again contested the party leadership, with the backing of the overwhelming majority of the cabinet. But once again he lost, this time to Haughey, who was supported by a majority of backbench TDs. The vote was 44 to 38. Haughey included him in his first cabinet as Minister for Energy, although Colley publicly indicated that he gave only qualified loyalty to the new party leader. He was not appointed to Haughey's second cabinet in 1982. He died in a London hospital on 17 Sept. 1983 while being prepared for heart surgery. His daughter Anne was a TD (PD Dublin South County) 1987–9.

COLLINS, Gerard (1938–), politician, b. Abbeyfeale, Co. Limerick, Oct. 1938, ed. St Ita's College, Abbeyfeale, Patrician College, Ballyfin, Co. Laois and UCD. Vocational school teacher. TD (FF Limerick West) since 1967. Parliamentary secretary to Ministers for Industry and Commerce and for the Gaeltacht 1969–70. Minister for Posts and Telegraphs 1970–73, as which he issued the first order under section 31 of the Broadcasting Authority Act, prohibiting broadcasts likely to promote the cause of organisations committed to violence. In 1972 he dismissed the RTÉ Authority because of a radio broadcast which he considered to have contravened this order. Minister for Justice 1977–81 and for Foreign Affairs in 1982 from Mar. to Dec., when the Fianna Fáil government went out of office. On its return in 1987 he became Minister for Justice again until his reappointment as Minister for Foreign Affairs in 1989. President of the EC Council of Ministers Jan.–June 1990 and joint co-chairman of the Anglo-Irish Conference 1989–92. He publicly pleaded with ALBERT REYNOLDS to desist from his effort to depose CHARLES HAUGHEY as FF leader in 1991. He lost his cabinet post when Reynolds succeeded as Taoiseach in Feb. 1992 but was elected MEP in 1994.

COLLINS, John (1883–1954), public servant, b. Waterford, ed. Mount Sion. Joined civil service 1902 and was assigned to London. Returned to Dublin in 1906 to the Office of the Inspectors of Lunacy at Dublin Castle. In 1923 he was transferred to the new Department of Local Government in the Custom House, from which department he retired as secretary in 1948. Shortly after the outbreak of World War II he was appointed regional commis-

sioner for Cos. Kildare, Dublin and Wicklow to operate the machinery of government in the event of an invasion. He was also for a period county manager of Mayo, and acted as commissioner in both Roscommon and Kerry following the abolition of the county councils there. When in 1945 the board of the Fever Hospital in Cork Street, Dublin was abolished after a controversial sworn inquiry, he found himself in the unpopular role of commissioner responsible for the hospital. Following his retirement he was retained in a temporary capacity to work on the modification of local government law, in which he was acknowledged to be an expert. His *Local Government*, published posthumously, was regarded as the definitive work on the local government system in Ireland.

COLLINS, Michael (1890–1922), revolutionary and statesman, b. Cork, 16 Oct. 1890, ed. Lisavaird NS, Co. Cork. Went to work in the British Post Office at the age of 15 and lived in London until 1916. There he became involved in Irish cultural organisations – including the GAA and the Gaelic League – and more revolutionary groups, such as the IRB, heirs of the Fenian tradition. He was leader of the IRB throughout the War of Independence and up to his death. Leaving London for Dublin when he heard of plans for the Easter Rising, he fought in the GPO, was arrested and interned in Frongoch camp in Wales. On release he rose quickly through the ranks of the independence movement. At the 1918 elections to the Westminster parliament he was elected in the South Cork constituency and took his seat in the independent Dáil Éireann.

Collins became Minister for Finance in the republican government formed by EAMON DE VALERA. With de Valera away in the USA for much of the subsequent period raising funds and political support for Irish independence, he became de facto leader of the movement. Although not in overall command of the armed struggle, as director of organisation and intelligence he was the central figure behind clandestine operations against the British authorities. These included penetration of British intelligence and the killing of many of its key operatives. In the course of this he became a folk hero, famous for his ability to escape detection by the authorities.

After the breakdown of talks in summer 1921 between de Valera and British Prime Minister Lloyd George, full negotiations between the two sides opened towards the end of that year. De Valera sent an Irish team headed by ARTHUR GRIFFITH, which included Collins but from which de Valera decided to absent himself. Griffith and Collins played a dominant role in the negotiation of terms, leading to resentment among colleagues at home. But the Corkman believed that an agreement was essential and that the Treaty finally settled upon, if not the full recognition of an all-Ireland republic, was the stepping stone to total independence and the maximum which could be obtained. The terms, however, were rejected by a minority of the Dáil cabinet and a sizeable minority in Dáil Éireann. The ensuing civil war was a bitter conflict, shorter but bloodier than the War of Independence. Collins became commander-in-chief of the forces of the newly created Irish Free State. At the conclusion of the talks in London Collins had told one of the British signatories to the Treaty, Lord Birkenhead, that he was signing his own death warrant. So it proved. He was killed in an ambush in Béal na mBláth, west Cork, 22 Aug. 1922, by anti-Treaty forces.

A complex character with outstanding organisational abilities and a penchant for covert activities, Collins for many remains a towering figure of 20th-century Irish history.

COLLINS, Patrick (1909–), painter, b. Dromore West, Co. Sligo, ed. CBS, Dublin. Insurance company employee before becoming a full-time artist. Largely self-taught, he represented Ireland at the Guggenheim Award Exhibition (New York) 1958, where he won the national award. He has exhibited widely nationally and internationally and is represented in every important collection. Member of Aosdána and a Saoi – the highest honour Ireland bestows for distinction in the arts.

COLLINS, Steve (1964–), boxer, b. Dublin, 21 July 1964. He won Irish titles at junior heavyweight, light-heavyweight and middleweight as an amateur before turning professional in Massachusetts in 1986. In Boston in 1988 he beat Sam Storey to win the Irish middleweight title, then defeated world number five Kevin Watts, and he had won 16 successive fights before Mike McCallum outpointed him over 12 rounds in the WBA world middleweight title fight in Boston in 1990. In 1992 he lost at the same weight to Reggie Johnson and to Sumbu Kalumbay in the EBU decider, before beating Gerhard Botes of South Africa to win the WBC Penta Continental title in 1993.

COLLIS, John Stewart (1900–1984), writer and naturalist, b. Dublin, brother of MAURICE and ROBERT COLLIS, ed. Aravon School, Bray, Co. Wicklow, Rugby and abroad. His childhood and, to some extent, later life were soured by his mother's preference for Robert, his twin. He embarked first upon a literary life in London, where he moved in the same circles as W.B. YEATS and GEORGE BERNARD SHAW, but soon grew weary of it, choosing instead a rural existence. Collis gained a solid reputation as an enlightened naturalist; he also published some flawed biographical works. Books include *Shaw* (1925), *Forward to Nature* (1927), *Farewell to Argument* (1935), *An Irishman's England* (1937), *While Following the Plough* (1946), *Down to Earth* (1947), *The Triumph of the Tree* (1950), *The Moving Waters* (1955), *Bound upon a Course*, autobiography, and *The Carlyles, Thomas and Jane* (1971), *The Worm Forgives the Plough* (1973), *Christopher Columbus* (1976) and *Living with a Stranger: A Discourse on the Human Body* (1978).

COLLIS, Maurice Stewart (1889–1973), writer, b. Dublin, brother of JOHN and ROBERT COLLIS, ed. Rugby and Oxford. He joined the Indian civil service 1911 and became district magistrate of Rangoon in 1928. His championing of Burmese nationalism brought him into disfavour with the Crown and he was obliged to take early retirement in 1934. Collis quickly earned recognition as a biographer and perspicacious historian. His 29 books include *Siamese White* (1934), *Foreign Need: Being an Account of the Opium Imbroglio at Canton in the 1830s and the Anglo-Chinese War that Followed* (1946), *Marco Polo* (1950), *Discovery of L.S. Lowry* (1951), *Journey Outward*, autobiography (1952), *Into Hidden Burma* and *Land of the Great Image* (1953), *Cortés and Montezuma* (1954), translated into six languages, *Last and First in Burma* (1956), *Nancy Astor: An Informal Biography* (1960) and *Somerville and Ross: A Biography* (1968). Wrote several good novels, a play and a volume of verse. He took up painting and art criticism in 1957 and was founder member of the International Association of Art Critics.

COLLIS, William *Robert* **Fitzgerald** (1900–1975), paediatrician and author, b. Dublin, son of a wealthy Dublin lawyer, brother of JOHN and MAURICE COLLIS, ed. Aravon School, Bray, Co. Wicklow, Rugby, Cambridge and King's College Hospital, London. He graduated MRCS (England), LRCP (London) in 1924, MB (Cantab.) in 1925 and was admitted MRCP in 1927. Meanwhile he was Sir Frederick Still's resident at the Hospital for Sick Children, Great Ormond Street and decided to be a paediatrician. His research dealt with rheumatic fever. Cambridge blue, Irish rugby international 1924–6. His family served the Meath Hospital for generations as surgeons or governors: he joined as assistant physician. He was also neonatologist to the Rotunda Hospital. Awareness of a relationship between poverty and disease compelled him to join the Citizens' Housing Council and to write a play, *Marrowbone Lane*, staged at the Gate Theatre. His wife, Phyllis, was Cornish; they had two sons, Dermot and Robert. His first volume of autobiography, *The Silver Fleece* (1936), is an idyll enriched by the happiness of youth. The second, *To Be a Pilgrim* (1975), has a foreword by CHRISTY BROWN, who owed much to Collis. It presents more sombre situations: Belsen, which Collis entered with a Red Cross team in 1945; Ibadan, where kwashiorkor was a common cause of death in children; apartheid in South Africa. Collis's move from Dublin to a larger stage was occasioned by domestic problems, ennui, professional jealousy and the conviction that broader measures must have larger rewards. This phase of his career was devoted to medical education in Africa. He separated from Phyllis and married Han Hogerzeil; their son, Sean, died suddenly in 1969. They retired to Bo-Island in Co. Wicklow and there, in May 1975, he met his death, thrown by a young horse.

COLUM, Mary (1887–1957), née Maguire, teacher, critic and essayist, b. Collooney, Co. Sligo, ed. UCD. Taught at St Ita's, PATRICK PEARSE's school for girls in Dublin. M. PÁDRAIC COLUM 1912 and moved with him to the USA, where she spent much of the remainder of her life. She became an important critic, wrote

book reviews for *The New York Times* and *Tribune*, was literary editor of *Forum*, and contributed essays to literary journals in both the USA and Ireland. She was a superb anecdotalist: her autobiography, *Life and the Dream* (1928), is still a very readable – if at times naïve – first-hand account of the people and events that shaped the Irish literary revival, while *Our Friend James Joyce* (1958), co-written with her husband and published after her death, remains one of the best and most intimate portraits of the artist. Her most important essays on modernism are collected in *From these Roots* (1938).

COLUM, Pádraic (1881–1972), poet and playwright, b. Longford, 8 Dec. 1881. Colum worked for five years as a railway clerk in Dublin before a scholarship from a wealthy American enabled him to study and write. He wrote several plays for the Abbey Theatre 1905–10, including *The Land*, *The Fiddler's House* and *Thomas Muskerry*. He also wrote his famous lyrics, 'She Moved through the Fair' and 'A Cradle Song', around this time, and he co-founded the *Irish Review* with THOMAS MACDONAGH and JAMES STEPHENS. In 1914 Colum left for America with his wife, MARY COLUM. He produced translations and children's books and recorded native Hawaiian myths and folklore, and they both lectured at Columbia University in New York. After Mary's death Colum divided his time between Ireland and the USA. He continued to write and lecture, and received honorary doctorates from UCD and Columbia in 1958. He died in Enfield, Connecticut, 11 Jan. 1972, and is buried in St Finian's Cemetery, Dublin.

COMISKEY, Brendan (1935–), Roman Catholic bishop, b. Co. Monaghan, ed. St Macartan's College, Monaghan. Entered Sacred Hearts Congregation, studied for priesthood in the USA, ordained 1961. Taught moral theology in America prior to becoming provincial of his congregation for Ireland and Britain 1971, secretary-general of the Conference of Major Religious Superiors of Ireland 1974. Auxiliary Bishop of Dublin 1980, Bishop of Ferns 1984. Came to public prominence through his interest in the media of communication both as social phenomena and as carriers of criticism of, or support for, the Church. Preached on media issues, engaged media commentators in debate, wrote a regular column in the *Irish Catholic* newspaper, founded the ecumenical Christian Media Trust for the Catholic and Protestant churches of Co. Wexford with its own radio studio and a 25 per cent holding in a local broadcasting company, South East Radio.

Bishop Comiskey became the focus of controversy in 1995 when he said that the question of clerical celibacy should be open to discussion. An altercation with Cardinal CAHAL DALY followed and a reprimand from the Vatican. Shortly afterwards Bishop Comiskey left suddenly for a protracted visit to the USA, represented as a sabbatical but soon admitted to be for treatment of alcoholism. During his absence some newspapers printed rumours of allegations charging him with extravagance, mishandling of diocesan funds and other improper behaviour. At a press conference upon his return in early 1996 he refuted a number of these stories but admitted to having dealt incompetently with cases of alleged child abuse by priests in his diocese. Controversy continued on this matter while many Catholics welcomed the bishop's stance on celibacy and his press conference statement as evidence of a new openness within the Irish ecclesiastical hierarchy.

COMYN, Sir James (1921–), lawyer, b. Dublin, s. of James Comyn QC of Clare, ed. Oratory School, England and Oxford. Held posts in journalism (his employers including the BBC and *The Irish Times*) during World War II. Called to English Bar 1942, to Irish Bar 1947 and to Hong Kong Bar 1961; QC (England) 1969; chairman of (English) Bar Council 1973–4. Among his clients at the English Bar was Lord Lucan. High Court judge (England) 1979–85. Has written four books on various aspects of the law as well as volumes of verse.

CONLON, Evelyn (1952–), fiction writer, b. Rockcorry, Co. Monaghan, ed. St Louis Convent, Monaghan; took a BA and H.Dip.Ed. at Maynooth, where (she takes great pride in noting) she founded a crèche. Travelled for several years in Australia, New Zealand, Asia and Russia. She joined Irishwomen United and was a founder member of the Dublin Rape Crisis Centre. Her writing won her a European script award in 1984 and an Arts Council bursary in 1988, and she has been a writer in residence in Dublin City Library, Co. Kilkenny and Co. Cavan. Her publications include a book on sex education for children, entitled *Where Did I Come From?* (1982), a novel, *Stars in the Daytime* (1989), and two books of short stories, *My Head is Opening* (1987) and *Taking Scarlet as a Real Colour* (1993). A board member of the Tyrone Guthrie Artists' Centre, she is much in demand as a reviewer and broadcaster.

CONNER, Patrick Rearden (1907–1991), novelist, b. Dublin, ed. Presentation College, Cork. He emigrated to England in his teens and took employment as a manual labourer, principally as gardener, while working on a novel. This was *Shake Hands with the Devil* (1933), his best-known book: a dark tale of treachery among Irish freedom fighters in the time of the Black and Tan war. Conner was never to surpass this achievement, though his autobiographical *A Plain Tale from the Bogs* (1937), which embraces the same period, as well as Depression-era London, is first-rate. His other novels, some published under the name of Peter Malin, include *Rude Earth* (1934), *I am Death* (1936), *Men must Die* (1937), *The Sword of Love* (1938), *Wife of Colum, To Kill is my Vocation* and *River, Sing me a Song* (1939), *The Devil among the Tailors* (1947), *My Love to the Gallows* (1948), *Hunger of the Heart* and *Kobo the Brave* (1950), *The Singing Stone* (1951) and *The House of Cain* (1952).

CONNOLLY, James (1868–1916), socialist, revolutionary, trade unionist and journalist, b. Edinburgh, largely self-educated. He came under the influence of the Scottish socialist John Leslie and, after a period in the British army, came to Dublin in 1896 as organiser of the Dublin Socialist Society (later the Irish Socialist Republican Party). Until at least 1899 his support for syndicalist socialism eschewed recourse to physical force, but his pungent journalism, based on an internationalist and class-based political analysis, notably in periodicals such as the *Workers' Republic* (1898–9), won him a small but dedicated following. He went to the USA 1903–10 and by 1911 was organiser in Belfast for the ITGWU. In 1912 he came to Dublin to assist JAMES LARKIN, and in the same year was one of those successfully working within the Irish Trades Union Congress for the conversion of the Irish Socialist Republican Party into the Independent Labour

Party of Ireland, forerunner of the present Labour Party. He returned permanently in 1914, both as a trade union organiser and as editor of the revived *Workers' Republic* 1914–15. When Larkin went to the USA he became acting general secretary of the ITGWU. His feeling that the British labour movement had betrayed Irish workers was accentuated by the outbreak of World War I and the ensuing mobilisation; thereafter his involvement with the Irish Citizen Army presaged the outcome of the revolutionary struggle. The Citizen Army joined forces with the Irish Volunteers in Jan. 1916, and, after some tactical disagreements about timing, the rebellion – in which Connolly acted as a commandant in the GPO and was wounded – took place that Easter. The last of the Rising's leaders to be executed, he was shot on 12 May 1916. His published books include *Erin's Hope* (1897), *Labour in Irish History* (1910) and *The Reconquest of Ireland* (1915).

CONNOLLY, Sybil (1921–), designer, ed. Convent of Mercy, Waterford. After studying dress design in London she returned to Ireland in 1940. In Dublin she worked in the Richard Alan shop and became a director in 1943. Ten years later she set up her own couturier business. For over 30 years she designed dresses for high-profile women internationally, including Jackie Kennedy while she was America's First Lady. Expanding her repertoire she moved into designing fabrics and interiors. She also designs china, crystal and pottery for Tiffany's store in New York. Publications include *In an Irish Garden* (coauthor) and *In an Irish House*.

CONNOLLY O'BRIEN, Nora (1893–1981), political organiser and trade unionist. Daughter of JAMES CONNOLLY, she came under his influence from a young age. While still a child, she attended his Irish Socialist Republican Party meetings in Dublin and accompanied him on a lecture tour to England and Scotland. When the family moved to the USA in the early 1900s, James Connolly founded a small journal called the *Harp*, of which Nora became manager. The Connollys returned to Ireland in 1910 and lived in Belfast, where she became active in revolutionary politics. She founded the Young Republican Party with a group of friends, organised the Belfast branch

of Cumann na mBan and was involved in the anti-recruitment campaign during World War I. During the week of the Easter Rising she travelled between Belfast and Dublin, bringing word to the North of EOIN MACNEILL's cancellation of the rebellion. Later that year she went to the USA, speaking about the Rising at mass meetings. She was active in the 1918 Sinn Féin general election campaign and imprisoned during the Civil War. Senator for 15 years, as Taoiseach's nominee of EAMON DE VALERA and SEÁN LEMASS.

CONNOR, Jerome (1876–1943), sculptor, b. Patrick Jeremias Connor near Anascaul, Co. Kerry, 12 Oct. 1876, d. Dublin, Aug. 1943. His family moved to the USA when he was a young boy. At 13 he ran away from home and worked in various jobs, one of which introduced him to the world of stonecutting and sculpture. By 1903 he was settled in Syracuse, New York, where he had his own studio. He gained a number of important commissions, including the Walt Whitman Memorial and a statue of Robert Emmet for the Smithsonian Institution in Washington, a cast of which stands on the west side of St Stephen's Green in Dublin. He returned to Ireland in 1925 to work on a memorial to those drowned in the sinking of the *Lusitania* off Co. Cork during World War I. His monument to four Kerry poets – Piaras Feiritéir, Seafradh Ó Donnchadha, Aodhagán Ó Rathaille and Eoghan Rua Ó Súilleabháin – was erected in Killarney in 1940, but it resulted in a legal action which left him bankrupt.

CONNOR, Matt (1959–), Gaelic footballer, b. 9 July 1959. From the Walsh Island club, he made his senior début with Offaly in 1978, and won one All-Ireland senior football medal in the team which in 1982 thwarted Kerry's bid for five consecutive wins. Earlier he had won six successive Offaly Senior Championship medals with his club, as well as Leinster senior medals in 1980 and 1981. He was national top scorer for a record five years in a row, and in the 161 matches he played for Offaly his haul was 906 points, from 82 goals and 660 points. He won three All-Star awards, in 1980 (right corner-forward), 1982 (left-half forward) and 1983 (centre-half forward). In 1984 a motor accident brought his sporting career to a premature end.

CONOLLY, Thomas J. (1902–1992), lawyer, b. Dublin, ed. UCD and King's Inns, d. 21 Sept. 1992. Called to Bar 1927, Senior Counsel 1945, was a pupil in Law Library of GEORGE GAVAN DUFFY. Became one of the most brilliant constitutional lawyers of his time, and for almost half a century appeared in one major constitutional case after another, acting for either the state or the plaintiff citizen. The list of cases he figures in reads almost like a history of Irish constitutional law from the 1940s to the 1980s. He has been described as 'the founder of constitutional law in Ireland'.

CONOR, William (1884–1968), painter, b. Belfast, 6 May 1884, d. 6 Feb. 1968. After some graphics training at the government School of Design, he became an apprentice poster designer and managed to save enough money to go to Dublin and Paris for further study. He first exhibited in 1914 and became a war artist. Though a skilled and popular portraitist, his lifelong interest was the rendering of his native city: shipyard workers, shawlies, the City Hall under snow. He was an obvious Bohemian in a very sedate society, easily recognisable with soft felt hat, large bow tie and cascading silk handkerchief. MRHA 1947, OBE 1952, granted a civil list pension in 1959.

CONROY, Susan *Sheila* (1917–), trade unionist, b. Bantry, 4 Apr. 1917, m. late John Conroy, general president of the ITGWU. Sheila Conroy served on all committees of ITGWU and became the first woman member to be elected to its national executive. Chairwoman RTÉ Authority 1976–81. She was also chairwoman of the national executive of the Widows' Association, member of the Commission on the Status of Women, government appointee to the committee of St Patrick's Institution and vice-chairwoman of Aontas, the National Association for Adult Education.

CONWAY, Arthur William (1875–1950), FRS, theoretical physicist, b. Wexford, 2 Oct. 1875, s. of Myles Conway, ed. UCD and Corpus Christi College, Oxford, m. Daphne Bingham, one s. three d., d. 11 July 1950. MA (RUI and Oxon.), Hon. D.Sc. (RUI) 1908. Hon. Sc.D. (TCD). Hon. LL D (St Andrews). Pontifical Academy of Sciences 1938. Registrar and Professor of Mathematical Physics UCD 1909–40. President UCD 1940–47. President of the RIA and the RDS. Principal research

interests: relativity and quantum theory, and particularly the application of quaternions to these subjects.

CONWAY, Edward (1894–1968), physiologist and biochemist, b. Nenagh, 3 July 1894, ed. Blackrock and UCD, d. Dublin, 29 Dec. 1968. Joined UCD's physiology department. In 1928 moved to Germany, where he spent a year studying muscle physiology. Returned to UCD to work on the physiology of electrolytes (substances that dissolve into their charged constituents in fluids), focusing on the exchange of cations (positively charged atoms) between the cell and its environment.

Conway was appointed to the chair of biochemistry and pharmacology in 1932, which he occupied until his retirement in 1964. The quality of the work of his research team there is reflected in the remarkable statistic that ten former students had attained the rank of professor by the time of his death.

Elected MRIA 1936, FRS 1947, honorary fellow of the RCPI 1953 and fellow of the Institute of Chemistry 1957. He was nominated to the Pontifical Academy of Sciences in 1961 and awarded the Boyle medal in 1967.

CONWAY, William (1913–1977), cardinal, b. Belfast, 22 Jan. 1913, ed. CBS, QUB, Maynooth and Gregorian University, Rome, d. Armagh, 17 Apr. 1977. Ordained priest 1937. Professor of Moral Theology Maynooth 1942–58 and of Canon Law 1943–58. Auxiliary Bishop of Armagh 1958, Archbishop of Armagh 1963, Cardinal 1965. He was a teacher of impressive clarity, with a memorable command of English, and was a compulsive traveller, given to exploring Europe on his vacations. He read widely and his interests ranged from space travel to existentialist philosophy: as cardinal he spoke movingly of his pleasure at the news that SAMUEL BECKETT had been awarded the Nobel prize for literature. He had a special talent for organisation.

These characteristics served him well as primate. He made a number of interventions, spoken and written, at the Second Vatican Council. Unlike other Irish bishops, the cardinal understood very well both the liberal and the conservative sets of mind. He also understood the media and their wants. This modernity, combined with an iron caution which restrained him from parting any distance in public from the values of traditional Catholicism, marked him out as a sophisticated but prudent ecclesiastic of the type admired by Pope Paul VI. The pope signalled his respect by making him one of the three presidents of the first Synod of Bishops in Rome in 1967.

At home, caution predominated as he led the Irish Church into the post-conciliar era. It was a calculated caution, paced to achieve as much change as possible in liturgy, ecumenism and promoting the concept of the People of God without causing excessive distress to Catholics suspicious of new ways. Under his guidance the Irish Episcopal Conference published a number of pastoral letters on subjects ranging from *Christian Marriage* (1969), which repeated the papal teaching against artificial birth control, to *The Work of Justice* (1977), which spoke in strongly conciliar terms about society's obligation to the unemployed.

He was also the principal signatory to three joint statements by the bishops of Northern Ireland (1970, 1971), condemning paramilitary violence but also the 'interrogation in depth' of people imprisoned without trial. The prolonged violence in the North, not least in his native west Belfast, greatly troubled the cardinal in his later years.

COOGAN, Eamonn (1896–1948), deputy commissioner Garda Síochána, b. Castlecomer, Co. Kilkenny, d. 22 Jan. 1948. B.Sc., B.Comm., BL. Principal Limerick School of Commerce; Irish Volunteers 1914; inspector Department of Local Government, under W.T. COSGRAVE. Appointed by Cosgrave second in command of the Civic Guard in May 1922.

Deputy Garda commissioner 1922. Coogan assumed the duties of chief commissioner for lengthy periods during the critical early years in the formation of the Garda Síochána: when EOIN O'DUFFY was out of the country at meetings of the International Association of Chiefs of Police in 1923 and 1925; and in 1924 during O'Duffy's absence as inspector-general of the defence forces. He was one of those who steered the unarmed force through the crisis of the Civil War. Removed from office in controversial circumstances 1936; reappointed as a chief superintendent, he retired in 1941. Entered politics, Dún Laoghaire Borough Council; elected Dáil Éireann as Fine Gael deputy for Carlow–Kilkenny 1944, and had

been nominated for his constituency in the 1948 general election at the time of his death. Father of TIM PAT COOGAN.

COOGAN, Tim Pat (1935–), journalist, historian and biographer, b. Co. Dublin, s. of EAMONN COOGAN, ed. Blackrock. Joined the *Evening Press* in 1954 and worked his way up from copy-boy to become editor of the *Irish Press* 1968–87. He brought new life to the paper, distancing it from rigid adherence to Fianna Fáil and engaging DAVID MARCUS, as literary editor, to edit a weekly page under the title 'New Irish Writing', which proved to be an important launching pad for literary talent. Coogan himself has made a significant contribution to Irish history with major reflective or investigative books like *Ireland since the Rising* (1966) and *The IRA* (1970), a fine biography, *Michael Collins* (1990), and a surprisingly critical one, *De Valera* (1993). He is also a frequent participant in Irish, English and American broadcast discussions on contemporary political developments, especially in relation to Northern Ireland.

COOKE, Barrie (1931–), artist, b. Cheshire, raised in the USA and Jamaica, ed. Harvard. After graduating with a degree in art history, he studied art with Rattner and Levine in New York. His first one-man show was held there in 1950. In 1954 he came to live in Ireland and the following year was awarded a scholarship to study under Oskar Kokoschka in Salzburg. He was very influential in introducing the style of the American abstract expressionists to Ireland. His later paintings offer a more representational exploration of the subject but retain the vigour and the exciting exploration of colour evident in his abstract work. A highly respected painter, he has had three major retrospectives: in Dublin 1971 (jointly with CAMILLE SOUTER), Belfast 1986 and the Haags Gemeentemuseum, Holland 1992. Cooke's work has been included in a number of group shows of major Irish artists both in Ireland and abroad. He also represented Ireland at the Paris Biennale in 1963 and at Rosc '84.

COOKE, Emma (1934–), novelist and short story writer, b. Portarlington, Co. Laois, ed. Alexandra; diploma in philosophy at Mary Immaculate Training College, Limerick. She began writing in the early 1970s and her fiction has appeared in magazines, newspapers and anthologies in Ireland, Europe and the USA. She also makes frequent radio broadcasts. Cooke is very active in creative writing workshops, as well as the Listowel Writers' Week, the Killaloe Writers' Group and the Arts Council's writers in schools project. She lives near Limerick and teaches at the Limerick Adult Education Institute. A collection of short stories, *Female Forms*, was published in 1981, and she has written three novels: *A Single Sensation* (1982), *Eve's Apple* (1985) and *Wedlocked* (1994).

COONEY, Joe (1964–), hurler, b. Bullaun, Loughrea, Co. Galway, 17 Mar. 1964. He played major roles in Galway's All-Ireland hurling final successes of 1987 and 1988, having been on the teams defeated in the finals of 1985 and 1986. He captained the side which lost the 1990 final, and again was on the losing team in 1993, his sixth All-Ireland final. One of hurling's great half-forwards, he won two National Hurling League medals, two Railway Cup medals with Connacht, and five All-Star awards, in 1985 and 1986 at left-half forward, and in 1987, 1989 and 1990 at centre-half forward. With his club, Sarsfields, he won Galway senior hurling medals in 1989 and 1992, and won the All-Ireland Club Championship in 1993.

COOPER, Robert George (1936–), chairman Northern Ireland Fair Employment Commission (formerly Agency) since 1976, b. 24 June 1936, eldest s. of William Hugh and Annie Cooper, ed. Foyle College, Derry and QUB (LL B). After graduating, he worked in industrial relations and was assistant secretary of the Engineering Employers' Federation of Northern Ireland 1963–72. Active in the Alliance Party for a number of years, he was appointed its general secretary 1972–3. Elected member for West Belfast in the Assembly elections of 1973 and served as Minister of Manpower Services in the NI Executive 1974.

CORISH, Brendan (1918–1990), politician, b. Wexford, 19 Nov. 1918, s. of RICHARD CORISH, ed. CBS, Wexford, m. Phyllis Donoghue 1949, d. 17 Feb. 1990. He succeeded his father in the Dáil at a by-election in 1945 and became a junior minister in the first inter-party government 1948–51. In the second inter-party government 1954–7 he was

Minister for Social Welfare. When WILLIAM NORTON resigned as leader of the Labour Party in 1960, Corish was the only realistic leadership candidate with ministerial experience and he was selected unanimously. The party of which he became leader had assumed an anti-coalition policy, one which Corish himself echoed. Despite his social conservatism he encouraged new blood in the party and, in tandem with the general secretary, BRENDAN HALLIGAN, went about nudging the party towards a more left-wing stance and attracting support both from smaller parties on the left and from individuals who had heretofore looked askance at Labour's strongly trade union image. By 1969 the combination of the party's left-wing stance and its anti-coalition policy had set it firmly on a new course. That course faltered as the electorate failed to respond, and Corish took personal responsibility for engineering a change in the anti-coalition platform before the 1973 election. The result – a pre-election pact with Fine Gael – saw him in office again as Minister for Health and Social Welfare 1973–7.

He continued to support and encourage newcomers to the party such as JUSTIN KEATING and CONOR CRUISE O'BRIEN, but it was to some extent a false dawn: when the party lost two seats in the 1977 election he resigned as leader and was succeeded by FRANK CLUSKEY. He stood down from the Dáil at the 1981 election.

CORISH, Richard (1889–1945), politician, b. Wexford, ed. CBS, Wexford. Trade union official. TD (SF 1920, Labour 1921–45, Wexford), Mayor of Wexford 1920–45. Father of BRENDAN CORISH.

CORKERY, Daniel (1878–1964), writer and teacher, b. Cork, 14 Feb. 1878, ed. Presentation Brothers, Cork and St Patrick's College, Dublin, d. Passage West, Co. Cork, 31 Dec. 1964. Taught in Cork for a number of years. He co-founded the Cork Dramatic Society (1908) with his friends TERENCE MACSWINEY and Con O'Leary and wrote plays in Irish and English for it. Professor of English UCC 1930–47. Member of Seanad Éireann 1951–4. Publications include collections of short stories: *A Munster Twilight* (1916), *The Hounds of Banba* (1926), *The Stormy Hills* (1929) and *Earth out of Earth* (1939); a novel,

The Threshold of Quiet (1917); plays, *The Labour Leader* and *The Yellow Pattern* (1920), *Resurrection* (1924). Also wrote the seminal book *The Hidden Ireland* (1924), which explored Ireland's long-forgotten cultural heritage and Gaelic poetry from the 18th century. Other works include *Synge and Anglo-Irish Literature* (1931) and *The Fortunes of the Irish Language* (1954).

CORRIGAN-MAGUIRE, Mairead (1944–), co-founder of the Peace People, b. 27 Jan. 1944. Initiator of the Peace Movement in Northern Ireland in Aug. 1976, the year in which she and BETTY WILLIAMS were jointly awarded the Nobel peace prize. Chair of the Peace People Organisation 1980–81. Director of Peace People's Commitment to Active Non-Violence. Inspired to launch the Peace People after her sister's three children were struck and killed by a runaway car whose IRA driver had been shot dead by the army. Her sister died in 1980 and a year later Corrigan married her former husband, Jackie Maguire. Still a fervent campaigner for peace, she commented at the launch of 'Initiative '92': 'We live in a society where people are afraid – but it's all right to be afraid. But we must overcome that fear and overcome apathy. Apathy is the greatest enemy facing us today. Apathy will kill our society.'

COSGRAVE, Liam (1920–), politician, b. 13 Apr. 1920, s. of W.T. COSGRAVE, ed. Synge Street, Castleknock and King's Inns, m. Vera Osborne, two s. one d. Served in the army during the Emergency and practised at the Bar. First elected to the Dáil in 1943 (FG Dublin County, later Dún Laoghaire–Rathdown) and for the rest of his career never lost an election. A parliamentary secretary 1948–51, he became Minister for External Affairs 1954–7. Following the resignation of JAMES DILLON, consequent on Fine Gael's failure to regain office at the election of 1965, Cosgrave became leader of the party. His questions to Taoiseach JACK LYNCH in 1970 were the first public hint of the subsequent Arms Crisis and the dismissal from cabinet of CHARLES HAUGHEY and NEIL BLANEY, but, to the surprise and disappointment of many in FG, the Fianna Fáil government managed to hold on to power despite its internal divisions.

Gradually, the more liberal wing of FG began to distance itself from Cosgrave and he came close to being ousted late in 1972 when, dramatically, his tough approach to law and order seemed vindicated by the explosion of loyalist bombs in Dublin city centre. When a general election was called in 1973 he negotiated an election pact with the Labour Party, which had previously declared it would not enter another coalition with FG. The coalition narrowly won the election and Cosgrave became Taoiseach. Although he had no great public charisma and his liberal critics within FG never fully accepted him, he drew much praise from Labour ministers for his skill in holding the coalition together at a time of severe inflationary pressures and economic disorder occasioned by the international oil crisis, with ensuing tensions in Irish industrial relations. But he never compromised on what he considered to be matters of principle; despite his known conservatism on social issues, he caused consternation among his colleagues when, on a free vote, he vetoed his own government's bill to liberalise the laws on contraception.

During his first year in power Cosgrave led the Irish government side in the negotiations with the British government and a number of the Northern Ireland parties which culminated in the Sunningdale Agreement. This provided for a power-sharing Executive in the North and a Council of Ireland similar to that which had been envisaged in the early 1920s. The former was to collapse within six months while the latter never got off the ground. It was an omen, for throughout Cosgrave's term of office the Northern situation was to pose problems for his government, especially when violence spilt over in the most horrific way into the Republic. In the worst single day's atrocity of the entire Troubles, 34 people were killed by bombs in Dublin and Monaghan on 17 May 1974. On 21 July 1976 the British ambassador, Christopher Ewart-Biggs, and an embassy secretary were murdered outside the embassy residence near Dublin. The Taoiseach did not hesitate to seek and enforce the powers he felt were necessary to cope with such violence.

The coalition parties conducted a lacklustre campaign in the 1977 general election, believing that their record would guarantee their survival and that any fall in popular support would be offset by the effects of a revision of constituency boundaries completed under their aegis. In the event, the FF opposition mounted a clever campaign focused on grievances over living costs and high taxation, much of which it promised to reduce or abolish. A huge swing to FF resulted and put an end to the coalition government. As soon as the scale of defeat became clear, Cosgrave with characteristic directness resigned as leader of FG. He retired from the Dáil in 1981 and took little further part in political life. In the judgment of many civil servants and professional politicians, including a number of his opponents, he was a model head of government, able to control and direct the energies of a very diverse group of colleagues while retaining to himself the authority to make major decisions.

COSGRAVE, William Thomas (1880–1965), revolutionary and statesman, b. Dublin, 6 June 1880, ed. CBS, d. 16 Nov. 1965. The separatist policies of Sinn Féin attracted him as a young man and he had been promoting the movement for several years before his election to the Dublin City Council in 1909. He joined the Irish Volunteers in 1913; when they split he took the side opposed to the recruitment of Irishmen for the British army. In the Easter Rising he served as adjutant to EAMONN CEANNT at the South Dublin Union, for which he was sentenced to death. The sentence was commuted and after a period of internment in Wales he won a by-election in Kilkenny for Sinn Féin. He was Minister for Local Government in the First Dáil, a post in which his City Council experience proved invaluable. He induced most of the county councils to acknowledge the authority of the Dáil ministry.

He supported the Anglo-Irish Treaty and became chairman of the Provisional Government of the Irish Free State after the death of MICHAEL COLLINS in Aug. 1922. He prosecuted the tragic Civil War to the end with profound distress but an unflinching sense of duty, even to the extent of approving the action for which he would be most reviled, the execution of four republican leaders as a deterrent against further killings of public representatives after the assassination of a Dáil deputy. When in Dec. the Free State came formally into being as a Commonwealth dominion, Cosgrave took office as President of the Executive Council (Prime Minister) and set about consolidating the new state. He made maximum use of the civil service inherited from the British regime, which gave a conservative character to fiscal and social policy but also ensured remarkable stability in a country emerging from a decade of unprecedented turmoil. Cosgrave also took care to reassure Protestants and unionists, appointing a number of them to the Seanad and leaving their extensive business enterprises fully under their own control.

A stoic quality marked the young but exceptionally able members of Cosgrave's governments. Their firm maintenance of law and order and their fiscal rectitude did not make for popularity, but they copper-fastened the stability which the state needed above all else. The maximum advantage was extracted from the Treaty. The Free State joined the League of Nations, issued passports, established diplomatic missions abroad and repudiated any role for UK authorities in Irish international relations. Much of this was done in the teeth of British disapproval but with the support of other Commonwealth countries, South Africa and Canada especially. At home important economic initiatives were undertaken – both for agriculture and, through the construction of the Shannon Hydroelectric Scheme, for future industrial development.

It was greatly to Cosgrave's credit that he established the new state so effectively notwithstanding a background of potential violence, typified in the attempted 'Army Mutiny' of 1924 and the assassination of KEVIN O'HIGGINS in 1927. Parliamentary procedures had to be developed initially in the absence of a normal opposition since the republicans who lost the Civil War commanded up to 40 per cent of the vote but refused to sit in the Free State Dáil until 1927; EAMON DE VALERA's Fianna Fáil party, which many of them joined, then took its seats after much argument over the oath of allegiance to the king required of TDs. Many consider it Cosgrave's finest achievement that, when his Cumann na nGaedheal lost the general election of 1932, he accepted the people's verdict and relinquished power democratically to de Valera. He founded a new party, Fine Gael, in 1933 and remained leader of the opposition until his retirement from politics in 1944. Father of LIAM COSGRAVE.

COSTELLO, Charles, KPM, sergeant RIC, b. Westport. RIC 1881, stationed at Croghan, Boyle. On duty at Boyle Races 7 June 1911; during the Hunt Race, when two children strayed onto the course, he ran out to save them and was badly injured himself. King's Police Medal, award from Carnegie Hero Fund and Certificate of Order of St John of Jerusalem. Costello's KPM may be taken as epitomising many deeds of bravery in the RIC in its role as a civil police force. (See JAMES MULROY.)

COSTELLO, Declan (1927–), politician, lawyer and judge, b. Dublin, s. of JOHN A. COSTELLO, ed. Xavier's School, Dublin, UCD and King's Inns. Barrister. TD (FG, Dublin North-West 1951–69, Dublin South-West 1973–6). Drafted and promoted a radical socio-political programme, *The Just Society*, to redirect state policy towards an emphasis on wide-ranging reform of the health services, social security and other areas of concern to the underprivileged. Although strongly supported by some senior members of Fine Gael such as THOMAS O'HIGGINS, ALEXIS FITZGERALD and future Taoiseach GARRET FITZGERALD, he had difficulty in winning wholehearted backing from the influential party hierarchy. He was appointed Attorney-General in 1973 in the incoming FG–Labour coalition, to the surprise of many who had expected him to receive a major portfolio like Health or Social Welfare, where he could give effect to his thinking. As Attorney-General he carried through an important reform in the administration of justice by creating the non-political office of Director of Public Prosecutions, to which virtually all of the Attorney-General's prosecuting function was transferred. In 1976 he became a High Court judge and in 1995 President of the High Court.

COSTELLO, John Aloysius (1891–1976), lawyer and politician, b. Dublin, 20 June 1891, ed. O'Connell School, UCD and King's Inns, m. Ida Mary O'Malley, three s. two d., d. 5 Jan. 1976. Called to Bar 1914. He became assistant to the Attorney-General in 1922, in which capacity he helped to devise the political and administrative structures of the newly established Irish Free State. He succeeded as Attorney-General in 1926 and contributed to the expansion of Irish independence through his efforts at Commonwealth conferences and the League of Nations to ensure that the freedoms implicit in the Anglo-Irish Treaty of 1921 were fully implemented. Much of what he sought was incorporated in the Statute of Westminster 1931, which recognised the complete freedom of action open to all Commonwealth dominions.

With the defeat of the Cumann na nGaedheal government in 1932 Costello returned to the Bar, where he built up an impressive practice and appeared in many of the major cases of the day. In 1933 he also entered politics as a TD (C. na nG., later FG; Dublin County, later Dublin South-East). In the Dáil he was a trenchant debater, especially when in 1937 he criticised the proposals for a new constitution, in part because he regarded as excessive the powers to be conferred upon the Taoiseach. After the general election of 1948 the disparate parties and independent TDs in the Dáil, who between them outnumbered Fianna Fáil and were determined to form a government, needed a leader around whom they could unite. Under much pressure, not least from his own indomitable sense of duty, Costello reluctantly agreed to be Taoiseach and on 18 Feb. became head of the first interparty or coalition government in the history of the state. It continued in office until 1951 and returned for a further three years in 1954, again with Costello as Taoiseach.

The achievements of the Costello governments included the establishment of the Industrial Development Authority and the Irish Export Board, rapid progress in the provision of municipal housing, the virtual elimination of tuberculosis, and the removal of lingering constitutional ambiguities by the Republic of Ireland Act, which took the state out of the Commonwealth in 1949. The Taoiseach gave special priority to the promotion of modern economic thinking, which came to fruition in creative plans for the national economy after he had left office in 1957. That so much could be put in hand by governments which included republican, socialist and right-wing elements was seen to be the personal achievement of John Costello, whose sensitivity to the various attitudes within the coalition held the alliance together even under the strain of controversy over the abandonment of NOEL BROWNE's

'Mother and Child' scheme. Costello continued to serve as a TD until 1969 and maintained his legal practice almost until his death.

COSTELLO, Michael Joseph (1904–1986), soldier and businessman, b. Cloughjordan, Co. Tipperary, ed. CBS, Nenagh, m. Mary Kennedy, eight s. one d. Son of teachers, godson of THOMAS MACDONAGH. Joined the IRA 1920. Supported the Treaty, joined National Army in Feb. 1922 and during the Civil War was given the rank of colonel-commandant by MICHAEL COLLINS. He was 18. Appointed director of intelligence 1923 and chief staff officer 1925. The following year he was sent to US army installations with HUGO MACNEILL and other officers to learn how to set up the Military College: they were the first officers of a foreign army thus facilitated. Director of military training 1930. Assistant chief of staff 1938. Arms-purchasing mission to USA 1939; aborted after three months. In Nov. 1939 he was appointed GOC Southern Command.

General manager Irish Sugar Company 1945. Beset by labour disputes since 1933, the company was soon involved in the major confrontation of 1945–6, after which industrial peace reigned for 30 years. Member of the Capital Advisory Committee 1956. Differences between Costello and the Department of Finance, which criticised the Sugar Company for 'salting away reserves', led to him offering his resignation in 1961. Taoiseach SEÁN LEMASS, however, advised him to 'pay no attention to the Department of Finance'. Further differences arose between Costello and Minister for Agriculture CHARLES HAUGHEY about the Sugar Company's right to grow potatoes. Lemass encouraged Costello to establish Erin Foods (1964) but the promised funding, autonomy and linkage to the co-operatives did not materialise. In 1966 Costello finally resigned, to be replaced by A.J.F. O'REILLY.

A practical patriot, Costello initiated and guided co-operatives in many fields. He oversaw the introduction of worker participation and diversification into machinery, fertilisers, accelerated freeze-dried foods and the reclamation of bogland for food-growing. In retirement Costello farmed in Co. Roscommon and was prominent in the campaign to prevent the army from participating in Remembrance Day ceremonies organised by the British Legion: he was unhappy about the compromise reached in this matter.

COSTELLOE, Paul (1945–), designer, b. Dublin, ed. Blackrock and the Chambre Syndicale de la Haute Couture in Paris. He worked in Paris, Milan and New York before returning to Ireland, from where he has established an international reputation as a fashion designer renowned for his beautifully tailored clothes and the use of fine-quality fabrics, particularly Irish linens and tweeds. His clothes are worn by many prominent women, including the Princess of Wales, a regular patron who has been photographed in several of his creations.

COSTIGAN, Daniel (1911–1979), commissioner Garda Síochána, d. 10 Sept. 1979. Entered civil service 1929. As assistant secretary Department of Justice he was a member of an interdepartmental committee of inquiry into the police service 1950. Appointed Garda commissioner 1952 at the age of 41, replacing another civil servant, MICHAEL JOSEPH KINNANE, who died in office. His appointment was greeted with dismay by some ambitious senior officers of long service. A brilliant administrator, Costigan accelerated the policy of amending outmoded regulations inherited from the RIC. He had to contend – practically alone – with the crisis in the 1950s brought about by the wholesale retirement of the founding generation of Gardaí recruited in the 1920s, including the loss of the older experienced officers and of the entire cadre of confident sergeants promoted by the first commissioners. Addressing himself single-mindedly to the modernisation of the Garda Síochána, he was opposed by disappointed officers and the deeply rooted conservatism in the force. He was isolated and finally defeated in the conflict between the rank and file and the Department of Justice in the 'Macushla' revolt in 1961, dismissing and then having to reinstate the suspected ringleaders, including JACK MARRINAN. Costigan, who served as commissioner until 1965, recruited the first women members of the Garda Síochána (1959).

COTTER, Maud (1954–), stained-glass artist, ed. St Patrick's Secondary School and Crawford Municipal School of Art, Cork. She started exhibiting in 1974 and went on to perfect the craft and technique of glass in association with JAMES SCANLON. Humour, strength, imagination, experimentation, energy and an interest in oriental art distinguish her work.

COUGHLAN, Eugene (Eudie, Hudie) (1900–), hurler. Having been a non-playing substitute in Cork's All-Ireland winning team in 1919, he captained the county to similar success 12 years on, in 1931. Cork defeated Kilkenny after two replays and his brother, John, was the goalkeeper. In between he had won further All-Ireland medals in 1926, 1928 and 1929, and was on the losing team of the 1927 final. He won an inaugural National Hurling League medal with Cork in 1926, another in 1930, as well as Railway Cup medals with Munster in 1928 and 1929. Though long retired he won his last medal, aged 54, in an inter-firm competition. In 1985 he and JACK LYNCH became the first two Corkmen to receive All-Time All-Star awards for hurling.

COULTER, Phil (1942–), songwriter, b. Derry, Feb. 1942. He has had a highly successful and enduring career as a musical arranger and producer, and as a writer of hit pop songs. With his partner, Bill Martin, he penned the winner of the 1968 Eurovision Song Contest, 'Puppet on a String', sung by Sandie Shaw, and the 1969 runner-up, Cliff Richard's 'Congratulations'. He also arranged DANA's 1970 winner, 'All Kinds of Everything'. In the mid-1970s the partnership supplied pop bands the Bay City Rollers, Kenny and Slik with a series of hit singles. However, Coulter did not confine his musical interests to pop, and during the same period he produced a number of records for folk bands THE DUBLINERS and Planxty. In 1983 he moved into another musical area with his first orchestral recording, *Classic Tranquility*. He has recorded several more albums in the same romantic, easy-listening style comprising a mixture of well-known tunes and his own compositions.

COUSINS, James Henry Sproull (1873–1956), writer, educator and art critic, b. Belfast, left school at 13 yet was later appointed private secretary to the Lord Mayor of Belfast. Moved to Dublin in 1897, where he befriended the prime movers of the literary revival. Met Frank and WILLIAM FAY in 1901 and introduced them to AE (GEORGE RUSSELL), whose *Deirdre* they performed 1902. Cousins wrote several plays for the fledgling Irish National Theatre Society, including *The Sleep of the King* (1902), *The Racing Lug* (1902) – a tragedy similar to J.M. SYNGE's later *Riders to the Sea* – and *The Sword of Dermot* (1903). Was for a time a member of the Theosophical Society. In 1915 he and his wife, MARGARET COUSINS, moved to India, where they made an enormous contribution to that nation's educational and literary life, art and philosophy. He wrote over 100 books, contributed hundreds of articles to Indian periodicals, and founded India's first art gallery at Travancore, later another at Mysore.

COUSINS, Margaret E. (1878–1954), née Gillespie, educator and feminist, b. Belmont, Boyle, ed. locally, Derry, RIAM and RUI (B.Mus.). M. JAMES COUSINS 1903. A women's rights activist from 1908, she was a delegate to a suffragist parliament in 1910 and imprisoned for throwing stones at 10 Downing Street. She left for India with her husband in 1915, became the first non-Indian member of the Indian Women's University at Poona 1916, was co-founder of the Women's Indian Association 1917 and foundation headmistress of a girls' school. She also did valuable social work, contributed numerous articles to Indian journals on theosophy, education, art and philosophy, and published many books, including a joint biography with her husband, *We Two Together* (1950). An accident in 1943 left her paralysed. She was honoured by the Madras government and Pandit Nehru for promoting Indian independence.

COX, Arthur (1891–1965), lawyer, b. Dublin, ed. Belvedere and UCD (BA 1912, MA 1913), d. 11 June 1965. Qualified as solicitor 1916; became senior partner in Dublin firm still bearing his name. Adviser to members of the committee drafting the constitution of the IFS, 1922. Member of council of Law Society 1941–61 and its president 1951–2; expert on company law and member of government committee whose report led to the Companies Act 1963. Married widow of KEVIN O'HIGGINS; retired 1961 after 46 years in practice. Ordained Catholic priest by Archbishop JOHN CHARLES MCQUAID 1963. Volunteered for missionary work with the Irish Jesuits in northern Rhodesia (now Zambia), where he died after a road accident.

CRAIG, James, first Viscount Craigavon (1871–1940), politician, b. 8 Jan. 1871, son of the millionaire owner of Dunville's Distillery, ed. local preparatory school and Merchiston Castle, Edinburgh. He set up his own stock-broking business in Belfast, then, unable to resist the excitement of the Boer War, served with the Royal Irish Rifles in South Africa 1900–1. Returning home he was attracted to politics and, with the help of a legacy from his father, was elected Unionist MP for East Down in 1906.

Craig joined his fellow unionists, mostly from Northern Ireland, in a parliament where the Union was under threat from an alliance of Irish Nationalists and British Liberals. He took the lead in organising the campaign against the third Home Rule bill. It was at his house, Craigavon, that EDWARD CARSON was persuaded to become leader of the Ulster Unionists in 1910. In 1912 Craig was deeply involved in the Ulster Covenant and in 1914 he helped with the landing of arms at Larne for the UVF. With the coming of war, Craig suggested that the UVF become the 36th (Ulster) Division. Not fit enough to serve at the front, he stayed in parliament, where he held minor government office. He used his influence to ensure that under the Government of Ireland Act 1920 a manageable six counties of Ulster would remain within the UK.

Craig felt it his duty to become first Prime Minister of Northern Ireland, 1921, after the ageing Carson, as expected, refused the post. As Prime Minister he was constructive in his relations with the new Free State under MICHAEL COLLINS and W.T. COSGRAVE. At home he appointed a reasonably talented cabinet which oversaw the government of the Northern Ireland state and its defence against attack from the IRA. But when the initial crises were surmounted he let things drift. He allowed Sir RICHARD DAWSON BATES at Home Affairs to pursue a harsh security regime. Under pressure from the Protestant Churches he amended the new Education Act and he safeguarded unionist political power by abolishing proportional representation and gerrymandering local government boundaries.

In all of this he showed no sense of the need to reassure the Catholic minority. The weakness he demonstrated in handling his supporters was also evident in his dealings with the Westminster government. Though he spent much time at his house at Cleere Court near London and flattered himself that he took a broad UK view, in fact he let the Northern Ireland case for preferential treatment in matters of finance go by default.

He continued as premier long after he was able to do the job because he needed the salary and liked the honours (he became Viscount Craigavon in 1927). He died at home on 24 Nov. 1940 in the company of his wife, Cecil Mary Tupper (with whom he had three children). At the time, unionist Ulster mourned a hero but a recent biographer sees him as 'a very ordinary man, mastered by and not master of circumstances and events'.

CRAIG, Maurice (1919–), Ireland's foremost architectural historian and author, ed. at Castle Park, Dublin, Shrewsbury School, England and, on a scholarship, Magdalene College, Cambridge. He has written extensively on matters relating to Ireland's history and heritage, particularly its architecture, with publications ranging from *The Volunteer Earl* (1948), on Lord Charlemont and his buildings, to *The Architecture of Ireland from the Earliest Times to 1880* (1982), on pre-modern Irish architecture. Most notable is *Dublin 1660–1860* (1952), arguably the most significant volume this century on Irish architecture. He later worked with An Taisce and on government projects, though his most important work remains his personal promotion of Ireland's architectural heritage.

CRAIG, William (1924–), politician, b. 2 Dec. 1924. Stormont MP for Larne from 1960. Government chief whip 1962–3. Minister of Home Affairs 1963–4, Health and Local Government 1964–5, Development 1965–6, Home Affairs 1966–8. Craig banned the civil rights march in Derry of 5 Oct. 1968, events surrounding which are usually seen as the start of the Troubles. He was sacked in Dec. of that year following disputes with Prime Minister TERENCE O'NEILL. In 1972 he helped to organise a 48-hour strike and a demonstration against the abolition of the Northern Ireland parliament. At the same time he formed the Ulster Vanguard Movement (after Mar. 1973 the Vanguard Unionist Progressive Party), which toyed with the idea of independence for NI. Elected to the NI Assembly for North Antrim in 1973 and for East Belfast in Feb.

1974. Craig was the first political leader to give his support to the loyalist strike of May 1974, which brought down the NI power-sharing Executive. Elected to the NI Convention in 1975, his proposal for a voluntary coalition of parties as the basis of an NI administration was almost accepted. The eventual refusal of other Unionists to support Craig's plan led to a split in Vanguard and the decline in the party. He rejoined the Ulster Unionist Party but narrowly lost his Westminster seat in 1979. A controversial political figure, Craig stated at a rally in Mar. 1972, 'If and when the politicians fail us, it may be our job to liquidate the enemy.'

CRANBERRIES, The, rock band, originated in Limerick. *Everybody Else Is Doing It, So Why Can't We?* (Island Records 1993) became the most successful début album ever by an Irish band, selling three million copies worldwide, while the single 'Linger' was a top ten hit in both the USA and the UK. The follow-up, *No Need to Argue*, went platinum within weeks of its release. With her sweet, soaring voice and highly personal lyrics, Dolores O'Riordan became a worthy successor to SINÉAD O'CONNOR.

CRAWFORD, Major Frederick Hugh (1861–1952), soldier, b. Belfast, 21 Aug. 1861, ed. Methodist College, Belfast and University College School, London. Fred Crawford worked as an apprentice at Harland and Wolff and later in the family starch-manufacturing business. He enlisted in the Mid-Ulster Artillery, later transferring to the Donegal Artillery, in which he was promoted captain in 1896. During the Boer War he served as adjutant of the Irish Division Militia Artillery. Mentioned in dispatches, he was awarded the Queen's Medal with three clasps. Served in the Royal Army Service Corps during World War I, and in the 1920s in the Northern Ireland Special Constabulary. Renowned as the organiser of the 1914 UVF gun-smuggling operation, a story which he detailed in *Guns for Ulster* (1947), Crawford had, at the time of the second Home Rule bill, even considered kidnapping British Prime Minister Gladstone. BASIL BROOKE described Crawford as 'a fearless figure in the historic fight to keep Ulster British'.

CREAN, Thomas (1877–1938), Antarctic explorer, b. Anascaul, Co. Kerry. Joined Royal Navy 1893 and took opportunity to go with Robert Scott's *Discovery* expedition to Antarctica in 1901. Returned with Scott on fated 1910 expedition, and in a clearly heroic episode with another seaman, W. Lashly, in Jan. 1912 hauled the sick Lieutenant (later Admiral) E. Evans across Antarctic waste to safety, as the three returned from helping Scott to embark on the last stage of the march to the South Pole. Crean and Lashly were each later awarded the Albert medal.

Crean returned to the Antarctic in 1914 as second officer on the *Endurance* in ERNEST SHACKLETON's epic expedition. Back in England and the navy, Crean was promoted but his eyesight had been affected by snow-blindness in the Antarctic and he retired in Mar. 1920. He returned to Anascaul with his wife, Ellen Herlihy, and died on 27 July 1938, a man who had shown great fortitude and courage in remarkable circumstances.

CROFTS, Ambrose (1894–1963), Dominican priest, b. Cork, 5 May 1894, ed. North Mon., d. 28 Sept. 1963. Entered Dominican order, ordained Rome 1919. From 1920 to 1933 attached to St Saviour's, Dublin. He was invited to join the St Columba's branch of the CYMS, North Frederick Street, Dublin, in 1926 and proved the vital personality in reviving that organisation into a significant body within Catholic Action. In 1932 he was instrumental in establishing a nationwide federation of CYMS branches and persuaded JOHN MCCORMACK to be its patron. That same year he formed the central study circle of the body, which emerged as a key force opposing left-wing groups in Dublin during the early 1930s. He became national organiser of the CYMS for a time but his influence over it declined and he was sent to Melbourne in 1938 as vicar provincial of Dominicans in Australia and New Zealand, a position he held until 1946. He returned to Ireland in 1949 as manager of Dominican Publications, devoting much of his time to writing and lecturing. In 1962 he became prior at Holy Cross, Sligo, where he died.

CROKER, Richard (1841–1922), Tammany Hall 'Boss', b. Clonakilty, Co. Cork, 23 Nov. 1841, d. New York, 29 Apr. 1922. His family emigrated to the USA when he was three. He began his working life at 13 but soon got involved with Democratic Party politics in

New York City, centred on Tammany Hall. He became an alderman in 1868 and five years later was appointed city coroner. In 1886 he became Democratic Party leader in the city and head of the Tammany organisation. He held this position until 1903, during which time he acquired considerable personal wealth. On retirement he lived briefly in England, then in Co. Dublin 1907–19. He returned to New York in the latter years of his life. In 1907 his colt Orby became the first Irish-trained winner of the Epsom Derby.

CROMIEN, Sean (1929–), economist and public servant, b. Dublin, ed. CBS, North Brunswick Street, Dublin and UCD (BA Econ., first class honours). After a short period as an executive officer in the OPW, in 1952 he joined the Department of Finance, of which he was appointed secretary in 1977. At various times director of the Central Bank and member of the NESC, the advisory committee of the National Treasury Management Agency, the executive committee of the ESRI and the council of the Statistical and Social Inquiry Society of Ireland. Chairman and subsequently president of the Institute of Public Administration. Fellow of the Irish Management Institute. Alternate governor for Ireland on the boards of the World Bank and the European Bank for Reconstruction and Development. Chairman of the OECD Senior Budget Officials Group.

CRONE, Anne (1915–1972), teacher and novelist, b. Dublin, ed. Belfast and Oxford. She wrote a series of novels in the 1940s and 1950s which are characterised by being narrated by young women, and whose principal themes are land, romance and the fortunes of rural Ulster families. They are: *Bridie Steen* (1948), *This Pleasant Lea* (1951) and *My Heart and I* (1955). Her first book has been the most popular; Lord DUNSANY, who wrote the introduction, called it 'one of the great novels of our time' and applauded Crone's rendering of Co. Fermanagh, 'smiling at times with the Christian charity of its people, and sometimes darkened with bigotry'. *Bridie Steen* enjoyed two reprints, the second as late as 1984. Nevertheless, Crone's work has not weathered well, is dated and mannered, and occupies only a minor position in Irish romantic fiction.

CRONE, John Smyth (1858–1945), physician, academic and bibliophile, b. Belfast, ed. Royal Academical Institution and QUB. Qualified in medicine, Apothecaries Co. and RCPI. He practised medicine in Willesden, London for 40 years and received many honours from the local authority. He founded the *Irish Book Lover* in 1909 and edited it until 1924. Elected MRIA in 1916. President 1918–25 of the Irish Literary Society, London, founded by W.B. YEATS in 1891. He is best remembered for his *A Concise Dictionary of Irish Biography* (1928), the first such compilation since Alfred John Webb's *Compendium of Irish Biography* (1878). He also wrote a well-received biography, *Henry Bradshaw: His Life and Work* (1931), and he and F.J. Bigger – the Irish-language revivalist (1863–1926) – edited Bigger's biographical, archaeological and historical writings as *In Remembrance* (1927).

CRONIN, Anthony (1926–), poet and novelist, b. Co. Wexford, ed. Blackrock, UCD and King's Inns, associate editor the *Bell* and literary editor *Time and Tide*. Publications include: *Poems* (1957), *The Life of Riley* (1964), *Collected Poems 1950–73* (1973), *Dead as Doornails* (1976), *Identity Papers* (1979), *Reductionist Poem* (1980), *Heritage Now: Irish Literature in the English Language* (1982), *An Irish Eye* (1985) and *The Life and Times of Flann O'Brien* (1989). His status as a literary critic of considerable authority was borne out by *A Question of Modernity* (1966) and a regular column in *The Irish Times* during the 1970s, but he chose to continue diversifying his activities between novel-writing, poetry and highly enjoyable, if acerbic, reminiscences. He was cultural adviser to Taoiseach CHARLES HAUGHEY and prime mover in the establishment of Aosdána. He was also racing correspondent for the *Sunday Tribune*. A writer of instinctive fluency and dry wit, he is a mordant observer of his country, its posturings and foibles.

CROSS, Eric (1903–1980), writer, b. Newry, d. at his home near Westport, 5 Sept. 1980. Although a research chemist by profession, his fame rests on the publication in 1942 of *The Tailor and Ansty*, in which he recorded the conversation of the remarkable Tim Buckley, the Tailor of Gougane Barra, Co. Cork, and his wife, Anastasia. Salty, demotic and colloquial, the Tailor's language caused the book to be banned under the Censorship Act. There followed an enormous public controversy, which culminated when a delegation of priests forced the Tailor to burn his own copy of the book in his fireplace. Cross continued to write for the rest of his life but never again achieved the same celebrity.

CROTTY, Elizabeth (1885–1960), née Markham, concertina player, b. Gower, Cooraclare, Co. Clare. Her older sister Margaret was a well-known local musician and the family home a venue for house dances. In 1914 she married Miko Crotty and both were to be active in the War of Independence. Later they bought a house in Kilrush, setting up business in the licensed trade. Her outstanding ability as a player was to become nationally recognised. She was recorded by SEÁN MAC RÉAMOINN for Radio Éireann, and in 1955 by CIARÁN MACMATHÚNA. Although examples of the work of Mrs Crotty, as she was universally referred to, may be heard on the RTÉ compilation album marking 50 years of radio and on an RTÉ cassette made by MacMathúna featuring his fieldwork in Clare and Kerry, there is no commercial recording of her playing.

CROTTY, Raymond B. (1925–1994), agricultural economist, b. Kilkenny, 22 Jan. 1925, ed. Albert Agricultural College, Glasnevin, Dublin and London School of Economics. From a Kilkenny baking family, he farmed in the county as a young man, developing a keen interest in the economics of agriculture. However, disillusionment with rural life led him towards an academic career. He lectured in agricultural economics at University College Wales at Aberystwyth and worked in Kuala Lumpur for the UK Overseas Development Agency. He later became a consultant with the World Bank/IMF in Washington, the Caribbean, South America and southern Africa. On returning to Ireland he became prominently identified with opposition to Ireland's membership of the European Community. A highly articulate and formidable campaigner, he was joint secretary of lobbying groups which opposed the decisions to join the Community in the 1972 referendum and to approve the Maastricht treaty in 1992. In 1987 he had almost single-handedly provoked the referendum on the Single European Act while researching in the TCD Department of Statistics. His hatred of emigration – four of his seven children joined the diaspora – fuelled his arguments against the prevailing economic orthodoxy, which he regarded as opportunist and short-term, favouring the business and political elite against the national interest. His published work includes the seminal *Irish Agricultural Production* (1966), *Cattle, Economics and Development* (1980), *Ireland in Crisis* (1986) and *Japan and Ireland: A Comparative Study* (1991). He was revising the final chapter of *Our Enemy the State* when he died on 1 Jan. 1994.

CROWLEY, Bob (1955–), designer, b. Cork, 10 June 1955, ed. Coláiste Críost Rí and Crawford Municipal School of Art, Cork and Bristol Old Vic. Associate designer with Britain's Royal National Theatre and with the Royal Shakespeare Company, Bob Crowley is among the world's foremost theatre and opera designers. Major productions include *The Plantagenets* and *Les liaisons dangereuses*, for which he won an Olivier award in 1985 for the RSC, and *Richard III*, *The Importance of being Earnest* and *Carousel* for the National Theatre, the latter transferring to New York's Lincoln Center in spring 1994. In Ireland Crowley has designed *Three Sisters* at the Gate Theatre, which transferred to the Royal Court Theatre in London, and *St Oscar* for Field Day Theatre Company. Also for Field Day he designed and co-directed SEAMUS HEANEY's *The Cure at Troy*.

CROWLEY, Eugene Christopher (1926–), commissioner Garda Síochána, b. Ballineed, Co. Cork, ed. St Ronan's College, Dunmanway, Co. Cork. Joined the force from school 1945 and rose through the ranks. Wide experience in operations and administration; personal assistant to EDMUND GARVEY. Garda commissioner 1988–91. As head of security, personally conducted unprecedented investigation into the 1988 shooting of Aidan McAnaspie at a British army checkpoint, Aughnacloy, Co. Tyrone. Directed the preparations for the departure of the first Garda contingent for duty with the UN (in Namibia) in Mar. 1989, which included STEPHEN FANNING and international commissioner and chief superintendent Noel Anderson as commander Garda contingent. Member Mater Dei Drug Awareness Group.

CROZIER, Frank Percy (1879–1937), British soldier, Auxiliary commander and author, born of army family with Irish connections and spent time as a child with relatives in Ireland, d. 31 Aug. 1937. Eventually commissioned in army and served in South African War, in campaign against Hausa in west Africa 1902–3 and later in Zululand, resigning commission in 1909. Employed in 1913 to train UVF group, he became an officer in the 36th (Ulster) Division and commanded a battalion of the Royal Irish Rifles on 1 July 1916 at the Somme. A hard-driving brigadier in the 40th Division 1916–19, he then took a post in the Lithuanian army, returning to become commandant of the Auxiliary Division of the RIC 1920–21. Resigned amid controversy about his attitude to the behaviour of Auxiliaries in Cork and Trim, and was later involved in long disputes with official circles about his service record. Wrote a widely read book about his time in Ulster and in World War I, and others such as *Ireland For Ever* (1932) and *The Men I Killed* (1937). His writings and attitudes provoked criticisms before and after his death.

CULHANE, John Leonard (1938–), FRS, scientist, s. of John Thomas and Mary Agnes Culhane, ed. Clongowes, UCD (M.Sc. 1960) and University College London (Ph.D. 1966), m. Mary Brigid Smith. Lecturer UCL 1967, reader 1976, professor 1980. Director Mullard Space Science Laboratory, University of London, since 1983. Visiting senior scientist Lockheed, Palo Alto. Chair SERC National Space Science Council; British delegate Space Science Progress Board 1989. Publications include *X-Ray Astronomy* (1981) and numerous papers.

CULLEN, James Aloysius (1841–1921), Jesuit priest, b. New Ross, 28 Oct. 1841, ed. Clongowes and St Patrick's College, Carlow, where he was ordained for the diocese of Ferns 1864, d. 6 Dec. 1921. After a successful career in the organisation of parish missions, he entered the Society of Jesus in 1881. Following studies in France he returned to Ireland in 1883 and carried on mission work for the Jesuits in schools and religious houses (the sermon in *A Portrait of the Artist as a Young Man* was long thought to be based on a retreat given by Cullen at Belvedere in 1896 which JAMES JOYCE attended, but this has been disputed in recent years). In 1887 he was appointed director for Ireland of the Apostleship of Prayer,

which encouraged devotion to the Sacred Heart as an antidote to religious anxiety and pessimism, failings from which Cullen himself suffered. In 1888 he launched the *Irish Messenger* to promote this devotion. Its circulation grew rapidly and reached 73,000 copies a month by 1904.

However, it is in connection with the temperance movement that his name is best remembered. In 1898 he founded the Total Abstinence League of the Sacred Heart. What in time became the Pioneer Total Abstinence Association claimed a membership of over 277,000 by 1919. Much of this success was due to Cullen's outstanding ability as an organiser and the manner in which he identified the temperance movement with the new cultural movements of the period, such as the Gaelic League.

CULLEN, Patrick (Paddy) (1944–), Gaelic footballer, b. Dublin, 18 Oct. 1944. A junior soccer player in the 1960s, he became an outstanding goalkeeper for Dublin in the 1970s, and starred in their three All-Ireland winning sides in that period, against Galway (1974), Kerry (1976) and Armagh (1977). He was also on the Dublin teams defeated by Kerry in the All-Ireland finals of 1975, 1978 and 1979, but won National League medals in 1976 and 1978 and four All-Star awards. He was Dublin's manager 1990–92, guiding them to victory in the National League in 1991 and to the All-Ireland final of 1992.

CULLEN, Thomas Joseph (1880–1947), architect, ed. Clongowes 1896–7, d. 22 Jan. 1947. Apprenticed to Ashlin and Coleman, a leading practice at the end of the last century, then in 1908 set up his own practice at 25 Suffolk Street, Dublin. In the same year he was elected a member of the RIAI, being raised to a fellow in 1922. Early projects of note include his design in the competition for UCD, Earlsfort Terrace, 1912. He was given responsibility for completing work on St Patrick's, Lough Derg, after the death of WILLIAM A. SCOTT, and he gained significant success with hospital buildings, including those at Galway 1932 and Castlepollard, Co. Westmeath 1940–42. In 1935 he sat on the board of assessors for the competition for the Department of Industry and Commerce, Kildare Street, Dublin.

CULLIGAN, Patrick Joseph (1936–), commissioner Garda Síochána, b. Limerick, son of a Garda sergeant, ed. St Brendan's College, Killarney. Garda 1957 and rose through the ranks. Wide experience of operations and administration; distinguished himself in the Technical Bureau (investigation of serious crimes). Garda commissioner 1991–6. Past president Bohemian Musical Society.

CUNNINGHAM, Larry (1938–), singer, b. Granard, Co. Longford, 13 Feb. 1938. His first band, the Mighty Avons, were the most popular country and western group on the ballroom scene during the 1960s and enjoyed consistent chart success with a mixture of Jim Reeves covers and original songs. Cunningham's recording of 'Lovely Leitrim' sold over a quarter of a million copies in Ireland and the UK. In 1968 he formed a new backing group, the Country Blue Boys, and he continued to have a highly successful performing and recording career until his retirement in 1985. During the 1970s he completed a number of recordings for his label, Release, in Nashville, and he was voted Europe's Top Country Singer at the Wembley International Festival in 1974.

CURRAN, Constantine Peter (1880–1975), architectural and literary historian, ed. O'Connell School, UCD and King's Inns. Barrister. Registrar Supreme Court 1946–52. Friend of JAMES JOYCE at UCD and afterwards. Outstanding authority on art and architecture of Georgian Dublin. Publications include *Dublin Decorative Plasterwork of the 17th and 18th Centuries* and *James Joyce Remembered*.

CURRIE, Austin (1939–), politician, b. Coalisland, Co. Tyrone, ed. St Patrick's Academy, Dungannon and QUB. Research fellow TCD 1976. Stormont MP (Nationalist East Tyrone) 1964–72. Active in Civil Rights Association, taking part in housing protest at Caledon, Co. Tyrone 1968 and later that year organising first civil rights march, from Coalisland to Dungannon. Founder member of the SDLP 1970; member NI Assembly 1973–5 and Convention 1975–6; local government minister in the NI Executive 1974. Chief whip SDLP 1974–9. Many attacks were made on his home in the 1970s and 1980s. TD (FG

Dublin West) since 1989. FG candidate in the presidential election 1990, coming third behind MARY ROBINSON and BRIAN LENIHAN, a result attributable in part to his then very recent arrival in Southern politics and the limited campaign he could conduct because of the tardiness of FG in deciding whom to nominate. Minister of State at the Departments of Education, Justice and Health (with special responsibility for co-ordinating children's affairs across the three departments) Dec. 1994.

CUSACK, Cyril James (1910–1993), actor, b. Kentani, Kenya, 26 Nov. 1910, s. of James Walter Cusack, colonial police sergeant, and Alice Violet Cole, actress, ed. several different national schools while on tour with theatre companies in Ireland, Dominican College, Newbridge, Co. Kildare, Synge Street and UCD. One of Ireland's most famous actors, he appeared in a huge number of stage productions and films. He performed with most of the major theatre companies in Britain and Ireland, including the Abbey and Gate companies in Dublin, the Royal Shakespeare Company and the English National Theatre. He was the recipient of numerous awards for his stage work, including the international critics' award 1960. His film career spanned an extraordinary 73 years, beginning with the Irish-made silent film *Knocknagow* in 1917 and ending with *My Left Foot* in 1990. He also starred in several major Hollywood films, including *Sacco and Vanzetti* (1974) and *True Confessions* (1981). In 1990 he played alongside his three daughters in the Gate's production of Chekhov's *Three Sisters*.

CUSHNAHAN, John (1948–), politician, b. Belfast, 23 July 1948, ed. St Mary's CBS and St Joseph's College of Education, Belfast and QUB. Teacher and PR consultant. Alliance Party whip Northern Ireland Assembly 1982–4; leader Alliance Party 1984–7; withdrew the party from the Assembly because of that body's refusal to accept the Anglo-Irish Agreement of 1985, which he fully supported. Having failed to secure a parliamentary seat at Westminster, he came south and was elected MEP (FG Munster) in 1989. He was re-elected in 1994.

D

DALTON, Emmet (1898–1978), revolutionary, b. Dublin, 4 Mar. 1898, d. 4 Mar. 1978. Enlisted in the British army 1915, rose to rank of major, won the MC. Joined the IRA 1919 and became special adviser to MICHAEL COLLINS. Supported the Treaty and was with Collins at Béal na mBláth, west Cork when he was killed. After the Civil War he made a career in the film industry in Hollywood and London.

D'ALTON, John (1883–1963), cardinal, b. Claremorris, Co. Mayo, 11 Oct. 1883, ed. Blackrock and Clonliffe 1901, d. 1 Feb. 1963. Received doctorate in divinity in Rome 1908; also studied in Oxford and Cambridge. Wrote *Horace and his Age* (1917), for which he received an honorary doctorate of literature from QUB; also *Roman Literary Theory and Criticism* (1931). President Maynooth 1936, made a monsignor two years later. Appointed Bishop of Meath 1943, Archbishop and Primate of All Ireland 1946, Cardinal 1953. In 1960 Pope John XXIII appointed him member of Central Preparatory Commission of Second Vatican Council. In 1961 celebrated the special mass in Armagh for the 15th centenary of St Patrick's arrival in Ireland.

DALY, Cahal Brendan (1917–), cardinal, b. Loughguile, Co. Antrim, 1 Oct. 1917, ed. St Malachy's College, Belfast, QUB, Maynooth and, after ordination, Institut Catholique, Paris. Lecturer in scholastic philosophy QUB 1946; Bishop of Ardagh and Clonmacnoise 1967; Bishop of Down and Connor 1982; Archbishop of Armagh 1990; Cardinal 1991. At QUB he became concerned with the social problems of Ireland as a whole, and through the Christus Rex movement helped to encourage new ideas on unemployment, economic planning and – a question which would face him as the bishop of a rural diocese in the Republic – the consequences of emigration. As bishop he also promoted new standards in church art and architecture when making the changes required by the Vatican Council's decree on the liturgy. He invoked the theme of ecumenism effectively to analyse the proliferating violence in Northern Ireland. With a Methodist scholar, Revd Eric Gallagher, he wrote a report in 1976 which recommended that Catholics and Protestants should work together to resolve the divisions on which violence thrived.

The need for reconciliation and co-operation, as well as bravely reiterated protests against paramilitary violence, was the consistent message of his many public statements when he returned to Belfast as bishop of the local diocese, Down and Connor. In 1984 he told the New Ireland Forum that the Catholic bishops would resist constitutional proposals likely to imperil civil or religious rights of Northern Protestants. His promotion to Armagh was widely welcomed because of this unrelenting advocacy of peace, which he continued as Irish primate, often sharing platforms and pulpits with the leaders of other Churches to do so at home and abroad.

In contrast to this stance, and some would say in contradiction of it, he held rigidly to the view that any deviation by the state from Roman Catholic attitudes on the socio-ethical questions of contraception, abortion and divorce would put the common good at risk. This was to leave him at odds more than once with Irish governments attempting to accommodate the laws to an increasingly pluralist society. His refusal to accept that the question of priestly celibacy should, or even could, be discussed conflicted with the opinion of a number of Irish Catholics, including notably Bishop BRENDAN COMISKEY. His term as primate was clouded by distressful scandals in the Irish Church – cases of clerics involved in paedophilia and covert relationships, both heterosexual and homosexual – in coping with which the Church authorities were widely judged to have reacted inadequately or improperly.

DALY, Edward (1891–1916), revolutionary, b. Co. Limerick, 25 Feb. 1891, ed. CBS. Joined the Irish Volunteers in 1913. Fought in the North King Street area during the Easter Rising. Executed in Kilmainham, 4 May 1916.

DALY, Fred (1911–1990), professional golfer, b. Portrush, Co. Antrim, 10 Oct. 1911, d. 18 Nov. 1990. In 1947 at Hoylake he became the only Irish golfer to date to win the British Open Championship, winning by one stroke, and he went on to capture the PGA Match Play, repeating that success in 1948 and 1952. In subsequent British Opens he has come second (1948), joint third (1950), joint fourth (1951) and third (1952). The first Irishman to attain Ryder Cup honours, he played four times (1947–53), with three wins, four losses and one half. He won the Ulster Professional Championship 11 times (1936, 1940–43, 1946, 1951, 1955–8) and the Irish Professional Championship three times (1940, 1946, 1952). Daly started his career as a caddie at Portrush, became the professional at Mahee Island and in 1944 at Balmoral in Belfast, a position he held for 30 years. Awarded the MBE in 1983.

DALY, Ita (1944–), fiction writer, b. Drumshanbo, Co. Leitrim, ed. St Louis High School, Rathmines, Dublin and UCD, where she took a BA and a diploma in education, m. DAVID MARCUS. Winner of an *Irish Times* short story competition and two Hennessy awards. Daly's work for adults is analytic and introspective, delving into the consciousness of mainly solitary protagonists. She has published five excellent novels: *Ellen* (1986), *A Singular Attraction* (1987), *Dangerous Fictions* (1989), *All Fall Down* (1992) and *Unholy Ghost* (1996); a volume of short stories, *The Lady with the Red Shoes* (1980); and children's fiction: *Candy on the DART* (1989) and *Candy and Sharon Olé* (1991). Her work has been translated into German, Danish and Swedish.

DANA (1951–), singer, b. Rosemary Brown, Derry, 30 Aug. 1951. In 1970 she became the first Irish winner of the Eurovision Song Contest with the ballad 'All Kinds of Everything'. The song reached number one in the pop charts of several countries and sold over a million copies worldwide. She never repeated this success but had minor hits in the UK during the 1970s and 1980s with the singles 'Who Put the Lights Out?', 'It's Gonna be a Cold, Cold Christmas' and 'Fairy Tale', and the albums *Everything is Beautiful* (1981), *Please Tell Him I Said Hello* (1984) and *Let there be Love* (1985). From the late 1980s she has pursued a career in acting and pantomime.

DAVEY, Shaun (1948–), composer, b. Dublin, ed. TCD and Courtauld Institute of Art, London. Initially a lecturer in the history of art but since 1977 has devoted himself to music. His work is characterised by melodic patterns based on the traditional Irish form with modern orchestration and arrangement. The hugely popular *Brendan Voyage*, for orchestra and uilleann pipes, is his best-known work.

DAVITT, Cahir (1894–1986), lawyer, b. Dublin, s. of Michael Davitt (Fenian revolutionary and founder of Irish National Land League), ed. Dublin in CBS, Dún Laoghaire, Presentation College, Glasthule, O'Connell School and UCD, d. 1 Mar. 1986. BA 1914, LL B 1916, called to the Bar 1916. Judge of Dáil courts 1920–22, member of Judiciary Committee 1923 which organised the new court system. Judge Advocate General of the Defence Forces 1922–6. Temporary Circuit Court judge 1926–7, appointed permanently 1927, High Court judge 1945–51, President of the High Court 1951–66. Chaired government committee 1961–3 whose report led to the amendment of traffic laws to introduce breathalyser system.

DAVITT, Michael (1950–), poet, broadcaster and editor, b. Cork, ed. UCC, degree in Celtic studies 1971. Founder and editor of the poetry journal *Innti*, manager of the Slógadh music festival, works in broadcasting. Publications include: *Innti* (1970–), *Gleann ar Ghleann* (1982), *Bligeárd Sráide* (1983) and *Rogha Dánta 1968–84* (1987).

DAWE, Gerald (1952–), poet and essayist, b. Belfast, ed. New University of Ulster, Coleraine and UCG, where he was later a tutor in the English department. He has always been acutely aware of the poet's traditional role in society, and has worked with young and old at many levels. He was involved with the Lyric Youth Theatre in Belfast and has been highly vocal in ecology, producing *The Urban Environment: A Sourcebook for the 1990s* (1990). He was awarded a Macaulay fellowship for literature in 1984, is founder editor of the arts review *Krino*, and lectures at TCD. His poetry includes *Heritages* (1976), *Sheltering Places* (1978), *The Lundys Letter* (1985), *The Water Table* (1990), *Sunday School* (1991) and *Heart of Hearts* (1995). He has also edited anthologies and published books of criticism, as well as collections of essays, addressing issues central to people, poets and places.

DEALE, Kenneth Edwin Lee (1907–1974), lawyer and writer, b. Dublin, ed. Christ Church Cathedral Grammar School, Wesley and King's Inns, d. 21 Oct. 1974. Called to Bar 1935, Senior Counsel 1950, Circuit Court judge 1951–74, sat mostly on NE circuit. Appointed High Court judge 1974, but died less than a year later. Popular with legal profession, perhaps because of his extrovert personality. Prolific author, broadcaster and playwright, his output included legal textbooks, popular accounts of Irish trials and a play accepted by the Abbey Theatre.

DEANE, Raymond (1953–), composer, pianist and novelist, b. Achill Island, ed. Dublin, Switzerland and Germany. Member of Aosdána. He has written pieces for orchestra, piano, voice and chamber ensembles, a film score, *Alembic* (1992), for symphonic wind band, and the chamber opera *The Poet and his Double* (1991). His music has been performed widely in Ireland and abroad. Recipient of the Varming prize, the Macaulay fellowship and the Marten Toonder award, as well as awards from Germany and Switzerland. His novel, *Death of a Medium*, was published in 1991.

DEANE, Seamus (1940–), academic and writer, b. Derry, ed. St Columb's College, Derry, QUB and Cambridge. Lectured extensively in the USA, England, France, Italy, Russia and Canada. Professor of Modern English and American Literature in UCD 1980–93, when he left to take up an academic appointment in the USA. His collections of poetry include *Gradual Wars* (1972), which won the AE literary award 1973, *Rumours* (1977), *History Lessons* (1983) and *Selected Poems* (1988). Published works of criticism include *Celtic Revivals* (1985) and *A Short History of Irish Literature* (1986). He edited the three-volume *Field Day Anthology of Irish Writing* (1991), which was criticised for its lack of female writers, and the *Penguin Twentieth Century Classics: James Joyce* (six vols. 1992). Received the Ireland Fund award for literature 1989. Member of the RIA and Aosdána; director Field Day Theatre Company; guest editor of the *Crane Bag* 1980.

DEASY, Richard (1916–), farmers' leader, b. Co. Tipperary, 13 Mar. 1916, s. of Major H.H.P. Deasy, explorer and industrialist, ed. Ampleforth and Oxford (BA economics/politics). He was the central figure in the militant campaign by farmers to secure price increases for agricultural products during the 1960s. He returned to farm his holding in Carrigahorig, Co. Tipperary in 1945 after serving as an artillery officer in the Irish army during World War II. He helped to found the National (later the Irish) Farmers' Association in 1956 and was elected its president in 1962, a position he held until 1967. After retiring from the IFA he was briefly involved in politics with the Labour Party. He is involved with the Glenstal and Greenhills ecumenical conferences and maintains a strong interest in politics, particularly issues of reconciliation in Northern Ireland.

de BARRA, Leslie Mary (1893–1984), née Price, relief agency organiser, b. Dublin. Teacher by profession. Participated in Easter Rising as a member of Cumann na mBan, of which she was director 1916–23. Lived in Cork after she married TOM BARRY 1921. She was among the first members of the Irish Red Cross Society 1939, and its chairwoman from 1950 for more than 20 years. Chairwoman Irish National Committee for Refugees 1955–60. President of Gorta 1960–65. Her inspirational commitment to international relief work in the decades following World War II was acknowledged in an honorary LL D (NUI) and a number of European awards, culminating in the Dunant medal, the highest honour of the International Red Cross Committee, 1978.

de BHALDRAITHE, Tomás (1916–1996), scholar and lexicographer, b. Co. Limerick, ed. Dublin and Paris. Professor of Modern Irish Language and Literature UCD 1960. Sometime editor of *Comhar*. Publications include *English–Irish Dictionary* (1959), for which he was best known, and *Gaeilge Chois Fhairrge: An Deilbhíocht* (1953). Edited *Nuascéalaíocht* (1952), PÁDRAIC Ó CONAIRE's *Scothscéalaíocht* (1956) and *Seacht mBua an Éirí Amach* (1967), and various documents of local Irish history. Editor (with Niall Ó Dónaill) *Irish–English Dictionary* (1978), editor *Pádraic Ó Conaire ar a Charn* (1982).

de BLACAM, Aodh (1890–1951), journalist and writer, b. London to Ulster parents,

d. Jan. 1951. He joined the staff of the *Enniscorthy Echo* in 1915. A member of Sinn Féin, he wrote nationalist propaganda during the War of Independence and was interned in 1922. He edited the literary journal *Commonweal* and contributed to newspapers and periodicals, including *The Irish Times*. He became editor of the *Standard* and later moved to the *Irish Press*, for which he wrote the hugely popular daily feature 'Roddy the Rover'. Member of Fianna Fáil's national executive until Dec. 1947, when he left to join Clann na Poblachta. Appointed director of publicity for the Department of Health in 1949. Publications include: *Towards the Republic* (1919), *The Story of Colmcille* and *Gaelic Literature Surveyed* (1929), *The Life of Wolfe Tone* (1935) and *The Black North* (1938). Plays include *King Dan* and *Two Kingdoms*.

de BRÚN, Pádraig (1889–1960), priest, academic, translator and poet, b. Grange-mockler, Co. Tipperary, ed. Rockwell, Clonliffe, UCD, Paris (D.Sc. Sorbonne) and Göttingen, d. 5 June 1960. Ordained Roman Catholic priest 1913. Professor of Mathematics Maynooth 1914–45. Translated much classical, French and Italian literature into Irish, including *Antigone* (1926), *Oedipus Rex* (1928) and *Athalie* (1930). Co-author of a life of Christ in Irish, *Beatha Íosa Críost* (1929). His translations of Dante's *Inferno* and an extended poem, *Miserere*, were published posthumously. President of UCG 1945, monsignor 1950, director of the Arts Council 1959. Chairman of the DIAS. Brother of MICHAEL BROWNE.

de BUITLÉAR, Eamon (1930–), naturalist, writer and film-maker, b. Dublin, moved to Wicklow when he was three months old, ed. Blackrock. De Buitléar nurtured an appreciation of Ireland's flora and fauna in more than one generation of television viewers, beginning in 1962 with the long-running series *Amuigh faoin Spéir*, with Dutchman Gerrit van Gelderen. Since then he has been a regular contributor of wildlife documentaries; recent series were *Lost Ireland* and *Ireland's Wild Countryside*. Publications include *Out and About* (1974), translated as *An Saol Beo* (1976), and *Ireland's Wild Countryside* (1993). For children: *Coinín the Rabbit: A Bilingual Story*, *Detective in the Wild: A Bilingual Field Book* and *Wild in the Garden: Adventure on your Doorstep* (1982) and *Wildlife* (1985). He

edited *Wild Ireland* (1984), *Irish Rivers* (1985) and Clive D. Hutchinson's *Watching Birds in Ireland* (1986). Hon. D.Sc. (UCD).

de BURGH, Chris (1948–), musician, b. Argentina, ed. Marlborough School, England and TCD. He developed his singing and songwriting by entertaining guests at his family's 12th-century castle in Co. Wexford. Signing to A&M Records in 1974, he made his UK début as support act with Supertramp. He had his first hit in Brazil, where he topped the charts for 17 weeks with his second single, 'Flying', but much of his 1970s success came from live work. The 1980s saw increasing chart action for de Burgh, culminating in his biggest-selling single to date, 'Lady in Red', in 1986. The song, written for his wife, reached number one in Britain and number three in the USA, and has since become a perennial wedding favourite.

de COURCY IRELAND, John (1911–), maritime historian, linguist, teacher and author, b. Lucknow, India, 19 Oct. 1911, son of a British army major from a Co. Kildare family, ed. Marlborough School, England, New College, Oxford (BA) and TCD (Ph.D.). Ran away to sea aged 17 but accepted Oxford scholarship. Returned to Ireland 1938. Taught in Newpark School, Blackrock, Co. Dublin 1968–86. He joined the Maritime Institute in 1943, undertaking extensive pioneering research into Ireland's maritime history. All his life he has campaigned for recognition of the country's maritime heritage. Saved Dún Laoghaire lifeboat station from closure 1956 and was its honorary secretary until 1983. One of the founders of the Maritime Museum 1959. Honorary secretary of the RNLI (Ireland) 1957–83, chairman until 1990; given its highest award, honorary life governor, 1995. The first Irishman to receive the Caird medal from the British National Maritime Museum (1996), he has been decorated by the governments of France, Portugal, Spain, Argentina and Yugoslavia. His books include *Ireland and the Irish in Maritime History* (1986). Mastered numerous foreign languages. Unsuccessful Democratic Socialist candidate for the European Parliament.

DEENY, James Andrew Donnelly (1906–1994), medical adviser, b. Lurgan, Co. Armagh, ed. Clongowes and QUB. Graduated MB in 1928, proceeding MD in 1931 with additional qualifications B.Sc., DPH and MRCPI. Elected FRCPI 1942. In medical practice in Lurgan his careful attention to individual patients led to some brilliant diagnoses but he was equally concerned to recognise major factors like poverty which affected community health.

Deeny left Armagh for Dublin when appointed chief medical adviser to the Department of Local Government and Public Health and immediately accepted the challenge of combating tuberculosis and reducing high infant mortality. He was chairman of the interdepartmental committee on the health services in 1945 which led to the establishment of the Department of Health in 1947.

A White Paper on tuberculosis published in 1946 marked the beginning of a period of intense activity in the battle against the disease, joined in 1948 by NOEL BROWNE, who became Minister for Health on his first day in the Dáil. It was not found possible, however, for the two single-minded emotionally involved doctors – with the same aims but with different views about how to achieve them – to live together. In 1950 Deeny was seconded to the Medical Research Council as director of the National Tuberculosis Survey.

He later undertook tuberculosis surveys for WHO in Sri Lanka and British Somaliland, and for two years was chief of mission in Indonesia. He spent the years 1971–2 in Rome as scientific adviser to the Holy See. His autobiography, *To Cure and to Care* (1989), was a memoir of exceptional frankness, in which he took serious issue with Browne's account of events in the 1948–51 period.

DEEVY, Teresa (1894–1963), playwright, b. Waterford, 31 Jan. 1894, d. Waterford, Jan. 1963. Deevy's first play, *Temporal Powers*, was performed at the Abbey Theatre in 1932. She contributed another three during the mid-1930s, *The King of Spain's Daughter*, *Katie Roche* and *The Wild Goose*, but turned her attention to radio from 1936. *Within a Marble City* was widely regarded as a masterpiece when first broadcast. Although she suffered from deafness, Deevy's work was characterised by a strong feeling for the sound as well as the meaning of language. MIAL 1954.

DELANEY, Edward (1930–), sculptor, b. Claremorris, Co. Mayo, ed. St Colman's College, Claremorris, National College of Art, Dublin and Academy of Fine Art, Munich. He represented Ireland at the 1959 and 1961 Paris Biennales, and has had shows in several countries, including Japan, the USA, Argentina and Hungary. Among the prizes and bursaries he has been awarded are the DOUGLAS HYDE gold medal at the Oireachtas 1972, first prize at the Art in Context exhibition in Belfast 1973, the West German fellowship of sculpture 1956–7 and the Irish Arts Council scholarship for sculpture and bronze casting 1964. He is a member of Aosdána. While Delaney is best known for a number of monuments which have been commissioned by the Irish government, including the Thomas Davis statue in College Green and the Wolfe Tone monument in St Stephen's Green, Dublin, he has also produced many small, figurative bronze works, which are expressionist in style and display both his control of the material and his sensitivity to the subject.

DELANEY, Frank (1942–), novelist, literary critic and broadcaster, b. Tipperary, 24 Oct. 1942, ed. Abbey School, Tipperary. After early banking career, worked in RTÉ continuity and newsreading in the early 1970s, became a news reporter with Radio Ulster, the BBC World Service and BBC Radio 4, where he created (1978) and for five years presented the award-winning programme *Bookshelf*. Better known in Britain than in Ireland because of BBC work. He is an outspoken critic of early 20th-century Ireland's social and moral attitudes.

Extensive broadcasting work includes *The Frank Delaney Series* (BBC 2), contributions for *Omnibus* (BBC 1), *Word of Mouth* (Radio 4) and *The Celts*, also a successful book. Presents weekly programme *The Bookshow*, Sky TV (1993–). An engaging broadcaster and populariser of literature, member of the Booker prize selection committee 1982. He has written fiction and non-fiction and has edited volumes of essays and poetry. *My Dark Rosaleen* (1988) was his first novel. The bestselling *The Sins of the Mothers* (1992) was the first of a five-novel sequence. Non-fiction books include *James Joyce's Odyssey* and *A Walk in the Dark Ages*.

DELANY, Ronald Michael (Ronnie) (1935–), athlete, b. Arklow, Co. Wicklow, 6

Mar. 1935. Delany graduated from Villanova University, Pennsylvania with a B.Sc., having been coached by Jim ('Jumbo') Elliott, and aged 18 reached the European Championship 1,500 m final in 1954. At Crampton, California early in 1956 he became the seventh man in history to run a sub-four-minute mile (at 3:59.0), then he lost form and was beaten twice by Brian Hewson, which meant that he just about scraped into Ireland's team for the Melbourne Olympics that year. But he set a new Olympic 1,500 m record with 3:41.2, covering the last 300 m in the unprecedented time of 38.8 seconds and the final 100 m in 12.9, winning by almost 4 m. He was undefeated indoors in the USA throughout a career of 40 races, including 34 at the mile, at which distance he set three indoor world records and won four successive AAU titles 1956–9. Previously, he won four successive Irish 800 yards titles, and at Villanova won the NCAA 1,500 m in 1956, the mile in 1957 and 1958 and the 800 yards in 1958. His best for the 800 yards was 1:47.8 in 1957, and his best mile was 3:57.5 in 1958 when he came third to Herb Elliott's world record 3.54.5 in Dublin.

DELANY, Vincent (1925–1964), lawyer, b. Longford, ed. Clongowes, TCD and King's Inns. Called to Bar 1950, lecturer in law QUB 1953, reader in law QUB 1960, Professor of Law TCD 1962. Author of textbook on law of charities in Ireland and of biography of CHRISTOPHER PALLES. A book on inland waterways in Ireland, on which he was working at his death, was published posthumously with his widow, Ruth, as co-author.

DEMPSEY, Jeremiah Francis (1906–), airline manager, b. Dublin, ed. CBS, Westland Row, Dublin and UCD, where he studied commerce. Chartered accountant; first secretary/accountant of the new national airline, Aer Lingus, in 1937. Until his retirement as general manager in 1967 he was actively involved in all aspects of the company's development. He sought to identify personally with his colleagues and maintained a deep interest in human relations. President International Air Transport Association 1962, chairman Irish Management Institute 1963–5. LL D (LC) (NUI) 1964. Throughout his life he has been a keen follower of soccer, having played at junior level for Ireland.

DENHAM, Susan (1945–), High Court judge, ed. Alexandra, TCD and Columbia University, New York. She qualified as a barrister in 1971, becoming a Senior Counsel in 1977. In 1991 she became only the second woman, after MELLA CARROLL, to be appointed judge of the High Court, and in 1993 the first – and to date the only – woman to be appointed to the Supreme Court.

de PAOR, Liam (1926–), archaeologist and historian, b. Dublin, ed. UCD. He has excavated sites in Ireland and on the Continent. With his wife, MÁIRE DE PAOR, he wrote *Early Christian Ireland* (1958). He was UNESCO adviser to the government of Nepal and has lectured widely in the USA, Canada and Ireland. Lecturer in history UCD 1964. He has drawn on archaeology and history to elaborate his views on the Irish national identity. His later publications include *The Peoples of Ireland: From Prehistory to Modern Times* (1986) and *Saint Patrick's World* (1993).

de PAOR, Máire (1925–1994), née McDermott, archaeologist, ed. Convent of Mercy, Buncrana, Co. Donegal and UCD, d. Dublin. On the staff of the archaeology department UCD for 12 years. Lectured and wrote widely. Went on to work as a researcher and producer in RTÉ television, through which she further promoted a popular understanding of the Celtic world. Member of the Arts Council. Co-author with her husband, LIAM DE PAOR, of *Early Christian Ireland* (1958).

de ROBECK, Sir John Michael (1862–1928), naval commander, b. 10 June 1862, s. of Baron de Robeck of Gowran Grange, Naas, Co. Kildare, ed. HMS *Britannica*, d. 20 Jan. 1928. Entered Royal Navy 1875. De Robeck was one of the few British commanders to emerge from the disastrous Dardanelles campaign of World War I with his reputation intact. After taking over from Sir Sackville Carden in Mar. 1915 he successfully oversaw the evacuation of the British naval forces there. Appointed vice-admiral commanding 2nd Battle Squadron in 1916; commander-in-chief Mediterranean Fleet 1919–22, Atlantic Fleet 1922–4. Admiral of the Fleet 1925.

de ROSSA, Proinsias (1940–), politician, b. Dublin, 15 May 1940, ed. Marlborough Street NS and Kevin Street College of Technology, Dublin. Interned in the Curragh

1956–9. Dáil Éireann deputy since Feb. 1982, MEP 1989–92, member of Dublin County Council since 1985. De Rossa worked in his family's fruit and vegetable business before becoming a full-time public representative. He succeeded TOMÁS MAC GIOLLA as leader of the Workers' Party in 1988. In early 1992 he was among the six of the party's seven Dáil deputies who founded a new party, provisionally known as New Agenda but later renamed Democratic Left. He became Minister for Social Welfare in the coalition government formed in late 1994. De Rossa has consistently been one of the Dáil's most energetic and impressive performers.

DESMOND, Barry (1935–), politician, b. Cork, May 1935, ed. Presentation Brothers, Coláiste Chríost Rí and School of Commerce, Cork and UCC. Trade union official (ITGWU and ICTU). TD (Labour Dún Laoghaire) 1969–89. Minister of State at the Department of Finance 1981–2. Minister for Health 1982–7 and for Social Welfare 1982–6. Deputy leader Labour Party 1982–9. MEP (Labour Dublin) 1989–94. Member European Court of Auditors since 1994.

DESMOND, Eileen (1932–), politician, b. Old Head, Kinsale, 29 Dec. 1932, ed. Convent of Mercy, Kinsale. Following death of her husband, Dan Desmond TD, became TD (Labour Mid-Cork, later Cork South-Central) 1965–9, 1973–87. MEP (Munster) 1979–81. Minister for Health and Social Welfare 1981–2.

DESPARD, Charlotte (1884–1939), suffragist and revolutionary, b. Edinburgh, daughter of a naval commander, sister of Lord French, Lord Lieutenant of Ireland 1918–21, m. Maximilian Despard. Known as 'Mrs Desperate' by Dublin working-class people, she devoted her life to radical causes and the emancipation of women. She supported the workers during the 1913 Lock-out and was active in the campaign for the release of republican prisoners after the Civil War.

de VALERA, Eamon (1882–1975), revolutionary, national leader and statesman, b. New York, 14 Oct. 1882, s. of Vivion de Valera, a Hispanic American, and Kate Coll, an immigrant from Co. Clare; ed. Bruree NS, Co. Limerick, Charleville, Co. Cork, Blackrock and UCD; m. Sinéad Ní Fhlannagáin (SINÉAD DE VALERA), five s. two d.; d. 29 Aug. 1975. Following the death of his father, when he was less than three years old, his mother sent him back to be brought up by relatives in Co. Limerick. Until his entry into public life he was called by the English version of his name, Eddie. During his time in UCD he was regarded as conservative and anti-republican. He became a mathematician and teacher of repute. De Valera joined the Gaelic League in 1910 and in 1913 the Irish Volunteers, a then unarmed but nascent paramilitary force opposed to British rule in Ireland. He reluctantly agreed to become a member of the secretive IRB, which controlled the Volunteers' executive, but took little or no part in its activities and maintained a lifelong distrust of secret organisations. In the Easter Rising he commanded a key section of the revolutionary forces at Bolands' Mills in the south of the city. He seems to have been ill equipped for a military role and it was his last period of involvement in armed struggle. Sentenced to death by a British military court, he was reprieved after the first wave of executions provoked public disgust. As the senior surviving figure from the Rising, he came to symbolise for many the Irish republic which was their goal.

In 1917, a month after his release from a British detention camp, he was elected as a member of parliament for Sinn Féin in Co. Clare. It was one of a series of blows which led to the demise of the Irish Parliamentary Party, which had sought Home Rule for Ireland. He was elected president of Sinn Féin after ARTHUR GRIFFITH stepped down in his favour. Having been arrested in May 1918 and deported to Lincoln Jail in England, he held his seat, unopposed, in the general election of that year. MICHAEL COLLINS and HARRY BOLAND, from outside, with de Valera doing the planning inside, engineered his escape in Feb. 1919, and when the Sinn Féin MPs boycotted Westminster and took seats in Dáil Éireann (which they declared to be the parliament of the Irish Republic), de Valera became Príomh-Aire or Prime Minister. The title was popularly translated as President.

From June 1919 to Dec. 1920 de Valera toured the USA seeking money for the new republic and recognition from American political leaders. In July 1921, when a truce had been called in the War of Independence, he went to London for talks with British Prime Minister Lloyd George. These produced one of de Valera's most famous comments: when Lloyd George complained that dealing with Dev was like trying to lift mercury with a fork, 'Why doesn't he try a spoon?' was the riposte. The talks did not produce a settlement. Later that year the cabinet in Dublin sent a team to open formal negotiations with British ministers. De Valera declined requests to participate himself and the delegation was led by Griffith and Collins. The negotiations produced a Treaty, signed by all members of both teams, but this was vehemently opposed back at home by de Valera and many of his colleagues. His grounds were the failure to submit the document for prior approval by the cabinet in Dublin, the oath of allegiance which all members of the Dáil would have to swear to the British monarch, and the failure to secure adoption of the scheme for external association with Britain. The Dáil approved the Treaty by a narrow majority. Continuing resistance from militant opponents led to a bitter civil war, during which de Valera was marginalised.

After the war, Eamon de Valera began to construct a political way forward for republicans. He quitted Sinn Féin and in May 1926 founded Fianna Fáil, which rapidly became the dominant political party in the state. The pro-Treaty government acted to force the new party's TDs to take their seats in Dáil Éireann, instead of abstaining, as they had done initially. When they entered the Dáil they took the oath of allegiance but denounced it as 'an empty formula'. In 1932 Fianna Fáil won power and did not lose it again until the general election of 1948. As head of government de Valera had a turbulent few years dealing with the British over inherited obligations, in particular the payment of land annuities, a battle that led to an economic 'war' of mutually prohibitive tariffs. But gradually the two sides began to bury their differences and in 1937 de Valera devised and had passed at referendum a constitution that was republican in all but name. A year earlier he had used the British abdication crisis to remove all references to the monarchy in the existing constitution. During World War II de Valera held Ireland to a policy of neutrality that had over-

whelming support from political parties and voters alike. His dignified response to an attack by British Prime Minister Churchill after Allied victory in that conflict remains one of the most famous Irish speeches of the century.

Although a revolutionary in constitutional matters, he was conservative on most economic and social issues, his vision of Ireland deriving mainly from his childhood days in Limerick, and he was a devout Catholic. He was Taoiseach 1932–48, 1951–4 and 1957–9. From the mid-1950s his eyesight began to weaken and his political powers started to wane. He failed in his attempt to get the electorate to abandon the voting system of proportional representation used in all elections. He was persuaded by colleagues to hand on political leadership and run for the presidency, which he did successfully in 1959. Re-elected by a small margin in 1966, he retired from all public life on completion of that term in 1973. He was father of VIVION DE VALERA and grandfather of SÍLE DE VALERA.

Among Eamon de Valera's legacies are the country's largest political party, the constitution, the *Irish Press* group of newspapers – which he founded in 1931 but which collapsed in financial crisis in 1995 – and a reputation as the country's most famous figure on the world stage.

de VALERA, Síle (1954–), politician, b. Dublin, d. of Terry de Valera and granddaughter of EAMON DE VALERA, ed. Loreto Convent, Foxrock, Co. Dublin and UCD. Career guidance teacher. TD (FF Dublin Mid-County) 1977–81. MEP 1979–84. TD (FF Clare) since 1987. Has served on the Oireachtas and European Parliament committees concerned with women's rights. Resigned the Fianna Fáil party whip in July 1993 in protest against the government's removal of the obligatory stopover at Shannon Airport, Co. Clare for transatlantic flights to and from Ireland. Rejoined the party 1994 and in Dec. BERTIE AHERN appointed her to the front bench as spokesperson on arts and culture.

de VALERA, Sinéad (1878–1975), née Flanagan (Ní Fhlannagáin), b. Balbriggan, Co. Dublin. National school teacher. Taught Irish to EAMON DE VALERA at the Gaelic League college in Parnell Square, Dublin and married him in 1910. Carried responsibility for rearing their family in the aftermath of the Easter Rising and during the War of Independence while her husband was variously imprisoned, in hiding or abroad on national business. Was rumoured to have favoured the Anglo-Irish Treaty but never said so publicly. Later wrote a number of well-regarded stories, plays and poems for children in both Irish and English. She died in Co. Dublin in 1975, eight months before her husband.

de VALERA, Vivion (1910–1982), scientist, lawyer, businessman and politician, b. Dublin, s. of EAMON DE VALERA, ed. Blackrock, UCD (M.Sc., Ph.D.) and King's Inns. Called to Bar 1937. After Emergency military service, retired from army with rank of major. TD (FF Dublin North-West, later North-Central and Central) 1945–81. Managing director Irish Press Ltd 1959–81.

de VALOIS, Dame Ninette, ballet dancer, choreographer and architect of British ballet, b. Edris Stannus, Blessington, Co. Wicklow, 6 June 1898, moved to England in 1905, m. Arthur Connell. Principal dancer in the 1919 Covent Garden Opera season, soloist with the Diaghilev Ballet Company 1923. Stopped dancing in her thirties. Set up the Academy of Choreographic Art in London 1926. Together with Lilian Baylis, created the Vic-Wells Theatre Company and started Sadler's Wells, which became the Royal Ballet 1956. Masterminded the partnership of Rudolf Nureyev and Margot Fonteyn. A friend of W.B. YEATS, she established Dublin's short-lived Abbey School of Ballet in 1928. Awarded a CBE 1947, made a Dame in 1951, OM 1992. She retired in 1972 but remained a governor of the Royal Ballet. Her early memoirs, *Come Dance with Me*, were first published in 1957.

de VERE WHITE, Herbert *Terence* (1912–1994), man of letters, b. Dublin, ed. TCD. MIAL. Practised as a solicitor for almost ten years before turning to writing in 1943. Literary editor *The Irish Times* 1963–78. His first books were biographical and socio-historical, beginning with a life of Isaac Butt – *The Road to Excess* – in 1946. There followed a controversial biography of KEVIN O'HIGGINS (1948); *A Fretful Midge*, an autobiography, considered his best work (1957); *A Leaf from*

the *Yellow Book* (1958); *The Parents of Oscar Wilde* (1967); *Tom Moore, The Irish Poet* (1977). He wrote a dozen novels, including *An Affair with the Moon* (1959), *The Remainderman* (1963), *Lucifer Falling* (1966), *Tara* (1967), *The Lambert Mile* (1969), *Mr Stephen* (1971), *The Distance and the Dark* (1973), *My Name is Norval* (1978) and *Chat Show* (1987). Short stories: *Big Fleas and Little Fleas* (1976), *Chimes at Midnight* (1978) and *Birds of Prey* (1980). Also societal history: *The Story of the Royal Dublin Society* (1955), *Leinster and Ireland* (1968) and *The Anglo-Irish* (1972).

DEVLIN, Bernadette. See under McAliskey.

DEVLIN, Denis (1908–1959), poet, b. Scotland, ed. UCD and Sorbonne, d. Dublin. He spent some years in Paris before joining the Department of External Affairs in 1935. He served in Washington 1938–46 and was appointed ambassador to Italy 1950. Publications include: *Intercession* (1937), *Lough Derg* and *Collected Poems* (1964) and *The Heavenly Foreigner* (1967).

DEVLIN, Joe (1871–1934), politician, b. Belfast, 13 Feb. 1871, ed. CBS, Divis Street, Belfast. He worked as a barman before becoming a journalist and, in 1902, unopposed Irish Parliamentary Party MP for North Kilkenny. He developed a very effective political machine with himself as boss, reorganising the nearly defunct Ancient Order of Hibernians along masonic lines. His political control of the Ulster section of the IP enabled it to defeat Sinn Féin candidates, elsewhere invincible, in the 1918 election. He himself held Falls against EAMON DE VALERA. After the Northern Ireland settlement, realisation of nationalist ineffectuality in the Stormont parliament caused him to abstain except on matters of Catholic interest. Though he continued to be an MP at Stormont and Westminster until his death on 18 Feb. 1934, his main energies were directed to improving the lot of his beloved Belfast Catholic working class.

DEVLIN, Joseph Francis (Frank) (1900–1988), badminton player, b. Dublin, 16 Jan. 1900, d. Clane, Co. Kildare, 27 Oct. 1988. He was the leading player of his time, winning five successive All-England singles titles 1925–9 and a sixth in 1931. He won his first men's doubles title with George Sautter of England in 1922 and six more with his compatriot Gordon 'Curly' Mack; he also won five mixed doubles, the first two with tennis player Kitty McKane (Godfree). He became a teaching professional at Winnipeg in Canada, toured Australasia and Malaysia, then settled in New York and later Baltimore. His daughters Susan (Peard) and Judith (Hashman) were outstanding players for the USA – Judy becoming the most successful player in the history of the All-England Championships – and Susan directed badminton coaching for Irish children 1960–84.

DEVLIN, Paddy (1925–), republican socialist, b. Belfast, 8 Mar. 1925, ed. locally until age 14, m. Theresa Duffy, 26 Oct. 1950. Progressed through Fianna Éireann into the IRA; interned 1942–5. In 1949 he joined the Belfast-based Irish Labour Party and by the early 1950s had become an active trade unionist. He defeated GERRY FITT in 1956 in a by-election to Belfast City Council. Joining the Northern Ireland Labour Party in 1958, he became its chairman in 1967. Also in 1967 he won the Falls seat in the Stormont parliament, held by Harry Diamond since 1945. Took part in the civil rights movement and in the formation of the Social Democratic and Labour Party in 1970. Responsible for health and social services in the short-lived power-sharing Executive 1974. In Aug. of that year he was expelled from the SDLP after resigning as chairman of the parliamentary group in a dispute over the party's policy stance in relation to the Dublin government. In 1978 he became Northern organiser for the ITGWU. The following year he stood unsuccessfully as an independent socialist candidate in the European Parliament elections.

DEVLIN, Polly (1941–), broadcaster, journalist and writer, b. Ardboe, Co. Tyrone, on the shore of Lough Neagh, whose environs have been inspirational for at least two of her books. She won a talent competition organised by *Vogue* in 1964, enabling her to work for the magazine in its London and New York offices. She quickly made a name for herself as a genial, though probing, interviewer, and met a host of music celebrities, as well as movers and shakers of the 1960s and later. Her writing won her an OBE in 1972. She works in London and divides her time between Somerset, London and Ireland. Publications: *The Vogue History of Photography* (1979); *All of Us There*, a childhood memoir, and *The Far Side of the Lough*, children's stories (1983); *Dora, or the Shifts of the Heart*, a novel, and *Polly Devlin Visits the Museum*, a guide booklet (1990); and *Dublin*, a travel booklet (1993).

DEVOY, John (1842–1928), Fenian, b. Kill, Co. Kildare, 3 Sept. 1842, son of a small tenant farmer, childhood mainly in Dublin, d. Atlantic City, New Jersey, 29 Sept. 1928. He devoted his entire adult life to the cause of revolutionary separatism, first as a member of the Fenian movement in Ireland in the 1860s, and later as the chief organiser of Irish-American support groups. After serving five years in prison for Fenian activities, he emigrated to the USA in 1871 and soon became a central figure in the most important Irish-American organisation, Clan na Gael. He favoured the policy of incorporating the land question in the nationalist agenda and was able to rally American support for this 'new departure', despite strong opposition from fellow Clan members. He founded two newspapers in the USA, the *Irish Nation* and the *Gaelic American*, and helped to raise funds for Sinn Féin and the Irish Volunteers. He enthusiastically backed EAMON DE VALERA's visit to the USA 1919–20 but strongly opposed his attempts to dominate Irish nationalist organisations there. *Recollections of an Irish Rebel* was published in 1929.

DILL, John Greer (1881–1944), British field marshal, b. Lurgan, Co. Armagh, 25 Dec. 1881, ed. Cheltenham College and Sandhurst, d. Washington. Commissioned into the Leinster Regiment 1901. Served in the Boer War and World War I; commanded the British forces in Palestine 1936–7. Chief of staff 1940, thought overcautious by Winston Churchill. He resigned his position in 1941 but accompanied Churchill to the USA in Dec. of that year and remained there as senior British representative on combined chiefs of staff committee in Washington.

DILLON, Eilis (1920–1993), author, b. Galway, 7 Mar. 1920, d. of Geraldine and Thomas Dillon, Professor of Chemistry UCG, ed. Ursuline Convent, Sligo. A prolific and very successful writer of books for children and adults in both Irish and English. Her best-known work is the historical romance *Across the Bitter Sea* (1973), to which a sequel, *Blood Relations*, was published four years later. The most popular of her children's books are *The Lost Island* (1952) and *The Singing Cave* (1959). She also lectured on children's literature in several American universities and in TCD. Her first husband was Cormac Ó Cuilleanáin, Professor of Irish Literature at UCC, and the poet EILÉAN NÍ CHUILLEANÁIN is their daughter. After his death in 1970 she married Vivian Mercier.

DILLON, Gerard (1916–1971), artist, b. Belfast, ed. CBS, d. Dublin. At 14 he was apprenticed to a painting and decorating contractor. A prolific and versatile artist, he moved with ease through several media, including oils, tapestry and murals, and also worked as a set designer for the Abbey Theatre. He began to paint seriously after moving to London in 1934 but became recognised only after the war. Most of his best-known early works were primitive oils of the landscape in Connemara, a part of Ireland he visited often. Dillon represented Ireland at the Guggenheim International Exhibition and Britain at the Pittsburgh International Exhibition. He also wrote a collection of short stories.

DILLON, James (1902–1986), politician, b. 26 Sept. 1902, s. of JOHN DILLON and Elizabeth Matthew, ed. Mount St Benedict, Gorey, Co. Wexford, UCD and King's Inns. He also studied business organisation – his family were rural merchants – in Britain and the USA. M. Maura Phelan, one s. Lived most of his life in Ballaghaderreen, Co. Roscommon. First elected to Dáil Éireann in 1932 as an Independent, he initially represented the Donegal constituency. That year he voted for Fianna Fáil's EAMON DE VALERA as President of the Executive Council, something for which he would self-mockingly reproach himself in later years. In the autumn of 1932 he joined with others to form the National Centre Party. A year later it coalesced with other small groups to create the United Ireland Party, the precursor of Fine Gael. Dillon switched constituencies to Monaghan in 1938 and represented the area until his retirement in 1969. During World War II he was expelled from Fine Gael, having been the sole TD to advocate Irish participation on the side of the Allies.

As an Independent he became Minister for Agriculture in the 1948–51 multi-party coalition government, and he held that post in the government of 1954–7, by which time he had rejoined Fine Gael. Became leader of that party in 1959. Fianna Fáil retained power at the subsequent two general elections, and after the 1965 contest Dillon resigned. He was an imposing orator, his broad-brimmed hats and dark coats enhancing his reputation for eccentricity. He was one of the last party leaders to hold eve-of-election rallies in Dublin before polling day – thereafter television became the main forum.

DILLON, John (1851–1927), politician, b. Blackrock, Co. Dublin, 4 Sept. 1851, s. of John Blake Dillon, ed. Cecilia Street Medical School, Dublin, m. Elizabeth Matthew, daughter of a former Lord Chief Justice of Ireland, d. London, 4 Aug. 1927. Qualified as a medical doctor but chose to concentrate on politics instead. Succeeded John Mitchel as member of parliament for Tipperary 1880; later represented Mayo East. Took a major part in the struggle to better the circumstances of tenant farmers in the 1880s through the Land League and through the Plan of Campaign, which he organised together with Timothy Harrington and WILLIAM O'BRIEN (1852–1928). Denounced interference by the Vatican in Irish public affairs when Rome condemned the campaign. Went to prison more than once for his activities and suffered ill health as a result. Broke with Charles Stewart Parnell at the time of the 'split', succeeded Justin McCarthy at the head of the anti-Parnellite party 1896 but stood down to allow JOHN REDMOND to become leader of the reunited Irish Parliamentary Party in 1900.

Dillon always looked with suspicion on landlords favourable to land reform; he attacked the Wyndham Act of 1903 because of the financial provisions it made for landlords, and more generally because he feared that Tory-inspired reforms could undermine popular support for Home Rule. Although opposed to what he saw as the extremism of Sinn Féin when Home Rule was about to be achieved – not least as the result of negotiations in which he had been closely involved – he persistently criticised government efforts in the early years of World War I to prevent the expression of strongly nationalist sentiments. After the Easter Rising he courageously praised the insurgents in a House of Commons speech: they had fought 'a clean fight, a brave fight, however misguided', he said. Opposed the application of conscription to Ireland. After Redmond's death in Mar. 1918 he became leader of the IP, only to lose his own seat in the collapse of the party's support at the general election in Nov. of that year. Father of JAMES and MYLES DILLON.

DILLON, Myles (1900–1972), Celtic scholar, b. Dublin, s. of JOHN DILLON and Elizabeth Matthew, ed. Mount St Benedict, Gorey, Co. Wexford, UCD and Bonn, d. Dublin, 18 June 1972. Lectured in English, Sorbonne, 1925; in Sanskrit, TCD, 1928–30, UCD, 1930–37. Professor of Irish, Wisconsin, 1937–46, of Celtic Philology, Chicago, 1946. Attached for a time to the US diplomatic service but returned to Ireland as a senior professor, School of Celtic Studies, DIAS, 1960–68. Wrote and lectured widely in his fields of Sanskrit and Celtic studies.

DINNEEN, Patrick (1860–1934), priest and lexicographer, b. Co. Kerry, ed. locally and at UCD. He became a leading member of the Gaelic League and in 1904 produced his *Foclóir Gaedhilge agus Béarla*, the most complete Irish–English dictionary yet prepared. A revised edition was published in 1927 under the imprint of the Irish Texts Society. Dinneen produced numerous plays and translations but his fame rests on his dictionary. His scholarship was frequently satirised by Myles na gCopaleen (see FLANN O'BRIEN) in *The Irish Times*.

DIXON, Henry Horatio (1869–1953), FRS, botanist, b. 19 May 1869, ed. TCD, d. 20 Dec. 1953. Professor of Botany TCD 1904–49. Best known for his cohesion theory of the rise of water in trees. Boyle medallist 1916. His calculations of the rate of mutations produced by cosmic rays are classics of early radiobiology. Much of his effort in his first years as professor went into the design of the new botany building in TCD.

DIXON, Kevin (1902–1959), lawyer, b. Dublin, ed. Belvedere, King's Inns and UCD, d. 25 Oct. 1959. Called to the Bar 1926, Senior Counsel 1940, Attorney-General 1942–6. Author of a book on Landlord and Tenant Act (1931). His early death deprived the Irish judi-

ciary of one of its more promising members, who would probably have been promoted to the Supreme Court. His judgment against the plaintiff in the unprecedented action (O'Byrne v. Minister for Finance 1959) brought by the widow of Mr Justice John O'Byrne, for the recovery of income tax which she claimed had been unconstitutionally deducted from her husband's salary, was upheld by a 3–2 majority of the Supreme Court.

DOCKRELL, Henry Morgan (1880–1955), businessman and politician, b. Dublin, s. of Sir Maurice Dockrell, Unionist member of parliament and chairman of the recruiting committee for the British army, m. Alice Evelyn Hayes, four s. one d. TD (FG County Dublin) 1932–48. Member of the Seanad 1948–51. Managing director and chairman of Thomas Dockrell, Sons and Co. Ltd, merchants and contractors; chairman of Celtic Insurance; trustee of Dublin Savings Bank; chairman of Sherwin Williams (Ireland); chairman Metropolitan Building Society. President of the Dublin Chamber of Commerce 1933. Two sons, Maurice E. and H. Percy Dockrell, were TDs and councillors in the Fine Gael interest.

DODDS, Edwin *Eric Robertson* (1893–1979), classical scholar and editor, b. Belfast, ed. St Andrew's College, Dublin, Campbell College, Belfast and Balliol College, Oxford. He lectured in classics at Reading University and the University of Birmingham, Professor of Greek at Oxford 1936–60. President of Society for Psychical Research 1961–3. Lecturer on Swan's Hellenic Cruises in 1960s. He was a friend of STEPHEN MACKENNA, edited his *Journals and Letters* (1936) and wrote a 'Memoir'. Literary executor of LOUIS MACNEICE, editor of his autobiography, *The Strings are False* (1965), and *Collected Poems* (1966). He also had a close friendship with W.H. Auden, whom he greatly admired. Other works include: *Select Passages illustrating Neoplatonism* (1923), *Proclus, The Elements of Theology* (ed.) (1933), *The Greeks and the Irrational* (1951), *The Ancient Concept of Progress and Other Essays on Greek Literature and Belief* (1973) and *Missing Persons* (1979), a lively and scholarly autobiography that won the Duff Cooper memorial prize.

DOHERTY, Edward Joseph (1923–), commissioner Garda Síochána, b. Buncrana, Co. Donegal, ed. St Columb's College, Derry.

Clerical officer. Joined as a guard and rose through the ranks; as sergeant, selected to assist DANIEL COSTIGAN in implementing reforms; graduate of command and staff course, Federal Bureau of Investigation, Washington, DC; member of interdepartmental committee on Garda training; headed interdepartmental committee on Garda communications and command and control systems. Garda commissioner 1987–8. President Coiste Siamsa, the governing body for sport in the Garda Síochána; head of the national sports body, Cospóir.

DOHERTY, John (1900–1979), fiddler, b. Glenfinn, Co. Donegal. He was a musician of exceptional brilliance, and like all the members of his family a performer whose playing suggested an underlying mystical quality. A travelling man most of his life, it is reckoned that he ventured beyond the boundaries of his native county on at most three occasions. Brother of MICKEY DOHERTY.

DOHERTY, Mickey (1894–1970), fiddler, b. Glenfinn, Co. Donegal. Of his seven siblings, four brothers (Charlie, Simon, Hugh and JOHN DOHERTY) were fiddlers, as was his father, 'An Dochartach Mór'; a sister, Mary, also played the instrument. The Dohertys were of a dynasty of musicians, Irish-speaking, travelling folk and exponents of the distinctive Donegal idiom – kin of similar families such as the McConnells and the MacSweeneys. By trade a travelling tinsmith, Mickey was influenced by his friend and fellow musician Neil O'Boyle from the Dungloe area. His playing is recorded on a double cassette released by Comhairle Bhéaloideas Éireann. This was the result of a spontaneous session recorded in 1949 by the folklorists Kevin Danaher and Seán Ó hEochaidh.

DOHERTY, Paddy, Gaelic footballer. An exceptional left-half forward, he won minor All-Ireland medals with Down in 1961 and in 1962, when he was captain; three All-Ireland senior medals, 1960, 1961 and 1968; Ulster SFC medals, 1963 and 1965; five Railway Cup medals, including the four successive victories 1963–6.

DOHERTY, Peter Dermot (1913–1990), international footballer, b. Magherafelt, Co. Derry, 5 June 1913, d. Fleetwood, Lancashire, 6 Apr. 1990. Having moved from Glentoran to Blackpool in 1933, he won the first of his 16 Northern Ireland caps in 1935. The following year he moved to Manchester City, where he won a League Championship medal and scored 30 goals. After service overseas he joined Derby County in 1945, having guested for the club earlier, and in 1946 he won an FA Cup medal with them. He moved to Huddersfield Town and was later player-manager of Doncaster Rovers. Doherty won his last international cap in 1950 and became manager of the Northern Ireland squad, taking them to the 1958 World Cup finals.

DOHERTY, Seán (1944–), politician, b. Co. Roscommon, 29 June 1944, ed. Presentation Brothers, Carrick-on-Shannon, UCD and King's Inns. Member of the Garda Síochána 1965–73. TD (FF Roscommon) 1977; Minister of State, Department of Justice, 1979; Minister for Justice 1982. After the Fianna Fáil government left office in Dec. 1982 it was revealed that he had ordered the tapping of two journalists' home telephones (they later successfully sued the state for damages). He resigned the party whip in consequence although it was restored late in 1984. Elected to the Seanad in 1989 and became its Cathaoirleach. In Jan. 1992 he called a dramatic news conference at which he said that he had handed transcripts of the tapped telephone conversations to CHARLES HAUGHEY while he was Taoiseach in 1982. Although Haughey rebutted the claim, the controversy forced his resignation as leader of the FF–PD coalition government. Doherty retained his Dáil seat at the 1992 general election in the new Longford–Roscommon constituency.

DONEGAN, Patrick (1923–), politician and businessman, ed. CBS, Drogheda and Castleknock. TD (FG Louth) 1954–7, 1961–81. Minister for Defence 1973–6, for Lands 1976–7, for Fisheries 1977. He was the central figure in a controversy which led to the resignation of President CEARBHALL Ó DÁLAIGH in Oct. 1976. In a speech on an official visit to a military base as Minister for Defence he described the president's referral of the Emergency Powers bill to the Supreme Court as 'a thundering disgrace'. Donegan's offer to resign was refused by the Taoiseach, LIAM COSGRAVE, and Ó Dálaigh resigned in order to 'protect the independence and dignity' of the office of president.

DONNELLY, Charles (1914–1937), poet and republican, b. Dungannon, 10 July 1914, ed. O'Connell School and UCD. While at college, he formed a left-wing society called Student Vanguard and contributed poems to *Comhthrom Féinne*, a university magazine edited by Niall Sheridan. The literary circle to which he belonged included FLANN O'BRIEN, DENIS DEVLIN, DONAGH MACDONAGH and CYRIL CUSACK. In 1936 Donnelly went to London and enlisted in the International Brigade to fight in the Spanish civil war. While in training there he wrote a thesis on military strategy in 19th-century Spain which was highly praised by his commanding officer. Donnelly's war was short-lived: he embarked for Spain in Jan. 1937 and died at the Jarama front on 27 Feb. Literary Ireland mourned the loss of a man likely to have become a major poet.

DONNELLY, Dervilla, academic, ed. Sacred Heart Convent, Leeson Street, Dublin, UCD and University of California. Lecturer in organic chemistry UCD 1957, Professor of Phytochemistry 1980. Visiting professorships/ fellowships at Institut de Chimie des Substances Naturelles, CNRS, Gif-sur-Yvette, France; Kunglia Tekniska Hogskolian, Stockholm; University of Oklahoma 1970; University of California 1976; University of Marseilles 1991. Member RIA, Phytochemical Society of Europe, Society of Pharmacognosy, Society of Chemical Ecology, Society of Chemical Industry; fellow Royal Society of Chemistry, Institute of Chemistry of Ireland. Has written over 125 scientific papers and is joint author of five books. Elected president of the RDS in 1991.

DONOGHUE, Denis (1928–), writer, critic and academic, b. Tullow, Co. Carlow, ed. CBS, Newry and UCD, fellow of King's College, Cambridge. Grew up in Warrenpoint, Co. Down, the son of an RUC policeman. He was a civil servant before joining the English department at UCD in 1953, becoming Professor of Modern English and American Literature 1967–80. He has held the Henry James chair of English and American letters at New York University since 1981. Publications include: *The Third Voice* (1959), *Connoisseurs of Chaos* (1966), *The Ordinary Universe* (1968), *Jonathan Swift* and *Emily Dickinson* (1969), *Yeats*

(1971), *Thieves of Fire* (1973), *The Sovereign Ghost* (1976). He gave the Reith Lectures (BBC) in 1982 and in 1983 was elected to the American Academy of Arts and Science.

DONOGHUE, Emma (1969–), writer and critic, ed. UCD and Cambridge, where she researched a Ph.D. on 18th-century literary friendships, published as *Passions between Women: British Lesbian Culture 1668–1801* (1993). She has published two novels, *Stir-fry* (1994) and *Hood* (1995), both set in contemporary Ireland. Her play, *I Know My Own Heart: A Lesbian Regency Romance*, was performed in Cambridge and the Project Theatre, Dublin in 1993.

DOOGE, James (1922–), engineer, academic and politician, b. Birkenhead, England, 30 July 1922, ed. Liverpool, CBS, Dún Laoghaire, Co. Dublin, UCD (BE, B.Sc., ME) and Iowa State University (M.Sc.). OPW 1942–6, ESB 1946–58 (1954–6, research associate, Department of Civil Engineering, Iowa). Professor of Civil Engineering UCC 1958– 70, UCD 1970–84. Consultant hydrologist Department of Engineering Hydrology UCG 1984–7, Centre for Water Resources Research UCD 1988–. Dooge has enjoyed a distinguished career in academia and in public life. He served on Dublin County Council 1948– 54 and was a member of Seanad Éireann 1961–77 and 1981–7, Cathaoirleach 1973–7. A close associate of GARRET FITZGERALD, he played an active role in the reorganisation of the Fine Gael party between 1978 and 1981. Minister for Foreign Affairs in the 1981–2 coalition government. Has received many awards and honorary degrees from international organisations and universities, including, most notably, the Bowie medal of the American Geophysical Union for his fundamental contributions to geophysics research. PRIA 1987–90.

DORAN, Johnny (1908–1950), traditional musician, d. Athy, Co. Kildare. With his brother Felix he was responsible for a long tradition of uilleann piping, developed by the travelling community, surviving and flourishing in the 20th century. Son of a piper and great-grandson of John Cash, an instrumentalist of almost mythical reputation and one of Francis O'Neill's *Irish Minstrels and Musicians*, he spent his early life in Rathnew,

Co. Wicklow. Later his parents took up permanent residence in Dublin. In the decade prior to World War II, accompanied by his wife and family, he opted for the life of a travelling professional piper, playing wherever crowds gathered for special occasions. His style, noted for its spontaneity and the constant use of regulators, was adopted by many younger pipers, such as Paddy Keenan, Finbar Furey and Davy Spillane. *The Complete Recordings of Johnny Doran*, a cassette of remastered recordings originally made by Kevin Danaher in 1947, was issued by Comhairle Bhéaloideas Éireann.

DORCEY, Mary (1950–), poet and fiction writer, b. Co. Dublin, ed. locally. She has lived in various parts of Ireland and spent long sojourns abroad, particularly in Britain, France, the USA and Japan. Her short stories have been published in many periodicals and anthologies in Ireland, Britain and the USA, and translated into Spanish, Italian, Dutch and Japanese. Both her prose and her poetry are strongly feminist and lesbian in character and explore universal themes from these platforms. Poetry: *Kindling* (1982) and *Moving into the Space Cleared by our Mothers* (1992). Novel: *The Tower of Babel* (1996). Short stories: *A Noise from the Woodshed* (1989), which won the Rooney prize in 1990. She also published a novella, *Scarlett O'Hara* (1988). Founder member of Irishwomen United.

DORGAN, Theo (1953–), poet and broadcaster, b. Cork, ed. UCC, where he also taught while working as literature officer at the Triskel Arts Centre. He has been co-director of the Cork Film Festival. Poetry collections include: *Slow Air* (1975), *A Moscow Quartet* (1989), *The Ordinary House of Love* (1990) and *Rosa Mundi* (1995). He has also edited a collection of essays, *Irish Poetry after Kavanagh* (1995), and was co-editor, with Máirín Ní Dhonnchadha, of *The Great Book of Ireland* and *Revising the Rising* (1991). He works in Dublin as a broadcaster and as director of *Poetry Ireland*.

DORMAN O'GOWAN, formerly Dorman Smith, **Eric Edward** (1898–1969), British general, b. Co. Cavan, childhood friend of JOHN CHARLES McQUAID, ed. Sandhurst. Associated with émigré literary circles in Paris after World War I. Regarded by many as the most brilliant military thinker of his day, he was responsible for the strategy which won

several important battles for Field Marshal Claude Auchinleck during the north African campaign. However, he fell victim to the sweeping changes in British senior command following the fall of Tobruk and was demoted from the rank of major-general to colonel. The shabbiness of his treatment became apparent only after the war when, under threat of legal proceedings for libel, Winston Churchill acknowledged that Dorman O'Gowan bore no responsibility for British defeats during the desert campaign. A remarkable man, he was a close friend of Ernest Hemingway, who used him as the model for Robert Cantwell, the hero of *Across the River and Into the Trees*. In his latter years, he acted as an occasional adviser to the IRA during the 1956–62 border campaign.

DOUGLAS, Barry (1960–), pianist, b. Belfast. Won the gold medal at the Tchaikovsky International Piano Competition in 1986, which launched his international career. Made his New York recital début at Carnegie Hall in 1988 and has performed with the Berlin Philharmonic, Israel Philharmonic, Cleveland and Philadelphia, all of the London orchestras, the National Symphony Orchestra of Ireland and the Bavarian Radio Symphony Orchestra, under conductors such as Ashkenazy, Masur, Previn, Rostropovich and Dutoit. Appeared at the London Proms, Edinburgh, Lucerne, Bergen, Tanglewood and the Hollywood Bowl. Worldwide performances include several extensive tours of Japan and New Zealand. Douglas has recorded piano concertos by Tchaikovsky, Brahms and Liszt, solo piano music by Beethoven, Tchaikovsky, Prokofiev, Liszt, Webern and Berg, and the Brahms Quintet with the Tokyo Quartet. Hon. D.Mus. (QUB).

DOUGLAS, James (1929–), writer, b. Bray, Co. Wicklow, ed. locally. He began writing drama and short stories when in his thirties. His first play, *North City Traffic Straight Ahead*, performed during the Dublin Theatre Festival of 1961, epitomised a renaissance in Irish theatre; *Carrie* (1963) and *The Ice Goddess* (1964) followed. *The Savages* was mounted in 1968 and *A Day Out of School* won the O.Z. Whitehead award for one-act plays in 1970. *What is the Stars?*, co-written with Robert Hogan, won an Irish Life award. Douglas has been very active in TV and radio drama; he devised the TV serial *The Riordans*, one of RTÉ's most successful soaps. Other dramatic works include: *The Bomb*, *The Hollow Field*, *How Long is Kissing Time?*, *Catalogue*, *Pay Now*, *Live Later* and *The Painting of Babbi Joe*, which was staged in New York in 1978. He co-authored, again with Hogan, the comic-historical novel *Murder at the Abbey Theatre* (1993).

DOUGLAS, James Green (1887–1954), businessman and senator, b. Dublin, ed. Friends' School, Lisburn; m. Ena Culley, two s. Treasurer and trustee of the White Cross in the War of Independence. Member of the committee that drafted the 1922 constitution. Vice-chairman of the Seanad 1922–5. A Quaker, Douglas was involved in the acrimonious debate on divorce in 1925. One result was that, although a principled believer in the indissolubility of marriage, he was characterised as having made 'an insidious move in the divorce game'. Chairman John Douglas and Sons Ltd and National City Bank; director Greenmount and Boyne Weaving Co.; clerk (chairman) Society of Friends Dublin 1921; chairman Postal Commission 1922. Lived at Brennanstown House, Cabinteely, Co. Dublin.

DOWLING, Joseph (1948–), theatre director, b. Dublin, ed. CUS and UCD. Director Peacock Theatre 1973–6; artistic director Irish Theatre Company 1976–8; artistic director Abbey Theatre 1978–85; managing director Gaiety Theatre 1985–9. Dowling has directed the work of Ireland's most prominent playwrights, including BRIAN FRIEL, TOM MURPHY, HUGH LEONARD and FRANK MCGUINNESS. At the Abbey he directed the premieres of Hugh Leonard's *Da* and Friel's *Aristocrats* and what many regard as the definitive production of the latter's *Philadelphia, Here I Come!* His acclaimed Abbey production of Friel's *Faith Healer* transferred to the Royal Court, London in 1991 and was nominated for an Olivier award for best revival. He has also worked extensively at the Gate; productions included *Our Country's Good*, *Twelfth Night*, *A Midsummer Night's Dream*, Friel's version of *A Month in the Country* and a hugely successful *Juno and the Paycock*. Dowling has worked with the Arena Stage in Washington, DC, with the Acting Company – America's only touring company – and with the Centaur Theater in Montreal.

DOWNES, Margaret (1934–), née Gavin, chartered accountant and businesswoman, ed. Loreto Abbey, Rathfarnham, Co. Dublin, UCD and Institute of Chartered Accountants in Ireland. Practised as an accountant London and Dublin. Partner Coopers and Lybrand 1964–84. In 1984 she became the first woman to be made a member of the court of the Bank of Ireland (i.e. a director). Holds numerous directorships in Ireland and the UK, is a trustee of the Chester Beatty Library and of the Douglas Hyde Gallery, Dublin. Hon. LL D (NUI).

DOWNEY, Angela (1957–), camogie player, b. Ballyraggett, Co. Kilkenny. Regarded as the top player of modern times, she won three All-Ireland Club Championships (1976, 1977 and 1988) with St Paul's, Kilkenny. She and her sister Ann are the only two players to have figured in all of Kilkenny's 11 O'Duffy Cup wins in the All-Ireland Senior Championship. Angela, who made her senior début aged 15 in 1972, has also won eight National League senior titles with the county, and has starred in many of Leinster's successes in the Gael-Linn Championship.

DOYLE, Jack ('**The Gorgeous Gael**') (1903–1978), boxer, b. Queenstown (Cobh), Co. Cork, 31 Mar. 1903, d. London, 13 Dec. 1978. A flamboyant character, he made his name as a heavyweight professional boxer (23 fights, 17 wins, six defeats) between 1932 and 1942, and later as a singer, vaudeville artist, occasional movie actor, and musical double act with his second wife, the Mexican starlet Movita, who subsequently left him for the young Marlon Brando. He never fought for a major title, apart from a disqualification against Jack Peterson in a challenge for the British Heavyweight Championship in 1933, but his good looks and 'celebrity' status drew huge crowds to his fights in London.

DOYLE, James (Jimmy) (1939–), hurler, b. Thurles. He won 11 County Senior Championships with Thurles Sarsfields, including five successive titles 1961–5, and also won one county football medal. He won three minor All-Ireland hurling medals, captaining the team in the third, in 1957. In a senior career that spanned the years 1957 to 1973, he captained the Tipperary sides which won the All-Ireland finals of 1962 and 1965, won a further four All-Ireland medals in 1958, 1961, 1964 and 1971, as well as playing on the teams which were defeated in the finals of 1960, 1967 and 1968, scoring a total of 46 points in his nine finals. His eight Railway Cup medals is a Tipperary record, and he also won six National League and five Oireachtas medals.

DOYLE, John (1930–), hurler, b. Holycross, Co. Tipperary. With CHRISTY RING he shares the record of winning eight All-Ireland Senior Hurling Championship medals, gained over 16 years in 1949, 1950, 1951 (all at left cornerback), 1958 and 1961 (both at left-half back), 1962, 1964 and 1965 (all at right cornerback). He was on the defeated sides of 1960 and 1967, and his ten All-Ireland final appearances is another record he shares with Ring. He won a record 11 National League medals with Tipperary, again over a 16-year period, as well as five Railway Cup medals and six Oireachtas medals.

DOYLE, Joseph (1891–1974), botanist, b. Glasgow, 25 Mar. 1891. Professor of Botany UCD. PRIA 1964–6. Boyle medallist 1942. He devoted most of his life to problems of the embryology of conifers. After graduation in 1911 from UCD he spent two years in Hamburg, and on returning joined the biology department. He became professor in 1924.

DOYLE, Lynn. See under Montgomery, Leslie Alexander.

DOYLE, Michael Gerard (Mick, 'Doyler') (1940–), international rugby player and coach, b. Castleisland, Co. Kerry, 13 Oct. 1940. At club level he played for Garryowen, Blackrock College, UCD, Cambridge University (where he won a blue in 1965) and Edinburgh Wanderers. Between 1965 and 1968 he won 20 consecutive Ireland caps as a flanker, three of them with younger brother Tommy on the other flank, and scored two international tries – the first on his début, against France at Lansdowne Road. He toured Australia with Ireland in 1967 and South Africa with the Lions the following year, playing in the 1st Test. He coached Leinster to Interprovincial Championship victories in 1979, 1980, 1981, 1982 (shared) and 1983, and as national coach guided Ireland to the Triple Crown and Five Nations Championship win of 1985. He later became a sports writer, and published a successful autobiography, *Doyler*, in 1991.

DOYLE, Paschal Vincent (1923–1988), hotelier, ed. CBS, Westland Row. A pioneer in Ireland of modern, well-appointed, medium-priced hotels, of which the Montrose, Skylon and Tara Towers in the suburbs of Dublin are typical. He later built the Berkeley Court and the Westbury in the luxury bracket and acquired hotels in the USA and London. Chairman of Bord Fáilte 1973–88.

DOYLE, Roddy (1958–), novelist, b. Dublin. Secondary teacher in Kilbarrack, Dublin for a number of years. Wrote satirical comedy plays for Passion Machine, a Dublin-based theatre company, including the highly successful *Brownbread* (1987). Novels: *The Commitments* (1987), which was made into a film, directed by Alan Parker; *The Snapper* (1990) and *The Van* (1991), also made into films, directed by Stephen Frears; *Paddy Clarke Ha Ha Ha*, for which he won the 1993 Booker prize; *The Woman who Walked into Doors* (1996). His comic outlook on life in the Rabbitte family in the fictional northside suburb of Barrytown stressed the human dimension of urban culture. *Family*, a television series broadcast on BBC and RTÉ in 1994, shocked Ireland with its raw portrayal of unemployed working-class Dublin family life, and the problems of alcoholism and wife-beating.

DOYLE, William Joseph Gabriel (1873–1917), Jesuit priest and military chaplain, b. Dalkey, Co. Dublin, 3 Mar. 1873, son of a legal official, ed. Ratcliffe College, Leicestershire, d. 16 Aug. 1917. Joined Society of Jesus, spent periods as a student or member of staff at Clongowes, Belvedere, Enghien in Belgium and Stonyhurst. Ordained a priest in 1907, he acquired a reputation as a giver of spiritual retreats and missions and his counsel was widely sought in person and by correspondence. He was also remarkable for his intense spirituality and asceticism, which later attracted criticism and controversy. Volunteering as a military chaplain in World War I, he went to France in 1916 with the 16th (Irish) Division of the British army and became a legend for his courage and persistence in providing the ministry of a Catholic priest to soldiers in the battle line. Involved at Loos, the Somme and Messines, he won the Military Cross and met his death during the Third Battle of Ypres. Accounts of his life gained extensive circulation after the war.

DREAPER, Thomas William (Tom) (1898–1975), horse trainer, b. Kilsallaghan, Co. Dublin, 28 Sept. 1898, d. Kilsallaghan, 28 Apr. 1975. He will always be remembered as the trainer of Arkle, but for 25 years beforehand he had produced a succession of notable steeplechasers from his stables at Greenogue, Kilsallaghan, the first of them being Prince Regent, winner of the 1946 Cheltenham Gold Cup. From Prince Regent in the 1940s to Flyingbolt in 1966, ten of his horses won the Irish Grand National, including seven in succession 1960–66, with PAT TAAFFE sharing in many of his triumphs. His son Jim (b. 1951) was a successful amateur jockey and now trains at the Greenogue stables, with many successes to his credit, including Brown Lad (the Irish Grand National winner in 1975, 1976 and 1978) and Ten Up (winner of the Cheltenham Gold Cup in 1975).

DRUMM, James (1896–1974), chemist and industrial technologist, b. Dundrum, Co. Down, 25 Jan. 1896, d. Dublin, 18 July 1974. Developed nickel-containing batteries that were capable of taking a very high charge. The Great Southern Railway Company took an interest and the so-called 'Drumm Train' was born. The first two came into service in the early 1930s; two more were built at the end of the decade. The battery-driven trains generally travelled on the old Bray–Harcourt Street line. They could carry 130 passengers, had a top speed of 47 m.p.h. and a range of 80 miles per charge.

DRURY, Michael Ivo (1920–1988), physician, b. Mountrath, Co. Laois, ed. locally by the Patrician Brothers and at UCD. Graduated in medicine in 1942. He joined the visiting staff of the Mater Hospital, where in 1947 facilities were meagre and record-keeping minimal. Refusing to take the line of least resistance, Drury provided himself with details of all his patients, especially those with diabetes and thyroid disorders. At St Michael's Hospital, Dún Laoghaire and the National Maternity Hospital he found the management of diabetes in pregnancy of particular interest and when his expertise in this field became apparent he was invited to attend the Coombe and Rotunda Hospitals and became an honorary FRCOG 1984. He was the author of *Diabetes Mellitus* (second ed. 1986). Elected president RCPI 1986.

DUBLINERS, The, folk group, one of the longest-surviving and most popular in Ireland. Formed in 1962 and initially known as the Ronnie Drew Group. The original line-up was Drew himself (b. 1935), Kieron Bourke (b. 1936, now deceased), Barney McKenna (b. 1939) and Luke Kelly (1940–84). Shortly afterwards they were joined by John Sheahan (b. 1939) on fiddle, and over the years there have been further personnel changes. In 1967 the Dubliners featured in the British top ten, and in time they were to draw large enthusiastic crowds abroad, especially in continental Europe; this they continue to do. Luke Kelly, a performer of exceptional presence, is possibly the only folk singer to have a bridge named in his memory by his native city.

DUFF, Frank (1889–1980), founder of the Legion of Mary, b. Dublin, 7 June 1889, ed. Belvedere and Blackrock, d. de Montfort House, Dublin, 7 Nov. 1980. Entered the Land Commission in 1908. Opted to join the civil service of the Irish Free State in 1922 and went on to work in the Department of Finance, from which he retired in 1934. His active role in Church affairs dates from 1913, when he joined the Society of St Vincent de Paul. A key influence on his religious outlook at this stage was de Montfort's *True Devotion to the Blessed Virgin*. In 1921, together with Fr Michael Toher, he founded the Legion of Mary in Dublin. In 1922 Duff established the Sancta Maria hostel for the rehabilitation of former prostitutes and in 1925 he was the driving force behind the closure of the 'Monto', Dublin's red-light district. In 1927 he set up the Morning Star hostel for homeless men and in 1939 the Regina Coeli for unmarried mothers. From 1925 onwards he oversaw the expansion of the Legion of Mary throughout Ireland and abroad. The Eucharistic Congress in Dublin in 1932 enabled him to introduce the Legion to overseas prelates, with the result that it was soon established in Australia, New Zealand and the USA. From 1935 he sent 'envoys' to Africa, China and South America, among them EDEL QUINN (east Africa), Fr Aedan McGrath (China) and Alphonsus Lambe (South America). But success abroad was overshadowed by strained relations at home with the Archbishop of Dublin, EDWARD BYRNE, who saw Duff as a maverick engaged in religious work without episcopal sanction. The result was that formal approval for the Legion in Dublin was withheld until 1935. A crucial factor in its survival in the city during this difficult period was the support Duff received from Cardinal JOSEPH MACRORY, papal nuncio Monsignor Robinson and W.T. COSGRAVE. In 1940 Duff welcomed the succession of JOHN CHARLES MCQUAID but was soon disappointed when the new archbishop required him to disband two Legion groups – the Mercier Society and the Pillar of Fire Society – which aimed at a dialogue with Protestants and Jews. It was not until the 1960s that Duff was to feel the Legion enjoyed Archbishop McQuaid's full support. In 1965 he was asked to attend the Second Vatican Council as a lay observer, but he was uncomfortable with the more relaxed theological climate that followed, which seemed to involve a swing away from Mariology.

He wrote extensively on the position of Mary in Church teaching. His more important writings included the pamphlet *Can We Be Saints?*, published in 1913 by the Catholic Truth Society of Ireland, *Legio Mariae – The Handbook of the Legion of Mary, Miracles on Tap* and *The Woman of Genesis*. His achievement in establishing the Legion of Mary was the formation of a body which was prepared to tackle some of the more difficult social problems of his time, such as prostitution and homelessness. In particular, as one commentator put it, he helped to change the climate where the 'established clerical order did not favour initiative from the laity'.

DUFFY, George Gavan (1882–1951), lawyer, b. Cheshire, s. of Sir Charles Gavan Duffy and brother of LOUISE GAVAN DUFFY, ed. at Petit Seminaire, Nice and Stonyhurst, d. 10 June 1951. Friend of ARTHUR GRIFFITH, whose early Sinn Féin movement he supported though critical of its conservative policies. Qualified as solicitor in England 1907, practising in London until 1916, when his partners effectively dismissed him for having defended ROGER CASEMENT. Duffy then took up residence in Ireland and was called to the Irish Bar in 1917. Elected Sinn Féin MP for South County Dublin 1918, attending open meeting of First Dáil the following year. With SEÁN T. Ó CEALLAIGH was unofficial delegate

of Republic of Ireland to Paris Peace Conference 1919; expelled from France at instigation of British government. Unofficial Irish envoy to Rome 1920. On Irish delegation to London 1921 for Anglo-Irish Treaty negotiations, he voted for the Treaty in Dáil ratification debates 1922. Minister for Foreign Affairs in the new Provisional Government of the Irish Free State, he resigned in 1922 in protest at the government's abolition of the republican courts. The following year he resigned his Dáil seat over the government's refusal to treat republican prisoners as prisoners of war. He resumed practice at the Bar, becoming Senior Counsel 1929. Appointed a High Court judge 1936 and consulted during the drafting of the new constitution, the principal draftsman, JOHN HEARNE, later saying that Duffy had a major input into article 40 (on fundamental rights). Promoted to presidency of the High Court 1946.

Duffy often equated Irish nationalism with Irish Catholicism, and tended to interpret the constitution in the light of Catholic teaching, as in the famous Tilson case of 1951 (on the father's right to control a child's education in a 'mixed' marriage). However, as a constitutional lawyer Duffy was ahead of his time, a defender of individual rights against the state, and is regarded by many authorities as the father of judicial review in Ireland.

DUFFY, Louise Gavan (1884–1969), teacher and revolutionary, b. Nice, 17 July 1884, d. of Sir Charles Gavan Duffy and sister of GEORGE GAVAN DUFFY, d. Dublin, 12 Oct. 1969. Among the first women to attend UCD (BA 1911). She taught in Scoil Íde, the all-girls school founded by PATRICK PEARSE. As a member of Cumann na nBan she worked in the kitchens of the GPO during the Easter Rising. With Annie McHugh in 1917 she founded Scoil Bhríde, an Irish-speaking school for girls. She left Cumann na mBan in 1922 because of its rejection of the Treaty but continued to devote her life to the education of girls. She received an honorary degree from the NUI for her pioneering work in this area.

DUGGAN, Eamonn (1874–1936), lawyer and nationalist, b. Longwood, Co. Meath, d. Dún Laoghaire, Co. Dublin, 6 June 1936. Solicitor to next of kin at the inquest on THOMAS ASHE. Elected TD for South Meath

1918. A signatory of the Anglo-Irish Treaty 1921, Minister for Home Affairs in the government of the Second Dáil to 9 Sept. 1922, and thereafter minister without portfolio in the Provisional Government of the Irish Free State, later parliamentary secretary to the Minister for Defence and the Executive Council. Senator 1933. First chairman of Dún Laoghaire Borough Council.

DUGGAN, Noel C. (1933–), entrepreneur, b. Millstreet, Co. Cork, 25 Dec. 1933. Left school at 13, served a hardware apprenticeship in Roscommon. Built up the family hardware business and developed it into a big, lucrative structural steel trade. Built a major equestrian centre, Green Glens (1990–93), which hosts the Millstreet International Horse Show, the Irish Showjumping Derby and various entertainment events, raising the profile of the Irish sport worldwide. In 1993, against a chorus of metropolitan cynicism, he succeeded in bringing the Eurovision Song Contest to Millstreet and running it with exemplary efficiency. Galvanised the local community to attract industrial investment into the remote Cork village. Planning a £10m hotel and leisure complex in Drishane Castle. National Endeavour Award, honorary degree in laws from NUI (1994). His wife, Maureen, and four children are all involved in the family business.

DUKES, Alan (1945–), politician and economist, b. Dublin, 20 Apr. 1945, ed. Coláiste Mhuire and UCD, m. Fionnuala Corcoran, two d. Worked as an economist for the IFA in its Dublin headquarters 1969–73. He then moved to Brussels to direct its EC operations. From 1977 to 1980 he was a member of EC commissioner RICHARD BURKE's cabinet. TD (FG Kildare) 1981. He joined a select number of TDs who became ministers on their first day in the Dáil, being given the Agriculture portfolio. That government collapsed in early 1982 but in the general election of Nov. that year it was returned to office and Dukes became Minister for Finance. He held the job until 1986, when he was appointed Minister for Justice in a major government reshuffle. After Fine Gael's poor performance in the 1987 general election and the consequent resignation of GARRET FITZGERALD as party leader, Dukes was voted in to take his place. Under his leadership the party made modest gains in the 1989 election but in the following year fared badly in the presidential election. Dukes was saddled with the blame and, although he fought hard, was forced to resign as leader. Involved in a later attempt to unseat his successor, JOHN BRUTON, he has been an outsider within his party, although widely regarded as one of its leading intellects and one of the foremost advocates of the benefits of EU membership.

DUNLOP, William Joseph (Joey) (1952–), motorcycle racer, b. Ballymoney, Co. Antrim, 25 Feb. 1952. With a record 15 TT wins between 1977 and 1994, as well as a record 29 victories on the road circuit at Castletown, he is the most successful rider ever in the Isle of Man TT races. He also won a record five Formula One world titles 1982–6 and was second in 1987, 1988 and 1990. He passed Mike Hailwood's record 14 Isle of Man TT wins in 1993, having equalled it the previous year. By recording three wins in a year at Senior, Junior and Formula One in both 1985 and 1988, he equalled another Hailwood record. A Formula One winner each year from 1983 to 1988, his other TT successes included Jubilee 1977, Classic 1980, 1987, Senior 1987 and Junior 1993, 1994. He was awarded the MBE in 1986. His brother Robert won the 125 cc in 1989 and the 250 cc in 1991.

DUNN, Joseph (1930–1996), Roman Catholic priest and broadcaster, ed. Belvedere, Clonliffe and UCD. Ordained priest 1955. Pastoral duties in Dublin until 1959 when Archbishop JOHN CHARLES MCQUAID sent him to England and the USA to take courses in television programme-making. In 1961 he formed a unit of priests with the archbishop's approval to make socio-religious documentaries in anticipation of the Irish television service, then about to commence broadcasting. This was the beginning of Radharc Films, which for more than 30 years under its founder's direction was to make hundreds of documentaries, covering all five continents and distinguished by searing criticism of oppressive regimes, as well as historical and informational programmes on matters related to religion, including many programmes on the challenges facing the modern Church. Subjects covered have been as various as Swedish Lutheranism, basic communities in Brazil and overpopulation in Indonesia, the problems of prostitution and unemployment in Ireland, Biafra during the Nigerian civil war and feminist issues in American Catholicism. Radharc programmes have been a feature of Irish television from its first month of broadcasting, have appeared on BBC and other services and won numerous awards, both Irish and international. Dunn's published work included *No Tigers in Africa* (1986), on 25 years of Radharc, and *No Lions in the Hierarchy* (1994) and *No Vipers in the Vatican* (1996), both of which were expressions of critical concern over what he saw as shortcomings in the structures and leadership of the Catholic Church, based on his worldwide experience of film-making.

DUNNE, Christopher *Lee* (1934–), novelist, playwright and scriptwriter, b. Dublin. Worked as a sailor, actor and taxi driver. He is best known for his first two novels, *Goodbye to the Hill* (1965), which pre-dates the work of hard realists like James Kelman in its portrayal of working-class life, and *A Bed in the Sticks* (1968), a semi-autobiographical account of a touring company of actors playing in halls in rural Ireland. He adapted *Goodbye to the Hill* for the stage in 1978, with astonishing popular success. Dunne is a prolific and entertaining writer with a distinct, colloquial style. His many novels include a series based on his taxi-driving experiences, such as *Midnight Cabbie* (1974), *The Cabbie Who Came In from the Cold* and *The Cabfather* (1975) and *Virgin Cabbies*. He has also written scripts for RTÉ radio and television.

DUNNE, Seán (1956–1995), poet and editor, b. Waterford, ed. UCC. Freelance writer and broadcaster and a regular contributor to *Sunday Miscellany* and *Poetry Choice* on Radio Éireann. Among his publications was a memoir entitled *In my Father's House* (1991), a sensitive and immensely readable account of his childhood in Waterford; particularly moving is the episode detailing his mother's death of heart failure and how he coped with his loss. Poetry collections: *Against the Storm* (1985), *The Sheltered Nest* (1992) and *Time and the Island* (1996). He edited *The Cork Anthology* (1993). Also edited *Poets of Munster: An Anthology* (1985) and an edition of the *Cork Review* (1991). He wrote a number of books on spirituality, including *The Road to Silence* (1994) and *Something Understood: A Spiritual Anthology* (1995). Other works: *An Introduction to Irish Poetry* (1992) and *The College: A Photographic History of University College Cork* (1995). Literary editor of the *Cork Examiner*.

DUNPHY, Eamon (1943–), international footballer, b. Dublin, 3 Aug. 1943. Apprenticed to Manchester United 1962, played in the English League for York City, Millwall (267 matches, 24 goals, 1965–73), Charlton and Reading. FAI Cup medal with Shamrock Rovers 1978. Won 23 Republic of Ireland caps 1966–77. Later became a sports writer and author, his book *Only a Game*, about the professional footballer's life, being highly acclaimed.

DUNSANY (Edward John Moreton Drax Plunkett), Lord (1878–1957), writer and dramatist, b. London, 18th Baron of Dunsany (the ancestral home in Co. Meath), ed. Eton and Sandhurst. Though at heart a British aristocrat, he contributed several plays to the Abbey during its formative years, including *The Glittering Gates* (1909) and *King Argimenes and the Unknown Warrior* (1910), which enjoyed success in Britain and the USA. He was a man of action, revelling in big-game hunting in Africa, and a seasoned army campaigner. His fame rests chiefly on his fiction, his short stories in particular, which were greatly admired by SEÁN O'FAOLAIN and PATRICK KAVANAGH, and on a raft of novels of a genre that nowadays would be categorised as 'swords and sorcery', such as *The Sword of Welleran* (1908), *The King of Elfland's Daughter* (1924) and *The Blessing of Pan* (1927). He discovered, encouraged and promoted the talents of his neighbour, the labourer-poet FRANCIS LEDWIDGE.

DUNWOODY, Thomas *Richard* (1964–), jump jockey, b. Comber, Co. Down, 19 Jan. 1964. He rode his first winner in 1983, finishing third in the amateur championship in 1983–4. After going professional he was runner-up (to Peter Scudamore) in the jockeys' championship in 1989–90 with 102 winners. He was champion himself in 1992–3 with 173 winners and record prize money of over £1m, and was awarded the MBE at the end of that season. He rode his 1,000th winner on 30 Jan. 1994. Other career highlights include Grand National wins in 1986 (on West Tip) and 1994 (on Minnehoma), the Cheltenham Gold Cup in 1988 (on Charter Party) and the Champion Hurdle (on Kribensis) in 1990.

DURCAN, Paul (1944–), poet and literary critic, b. Dublin, ed. Gonzaga and UCC, where he studied, and later tutored in, archaeology and medieval history. PATRICK KAVANAGH award 1974. Arts Council creative bursaries 1976 and 1980. Irish-American Cultural Institute award 1989. His works include *O Westport in the Light of Asia Minor* (1974), *Jesus, Break his Fall* (1980), *The Berlin Wall Café* (1985), *Going Home to Russia* (1987), *Daddy, Daddy* (1990), which won the Whitbread prize, *Crazy about Women* (1991), *New and Selected Poems* (1993). He is a best-selling poet in Ireland, quoted by President MARY ROBINSON in her inauguration speech. His work is intensely lyrical but also highly satirical.

E

EAMES, Baron Robert Henry Alexander (**Robin**) (1937–), Church of Ireland archbishop, b. 27 Apr. 1937, ed. Belfast Royal Academy, Methodist College, Belfast, QUB (Ph.D.) and TCD. Archbishop of Armagh since 1986. Tutor in the faculty of law at QUB 1960–63, curate in Bangor, Co. Down 1963–6 and rector in Belfast 1966–75. Bishop of Derry and Raphoe 1975–80, Down and Dromore 1980–86. He was consulted by Taoiseach ALBERT REYNOLDS in the period leading up to the publication of the Downing Street Declaration in Dec. 1993 and was instrumental in helping to draft elements of the document in regard to the Irish Republic's attitude towards Protestant concerns. He became a life peer in 1995 and in the same year told the Church of Ireland General Synod: 'True freedom in society is the freedom and obligation to order its affairs with justice, compassion and understanding so that all its traditions may respect each other without fear.'

EARLY, Dermot (1948–), Gaelic footballer, b. Castlebar, 24 Feb. 1948. A midfielder, he played on the first Roscommon team to win the All-Ireland under-21 title, in 1966, and in the 1966–7 season he set a record by becoming the first player to compete at every grade from county minor to senior as well as in the Railway Cup and the National League. In a career which lasted from 1965 to 1988 he starred in Roscommon's five Connacht Championship wins, helped the county to reach the All-Ireland final of 1980 (which was won by Kerry) and won National League and Railway Cup winners' medals. He was the game's top scorer in 1974 with 126 points in 25 matches, this average of 5.04 being a record for a Roscommon player. He was an All-Star twice, in 1974 and 1979, both at centre-field.

EASON, John Charles Malcolm (1880–1976), businessman, b. Dublin, ed. TCD, m. Eliza Beck Douglas, four d. In 1901 he joined the family firm of newsagents, bookshops, stationers and wholesale distributors, which his father, Charles, had founded by buying out W.H. Smith's Irish interests. Motorised the firm's fleet 1911. Staff numbered almost 700 at the time of the Easter Rising, when O'Connell Street was destroyed; he and his father supervised the building of the new premises. Joined the Dublin Chamber of Commerce 1918; active in the local government inquiry into the affairs of the city 1924, to which Eason made the case for the Chamber, a scathing examination of the City Council. The outcome was the Council's replacement by a commission which reigned until new elections were called in 1930. Eason, president of the Chamber 1927, successfully argued the case before this commission for the extension of the city boundaries to embrace the townships of Pembroke and Rathmines. In the Chamber, Eason formed a centre group with GEORGE N. JACOB and Lombard Murphy (whose fathers had come together to deal with the 1913 Lockout), Dissenter, Quaker and Catholic making common cause. Resigned from chairmanship of Eason's 1958. Hon. M.Comm. (TCD) 1960. Sat on the council of the Civics Institute; member of the Statistical and Social Inquiry Society of Ireland, president 1930–34.

EASTWOOD, Bernard Joseph (**Barney**) (1932–), businessman and boxing manager/promoter, b. Cookstown, Co. Tyrone. He is best remembered for his management of the boxers BARRY MCGUIGAN and DAVE MCAULEY. Eastwood married at 19 and he and his wife, Frances, moved to Carrickfergus, Co. Antrim. A gifted businessman, he amassed considerable wealth through his string of betting shops, public houses and other interests. He established himself as a boxing manager, achieving his greatest success when McGuigan won the world featherweight title in 1985. As a promoter he established the King's Hall, Belfast as a major championship venue. He also managed Paul Hodkins of Liverpool, who won the world featherweight title, and, from 1991 to 1993, STEVE COLLINS.

EDDERY, Patrick James John (**Pat**) (1952–), jockey, flat racing, b. Blackrock, Co.

Dublin, 18 Mar. 1952. He has been retained by Frenchie Nicholson, Peter Walwyn, VINCENT O'BRIEN and Prince Khaled Abdulla. Eddery has won three Epsom Derbys (1975 on Grundy, 1982 on Golden Fleece and 1990 on Quest for Fame), two 2,000 Guineas (1983 on Lomond and 1984 on El Grand Senor), two Epsom Oaks (1974 on Polygamy and 1979 on Scintillate), the 1,000 Guineas (1993 on Zaphonic) and two St Legers (1986 and 1991, both on Moon Madness). His Irish Classic wins include four Derbys, two 2,000 Guineas, two Oaks and the St Leger, and he has also won four Prix de l'Arc de Triomphe (a record which includes three in succession on Rainbow Quest, Dancing Brave and Trempolino), three French Derbys and the French Oaks. By 1993 he had been British champion jockey nine times.

EDGEWORTH-JOHNSTONE, Sir Walter, CB, lieutenant-colonel, commissioner DMP, ed. St Columba's, TCD and Sandhurst. 1st West India Regiment, Royal Irish Regiment. Resident magistrate 1904. Versatile athlete in many codes: swordsman, British army heavyweight boxing champion, played cricket with Gentlemen of Ireland. Commissioner of the DMP 1914. Survived the Easter Rising and subsequent unrest in the force. Succeeded in 1923 by W.R.E. MURPHY.

EDWARDS, Hilton Robert Hugh (1903–1982), actor and theatre director, b. Holloway, London, 2 Feb. 1903, ed. East Finchley Grammar School and St Aloysius's College, Highgate, d. Dublin, 18 Nov. 1982. After brief military service, acted with a touring theatre group in England and Ireland, spent a period with the Old Vic, then returned to Ireland in 1927 with ANEW MCMASTER's company, where he met McMaster's brother-in-law, MICHEÁL MACLIAMMÓIR. The two formed a partnership which was to last 50 years, to the great benefit of theatre in Ireland. The company they founded, the Gate Theatre, was launched in Dublin on 14 Oct. 1928 with a performance of Ibsen's *Peer Gynt* in the Peacock Theatre, the small auditorium attached to the Abbey Theatre; Edwards directed, and also played the title role. This production, together with other offerings in their first year – most notably DENIS JOHNSTON's *The Old Lady Says 'No!'*, which had been rejected by

the Abbey – established the group's intention to offer a cosmopolitan selection of classics and new plays, employing imaginative, even experimental techniques.

Although a fine actor, Edwards made his major impact in production and direction: his effective use of lighting was just one of the talents he brought to the theatre. These showed to even better effect when in Feb. 1930 the Gate moved to a permanent home in the Rotunda Assembly Rooms, Parnell Square, where the opening production was Goethe's *Faust*, with Edwards as Faust and MacLiammóir as Mephistopheles. There followed down the years innumerable new performances and revivals of plays by Wilde and SHAW, O'Neill, Koestler and Brecht, Maupassant and Shakespeare, MAURA LAVERTY, BRIAN FRIEL, Desmond Forristal and MacLiammóir himself. The Gate also saw the early appearances of such famous actors as Orson Welles, CYRIL CUSACK and RIA MOONEY. Productions were brought to many foreign countries, even to the Balkans and, famously, to Egypt.

Because of differences between the Edwards–MacLiammóir partnership and their patron, Lord LONGFORD, the company divided into two in 1936, the Gate and Longford Productions. They shared the Gate Theatre, each using it for half the year and touring when the other was in possession. The result was memorable productions by Edwards–MacLiammóir at Louis Ellman's Gaiety Theatre in Dublin as well as in the Cork and Belfast Opera Houses. In an interlude of this crowded career Edwards served as head of drama 1961–3 at the newly established Telefís Éireann (later RTÉ). In 1973 he and MacLiammóir became the first members of the theatrical profession to receive the freedom of the city of Dublin. They also received honorary doctorates from the NUI and TCD. Hilton Edwards survived his partner by four years.

EDWARDS, Robert Dudley (Robin) (1909–1988), historian, b. Dublin, ed. CUS, UCD and King's College, London. Lecturer in modern Irish history UCD 1942. His own special field was 16th-century Ireland, but more importantly, together with TCD history professor THEODORE MOODY, he was a powerful stimulator of fresh approaches in the research and interpretation of Irish history. In

1938 he and Moody founded the journal *Irish Historical Studies*, which set new standards for professional historians. His published work ranged from *Church and State in Tudor Ireland* (1935) to (with Mary O'Dowd) *Sources for Early Modern Irish History* (1985).

EGAN, Desmond (1936–), teacher, publisher and poet, b. Athlone, ed. Mullingar and UCD. One of the country's most idiosyncratic versifiers, he has been hailed by critics of the stature of Hugh Kenner and Brian Arkins as an important poet, in two separate studies which appeared in 1989 and 1992. He works largely in free verse, shunning traditional punctuation and standard syntactical forms. Egan set up the Goldsmith Press in 1972 and has since published and edited an impressive array of poets, including MICHAEL HARTNETT, DESMOND O'GRADY, Eugene Watters and Kevin Faller. He published a posthumous autobiographical novel by PATRICK KAVANAGH, *By Night Unstarred* (1977), and a biography of Kavanagh by his brother Peter in 1979. His own collections are: *Midland* (1972), *Leaves* (1974), *Siege!* (1977), *Woodcutter* (1978), *Athlone?* (1980), *Seeing Double* and *Collected Poems* (1983), *Terre et Paix* (1988), *A Song for my Father* (1989), *Snapdragon* (1992), *Selected Poems* (1993) and *In the Holocaust of Autumn* (1994). He won the Muir award 1983 and the American Society of Poetry award 1984.

ENGLISH, Nicholas (Nicky) (1962–), hurler, b. Cullen, Co. Tipperary, 20 Oct. 1962. After winning an All-Ireland minor medal in 1980 and an All-Ireland Under-21 Championship medal in 1981, he went on to captain the Tipperary team which was defeated in the All-Ireland senior final of 1988. He helped the county to win the final the next year, scoring two goals and 12 points, and won another All-Ireland medal in 1991. Other achievements include a National League medal in 1988, Railway Cup medals with Munster in 1984 and 1985 and six All-Star awards.

ENNIS, Seamus (1919–1982), musician. Occupies a unique role in the history of Irish traditional music in the 20th century because of the extent and diversity of his contribution. Unquestionably one of the foremost uilleann pipers of the era, he was also a whistle player, a singer and storyteller, and a collector of music, song and folklore of priceless cultural

importance. He was born in Jamestown in north Co. Dublin, the son of a highly respected piper, James Ennis, to whom he frequently expressed his indebtedness. He himself commenced learning the pipes at the age of 13; thereafter, due to his constant association with musicians from all over Ireland, he developed an individualistic style which was nevertheless totally within the traditional mould. His influence on a younger generation of pipers, such as LIAM O'FLYNN and Peter Browne, was considerable.

He had extensive collecting experience. In the 1940s he worked with the Radio Éireann mobile recording unit and with the BBC, joining the latter as a staff member in 1954. He also made frequent radio and later television broadcasts.

Apart from his many tangible achievements, his position in the musical world was in part due to his presence; while never strident, he was charismatic, with a visit by Ennis to a particular district invariably an *event*. His last years, plagued by ill health, were spent in Naul close to the place of his birth. His daughter Catherine is a professional organist of international reputation.

ENRIGHT, Anne (1962–), writer, b. Dublin, ed. Vancouver, TCD and University of East Anglia. Worked as an actress and writer; won the Rooney prize 1991. Producer/director with RTÉ. Short stories: *The Portable Virgin* (1991). Novel: *The Wig my Father Wore* (1995).

EOGAN, George (1930–), archaeologist, b. Nobber, Co. Meath, ed. locally, UCD and TCD. After a period as a research assistant at TCD he was appointed lecturer in archaeology at UCD in 1965, professor 1979. The Irish Later Bronze Age was a field he dominated for years, publishing 'The Irish Later Bronze Age in the Light of Recent Research' in 1964, followed by the *Catalogue of Irish Bronze Swords* (1965) and *The Hoards of the Irish Later Bronze Age* (1983); despite his other commitments he maintained this interest and in 1994 produced *The Accomplished Art: Gold and Gold-working in Britain and Ireland during the Bronze Age*. His excavations, mainly in his native Meath, culminated in the massive undertaking of the excavation of the great passage tomb at Knowth, with its satellites and occupation sites; the publication of the results (in three volumes) commenced in 1984 with *Excavations at Knowth, I.* He is a member of many learned bodies, including Academia Europea, and from 1987 to 1989 was a member of Seanad Éireann (Taoiseach's nominee).

ERVINE, St John Greer (1883–1971), playwright, critic and novelist, b. Ballymacarret, Belfast, d. Seaton, Devon, 24 Jan. 1971. After working for three years in an insurance company, went to live in London, from where he contributed several plays on Ulster themes to the Abbey Theatre in Dublin. Became manager of the Abbey 1915 but his regime was so controversial that he was removed the following year. Joined the Dublin Fusiliers and lost a leg as a result of combat wounds 1918. Continued to write occasionally for the Abbey while concentrating on plays for the London theatre and writing opinionated biographies of GEORGE BERNARD SHAW, Parnell and Wilde. Ervine's serious work mirrored the hard, honest, narrow-minded and survivalist Ulster character. His plays included *Mixed Marriage* (1914), *The First Mrs Fraser* (1929) and *Boyd's Shop* (1936). Drama critic of the *Observer* until 1939. Early member of the IAL.

ESPOSITO, Michele (1855–1929), composer, pianist, teacher, conductor, editor and music publisher, b. Naples, d. Florence. Came to Dublin 1882. Senior Professor of Piano at the RIAM for 46 years. Founded RIAM local centre examination system in 1894 and Dublin Orchestral Society in 1899. Instrumental in the inauguration of RDS music recitals. Hon. Mus.D. (TCD) 1917. Order of Commendatore of the Italian Republic 1923. Compositions include *An Irish Symphony*, a piano concerto and a musical setting of DOUGLAS HYDE's *The Tinkerbell and the Fairy*.

EVANS, Emyr Estyn, writer and academic, b. Wales. Joined geography department QUB 1928; retired as director Institute of Irish Studies 1970. Publications include: *Irish Heritage* (1942), *Mourne Country* (1951), *Irish Folk Ways* (1957), *Prehistoric and Early Christian Ireland* (1966) and *The Personality of Ireland* (1973).

EVERETT, James (1890–1967), politician, b. Co. Wicklow. An official of the Co. Wicklow Agricultural Union, which later amalgamated with the ITGWU. Elected to the Dáil in 1922 and held his seat until his death. A central figure in the Labour Party split in the mid-1940s, when the ITGWU disaffiliated, ostensibly on the grounds of 'communist infiltration'. The dispute was in fact related to the readmission of JAMES LARKIN and his son, James, to the Labour parliamentary party – both were successful Labour candidates in the 1943 general election. Everett headed a breakaway group of five TDs, all ITGWU members, to form National Labour. The new party contested the 1944 and 1948 elections as an independent entity, but Larkin's death in 1947 and the participation of both Labour groupings in the 1948–51 inter-party government led to an eventual rapprochement. Everett was Minister for Posts and Telegraphs 1948–51 and Minister for Justice 1954–7. LIAM KAVANAGH is his nephew.

EWING, Reginald Cecil (1910–1973), golfer, b. Rosses Point, Co. Sligo, 10 July 1910, d. Rosses Point, 27 Aug. 1973. One of the foremost amateurs of his day, he won the Irish Close Championship twice (1948, 1958) and the Irish Amateur Open twice (1948, 1951), won the West of Ireland ten times (1930, 1932, 1935, 1939, 1941–3, 1945, 1949–50) and was runner-up eight times. He was runner-up in the British Amateur Championship at Troon in 1938, played on the first Walker Cup-winning side of 1938 and was a selector when Great Britain and Ireland won their second Walker Cup in 1971. He played on six Walker Cup sides in all (1936, 1938, 1947, 1949, 1951 and 1953), in 92 home international matches for Ireland 1934–58, and was non-playing captain when Ireland won the European Team Championship in Sandwich (1965) and Turin (1967). President of the Golfing Union of Ireland in 1970.

F

FALLON, Padraic (1905–1974), poet and playwright, b. Athenry, Co. Galway, 3 Jan. 1905, ed. Cistercian College, Roscrea and Garbally Park. After school he joined the customs and excise service and served in Wexford for many years, where he also farmed. He wrote remarkable verse plays, broadcast on Radio Éireann, including his own versions of the legends *Diarmuid and Grainne* and *The Vision of Mac Conglinne*. His stage play *The Seventh Step* (1954) was performed in Cork and Dublin. Much of his poetry appeared in the *Dublin Magazine* in the 1950s and was later published in *Poems* (1973) and *Poems and Versions* (1983).

FALLON, Peter (1951–), poet, publisher and literary editor, b. Osnabrück, Germany to Irish parents and grew up on a farm in Co. Meath, ed. Glenstal and TCD. Ireland's most respected poetry publisher, he set up the Gallery Press in 1970. Poet in residence at Deerfield Academy, Massachusetts 1976–7, co-editor of *Ocarina*, the arts review. Arts Council bursary 1981. Fiction editor to the O'Brien Press 1980–85. He has published, among other works, *A Farewell to English* by MICHAEL HARTNETT (1978) and co-edited *Soft Day: A Miscellany of Contemporary Irish Writing* (1980). Fallon's own poetry celebrates with brio the rural life he knows so intimately; any ill-considered charges of provincialism are answered by incisive ripostes which contain more universality than most metropolitan poetry. His collections are: *Among the Walls* (1971), *Co-incidence of Flesh* (1972), *The First Affair* (1974), *A Gentler Birth* (1976), *Victims* (1977), *Finding the Dead* and *The Speaking Stones* (1978), *Winter Work* (1983), *The News and Weather* (1987) and *Eye to Eye* (1992).

FALLS, Cyril Bentham (1888–1971), military correspondent and historian, s. of Sir Charles Fausset Falls, ed. Portora and London University, d. 23 Apr. 1971. Served in Royal Inniskilling Fusiliers, later on divisional staffs and as a liaison officer with the French 1914–18. Became official historian of the 36th (Ulster) Division and joined staff of historical section of the Committee of Imperial Defence. Wrote official histories and many other works, becoming military correspondent of *The Times* 1939–53 and Chichele Professor of the History of War at Oxford 1946–53. His books included *Elizabeth's Irish Wars* and *The Birth of Ulster* and he became a vice-president of the Military History Society of Ireland, contributing articles to its journal.

FANNING, Stephen (1922–), assistant commissioner Garda Síochána, b. Boyle. Farmer. Joined the police force 1944. Seconded to the UN Transition Assistance Group supervising the transition to independence in Namibia. Retired 1987. Appointed commissioner international civil police force 1989.

FARRELL, Bernard (1939–), playwright, b. Dublin, ed. Monkstown Park College and People's College, Dublin. Farrell's sharply observed social comedies have enjoyed great popular success. Much of his work has been performed at the Abbey Theatre, including *I Do Not Like Thee Doctor Fell* (1979), *Canaries* (1980), *All the Way Back* (1985), *Say Cheese!* (1987) and *The Last Apache Reunion* (1993). *Forty-four Sycamore* (1992), produced by Red Kettle Theatre Company, won the *Sunday Tribune* Comedy of the Year award. Farrell has also written for television and radio. He received the Rooney prize for Irish literature in 1980 and became a member of Aosdána in 1989.

FARRELL, Brian (1929–), academic, author, journalist and broadcaster, b. Manchester, ed. Coláiste Mhuire, UCD and Harvard. In 1955 he joined the administrative staff of UCD, became director of extramural studies and in 1957 assistant to the registrar. From 1966 he lectured in the Department of Ethics and Politics at UCD, going on to become senior lecturer in politics, acting head of department and, in 1985, Associate Professor of Politics. He has written a number of books on Irish political history, including *Chairman or Chief?*, a pioneering analysis of the role of the head of government in independent Ireland, *The Founding of Dáil Éireann*, an analysis of the emergence and evolution of the First Dáil, and a biography of SEÁN LEMASS. He edited lectures in the RTÉ Thomas Davis series, *Communications and Community in Ireland* and *De Valera's Constitution and Ours*. In his parallel career as a media commentator he contributed to the *Irish Press*, *Irish Independent* and Radio Éireann in the 1950s and 1960s, and for more than 30 years presented RTÉ television's main programmes of comment and analysis, successively *Broadsheet*, *Newsbeat*, *Seven Days*, *Today Tonight* and *Prime Time*. He has also covered major news events at home and abroad, especially in the USA, and presented the results programmes for some ten Irish general elections. He now conducts interviews with leading politicians on a weekly television programme *Farrell* and analyses developments in the media on a weekly radio programme *Soundbite*. On retirement from UCD in 1994 he became director-general of the Institute for European Affairs.

FARRELL, Michael (1899–1962), physician and marathon novelist, b. Carlow, ed. locally and UCD, where he studied medicine. He was jailed for a small part played in the Troubles, travelled widely and was appointed marine superintendent in the Belgian Congo. He returned to Ireland in 1930 to study at TCD. In 1932 he gave up medicine, went to live in Co. Wicklow and embarked upon a predominantly autobiographical novel which, because of its non-appearance, became the stuff of literary pub legend. During World War II he wrote as 'Gulliver' for the *Bell* and worked for Radio Éireann as compère, scriptwriter and producer. He retired from journalism and continued his novel, which by the 1950s had assumed Tolstoyesque proportions. Farrell died before he could revise the MS, and his friend MONK GIBBON undertook the task of editing. It was published as *Thy Tears Might Cease* in 1963 and became a best-seller on both sides of the Atlantic.

FARRELL, Michael (1940–), painter, lithographer and engraver, b. Kells, Co. Meath, ed. St Martin's School of Art, London 1957–61. Awarded scholarships to Italy in 1964 and 1966. Has won numerous international arts awards and is a member of Aosdána. He is closely connected with pop art, and his nude self-portraits have also been highly commended.

FAUL, Denis (1932–), Roman Catholic priest, b. Louth. Leading campaigner against ill-treatment of people detained by the security forces in Northern Ireland. He first attracted public attention in 1969 when he criticised NI's judicial system and the actions of the police and army. He was chaplain to the Maze Prison during the H-block hunger strikes, which he strongly opposed, nevertheless urging the government to make concessions to prisoners. Although an outspoken critic of IRA violence, he has in recent years called for the early release of young and long-term prisoners as a means of diffusing tension in NI. Fr Faul is president of St Patrick's Academy, Dungannon.

FAULKNER, Arthur *Brian* **Deane** (1921–1977), politician, b. Helen's Bay, Co. Down, 18 Feb. 1921, ed. St Columba's, d. Mar. 1977 following a hunting accident in Co. Down. He was first elected MP for East Down in the Northern Ireland parliament in 1949. As Minister of Commerce from 1963, he proved especially competent in attracting foreign industry to NI. He resigned from TERENCE O'NEILL's cabinet in Jan. 1969 in protest at the conciliatory response to the demands of the Northern Ireland Civil Rights Association. The following May he rejoined the government under O'Neill's successor, JAMES CHICHESTER-CLARK, as Minister of Development. He succeeded Chichester-Clark as Prime Minister in Mar. 1971. In response to the continually deteriorating security situation, he introduced internment in Aug. 1971, a decision which exacerbated the crisis when it was directed almost entirely against the nationalist community. However, he was unable to maintain the support of the right wing of his party after the imposition of direct rule from Westminster in 1972. In Dec. 1973 he signed the Sunningdale Agreement, which provided for power-sharing within NI and a Council of Ireland, and he was chief of the Executive which it established. The furious opposition of many unionists culminated in the loyalist strike of May 1974, which brought down not only the Executive but Brian Faulkner himself. The Unionist Party of Northern Ireland, which he founded when the main party broke from him, won little support at the election of 1975 for the

Constitutional Convention. Faulkner quitted politics the following year and in 1977 became a life peer (as Lord Faulkner of Downpatrick).

FAY, William George (Willie) (1872–1947), actor, b. Dublin, 12 Nov. 1872, ed. Belvedere, d. London, 27 Oct. 1947. Willie and his brother Frank Fay joined W.B. YEATS and Lady GREGORY in founding the Abbey Theatre, where Willie worked as stage manager. Poor relations between him and Annie Horniman, the company's early benefactor, led to a disagreement with the Abbey's directors and in 1908 the two brothers left for the USA, where they produced a repertory of Irish plays. Willie Fay moved to London in 1914 and enjoyed a successful stage career, also appearing in several films.

FELL, Sir David (1943–), public servant, b. 20 Jan. 1943, ed. Royal Academical Institution and QUB. Joined the Northern Ireland civil service in 1969 and served in the Ministry of Agriculture until 1972. Held a number of posts in the areas of economic and industrial development, including deputy chief executive to the NI Industrial Development Board 1982 and permanent secretary at the Department of Economic Development 1984–91. In 1991 he became the youngest ever head of the NICS. He received a knighthood in 1995. At a conference organised by Northern and Southern trade unions in Feb. 1996 he referred to the ending of the IRA ceasefire and said, 'We are not in a hopeless state,' adding: 'Political partnerships and social inclusion are linked. Social partnership cannot but prepare the way for the partnership that will be required in a final political accommodation.'

FENNELL, Desmond (1929–), academic, journalist and author, b. Belfast, ed. Belvedere, UCD and Bonn. Aer Lingus sales manager in Germany before returning to Ireland in the 1960s to work as a freelance journalist. Wrote a weekly column for the *Sunday Press* and contributed widely to other national newspapers on political, religious and social issues as well as broadcasting on current affairs. Editor 1964–8 of *Herder Correspondence*, the autonomous English-language edition of a prestigious German Roman Catholic journal. Lectured in political science at UCG 1976–82. Lived in Connemara during the 1970s, from where he provided incisive comment on the changing character of Irish society. From 1983 lecturer in communications, College of Commerce, Rathmines, Dublin. Publications include *Mainly in Wonder, Sketches of the New Ireland* and *Beyond Nationalism*.

FERGUSON, Henry George (Harry) (1884–1960), engineer and inventor, b. Growell, near Hillsborough, Co. Down, 4 Nov. 1884, d. Stow-on-the-Wold, Gloucestershire, 25 Oct. 1960. At 16 he left the strict life of the family farm to become a mechanic in Belfast. He soon developed an effective sports motorcycle which he raced himself, earning the sobriquet 'The Mad Mechanic'. By 1909 he had built the first Irish aeroplane and flown it a creditable 130 yards on its maiden flight. During World War II he was asked by the government to devise machinery which would help in the 'Grow More Food' campaign. His response was to improve the speed and efficiency of ploughing by mounting the plough on a tractor, the first step in the sequence that led in 1939 to his perfection of the famous Fordson tractor, which more than any other device revolutionised modern farming. Until meeting Ferguson, Henry Ford had refused to take on partners but on the first demonstration of the prototype they made a 'handshake agreement' in 1939 to produce the world-famous and immensely profitable machine. In 1947, when Ford's grandson refused to honour the agreement, Ferguson opened his own very successful factory in Detroit and filed a suit against the company which resulted in an award of $9.25 million in 1952. After this, Ferguson's inventive genius was turned to the car and in particular to ideas of automatic transmission. He remained a man of great independence of mind and action, refusing a knighthood for service to the Allies during the war, and always claiming that the battle with Ford was not for financial gain but for the rights of the small inventor against the big corporation.

FERGUSON, Howard (1908–), composer, pianist, teacher and musicologist, b. Belfast, ed. Westminster School and RCM, London. Studied under R.O. Morris (composition), Harold Samuel (piano) and Sir Malcolm Sargent (conducting). With Myra Hess he established a series of wartime concerts which took place daily at the National Gallery, London. In 1948 he was appointed

Professor of Composition to London's Royal Academy of Music, where he lectured until 1963, his pupils including Richard Rodney Bennett and Cornelius Cardew. As a pianist he formed partnerships with Yfrah Neaman (violin) and Denis Matthews (piano) and subsequently performed worldwide. Emerged as a composer in the early 1930s. His output includes works for orchestra and chamber ensemble, a piano concerto and violin sonatas. After completing two large-scale choral works, *Amore Langueo* (1956) and *The Dream of the Rood* (1959) for the Three Choirs Festival, Gloucester, he stopped composing. Music editor, particularly for the Associated Board; author of *Keyboard Interpretation* (1975). Hon. D.Mus. (QUB) 1959.

FERGUSON, Richard (1935–), lawyer, b. 22 Aug. 1935, ed. Methodist College, Belfast, TCD and QUB. Leading defence counsel. Called to the NI Bar in 1956 and the Bar of England and Wales in 1972. Elected Ulster Unionist MP for South Antrim at a by-election in 1968 but resigned in 1970. Queen's Counsel 1973, in England and Wales 1986, and Senior Counsel in the Irish Republic 1983. Chairman of the NI Mental Health Review Tribunal 1973–84 and chairman of the Criminal Bar Association of England and Wales 1993–5. In the course of his career he has defended former Guinness boss Ernest Saunders, boxer Terry Marsh, the 'Birmingham Six' and Rosemary West.

FIACC, Padraic (1924–), poet, b. Patrick Joseph O'Connor, Belfast, ed. locally, emigrated with family, then attended Commerce and Haaren High Schools and St Joseph's Seminary, Yonkers, New York. In 1946 he returned to Belfast, where he has lived since. Fiacc is perhaps the only major poet of Northern Ireland whose work is a true microcosm of the horrors that have been visited upon that community. This is a man who has lost more than one dear friend to the bloodletting; to look for levity is to insult both the poet and the city that he still loves fiercely, though it has caused unutterable pain – and will, in all likelihood, continue to do so. Collections: *By the Black Stream* (1969), *Odour of Blood* (1973), *Nights in the Bad Place* (1977) and *Ruined Pages: Selected Poems of Padraic Fiacc* (1994). He also edited *The Wearing of the Black* (1974).

FIGGIS, Darrell (1882–1925), revolutionary and politician, b. Rathmines, Dublin, took his own life in London, 27 Oct. 1925. Worked in tea business in London and Calcutta prior to becoming a freelance journalist. Went to Germany in May 1914 with ROBERT ERSKINE CHILDERS to buy the arms subsequently landed at Howth and Kilcoole. Imprisoned in England after Easter Rising. Honorary secretary Sinn Féin 1917–19. Editor the *Republic* 1919. Acting chairman of the committee which drafted the constitution of the Irish Free State. TD (Pro-Treaty County Dublin) 1922–5. Figgis wrote novels and literary criticism under the pseudonym Michael Ireland.

FINLAY, Thomas (1922–), lawyer, politician and judge, ed. Clongowes, UCD and King's Inns. Called to Bar 1944, Inner Bar 1961. TD (FG Dublin Central) 1954–7. High Court judge 1971, President of the High Court 1974, Chief Justice 1985–94. As Chief Justice he delivered a number of major Supreme Court interpretations of the constitution, including the decision in 1990 that the reintegration of the national territory was 'a constitutional imperative' and that the declaration of the extent of the national territory (to include the whole island of Ireland) was 'a claim of legal right'. He also delivered the judgments in 1992 and 1993 confirming as constitutional the confidentiality of government meetings and the parliamentary privilege enjoyed by TDs in respect of statements made by them in the Dáil.

FINUCANE, Aengus (1932–), chief executive of Concern Worldwide, b. Limerick, 26 Apr. 1932, ed. Sexton Street CBS, Limerick, Holy Ghost novitiate, Kilshane, Co. Tipperary, 1949–50, UCD 1950–53, Swansea University (Dip.Soc.Admin.), Kimmage Seminary, Dublin 1955–9. After his ordination, in 1958, Fr Finucane spent several years working in eastern Nigeria as a teacher, missionary and social worker. In 1968, after the outbreak of the Nigerian civil war, he helped to set up Concern, along with several other Irish people, in order to alleviate the desperate situation faced by the people of Biafra. Although there was close co-operation between Concern and missionary groups from the outset, it remained a non-denominational organisation and adopted a comprehensive approach to its development programme in the many countries in which it became established in the following years. Fr Finucane helped to co-ordinate this work in Gabon, Bangladesh and the refugee camps of South-East Asia before being appointed Concern's chief executive in Dublin in 1981.

FINUCANE, Marian (1950–), broadcaster, ed. Scoil Chaitríona and College of Technology, Bolton Street, Dublin. Practised as an architect before joining RTÉ in 1974. After two years as an announcer she became a programme presenter, working mainly on programmes concerned with contemporary social issues, especially those concerning women. She won the Prix Italia for a documentary on abortion and also won a Jacob's award. *The Marian Finucane Show* on radio, a combined interview and phone-in chat show on weekday afternoons, attracted a large listenership from the outset and won for its presenter the Radio Journalist of the Year award in 1988. Her television work in later years has included major information programming on RTÉ such as *Consumer Choice* and the police investigation programme *Crimeline*.

FITT, Gerry (1926–), republican socialist, b. Belfast, 9 Apr. 1926, ed. CBS, Belfast, m. Susan Doherty 1947 (d. 1996). Archetypically Belfast Catholic working-class in origin, he served in the merchant navy 1941–53 and was first elected to Belfast City Council in 1958 as a member of the Belfast-based Irish Labour Party. He won a Stormont seat from the Unionist Party in 1962, and a Westminster seat for West Belfast (also from the Unionists) in 1966, by then as standard-bearer of the largely Belfast-based Republican Labour Party. He succeeded in interesting a number of British MPs in Northern Ireland and its problems; sympathetic UK parliamentarians were present at the civil rights march in Derry in Oct. 1968, where he was wounded in the course of a police baton charge. In Aug. 1970 he became the first leader of the loose coalition of civil rights and former nationalist leaders who created the Social Democratic and Labour Party.

He became deputy chief executive (under BRIAN FAULKNER) of the short-lived power-sharing Executive in 1974. His hostility to paramilitary forces led to unpopularity among republican sympathisers, some of whom attacked his home in Aug. 1976. His growing disillusion with British handling of the Northern issue led him to abstain in a crucial Commons vote in 1979 which brought down the then Labour government. Later that year he resigned from the leadership of the SDLP (to be succeeded by JOHN HUME) because of disagreement with the party's view that an 'Irish dimension' had to be a component of political progress. In 1981 he opposed the Maze hunger strikes, ensuring that his seat would be targeted by Sinn Féin. He lost the seat to GERRY ADAMS in June 1983 and was made a life peer (Baron Fitt of Bell's Hill) the following month.

FITZGERALD, Alexis (1916–1985), lawyer, economist and senator, b. Waterford, 4 Sept. 1916, ed. Clongowes and UCD, d. Dublin, 18 June 1985. Qualified as a solicitor in 1941, became a lecturer in economics in UCD the same year. An authority on commercial law, he was a founding partner in 1947 of McCann, White and FitzGerald, which became one of the biggest law practices in the state. He had a major influence on the thinking of his father-in-law, JOHN A. COSTELLO, whom he won over to Keynesian principles in the formulation of economic policy. He was a Fine Gael senator 1969–81 and made significant contributions to the discussion of financial and legal legislation. His philosophical approach to political questions owed much to his interest in contemporary theology with its emphasis on the Christian duty of service to others. On social questions he stood well to the left of many in FG, sharing as he did the 'just society' vision of DECLAN COSTELLO, but in reaction to the Northern Ireland crisis he favoured strong security measures because, as he put it, 'the security of the state is the protection of our weakest citizens'. He was appointed special adviser to the government by Taoiseach GARRET FITZGERALD (no relation) in the FG–Labour coalition of 1981–2.

FITZGERALD, Barry (1888–1961), actor, b. William Joseph Shields, Dublin, 10 Mar. 1888, ed. Merchant Taylor's School and Skerry's College, Dublin, d. Dublin, 4 Jan. 1961. Adopted the stage name Barry Fitzgerald because he worked in the civil service 1911–29 while playing in the Abbey Theatre at night. In 1929 the offer of the leading role in SEAN

O'CASEY's new play *The Silver Tassie*, which was to be produced in London, tempted Fitzgerald to resign from the civil service and become a full-time actor at the age of 40. During the early 1930s he toured the USA with the Abbey and he appeared in John Ford's film version of *The Plough and the Stars* in 1936. Thereafter he divided his time between Hollywood and Broadway, appearing in films such as *The Long Voyage Home* (1940), *How Green Was My Valley* (1941) and *None but the Lonely Heart* (1944), and in successful Broadway productions of *Juno and the Paycock* (for one of which he won a New York critics' award) and P.V. CARROLL's *The White Steed*. Most memorably, Fitzgerald, although a Protestant, played the part of Fr Fitzgibbon in the film *Going My Way* (1944), for which he won an Oscar as best supporting actor.

FITZGERALD, Ciaran Fintan (1952–), international rugby player, b. Galway, 4 June 1952. A hurler and boxer of note while at school, he shares (with KARL MULLEN, co-incidentally also a hooker) the distinction of captaining Ireland to two Triple Crown wins as well as captaining the Lions. He was first capped on Ireland's triumphant tour of Australia in 1979 and went on to make 25 appearances for his country, as well as playing in all four Tests for the Lions against New Zealand in 1983, when the tourists were whitewashed. He succeeded FERGUS SLATTERY as captain in 1982, when Ireland won the Triple Crown for the first time since 1949, and led the team to Five Nations Championship victory in 1983 and to a second Triple Crown and Championship in 1985. He captained Ireland 19 times and was national coach 1990–92.

FITZGERALD, Desmond (1888–1947), revolutionary, politician and philosopher, b. London to Irish parents, m. Mabel McConnell (Maedhbh Ní Chonaill), a Belfast Presbyterian nationalist, d. Dublin, 9 Apr. 1947. He grew up in London, learning Irish at Gaelic League classes. He and his wife lived in Brittany for two years in the company of writers and poets, with whom he had a strong affinity: Ezra Pound was to become a special friend. Settled in Co. Kerry 1913, where he joined the IRB and organised the Irish Volunteers. Imprisoned 1915 for sedition. He served in the GPO during the Easter Rising, together with his wife,

and was interned in England. Elected to parliament (SF Dublin Pembroke) 1918, director of publicity for the Dáil during the War of Independence. Supported the Anglo-Irish Treaty of 1921. Minister for External Affairs 1922–7, secured Irish membership of the League of Nations, registered the Treaty as an international agreement despite British objections, opened Irish legation in Washington – the first diplomatic mission of a Commonwealth country. Minister for Defence 1927–32. TD (C. na nG., later FG; Dublin County, later Carlow–Kilkenny) 1922–37, senator 1938–43. Co-founder Irish Academy of Letters 1923; maintained friendship with W.B. YEATS, JAMES JOYCE, Pound; wrote on the philosophy of politics (*Preface to Statecraft*, 1939) and lectured on Thomism in the USA. Father of DESMOND and GARRET FITZGERALD.

FITZGERALD, Desmond (1910–1987), architect, s. of DESMOND FITZGERALD, ed. on the Continent and at UCD. Graduated 1935. The following year, through the OPW, he was given responsibility for the most significant project of his career, and the most important Irish building of the decade, the new terminal building at Dublin Airport. He was awarded the RIAI triennial gold medal 1941–3 for its design, though its development appears to have been essentially a group project carried out within the OPW. More representative of FitzGerald's own style is the Moyne Institute, TCD of 1953. Appointed professor in UCD's School of Architecture in 1951, succeeding J.V. Downes, and in 1970 accepted the newly created chair of architecture and planning there. He remained in practice until soon before his death.

FITZGERALD, Garret (1926–), economist and politician, b. Dublin, 9 Feb. 1926, s. of DESMOND FITZGERALD (1888–1947), ed. Belvedere and UCD, m. Joan O'Farrell 1967, two s. one d. Worked in Aer Lingus 1947–58, becoming an authority on the economics of transport. Lecturer in economics UCD 1959–73; also a commentator on economic affairs in English as well as Irish media, and managing director of a consultancy for Irish enterprises which he set up jointly with the Economist Intelligence Unit of London. In 1969 he obtained his Ph.D. for a thesis later published under the title *Planning in Ireland*.

His entry to politics in 1964 was stimulated not only by his father's example but by his mother, Mabel, who, although an ardent nationalist herself, came of Ulster unionist stock. He would later describe his political objective as the creation of a pluralist Ireland where the Northern Protestants of his mother's family tradition and the Southern Catholics of his father's could feel equally at home. The radical socio-economic ideas of the Fine Gael TD DECLAN COSTELLO also inspired him and he served as an FG senator from 1965 until his own election as a TD (FG Dublin South-East) in 1969. Within FG he soon came to be seen as a progressive counterweight to the more conservative party leader, LIAM COSGRAVE.

When the coalition of FG and Labour took office in Mar. 1973 Cosgrave, as Taoiseach, appointed FitzGerald Minister for Foreign Affairs. Ireland had just become a member of the EEC, a milieu already familiar to the new foreign minister, who now became ex officio a member of the Community's Council of Ministers. His innovative views, energy and fluency in French won him – and through him, Ireland – a status in European affairs far exceeding the country's size and ensured that the first Irish presidency of the EEC (Jan.–June 1975) was a noted success. When the government fell in 1977 FitzGerald succeeded as leader of FG and at once undertook a major modernisation of the party. Following the election of June 1981 FG and Labour were again able to form a government, now under FitzGerald.

He first transpired to be what he himself described as a 'revolving door Taoiseach', losing office early the following year over a controversial budget proposal. The succeeding Fianna Fáil government, however, lasted only until Nov. 1982. By Christmas the FitzGerald administration was reinstalled with a comfortable majority which kept it in being for virtually a full term, although pursuit of 'fiscal rectitude' in order to reduce a high national debt required a firmer control of public spending than Labour found easy to accept. The harmonious relationship the Taoiseach developed with Tánaiste DICK SPRING sustained the coalition for more than four years, despite tensions between other ministers, and enabled a rational policy to be evolved whereby this and subse-

quent governments were able substantially to mitigate the country's financial problems.

The pluralist state of FitzGerald's vision proved more elusive. He was seen by influential senior churchmen as an opponent of Roman Catholic orthodoxy in spite of the fact that he was a committed Catholic and the only theologically literate head of government in the history of independent Ireland. He warned in 1983 against the wording of a proposed constitutional amendment to prohibit the legalisation of abortion, but his opinion was rejected by the Catholic bishops and fundamentalist pressure groups as well as by Fianna Fáil; the amendment was voted into the constitution by referendum – and within ten years resulted in a Supreme Court decision that in certain circumstances abortions could be legally performed. The government's attempt in 1986 to have the constitutional ban on divorce removed by referendum also failed, not only because of traditionalist opposition but because many felt that the government had not sufficiently clarified the consequences, especially regarding inheritance, of the envisaged legislation.

FitzGerald's most dramatic achievement as Taoiseach was in regard to Northern Ireland. The New Ireland Forum, which he set up in 1983, brought together representatives of the parties in the Republic and the nationalist SDLP from the North. Although the Unionist parties spurned his invitation to join, and the Forum's conclusions proposing various forms of association between NI and the Republic were rejected by British Prime Minister Margaret Thatcher, the Forum provided the impetus for the resumption of serious negotiations between the Irish and British governments, which culminated in the Anglo-Irish Agreement of Nov. 1985. The Anglo-Irish Conference thereby established made it possible for the Irish government to represent nationalist interests in ongoing contact with the British through a common secretariat and regular ministerial meetings. While vehemently repudiated by the Unionists, the Agreement became the basis for developing trust and common action between the governments, which in time would bring about the Downing Street Declaration of 1993 and the subsequent republican and loyalist ceasefires.

The FG–Labour coalition broke up amicably in Jan. 1987, when Labour was unable to accept the stringent budgetary measures insisted upon by the Taoiseach. After a general election, Fianna Fáil formed a government and FitzGerald resigned the leadership of FG. He took little part thereafter in active politics, from which he retired completely in 1992. His autobiography, *All in a Life*, appeared in 1991 and immediately became a best-seller. He resumed writing and lecturing widely at home and abroad on public affairs.

FITZGERALD, Garret A. (1950–), medical scientist, b. Dublin, ed. Belvedere and UCD. Graduated MB (1974), proceeding MD (1980), admitted MRCPI (1976), MRCP UK (1977), elected FRCPI (1982). After completing junior resident posts in Dublin, he held postdoctoral fellowships in London, Germany and the USA, and faculty positions of increasing responsibility to professorial level in departments of medicine and pharmacology at Vanderbilt University, Nashville, Tennessee. Returning to Ireland in 1991 as Professor of Medicine and Experimental Therapeutics at UCD, he established an active centre for cardiovascular research at the Mater Hospital. His principal research interest has been in the mechanisms and treatment of coronary vascular occlusion and the challenge of elucidating the role of lipid mediators in this process, integrating approaches involving both basic and clinical science. Garret FitzGerald is unrelated to his political namesake but has sometimes received his mail. In 1994 he accepted the post of Robinette Professor of Cardiovascular Medicine at the University of Pennsylvania.

FITZGERALD, Geraldine (1892–1967), librarian, ed. Alexandra and TCD, where she had a distinguished career, graduating with a gold medal in history, d. 26 Oct. 1967. Gave generations of history students the benefit of her tutoring, formally and informally. Awarded honorary MA on her retirement in 1962 for her contribution to learning as a librarian, initially at the RIA, then as first librarian of the Representative Church Body 1932–62. A keen though critical cinema and theatre goer, she was a member of the Film Censorship Appeals Board.

FITZGERALD, Mary (1956–), painter, graduated from NCAD 1977, Tama University

of Fine Art 1981. Has held solo exhibitions in Dublin 1982, 1984, 1986, and group exhibitions in Tokyo, Cork, Limerick, Kilkenny, Edinburgh, Brazil, Argentina. Her paintings are abstract and she blends the influences of Japanese traditions and Western, modernist practices.

FITZGERALD, Oliver (1910–1987), physician, b. Waterford, ed. Clongowes and UCD, m. Cleo Maiben. He was the eldest of a trio of brothers of luminous intelligence who shone in the medical school. Another brother was ALEXIS FITZGERALD. Oliver entered UCD in 1929, taking the B.Sc. (1933) and MB (1936) with first place and first class honours. A travelling scholarship in physiology enabled him to study in Basle and Cambridge. At St Vincent's Hospital, where he was visiting physician, his major interest was gastroenterology; he was among the comparatively few of his contemporaries who continued to conduct original research while carrying the responsibilities of a large consulting practice. His seminal paper, 'Studies on the Physiological Chemistry and Clinical Significance of Urease and Urea in Special Reference to the Stomach', was published in the *Irish Journal of Medical Science* in 1950.

A well-read man, he was for some years editor of the *Journal of the Irish Medical Association*. He held a chair of therapeutics at UCD, was the first chairman of the National Drugs Advisory Board, a council member of the Medical Defence Union and for a year president of the British Society of Gastroenterology.

FITZGERALD, William O'Brien (1906–1974), lawyer, b. Cork, ed. Belvedere and King's Inns, d. 17 Oct. 1974. Called to Bar 1927, Senior Counsel 1944. Over two decades from the mid-1940s he built up an enormous general practice, becoming one of the highest earners at the Bar and also one of the most skilful and beguiling of cross-examiners. A prominent Fine Gael supporter, his appointment straight from the Law Library to the Supreme Court in 1966 by fellow Corkman Taoiseach JACK LYNCH was a major surprise, as was his promotion to Chief Justice by the same administration in 1972. His judicial career proved unexciting; he dissented in some important judgments and usually took a conservative line on the constitution.

FITZGIBBON, Robert Louis Constantine (1919–), novelist and translator, b. Lenox, Massachusetts to a Northern Irish father and an American mother, ed. Munich University, Sorbonne and Oxford. Served with the British army and the US forces in World War II. He was a teacher in Bermuda before turning to writing and moving to Ireland, where he took citizenship. He has been a highly productive writer and translator from French and German. Fitzgibbon's non-fiction work is largely popular historical. He has also written biographies of EAMON DE VALERA and Dylan Thomas. His many novels include *High Heroic*, centring on MICHAEL COLLINS (1969), *Man in Aspic* (1977) and *When the Kissing had to Stop* (1978). Historical: *Out of the Lion's Paw: Ireland Wins her Freedom* and *Denazification* (1969), *The Blitz* (1970), *Red Hand: The Ulster Colony* and *London's Burning* (1971), *To Kill Hitler* (1972) and *Secret Intelligence in the Twentieth Century* (1976).

FITZMAURICE, Gabriel (1952–), poet, editor and teacher, b. Moyvane, Co. Kerry, ed. locally. He is the engine that drives Listowel Writers' Week, for which he is chairman and literary adviser. He won a Gerard Manley Hopkins Centenary poetry prize in 1989. Fitzmaurice is deeply committed to his native place and its poetic traditions, as his own verse – written in English and Irish – makes hauntingly clear. He is also an accomplished singer and musician, has performed on two albums and produced a third, *The Songs and Ballads of Kerry*, in addition to broadcasting frequently on RTÉ radio and television. His most recent collections are *The Space Between* (1993), *Nach Iontach mar atá Rainn do Pháistí* (1994) and *Ag Síobshiúl chun an Rince* (1995). He has edited *An Bealach 'na Bhaile, Rogha Dánta, Homecoming* by CATHAL Ó SEARCAIGH, *Irish Poetry Now: Other Voices* and *Kerry through its Writers* (1993) and *The Listowel Literary Phenomenon: North Kerry Writers, A Critical Introduction* (1994).

FITZMAURICE, James C. (1898–1965), aviator, b. Dublin, 6 Jan. 1898, ed. CBS, Maryborough (Portlaoise) and Rockwell. On the outbreak of World War I he joined the 7th Lancers, saw service on the Western Front, was wounded and decorated. He joined the Royal Flying Corps in 1917 but came back to Ireland following the Anglo-Irish Treaty and was one of the first officers commissioned in the new Army Air Corps. Commandant of the Corps 1927. He dreamed of making the first east-to-west transatlantic flight, and after an abortive attempt in 1927 he succeeded the following year. Leaving Baldonnel Aerodrome, Co. Dublin at dawn on 12 Apr. 1928 he piloted a German Junker (D. 1167), accompanied by his co-pilot, Capt. Koehl, and the sponsor of the enterprise, Baron von Huenefeld. It took them 36.5 hours to cover the 2,320 miles to Greenly Island off the coast of Newfoundland. Retired from the Air Corps 1929 and lived abroad until 1951. He died in Dublin in Sept. 1965.

FLACKES, William D. (Billy) (1921–1993), journalist and broadcaster, b. Co. Donegal, d. suddenly 1 Aug. 1993. Freelance reporter 1939–42, worked for a number of provincial newspapers in Northern Ireland 1942–5 and as Stormont parliamentary reporter for the *Belfast Newsletter* 1945–7. Press Association parliamentary reporter at Westminster 1947–57. Successively chief leader writer and news editor *Belfast Telegraph* 1957–64. Northern Ireland political correspondent BBC 1964–82. He frequently broadcast from Dublin and became one of the best-known television commentators in Britain and Ireland during the earlier years of the prolonged Northern Troubles. Awarded OBE 1981. Pursuant to the policy of most Irish governments from the early 1970s to have a Northern voice on the controlling body of the broadcasting service in the Republic, he was appointed a member of the RTÉ Authority 1985–90. Author of *Northern Ireland: A Political Directory* (1980, 1983), and with Sydney Elliott of the third edition of the same work (1989, 1994).

FLANAGAN, John J. (1873–1938), hammer-thrower and shot-putter, b. Kilbreedy, Co. Limerick, 9 Jan. 1873, d. Kilbreedy. He emigrated to New York in 1896 and went on to become the first athlete to win gold medals for the hammer at three successive Olympic Games – Paris 1900, St Louis 1904 and London 1908. He headed the world rankings in the hammer in all except three years between 1895 and 1910, won the British AAA title 1896, 1900, and seven successive AAU hammer titles. He won a silver medal for the shot in the 1904

Olympics, when he also came fourth in the discus, as well as five AAU titles.

FLANAGAN, Oliver J. (1920–1987), politician, b. 22 May 1920, ed. Mountmellick NS, Co. Laois, d. 26 Apr. 1987. First elected to Laois County Council in 1942, he successfully contested the 1943 general election standing on an independent Monetary Reform ticket: this involved a substantial anti-Jewish bias. He was re-elected as an Independent in 1948, joined Fine Gael in 1950 and contested all subsequent general elections for the party until his retirement at the 1987 contest. He topped the poll in Laois–Offaly in each general election from 1948 except those of 1977 and Feb. 1982. He was parliamentary secretary to the Minister for Agriculture 1954–7 and to the Minister for Local Government 1975–6. Appointed Minister for Defence in 1976 – succeeding PATRICK DONEGAN, who had been moved to the Department of Lands following his public attack on President CEARBHALL Ó DÁLAIGH – and held that post until the formation of the Fianna Fáil government in 1977. A member of the Knights of Columbanus, he was awarded the Knighthood of St Gregory the Great by Pope John Paul I in 1978. He was a resolute opponent of changes in the contraceptive law and of the attempts to allow civil divorce, and in the 1983 referendum a strong supporter of the 'pro-life' amendment. His son Charles has been FG TD in Laois–Offaly since 1987.

FLANAGAN, T.P. (1929–), artist, b. Enniskillen, raised in Sligo and Fermanagh, ed. Belfast College of Art 1949–53. He taught art in a number of secondary schools and at St Mary's College of Education, Belfast, where he became head of the art department in 1965. Flanagan has received many important awards, including the painting prize at the 1974 Oireachtas and the Royal Ulster Academy gold medal in 1977. His work has appeared in several significant group exhibitions of Irish artists, including Irish Art 1943–1973 (Rosc '80, Cork). He has had two retrospective exhibitions, organised by the Arts Council of Northern Ireland in 1977 and by the Ulster Museum in 1995. Appears in a number of major Irish art collections, including those of the Hugh Lane Municipal Gallery and the Irish Museum of Modern Art, Dublin, and

the Ulster Museum, Belfast. His skill as a draughtsman, and his ability to combine an expressionist style with a highly controlled, almost delicate approach to his work, have made him one of the most admired of contemporary Irish landscape painters.

FLANNERY, Austin (1925–), Dominican friar, editor and human rights activist, b. Co. Tipperary, 10 Jan. 1925; ed. St Flannan's College, Ennis; Dominican College, Newbridge, Co. Kildare; St Mary's, Tallaght, Co. Dublin; Blackfriars; Oxford; the Angelicum University, Rome. Baptismal name Liam, received name Austin on entering Dominican order 1943. Ordained priest 1950. Taught theology for two years at Glenstal. Editor 1957–88 of the Dominican journal *Doctrine and Life*, which he developed into a major source of information on the Second Vatican Council. Through the journal and informal discussion groups, he particularly influenced religious affairs journalists and Irish Catholic intellectuals. He has also been an enthusiastic promoter of new standards in church art and architecture as an expression of the liturgical reforms initiated by the Council. In 1975 his *Vatican Council II: The Conciliar and Post-Conciliar Documents* issued simultaneously from six publishing houses in Ireland, the UK and the USA and soon became the standard edition used when Council texts were cited in English. Among the causes to which he has given much time and energy in the field of social justice is the Irish Anti-Apartheid Movement, of which he was successively chairman and president.

FLEISCHMANN, Aloys (1910–1992), composer, teacher, administrator and author, b. Munich, d. Cork. Appointed Professor of Music UCC in 1934, a post he held until his retirement in 1980. Other positions included conductor of Cork Symphony Orchestra, which he founded, chairman Cork Orchestral Society and Cork Ballet Company, director Cork International Choral and Folk Dance Festival and vice-chairman Irish National Ballet. Founder of Cumann Náisiúnta na gCór. Member of Aosdána. Works include a symphony, song cycles, four ballets, including one based on the Táin, works for choir and orchestra, chamber and instrumental music. Author of *Music in Ireland* and *Sources of Traditional Irish*

Music, which he completed just prior to his death. Awarded doctorates in music from the NUI and TCD and Order of Merit of the German Federal Republic.

FLYNN, Padraig (1939–), politician and EU commissioner, b. Castlebar, 9 May 1939, ed. St Gerard's, Castlebar and St Patrick's College, Dublin. Teacher. Member of Mayo County Council 1967–86. First elected to Dáil Éireann in 1977 (FF Mayo West). He was Minister of State, Department of Transport and Power, 1980–81; Minister for the Gaeltacht Mar.–Oct. 1982; for Trade, Commerce and Tourism Oct.–Dec. 1982; for the Environment 1987–late 1991, when he resigned his post having decided to support a motion of no confidence in party leader and Taoiseach CHARLES HAUGHEY. Following Haughey's resignation the following year and the succession of ALBERT REYNOLDS, he became Minister for Justice, which post he held until Dec. 1992. He was appointed EU commissioner in 1993 and reappointed to that post in 1995 by the new Fine Gael–Labour–Democratic Left coalition. On each occasion he was given the Social Affairs portfolio.

FOGARTY, Francis (1899–1973), air chief marshal, b. Cork, 16 Jan. 1899, ed. Farranferris College, Cork, d. 12 Jan. 1973. He joined the RAF in 1918 and served in several squadrons before being appointed commander of 37th Bomber Squadron in 1939. As senior air staff officer of No. 4 Group Bomber Command, he played a central role in planning the Allies' aerial bombardment of Germany 1944–5. In 1945 he became air officer in command of Mediterranean Allied Air Forces. He also served as air aide-de-camp to Queen Elizabeth II before retiring in 1957.

FOLEY, Desmond (Des) (1940–1995), hurler, Gaelic footballer and politician, b. Dublin, younger brother of LAR FOLEY. He won four Dublin County Senior Hurling Championships with the St Vincent's club, having earlier captained the St Joseph's school team which in 1959 brought the All-Ireland Colleges football title to the capital city for the first time. He also captained the Dublin side which won the All-Ireland minor football final in 1958, and in 1962 became the only player to play in two Railway Cup finals, in hurling and football, on the same day, winning medals in both codes; he won Railway Cup hurling medals again in 1964 and 1965. He played on the Dublin hurling team 1958–69, and in 1963 captained the county football side which defeated Galway to win the All-Ireland title. TD (FF Dublin North County) 1965–70. Resigned his seat 4 Nov. 1970 in protest against the Northern policy of the Taoiseach, JACK LYNCH. KEVIN BOLAND resigned his seat on the same day.

FOLEY, Donal (1922–1981), journalist, b. Ring, Co. Waterford, 4 Sept. 1922, son of a schoolteacher and socialist, ed. St Patrick's College, Waterford, d. Dublin, 7 July 1981. He was brought up as a native Irish speaker at Ferrybank and maintained a lifelong love of the Irish language and the GAA. Emigrated to London in 1944 and got a job as a clerk on the LMS railway. He joined the Irish News Agency in London in a clerical grade but was soon covering news events. When the agency was closed down he was taken on by Terry Ward, London editor of the *Irish Press*, as a reporter and writer. He joined the London office of *The Irish Times* in 1955 and came to Dublin as news editor in 1963. Appointed deputy editor in 1977. The *Irish Times* style of journalism and coverage of events was changed significantly at least three times during this century: by ROBERT SMYLLIE in the 1930s and 1940s, by ALAN MONTGOMERY in the 1950s and by Foley and DOUGLAS GAGEBY in the 1960s and 1970s. Foley sought out a new type of reporter, more original and discursive, better educated, and – especially – women journalists, to whom he gave opportunities hitherto denied to them. He saw *The Irish Times* as a forum for discussion, a mouthpiece for minorities as well as the majority, and a newspaper with a clear-cut, radical viewpoint.

His own writing could be serious and concerned, but he was perhaps best known for his 'Man Bites Dog' satirical column, much of which was later published in book form. His autobiography, *Three Villages*, was published in 1977.

FOLEY, Liam (Lar) (1939–), hurler and Gaelic footballer, brother of DES FOLEY, b. Dublin, he played for the St Vincent's club and captained Dublin to All-Ireland minor football success in 1956, having also been in the winning team the year before. He made his senior county début in 1957, and the following year was at 19 the youngest member of the team which won the All-Ireland football final; he also shared in Dublin's success of 1963. A member of the Dublin side defeated by Tipperary in the All-Ireland hurling final of 1961, he won Railway Cup hurling medals in 1962 and 1964, and later trained the St Vincent's and Dublin senior hurlers.

FOSTER, John Wilson (1944–), academic, b. Belfast, ed. QUB and University of Oregon. He went to study aesthetics in Eugene, Oregon in the 1960s, married a Canadian and developed a love of North America that endures to this day. He returned for a spell to Belfast and in 1972 moved to Dublin on a Fulbright scholarship. In 1974 he joined the faculty of the University of British Columbia, Vancouver, where he is currently Professor of English. His critical work and robust polemics have assured his status as literary commentator par excellence on both sides of the Atlantic. His publications, aside from numerous papers and articles, include *Forces and Themes in Ulster Fiction* (1974), *Fictions of the Irish Literary Revival: A Changeling Art* (1987) and *Colonial Consequences: Essays in Irish Literature and Culture* (1991). He has also edited *The Poet's Place: Ulster Literature and Society* (with GERALD DAWE) (1991) and *The Idea of the Union: Statements and Critiques in Support of the Union of Great Britain and Ireland* (1995).

FOSTER, Robert Fitzroy (Roy) (1949–), historian and biographer, b. Waterford, ed. locally, USA and TCD, where he was a foundation scholar in history. He has held two visiting fellowships at St Anthony's College, Oxford and has read modern history at Birkbeck College, University of London. His work includes: *Charles Stewart Parnell: The Man and his Family* (1976), *Lord Randolph Churchill: A Political Life* and *Political Novels and Nineteenth-century History* (1981), *Modern Ireland 1600–1972* (1988) and *Paddy and Mr Punch: Connections in Irish and English History* (1993). Ed. *The Oxford Illustrated History of Ireland* (1989), *The Oxford History of Ireland* (1992) and *The Sub-Prefect Should Have Held His Tongue* by HUBERT BUTLER (1992). He also wrote 'Varieties of Irishness' in *Cultural Traditions in Northern Ireland*, ed. Jacques Darras

(1991). Foster has numerous articles, essays and book reviews to his credit, and is currently working on the authorised biography of W.B. YEATS. He is Carroll Professor of Irish History at Oxford.

FRASER, Sir Ian James (1901–), DSO, OBE, surgeon and soldier, b. Belfast, ed. Royal Academical Institution and QUB, taking medical degrees in 1923 and becoming in due course FRCSI (1926), FRCS England (1927), M.Ch. (1927), MD (1932). His first senior appointment was to the staff of Belfast's Hospital for Sick Children. During World War II he served in west Africa and with the Eighth Army in north Africa. He was with the Allied advance through Sicily and Italy and was present at the Battle of Salerno; joined later in the landings in France, going in on the beaches at Arromanches. Finally he was posted to Agra as consultant surgeon north India. He had the opportunity of directing the MRC/RAMC team which pioneered the use of penicillin in the forward area.

Fraser was appointed to the honorary staff of the Royal Victoria Hospital, Belfast and also resumed paediatric surgery. He has lectured throughout the world, and his numerous publications include an autobiography, *Blood, Sweat and Cheers* (1989), written at the invitation of the editor of the *British Medical Journal*.

FRENCH, William Percy (1854–1920), songwriter and painter, b. Cloonyquin, Co. Roscommon, ed. England, Foyle College, Derry and TCD, d. Formby, Lancashire. As a civil engineer he was appointed Board of Works surveyor of drains for Co. Cavan. Took up journalism briefly in 1887 but went on to devote himself solely to entertainment, writing libretti for musical comedies and his own inimitable light-hearted songs: 'Come Home, Paddy Reilly', 'The Mountains of Mourne', 'Are Ye Right There, Michael?' (which involved him in a libel action) and many more. He toured England, North America and the West Indies with his repertoire of songs and sketches. The songs were to remain popular throughout the 20th century and enjoyed a notable revival in the 1950s, when a musical on his life, *The Golden Years*, drew appreciative audiences, and the greater part of the canon was recorded by the tenor Brendan O'Dowda. French's watercolour landscapes were remarkably fine and suggested that he could have made painting a career had he wished.

FRICKER, Brenda (1944–), actress, b. Dublin, 17 Feb. 1944, ed. Loreto College, St Stephen's Green, Dublin and UCD. With stage and television experience in Ireland, she moved to London, where she got her first film role in Henry Hathaway's remake of *Of Human Bondage* (1964). In the 1970s and 1980s she built up a substantial body of TV work, including playing Bridie, a faded Irish countrywoman, in PAT O'CONNOR's *The Ballroom of Romance* (1981). Generally cast on screen as a mother figure, in 1989 she played Mrs Brown in JIM SHERIDAN's *My Left Foot*, for which she received an Oscar as best supporting actress. However, subsequent big-screen roles have been poorly chosen and it could be said that Fricker has utilised her talents better on television.

FRIEL, Brian (1929–), playwright and short story writer, b. Killyclogher, near Omagh, the son of a schoolteacher from Derry and a postmistress from Donegal, ed. St Columb's College, Derry, Maynooth and St Joseph's Teacher Training College, Belfast. Long before the Troubles erupted in Northern Ireland, Brian Friel was exploring what it meant to inherit a divided cultural and political experience on this island, first in short stories (two collections were published early in his career), more enduringly in the 20 original plays which have won him a position as one of the world's leading contemporary dramatists.

After a crucial sojourn studying production at the new Tyrone Guthrie Theater in Minneapolis, Friel returned to Ireland in 1964 to write his breakthrough play, *Philadelphia, Here I Come!*, which brought a sophisticated dramatic technique to bear on the dilemma of a young Donegal man emigrating to the USA. The play's genius was to dramatise the divided feelings of the character by using two different actors, one playing the public figure that everyone sees, the other representing the private self or alter ego. Their dialogue stands in marked contrast to the silence between father and son in a house where the mother has died. *Philadelphia* scored in both Dublin and New York, speaking to the historical legacy of emigration but doing so in a new, more revealing way. He followed it up with a series of plays through the 1960s, among them *The Loves of Cass McGuire* (1966), where we see the other half of the earlier play, an old Irish woman who has returned home after years in the USA, and *The Mundy Scheme* (1969), where the themes of Irish-Americanism and post-colonialism are satirically addressed.

By the end of the 1960s this first phase of Friel's playwriting career had run its course. In 1973 he began an association with the Abbey Theatre in its production of *The Freedom of the City*, Friel's most overtly political drama. It responded to the previous four years' events in Northern Ireland with an imaginative version of the shooting down of unarmed civil rights marchers in Derry's 'Bloody Sunday'. Throughout the 1970s four more Friel plays were staged at the Abbey, culminating in *Faith Healer* (1980). A failure in New York, this (possibly Friel's masterpiece) found an audience in Ireland. Examining the interrelated lives of a travelling faith healer, his wife and manager, the play dealt with the question of belief and its bearing on personal and national identity.

In 1980 Friel founded the Field Day Theatre Company with STEPHEN REA and premiered his new play, *Translations*, in Derry's mayoral Guild Hall before touring it to the remotest corners of Ireland. (This established the pattern for an annual Field Day production for over ten years.) *Translations* was set in a Donegal hedge school some years before the Famine and saw the arrival of a group of sappers with the schoolmaster's son to carry out work on the Ordnance Survey map of Ireland. The play dramatised memorably the culture shock arising out of the clash of two traditions, partly through the love affair between a British soldier and an Irishwoman, partly through a linguistic impasse where neither can speak or understand the other's language. *Translations* had a seismic impact on Irish audiences, articulating a painful race memory in a dramatically arresting way, but it was also acclaimed by people from equivalent multicultural situations the world over. Friel produced several more plays for Field Day in the 1980s.

With *Dancing at Lughnasa* (1990) he returned to the Abbey. Here the dramatic emphasis shifted from men to women, five of them, during a period in the 1930s when they were being written out of the public record and into the home. The resilience, interplay and shared hurt of these sisters spoke with particular eloquence to an Ireland which was about to elect MARY ROBINSON as president.

Friel served in the Seanad in the 1980s and has continued to write plays on into his sixties, including *Wonderful Tennessee* in 1993.

FRIERS, Rowel (1920–), Northern Ireland's most celebrated cartoonist, b. Belfast, ed. Park Parade School and the Belfast College of Art. Friers served as an apprentice lithographer before returning to study art. His first exhibition of paintings, drawings and cartoons was held in 1953, since when his work has appeared in numerous newspapers and magazines, such as the *Belfast Telegraph*, *The Irish Times*, *Belfast Newsletter*, *Daily Express*, *Punch* and *Radio Times*. He has designed sets for Belfast's Lyric Theatre and for Northern Ireland Opera. Nine published collections of cartoons include *Riotous Living*, *Pig in the Parlour*, *The Revolting Irish* and *On the Borderline*. He has also illustrated more than 30 books. Awarded an MBE in 1977 and an honorary MA from the Open University in 1981. Chairman of the NI Cystic Fibrosis Research Trust, president of the Royal Ulster Academy of Arts since 1993. His autobiography, *Drawn from Life*, was published in 1994.

FROMEL, Gerda (1931–1975), sculptor, b. Czechoslovakia to German parents, ed. art schools in Stuttgart, Darmstadt, Munich 1948–52. Came to Ireland 1956. Participated in the Irish Exhibition of Living Art 1957–75, the Salzburg Biennale of Christian Art 1960–62 and other festivals. Her work was admired for its refinement, sensitivity and reticence. She worked in bronze, stone and most media, except wood. Her best work includes heads of women and children, done mainly in bronze and alabaster.

G

GAFFNEY, Maureen (1947–), clinical psychologist, writer and broadcaster, b. Midleton, Co. Cork, ed. UCC and University of Chicago (master's in social science). Joined Eastern Health Board in 1973 as a clinical psychologist. At the University of Chicago she became an advocate of the 'life cycle' approach to developmental psychology, which sees the adult as constantly evolving. Research associate and organiser of the joint Eastern Health Board/TCD postgraduate training course in clinical psychology. Member of the Law Reform Commission since 1985, influential in changing the legal profession's perspective on rape, child sexual abuse and aspects of family law. In 1993 she was appointed chairwoman of the National Economic and Social Forum, one of whose major tasks was to develop new initiatives to tackle unemployment. Regular contributor to the GAY BYRNE radio show and author of *The Way We Live Now* (1996).

GAGEBY, Douglas (1918–), journalist and editor, b. Dublin, ed. Belfast Royal Academy and TCD. Army officer during the Emergency. Joined *Irish Press* 1945; assistant editor *Sunday Press* 1949; editor-in-chief Irish News Agency 1952; editor *Evening Press* 1954. Joint managing director *The Irish Times* 1959; editor 1963–74 and again 1977–86. Although the success of the *Evening Press*, for which he was largely responsible, would have been sufficient for him to earn a special place in the history of Irish newspapers, his remarkable resuscitation of *The Irish Times* must rank as the outstanding editorial achievement of the century.

His immediate predecessors had weaned the paper away from its position as the voice of Southern Protestantism and lingering unionist sentiment, but commercial difficulties had prevented its development into a truly national daily, integrated into the mainstream life of the country. Gageby made it precisely this with the aid of a brilliant news editor, DONAL FOLEY. New areas of social concern were investigated, prominence was given to women writers, JOHN HEALY's 'Backbencher' column was taken over from the defunct *Sunday Review*. Circulation quickly moved upwards, eventually doubled and continued to grow. The modern *Irish Times* is the creation above all of Douglas Gageby.

GALE, Martin (1949–), artist, b. Worcester, ed. National College of Art, Dublin. He has had several one-man shows in Ireland and represented the country in many exhibitions abroad, including the International Connection show at the Sense of Ireland Festival in London and the XIe Biennale de Paris, both in 1980. His work was shown at the Young Artists exhibition at the Union Carbide Building in New York 1973, and he won an Oireachtas Exhibitions prize in the same year. Member of Aosdána. He also works as a book illustrator and in 1985 won first prize in the Irish Book Design Awards. Gale's skill as an illustrator is evident in the manner in which he enlivens the unspectacular scenes of his paintings through a detailed observation of each of their components.

GALLAGHER, Frank (1898–1962), journalist and first editor of the *Irish Press*, b. Cork, d. Dublin, 16 July 1962. Joined the *Cork Free Press* while in his teens and was dispatched to London to cover the historic Home Rule debates in Westminster. He joined the Volunteers after 1916 and helped ROBERT ERSKINE CHILDERS produce the *Irish Bulletin* during the War of Independence. He took the republican side after the Treaty and was interned, during which time he survived a lengthy hunger strike. In 1931 EAMON DE VALERA appointed him editor of the *Irish Press*, a position he filled with great energy and flair. He left in 1936, following a clash with the directors, but remained close to de Valera, who appointed him deputy director of Radio Éireann in 1936, director of the Government Information Bureau 1938–48 and 1951–4. Publications include *Days of Fear* (1928) and, as David Hogan, *The Four Glorious Years* (1953).

GALLAGHER, Patrick (1873–1964), promoter of rural co-operation, b. Cleendra, Co. Donegal, 25 Dec. 1873, ed. local primary school. Hired out as a farm labourer from the age of ten, he worked in England and Scotland in a variety of labouring jobs until he had saved enough to buy a farm in Cleendra. In 1906, influenced by his experience of co-operatives in Scotland and by the promotional efforts of GEORGE RUSSELL and the Irish Agricultural Organisation Society, he set up a co-operative society with 14 subscribers, despite the opposition of traders and merchants to the bulk buying of fertilisers and foodstuffs. Became known as 'Paddy the Cope', 'cope' being the popular pronunciation of 'co-op'. He diversified and expanded the society in the succeeding years, securing outlets for its products at home and abroad, developing the weaving industry, opening a glove factory and providing an electricity generator for the town of Dungloe. His autobiography, *My Story*, was published in 1939.

GALLAGHER, Patrick Joseph (1901–1957), Garda representative, b. Ballaghaderreen, Co. Roscommon, d. 17 Nov. 1957. Farmer's son, primary school monitor. Sergeant Garda Síochána 1923. Secretary of Garda Representative Body for Inspectors and Sergeants and of Joint Representative Body from 1925 to his death in the service; secretary Benevolent Society and Medical Aid Society; managing editor *Garda Review*. Within the constraints of the regulations, he ably articulated the grievances of the first generation of rank-and-file members of the force. His death left the Representative Body rudderless until a young JACK MARRINAN emerged as leader in 1961.

GALLAGHER, Rory (1949–1995), bluesman, b. Ballyshannon, Co. Donegal, reared in Cork. He grew up listening to Lonnie Donegan, Jerry Lee Lewis, Chuck Berry and Muddy Waters, heroes to whom he always remained true; later he was to fulfil lifelong ambitions by recording with them. He came to prominence in 1965 with the power trio Taste. Their second album, *On the Boards*, reached the UK top ten in 1970. Gallagher went solo the following year, again making the top ten with *Live in Europe*, and was voted World's Top Guitarist by British music weekly *Melody Maker*. When he died

after an operation in June 1995 he was mourned by millions of fans throughout the world, who will remember him as a gentle and unpretentious check-shirted man with a passion for the blues, coaxing tasteful solos from his battered old Stratocaster. The four-CD set *Rory Gallagher Boxed* (1992) is a collector's item.

GALVIN, Edward (1882–1956), co-founder of St Columban's Foreign Mission Society (Maynooth Mission to China), b. Crookstown, Co. Cork, 21 Nov. 1882, ed. Classics School, Bandon, Farranferris Seminary, Cork and Maynooth. Ordained 1909, appointed to Brooklyn, New York. In 1912 he volunteered for missionary work in China in Chekiang province. An acute shortage of priests there convinced him to return to Ireland in 1916 to seek recruits. A meeting with JOHN BLOWICK, Professor of Theology at Maynooth, followed and in Oct. 1916 the two founded Ireland's first native missionary body of secular priests, the Maynooth Mission to China. In 1918 they adopted the name St Columban's Foreign Mission Society, with Fr Blowick as superior-general.

In 1920 Fr Galvin led the first party of Columbans to China and established Ireland's first mission territory there at Hanyang in Hupeh province. In 1924 he became prefect apostolic for the area and in 1927 vicar apostolic. In the same year he was consecrated bishop. The capture of Hanyang by the Japanese in 1938 confronted Bishop Galvin and his priests with considerable obstacles to their work. His missionary efforts were finally curbed in 1949 when the communists came to power. He was placed under house arrest until Sept. 1952, then expelled from China. He returned to Ireland, where he died on 23 Feb. 1956.

GALWAY, James (1939–), musician, b. Belfast, 8 Dec. 1939, son of a shipyard riveter, ed. St Paul's School, Mountcollver Secondary Modern School, Belfast, RCM and Guildhall School of Music, London and Conservatoire National Supérieur de Musique, Paris. Internationally famous classical flautist. His numerous recordings and the eloquent and amusing style in which he describes his work have helped to make him very popular with the general public. Principal flute with the London Symphony Orchestra 1966 and the Royal Philharmonic Orchestra 1967–9, and principal solo flute with Berlin Philharmonic Orchestra 1969–75 under Herbert von Karajan. Since 1975 he has pursued a solo career. Awards include the Officier des arts et des lettres, France 1987. He published his autobiography in 1978 and had his own television series, *James Galway's Music in Time*, in 1983.

GARVEY, Edmund Patrick (1915–1989), commissioner Garda Síochána, b. Ballinlough, Co. Roscommon, d. 29 Nov. 1989. Motor mechanic; joined Taca Síochána, the auxiliary police, as a guard in 1940 and rose through the ranks; in the Central Detective Unit earned a reputation as an effective investigator of serious crime. Energetic in promoting welfare in the force, founded the Garda Club and Stackstown Golf Club. Garda housing officer. Assistant commissioner Crime Branch, later head of the force (1975–8), during a period of paramilitary activity in the state. Decorated as a member of the Orange Order by the government of the Netherlands for the rescue of the kidnapped industrialist Tiede Herrema 1975. His assertive style of leadership brought him into conflict with the representative associations. Removed from office; believing his integrity impugned, he fought a successful action in the courts against the state.

GARVEY, Philomena K. (1927–), golfer, b. Drogheda, 26 Apr. 1927. She won the British Ladies Amateur Open in 1957 and was runner-up four times, in 1946, 1953, 1960 and 1963. She played six times in the Curtis Cup, winning two matches, losing eight and halving one. Having turned professional in 1964, she was reinstated as an amateur in 1968. Her 15 wins over a 25-year period (1946–8, 1950–51, 1953–5, 1957–60, 1962–3 and 1970) in the Irish Ladies Amateur Open is a record, and she was never defeated in the final. She reached the quarter-finals of the US Ladies Championship in 1950, and played for Ireland in the home international series 18 times between 1947 and 1969, being captain on six occasions.

GARVIN, John (1904–1986), public servant and Joycean scholar, b. Ballinfad, Co. Sligo, ed. St Nathy's College, Ballaghaderreen, Co. Roscommon, UCG (BA, B.Comm.) and UCD (LL B). One of the first administrative officers recruited for the service of the new state in 1925. He was assigned to the Department of Local Government and Public Health, from which he retired as secretary in 1966. During his time there he was secretary of the Local Government (Dublin) Tribunal in 1938 and a member of the three-person Local Appointments Commission 1949–66. After retirement he was appointed chairman of the Library Council and was deputy chairman of the Higher Education Authority. When the members of Dublin Corporation were removed from office in 1969 by the Minister for Local Government, for failure to carry out their statutory duty in regard to the striking of a rate, Garvin was called back into public service and appointed Dublin city commissioner, a post he held until 1973.

For most of his life he immersed himself deeply in the work of JAMES JOYCE and he became an internationally recognised interpreter of its more obscure areas. He contributed many articles to learned journals and lectured both at home and abroad on Joyce and on Anglo-Irish literature in general. In 1966, on the occasion of the burial of Nora Joyce alongside her husband in Fluntern Cemetery, he delivered the James Joyce memorial lecture in the University of Zurich. His schooling had laid the foundations of a deep knowledge of Greek and Latin and he was an Irish speaker. He had a great interest in the innovative use of words. The pen-name Andrew Cass, under which he usually wrote on Joyce, derived through a typical Joycean inversion from Cassandra, the Trojan prophetess to whom no one would listen. *James Joyce's Disunited Kingdom and the Irish Dimension* was published in 1976.

GATENBY, Peter Barry Bronte (1923–), physician, b. Dublin, eldest s. of Professor J. Bronte Gatenby of TCD, a native of New Zealand, ed. St Andrew's College, Dublin and TCD. He graduated in medicine in 1946 and after experience at the Middlesex Hospital became physician to Dr Steevens's and the Meath Hospitals. Appointed to TCD's chair of medicine in 1960, he was the first to hold the professorship on a full-time basis. He reorganised teaching, conducted research into the anaemias of pregnancy and the malabsorption syndrome, and as WHO consultant in India established a medical school in Delhi.

Appointed medical director of the UN Medical Services, Gatenby lived in New York City 1974–82, travelling widely in Europe, Africa and Asia in a supervisory capacity; later he was chief medical officer to FAO in Rome, returning to Ireland in his retirement. Subsequently an international civilian physician for UNPROFOR in Zagreb. Hon. FTCD.

GEARY, Frank J. (1896–1961), journalist, b. Co. Kilkenny, ed. CBS, Kilkenny, d. 21 Dec. 1961. Reporter for *Kilkenny People* under its colourful and often controversial editor E.T. Keane (an early supporter of Sinn Féin and later a lifelong critic of EAMON DE VALERA), later on editorial staff of *Midland Tribune* (Birr) and *Carlow and Leinster Nationalist*. Joined *Irish Independent* in 1922 and covered the Civil War in Munster, frequently working under conditions of great personal danger. In 1927 became a sub-editor on *Irish Independent*, in 1931 its assistant editor and in 1935 its editor, until his retirement 26 years later. Geary's regime as *Independent* editor coincided with the growth of its rival *Irish Press* and was marked by an editorial policy of persistent criticism of and at times hostility to the Fianna Fáil administration, which was not, however, accompanied by subservience to the main opposition party, Fine Gael. A close friend of several members of the Catholic hierarchy, Geary, who adhered to the highest standards of journalistic ethics, made the *Irish Independent* of his time into a family paper with a strong Catholic bias.

GEARY, Robert Charles (Roy) (1896–1983), statistician, b. Dublin, 11 Apr. 1896, ed. O'Connell School, UCD and Sorbonne, d. Dublin, 8 Feb. 1983. Hon. degrees: NUI, QUB, TCD. Boyle medallist of the RDS. Working initially in the statistics branch of the Department of Industry and Commerce, he was appointed in 1949 as first director of the Central Statistics Office. In 1957 he went to New York to head the UN national accounts branch of the Statistical Office. Returning in 1960 he became first director of the Economic Research Institute (now the ESRI). His statistical interests were wide, perhaps the best-known being his suggestion of tests for normality and on the sampling theory of ratios.

GEDDES, Wilhelmina (1887–1955), stained-glass artist, ed. Methodist College, Belfast, Belfast School of Art 1903 and Metropolitan School of Art, Dublin under WILLIAM ORPEN 1910. In 1914 her work was included in the Exposition des arts décoratifs in the Louvre; in 1913 her work was exhibited at the RHA. She also designed stamps, posters, bookjackets, bookplates, graphics and book illustrations, some of which she translated into glass.

GELDOF, Bob (1954–), singer, b. Dún Laoghaire, Co. Dublin, 5 Oct. 1954, ed. Blackrock. After a brief spell as a journalist in Canada, he helped to establish the rock band THE BOOMTOWN RATS in Dublin in 1975. In 1984, after witnessing the plight of starving people in Ethiopia, Geldof brought the UK's leading pop stars together, along with members of the Rats, to record 'Do They Know It's Christmas?' under the collective name Band Aid. The song became the biggest-selling single in British pop history and provided the springboard for Live Aid in 1985, a huge charity concert held simultaneously in London and Philadelphia which raised over £50m. Geldof received an honorary knighthood for his humanitarian work and wrote a best-selling autobiography, *Is That It?*

GEOGHEGAN, Trevor (1946–), artist, b. London, ed. Worthing College of Art, Sussex and Chelsea School of Art, London. He moved to Ireland in 1971 and now teaches in the NCAD. In 1989 he was chosen to represent Ireland at the 25th International Festival of Painting in Cagnes-sur-Mer, France. Geoghegan paints the landscapes of Wicklow and the Burren region of Co. Clare in a realist style. There is great attention to detail both in the manner in which the various aspects of the landscape are rendered and in the composition of the paintings.

GEOGHEGAN-QUINN, Máire (1950–), politician, b. 5 Sept. 1950, ed. Coláiste Mhuire, Mayo and Carysfort College, Dublin. Her father, Johnny Geoghegan, was Fianna Fáil TD for Galway West from 1954 until his death in 1975. Máire Geoghegan successfully contested the subsequent by-election and each general election since. She was parliamentary secretary/Minister of State at the Department of Industry, Commerce and Energy 1977–9. From 1979 to 1981 she was Minister for the Gaeltacht – the first woman to hold a cabinet post since Countess MARKIEVICZ. Minister of State at the Department of Education 1982 and the Department of the Taoiseach (with special responsibility for co-ordinating EC policy) 1987–Nov. 1991, when she resigned in opposition to CHARLES HAUGHEY's leadership. When ALBERT REYNOLDS succeeded Haughey early the following year she was appointed Minister for Tourism, Transport and Communications and in Jan. 1993 she became Minister for Justice, losing office in Dec. 1994 after the collapse of the FF–Labour government. Member of Galway Corporation 1985–91.

On social issues she has been on the liberal wing of FF and as Minister for Justice undertook substantial law reform legislation. After the resignation of Reynolds as party leader she announced that she would challenge BERTIE AHERN for the post but withdrew on the day of the planned ballot. She was appointed to his new FF front bench.

GIBBON, William *Monk* (1896–1987), poet, critic and scholar, b. Dublin, ed. St Columba's and Oxford. After World War I he studied agriculture but took up teaching instead. He won a silver medal for poetry at the Tailteann Games 1928, being narrowly beaten by OLIVER ST JOHN GOGARTY, who took gold at W.B. YEATS's recommendation. MIAL and fellow of the Royal Society of Literature. He was very much a minor, conventional poet who would turn a poor Swinburne on a bad day, yet could sometimes rise to unexpected heights. His collected poetry was published as *This Insubstantial Pageant* (1951). Gibbon's prose was of a miscellaneous nature, ranging from some excellent autobiography – *The Seals* (1935), *Mount Ida* (1948) and *The Climate of Love* (1961) – to travel books, ballet and film criticism. His memoir of Yeats, *The Masterpiece and the Man: Yeats as I Knew Him* (1959), is a personal, if curiously unflattering, sketch of the great poet.

GIBSON, Cameron Michael Henderson (Mike) (1942–), international rugby player, b. Belfast, 3 Dec. 1942. He is Ireland's most capped rugby player, with 69 (40 at centre, 25 at outside half and four on the wing) and with TONY O'REILLY he shares the Irish record for the longest international career, 16 seasons, 1964–79. He played for Dublin

University, Wanderers, Cambridge University (three blues) and NIFC, made five Lions tours, including the series-winning visits to New Zealand in 1971 and to South Africa in 1974, and won 12 Test caps. With Ireland he toured Australia in 1967, New Zealand in 1976 and Australia again in 1979, when he made his last international appearance in the second Test at Sydney. Among the greatest players produced by this or any other country, he is one of five Irish players to have surpassed 100 points in international rugby.

GILES, Michael John (Johnny) (1940–), international footballer, b. Dublin, 6 Jan. 1940. He moved from Home Farm to Manchester United as a 17-year-old and won an FA Cup medal with them in 1963, having made his League début with the club in 1959. Thanks to the influence of Don Revie he moved to Leeds United in 1963, and in 12 seasons scored 115 goals in 525 matches and helped the club to win the League title twice (1969 and 1974), the League Cup (1968), the FA Cup (1972) and two Fairs Cups (1968 and 1971). Between 1959 and 1979 he won 59 caps for the Republic of Ireland and scored five international goals. In his later career he played and coached in the USA and Canada, was player-manager of West Bromwich Albion 1975–7 and Shamrock Rovers 1977–8 – winning an FAI Cup medal in 1978 – and was player-manager of the Republic of Ireland team 1973–80.

GILL, Michael (1940–), publisher, b. Dublin, 5 Feb. 1940, ed. Belvedere and UCD. Worked in publishing houses in London, Paris and New York before returning to Ireland in 1963 to the family firm, M.H. Gill & Son. In 1968 he became the first – and to date the only – managing director of Gill & Macmillan as the company entered an association with Macmillan of London. President of the Irish Book Publishers' Association 1974–6 and 1992–3.

GILLEN, Gerard (1942–), organist, teacher and academic, b. Dublin, ed. Dublin, Antwerp and Oxford. Titular organist Pro-Cathedral, Dublin since 1976. Lecturer in music UCD 1969–85. Appointed Professor of Music Maynooth 1985. Artistic director Dublin International Organ Festival. Has performed in Europe, USA and Canada and made numerous recordings and contributions to international music journals. Edited *Irish Music Studies*.

GILMARTIN, Thomas James (1905–1986), anaesthetist, b. Ballymote, Co. Sligo, ed. Summerhill College, Co. Sligo, Belvedere and the RCSI, m. Margaret (Peggy) Maiben. Graduated LRCP&SI 1929. After gaining clinical experience in England he became anaesthetist to Mercer's Hospital, remaining on the staff until the hospital's closure in 1983. During the intervening years Gilmartin was a major influence in raising his speciality from a haphazard art to a skilled science. A founder member of the Association of Anaesthetists of Great Britain and Ireland 1932, he was first in Ireland to use curare as a relaxant, and was chairman of a steering committee that established the faculty of anaesthetists of the RCSI in 1959. He was dean of the faculty and the first in the country to hold a chair of anaesthesiology.

GILMORE, George (1898–1985), republican socialist, b. Belfast, son of an accountant, childhood spent in Howth and Foxrock, Co. Dublin, d. Dublin, 20 June 1985. He joined the IRA during the War of Independence and took the anti-Treaty side in the Civil War. He remained active in the IRA and was imprisoned in 1931. A central figure in the movement that sought to combine the efforts of republicans and socialists in one organisation during the 1930s. In 1934, along with fellow IRA members FRANK RYAN and PEADAR O'DONNELL, he established the Republican Congress, an organisation dedicated to the creation of a workers' republic. The Congress, suffering from internal division and strong opposition from the IRA, was dissolved in 1935.

GILROY, Frederick (Freddie) (1936–), boxer. b. Belfast, 7 Mar. 1936. In 1956 he won the Irish National Senior Championship bantamweight title and won a bronze medal at the same weight in the Melbourne Olympic Games. Going professional in 1957, he was European bantamweight champion 1959–60, British Empire champion 1959–62 and British champion 1959–63. In his five-year professional career he won 28 of 31 bouts, 18 of them inside the distance, and was also a Lonsdale Belt winner.

GIVENS, Don (1949–), international footballer, b. Castleconnell, Co. Limerick,

9 Aug. 1949. He started his career with Manchester United but played only five games for them. His other clubs were Luton Town (19 goals, 83 matches, 1970–72), Queen's Park Rangers (76 League goals, 242 matches, 1972–7), Birmingham City, Bournemouth and Sheffield United. He scored 113 League goals and another nine in European competitions. His last six seasons were spent with Neuchâtel Xamax in Switzerland, where he scored 34 Swiss League goals and captained the club to its first League Championship. In 56 international appearances for the Republic of Ireland over 13 years, he scored 18 goals – three against the USSR in 1974 and four against Turkey in 1975, both matches at Dalymount Park in Dublin.

GOGARTY, Oliver St John (1878–1957), surgeon, poet and writer, b. Dublin, 17 Aug. 1878, ed. Mungret College, Co. Limerick, Stonyhurst, Clongowes, TCD and Oxford, d. New York. As a student he became a friend of JAMES JOYCE, with whom he briefly shared lodgings in the Martello Tower at Sandycove near Dublin, thereby achieving immortality as 'stately plump Buck Mulligan' in *Ulysses*. Went on to become a fashionable nose and throat surgeon but also wrote verse, plays, novels and finely crafted memoirs (*As I Was Going Down Sackville Street*, 1937; *It Isn't This Time of Year at All!*, 1954). His irrepressible wit, often directed against sacred cows, to a degree obscured his deeply serious commitment to the country and its future. He supported the Anglo-Irish Treaty of 1921, was captured by republicans in the Civil War but escaped by swimming the Liffey – to which he presented a pair of swans in gratitude. He tended his friend ARTHUR GRIFFITH in the days before his death and performed the autopsy on MICHAEL COLLINS. When his house in Renvyle in Connemara was burned down in the Civil War he rebuilt it as a hotel. He was a senator 1922–36 and, having an interest in many sports, organised the Tailteann Games of 1924. He spent his later years in New York.

GONNE, Maud. See under MacBride.

GOODMAN, Larry (1939–), businessman, b. Co. Louth, ed. Marist College, Dundalk. Chief executive of Irish Food Processors. He began his business career as a trader in hides and other animal by-products before getting involved in the meat-processing industry. By the mid-1980s he had become the largest processor and exporter of beef in Europe. In 1992 Goodman International, the group of companies which formed his beef and dairy empire, went into examinership with debts of over £500m. The group also came under the scrutiny of a major tribunal set up to investigate fraud, tax evasion and the use of political influence to secure state-backed export credit insurance. However, in less than three years Larry Goodman had made a remarkable recovery and regained control of the group through an agreement with its creditors.

GORE-BOOTH, Eva Selena (1870–1926), poet, verse dramatist and feminist, b. Lissadell, Co. Sligo, sister of Countess CONSTANCE MARKIEVICZ. W.B. YEATS, who knew them both, described Eva in a poem as 'beautiful . . . a gazelle' – though perhaps only to achieve a rhyme to 'Lissadell'. At age 22 she went to live with her lifelong friend Esther Roper in Manchester, where she threw herself into social and political work for women, befriending and influencing the suffragist Christabel Pankhurst in 1901. In 1913 Eva's ill health forced the friends to move to London, where Gore-Booth worked for the Women's Peace Crusade, then from 1916 for Irish independence. She wrote three verse dramas – *Unseen Kings* (1904), *The Death of Fionavar* (1916) and *The House of Three Windows* (1926) – none of which was successful. Her poems were numerous and compare favourably in quality with those of her peers. She is remembered chiefly for 'The Little Waves of Breffny'. Her *Complete Poems* were published in 1929.

GORHAM, Maurice Anthony (1902–1975), journalist, broadcaster and author, b. London, son of a doctor from Clifden, Co. Galway, ed. Stonyhurst and Balliol College, Oxford, d. Dublin, 9 Aug. 1975. Joined the BBC's programme journal *Radio Times* in 1926, becoming editor 1933–41. Moved into broadcasting 1941 to direct BBC services to North America; founded and directed the Allied Expeditionary Forces Programme (1944) and the Light Programme (1945), relaunched and headed BBC television (1946). Resigned in 1947 to become a freelance writer and broadcaster. Appointed director of broadcasting (chief executive of Radio Éireann) 1953, as which he guided the service through its interim phase as a semi-autonomous body under its own council (Comhairle Radio Éireann), no longer controlled directly by the Department of Posts and Telegraphs but not yet a state company. He expanded the Radio Éireann orchestras, introduced listenership surveys, extended the hours of broadcasting, opened new studios in Cork and initiated major live broadcasting from abroad. Preliminary arrangements were in hand for the introduction of television and the conversion of the broadcasting service into a public authority when Gorham resigned in 1959 because he disliked the thought of adapting to a new system and doubted the possibility of achieving a good combined service of radio and television on the available resources. He wrote several books, including the official history of Radio Éireann, *Forty Years of Irish Broadcasting* (1967).

GORT (John Standish Vereker), sixth Viscount (1886–1946), British field marshal, b. July 1886, ed. Harrow and Sandhurst, d. London. Commissioned into Grenadier Guards 1905. Won VC during World War I. Chief of the Imperial General Staff 1937. Commander-in-chief of the British Expeditionary Force during the fall of France in 1940. His major achievement was overseeing the successful retreat and evacuation of the bulk of the BEF. However, he was not rated highly by either Bernard Montgomery or Viscount ALANBROOKE and Dunkirk was to be his last significant engagement. He was made a field marshal in 1943.

GOSSET, William Sealy ('Student') (1876–1937), statistician, b. Canterbury. He worked for Guinness's 1899–1935, becoming in due course a brewer. Company rules at the time prohibited publication under the individual's own name so he chose the pseudonym 'Student'. He had extensive interests but especially – arising from the problems of barley selection – the statistics of small samples. His invention of 'Student's t-test' remains important for a wide variety of statistical applications today.

GOUGH, Sir Hubert de la Poer (1870–1963), British general and Irish unionist, b. Gurteen, Co. Waterford, 12 Aug. 1870; s. of General Sir Charles Gough of Marfield, Co. Tipperary, from a family famous in Anglo-

Indian military history, and Harriette de la Poer of Gurteen; ed. Sandhurst; d. 18 Mar. 1963. Commissioned in the cavalry and served in India and in the South African war 1899–1902. Noted for his success as a horseman, he was a brigadier at the Curragh in 1914 and the leading figure in the 'Curragh Mutiny', where army officers resigned rather than participate in a show of force against the Ulster Volunteers, who were arming themselves to oppose Home Rule. Restored to command because the Asquith government was ready to concede that there had been procedural misunderstandings and because of the powerful support of high-ranking officers, Gough substantially gained his way over Ulster and went on to win rapid promotion in the early phases of World War I.

As a lieutenant-general he commanded the Fifth Army in harsh and costly battles at the Somme in 1916, at the Third Battle of Ypres in 1917, and during the attack of Mar. 1918, when the early success of the German offensive resulted in his dismissal. Serving in the Baltic in 1919 and a full general in 1922, he left the army and became active in industry. He was awarded the GCB in 1936, his reputation vindicated against blame for the fate of the Fifth Army in 1918. A zone commander of the Home Guard in his seventies (1942), he promoted a wartime club for Irish soldiers in London.

GOULDING, Cathal (1922–), chief of staff of the Official IRA, b. Dublin. His family background was strongly republican and he joined the IRA at a young age. Interned by the Irish government during World War II but active in the reorganisation of the IRA in the immediate post-war period. During the 1960s he was one of the most influential figures among that section of the IRA which emphasised political, as opposed to military, action as a means of furthering the republican cause. His broadly Marxist outlook was reflected in the policy of the newly formed Official Sinn Féin, which emerged from the 1970 split in the republican movement. He was leader of the OIRA when it declared a ceasefire in 1972.

GRAHAM, Patrick (1943–), artist, b. Mullingar, ed. National College of Art, Dublin. After spending a number of years in the USA he returned to live in Ireland in 1972. He has exhibited widely in Ireland, England and the USA, and his work is represented in several important collections both in Ireland and abroad. Among the awards he has received for his work are the Independent Artists Award for Painting of Outstanding Merit 1981, the president's gold medal at the Oireachtas Exhibition 1987 and the painting award at the International Cultural Fair, Iraq, 1987. Graham's skill as a draughtsman was acknowledged early in his career and drawing continues to be an important aspect of his work. While many of his expressionist paintings and drawings appear overtly erotic, the figure is often depicted as wounded and vulnerable and the overriding mood is one of melancholy and fear.

GRAY-STACK, Charles Maurice (1912–1985), Church of Ireland cleric and ecumenist, b. 12 May 1912, d. 25 July 1985. Following service in several parishes in the dioceses of Limerick and Ardfert, appointed dean of Ardfert in 1966. Advocate of 'Parish and People' in the 1960s, an Anglican movement committed to lay involvement in liturgy and Christian service. A prominent ecumenist, especially in the early days of the Glenstal and Greenhills conferences.

GREACEN, Robert (1920–), poet, b. Derry, ed. Belfast and TCD. He published three collections of poetry in the 1940s. In 1948 he emigrated to London, where he worked as a teacher. He published some critical work and a memoir following the death of his wife – *Even Without Irene* (1969) – but did not return to poetry until 1975, since when four volumes have appeared.

GREENE, David William (1915–1981), Celtic scholar, b. Dublin, ed. St Andrew's College, Dublin and TCD. Following postgraduate work in Oslo, he taught in Glasgow University before returning to Ireland as assistant librarian in the National Library 1941–8. Professor in the DIAS 1948–55 then Professor of Irish in TCD. He returned to the DIAS in 1967 as senior professor in the School of Celtic Studies. A formidable and rigorous scholar, he was also well known as a trenchant contributor to cultural debate.

GREEVY, Bernadette (1940–), mezzo-soprano, b. Dublin, ed. Dublin and London. Has performed throughout the world. She is especially renowned as an exponent of the music of Mahler and of Elgar, in particular the role of Angel in *The Dream of Gerontius*, which she first performed with Sir John Barbirolli. Made her operatic début at the Wexford Festival in 1962 as Beppe in Mascagni's *L'Amico Fritz*, and her Covent Garden début in 1982 as Geneviève in Debussy's *Pelléas et Mélisande*. Commercial recordings include music by Handel, Brahms and Haydn; *Nuits d'été* by Berlioz; the songs of Henri Duparc; and the prizewinning 1981 recording of Elgar's *Sea Pictures* with the London Philharmonic, conducted by Vernon Handley. She has also given first performances of many works by Irish composers, including several written specially for her, such as the two SEOIRSE BODLEY song cycles, *A Girl* and *The Naked Flame*. Awards include the Harriet Cohen international music award, the Order of Merit of Malta, the 'Pro Ecclesia et Pontifice' (conferred on her by the Holy See) and honorary doctorates of music from both the NUI and TCD.

GREGG, John Allen Fitzgerald (1873–1961), Church of Ireland archbishop, b. Gloucestershire, 4 July 1873, though his family was Irish (a grandfather was Bishop of Cork), ed. Cambridge, graduating in classics, and TCD, d. 2 May 1961. Ordained deacon 1896, priest 1897. Having served in parishes in Ballymena and Cork, he was appointed Archbishop King's Professor of Divinity in TCD 1911–15. Elected Bishop of Ossory, Ferns and Leighlin 1915. Archbishop of Dublin 1920, Archbishop of Armagh 1939–59.

His period in Dublin coincided with vast political change, and the Church of Ireland was fortunate at that time in having an archbishop with Gregg's statesmanlike and diplomatic skills. These were particularly evident when he was consulted by EAMON DE VALERA as the 1937 constitution was being drafted. In 1949, when he was primate and the 26-county state left the Commonwealth, Gregg unhesitatingly told the Church of Ireland that 'in our prayers, above all, there must be reality', and so new state prayers were introduced to the *Book of Common Prayer* for use in the Republic.

Gregg's primacy in Armagh included the years of World War II (his elder son died a Japanese prisoner of war) and he presided over a Church that spanned two jurisdictions, one of them neutral. While his addresses to the General Synod had a considerable theological

and, indeed, admonitory content, he was practical too, and the Church's financiers held his business acumen and legal competence in high regard.

GREGORY, Lady Augusta (1852–1932), née Persse, author, playwright and theatre administrator, b. Roxborough, Co. Galway, 15 Mar. 1852, of a unionist family of landed gentry, ed. privately, d. Coole Park, Co. Galway, 22 May 1932. Showed an early interest in agrarian reform but remained attached to many of the values of her family background until after the death in 1892 of her elderly husband, Sir William Gregory, a former Governor of Ceylon and MP for Galway City, from whom she inherited the estate of Coole Park near Gort. Sir William had shared her concern for tenant rights and encouraged her to develop her literary talent. Her early writings were quasi-political, advocating economic policies to meet specific Irish needs but opposing Home Rule. In the mid-1890s she changed her views fundamentally, becoming a convinced nationalist, and, under the influence of W.B. YEATS and her Co. Galway neighbour EDWARD MARTYN, began to collect and publish folklore and learn the Irish language in order to translate Gaelic sagas and poetry into English. *Cuchulain of Muirthemne* (1902) and *Gods and Fighting Men* (1904) resulted from these endeavours, as well as *The Kiltartan Poetry Book: Translations from the Irish* (1919) and *Visions and Beliefs in the West of Ireland* (1920).

The theatre meanwhile became Lady Gregory's primary concern. Together with Yeats, Martyn and DOUGLAS HYDE she founded the Irish Literary Theatre in 1899, from which the Abbey Theatre developed in 1904, with her, Yeats and J.M. SYNGE as co-directors. She now turned to playwriting, composing no fewer than 27 plays for the Abbey, most of them of high dramatic quality, making full use of her ear for dialogue and her sympathetic understanding of the lives of Irish country people. She drew on her knowledge of history and folklore to create plays that stood the test of time and were to be revived again and again throughout the century. Her special genius was for short, often one-act, comedies, although she could also write more extended tragedies and translate from French into the Galway dialect of English which became known from the name of her local village as 'Kiltartan' or 'Kiltartanese'. The most popular of her plays proved to be *Spreading the News* (1904), *The Gaol Gate* (1906), *The Rising of the Moon* (1907) and *The Workhouse Ward* (1908). Her close collaboration with Yeats caused him to seek her advice and assistance in the composition of a number of his own plays. She spent much time in directing the affairs of the Abbey, and identified and encouraged the talents of the young SEAN O'CASEY. She also worked hard to recover for Ireland the collection of Impressionist paintings bequeathed by her nephew Sir HUGH LANE, in an unwitnessed and therefore inoperative codicil to his will.

GREGORY, Tony (1947–), politician, b. Dublin, Dec. 1947, ed. O'Connell School and UCD (BA, H.Dip.Ed.). Independent TD since 1982; member Dublin City Council since 1979; chairman North Centre City Community Action Project. Former secondary school teacher. On his election in Feb. 1982 he immediately achieved national prominence through the famous 'Gregory Deal', which he negotiated with Fianna Fáil leader CHARLES HAUGHEY. In return for supporting Haughey as Taoiseach, he was guaranteed a massive cash injection for his inner-city Dublin constituency, an area beset by poverty and neglect. Although he was reviled in certain quarters for effectively holding a government to ransom, Gregory's uncompromising commitment to the poor was widely admired.

GRENNAN, Eamon (1941–), poet and translator, b. Dublin, ed. Cistercian College, Roscrea, UCD and Harvard, where he took his Ph.D. in 1972. He lived in Italy for a time, in 1991 received a fellowship from the National Endowment for the Arts, a Guggenheim fellowship and appointment as writer in residence at UCD. He has also taught at the City University of New York. Grennan has published critical studies covering a wide field of literature, from Shakespeare and Spenser to the modern poets. His own verse is a fine mélange of lyricism and meditation which, though focusing sharply and consistently on the commonplace, seldom neglects the big issues that affect us all. His collections include *Wildly for Days* (1983), *What Light There Is* (1987), *As If It Matters* (1991) and *So It Goes*

(1995). He has translated *Selected Poems of Giacomo Leopardi* (1995). At present he teaches English at Vassar College, Poughkeepsie, New York, dividing his time between the USA and Ireland.

GRIFFIN, Victor (1924–), Church of Ireland dean, b. Carnew, Co. Wicklow, ed. Kilkenny College, Mountjoy School, Dublin and TCD. Ordained Church of Ireland priest 1947. Curate, later rector, of parishes in Derry city 1947–68; active in protests over the neglect of Derry by Stormont; encouraged ecumenical relations with Roman Catholic clergy. His liberal views drew abuse from the loyalist extreme but found support among moderate unionists. Elected dean of St Patrick's Cathedral, Dublin, Nov. 1968. Became prominently associated with progressive opinion in the Republic, continuing his ecumenical commitment while also criticising what he saw as undue Roman Catholic influence on the civil law. He publicly endorsed the anti-apartheid movement, canvassed for MARY ROBINSON and DAVID NORRIS in their campaigns for election to the Seanad, opposed the wording of the 1983 constitutional amendment prohibiting abortion and backed the 1986 proposal to remove the constitutional ban on divorce. He took a leading part in campaigns to preserve the old Liberties quarter of Dublin for its people and conducted a successful appeal for the renovation of St Patrick's, although he failed in his effort to persuade churchmen of other denominations to consider using the cathedral for services according to their own rites as a witness to 'brotherhood and reconciliation in Christ'. He retired in 1991.

GRIFFITH, Arthur (1871–1922), journalist, politician, political theorist and founder of the independent Irish state, b. Dublin, 31 Mar. 1871, ed. CBS, Strand Street. A printer by trade, co-founder of Celtic Literary Society 1893, member of the Gaelic League and the IRB. After three years in South Africa, returned in 1899 to edit the weekly *United Irishman*. Denounced what he saw as the growing adoption of English tastes in literature, sport and social mannerisms by the Irish Catholic middle classes but soon concentrated on seeking a political means of national self-expression. He considered Home Rule to be insufficient and, citing the precedent of the Austro-

Hungarian dual monarchy in *The Resurrection of Hungary* (1904), proposed instead that Irish members of parliament should withdraw from Westminster and come together as a national assembly in Dublin which would legislate for Ireland and set up its own law courts: in short, the repeal of the Union sought in the past by Daniel O'Connell but implemented unilaterally by the Irish rather than extracted as a concession from the British government. The self-help element of the proposal was caught in the name Griffith gave to the movement and to the newspaper he founded to propagate it, *Sinn Féin* ('we ourselves').

Griffith supported the Irish Volunteers, opposed recruitment to the British army at the outset of World War I, and was imprisoned for a time after the Easter Rising although he had not been involved. He was elected to parliament (SF Cavan East) in 1917 and again in the 1918 general election, when SF won an overwhelming victory. In his absence (he was interned in 1918) the SF members implemented Griffith's plan, meeting in Dublin on 21 Jan. 1919 as an Irish parliament under the name Dáil Éireann, calling themselves *Teachtaí Dála* (deputies of the Dáil or TDs), proceeding to take over the local authorities in the counties and set up their own courts. They also endorsed the Proclamation of the Republic made in 1916. The War of Independence followed. Griffith led the delegation which negotiated a settlement with the British (the Treaty of 1921). When this was rejected by EAMON DE VALERA and a substantial minority of TDs, Griffith became president in place of de Valera. He had the immensely difficult task of consolidating the new state against the resistance of the anti-Treaty party, which in months escalated into a hateful civil war. The bitterness it engendered was the last intolerable strain on an already sick man and Griffith died on 12 Aug. 1922.

GRIMSHAW, Beatrice (*c.* 1870–1953), writer and traveller, b. Cloona, Co. Antrim, ed. Belfast, London and Normandy. A champion cyclist, she felt circumscribed by her work as a journalist in Dublin and London. She visited Tahiti in 1906 and later settled for a time in New Guinea. She supported herself by freelance journalism and travel books, which included *In the Strange South Seas* (1907)

and *From Fiji to the Cannibal Islands* (1917). She also published numerous novels.

GRUBB, Sir Howard (1844–1931), FRS, astronomical instrument maker, d. 16 Sept. 1931. Cunningham medal 1881, knighted 1887, Boyle medal 1912. Hon. ME (TCD). Governor RDS.

GUERIN, Veronica (1958–1996), journalist, b. Dublin, 5 July 1958, m. Graham Turley 1985, one s., d. 26 June 1996. Veronica Guerin, in a journalistic career that spanned only half a dozen years, left an indelible mark on her profession as an investigative reporter of rare courage, enterprise and dedication. She originally trained as an accountant and later started her own PR agency. She was also politically active, serving as a researcher to CHARLES HAUGHEY at the New Ireland Forum, and was appointed by Fianna Fáil to the governing body of the NIHE, Dublin for two terms. In 1990 she made a successful career change into journalism, working in turn for the *Sunday Business Post*, the *Sunday Tribune* (1993–4) and the *Sunday Independent* (1994–6). For the *Tribune* her most celebrated coup was an interview with Bishop EAMONN CASEY, then in hiding. For the *Sunday Independent* she specialised in crime and drug-related investigations, for which she received a number of national and international awards. These investigations also prompted three gun attacks on her – the third, fatal one carried out in broad daylight by professional killers.

GUINEY, Denis (1893–1967), businessman, b. Brosna, Co. Kerry, ed. Knockaclarig NS. Worked in Ireland and England at the drapery trade and in 1921 opened his first shop at 79 Talbot Street, Dublin. By 1931 Guiney & Co. had the enlarged shop refurbished in art deco style. Turnover was 30 times that of ten years previously and Guiney offered to refund country customers their rail fares if they spent over £5; he also ran his own excursion trains. He made wide use of newspaper advertisements and by 1941 his turnover was £1m. When Clery's had to bring in a receiver, Guiney, without valuing stock or premises, bought the store for £250,000. He opened on 29 Nov. 1940 with a sale that realised £54,000 in its first week. The old board, under Sir Christopher Nixon, tried to stop the purchase but Mr Justice GAVAN DUFFY ruled in favour of the receiver. The phenomenal success of Clery's under Guiney's management made him a household name and one of the most successful retailers in modern Ireland.

GUINNESS, Desmond (1931–), author and conservationist, b. 8 Sept. 1931, ed. Gordonstoun School and Oxford. A leading member of the Irish Georgian Society, of which he has been president, his career has been focused on the conservation and preservation of Ireland's Georgian architecture. Author and co-author of numerous works on the subject.

GUINNESS, May (1863–1955), artist, ed. at home by French and German governesses. Studied art seriously for the first time in Paris c. 1905–7 with Van Dongen, André Lhote and later with Spanish artist Aglada. During World War I she joined the French army as nurse and was decorated. Visited France every year thereafter. Influenced by Matisse and the post-Impressionists as well as by Picasso, Dufy and the gentle style of Marie Laurecin.

GUTHRIE, William *Tyrone* (1900–1971), theatre producer and benefactor, b. Tunbridge Wells, ed. Wellington College and St John's College, Oxford, d. Annaghmakerrig, Co. Monaghan, 15 May 1971. Early career in broadcasting with BBC (Belfast and London) and CBC (Canada). Directed theatrical productions in Glasgow, Cambridge and London, becoming administrator Old Vic and Sadler's Wells 1939–45; director Old Vic 1950–51. Produced plays in many countries, including the USA, Finland, Australia and Israel; founded the Tyrone Guthrie Theater in Minneapolis 1963. Knighted 1961. Chancellor QUB 1963–70 and chairman of the Ulster Theatre Council. To counter emigration, set up preserves factory at Newbliss, Co. Monaghan, near his home, Annaghmakerrig House. Left the house after his wife's death to the Irish state, to be used by writers and artists as a residence at times when they needed to concentrate on their work in tranquillity.

GWYNN, Aubrey (1892–1983), historian and Jesuit, s. of STEPHEN GWYNN, ed. Clongowes, UCD, Queen's College, Oxford and Louvain, d. Dublin. The first student to sign the register of UCD when it became a college of the newly founded National University in 1909. Ordained a Jesuit priest 1924. Lecturer in ancient history UCD 1927; in medieval history 1930; Professor of Medieval History 1949–62. Although his academic training was in the classics, Gwynn became the leading authority of his day on the medieval Irish Church. Among his most important publications are *The Medieval Province of Armagh 1470–1545* and *The Writings of Bishop Patrick 1074–1084*.

GWYNN, Stephen (1864–1950), author, parliamentarian and soldier, distinguished member of a remarkable Irish family, b. Rathfarnham, Co. Dublin, 13 Feb. 1864, ed. St Columba's and Brasenose College, Oxford (first in Greats), d. Dublin, 11 June 1950. Grandson of William Smith O'Brien, Young Ireland leader, he was brother of a Provost of TCD and father of notable historians Denis and AUBREY GWYNN. He left schoolmastering for a long and productive career as an author, writing biographies, memoirs, poetry, travel and historical works. Biographies include studies of Swift, Grattan, Thomas Moore, Scott of the Antarctic and an important work on his political leader, John Redmond (1919).

Member of the Irish Parliamentary Party, he was MP for Galway City 1906–18; he strongly supported Redmond's decision to urge nationalist Ireland into involvement in World War I, enlisting himself in the 16th (Irish) Division and serving as an officer of the Connaught Rangers in France at Messines, the Somme and elsewhere. He never repudiated his wartime service, and later expressed in verse his appreciation of those Irish who participated in World War II. His life bridged several streams of Irish tradition: he came from an old Protestant family and sent his sons to school to PATRICK PEARSE, stood firmly for Home Rule and preserved a deep love for the literature of England. A Chevalier of the Légion d'honneur, he was honoured by the IAL in 1950.

H

HALL, Frank (1921–1995), journalist and broadcaster, b. Newry, ed. CBS, Newry. Waiter in London before joining Independent Newspapers, where he worked in the art department, wrote a column for the *Evening Herald* and reviewed books for the *Irish Independent*. Became a news reporter with Telefís Éireann (later RTÉ) upon its establishment in 1961. He scripted the magazine programme *Newsbeat* and gave it a uniquely humorous flavour which he further developed in the series by which he would be best remembered, *Hall's Pictorial Weekly*. With a small group of talented actors, he reproduced in television format the interests, obsessions, opinions and style of an Irish provincial newspaper, all exaggerated to a level of zaniness which drew the sting from the programme's often incisively critical comment on contemporary political and social attitudes. He later presented a regular analysis on RTÉ radio of the (actual) provincial press and served for a time as film censor, a post from which he retired in 1986.

HALLIGAN, Brendan (1936–), economist and politician, b. Dublin, 5 July 1936, ed. St James's CBS and Kevin Street College of Technology, Dublin, m. Margaret Brennan, July 1964. His early career was as an economist 1963–7, notably with the burgeoning Irish Sugar Company under M.J. COSTELLO; in 1967 his trajectory altered dramatically when he became general secretary of the Labour Party under BRENDAN CORISH, who relied significantly on his intellectual and political skills. The first few years saw an energetic reorganisation of Labour's structures and policies, coinciding with the party's leftward policy shift and a pronounced anti-coalition stance. Halligan was a staunch advocate of both, but was instrumental in securing the eventual, and somewhat unwilling, acceptance by the party of the reversal of anti-coalitionism after the disappointing 1969 general election results. Appointed a member of Seanad Éireann in 1973, he won a by-election to the Dáil in 1976 in Dublin South-West but failed to hold the seat in the general election the following year. In 1980 he resigned as secretary of the party but was nominated briefly to the European Parliament 1983–4. Since 1985 he has been managing partner in a public affairs consultancy. He is also Adjunct Professor in European Affairs at the University of Limerick and was chairman of Bord na Móna 1985–95. His commitment to Europe, necessarily veiled during the party's campaign against the EC referendum in 1972–3, has led to his membership of the Irish Council of the European Movement and to the creation of the Institute of European Affairs, of which he is chairman.

HAMILTON, Hugo (1953–), novelist and short story writer, b. and reared in Berlin, half-German, half-Irish. He has travelled far and wide in Europe and elsewhere. His novels – beautifully crafted, suspenseful and 'deeply satisfying' fictions – are set mainly in Germany and are not immediately identifiable as the work of an Irish writer. They are: *Surrogate City* (1990), *The Last Shot* (1991) and *The Love Test* (1995). Hamilton has also published a volume of short stories: *Dublin Where the Palm Trees Grow* (1996), which perhaps reflects the fact that he has resided in the capital now for a number of years. He has also contributed stories to *The Irish Times*, *Soho Square* (1993) and *First Fictions: Introduction 10* (1989). He won the Rooney prize for Irish literature in 1992.

HAMILTON, Letitia (1876–1964), artist, b. Hamwood, Co. Meath, ed. Alexandra and Metropolitan School of Art, Dublin. She studied under WILLIAM ORPEN in Dublin and later under Frank Brangwyn in Belgium. She travelled widely on the Continent and her development as an artist was heavily influenced by the late French Impressionists, especially Raoul Dufy, and the Irish artists PAUL HENRY and Roderic O'Connor. Her landscapes are painted in subtle tones but use a wide range of colours and shades to enliven the surface. She was made a member of the RHA in 1944 and often exhibited in the Academy's gallery.

Founder member of the Society of Dublin Painters. Her work can be found in the collections of the National Gallery of Ireland, the Hugh Lane Municipal Gallery, Dublin and the Ulster Museum, Belfast.

HAMILTON, Liam (1928–), lawyer and judge, b. Mitchelstown, Co. Cork, ed. CBS, Mitchelstown, UCD and King's Inns. Called to Bar 1956, Inner Bar 1968. Active in Labour Party and a candidate at several municipal elections in Dublin. High Court judge 1974, President of the High Court 1985, Chief Justice 1994. Sole member of the tribunal of inquiry into the beef industry 1991–4 and author of its exhaustive report. Presided over notable trials in the Special Criminal Court, including the Mountbatten murder and the *Eksund* gun-running cases. As Chief Justice delivered Supreme Court judgments rejecting the natural law as a basis for interpreting Irish constitutional law and approving the irretrievable breakdown of marriage as a ground for judicial separation without reference to the cause of breakdown – a decision which influenced the form of amendment proposed in 1995 to permit the introduction of divorce.

HANAHOE, Tony, Gaelic footballer, b. Dublin. He captained the St Vincent's club to its All-Ireland championship win in 1976. He played a major role in the Dublin revival, as a member of the team that beat Galway in the All-Ireland final of 1974 and captain of the teams that won again in 1976 and 1977. He also played on three losing All-Ireland final teams and captained Dublin in the National League victories of 1976 and 1978, later coaching the county's senior squad.

HANLY, David (1944–), broadcaster, b. Limerick, ed. CBS, Sexton Street, Limerick. Civil servant 1962; Radio Éireann (later RTÉ) journalist 1963–70; publicity officer Bord Fáilte 1970–76; freelance writer 1976–81. Rejoined RTÉ and launched the radio news feature breakfast programme *Morning Ireland*, on which he has been from the outset the principal interviewer-presenter. Also presented his own personality interview programme on television, *Hanly's People*. Awards: Jacob's (1985), Benson & Hedges (1986), *Sunday Independent/Irish Life* (1988). Publications: *In Guilt and in Glory* (1979) and a weekly column in the *Sunday Tribune*. Brother of MICK HANLY.

HANLY, Mick (1949–), singer and songwriter, b. Limerick, 3 July 1949. He was one of a group of Irish country music performers that emerged during the 1980s and that differed from their showband predecessors in that they wrote most of their own music and adhered to a 'country-rock' style of playing. Hanly has been by far the most commercially successful of these singer/songwriters. In 1992 the Hal Ketchum recording of his song 'Past the Point of Rescue' reached number two in the American charts and won him a BMI award for the most played country song on American radio. After a year with Moving Hearts he formed his own band, Rusty Old Halo, with whom he recorded the critically acclaimed album, *Still Not Cured* in 1986. Since then he has recorded three solo albums with Round Tower Music, *All I Remember* (1989), *Warts & All* (1991) and *Happy Like This* (1993). Brother of DAVID HANLY.

HANNON, Mary Josephine (1865–1935), early woman doctor, b. Riverstown, Killucan, Co. Westmeath, ed. RCSI, which on 10 Jan. 1885 had decided to extend its facilities to women. The first woman student on the college's books was Miss Agnes Shannon, who did not persist with her studies. Hannon was the first Irishwoman to graduate (LRCP&SI) having studied in an Irish medical school. She registered as a medical practitioner on 30 July 1890 and worked in India at Dufferin Hospital, Ulwar State, Rajputana. She returned to Europe but settled in the Transvaal at Pretoria.

HANSON, Anthony Tyrrell (1916–1991), Church of Ireland biblical scholar and systematic theologian, b. 24 Nov. 1916, d. 28 May 1991. Ordained deacon 1941, priest 1942. Held several lecturing posts in India before being appointed canon theologian St Anne's Cathedral, Belfast 1959–62. Professor of Theology, Hull 1963–81. Publications include *Reasonable Belief: A Survey of the Christian Faith*, with his twin RICHARD HANSON (1980), and *The Bible without Illusions* (1989)

HANSON, Richard Patrick Crosland (1916–1988), Church of Ireland bishop and theologian, b. 24 Nov. 1916, ed. Cheltenham and TCD, scholar in classics. Ordained deacon 1941, priest 1942, bishop 1970. Head of Department of Theology, Nottingham 1964–70. Bishop of Clogher 1970–82. Assistant Bishop of Manchester. Publications include *St Patrick: His Origins and Career* (1965), *Reasonable Belief: A Survey of the Christian Faith*, with his twin ANTHONY HANSON (1980), and *The Life and Writings of the Historical St Patrick* (1983). Edited *The Pelican Guide to Modern Theology*.

HARBISON, Peter Desmond (1939–), archaeologist and art historian, b. Dublin, ed. Glenstal, UCD, Freiburg, Kiel and Marburg (Ph.D. 1964). Excavated in Spain and Portugal, an authority on the weapons and artefacts of the Early Bronze Age in Ireland and on the Celtic high crosses. Archaeological officer with Bord Fáilte since 1966 and editor until 1995 of its magazine, *Ireland of the Welcomes*. Publications include: *A Guide to the National Monuments in the Republic of Ireland* (1970), *Irish Art and Architecture from Prehistory to the Present*, with Jeanne Sheehy and Homer Potterton (1978), *Pre-Christian Ireland* (1988) and *The High Crosses of Ireland* (1992).

HARDIMAN, Thomas Patrick (1929–), public servant, engineer, broadcaster and company director, b. Dublin, ed. Coláiste Mhuire and UCD (BE Mech. and Elec., B.Sc.). Joined Department of Posts and Telegraphs 1952 and Radio Éireann 1955. Served in many areas of the broadcasting service, becoming director of engineering of RTÉ in 1967 and director-general in 1968. He left in 1975 and became extensively involved in the private sector, serving on the boards of various companies, including the Bank of Ireland, while at the same time undertaking a number of public sector responsibilities, being first chairman of the National Board for Science and Technology and chairman of the Irish Goods Council. Director of the National Planning Board 1983–5. Chairman of the Technological Education Review Commission 1986–8, which led to the establishment of the two new universities in Dublin and Limerick. A member of the EC's committees on research and development and on telecommunications research. President of the Confederation of Irish Industry 1982–4, of the Marketing Institute 1984–7 and of the Dublin Chamber of Commerce 1988–9; of the industrial affairs committee of the Confederation of European Industry, Brussels 1984–8, and of the International Institute of Communications 1983–8. Frequent contributor to national and international journals on various topics, includ-

ing industrial policy, higher education, telecommunications, Euro-Japanese relations. MRIA 1980. Order of the Rising Sun, Japan 1986. LL D (NUI) 1990. Supervisory Board of the EU–Japan Centre for Industrial Co-operation 1994.

HARNEY, Mary (1953–), politician, b. Ballinasloe, Co. Galway, 11 Mar. 1953, to parents from a small farm background, brought up mainly in Newcastle, Co. Dublin, ed. Convent of Mercy, Inchicore, Coláiste Bríde, Clondalkin, Dublin and TCD – where she became the first woman auditor of the College Historical Society. It was in that role that she came to the attention of Fianna Fáil leader JACK LYNCH, who secured her a party nomination in the Dublin South-East constituency at the 1977 general election. She was unsuccessful, but when Lynch became Taoiseach after that election she was one of his Seanad nominees.

She won a Dáil seat in Dublin South-West in 1981 and at each subsequent general election. Had a number of difficulties with FF following the election of CHARLES HAUGHEY as leader and finally quitted, having defied the party whip by voting in favour of the Anglo-Irish Agreement of 1985. She was instrumental in the establishment of the Progressive Democrat party in Dec. of that year.

On the formation of the FF–PD coalition government in 1989 she was appointed Minister of State at the Department of the Environment. Responsible for legislation outlawing the sale and use of bituminous fuel in the Dublin area and for legislation that led to the establishment of an independent environmental agency. She became leader of the PDs after DESMOND O'MALLEY's resignation in Oct. 1993, the first woman to lead a party in Dáil Éireann.

HARPER, Charles (1942–), artist, b. Valentia Island, Co. Kerry, 30 July 1942, ed. Crescent College, Limerick, National College of Art, Dublin, Limerick School of Art and Fisherkoesen Film Studio, Bonn. He has been head of fine arts at the Limerick School of Art and Design since 1975, and has for several years been a member of the fine art committee in the Project Arts Centre, Dublin. Awards include the Carroll's open award at the Irish Exhibition of Living Art in 1971. His work has been shown in several European countries, the USA and India. A retrospective exhibition was held in Kilkenny in 1980. His experience with a range of visual media, including printing and film-making, has helped him to bring a breadth of vision to the subjects of his work, which are painted in an expressionist manner.

HARRIS, Richard (1930–), actor, b. Limerick city, 1 Oct. 1930, ed. Crescent College, Limerick and London Academy of Music and Dramatic Art. Made his stage début in 1956 in Joan Littlewood's production of BRENDAN BEHAN's *The Quare Fellow*. After his first screen role in 1958 (Cyril Frankel's *Alive and Kicking*), he progressed through some typecast Irish parts until his breakthrough as the Rugby League player Frank Machin in Lindsay Anderson's *This Sporting Life* (1963), for which he received an Oscar nomination as best actor. Despite some fine performances subsequently, he never attained superstar status. In 1969 he recorded 'MacArthur Park', which sold over five million copies. Besides his definitive performance as King Arthur in the stage version of *Camelot* in the early 1980s, his most impressive role in recent years has been as Bull McCabe in JIM SHERIDAN's *The Field* (1990), for which he was again nominated for an Oscar.

HARTNETT, Michael (1941–), poet and translator, b. Croom, Co. Limerick, ed. Newcastle West, UCD and TCD. Co-editor of *Arena* 1963–5 and poetry editor of *The Irish Times*. Held diverse jobs before returning to Co. Limerick to live and write in Irish. Won the Irish-American Cultural Institute award 1975; lecturer in creative writing at Thomond College, Limerick 1976–8. Hartnett bestrides the English–Gaelic divide, having acquired his poetic heritage from 18th-century ancestors. He bade 'A Farewell to English' in a 1975 poem and kept his vow for ten years. He has published 12 books of English poetry, four of Irish, and translations from Irish, Spanish and Chinese, including *The Hag of Beare* (1969), *Gypsy Ballads* by García Lorca (1970), *Tao* (1971), *Cúlúíde: The Retreat of Ita Cagney* (1975), *Selected Poems of Dáibhí Ó Bruadair* (1985), *Portrait of the Artist as an Abominable Snowman*, selected poems of GABRIEL ROSENSTOCK (1989), *The Midnight Verdict* (1993). He is a member of Aosdána.

HARTY, Hamilton (1879–1941), composer, conductor, pianist and organist, b. Hillsborough, Co. Down, d. Brighton. Taught viola, piano and counterpoint by his father. Advised and helped by MICHELE ESPOSITO in Dublin. In 1900 he went to London, where the Comedy Overture, performed at the Promenade Concerts in 1907, established him as a composer. *With the Wild Geese* was first performed in 1910 at Cardiff. He conducted the Hallé Orchestra in Manchester frequently during World War I, was appointed its permanent conductor in 1920 and made it probably the best orchestra in England. Champion of Bax, Walton, Constant Lambert and E.J. Moeran, among others. He conducted the first performance in England of Mahler's Ninth Symphony in 1930 and of Shostakovich's First Symphony in 1932. His own Irish Symphony was written during this period. His flamboyant orchestrations of Handel's *Water Music* and *Music for the Royal Fireworks* have become standard works. Harty's career with the Hallé ended in resignation and some acrimony in 1933; after this he was principally associated with the London orchestras. Honours and awards included a knighthood in 1925 and the gold medal of the Royal Philharmonic Society in 1934.

HAUGHEY, Charles (1925–), politician, b. Castlebar, 16 Sept. 1925, ed. St Joseph's CBS, Dublin, UCD and King's Inns, m. Maureen Lemass, d. of SEÁN LEMASS, three s. one d. His father, Sean, and mother, Sara Williams, both originally from Swatragh, Co. Derry, were involved in the War of Independence. At the time of Charles's birth Sean Haughey was serving in the army but, suffering from multiple sclerosis, he was forced to retire and the family lived on his army pension in Donnycarney, north Dublin. Initially unsuccessful in his bids for public office, Charles Haughey was eventually elected to the Dáil for Fianna Fáil in 1957. At this stage he was employed in the accountancy firm Haughey, Boland. He topped the poll in his constituency at each subsequent general election. His first ministerial appointment was as parliamentary secretary to justice minister OSCAR TRAYNOR in 1961. Later that year he entered the cabinet as Minister for Justice himself. There, he was responsible for a major piece of law reform in the Succession Act, which guaranteed financial entitlement for widows. He also introduced military courts shortly before the IRA called off its sporadic and unsuccessful military campaign against British border installations. Minister for Agriculture 1964–6 and for Finance 1966–70. His ministerial successes and brash manner upset some party traditionalists. When Seán Lemass retired as Taoiseach in 1966 Haughey was one of the main contenders but withdrew in favour of a compromise candidate, JACK LYNCH. The frustration caused by this forced compromise was to have repercussions in later years.

In the late 1960s a civil rights campaign for Catholics in Northern Ireland provoked repression by security forces and loyalist attacks on Catholic targets. Nationalists and Catholics demanded aid from the government of the Republic. Few were aware of Haughey's family background and his instinct to support those seeking help. Taoiseach Jack Lynch accused Haughey and NEIL BLANEY of not fully subscribing to government policy on Northern Ireland and dismissed them. Sensationally, in May 1970 Haughey was arrested and charged before the courts with conspiring to import arms illegally: a jury finally acquitted him of all charges. The events led to five years in the political wilderness as he tried to build himself a new base in the party. In 1975, with FF performing poorly in opposition having lost power in 1973, Lynch bowed reluctantly to party pressure and invited Haughey back on to his front bench. After FF's sweeping success in the 1977 general election, Lynch appointed Haughey Minister for Health. With many of the newly elected FF TDs nervous about holding on to their seats at the next general election, Lynch came under significant political pressure and in 1979 decided to retire. Against most media predictions, Haughey defeated his old rival GEORGE COLLEY for the post of party leader, and, after an acrimonious Dáil debate in which he was subjected to unprecedented attacks on his character, was duly elected Taoiseach.

His government failed to come to grips with serious problems in the public finances and he lost office in 1981, but the incoming Fine Gael–Labour coalition fell on its 1982 budget. A general election ensued and Haughey once again became Taoiseach, this time of a minority FF administration, the first of several bids to oust him as leader having failed.

Beset by a number of political controversies, he too soon lost power and the previous coalition returned with a secure overall majority after another general election in Nov. of the same year. Haughey had an undistinguished period as leader of the opposition but at the general election of 1987 scraped back into power, once again leading a minority administration. That government was, perhaps, his most successful, especially in the progress it made towards restoring balance to the public finances. Two years later, frustrated by a number of minor parliamentary defeats and tempted by encouraging opinion polls, he called a snap election. Instead of gaining, FF deteriorated further in strength and Haughey, to the amazement of many, became the first leader of his party to enter a coalition – this time with the Progressive Democrats, one of whose reasons for existing had been the inability of some former FF TDs to accept Haughey's iron control of his party. He skilfully steered that government through uncharted waters but renewed pressure on his leadership arose, this time from those who had once been his most enthusiastic supporters. Early in 1992 his former justice minister SEÁN DOHERTY said that Haughey had been aware of phone taps on two political writers while Taoiseach in the brief 1982 government. Haughey denied this but, bowing to the inevitable, decided to resign, and was succeeded by ALBERT REYNOLDS.

Haughey was among the most controversial of Irish political leaders – being loved and loathed in almost equal proportions. He had mixed success as Taoiseach, typified in an early good relationship with British Prime Minister Margaret Thatcher, which later soured. His son Seán succeeded him as TD for Dublin North-Central in 1992.

HAUGHTON, William Steele (1869–1951), surgeon and radiologist, b. Dublin, youngest s. of Samuel Haughton FTCD, a noted polymath, ed. Portora and TCD, m. Jane Eliza Halahan, one s. one d., d. Dublin, 12 Oct. 1951. Graduated in medicine in 1891. He joined the staff at Sir Patrick Dun's Hospital in 1895 but in 1899 moved to Dr Steevens's Hospital, which he served for more than 50 years, known to generations of students as 'Baldy' Haughton.

He is generally regarded as the pioneer of clinical radiology in Ireland. He spoke to the Academy of Medicine on 'Some Applications of the X-Rays: Diagnosis' on 7 May 1897. At classes held for colleagues, he hid coins in bread and required his pupils to locate them by X-rays in three dimensions. Speaking again to the Academy in Mar. 1902 he encouraged physicians to use X-rays, which they neglected due to 'a natural diffidence to adopt a new method of examination whose utility was unproven'. He supplied many instances of its usefulness. First president of the Radiological Society of Ireland.

Numerous publications include *Mechanical Structure and Bone Demonstrated by Röntgen Stereoscopy* (1901) and *Aseptic versus Antiseptic Methods* (1904).

HAYES, Joanne (1959–), b. Abbeydorney, Co. Kerry. She was the figure at the centre of the famous 'Kerry babies' case during the mid-1980s. In Apr. 1984 she gave birth secretly to a boy who died very soon afterwards. Later, under police interrogation, she confessed to the murder, by stabbing, of another baby, even though medical evidence showed that the murdered child was not hers. A tribunal set up to investigate why she had confessed to this crime involved a detailed examination of her sexual history and personal life in order to test the Garda hypothesis that she had had twins by two different men. Her treatment during the tribunal became a cause célèbre for Irish feminists and was the subject of a book by NELL MCCAFFERTY, *A Woman to Blame*.

HAYES, John M. (1887–1957), canon, churchman and social reformer, b. Murroe, Co. Limerick, 11 Nov. 1887, ed. Crescent College, Limerick, St Patrick's College, Thurles and Irish College, Paris, d. 22 May 1957. Ordained priest 1913. As a curate in the rural parish of Castleiny, Co. Tipperary, and as the son of a small farmer, he sympathised with the problems of the agricultural community at a time of economic recession. Influenced by Pope Leo XIII's encyclical *Rerum Novarum*, he founded the self-help body Muintir na Tíre in 1931. At first a marketing co-operative, it developed in line with the 'vocational' theory then widely favoured, not least in the Roman Catholic Church, that society should be organised into groups representing different interests and activities. A Muintir parish guild typically comprised farmers, farm labourers, professional people and the unemployed. This echoed the teaching of a new encyclical, *Quadragesimo Anno*, fortuitously published by Pope Pius XI a week after the foundation of Muintir and promoted energetically by Fr Hayes.

Under the guidance of its founder, Muintir ran weekend and week-long seminars in various parts of the country at which delegates from the parishes discussed ideas for rural development with experts in appropriate subjects; Fr Hayes often addressed these 'Rural Weeks' himself. The guilds meanwhile undertook house repairs, tree-planting, the provision of group water schemes and much else. Canon Hayes, as he ultimately became (having been appointed parish priest of Bansha, Co. Tipperary, 1946), increasingly denounced state intervention in the lives of citizens, although the state was happy to have his services as a member of its Commission on Vocational Organisation 1939–43. He lectured widely in Ireland and the USA, and can fairly be considered the most effective advocate of Catholic social thinking in 20th-century Ireland.

HAYES, Richard (1882–1958), medical doctor, revolutionary, historian and film censor, b. Bruree, Co. Limerick, ed. Catholic University Medical School, Dublin. Dispensary doctor, Lusk, Co. Dublin. Commanded Fingal Battalion, Irish Volunteers, but served as medical officer under THOMAS ASHE and RICHARD MULCAHY at Ashbourne, Co. Meath, where the battalion achieved the insurgents' only military success during the Easter Rising. Received death sentence (commuted), was released and rearrested. TD (SF Limerick) in First Dáil and subsequently; supported Anglo-Irish Treaty 1921. Retired from politics 1924. Dispensary doctor, Donnybrook, Dublin. Film censor 1940–54. An authority on Irish connections with France, especially in the 18th and 19th centuries; publications included *Irish Swordsmen of France* (1934) and an account of the Humbert expedition of 1798, *The Last Invasion of Ireland* (1937). Member RIA and Légion d'honneur, hon. D.Litt. (NUI).

HAYES, Richard James (1902–1976), librarian and scholar, b. Abbeyfeale, Co. Limerick, ed. Clongowes and TCD, d. Dublin, 21 Jan. 1976. After a brilliant undergraduate career in Celtic studies, languages and philosophy, he joined the National Library in 1926, rising to the position of director in 1940. His fame rests on his achievement as a bibliographer. In *Clár Litrídheachta Nua-Ghaedhilge* (three vols. 1938–40) he catalogued a vast array of modern material in the Irish language. His magnum opus, however, was his cataloguing and copying of Irish documents from all over the world under the title *Manuscript Sources for the History of Irish Civilisation* (11 vols. 1965). Drawing on some 1,300 archives, both public and private, in 30 different countries, the whole work contains more than 300,000 entries. His final book, *Sources for the History of Irish Civilisation: Articles and Periodicals*, appeared in 1970, three years after his retirement.

HAYES, William (1913–1994), FRS, microbial geneticist, b. 18 Jan. 1913, ed. St Columba's and TCD. Lecturer TCD 1947–50, senior lecturer in bacteriology University of London Postgraduate Medical School 1950–57. Director Microbial Genetics Unit, Edinburgh 1957–68; Professor of Molecular Genetics Edinburgh 1968–73; professor and head of genetics department, School of Biological Sciences, Australian National University, 1974–8. Fairchild Distinguished Scholar, Biology Division, California Institute of Technology, 1979–80; visiting fellow, Department of Botany, Australian National University, 1980–86; Emeritus Professor of Genetics Australian National University since 1979. Publications include *The Genetics of Bacteria and their Viruses* (1964, 1968) and *Experiments in Microbial Genetics* (1968).

HAYES, William (1930–), academic, b. Killorglin, Co. Kerry, 12 Nov. 1930, s. of Robert and Eileen Hayes, ed. Synge Street, UCD (M.Sc., Ph.D.) and Oxford (MA, D.Phil.) 1951. Overseas scholar St John's College, Oxford 1955–7, official fellow and tutor 1960–87, principal bursar 1977–87, president since 1987. University lecturer in physics 1962. Director and head of the Clarendon Laboratory 1985–7, senior research fellow of the laboratory since then. Member of the general board of the faculties 1985–8, member of the Hebdomadal Council since 1989 and Pro-Vice Chancellor of Oxford University 1990. Chairman of the Curators of University Chest since 1992, delegate of Oxford University

Press since 1991 and chairman of the trustees of the Oxford Institute of Legal Practice 1993. Visiting fellowships and professorships at the Argonne Laboratory, Purdue University, RCA Laboratories, Princeton, University of Illinois and Bell Laboratories. Hon. D.Sc. (NUI) 1988.

HAYES-McCOY, Gerard Anthony (1911–1975), historian, b. Galway, ed. Patrician Brothers, Galway, UCD, Edinburgh and London. Attached to National Museum 1939–58. Professor of History UCG 1958–75. For many years the leading authority on Irish military history, co-founder of the Military History Society, editor of the *Irish Sword* 1949–60. Wrote extensively on Irish battles, weapons, flags and related subjects.

HEALY, Cahir (1877–1970), politician and journalist, b. Mount Charles, Co. Donegal, Healy moved to Enniskillen at the age of 18. He worked as a journalist on several local papers as well as in a solicitor's office and as a land agent. Joined Sinn Féin in 1905 and in May 1922 was arrested and interned. Elected to Westminster parliament as MP for Fermanagh–Tyrone in 1922 while still interned, his case led to heated exchanges in the House of Commons. On his release he returned to Enniskillen, from where he was excluded, and was immediately rearrested. British pressure once more led to his release in Mar. 1924. Retired in that year but was elected for Fermanagh–Tyrone again at a by-election in 1931, holding the seat until 1935, and was MP for Fermanagh–South Tyrone 1950–55. Elected for Fermanagh and Tyrone to Stormont parliament 1925 and for South Fermanagh 1929–65.

A founder member of United Irish League and Irish Anti-Partition League, Healy wrote numerous articles for the *Weekly News* and the *Irish News*, of which he was a director, and collaborated with Cathal O'Byrne on a book of verse, *The Lane of the Thrushes*. Campaigned with ARTHUR GRIFFITH in the first election contested by Sinn Féin in North Leitrim. An associate of W.B. YEATS, ALICE MILLIGAN and ETHNA CARBERY. His obituary in the *Irish News* noted: 'Though a bitter opponent of discrimination and injustice and an unrepentant Republican, he was esteemed for his ability and gentle manner by every member at Stormont, without exception.'

HEALY, Dermot (1947–), writer, editor, poet and dramatist, b. Finea, Co. Westmeath. Long an important presence in western Ireland, he edited for a time the Cavan-based literary and local history magazine the *Drumlin*, and later the community arts journal *Force 10*. Healy's short stories won him Hennessy literary awards in 1974 and 1976, and he has published a collection, *Banished Misfortune and Other Stories* (1982). From the 1980s to the present he has divided his time between drama and fiction. He wrote the film script for *Our Boys* (1980) and the stage plays *The Long Swim* (1986), *Here and There* and *Going to America* (1987), *Blood Wedding*, an adaptation (1990), and *On Broken Wings* (1992); he has also directed and acted in several plays and films. Won the Tom Gallon award 1983. He has published two superb novels so far: *Fighting with Shadows, or Sciamachy* (1984) and *A Goat's Song* (1994), and a collection of poems, *The Ballyconnell Colours* (1992). He lives in Maugherow, Co. Sligo.

HEALY, John (1930–1991), journalist, broadcaster and reporter, b. Charlestown, Co. Mayo, ed. St Nathy's, Ballaghaderreen, Co. Roscommon, d. 6 Jan. 1991. Joined *Western People* as a reporter in 1948 and came to Dublin in 1950 to join the newly formed Irish News Agency. When it closed down he joined the *Irish Press* and *Evening Press* under DOUGLAS GAGEBY. Editor of the *Sunday Review* from 1959 until its demise in 1963, then moved briefly to the *Evening Mail*, which had been acquired by *The Irish Times*. He launched the 'Backbencher' column in the *Sunday Review* with TED NEALON, and it soon became compulsive reading for anyone interested in Irish politics. The two men found conduits to senior politicians, especially among the thrusting young Turks of the new-style Fianna Fáil party, and were able to write with great authority of political rumours and predictions. The column transferred to *The Irish Times* when the *Sunday Review* closed down, and remained for many years an influential font of political information.

Politics and the day-to-day chores of journalism and reporting were the abiding interests of Healy's life. He wrote – sometimes at inordinate length – of the happenings in the smoke-filled rooms of political parties, often imaginatively, always entertainingly. He liked to see himself as the cool observer, knowledgeable, incorruptible, but he was too deeply immersed in the sheer joy of politicking in the old, almost American style, to be always totally impartial. He won a Jacob's award for his television programme *Headlines and Deadlines* and inaugurated the programme *The Hurler on the Ditch*. A committed regionalist, it was natural that he should have returned to his Connacht roots in 1975 to co-found and edit the weekly *Western Journal*. He was a champion of the people of rural Ireland, especially the west. His articles about the history and his experiences of Mayo were later published as a book, *Nobody Shouted Stop – The Death of an Irish Town*, which became a classic.

In 1979 he spent six months in Strasbourg observing the European Parliament and subsequently used his expertise in writing many articles on Europe for *The Irish Times*, with which he had an on-and-off relationship for most of his professional life.

HEALY, Michael (1873–1941), illustrator and stained-glass artist, b. Dublin, 14 Nov. 1873, d. 22 Sept. 1941. Left school at a young age, worked in several Dublin businesses before going to the Metropolitan School of Art in 1897 and then to the RHA school, where he received first prize for drawing from life: perhaps not surprisingly, as he had already made many acutely observed sketches of the people in the streets of his native city. His first commission came from the Dominican fathers, for whose journal, the *Irish Rosary*, he did a number of illustrations. The Dominicans then helped him to study in Florence for a time before employing him as an art teacher at Newbridge College, Co. Kildare. In 1903 he joined SARAH PURSER's stained-glass window workshop, An Túr Gloine, which was to be his base throughout his working life.

Healy's brilliant handling of strong colours, his graceful figure work and his technical skill show to perfection in the glorious sequence of windows which he made for Loughrea Cathedral (Co. Galway), but can also be admired in many other church buildings, among them the Capuchin church at Rochestown (Co. Cork), the Catholic parish church of Dundrum (Co. Dublin), and the Church of Ireland churches of Rathmines

(Dublin), Gowran (Co. Kilkenny) and St Mark's (Dundela, Belfast). He made windows also for the school chapels in Blackrock and Clongowes – including, for the latter, three of the seven windows on the theme of the Seven Dolours of Our Lady, the rest of which were completed after his death by EVIE HONE. Together with Hone and HARRY CLARKE, Michael Healy must be counted among the finest 20th-century artists in stained glass.

HEALY, Timothy (1855–1931), politician, b. Bantry, Co. Cork, 17 May 1855, ed. CBS, Fermoy, Co. Cork, d. 26 Mar. 1931. Emigrated to England, covered parliament for the *Nation* newspaper. MP (IP Wexford 1880; later successively Monaghan, Londonderry South, Louth North, Cork North-East). Called to Bar 1884. Active in the Parnellite politics of the 1880s but bitterly opposed to Parnell at the 'split': his invective was long remembered and resented by those loyal to the leader. Quarrelled with the leadership of the reunited Irish Parliamentary Party, from which he was expelled in 1902, but retained a seat in parliament with the help of his friends WILLIAM MARTIN MURPHY and WILLIAM O'BRIEN. In 1918 he vacated his seat in Cork to facilitate the election of a Sinn Féin prisoner, having himself become converted to the political objectives of Sinn Féin after the Easter Rising. In spite of criticism from anti-Treatyites as well as his former opponents within the Irish Party, he was appointed first Governor-General of the Irish Free State in 1922 and served until 1928.

HEANEY, Seamus (1939–), poet and Nobel laureate, b. Castledawson, near Mossbawn, Co. Derry, ed. St Columb's College, Derry and QUB. If W.B. YEATS was the premier poet in these islands during the first half of the 20th century, then there were three candidates tipped to succeed him: Philip Larkin, Ted Hughes and Seamus Heaney. Larkin died in 1985; Hughes became the Poet Laureate; Heaney, in 1995, took the trophy that brought him close to Yeats in stature: the Nobel prize for literature. And Heaney, like Yeats before him, has done more than most to bring poetry under the gaze of the general public. Yet a list of the resemblances between the two must end here, for the Derryman is a different kind of poet. He grew up among a people whose rural life was harsh and unremitting, married totally to the soil. Heaney brought some of their attitudes and aspirations with him when he studied at QUB. Belfast changed him; there was no escaping the politics, and Heaney was conscious of pressure to become a spokesman for the Catholic community. Instead, he chose to move south with his family, taking a cottage in Ashford, Co. Wicklow, 1972–6. The sojourn produced *Wintering Out* (1972) and *North* (1976), collections that set the tone for much of Heaney's future work. He delves down deep in the boglands of Ireland and Europe, seeking to find among the Viking bones and old Irish place names clues to the nature of the madness that has gripped his compatriots. Excavation – of the land, of the past, of the self – remained a leitmotiv in his work. In the course of the next two decades he held teaching posts in Dublin, then Belfast, and the University of California, Berkeley. He was Professor of Poetry at Oxford 1989–94 and is now Boylston Professor of Rhetoric at Harvard. Heaney has been accorded most of the literary honours to be won in Ireland and the UK.

Other important collections include: *Death of a Naturalist* (1966), *Door into the Dark* (1969), *Field Work* (1979), *Hailstones* (1984), *Station Island* (1985), *The Haw Lantern* (1987), *Seeing Things* (1991) and *Sweeney's Flight* (1992).

HEARNE, John (1893–1968), lawyer and public servant, b. Waterford, ed. Waterpark, NUI and King's Inns, m., three children. Assistant parliamentary draftsman 1923–9, legal adviser to the Department of External Affairs 1929–39. In 1935, at the request of EAMON DE VALERA, he drew up the heads of a new constitution and he is accepted as the main contributor to the formulation of that document in drafting the articles and in co-ordinating the submissions from outside the government. High commissioner to Canada in 1939 and ambassador to the USA in 1950.

HEDERMAN O'BRIEN, Miriam (1932–), policy consultant, b. 6 June 1932, née Hederman, ed. Mount Anville, UCD, King's Inns (BL) and TCD (Ph.D.). Irish secretary European Youth Campaign 1954–7; later honorary secretary Irish Council of the European Movement, chairperson and vice-president. Frequent broadcaster, especially on east–west European affairs; member (later chairwoman) Broadcasting Complaints Commission 1977–80. Chaired the Commission on Taxation 1980–85; also the Foundation for Fiscal Studies, the international executive of the European Cultural Foundation and the Commission on Funding the Health Services (1987–9). Member of many other bodies, including the Irish Centre for European Law and the NESC (1984–94). Director AIB from 1986. Killeen fellowship for research into exchange training, education and professional formation between Ireland and Czechoslovakia, Hungary and Poland (1990–92). Published work includes *The Road to Europe: Irish Attitudes to European Integration 1948–61* (1983) and *Eastern Exchanges* (1992), as well as numerous contributions to professional journals. European Order of Merit (1984), gold medal and Order of Merit of the President of Poland (1992).

HEFFERNAN, Kevin ('Heffo'), Gaelic footballer and trainer, hurler, b. Dublin. He will always be associated with the great Dublin football teams of the 1970s which he coached to All-Ireland successes in 1974, 1976 and 1977 and to National League titles in 1976 and 1978, the era when the side's ecstatic followers were dubbed 'Heffo's Army', and in 1974 he became the only non-player to be nominated Texaco Footballer of the Year. But his playing days were also distinguished: he captained Dublin to All-Ireland victory in 1958, was in the National League-winning teams of 1953, 1955 and 1958, and won seven Railway Cup medals with Leinster. He played for Dublin at minor, junior and senior levels in both hurling and football, and also helped his club, St Vincent's, to win the County Championship in both sports.

HEITLER, Walter (1904–1981), FRS, theoretical physicist, b. Karlsruhe, 2 Jan. 1904, d. Zurich, 15 Nov. 1981. Although he lived in Ireland only from 1941 to 1949, he became an Irish citizen and remained one for the rest of his life. He was appointed at quite a junior level to the new Dublin Institute for Advanced Studies, but soon built up an active and productive group which in certain respects led the world. Promoted to senior professor in 1945. His main work was in the quantum theory of radiation, and he wrote what became – and to some extent still is – the standard

reference book on the subject. He also took a close interest in the new mesons. Appointed to a professorship in Zurich in 1949.

HENCHY, Seamus (1927–), lawyer and judge, b. Co. Clare, ed. St Mary's College, Galway, UCG, UCD and King's Inns. MA, LL B and Ph.D. (NUI). Called to Bar 1942, Senior Counsel 1959; Professor of Roman Law, Jurisprudence and Legal History UCD 1948–62. High Court judge 1962–72, Supreme Court judge 1972–88, retiring to become chairman of the Independent Radio and TV Commission 1988–93. Chaired Commission on Mental Illness 1962–6, member of Anglo-Irish Commission on Law Enforcement 1974. On the retirement in 1972 of Chief Justice CEARBHALL Ó DÁLAIGH, Mr Justice Henchy became with Mr Justice BRIAN WALSH a member of the liberal wing of the Supreme Court. Among the major constitutional cases he was involved in as a judge were the McGee case (1974) on marital privacy, the DAVID NORRIS case (1984) on homosexuality and the RAYMOND CROTTY case (1987) on the Single European Act, probably the most controversial Supreme Court decision for 50 years.

HENDERSON, Robert *Brumwell* (1929–), television executive, b. Hillsborough, Co. Down, 28 July 1929, ed. Brackenber House School, Belfast, Bradfield College School, Berkshire and TCD (BA 1951, MA 1959). Worked as a journalist for several years in London, Liverpool, Glasgow and Belfast. Appointed managing director of UTV in 1959, chairman 1983–91. He has been vice-president of Co-operation North since 1984 and was president of the Northern Ireland Chamber of Commerce and Industry 1980–81. His publications include *Midnight Oil* (1961), *A Television First* (1977) and *Amusing* (1984).

HENN, Thomas Rice (1901–1974), academic, critic and W.B. YEATS scholar, b. Sligo, ed. Manor School, Fermoy, Co. Cork, Aldenham and St Catharine's College, Cambridge, where he took modern languages. He later taught at his Alma Mater: as fellow of St Catharine's and lecturer 1926, senior tutor 1945–57 and president 1951–61. Taught in Burma 1923–5 and TCD 1965. Henn took a commission in the British army in 1939, was promoted to brigadier, awarded military CBE and American Legion of Merit, and twice mentioned in dispatches. He devoted the rest of his life to Anglo-Irish literature and was instrumental in the foundation of the Yeats International Summer School, of which he was director until 1969, becoming its patron in 1972 on the death of PÁDRAIC COLUM. His published work includes critical studies, notably of Yeats – *The Lonely Tower* (1950) – and *The Plays and Poems of J.M. Synge* (1963), some biography, as well as anglers' guides and manuals on automatic weapons. His lively prose illuminated many areas of Irish society.

HENNESSY, Patrick (1915–1981), artist, b. Cork, ed. Dundee College of Art. He returned to Ireland from Scotland in 1939 and lived in Dublin and Cork. In the early 1970s he went to live on the Continent but spent long periods in Morocco. He had several solo exhibitions in Dublin and London and was the subject of a retrospective exhibition in the RHA in 1952 and a tribute exhibition in Cork in 1981 shortly after his death. MRHA 1949. Hennessy's early work was heavily influenced by the surrealists but he later adopted a more literal style. While there is obviously a concern with precise rendering and minute attention to detail in his landscapes, especially the later photorealist work, the paintings retain the depth and sense of unease characteristic of the surrealist approach.

HENRY, Arnold Kirkpatrick (1886–1962), surgeon and author, b. Dublin, ed. Trent College, England and TCD. MB (1911), FRCSI (1914). He served as surgeon in the Serbian and French armies and the RAMC. After the war he joined the staff of the Richmond Hospital and edited the *Irish Journal of Medical Science*. He resigned from those posts in 1925 when appointed Professor of Surgery in the University of Cairo. His classic work on limb surgery, *Extensile Exposure*, was published in 1927. The emeritus professor left Egypt 11 years later to take a teaching post in London at the Postgraduate Medical School, Hammersmith. He returned to Dublin in 1947 as Professor of Anatomy RCSI. He is honoured by the annual 'A.K. Henry Lecture' in the college.

HENRY, Grace (1868–1953), artist, b. Emily Grace Mitchell, Aberdeenshire, ed. privately. She did not begin her formal education in art until 1900, then studied in Brussels and Paris, where she married PAUL HENRY 1903. They lived for several years in Achill, Co. Mayo but her career began to flourish only when she moved to Dublin in 1920. She studied in France under André Lhote and had her first solo exhibition in the Magee Gallery, Belfast in 1923. Henry travelled extensively in Italy and the south of France and the bold, colourful style she had developed in Achill was adapted to capture the sunlit Mediterranean landscapes. She had frequent exhibitions in Dublin galleries and at the RHA.

HENRY, Paul (1877–1958), artist, b. Belfast, the son of a Baptist minister, ed. Royal Academical Institution, Belfast School of Art and the Académie Julian in Paris, m. GRACE HENRY, d. Enniskerry, Co. Wicklow, 28 Aug. 1958. Henry is best known for his oil paintings of the landscape of the west of Ireland, where he lived for seven years. The influence of Whistler, with whom he studied while in Paris, is very evident in the subtle colouring of these works. He moved to Dublin in 1920 and was elected to the RHA in 1929. Henry was originally trained as a designer and undertook a number of poster commissions for the Irish Tourist Board and the London & Scottish Railway.

HENRY, Sam (1878–1952), folk song collector. By profession a public servant, working in the sphere of inland revenue and pensions. The nature of his employment allowed him to indulge his passion for collecting folk songs directly from the ordinary people who sang them. Many of these were published by the Coleraine newspaper the *Northern Constitution*, which ran a series entitled 'Songs of the People' 1923–39, in which readers were provided with both words and music. Henry submitted the largest proportion of these, in all well over 600 songs, sourced mainly in Co. Derry and north Co. Antrim. Many have been reprinted in book form, *Songs of the People*, compiled by John Moulden.

HERBERT, Victor (1859–1924), composer, cellist and conductor, b. Dublin. Grandson of the Irish novelist, poet and composer Samuel Lover. Went to New York in 1886 and played as a cellist in the Metropolitan Opera Orchestra. Wrote operas, cello concertos, instrumental music and a symphonic poem, *Hero and Leander*, but it was through his operettas – he wrote over 40 – that he achieved lasting fame. They include *Naughty Marietta* and *Babes in Toyland*.

HERMON, Sir John Charles (1928–), chief constable RUC, b. Larne, Co. Antrim. John Hermon was a lifelong RUC officer. In 1963 he became the first RUC member to attend Bramshill police training college in England. In 1966 he was district inspector in charge of the Cookstown area, Co. Tyrone, in 1967 deputy commandant of the RUC training station in Enniskillen. Promoted chief superintendent in 1970, he became assistant chief constable in 1974 and in 1976 deputy chief constable, having also been awarded an OBE the previous year. He went on attachment to Scotland Yard in 1979, became chief constable of the RUC in 1980 and was knighted in 1982. During his period as chief constable he faced the controversies surrounding the H-block hunger strikes, the 'supergrass' system, 'shoot to kill' allegations, the sacking of women officers and the hostile unionist reaction to the Anglo-Irish Agreement. He has been a consultant to Securicor since his retirement from the RUC in 1989.

HERON, Hilary (1923–1977), artist, b. Dublin, spent most of her childhood in New Ross and Coleraine, ed. one-teacher school and National College of Art, Dublin. Won three of the Taylor prizes. Awarded the first MAINIE JELLETT memorial travelling scholarship 1947 for work in carved wood, limestone and marble. First exhibited at the Irish Exhibition of Living Art, of which she was a founding member. Represented Ireland with LOUIS LE BROCQUY at the Venice Biennale 1956. Second wife of Celtic scholar DAVID GREENE.

HEWITT, John (1907–1987), poet, b. Belfast, Oct. 1907, ed. Methodist College, Belfast and QUB, d. Belfast, 27 June 1987. Worked in Ulster Museum 1930–57; director of Coventry's Herbert Art Gallery and Museum 1957–72 before retiring and returning to Belfast. Publications include *Collected Poems* (1968), *Out of my Time* (1974) and *Time Enough* (1976), which won the Poetry Society book award. Edited William Allingham's poems and wrote a short book on painter COLIN MIDDLETON. MIAL 1960. Hon. D.Litt.

(NUU). Worked as an art critic for the *Belfast Telegraph*, *The Irish Times* and *Birmingham Post*. Poet in residence QUB. Hewitt chose the Ulster farmland as the *mise en scène* for many of his poetic reflections on the relationship between the people of his own planter stock and the descendants of the native Irish whom they displaced. In such poems as 'Once Alien Here' and 'The Colony', he bore witness to the affinity based on a shared landscape which he felt should link these people of different origins and faiths.

HEWSON, George Henley Phillips (1881–1972), musician. Professor of Music TCD and Professor of Organ RIAM. Organist and choirmaster of St Patrick's Cathedral, Dublin 1920–60. He was a noted teacher and arranger and some of his pieces remain in the repertoire.

HICKEY, John D. (1911–1977), journalist, b. Thurles, ed. local CBS, d. 10 June 1977. Became news reporter with *Tipperary Star* on leaving school. Joined *Irish Press* as a news sub-editor in 1943, transferring to *Irish Independent* in 1947, where he eventually settled in the sports department. For over 25 years Hickey was the paper's chief GAA correspondent, covering 50 All-Ireland finals. His period as a Gaelic games specialist coincided with the GAA's period of greatest popularity, with attendances of 80,000–90,000 at some finals. Hickey's flamboyant style of writing, which produced colourful, detailed and often hard-hitting reports of major fixtures, made him a controversial figure in Irish journalism. He frequently clashed with the GAA authorities and boasted of having received 'expulsion orders' from at least 11 counties, including his native Tipperary, to whose prowess on the hurling field he always paid special, if partisan, attention.

HICKEY, Patrick (1927–), artist, b. India. He did not come to Ireland until he was 21; studied architecture at UCD and later went to Italy to study printmaking at Urbino. On his return he taught in the School of Architecture at UCD and developed his career as a painter. Head of painting at the NCAD 1986–90. Founder member of the Graphic Studio, Dublin 1961. Widely respected for his technical mastery, he has exhibited internationally.

HICKS, Frederick (1870–1965), architect, b. Banbury, Oxfordshire, ed. Taunton School, later studying design in the Architectural Association School and at Finsbury Technical College. He took his articles with F.W. Stevens of London and came to Dublin in 1890 as temporary assistant in the offices of J. Rawson Carroll. Here he worked alongside his future partner, Frank Batchelor, before briefly joining the offices of William H. Byrne and later becoming chief assistant in the offices of Sir Thomas Drew. With R.M. BUTLER he assisted in the revival of the AAI, acting as its president in 1896. In 1898 he established his own practice in Dublin. In the same year he became a member of the RIAI, later being raised to a fellow; president 1929–31. In 1904 he was appointed architect for the Irish section of the Louisiana Purchase Exposition. The following year he gained his first significant public success, winning the competition for the public library in Rathmines, after which he entered partnership with Batchelor. He was appointed architect to the Marino housing scheme by Dublin Corporation in 1923. First recipient of the RIAI triennial gold medal 1932–4, awarded for his church of St Thomas, Marlborough Street, Dublin. He retired from private practice in 1945–6, by which time he was in partnership with ALAN HOPE.

HIGGINS, Aidan (1927–), writer, b. Celbridge, Co. Kildare, ed. Clongowes. He held a series of temporary jobs in Ireland, moved to England, married in London, and toured Europe, Rhodesia and South Africa with a marionette company. From South Africa he and his wife went to Germany, then London, before settling in Connemara. He is best known for his fiction and travel books and has won many prizes, including the James Tait Black memorial prize, an IAL award, the Daad scholarship of Berlin and the American Foundation literary award. His novels include: *Langrishe, Go Down* (1966), *Balcony of Europe* (1972), *Scenes from a Receding Past* (1977), *Bornholm Night-ferry* (1983) and *Lions of the Grunewald* (1993). Short stories: *Felo de Se* (1960), *Asylum and Other Stories* (1978), *Helsingor Station and Other Departures* (1989) and *Selected Fictions* (1993). He has also written plays for radio and in 1995 published an autobiography, *Donkey's Years*.

HIGGINS, Alexander Gordon (**'Hurricane'**) (1949–), professional snooker player, b. Belfast, 18 Mar. 1949. Having won the Northern Ireland Amateur Snooker Championship in 1967, he turned professional in 1971, and a year later became the youngest world champion, at 23, beating John Spencer in the final at Birmingham. Though he was the game's biggest attraction because of his emotional nature, he did not win the title again until 1982, when he defeated Ray Reardon. His other notable successes include the British Gold Cup (1980), the UK Open (1983), the Benson & Hedges Masters (1978, 1981) and the B. & H. Irish Masters (1989). He also played on the Ireland team which won the World Cup 1985–7, and won the Irish national title four times (1972, 1978, 1979 and 1983).

HIGGINS, Frederick Robert (1896–1941), poet and theatre director, b. Foxford, Co. Mayo. He worked in Dublin as an office boy from the age of 14 and was an early labour activist. He founded a clerical workers' union and set up the trade paper the *Irish Clerk*. From 1920 on he edited journals, including Ireland's first – if painfully short-lived – women's magazine, and was co-editor with W.B. YEATS of *Broadsides*, a poetry magazine, which included sumptuous colour artwork by JACK B. YEATS. He was a founder member of the IAL and business manager of the Abbey Theatre, a director in 1935. He produced one mediocre play, *A Deuce of Jacks* (1935), and is best remembered for his poems, some of which were strong enough to merit reprinting in 1992 as *The 39 Poems*. His collections were: *The Salt Air* (1923), inspired by folk songs of Connacht, *Island Blood* (1925), *The Dark Breed* (1927), *Arable Holdings* (1933) and *The Gap of Brightness* (1940).

HIGGINS, Michael D. (1941–), politician and academic, b. Limerick, Apr. 1941, ed. St Flannan's College, Ennis, UCG, Indiana University and Manchester University (BA, B.Comm. and MA). Labour TD 1981–2 and since 1987; senator 1973–7 (Taoiseach's nominee) and 1982–7 (NUI). Member Galway City Council 1985–93; alderman Galway Borough Council 1974–85; member Galway County Council 1974–85; Mayor of Galway 1982–3 and 1991–2. Former lecturer in sociology and politics UCG. A passionate and intellectual politician with a strong commitment to human rights and Third World issues, Higgins was appointed Minister for Arts, Culture and the Gaeltacht in Jan. 1993. As such, he allowed the ministerial order issued under section 31 of the Broadcasting Act to lapse, thereby granting members of Sinn Féin and other organisations access to the airwaves. He also re-established the Irish Film Board. In addition to his academic writings, he has produced two poetry collections, *The Betrayal* (1990) and *The Season of Fire* (1993). He was a columnist with *Hot Press* magazine for 13 years.

HIGGINS, Rita Ann (1955–), poet and playwright, b. Galway, ed. locally. She contracted tuberculosis in 1977, read voraciously during her confinement in a sanatorium, and joined a Galway writers' workshop in 1982. She was awarded Arts Council bursaries in 1986 and 1989, was writer in residence in Galway Library in 1987 and received a PEADAR O'DONNELL award in 1989. She has read her poetry on television, at universities and in prisons, at festivals in Ireland, England and on the Continent, and is a frequent contributor to literary journals and newspapers. She was recently writer in residence at UCG. There are four collections of her poetry, two of which have been reissued in one volume: *Goddess on the Mervue Bus* (1986), *Witch in the Bushes* (1988), *Philomena's Revenge* (1992), *Higher Purchase* (1996). Her play *Face Licker Come Home* was a resounding success at the 1991 Galway Arts Festival. Two more followed: *God of the Hatch Man* and *Colie Lally Doesn't Live in a Bucket* (1993).

HILL, Derek (1916–), artist, b. Southampton. During the 1930s he spent several years travelling, working and studying the craft of theatre design in Great Britain, France, Germany and the USSR. Returning to live in Britain in 1939, he concentrated on painting and drawing, and in 1954 he moved to Donegal. He is best known for his portraits of noted British and Irish figures, but he has also written and lectured extensively and organised numerous exhibitions, including the Degas show at the Tate Gallery in 1952. He has had retrospective exhibitions in London 1961, Belfast 1970, at the Royal Hospital,

Kilmainham in Dublin 1989 and at Colnagi's in London 1994.

HILL, Dick (1938–), broadcaster, ed. Midleton College, Cork and TCD. Worked as a scientist with industrial firms before going to BBC television and then (1964) to RTÉ as a researcher and reporter, becoming deputy programme editor (1965) and first producer of the *Seven Days* current affairs television programme (1966). Held a succession of senior posts in television programming and in 1977 was appointed first controller of programmes for the second channel, RTÉ 2, launched the following year. Director of television 1980–86. After retiring from RTÉ he became a director of the COCO television production company, Cork.

HILL, Hugh *Allen* Oliver (1937–), academic, b. 23 May 1937, ed. Royal Academical Institution, QUB and Oxford. Departmental demonstrator Oxford 1965–7, lecturer in inorganic chemistry 1967–90, reader in bioinorganic chemistry 1990–92, Professor of Bioinorganic Chemistry 1992. Visiting appointments Harvard, University of Sydney and University of California. Co-editor-in-chief *Journal of Biochemistry.*

HILLERY, Patrick (1923–), politician, EEC commissioner and President of Ireland, b. Miltown Malbay, Co. Clare, 2 May 1923, ed. Rockwell and UCD, m. Maeve Finnegan. Medical doctor. TD (FF Clare) 1951–73. Minister for Education 1959–65, Industry and Commerce 1965–6, Labour 1966–9, Foreign Affairs 1969–73. In his first three elections he was running mate in Clare with his party's founder, EAMON DE VALERA. As Minister for Education he was responsible for much innovative thinking, preparing the ground for the introduction of comprehensive schools, regional technical colleges and higher technical education. Under his aegis the local authorities' scholarship system was also extended. The developing crisis in Northern Ireland demanded much of his attention during his term at Foreign Affairs. He was able nonetheless to lead the successful negotiations for Irish entry to the EEC, following which he served as the country's first commissioner 1973–6, holding the Social Affairs portfolio.

When President CEARBHALL Ó DÁLAIGH resigned in 1976 after being verbally assaulted by the Fine Gael Minister for Defence, PATRICK DONEGAN, Hillery reluctantly yielded to Fianna Fáil entreaties to make himself available to fill the vacancy and became President of Ireland by all-party agreement in Dec. of that year. He was again unopposed upon his renomination seven years later and shared the distinction, with de Valera and SEÁN T. Ó CEALLAIGH, of serving two full terms as head of state. As president he kept a low profile but became involved in unwelcome publicity in 1982, when he declined to accept FF telephone calls urging him to consider refusing a dissolution of the Dáil to the FG Taoiseach GARRET FITZGERALD, whose government had been defeated on a budgetary proposal. Hillery withdrew completely from public life on his retirement.

HOBSON, Bulmer (1883–1969), revolutionary, b. Holywood, Co. Down, ed. The Friends' School, Lisburn, Co. Antrim, d. Aug. 1969. Secretary of the first Antrim GAA county board, founder of the Ulster Literary Theatre and (with DENIS McCULLOUGH) the Dungannon Clubs, which promoted republicanism and consideration of the implications of national independence. He launched the *Republic* as a weekly newspaper in 1906 and the following year became vice-president of Sinn Féin; he later left the organisation over disagreements with ARTHUR GRIFFITH. He had been active in the IRB but disapproved of the planned Easter Rising and was kept in detention by his colleagues until the fighting had begun. Under the Irish Free State he joined the revenue commissioners' office in Dublin Castle, retiring in 1948. Publications include *The Life and Times of Wolfe Tone* (1919), *A National Forests Policy* (1923) and *Ireland Yesterday and Tomorrow* (1968).

HOGAN, Desmond (1950–), novelist, dramatist and short story writer, b. Ballinasloe, Co. Galway, ed. Garbally Park and UCD. He began writing and acting at an early age, worked with a children's theatre group in Dublin 1975–7 and taught in London 1978–9. He won a Hennessy award 1971, Rooney prize 1977, Rhys memorial prize 1980. Hogan sets his work in both London and rural Ireland, and has done for the latter what DERMOT BOLGER's novels did for Dublin: revealed its dark and terrifying facets. His novels include: *The Ikon*

Maker (1976), *The Leaves on Grey* (1980), *A Curious Street* (1984), *A New Shirt* (1986) and *A Farewell to Prague* (1995). Plays: *A Short Walk to the Sea* (1975), *Sanctified Distances* (1976), *Jimmy*, a BBC radio play (1977), *The Ikon Maker* (1980) and *The Mourning Thief*, a television play (1984). Short stories: *The Diamonds at the Bottom of the Sea* (1979), *Children of Lir: Stories from Ireland* (1981), *The Mourning Thief* (1987) and *Lebanon Lodge* (1988). Collected journalism: *The Edge of the City* (1993).

HOGAN, James (1898–1963), academic and politician, b. Kilrickle, Co. Galway. Professor of History UCC 1933. Vice-president Fine Gael on founding of party 1933; resigned 1934 in protest at what he saw as the destructive leadership of EOIN O'DUFFY. Prominent advocate of corporate state. Brother of Patrick Hogan, Minister for Agriculture in government of W.T. COSGRAVE.

HOGAN, Patrick (1886–1969), politician, b. Kilmaley, Co. Clare, d. Mullingar, 24 Jan. 1969. Hogan joined the Volunteers in Limerick and was deported for a time to prison in England, where he composed the song 'The Shawl of Galway Grey'. Active in Clare during the War of Independence and after the Treaty became a full-time official of the ITGWU. Labour TD for Clare 1923–38, senator 1938–42 and TD again from 1943. He served as Ceann Comhairle from 1951 until 1967 and was still a TD at the time of his death. Called to the Bar in 1936.

HOLLAND, Mary (1936–), political journalist, b. London, 19 June 1936, ed. Loreto Abbey, Rathfarnham, Co. Dublin, schools in England and London University. A columnist with *The Irish Times* and a regular contributor to the *Observer*, Holland has worked for a wide variety of British and Irish publications, including *New Statesman*, *Vogue*, *Sunday Press* and *Magill*. She has also worked in television, presenting *Weekend World* for LWT during the 1970s and appears regularly on RTÉ. Particularly renowned for her coverage of Northern Ireland, for which she was nominated Britain's Journalist of the Year in 1970. Her ITV television documentary *Creggan* won the 1980 Prix Italia award, and in 1989 she shared with fellow journalist David McKittrick the tenth Christopher Ewart-Biggs memorial prize for her contribution to a better understanding between Britain and Ireland.

HOLLOWAY, Joseph (1861–1944), diarist, b. Dublin, the son of a baker, ed. Castleknock and the Metropolitan School of Art, Dublin. He became an architect; when the Irish National Theatre Society bought the Mechanics' Institute, Dublin in 1903 Holloway was engaged to convert it into the Abbey Theatre. His passion for theatre was already well developed and it deepened even further over time, especially following his retirement from his architectural practice in 1914. He was reputed to have attended every play staged in Dublin over a 50-year period, as well as joining every society and group connected to the theatre. He left a journal of more than 200 volumes describing his theatregoing, selections of which were published as *Joseph Holloway's Abbey Theatre* (1967) and *Joseph Holloway's Irish Theatre* (three vols. 1968–70).

HOLMES, Sir Gordon Morgan (1876–1965), neurologist, b. Castlebellingham, Co. Louth, ed. TCD, m. Captain Rosalie Jobson, a doctor, three d., d. 29 Dec. 1965. Graduated MB 1898, proceeding MD 1903. After a voyage as ship's surgeon to New Zealand, he used a travelling scholarship to study neuro-anatomy under Ludwig Edinger and opted for a career in neurology. Many Irish doctors have excelled in this speciality, both at home and abroad, including Frank Purser, Hugh Staunton, Robert Foster Kennedy (New York) and James Purdon Martin (London).

Early in the century Holmes was RMO at the National Hospital, Queen Square, London, where his masters were John Hughlings Jackson and Sir William Gowers, respectively neurology's philosopher and its most consummate diagnostician. Within a few years he was honorary physician to the National Hospital and to Charing Cross and Moorfields Hospitals. During World War I he worked at a Red Cross field hospital and carried out research on dysfunction of the occipital lobes and cerebellum due to gun-shot wounds.

A great teacher, he attracted students to London from abroad. His publications, now regarded as classics, include *Introduction to Clinical Neurology* (1946) and *Selected Papers of Gordon Holmes* (1956).

HONE, Evie Sydney (1894–1955), artist, b. Dublin, 22 Apr. 1894, ed. London and Paris. Descended from Joseph, brother of 18th-century portrait painter Nathaniel Hone. Crippled by infantile paralysis. Started her formal training as an artist shortly before World War I at the Byam Shaw School of Art in London. In Paris she and MAINIE JELLETT studied under André Lhote, mastering the principles of cubism, and Albert Gleizes. In 1924, with Jellett, she first exhibited her abstract paintings in Dublin. Hone began to make stained glass at SARAH PURSER's An Túr Gloine around 1933, her first commission being for a window in St Naithi's Church, Dundrum, Co. Dublin. During her career she completed about 48 windows, the most famous being the east window for Eton College Chapel 1948–52. The strong devotional images of Georges Rouault had a direct influence on her work. Other influences were medieval Irish carvings and Italian primitives, as well as the glass of her French contemporaries, which she saw during regular visits to the Continent.

With Jellett she was a founder member of the Irish Exhibition of Living Art in 1943. She died at her home in Rathfarnham, Co. Dublin on 13 Mar. 1955.

HONE, Nathaniel (1831–1917), artist, b. 26 Oct. 1831, ed. TCD, d. Dublin, 14 Oct. 1917. Railway engineer until he decided to study painting. Worked at Barbizon with Millet and others. From 1875 lived at Malahide, Co. Dublin, making the neighbouring country-side the subject of many landscapes, seascapes and studies of grazing animals, in which he captured effectively the elusive Irish light. MRHA 1880, Professor of Painting RHA 1894–1917.

HOPE, Alan Hodgson (*c.* 1909–1965), architect, came to Ireland after qualifying at the Liverpool School of Architecture and joined the offices of FREDERICK HICKS in the late 1930s. On Hicks's retirement in 1945–6 Hope carried on work on his own account, developing his practice particularly in the areas of hospitals and factories. He gained public recognition with the award of the 1947–9 RIAI triennial gold medal for his innovative and typically expressive Aspro factory, Inchicore, Dublin, sadly later demolished. However, despite Hope's undoubted talent he was unfortunate in the small number of major projects brought to fruition before his early death. He was an associate of the RIBA, an active member of the RIAI and had been a vice-president of the AAI.

HOPKIRK, Patrick (Paddy) (1933–), international rally driver, b. Belfast, 4 Apr. 1933, ed. Clongowes and TCD. He had established himself as the world's most notable rally driver by the end of the 1960s. He had won a Coupe d'Argent on the Alpine Rally, the results of Coupes earned with a Triumph TRS in 1956, a Sunbeam Rapier in 1959 and a Mini Cooper in 1965. He began the notable Mini Cooper successes when he won (with Henry Liddon) the 1964 Monte Carlo Rally. Other achievements include wins in the Acropolis and Alpine Rallies in 1967, second in the 1968 London to Sydney Rally, and a record five wins in the Circuit of Ireland in a Triumph TR3 (1958), Sunbeam Rapier (1961, 1962) and Mini Cooper (1965, 1967).

HORAN, James (1912–1986), monsignor and airport developer, b. Partry, Co. Mayo, ed. St Jarlath's College, Tuam and Maynooth. Following his ordination in 1935 he served as a curate near Glasgow before returning to the west of Ireland. He went to Knock, Co. Mayo in 1963 as senior curate and became parish priest in 1967. Within a decade he had transformed the village – a traditional site of Marian pilgrimage following a reported apparition of the Virgin Mary there in 1879 – into a modern pilgrimage centre, complete with new basilica. Pope John Paul II visited Knock during his Irish visit in 1979. Two years later Monsignor Horan's ambitious plan to build an international airport nearby was approved by the then Fianna Fáil government, but following the victory of the Fine Gael–Labour coalition under GARRET FITZGERALD in 1982 further funding was withdrawn. Undeterred, Monsignor Horan raised the remaining money privately and the airport was officially opened by CHARLES HAUGHEY in May 1986. Only a few weeks later, on 1 Aug., he died suddenly while on a pilgrimage to Lourdes. His mixture of business flair, vision and political cunning made him one of the most unusual Irish people of his time.

HORGAN, John (1940–), journalist, politician and academic, b. Tralee, 26 Oct. 1940, ed. Glenstal, UCD, UCC and Harvard. Religious affairs and then education correspondent of *The Irish Times* 1964–73. Reported perceptively on the Second Vatican Council, subsequent Synods of Bishops, the World Council of Churches and the Nigerian civil war in Biafra; later opened to popular discussion the debate on the future of education. Editor of the *Education Times*, a subsidiary of *The Irish Times*, 1973–6. Elected to the Seanad for the NUI constituency 1969 and a TD (Labour Dublin South County) 1977–81. MEP (Labour Dublin) 1981–3. Successively lecturer and senior lecturer (directing the postgraduate courses in journalism), School of Communications, DCU, from 1983. Publications include *The Church among the People* (1969) and *Labour: The Price of Power* (1985).

HORSLIPS, rock band. Ireland's most famous 'progressive' group, Horslips blended traditional Irish music with full-on rock and roll to create an epic, sword-and-sorcery style of Celtic rock. Their début album, *Happy to Meet, Sorry to Part*, combined gentle Irish airs with lengthy electric guitar passages and was recorded in the Rolling Stones' mobile studio in 1972. Their next, *The Táin*, was a concept album based on the famous Irish legend of the cattle raid of Cooley, perfectly suiting the band's music. In a bid for world domination, Horslips signed to RCA and released *Dancehall Sweethearts* (1974), following that with *The Unfortunate Cup of Tea* (1975), *Drive that Cold Winter Away* (1975), finally scraping the top 40 with another concept album, *The Book of Invasions* (1976). Despite their lack of chart success Horslips were a consistent live draw, and their Celtic-style stage sets and sophisticated musicianship guaranteed sell-out concerts in both Europe and the USA. As the 1970s drew to a close, however, the band became splintered creatively and broke up amid disagreements about musical direction. They had created the genre of Celtic rock but were unable to bring their vision to fruition.

HOTHOUSE FLOWERS, rock band. A whole crop of new Irish bands emerged in the wake of U2's international success. Of these 'second generation' acts of the mid to late 1980s, the most successful were Hothouse Flowers, a Dublin five-piece led by Liam Ó Maonlaí. Originally a busking duo consisting of Ó Maonlaí and guitarist Fiachra Ó Braonáin, Hothouse Flowers blended the soulful R & B style of VAN MORRISON with a distinctive Irish identity, and their exuberant live shows made them a major attraction at home. Their second single, 'Don't Go', reached number 11 in the British charts, while their début album, *People*, hit number two. In 1988 Hothouse Flowers co-headlined an open-air concert in Dublin with Tracy Chapman, attracting a crowd of over 30,000. Subsequent albums, *Home* (1990) and *Songs from the Rain* (1993), also made the UK top ten, and the group have enjoyed successful tours in the USA and Australia.

HOULIHAN, Con (1925–), sports journalist, b. Castleisland, Co. Kerry, 6 Dec. 1925, ed. Castlemartyr College, Co. Cork and UCC. Worked as a labourer in England during World War II and then studied at UCC, gaining a first class honours BA (1948) and MA (1949). Returned to England in 1950 to work as a PT teacher in Hastings, Essex. By the mid-1950s he was back in Castleisland, where he worked as a butcher, teacher and turf accountant. He also became involved in journalism, contributing pieces to Radio Éireann and editing a monthly newspaper called the *Taxpayer's News*. A libel case finished the latter in the mid-1960s, but he was then offered a political column by the *Kerryman* newspaper. In the early 1970s he moved to Dublin, establishing what became an institution in Irish journalism, his back page sports column in the *Evening Press*.

HUME, John (1937–), politician, b. Derry, 18 Jan. 1937, ed. St Columb's College, Derry and Maynooth. Since the beginning of the conflict in Northern Ireland in 1969 he has been the most prominent and influential representative of its nationalist population. He has played a central role in all of the various political initiatives that have been attempted to resolve this conflict, and has had a direct impact on official policy towards Northern Ireland in the USA, in Europe and especially in the Republic of Ireland. He became active in the Northern Ireland Civil Rights Association in Derry in the late 1960s. In Oct. 1968, following police attacks on NICRA members, he was elected vice-chairman of Derry Citizens' Action Committee and deter-

minedly pursued a policy of non-violent protest. He took the Foyle seat in the NI parliament elections in 1969 and the following year co-founded the Social Democratic and Labour Party. Elected to the NI Assembly 1973–4, the NI Convention 1976–7 and the new Assembly 1982–6; served as Minister for Commerce in the power-sharing Executive 1974.

In 1979 he won a seat in the European Parliament, and replaced GERRY FITT as leader of the SDLP. He also became MP for Foyle in the UK parliament in 1983. Unlike Fitt, he stressed the importance of the 'Irish dimension' to any settlement in Northern Ireland. However, he did not cling to the shibboleths of Irish nationalism, but called on politicians in the Republic to try to describe their vision of a future united Ireland to which unionists could belong. Hume's suggestion, made at a time when Sinn Féin was posing a serious threat to the SDLP's electoral base, led to the setting up of the New Ireland Forum in 1984. The articulation of a tentative new nationalist consensus in the South, and Hume's assiduous work in the European Parliament and the USA, were important elements in the process that led to the signing of the historic Anglo-Irish Agreement in 1985.

A series of discussions with SF president GERRY ADAMS beginning in 1988 angered unionists, were viewed with suspicion in London and with cautious approval in Dublin. In the wake of the Downing Street Declaration by the Irish and British governments (Dec. 1993), the Hume–Adams dialogue was instrumental in eventually persuading the IRA to call a ceasefire in Aug. 1994. Thereafter Hume argued for a speedy start to all-party talks on the future of NI. These began eventually in June 1996 but without SF, who were excluded because the IRA ceasefire had collapsed in Feb. of that year. Despite his scepticism about the elections to an NI Forum which preceded the talks, Hume led the SDLP to achieve a strong renewal of its mandate as the principal voice of Northern nationalism.

HUMPHRIES, Carmel Frances (1909–1986), academic, b. Waterford, 3 June 1909, ed. Ursuline Convent, Waterford, Loreto College, St Stephen's Green, Dublin and UCD (B.Sc. 1932, M.Sc. and H.Dip.Ed. 1933, Ph.D. 1938, D.Sc. 1956), d. Dublin. Postgraduate research at Freshwater Institute, Ambleside, England, 1934–6 and at the Hydrobiologische Anstalt Plon/Holstein, Germany, 1936–8. From 1938, assistantships in zoology UCD, QUB; lecturer in zoology UCD 1948 and professor 1956. Member of RIA Committee of Science and its Industrial Application, RDS, Institute of Biology, and Irish representative for the International Limnological Association and the Freshwater Association, England. Principal research interest: the area of limnology (freshwater biology), particularly the taxonomy of chironomidae or non-biting midges.

HUNNIFORD, Gloria (1940–), broadcaster, b. Portadown, Co. Armagh, 10 Apr. 1940. From a family of amateur entertainers, she was named after Hollywood actress Gloria Swanson. Professional singer in the 1960s, in 1969 hosted a radio show in Canada. Made a weekly radio programme for British forces in West Germany 1969–81. In 1982 she became the first woman to host a daily radio show for BBC Radio 2. She has made numerous television appearances and hosted a number of television chat shows in Northern Ireland and in Britain. Awards include the Variety Club Radio Personality of the Year 1982 and *TV Times* TV Personality of the Year 1987. Her autobiography, *Gloria*, was published in 1993.

HUNT, John (1900–1976), scholar and antiquarian, b. Limerick, 25 May 1900. He spent most of his adolescence and early manhood in London before returning to Limerick in 1940, by which time he had an international reputation as a medievalist. He helped to restore Bunratty Castle from its neglected condition and was the founder of the Bunratty Folk Park. He also supervised the restoration of Craggaunowen Castle and the building of its replica crannog. The Hunt Museum in the University of Limerick is named for him: he donated the core of its collection. Author of *Irish Medieval Figure Sculpture* (two vols. 1974).

HUNTER, Richard Henry (*c.* 1892–1970), anatomist and artist, b. Berbice, British Guiana, ed. Ballymena Academy and QUB (MB 1920, MD 1923, Ph.D. 1928). Studied art in Belfast and Paris; held a Rockefeller fellowship. Stretcher-bearer with French Red Cross 1914–15. Lecturer in Department of Anatomy and secretary QUB; editor *Ulster*

Medical Journal. Hunter remained a bachelor; he died at a Cistercian monastery, a convert to Catholicism.

HUTCHINSON, William Patrick Henry *Pearse* (1927–), poet, b. Glasgow to Irish parents, ed. St Enda's, Synge Street, UCD and Salzburg. Translator in Geneva 1951–3, lived in Barcelona 1954–7 and 1961–7. Drama critic for RTÉ radio and television 1957–70. Won Butler award for Irish writing 1969, Gregory fellow in poetry University of Leeds 1971–3. His verse owes not a little to his Mediterranean sojourns and pulsates at times with Catalonian rhythms. When not taking the scalpel to his past he can be found dissecting the pathology of madness. His volumes are: *Tongue without Hands* (1963), *Expansions* (1969), *Watching the Morning Grow* (1972), *The Frost is All Over* (1975), *Selected Poems* (1982), *Climbing the Light* (1985), *The Killing of Dreams* (1992), *Barnsley Main Seam* (1995); and in Irish: *Faoistin Bhacach* (1968), *Le Cead na Gréine* (1990). Translations: *Poems* by Josep Carner (1962), *Friend Songs: Mediaeval Love-songs from Galaico-Portuguese* (1970), *Antica Lirice Irlandese*, with Melita Cataldi (1982), *The Soul that Kissed the Body: New and Selected Poems in Irish* (1990).

HYDE, Douglas (1860–1949), translator, academic and President of Ireland, b. Castlerea, Co. Roscommon, 17 Jan. 1860, son of a Church of Ireland rector, ed. TCD, d. Dublin, 12 July 1949. Multilingual, knowing Greek, Latin, Hebrew, French, German and Irish. LL D 1888. Lectured in modern languages University of New Brunswick 1891. Back in Roscommon, concentrated on the collection and translation of Irish folklore and poetry. Co-founded the Irish Literary Society in London 1891 and became president of the National Literary Society in Dublin 1892. *Love Songs of Connacht*, with verse translations into English, was published 1893, the same year that he co-founded the Gaelic League and became its first president.

In the following years he made the League his primary commitment, encouraging its promotion of the Irish language, music, dancing and games. He continued to write, often under his pseudonym, 'An Craoibhín Aoibhinn' ('The Lovely Little Branch'); his *Literary History of Ireland* appeared in 1899, *Religious Songs of Connacht* in 1906. The Irish Literary Theatre staged his play *Casadh an tSúgáin* in 1901: the first known professional production in the Irish language. His writings were an important influence on W.B. YEATS and others associated with the Irish literary revival of the day and the early Abbey Theatre. Member of the Commissions for Irish Secondary and University Education 1901 and 1906. Hyde became increasingly unhappy with the involvement of the Gaelic League in separatist politics and resigned from its presidency in 1915. Professor of Modern Irish at UCD from 1909, he retained the post until his retirement in 1932. He was briefly (1925–6) a senator. His autobiographical *Mise agus an Conradh* appeared in 1931. By all-party agreement he was chosen to be first President of Ireland under the 1937 constitution and served an uncontroversial full term 1938–45.

HYLAND, Aine (1942–), educationalist, b. Athboy, Co. Meath, 1 Mar. 1942, ed. Convent of Mercy Secondary School, Ballymahon, Co. Longford. Entered Department of Education in 1959. Became research assistant with the Investment in Education team but when she married the team statistician, William J. Hyland, the marriage bar then in operation required her to resign. After two years with the International Labour Office in Geneva, she returned to Dublin in 1966. BA, H.Dip.Ed., M.Ed. (1975), Ph.D. (1982) for her thesis on the administration and financing of Irish education. Re-entered the public domain through her involvement in the multidenominational primary school movement.

A founder member of the Dalkey School Project in the mid-1970s, since the 1980s she has served on Educate Together, the national co-ordinating committee for multidenominational schools. Has written on educational history and comparative education. Admissions officer and senior lecturer in education in Carysfort College, Dublin 1980. On its closure in 1988 she joined the education department of UCD and in 1993 was appointed to the chair of education at UCC.

HYNES, Garry (1953–), theatre director and founder of the Druid Theatre Company, b. Roscommon, 10 June 1953, ed. Dominican College, Galway and UCG (BA). On graduation in 1975 set up Druid Theatre with Marie Mullen and MICK LALLY and was its artistic director. The pioneering company brought theatre to rural Ireland and toured its productions in Europe and Australia. Druid's survival based outside Dublin set an important precedent. As its inspirational force Hynes has made a unique contribution to Irish theatre. Artistic director in the Abbey Theatre 1990–93, she returned to Druid in a consultant capacity 1994. In 1988–9 she directed with the Royal Shakespeare Company at Stratford and London. A forceful, creative woman with a passionate commitment to excellence, she was awarded the Harvey's Director of the Year (1983, 1985), the *Time Out* London award for direction (1988), and an honorary doctorate of laws (1988) for her services to Irish theatre. Her brother Jerome Hynes is chief executive of the Wexford Opera Festival.

I

INGLIS, Brian St John (1916–1993), author, broadcaster and journalist, b. Dublin, 31 July 1916, only child of Sir Claude Inglis, a civil engineer who spent much of his life in the Indian civil service, ed. Bexhill, Shrewsbury School, Magdalen College, Oxford and TCD, d. London, 11 Feb. 1993. He spent the first two years of his life in Ireland before joining his parents in India at the end of World War I. His mother returned with him to Ireland before he was five and it was then that he got to know the village of Malahide, Co. Dublin, of which he wrote much in two autobiographies: *West Briton* (1962) and the much fuller *Downstart* (1990). Joined the RAF during World War II. Worked with *The Irish Times* as a freelance journalist in England. Editor of the *Spectator* 1954–9. Well-known television presenter: he inaugurated *What the Papers Say* and *All Our Yesterdays*.

He wrote a biography of Sir ROGER CASEMENT (1973). Among his other publications, including many on the paranormal and fringe medicine, are: *Revolution in Medicine* (1958), *Fringe Medicine* (1964), *Abdication* (1966), *Poverty and the Industrial Revolution* (1971), *Natural and Supernatural* (1979), *The Diseases of Civilisation* (1981) and *Science and Parascience* (1984).

INGRAM, Rex (1893–1950), filmmaker, professional cognomen of Reginald Ingram Montgomery Hitchcock, b. Rathmines, Dublin, 10 Jan. 1893, ed. St Columba's and Yale School of Fine Arts, USA, d. Hollywood, 22 July 1950. Became a cinema actor and scriptwriter, going on to make several productions before joining the Metro company in Hollywood, for which he directed the hugely successful *Four Horsemen of the Apocalypse* (1921), starring the hitherto unknown Rudolph Valentino. Among the best-known of Ingram's 25 other films were *The Prisoner of Zenda* (1922), *Scaramouche* (1923) and the early sound film *Baround*, made at the Victorine Studios, which he founded at Nice after he left Hollywood in the mid-1920s. Although ranking among the greatest directors of his day, he gave up film-making in 1933 to concentrate on sculpture, writing and travel.

IRELAND, Denis (1894–1974), writer and broadcaster, b. Belfast, ed. Royal Academical Institution and QUB, d. Belfast, 23 Sept. 1974. After military service during World War I in France and Greece, worked in family linen firm, later becoming a freelance journalist and political commentator. Advocate of Irish unity based on what he saw as the republican tradition of Ulster Presbyterianism. Nominated to the Seanad 1948–51 by the Taoiseach, JOHN A. COSTELLO, at the instigation of SEÁN MACBRIDE's Clann na Poblachta party, and a member of the Irish delegation to the Council of Europe. Publications include: *From the Irish Shore* (1936) and *Statues round the City Hall* (1939), both autobiographical, *Patriot Adventurer* (1936), a life of Wolfe Tone, and *Six Counties in Search of a Nation* (1947).

IREMONGER, Valentin (1918–1991), poet and diplomat, b. Sandymount, Dublin, ed. Synge Street and Coláiste Mhuire. He trained as an actor and played with the Abbey and Gate companies in early 1940s, wrote verse and won an AE memorial award in 1945. He entered diplomatic service in 1946 and was ambassador to Norway, Sweden, Finland, Luxembourg, Portugal and India in the course of a career that lasted until 1980. Robert Hogan thought him 'a thoroughly glum poet' yet he could enthral, and was inspirational for younger practitioners. His poetry includes *Reservations* (1950), *Horan's Field and Other Reservations*, collected poems (1972), and *Sandymount, Dublin* (1988). He translated Rilke into Irish (1955) and two Irish novels into English: Michael MacGowan's *The Hard Road to Klondyke* (1962) and DÓNALL MAC AMHLAIGH's *An Irish Navvy* (1964). Co-editor of *Contemporary Irish Poetry* (1949), poetry editor of JOHN RYAN's *Envoy* (1949–51), editor of *Irish Short Stories* (1960) and wrote the play *Wrap up my Green Jacket* (1948).

J

JACKSON, Robert Wyse (1908–1976), bishop, historian and writer, b. 12 July 1908, d. 21 Oct. 1976. Ordained Church of Ireland deacon 1934, priest 1935. Dean of Cashel; Bishop of Limerick, Ardfert and Aghadoe 1960–70. Contributed to many periodicals, including the *Bell*. He also wrote extensively for local historical and archaeological society journals, particularly on Jonathan Swift, and was an expert on early Irish silver, on which he wrote a monograph.

JACOB, George N. (1854–1940), biscuit manufacturer, b. Dublin. Worked for over 70 years and invented the cream cracker. President of Dublin Chamber of Commerce 1926. Active in Chamber's campaign to prevent the completion of the Shannon Scheme and the establishment of the ESB. L.M. Cullen writes, 'It was in reality the crucial test of relationships between relatively conservative businessmen, many of them still doubtful about the state politically as well as economically, and a government still feeling its way uncertainly amid the complex problems of the post-war world.' Government lobbying brought the Chamber around and the ESB successfully took over the existing municipal power stations throughout the country as well as in Dublin.

JAFFÉ, Sir Otto (1846–1929), only Jewish Lord Mayor of Belfast, b. Hamburg, 13 Aug. 1846, s. of Daniel Joseph Jaffé, who came to Belfast to establish a linen-exporting business, ed. Mr Tate's, Holywood, Co. Down, d. London, 29 Apr. 1929. He established a reputation for himself in Belfast as an able businessman and entered local government in 1894 as a city councillor. Lord Mayor in 1899 and again in 1904, also served as high sheriff of the city in 1904. Jaffé was a devout Jew and helped to pay the cost of building Belfast's synagogue and a school for Jewish children. He was life president of the Belfast Hebrew congregation.

JAMESON, Rt. Hon. Andrew (1855–1941), distiller and banker, b. Alloa, Scotland, ed. Cambridge and TCD. Joined his brother John at Bow Street distillery at an early age;

became chairman 1905. High sheriff for Sligo 1898 and for Co. Dublin 1902. Member of the court of directors of the Bank of Ireland for a record 54 years 1887–1941 and governor 1896–8. Went big-game hunting in Texas with Theodore Roosevelt 1876. Member of the Irish Convention 1917 and of the Irish Privy Council. President Dublin Chamber of Commerce 1921. Advocated Southern unionist participation in the new state and was nominated to the Seanad 1922–36.

JELLETT, Mary Harriet (Mainie) (1897–1944), artist, b. Dublin, ed. National College of Art, Dublin. Went to London 1919 and then to Paris, where she joined EVIE HONE to study the nature of form and the relationship of shape to colour under André Lhote and Albert Gleizes. The technique which she evolved to convey balanced movement, with the composition of the whole picture reflected in its various segments, put her in the forefront of cubist artists – so much so that she became an influence on her sometime master, as Gleizes himself acknowledged in paying tribute to what he learned in collaboration with Hone and Jellett. It took some years for her special talent to be recognised in her native city but eventually, after exhibiting in Dublin and Paris, she settled in Ireland 1930, where her work, together with Hone's, encouraged the development of a school of abstract painting in the country. This was soon to be represented in the annual Irish Exhibition of Living Art, of which Jellett and Hone were founding members in 1943, Jellett becoming its first president.

JENKINSON, Biddy (1929–), poet and critic, published widely in such literary journals as *Innti*, *Comhar* and *Irish University Review*. An assured feminist voice among contemporary poets. Publications include *Baisteadh Gintlí* (1987) and *Uiscí Beatha* (1988).

JENNINGS, Patrick Anthony (Pat) (1945–), international footballer, b. Newry, 12 June 1945. A brilliant goalkeeper, he is Northern Ireland's most capped player, with

119 (then a world record) earned between 1964 and 1986, when he retired after the World Cup in Mexico. He began his career with Newry Town, moved to Watford in 1963 but after a year transferred to Tottenham Hotspur, where he stayed for the next 13 seasons, before switching to Arsenal in 1977. With Spurs he won an FA Cup medal (1967), two League Cup medals (1971 and 1973), a European Cup Winners' medal (1968) and a UEFA Cup Winners' medal (1972). He won another FA Cup medal with Arsenal (1979) and two runners-up medals (1978 and 1980). Football Writers' Association Player of the Year 1973, Professional Footballers' Association Player of the Year 1976, awarded the MBE 1976 and the OBE 1987.

JOHNSON, Thomas Ryder (1872–1963), socialist, trade unionist and parliamentarian, b. Liverpool, 17 May 1872, the son of a sailmaker, ed. locally until 1885, m. Marie Ann Tregay, 24 Mar. 1898, d. 17 Jan. 1963. He was a classic product of the late 19th-century English socialist tradition who adopted Ireland as his country and spent most of his working life as a committed advocate of social and economic progress. He first visited Ireland in 1892, when he worked for a firm of fish merchants, buying fish in Kinsale and Liverpool. In 1893 he joined the Independent Labour Party in Liverpool and the following year he met JAMES LARKIN snr, whose birthplace was only a few streets away from his own. In 1903 he became a traveller for a firm selling veterinary medicines and animal foodstuffs in Ireland, moved to Belfast and joined the National Union of Shop Assistants and Clerks. A supporter of Home Rule, he stood unsuccessfully for election in Belfast in Jan. 1908. He became honorary secretary of the Belfast Socialist Society in 1911 and helped to arrange JAMES CONNOLLY's return to that city. In Sept. 1913 he moved to Dublin to assist Connolly and Larkin, joined the Socialist Party of Ireland and was active in the early years of the Irish Labour Party and Trades Union Congress. He was president of the Irish Trades Union Congress 1914–16, and in the latter year intervened with the authorities on behalf of trade unionists who had been involved in the Easter Rising. He was editor of *Irish Opinion: The Voice of Labour* 1917–18 and rejected English

offers of financial help; he proposed that Labour candidates cede to Sinn Féin candidates for the 1918 election.

Instrumental in the drafting of the Democratic Programme of the First Dáil (1919), he was elected to the Dáil as TD for South Dublin in 1922, becoming leader of the group of 17 Labour TDs and of the official opposition until 1927. He helped to secure a Labour–Fianna Fáil pact – in which he would have become a government minister – after the first 1927 election, but the Cumann na nGaedheal government survived. He lost his seat in the second election of that year to James Larkin and resigned as Labour Party secretary in 1928. He was a member of Seanad Éireann 1928–38 and acted as general secretary of the ITUC until 1945. In 1946 he was appointed to the newly established Labour Court, where he remained until his retirement in 1955. Despite his conflicts with Larkin snr, he admired his son, and played a not insignificant part in healing some of the splits to which the political and industrial labour movement was particularly prone. Politically active until the 1961 general election.

JOHNSTON, Denis (1901–1984), playwright, b. Dublin, 18 June 1901; ed. St Andrew's College, Dublin, Merchiston School, Edinburgh, Cambridge and Harvard; m. first SHELAH RICHARDS, one s. one d.; m. second actress Betty Chancellor, two s.; d. Ballybrack, Co. Dublin, 8 Aug. 1984. Johnston's first play, *The Old Lady Says 'No!'*, was produced at the Gate Theatre in 1929, when he was working as a scriptwriter for BBC Northern Ireland. It was followed by *The Moon in the Yellow River*, produced at the Abbey Theatre in 1931. Around this time Johnston joined the staff of the Gate, working as director until the mid-1930s, when he moved to London to become a drama producer for the new BBC television service. During World War II he was a BBC war correspondent, for which he later received the OBE. After the war he moved to the USA, where he worked as a professor in several universities. Other plays include *A Bride for the Unicorn* (1933), *Storm Song* (1934), *The Golden Cuckoo* (1939), *The Dreaming Dust* (1940), *A Fourth for Bridge* (1948), *Strange Occurrence on Ireland's Eye* (1956) and *The Scythe and the Sunset* (1958). His autobiographical writings include *Nine Rivers from Jordan* and *The Brazen Horn*. Father of JENNIFER JOHNSTON.

JOHNSTON, Jennifer (1930–), novelist and playwright, b. Dublin, d. of DENIS JOHNSTON and SHELAH RICHARDS, ed. Park House School, Dublin and TCD. Her novels include *The Captains and the Kings* (1972), *The Gates* (1973), *How Many Miles to Babylon?* (1974), *The Old Jest* (1979) and *The Railway Station Man* (1984), which was made into a film in 1991. Among her published plays are *Indian Summer* (1984) and *The Porch* (1986). Member of Aosdána. Honours include Robert Pitman award, *Yorkshire Post* award, Whitbread award. *Shadows on our Skin* was shortlisted for the Booker prize and for the *Daily Express* Best Book of the Year 1992. Many of her novels deal with the era of the 'Big House' Anglo-Irish ascendancy and its demise. This gives her a basic theme in the contrast between a new Ireland and an old, between youth and age, between crumbling manners and assertive prejudices. Within such contexts her stories tell of human relationships attempted, achieved or thwarted. A writer sensitive equally to her subjects and to the language in which she writes.

JOHNSTON, Joseph (1890–1972), academic and senator, b. Castlecaulfield, Co. Tyrone, ed. Dungannon, TCD and Lincoln College, Oxford. Researched economic conditions in India and the Far East before appointment as a lecturer at TCD. Adviser on regional economics to the Free State side in the Boundary Commission negotiations 1925. Rockefeller fellow for economic research in Europe 1928–9; Professor of Applied Economics TCD 1939. Senator (Ind. DU) 1938–43, 1944–8, 1951–4. His special interest was in agricultural economics, on which he wrote widely in the press and elsewhere, being especially critical of Fianna Fáil agricultural policy. He also argued for the continuing relevance of George Berkeley's theories to modern Irish economic development. He was awarded a D.Litt (TCD) for his *Berkeley's Querist in Historical Perspective* (1970).

JOHNSTON, Margaret (Maggie) (1943–), bowls player, b. Bellaghy, Co. Derry, 2 May 1943. A member of Ballymoney Bowling Club, she won her first national title with the Irish fours in 1983, and a year later captured both the singles and the pairs. In 1985 she won the singles and pairs titles in the British Isles Championship. She and Phyllis Nolan won the World Championship pairs for Ireland in 1988, and in 1992 she retained the title and also won the singles. She won a Commonwealth Games bronze medal in the singles in 1990, was world indoor champion in 1988 and 1989 and lost in the final in 1991. Awarded the MBE 1991.

JOHNSTON, Roy (1936–), artist, b. Pomeroy, Co. Tyrone, ed. Dungannon Royal School, Stranmillis College, Belfast and Belfast College of Art. He had his first one-man show in the Arts Council of Northern Ireland Gallery, Belfast in 1971, and won the Carroll's award at the Irish Exhibition of Living Art in 1973. He won the DOUGLAS HYDE gold medal at the Oireachtas in 1979. Johnston has taught art in several third-level colleges and in 1974 became principal lecturer in the School of Fine Art, Art and Design Centre, Ulster College. His work is largely abstract formalist in style with an emphasis on the interaction between geometric shapes rather than on tone or light. However, this hard-edged austerity is often relieved by a rich brush stroke or the use of vivid colours.

JORDAN, Edmund (Eddie) (1948–), motor racing team owner, b. Dublin, ed. Synge Street. After a successful career as a racing driver at all levels except Formula One, he formed his own racing team in 1987 at junior level. The Jordan Team entered the Formula One Championship for the first time in 1991, making him the first Irish person to own a Formula One team. In 1995 Jordan concluded an agreement with Peugeot for the supply of engines for its Formula One cars.

JORDAN, John Edward (1930–1988), literary critic, poet and short story writer, b. Dublin, ed. Synge Street, UCD and Oxford. He lectured at UCD from 1959 and resigned 1969 to pursue a career in the theatre. Having worked with such luminaries as MICHEÁL MACLIAMMÓIR, HILTON EDWARDS and Lord LONGFORD at the Gate, he turned to literary criticism in the 1950s, was a book critic for *The Irish Times*, and earned a fine reputation as cultural commentator through a column in *Hibernia*. Jordan was less well known for his poetry, though some of his verses – particularly his revised 'Patrician Stations' in *Blood* *and Stations* (1976) – display the satirical edge one associates with the like of PATRICK KAVANAGH. His other collections were: *Patrician Stations* (1971), *A Raft from Flotsam* (1975) and *With Whom Did I Share the Crystal?* (1980). He published short stories: *Yarns* (1977), co-translated *Fifteen Short Stories by Pádraic Ó Conaire* (1982) and edited *The Pleasures of Gaelic Literature* (1977).

JORDAN, Neil (1950–), writer and cineaste, b. Co. Sligo, ed. St Paul's, Raheny, Dublin and UCD. He published a collection of short stories, *Night in Tunisia*, in 1978, which won the *Guardian* prize for fiction. It was followed by the novels *The Past* (1980) and *The Dream of a Beast* (1983). Gaining his first film experience on John Boorman's *Excalibur* in 1981, he directed *Angel* (1982) and won the British Critics' Circle best director award for *The Company of Wolves* (1984). His next film, *Mona Lisa* (1986), took a Palme d'Or at Cannes as well as a De Sica award at the Sorrento Film Festival. Yet it was not until 1992 that Jordan's talents came to full fruition, with the stunning thriller *The Crying Game*, which won him an Oscar for best screenplay. His latest work is *Michael Collins* (1996). He published a novel, *Sunrise with Sea Monster*, in 1994.

JORGENSEN, Ib (1935–), dress designer and art dealer, b. Denmark, ed. Denmark, Morgan School, Castleknock, Co. Dublin and Grafton Academy of Dress Design. He and his family moved to Ireland in 1950 to join his father, who had come here three years earlier to work with the Department of Agriculture. At the top of the couture profession for nearly 40 years, having opened his own couture house in Dublin when he was 23. In 1991 he opened the Jorgensen Fine Art Gallery. He presented his last fashion collection in Feb. 1994, citing the VAT rate of 21 per cent on clothing as one of the main reasons for his exit from the fashion scene to become an art dealer.

JOURDAN, Georges Viviliers (1867–1963), Church of Ireland cleric and historian, b. Apr. 1867, d. 8 Dec. 1963. Ordained deacon 1894, priest 1895. Served in several parishes before and after his tenure as Beresford Professor of Ecclesiastical History in TCD 1933–55. Fellow of the Royal Historical Society and the RIA. Author of a number of books, but it is perhaps the chapters he contributed to W. Alison Phillips's *History of the Church of Ireland* in the 1930s that have best stood the test of time.

JOYCE, James (1882–1941), writer, b. 41 Brighton Square, Rathgar, a fashionable suburb of Dublin, 2 Feb. 1882, first child to a comfortably-off middle-class Catholic couple. His father, John Stanislaus Joyce, came from a Cork family which had left him with substantial wealth in money and property, while his mother's folk, the Murrays, were prosperous farmers and merchants from Co. Longford. Though John Joyce's spendthrift ways were soon to plunge his family into abject poverty – 16 changes of address within 20 years – the first decade of the writer's life was happy and secure.

In the most intensely autobiographical of Joyce's fictions, *A Portrait of the Artist as a Young Man* (1916), this period is covered in chapter one, with the Dedalus family living in the sunlit felicity of 1 Martello Terrace, Bray, Co. Wicklow, 1887–91, their eldest son enlisting as a boarder at Clongowes. The subsequent decline of the family and the growth of the artist's consciousness are rendered in the next four chapters of this remarkable *Bildungsroman*. Having completed his education with the Jesuits at Belvedere and UCD, the young hero leaves Ireland to 'forge in the smithy of my soul the uncreated conscience of my race'.

The biographical facts differ from the fiction only in detail and emphasis. After Clongowes the writer and his brother, Stanislaus, spent a short time with the Christian Brothers in O'Connell School, before being accepted by the legendary Fr John Conmee at Belvedere. Joyce entered UCD in 1898, emerging with an indifferent degree in modern languages in 1902. Shabby but disdainful, he neglected his studies while making a reputation for himself as a daring intellectual, rejecting nationalism, professing atheism and promoting the merits of Bruno, d'Annunzio and Ibsen. While a student he wrote 'Ibsen's New Drama' (1900), published in the *Fortnightly Review*, a pamphlet attacking Yeats's movement, *The Day of the Rabblement* (1901); and the essay 'James Clarence Mangan' (1902), which appeared in the college magazine, *St Stephen's*. In Dec. 1902 Joyce took up the study of medicine, first at

St Cecilia's Medical School, Dublin, then at the Sorbonne, Paris, where he met J.M. SYNGE. In Apr. 1903 he returned to Dublin for his mother's last illness and was present at her death in Aug. of that year, an event that haunts the mind of his alter ego, Stephen, in *Ulysses* (1922). In 1904 Joyce began the writing of *Stephen Hero*; wrote the essay-story 'A Portrait of the Artist', which was refused publication by the journal *Dana*; had the stories 'The Sisters', 'Eveline' and 'After the Race' published in the *Irish Homestead*; and wrote the satiric poem *The Holy Office*. He stayed briefly with OLIVER ST JOHN GOGARTY at the Martello Tower, Sandycove, setting for the first episode of *Ulysses*, and worked at the Clifton School, Dalkey, setting for the second. He walked out with Nora Barnacle for the first time on 16 June of that year – now immortalised as 'Bloomsday' – and on 18 Oct. departed with her to the Continent, fetching up as a Berlitz teacher at Pola.

The Joyces moved to Trieste in June 1905 and remained there – apart from six unhappy months 1906–7 in Rome – until June 1915, when they retired to the neutrality of Zurich. During the Trieste period Joyce wrote *Chamber Music* (published 1907), completed and had published as a volume the stories of *Dubliners* (1914), abandoned *Stephen Hero* and recast it as *A Portrait of the Artist as a Young Man*, which was published serially in Ezra Pound's *The Egoist* (1914). He also wrote several articles for the Triestine newspaper *Il Piccolo della Sera* and gave public lectures on Irish literature and politics. In Trieste his two children were born, Giorgio (1905) and Lucia (1907). He was joined by Stanislaus, whose teaching helped to support the family, until he was imprisoned as an alien by the Austrian authorities in 1915.

In Zurich Joyce completed his play *Exiles* (1918) and began serious work on *Ulysses*, which earlier he had thought of as a story for *Dubliners*. He received pensions from both the Royal Literary Fund and the civil list in 1915; in 1917 he received his first subvention from Harriet Shaw Weaver, who was to be his patron for the rest of his life. He underwent the first of his many eye operations in the same year. From Mar. 1918 to Dec. 1920 episodes of *Ulysses* were published in the *New York Little Review*, only to be halted by a prosecution for obscenity.

In 1920, on the advice of Ezra Pound, the Joyces moved to Paris, where Joyce became the centre of a famous literary circle which included his townsman SAMUEL BECKETT. *Ulysses* was published by his friend Sylvia Beach at her bookshop, Shakespeare and Company, on his birthday, 2 Feb. 1922. Despite almost universal censorship, the book, charting the life of Dublin over a single day, was quickly recognised as perhaps the finest novel of its time.

In 1923, despite failing eyesight, Joyce began writing 'Work in Progress', which was eventually to appear as *Finnegans Wake* (1939). A section from it bewildered readers of *Transatlantic Review* in 1924. Further sections such as 'Anna Livia Plurabelle' (1928) and 'Tales of Shem and Shaun' began to attract an avant-garde readership to the great experiment. In 1931 Joyce and Nora were married in England in order to legitimise their children; John Joyce died. The next year James saluted the birth of his first and only grandchild, James Stephen, with an exquisite poem, 'Ecce Puer', while Lucia suffered the first onset of the schizophrenia which was to cast such a shadow over her father's life. In 1933 a New York court in a famous judgment removed the ban from *Ulysses*, which was published by Random House in the following year. With the outbreak of World War II the Joyces were forced to flee to Switzerland, where he died in Zurich, 13 Jan. 1941, of a perforated duodenal ulcer. Ten years later Nora Joyce died in the same city, where she was buried beside her husband.

JOYCE, Patrick Weston (1827–1914), collector, b. Glenosheen, Co. Limerick. His work in Irish music was only one facet of a commitment to scholarship including research into place names, cartography and the usage of the English language in Ireland. His brother, Robert Dwyer Joyce, became an eminent academic in Boston and supporter of the Fenian movement in the USA. Joyce's collection *Ancient Music of Ireland* appeared in two parts in 1875 and 1888. In 1909 *Old Irish Folk Music and Songs* was published under the patronage of the Royal Society of Antiquaries of Ireland. This volume also encompasses the

19th-century collections of Samuel Forde and John Edward Piggott.

JOYCE, William Brooke (1906–1946), propagandist and broadcaster, b. Brooklyn, New York, 24 Apr. 1906, ed. St Ignatius's College, Galway and Birkbeck College, University of London. Joined the British Union of Fascists 1933, broke with it in 1937 and founded the pro-Nazi National Socialist League. Went to Germany 1939, staying there after the outbreak of war. One of several broadcasters of Nazi propaganda to Britain, where they were known collectively as 'Lord Haw-Haw' because of their supposedly exaggerated upper-class accents. The derisive nickname soon attached to Joyce alone as he became the most prominent of the broadcasters in English. On foot of his British passport he was condemned to death as a traitor after the war and hanged in Wandsworth Jail on 3 Jan. 1946.

K

KAVANAGH, Liam (1935–), politician, b. Wicklow, 9 Feb. 1935, ed. De La Salle School, Wicklow and UCD. Entered the Dáil as a Labour deputy in 1969; Minister for Labour and the Public Service 1981–2, Labour 1982–3, the Environment 1983–6, Tourism, Fisheries and Forestry 1986–7. MEP 1973–81; member Wicklow County Council 1974–81 and since 1987. Before entering politics Kavanagh worked as an accountant and in local government. He is a nephew of JAMES EVERETT.

KAVANAGH, Muiris ('Kruger') (1894–1971), publicist and publican, b. Dún Chaoin, Co. Kerry, d. 15 Apr. 1971. At national school he displayed his spirited and independent temperament by loudly declaring his support for Kruger and the Boers in the Boer War, thus earning himself the nickname which he carried for the rest of his life. When he was 19 he left for the USA, where he obtained the rudiments of an education before making his way in the movie business. His self-assurance and chutzpah brought him the job of publicity manager for MGM and he was familiar with many of Hollywood's top stars and producers. Then, at the age of 26, he threw it all up and returned to Dún Chaoin, opening a guest house and pub which became one of the most famous hostelries in Ireland. Despite its location at the farthest tip of the Dingle peninsula it was the haunt of many celebrities, attracted by its proprietor's relaxed and fluent bonhomie.

KAVANAGH, Patrick (1904–1967), poet, b. townland of Mucker near Inniskeen, Co. Monaghan, ed. Kednaminsha and Rocksavage NS, m. Katherine Barry Maloney 1967. Kavanagh began writing while working in his home county as a small farmer and shoemaker. Some of his earliest verses were published in a local newspaper, the *Dundalk Democrat*. He was introduced to contemporary poetry by the *Irish Statesman*, which published him in 1930. Its editor, GEORGE RUSSELL (AE), had encouraged the young poet and in 1931 Kavanagh walked the 60 miles between Inniskeen and Dublin to visit him. From this date onwards he played a part in the literary life of the country and his days as a naïve ploughman poet were over. In 1936 Macmillan in London published a short collection entitled *Ploughman and Other Poems*, and in 1937 he moved to England to seek his literary fortune. There he met HELEN WADDELL, who urged him to write an autobiographical prose account of his childhood and youth. This appeared in 1938 as *The Green Fool*. A bucolic, genial recollection of his rural roots, this work had a sad fate for in 1939 OLIVER ST JOHN GOGARTY took offence at an obviously innocent remark in the book and sued for libel. Kavanagh's publishers lost the case and the book was withdrawn. In 1939 Kavanagh settled in Dublin, where he resided for the rest of his life. He supported himself by means of occasional journalism and rarely enjoyed a steady income. His reputation in the early Dublin years was that of a peasant-poet, whose work, under AE's influence, had exploited a rich vein of romantic pastoral feeling about the Irish countryside. Always a partial reading, this view of Kavanagh was definitively complicated by the publication in 1942 of his best work, *The Great Hunger*. This long poem in 14 sections explored the life of a Monaghan small farmer not as a pastoral idyll but as a destructive round of menial labour in an emotional and cultural environment marked by deprivation and sexual repression. It represented a frank new realism in Kavanagh's oeuvre which was consolidated in 1949 by the publication of *Tarry Flynn* (a more exacting study of his origins than *The Green Fool*), which was banned under the censorship laws then pertaining in Ireland. In 1952, with his brother Peter, Kavanagh edited, published and for the greater part wrote *Kavanagh's Weekly*, which for 13 issues inveighed against the mediocrity of Irish society in general and Irish writing in particular. In 1954 the poet sued the *Leader* for libel and lost the case amid unwelcome notoriety.

In 1955 he survived treatment for lung cancer, and in the years remaining to him he eschewed social criticism and satire for a lyrical celebration of ordinary life. *Come Dance with Kitty Stobling* (1960), which collected some of the finest of these poems, won wide admiration, and the appearance of his *Collected Poems* in 1964 established his reputation, especially among the generation younger than his own, as one of the most significant Irish poets of the post-YEATS period.

KEAN, Marie (1922–1993), actress, b. 27 June 1922, d. 31 Dec. 1993. Kean trained in the old Gaiety School of Acting and joined the Abbey Theatre in 1948. A generation of Irish radio listeners remembers her as Mrs Kennedy in *The Kennedys of Castle Ross*, RTÉ's long-running drama series in the 1950s and 1960s. Memorable stage roles included Mrs Tancred in SEAN O'CASEY's *Juno and the Paycock*, Winnie in SAMUEL BECKETT's *Happy Days* and her own one-woman show, *Soft Morning City*, a poetic evocation of Dublin with which she toured the USA in the 1960s. She joined the Royal Shakespeare Company for several years in the 1970s, but returned at the end of the decade to her first home, the Abbey, where her final performance was as Mrs Grigson in O'Casey's *The Shadow of a Gunman*. Film appearances included *Barry Lyndon*, *Rooney* and, finally, John Huston's *The Dead*.

KEANE, John B. (1928–), playwright, b. Listowel, Co. Kerry, 21 July 1928, ed. St Michael's College, Listowel. Apart from a number of years in the early 1950s working as a labourer in England and a chemist's assistant in Doneraile, Co. Cork, Keane has lived in his native town. His plays were first rejected by the Abbey Theatre in the 1960s but produced in Cork by Theatre of the South. During the 1980s he underwent something of a renaissance, and his work has since become an important element of the Abbey's repertoire. The revival of interest in Keane has been largely due to the work of director Ben Barnes, both at the Abbey and with Groundwork Productions. Although Keane's importance as a playwright has been questioned, his immense popularity throughout Ireland is undeniable. His major plays include *Sive* (1959), *Sharon's Grave* (1960), *The Man from Clare* (1962), *Many Young Men of Twenty* and *The Year of the Hiker* (1963), *The Field* (1965), *Big Maggie* (1969) and *Moll* (1972). Keane is also a prolific prose writer; among his collections are *Unlawful Sex* (1978), *Owl Sandwiches* (1985) and the humorous letters series (including *Letters of a Successful TD* and *Letters of an Irish Parish Priest*), and he has had three novels published, *The Bodhran Makers* (1986), *Durango* (1992) and *The Contractors* (1993).

KEANE, Molly (1905–1996), novelist and playwright, b. Co. Kildare, d. Co. Waterford, 22 Apr. 1996. Keane wrote ten novels between 1928 and 1952 under the pseudonym M.J. Farrell. She also wrote several plays, including *Spring Meeting* (1938) – a great West End success – *Ducks and Drakes* (1942), *Treasure Hunt* (1949) and *Dazzling Prospect* (1961), all of which were directed by John Gielgud. Gained a whole new audience when she re-emerged, writing under her own name, with the novel *Good Behaviour* in 1981, which was followed by *Time after Time* (1983), *Loving and Giving* (1988) and *Conversation Piece* (1991). All were worthy, but her masterpiece remained *Good Behaviour*, with its black-comedy depiction of an Anglo-Irish family in decline during the 1920s. 'Sharp', 'crisp', 'alert', 'wickedly alive' were among the reviewers' tributes, indicating the success with which she drew upon the world she knew as a young woman on the border of Cos. Waterford and Tipperary.

KEANE, Rita and **Sara**, singers, two sisters from Caherlistrane, Co. Galway, who have attracted enthusiastic attention in many countries. Although within the traditional mode, they perform in a uniquely personal way, singing in unison and creating an almost ethereal atmosphere. The family is widely known for musical talent and Rita and Sara were both associated with the Keane Céilí Band, which also involved their brothers Matt, Tom, John Joe and Paddy. Their niece Dolores Keane was the original singer with the group Dé Danann, which initially consisted of the acclaimed young fiddler Frankie Gavin along with Charlie Piggott, Alec Finn and Johnny McDonagh. As a soloist she has established an international reputation but, like other well-known Irish women singers such as MARY BLACK and Máire Brennan, no longer relies on material within the traditional vein.

KEANE, Roy Maurice (1971–), international footballer, b. Cork, 10 Oct. 1971. Having played with local clubs Rockmount and Cobh Ramblers, he was signed by Nottingham Forest in 1990 and was a member of the side defeated in the FA Cup final of 1991, when he was the youngest player on the field. Three years later he transferred to Manchester United for the then record British fee of £3.75 million and he was a major player in the team which achieved the League and Cup double in 1994. Having been capped for Ireland at under-15, under-16, youth and under-21 levels, he made his full senior début against Chile in 1991, and went on to play for the Republic in the 1994 World Cup finals in the USA.

KEARINS, Michael (Mickey) (1943–), Gaelic footballer. After winning seven Sligo county football medals with the Dromard club, he played for 17 successive seasons for the county, sharing in its only Connacht Senior Football Championship success (1975) and being on the team which lost the finals of 1965 and 1971. A notable marksman, he was Sligo's top scorer in competitive matches in four different years. He won two Railway Cup medals in a 13-year career with Connacht (1967, 1969) and won an All-Star award (at left full-forward) in the inaugural year of the scheme, 1971.

KEARNEY, Peadar (1883–1942), songwriter, b. Dublin, ed. Model School, Schoolhouse Lane and CBS, Marino, d. Dublin, Nov. 1942. Left school at 14 and worked in various jobs, eventually becoming a house painter. Joined the Gaelic League and the IRB. He wrote the words of 'A Soldier's Song' in 1907; set to music, it later became the Irish national anthem. Member of the Jacob's factory garrison under THOMAS MACDONAGH in the Easter Rising. Interned during the War of Independence.

KEARNEY, Richard (1954–), critic and academic, b. Cork, ed. CBS, Cork, Glenstal, Montreal and Paris. He lectured in philosophy at UCD 1981–9, professor since 1990. Won the American Library Association award 1989. Founder editor of the *Crane Bag Book of Irish Studies*. Kearney is one of Ireland's brightest and most erudite intellectuals, whose work is at the cutting edge of European philosophy.

Writings include: *Heidegger et la question de Dieu*, co-edited with Joseph Stephen O'Leary (1980), *Dialogues with Contemporary Continental Thinkers* (1984), *The Irish Mind* and *Modern Movements in European Philosophy* (1985), *Across the Frontiers* and *The Wake of Imagination* (1988), *Migrations* (1990), *Poetics of Imagining, From Husserl to Lyotard* (1991), *Visions of Europe* (1992), *Twentieth-century Continental Philosophy* (1994), *Poetics of Modernity* (1995). He has also published poetry: *Poétique du possible* (1984) and *Angel of Patrick's Hill*, a long poem (1991); a novel: *Sam's Fall* (1995). Member of the Arts Council, Higher Education Authority, RIA and Irish Philosophical Society.

KEATING, John (Seán) (1889–1977), artist, b. Limerick, 19 Sept. 1889, ed. St Munchin's College, Limerick, Limerick Municipal School of Art and Metropolitan School of Art, Dublin, where he was taught by WILLIAM ORPEN, d. Dublin, 21 Dec. 1977. Influenced, and was influenced by, his friend HARRY CLARKE: each included portraits of the other in various compositions. Clarke introduced him to the Aran Islands, the people of which he was to paint often and evocatively. MRHA 1923. In a series of pictures, he painted a record of the ongoing construction of the Shannon Hydroelectric Scheme in the late 1920s, a canvas for the New York World Fair in 1939 and a mural for the International Labour Office in Geneva in 1961. His fine Stations of the Cross in Clongowes show him simultaneously at his most dramatic and his most reverential; they also depict Keating himself as Christ, with his wife as the Virgin Mary.

KEATING, Justin (1930–), politician, broadcaster and veterinary surgeon, b. Dublin, 7 Jan. 1930, ed. UCD and London University. Lecturer in anatomy at UCD's veterinary college 1955–60, senior lecturer TCD 1960–65. RTÉ's head of agricultural programmes for two years before returning to TCD in 1967. Entered the Dáil as a member of the Labour Party two years later and was appointed Minister for Industry and Commerce in the 1973–7 Fine Gael–Labour coalition. He lost his seat in the 1977 election and subsequently became a member of the Senate 1977–80 and chairman of the Crafts Council of Ireland 1982–4. His television documentaries include *Surrounded by Water*, *Into Europe* and *A Sense of Excellence*.

KEATING, Michael (Babs) (1944–), hurler, Gaelic footballer and hurling trainer, b. Ardfinnan, Co. Tipperary, 17 Apr. 1944. A member of the Tipperary team which won the inaugural All-Ireland Under-21 Hurling Championship in 1964, he played senior county hurling 1963–73 and senior county football 1962–75. He won three All-Ireland senior hurling medals with Tipperary (1964, 1965 and 1971), two Railway Cup hurling medals with Munster (1968 and 1970) and a Railway Cup football medal (1972). He was a member of the inaugural All-Stars hurling team in 1971. As a trainer, he guided Tipperary to the All-Ireland victories of 1989 and 1991, five Munster championships and National League success.

KEATING, Séamus (1930–), public servant, b. Tipperary, ed. Rockwell, m., nine children. Served with the county councils of Waterford, Tipperary, Donegal and Kerry before becoming county manager of Galway in 1973 and in 1986 county and city manager and town clerk. Retired 1993. At various times chairman of the County and City Managers' Association, Kerry and Galway County Development Teams, Galway Task Force and the Leukaemia Trust. Board member of Ireland West, Galway Airport and Galway/ Boston Ventures. Played a large part in major infrastructural developments in Galway county and city, in an urban renewal programme in the city and in the Galway quincentennial celebrations in 1984.

KEAVENEY, James (Jimmy) (1945–), Gaelic footballer and hurler, b. Dublin, 12 Feb. 1945. While renowned as a football full-forward, he also played hurling at minor, underage and senior level for Dublin 1962–70, and won many honours with the St Vincent's club. His senior football début for Dublin came in 1964. He retired prematurely in 1972 but returned to play a starring role in Dublin's great successes in the 1970s, winning All-Ireland football medals in 1974, 1976 and 1977 and playing on the teams which lost the finals of 1975 and 1978. He was Dublin's top points-scorer in 1967 and again in three successive years 1976–8. His two goals and six points in the 1977 final against Armagh is a record individual score shared with Kerry's MIKEY SHEEHY, and he also won two National League medals with Dublin, in 1976 and 1978. He

won three All-Star awards, in 1974, 1977 and 1978, all at full-forward.

KEENAN, Brian (1950–), Beirut hostage, b. Belfast, left school at 15. Worked with a heating firm in east Belfast, studied for City and Guilds qualification as a heating engineer. Won several prizes for poetry, went to NUU (Coleraine), where he graduated with a degree in 19th- and 20th-century Irish, British and American literature, later completing MA in Anglo-Irish literature. Taught in Belgium and Spain as well as Belfast, where he also worked in community development. Went to Beirut as lecturer in English in 1986, was kidnapped and held captive there by fundamentalist Shi'ite militiamen for four and a half years (1,596 days) and released in Aug. 1990 following sustained diplomatic intervention by Irish foreign minister GERARD COLLINS on his behalf as an Irish citizen holding an Irish passport. His best-selling book, *An Evil Cradling* (1992), detailed how he and other hostages were beaten, humiliated and kept in darkness and squalor. In 1993 he won the *Irish Times* prize for non-fiction, the Christopher Ewart-Biggs memorial prize and the *Time/Life* international prize. Took up writer-in-residence post in TCD 1993. Awarded CBE with former hostages John McCarthy and Terry Waite in Mar. 1992.

KEHER, Edward Peter (Eddie) (1941–), hurler, b. Inistioge, Co. Kilkenny, 14 Oct. 1941. In a senior hurling career which lasted from 1959 to 1977 he won six All-Ireland medals with Kilkenny, in 1963, 1967, 1969, 1972, 1974 and 1975. He scored 14 points in the 1963 final, captained the team in 1969, and his 93 points (seven goals and 72 points) is a record in senior All-Ireland hurling finals. He also was on the losing Kilkenny sides in the finals of 1966, 1971 (when he scored a record 2–11) and 1973, and he was hurling's leading points-scorer an astonishing 11 times between 1963 and 1976. His nine Railway Cup medals is a Leinster hurling record, and he also won three National League titles with the county, in 1962, 1966 and 1976. He won five successive All-Star awards 1971–5, at left-half forward and at left full-forward.

KELLETT, Iris Patricia (1926–), international showjumper, b. Dublin, 8 Jan. 1926. Her first major win was the Queen Elizabeth

Cup in 1949 and she regained it in 1951 (both times on Rusty), having been placed second in 1950. Her major year was 1951, with four victories at the three top shows, but an injury in 1952 kept her out of the sport until the 1960s. In 1969 she became Ladies European Champion in Dublin with her defeat of Ann Drummond-Hay. She later ran a highly successful riding school.

KELLY, Charles E. (1902–1981), cartoonist and editor, b. Dublin, ed. Synge Street, d. 20 Jan. 1981. Worked in Department of Education while contributing cartoons to the humorous monthly *Dublin Opinion*, which he founded in 1922 with Arthur Booth and a colleague in the department, Thomas Collins, and which he and Collins edited 1926–68. It was virtually a national institution until the 1950s, when the competition of newer media and a sharper public taste in satire led to its decline. Gentle fun-poking, often amounting to subtly perceptive comment on the political institutions and personalities of the day, distinguished Kelly's many cartoons, all signed C.E.K. Some were long-remembered masterpieces of the art: 'The Night the Treaty was Signed', for example, and 'Ceilidh at the Kildare Street Club'. Kelly became deputy director of broadcasting in 1942, director 1948–52. Hon. doctorate (NUI).

KELLY, Henry (1946–), broadcaster, b. Dublin, 17 Apr. 1946, ed. Belvedere and UCD (BA). From 1968 to 1976 he was *Irish Times* reporter in Dublin and Belfast, where he wrote *How Stormont Fell*; Northern editor 1969–73. Also contributed to Press Association, *Observer*, *The Sunday Times* and various publications around the world. BBC Radio 4 reporter and sometime presenter for *The World Tonight* 1976–81. In the early 1980s he hosted London Weekend TV's *Game for a Laugh*, which earned ratings of 18 million and established him as a TV face. Presented editions of TV-AM and since 1987 the lunchtime BBC 1 TV quiz *Going for Gold*, which has a weekly viewership of 10–15 million. Joined the new commercial British radio station Classic FM 1992 and presents a three-hour morning programme every weekday, his flamboyant broadcasting personality now identified with the station. Sony Broadcaster of the Year 1994, *Irish Post* Man of Achievement 1994.

KELLY, John (1912–1989), fiddler and concertina player, b. Rehy Cross, Co. Clare, an area of the county where the Irish language had proved more lasting than elsewhere. From an early age he demonstrated exceptional gifts on both his instruments in the time-honoured style of Clare. His many musical friends included JOHNNY DORAN. Moving to Dublin at the age of 30, he established a shop in Capel Street where he dealt in everything from bicycles to fiddles. The premises became a required gathering point for visiting musicians and those resident in the city. Although widely acclaimed as a soloist, he gained much ensemble experience. SEÁN Ó RIADA enrolled him as a member of Ceoltóirí Cualann and he also played with the Castle Céilí Band. Later he recorded with Ceoltóirí Laigheann, the group formed by EAMON DE BUITLÉAR with some former members of Ceoltóirí Cualann and other musicians.

KELLY, John Maurice (1931–1991), lawyer and politician, b. Dublin, ed. Glenstal, UCD, Oxford, Heidelberg and King's Inns, d. 24 Jan. 1991. Doctorate in jurisprudence (Heidelberg), fellowship of Trinity College, Oxford, specialised in Roman law. Senator for NUI constituency 1969–73, then Fine Gael TD, chief whip and member of opposition front bench. Called to Bar 1957, became Senior Counsel 1977 on the day after he was appointed Attorney-General, a post he held for 48 days. On the government's defeat in July of that year he returned to UCD to the professorship of jurisprudence and Roman law he had held from 1965. A brilliant public speaker, probably the best since JAMES DILLON, Kelly often took an independent line on party issues and incurred the wrath of Fine Gael for persistently advocating a merger with Fianna Fáil. His honesty and frankness made him popular with the public and his opponents. Refusing to hold constituency 'clinics' because of his dislike of political 'clientelism', and declining the privilege of a state car when in office, his partisan attitude in the episode that led in 1976 to the resignation from the presidency of CEARBHALL Ó DÁLAIGH caused some surprise.

Appointed Minister for Industry and Commerce, he also held the foreign ministry post briefly. Although a member of the New

Ireland Forum, he refused to sign its report in 1984. He was against the FG–Labour coalition in 1982 but supported it in preference to an FF administration led by CHARLES HAUGHEY, whom he distrusted. He favoured the introduction of divorce and increased privatisation, even of education. A frequent, often controversial and always witty broadcaster on both radio and television, Kelly was also a prolific writer. As a young lawyer he wrote two novels, the second a political detective story that appeared posthumously. In the legal world he will be remembered principally for his two series of books on the constitution – the popular *Fundamental Rights under the Irish Constitution* (1961 and 1967), followed by his massive academic work, *The Irish Constitution* (1980 and 1984), a posthumous third edition of which (eds. Hogan and Whyte) appeared in 1994. He was also responsible for the 'new' *Irish Jurist*, which under his editorship became easily the best ever Irish legal academic periodical. Within a year of Kelly's death an anthology of his speeches and witticisms had also been published, under the title *Belling the Cats*.

KELLY, Maeve (1930–), fiction writer and poet, b. Dundalk, ed. locally. She trained as a student nurse in London and went on to work in Oxford and at several Irish institutions. After farming for a time in Co. Clare, she became involved in the Irish Women's Liberation Movement in 1974; she has been active for many years with ADAPT, the Limerick refuge for battered wives and their children. In 1972 she won a Hennessy literary award. Kelly's work is conventional and deals mainly with the problems which beset rural Irish women. Her short story collection, *A Life of Her Own* (1976), was highly praised, and she has written four novels to date: *Necessary Treasons* (1985), *Orange Horses* (1990), *Florrie's Girls* (1991) and *Alice in Thunderland (A Feminist Fairytale)* (1993), as well as a book of poetry, *Resolution* (1986). She gives frequent readings and workshops throughout the country.

KELLY, Oisín (Austin Ernest) (1915–1981), sculptor, b. Dublin, 17 May 1915, ed. St James's NS, Mountjoy School, Dublin and TCD. After graduation he continued his studies at the Goethe University in Frankfurt and later with Henry Moore at the Chelsea Polytechnic in London. He joined Kilkenny Design Workshops in 1966 but continued his private practice. His most celebrated public work is *The Children of Lir* in the Garden of Remembrance, Parnell Square, Dublin. His statue of the labour leader JAMES LARKIN, based on a famous photograph by Joseph Cashman, stands in O'Connell Street.

KELLY, Séamus Brian (1912–1979), journalist and critic, b. Belfast, Aug. 1912, the son of a civil servant, ed. St Mary's CBS, Belfast and at QUB and UCC, from neither of which he graduated, m. Aileen Murphy 1943, three children, d. Dublin, 31 May 1979. Boxing blue at QUB and while studying Anglo-Irish literature at UCC supported himself by means of occasional journalism. He joined the army as a gunner in 1940 and was commissioned the following year. While still in the army, he contributed reports and articles to a number of newspapers, including *The Irish Times*, which was subsequently to engage him in his journalistic career. He also wrote theatre notices, ballet notes and critiques. Member of the Aer Lingus public relations and publicity department 1946–9. By this stage he was the *Irish Times* theatre critic and was contributing more and more to the daily 'Irishman's Diary' column as one of the many Pro-Quidnuncs then employed. Appointed as Quidnunc in the autumn of 1949, he rapidly made the column essential reading for anyone who had aspirations of familiarity with Ireland's social or cultural scene. In 1954 John Huston chose him to play Flask, the third mate, in his film version of *Moby Dick*. It was a part in which Huston admitted that Kelly did not shine, but his wonderful face filled the screen as well as those of the professionals who played Queequeg or Ahab. He was a founding member of the JOYCE Society.

KELLY, Seán (1956–), cyclist, b. Curraghduff, Co. Waterford, 24 May 1956. Having won the Irish Junior Championship in 1972, he won his first professional race in 1977. He was ranked the world's number one cyclist from Oct. 1984 to May 1989, due mostly to his success in one-day classics, of which he won 12 in all. He won 32 races in 1984, 29 in 1986 and was the first World Cup series winner in 1989. An average climber, his biggest disappointment was failure to win the Tour de France, though he was points winner a record four times, in 1982, 1983, 1985 and 1989. His best placing was fourth in 1985, he had five stage victories between 1978 and 1982, and wore the yellow jersey once, in 1983. The Paris–Nice stage race, which he won an astonishing seven years in a row, was his major success; other achievements include Vuelta d'España (1980 – points jersey – 1985, 1986, 1988), Tour de Suisse (1983), Milan–San Remo (1986, 1992), Ghent–Wevelgem (1988), Paris–Roubaix (1984, 1986), Liège–Bastogne–Liège (1984, 1989), Grand Prix de Nations (1986), Paris–Tours (1984), Tour of Lombardy (1983, 1985, 1991).

KELLY-ROGERS, J.C. (1905–1981), captain and aviator, b. Co. Dublin, ed. Presentation College, Glasthule and Clongowes, d. Dublin, 29 Jan. 1981. He became a pilot in the RAF in 1927 and entered the world of civil aviation in 1935. Churchill's transatlantic pilot during World War II, he later became chief North Atlantic pilot for BOAC, which preceded British Airways. OBE 1941. Joined Aer Lingus 1947 as technical manager and rose to deputy manager before retiring in 1965. Prime mover behind the Irish Aviation Museum.

KEMMY, Jim (1936–), politician, b. Limerick, Sept. 1936, ed. CBS, Sexton Street and Municipal Technical Institute, Limerick and UCC (Dip.Soc.Sci.). Dáil deputy 1981–2 and since 1987 (elected as an Independent, he joined the Labour Party in 1991); chairman Labour Party since 1993. Member Limerick County Council since 1974 (alderman from 1979; mayor 1991–2). Kemmy worked as a stonemason with Limerick Corporation 1962–81; secretary of the Limerick branch of the Brick and Stonelayers' Trade Union since 1960 and of the Limerick Building Trades Group since 1968. He was a member of the Labour Party 1963–72 and in 1982 founded the Democratic Socialist Party, which merged with Labour in 1991. Editor of the *Limerick Socialist* 1972–81 and of the *Old Limerick Journal* since 1979.

KENNEDY, Hugh (1879–1936), lawyer, b. Dublin, ed. privately and at UCD and King's Inns, d. 12 Dec. 1936. Called to Bar 1902, Senior Counsel 1920, practised on Munster circuit. Honorary secretary, central branch, Gaelic League. Legal adviser to Irish delegation at Anglo-Irish Treaty negotiations 1921, law officer of Provisional Government of the Irish Free State 1922. The most influential member of the committee that drafted the IFS constitution, he was appointed first Attorney-General of IFS Dec. 1922, was on the Judiciary Committee that reorganised the courts system and on the first Irish delegation to the League of Nations. TD (C. na nG. Dublin City South) Oct. 1923, first Chief Justice of IFS June 1924, a post he filled with outstanding success for over 12 years. Inclined like many of his time to equate Irish nationalism with Irish Catholicism, he anticipated, in a famous dissenting judgment in 1935 (State, Ryan v. Lennon), the influence of natural law, which became the basis of major Supreme Court decisions 30 years later. Among his successors, history will probably record that only CEARBHALL Ó DÁLAIGH has so far equalled him for all-round judicial competence. Possessing a brilliant analytical mind, Kennedy was an intensely patriotic man, ideally qualified to oversee the replacement of the politicised pre-1922 Dublin Castle judiciary by one befitting the new independent Irish state, where the separation of judicial and executive powers is rigidly adhered to. Widely read, he was interested in all forms of Irish culture and characteristically left his substantial collection of papers to his Alma Mater, UCD, where it forms one of the most important private sources of the history of the modern Irish state.

KENNEDY, Jimmy (1902–1984), lyricist, b. Omagh, 20 July 1902, d. Cheltenham, 6 Apr. 1984. Reared in Portstewart, Co. Derry. After leaving TCD he worked in the colonial service until the success of 'The Teddy Bears' Picnic', which sold four million records, allowed him to become a full-time lyricist. The inferior position accorded by the trade to the wordsmith rankled, but 'South of the Border', 'The Isle of Capri' and 'Red Sails in the Sunset' are known to many who do not know the composer. Kennedy's career lasted until the 1960s, when a different kind of popular music took over. His citations include the Ivor Novello award (twice), D.Litt. (NUU) 1978 and an OBE granted in 1983.

KENNEDY, Kieran (1935–), economist, b. Newbridge, Co. Kildare, ed. NUI (M.Econ. Sc. 1960), Nuffield College, Oxford (B.Phil. 1963) and Harvard (Ph.D. in economics 1968). Executive officer in the Department of Industry and Commerce prior to joining the Department of Finance as an administrative officer in 1956. On loan to the ESRI from 1968, director 1971–96. Member of the RIA and of several government advisory bodies, including NESC and the Committee on Local Government Reorganisation and Reform. Member of the American Economic Association and of the International Association for Research on Income and Wealth. Involvement in ecumenical activities has included membership of the Pauline Circle for dialogue between the Irish Council of Christians and Jews. Author of over 70 published papers (sometimes in collaboration with others) on various aspects of economic development, of another 70 given at economic seminars and related occasions, and about 40 on religious and ecumenical topics. His books include *Economic Growth in Ireland: The Experience since 1947* and *The Economic Development of Ireland in the Twentieth Century*.

KENNEDY, Sister Stanislaus (1939–), founder and president of Focus Point, Focus Housing and Focus Ireland, campaigner for the homeless and disadvantaged, b. Treasa Kennedy, Dingle, Co. Kerry, 19 June 1939, ed. Presentation Convent, Dingle, UCD (B.Sc. social science, MA social policy) and Manchester University. Joined the Sisters of Charity 1958, in 1964 was sent to the Kilkenny Social Services Group, under guidance of Bishop Birch, became director 1970. Went to Dublin 1983 and undertook the first major study of homelessness. Created Focus Point in Eustace Street, one of the most active agencies for the deprived in the city; Focus Housing (1989), based in the Sisters of Charity's convent, Stanhope Street; and the national research, development and public awareness project Focus Ireland (1994). Chairperson of National Committee to Combat Poverty 1974–80. Books include *Who Should Care?* and *One Million Poor?* (1981); she has also written articles and papers. Frequent clashes with public figures because of her outspoken views on social issues. The

first nun to receive an honorary doctorate of laws from TCD (1982).

KENNELLY, Brendan (1936–), poet and academic, b. Ballylongford, Co. Kerry, 17 Apr. 1936, ed. St Ita's College, Tarbert, Co. Kerry, TCD and Leeds University. Has lectured in English literature in TCD since 1963, becoming Associate Professor of Modern Literature 1969, professor 1973. He has also lectured in US colleges, was Gildersleeve Professor of Literature at Barnard College, New York 1971 and taught in Pennsylvania 1971–2. Poetry collections include *My Dark Fathers, Good Souls to Survive, Dream of a Black Fox, Love Cry, The Voices, Shelley in Dublin, Islandman, The House that Jack Didn't Build, The Boats are Home, Cromwell* and *Judas*. Editor of *The Penguin Book of Irish Verse* and co-editor of *Ireland's Women: Writings Past and Present*. Received AE memorial prize for poetry 1967 and Critics' Special Harvey Award 1988. A national figure through his appearances on radio and television.

KENNY, John (1918–1987), lawyer and judge, b. Dublin, ed. CUS, Konsular Akademie, Vienna, UCD and King's Inns, d. 25 Mar. 1987. Called to the Bar 1940, Senior Counsel 1958, lectured in law in UCD and King's Inns. High Court judge from 1960, appointed to the Supreme Court 1975, retiring because of ill health 1981. Regarded as being of liberal outlook when on the bench, his seminal decision as a High Court judge in the fluoridation case (Ryan v. A.-G. 1965) established the doctrine of citizens' unenumerated or unspecified rights enforceable under the constitution.

KENNY, Mary (1944–), journalist, b. Dublin, ed. Loreto College, St Stephen's Green, Dublin. Closely involved in the founding of the Irish Women's Liberation Movement in the 1970s. She has worked as a journalist on newspapers and magazines in Dublin and in London, where she now lives. Her published work is largely serious non-fiction and concerns itself with motherhood, women in the workplace, and morality from a Roman Catholic viewpoint. Publications include *Woman x Two: How to Cope with a Double Life* (1978), about women and employment, *Why Christianity Works* (1981) and *Abortion: The Whole Story* (1986). She has also written a book of short stories, *A Mood for Love* (1989), set in Dublin, Budapest, Brussels and chiefly London.

KENNY, Pat (1949–), broadcaster, ed. O'Connell School, UCD (graduating in science) and Georgia Institute of Technology. Lecturer in Bolton Street College of Technology, Dublin 1970–72. Current affairs reporter-presenter on RTÉ from 1972. Involved in many programmes of topical social and political analysis, such as the TV series *Public Account* and *Today Tonight*, and the long-running midmorning *Pat Kenny Show* on radio. A television chat-and-music show, *Kenny Live*, has meanwhile given him a platform to deal with lighter matters. Glaxo award for scientific broadcasting 1979, Jacob's award 1982. Member RTÉ Authority 1985–90. Director of programme production firm Promedia Ireland Ltd.

KENNY, Sean (1933–1973), set designer, b. Portroe, Co. Tipperary. Trained as an architect, he studied in the USA with Frank Lloyd Wright, whose work he especially admired. He did not succeed in private architectural practice back in Ireland, however, and left for London, where he established himself as a theatre designer of outstanding originality and flair. His fame spread and architectural and theatrical commissions came from both sides of the Atlantic. He died with tragic suddenness in London on 11 June 1973.

KENT, Thomas (1867–1916), revolutionary, b. Castlelyons, Co. Cork, into a substantial farming family who had been prominent locally in the Land League. After a period in America he returned to Ireland, joined the Gaelic League and the Irish Volunteers. Waited at home in Co. Cork during Easter Rising in 1916, expecting further instructions following the attempted cancellation of the insurrection by EOIN MACNEILL. Together with his brothers and 80-year-old mother, he resisted arrest by armed police on 2 May in a fracas which resulted in the deaths of his brother Richard and the head constable in charge of the police unit. Court-martialled, executed Cork, 9 May 1916.

KEOGH, Sir Alfred (1857–1936), director-general British Army Medical Services, b. 3 July 1857, s. of Henry Keogh of Roscommon, ed. Queen's College, Galway, d. 30 July 1936. Qualified as a doctor in 1880 and joined the British army. Deputy director-

general of Army Medical Services 1902. As director-general 1905–10 and 1914–18 he helped to establish the Royal Army Medical College, Millbank and the Army School of Hygiene. Rector of the Imperial College of Science 1910–22.

KERNAN, Anne (1933–), scientist, b. Dublin, d. of Frederick and Annie Kernan, ed. King's Inn Street School, Dominican College, Eccles Street, Dublin and UCD (B.Sc., Ph.D. in physics). Assistant lecturer UCD 1958–62, postdoctoral researcher at Lawrence Berkeley Laboratory, California 1962–6 and at Stanford Linear Accelerator Centre, California 1966–7. Since 1967 a faculty member at University of California, Riverside (UCR); appointed Professor of Physics 1972 and served as physics department chair 1973–6. Since 1991 vice-chancellor for research and dean of the graduate division at UCR; currently serving as chair of the council of graduate deans of the University of California system. Throughout her career she has pursued research in elementary particle physics, the search for the ultimate constituents of matter and the forces which bind them. In experiments at high-energy particle accelerators she has investigated: the structure of the weak interaction through studies of K-meson decays; the quark structure of matter through measurements of the quantum numbers of baryon resonances; the creation of short-lived heavy quarks and the theory of the strong interaction. She led the US team on the multinational experiments at CERN (European Centre for Particle Physics) which in 1983 discovered the W- and Z-bosons, the long-sought carriers of the weak force. In 1984 she was named faculty research lecturer at UCR. She has served on many national committees in the USA, including the advisory committee for physics to the National Science Foundation 1978–81, the council of the American Physical Society 1985–9 and the High Energy Physics Advisory Panel 1986–90.

KERNOFF, Harry Aaron (1900–1974), artist, b. London, 9 Jan. 1900, moved to Dublin with his family in 1914. He was apprenticed to his father's trade as a cabinetmaker but attended evening classes at the Metropolitan School of Art, Dublin. In 1923 he won the Taylor art scholarship in both watercolour and oil painting. Kernoff adopted a strongly realistic approach to his figurative and landscape studies. His work is often colourful and witty, and is concerned more with detailed observation and rendering rather than attempting to convey the mood or atmosphere of a scene. This realism places him firmly in the academic tradition of painting, but his approach to his subject, usually the mundane and ordinary, is charming and original. His humour is also evident in his woodcuts and in his work as an illustrator and set designer. He exhibited at the RHA every year between 1926 and his death, on Christmas Day, in 1974.

KETTLE, Thomas Michael (1880–1916), essayist, orator and parliamentarian, b. Artane, Co. Dublin, 9 Feb. 1880, s. of Andrew Kettle, a leading associate of Parnell in the Land League, ed. CBS, North Richmond Street, Dublin, Clongowes and UCD, m. Mary Sheehy 1909, d. 9 Sept. 1916. He was called to the Bar but his interests lay more in public affairs. MP (IP East Tyrone) 1906–10, he spoke with verve and wit at Westminster and on public platforms. Publications include a collection of essays, *The Day's Burden* (1910), a booklet on Home Rule finance (1911) and *The Open Secret of Ireland*. In 1909 he had been appointed Professor of National Economics at UCD but this did not really suit his talents. Associates noted his phases of conviviality and melancholia and escapes into heavy drinking. His social concern was shown by his efforts to mediate in the 1913 Lock-out, and his deep religious sense was evident in his writings.

Active in the formation of the National Volunteers, he was in Belgium in 1914 at the outbreak of World War I. Taking a commission in the Royal Dublin Fusiliers, he recruited strenuously for the Irish regiments. Dismayed by the Easter Rising and the executions – some of personal friends – that followed, he was serving with the 16th (Irish) Division in France when killed at Guinchy on the Somme. Virtually on the eve of his death he wrote a famous sonnet dedicated to his infant daughter, Betty, and ending with the memorable lines:

Died not for flag, nor King, nor Emperor,
But for a dream, born in a herdsman's shed,
And for the secret Scripture of the poor.

KIELY, Benedict (1919–), writer, b. Dromore, Co. Tyrone, ed. CBS, Omagh and UCD. Journalist in Dublin 1940–65, including a spell as literary editor of the *Irish Press*. His published novels include *Land without Stars* (1946), *In a Harbour Green* (1949), *The Captain with the Whiskers* (1960), *Nothing Happens in Carmincross* (1985). Short story collections include *A Journey to the Seven Streams* (1963), *A Cow in the House* (1978), *A Letter to Peachtree* (1987). Editor of *The Penguin Book of Irish Short Stories* (1981). A prolific writer, he received the American-Irish Foundation award 1980, IAL award 1980, *Irish Independent* literary award 1985. D.Litt. (NUI and QUB).

KIERNAN, Thomas J. (1897–1967), diplomat and author, b. Dublin, ed. St Mary's College, Rathmines, Dublin, UCD (MA) and London University (Ph.D.), m. Delia Murphy, well-known ballad singer, three children. Inspector of taxes 1919. Appointed secretary to the office of the Irish high commissioner in London 1924, where he was a founder of the National University Club. Returned to Dublin in 1935 to become director of Radio Éireann in its new headquarters in the recently rebuilt GPO. The initial appointment was for one year, on secondment. It continued, however, until 1941, when he was appointed Minister to the Vatican. In 1946 he went to Australia to open Ireland's first mission to that country as high commissioner, becoming ambassador in 1950. Later Kiernan served as ambassador to West Germany 1955–6, Canada 1956–60 and Washington 1960–64, as which he discussed with John F. Kennedy the detailed arrangements for the US president's visit to Ireland in 1963, including the content of his speeches. Addressing a dinner of the Charitable Society of Boston on St Patrick's Day 1962, he made a successful appeal for an Irish-American foundation, and subsequently became its director. Publications include: *British War Finance, A Study of National Finance, A History of the Financial Administration of Ireland to 1817, The Irish Exiles in Australia* and a literary portrait of Pope Pius XII.

KIERNAN, Thomas Joseph (1939–), international rugby player, b. Cork, 7 Jan. 1939. Although originally a centre, he is Ireland's most capped full-back, with 54 international appearances 1960–73, being captain in 24 of them, which is an Irish record. He toured South Africa with the Lions in 1962, playing in the first Test, and returned as captain of the 1968 touring party, playing in all four Tests, scoring 17 points in the first and 35 of the 38 points scored by the Lions in the series. Ireland's national coach for three seasons, he coached the squad which in 1982 won the Triple Crown for the first time in 33 years and in 1983 won the Five Nations Championship. He also coached the 1978 Munster side which defeated the All Blacks, the only Irish team to beat New Zealand. He was president of the IRFU 1988–9 and is one of Ireland's representatives on the International Rugby Football Board.

KIGGELL, Launcelot Edward (1862–1954), British general, b. Ballingarry, Co. Limerick, 2 Oct. 1862, d. 23 Feb. 1954. Served in South African War 1899–1902, commandant of Staff College 1913–14. He became chief of staff to General, later Field Marshal, Haig in France 1915–18, a period covering the Battle of the Somme 1916, Third Ypres ('Passchendaele') 1917 and the March Offensive 1918. Strong supporter of Haig and Western Front generals against Lloyd George. Knighted and made lieutenant-general, he was later commanding officer in Guernsey 1918–20.

KILLANIN (Michael Morris), Lord (1914–), journalist, businessman and sports administrator, b. Melbourne, ed. Eton, Sorbonne and Magdalene College, Cambridge. Began his career in journalism as diplomatic and political correspondent of the *Daily Mail* and the *Sunday Dispatch*. Served in British army in World War II as brigade-major, 30th Armoured Brigade. Elected president of the Olympic Council of Ireland 1950; president of the International Olympic Committee 1970–80, overseeing the modernisation of the Games. On a number of company boards, also involved in the bloodstock industry. Has written several books and worked with John Ford in film production.

KILLEEN, Michael (1928–1986), public servant, b. Donegal, ed. Garbally Park, UCG and TCD. Executive officer in the Department of Industry and Commerce 1947–52. Joined Córas Tráchtála Teoranta (CTT) as manager of that body's first New York office 1952. Became secretary in 1957, deputy general

manager in 1963 and served as general manager 1967–9. During this period he was a lecturer in marketing in TCD. In Jan. 1970 he was appointed by the government as chief executive of the re-formed Industrial Development Authority; retiring in 1980, he was chairman of the Authority from the following year.

His exceptional blend of attractive personality, analytical capacity, sound judgment and persuasiveness enabled him to make a considerable contribution to the development of modern Irish industry. At the time of his death he was chairman of Co-operation North, endeavouring to bring Irish people closer together in business, social and educational matters. Throughout his career he held a number of part-time appointments. He was the first chairman of AnCO and served on the boards of the Central Bank, the Shannon Free Airport Development Company, the Institute of Public Administration and the ESRI. Hon. doctorate (NUI).

KILLORAN, Paddy (1904–1965), fiddler and band leader, b. Ballymote, Co. Sligo, he was one of eight siblings, all of whom were instrumentalists. These talents were inherited, their father playing the flute and their mother the concertina. Growing up in an area rich in musical tradition, Killoran emigrated to the USA in 1925, settling in New York. Having initially worked as a lift attendant, he eventually made a living through music. Highly regarded as a soloist, he is perhaps most vividly remembered as leader of the Pride of Erin Orchestra, attached to the ballroom of the same name. During the 1930s the orchestra frequently performed live on the Brooklyn radio station WBBC and recorded numerous 78s. Some of these early recordings were reissued on the Shanachie label, and in 1958 Colonial released an LP of him with flute player Michael Flynn.

KILROY, Thomas (1934–), playwright and academic, b. Callan, Co. Kilkenny, ed. UCD. Lecturer 1962–5 at Notre Dame University, Indiana and the Vanderbilt University, Tennessee; at UCD 1965–73; Professor of English UCG 1979–89. Plays include: *The Death and Resurrection of Mr Roche* (1968); *Tea, Sex and Shakespeare*, which was performed at the Abbey Theatre in 1976;

Talbot's Box, Peacock Theatre 1977 and the Royal Court Theatre, London; *Double Cross*, produced by Field Day Theatre Company in 1986; *Madam McAdam's Travelling Theatre* (1992), produced by the same company (of which he became a director in 1988). Adaptations include Chekhov's *The Seagull*, Royal Court 1981, and Ibsen's *Ghosts*, Peacock 1989. *The Big Chapel* (1971), a historical novel set in his native Callan, was shortlisted for the Booker prize and won the *Guardian* prize for fiction.

KINANE, Michael Joseph (1959–), jockey, b. Killenaule, Co. Tipperary, 22 June 1959. He rode his first winner at Leopardstown in 1975, was champion apprentice in 1978, and Irish champion jockey ten times between 1984 and 1994. His Irish Classics wins were the 2,000 Guineas (1982, 1986), the 1,000 Guineas (1988), the Oaks (1989) and the St Leger (1993, 1994, both on Vintage Crop). English Classics successes were the 2,000 Guineas (1990, on Tirol) and the Derby (1993, on Commander-in-chief). In 1989 he won the Prix de l'Arc de Triomphe on Carroll House and in the same weekend won the Cartier Million on The Caretaker, and in 1993 he won the Melbourne Cup on Vintage Crop, which was the first European-trained horse to win the Australian race. His father, Tommy Kinane, rode Monksfield to win the Champion Hurdle at Cheltenham in 1978.

KING, Brian (1942–), sculptor, b. Dublin, ed. National College of Art, Dublin. He participated in the Irish Exhibition of Living Art 1964–78 and won the Carroll's award in 1965. In 1969 he represented Ireland at the Paris Biennale and became the first Irish artist to win the major prize there. He has had solo exhibitions in several major galleries, including the Ulster Museum, Belfast 1973 and the Douglas Hyde Gallery, Dublin 1982. King has lectured in the NCAD for a number of years and is now head of the college's sculpture department. His large-scale public metal sculptures are abstract and minimalist in style, usually based on simple geometric patterns; among his commissions is the brilliant yellow structure outside the science block in UCG. His exhibition pieces, though far smaller in scale, are equally concerned with achieving simplicity and balance in design.

KING, Cecil (1921–1986), artist, b. Rathdrum, Co. Wicklow, 22 Feb. 1921, ed. Athlone and Dublin, d. Dún Laoghaire, Co. Dublin, 7 Apr. 1986. Businessman. His membership of An Óige (the Irish Youth Hostel Association) developed a natural taste for travel as well as for walking, which enabled him to see all the major international collections. At the age of 33, when building up a personal collection of modern paintings, he taught himself to paint. His first one-man show was held in Dublin in 1959, and two years later he designed stage scenery for *Les Sylphides*, performed by the Irish National Ballet Company at the Abbey Theatre. He painted some religious works in the early 1960s.

From 1964 King devoted himself to painting. Winning the Open Painting Competition in Belfast began a career which brought him international acclaim. His work had by now become completely abstract, though always with some allegorical significance and based on actuality. From 1965 to 1968 he was absorbed with the tension and excitement of acrobatic performances at the circus – a sickle shape representing a thrown rope, a taut band or flickering loop symbolising aspects of the trapeze act. A gift for poetic understatement was enhanced by touches of humour and subtle shifts of emphasis in detail. His 'Berlin' paintings were more sombre, simple yet profound in their condemnation of the restriction of man's freedom. The poetic concepts of these groups of paintings adapted well to small pastels, for which King was celebrated, and to tapestry.

His mature style altered little, other than by the work increasing in size. He acknowledged the influences of LOUIS LE BROCQUY, Roger Hilton and Victor Vasarely, while developing his own hard-edged manner.

KINNANE, Michael Joseph (1888–1952), commissioner Garda Síochána, b. Co. Galway, ed. Blackrock, d. 10 July 1952. LL B. Joined civil service in London 1908; principal officer Department of Home Affairs in Dublin 1922; assistant secretary Department of Justice 1928. Dealing directly with Garda matters, he gained valuable insights into the problems of the force. Appointed Garda commissioner 1938 and held the post until his death. On conditions of employment for the rank and file, Kinnane had a strong sense of fair play, trenchantly arguing their case with former civil service colleagues. He commenced the process of dismantling the structures and regulations inherited from the RIC in 1922. Following the political years of EAMONN BROY's stewardship, he adopted a low profile as an administrator, giving rein to the ambitions of his senior officers. Having proved themselves very successful commanders in the field during the Emergency, Kinnane's aides could reasonably have anticipated that one of their number would succeed him as commissioner; the government preferred instead another civil servant, DANIEL COSTIGAN.

KINSELLA, Thomas (1928–), poet, b. Dublin, ed. UCD. Civil servant in the Department of Finance 1948–65, leaving to become artist in residence at Southern Illinois University 1965–70. He later held a chair at Temple University, Philadelphia. Kinsella co-founded the Dolmen Press (with LIAM MILLER), the Cuala Press, and his own small house, Peppercanister, in Dublin. One of the most stimulating poets to emerge in the 1950s, he was fêted for his outstanding translations from the early Irish – *The Táin* (1969) being the masterpiece among them. His publications include: *Butcher's Dozen* and *Finistere* (1972), *Vertical Man* (1973), *One* (1974), *Fifteen Dead* (1979), *One Fond Embrace* (1981), *Her Vertical Smile* (1985), *Blood & Family* (1988), *From Centre City* (1990), *Madonna* and *Open Court* (1993) and *The Dual Tradition: An Essay on Poetry and Politics in Ireland* (1995).

KIRBY, Pat (1936–), handballer, b. Tuamgraney, Co. Clare, 14 Apr. 1936. One of seven handballing brothers, four of whom also won Irish titles. He won ten Irish senior softball singles titles, on both 60 x 30 and 40 x 20 courts, between 1974 and 1980, as well as five doubles titles. Living in the USA 1959–72 he won three American senior titles, three Canadian titles, became world champion in 1970 – retaining the title in the following two years – and was Handballer of the Year 1975–7. He won six over-40s titles in the 1980s and the world over-55 title in 1991. Kirby also played hurling for Clare at all levels, as well as for New York Selected 1959–72.

KIRKPATRICK, Thomas Percy Claude (1869–1954), physician and medical humanist, b. Dublin, ed. Foyle College, Derry and TCD. Graduating MB in 1895, he proceeded MD in the same year. Elected FRCPI in 1904, he served the College of Physicians for 44 years as registrar. He was a bibliophile and author and is remembered as a medical humanist, though he was also a physician to Dr Steevens's Hospital. He was, indeed, an anaesthetist early in his career and is honoured still in the faculty's 'Kirkpatrick Lecture'.

First publications dealt with medical matters but his *History of the Medical Teaching in Trinity College Dublin* (1912) was followed by *The Book of the Rotunda* (1913), *The History of Dr Steevens' Hospital Dublin 1720–1920* (1924) and other major contributions to medical history. An honorary chair in the history of medicine was created for him by TCD in 1936 and he was awarded the honorary degree of doctor of literature by both DU and the NUI. PRIA 1946, held presidential office in the Irish Historical Society 1948–51.

KITCHENER, Horatio Herbert, first Earl Kitchener of Khartoum (1850–1916), British field marshal, b. Ballylongford, Co. Kerry, 24 June 1850, ed. Royal Military Academy, Woolwich. Commissioned into Royal Engineers 1871. He commanded the British forces in Sudan during the war of 1892–6, recapturing Khartoum after annihilating the Khalifa's army at Omdurman. During the Boer War he became commander-in-chief South Africa and developed the tactics which led to defeat of the guerrillas. As Secretary of State for War in 1914 he was responsible for the reorganisation of the army to deal with the massive level of recruitment at the start of the war. Died 5 June 1916 in sinking of HMS *Hampshire*.

KNOWLES, Matilda (1864–1933), botanist, b. 31 Jan. 1864. Co-author of the internationally respected *The Lichens of Ireland*. Associated with the work of R.L. PRAEGER. Became head of the botanical collections in the National Museum 1923.

KYLE, John Wilson (Jackie) (1926–), international rugby player, b. Belfast, 10 Jan. 1926. In his day he was among the greatest out-halves in the world, and he is still Ireland's most capped player in that position, with 46 international appearances (then a world record) between 1947 (when he was a medical student at QUB) and 1958, having earlier played in the unofficial 'Victory' internationals in 1946, in which caps were not awarded. He was the inspiration in Ireland's only Grand Slam, in 1948, and again the following year, when the Triple Crown was won. He toured New Zealand and Australia with the Lions in 1950 and played in all six Tests, when, with the cream of four countries around him, his brilliance was constantly evident. In his Ireland career he played in 42 Five Nations Championship matches, was on the winning team 22 times – a better average than other top Irish players – and in 11 games was never on a losing side against Scotland. Elected to the Texaco Hall of Fame 1977 and to the Rugby Writers of Ireland–Digital Hall of Fame 1991, he was also awarded the OBE.

KYLE, Maeve Esther Enid (1928–), née Shankey, international athlete and hockey player, b. Kilkenny, 6 Oct. 1928. She won a record 41 Irish and Northern Irish track titles between 1955 and 1975, at distances which included 80 yards, 100 yards, 440 yards and 880 yards, and at long jump, high jump and pentathlon. She became the first woman to compete for Ireland in the Olympic Games when she ran in the 100 m and 200 m at Melbourne in 1956, and she competed – again without success – in the same disciplines in the Rome Olympics in 1960. She did better in the Tokyo Games of 1964, reaching the semi-finals of the 400 m and 800 m. As well as setting numerous Irish records in disciplines including the long jump and hurdles, she won the British WAAA 440 yards in 1961, and set world indoor records for both 440 yards and 400 m the same year. She won 58 international hockey caps for Ireland as a winger and shared in Ireland's Triple Crown victory at Wembley in 1950. Later she helped to establish the Ballymena club, with her husband, top athletics coach Sean Kyle, and became a prominent sports administrator.

L

LALLY, Mick (1945–), actor, ed. UCG. In 1975, together with GARRY HYNES and Marie Mullen, founded Galway's Druid Theatre. His television career started with GABRIEL BYRNE in *Bracken*, for which he received a Jacob's award. Since 1982 he has played Miley Byrne in the popular RTÉ drama series *Glenroe*. Among his stage roles are Michael Carney in TOM MURPHY's *A Whistle in the Dark* and Hiker Lacey in J.B. KEANE's *The Year of the Hiker*, screen work includes PAT O'CONNOR's *The Ballroom of Romance* (1981), and *A Man of No Importance* (1994).

LAMBERT, Eugene (1928–), puppeteer and variety artist, ed. Marist Brothers and Summerhill College, Sligo. Lambert brought joy to a generation of Irish children as the gormless but lovable O'Brien in *Wanderly Wagon*, which ran on RTÉ for 13 years; he also worked for 18 years on *Murphy agus a Cháirde*. He has appeared in pantomime and has for many years managed the family-owned Lambert Puppet Theatre and Museum in Monkstown, Co. Dublin.

LAMBERT, Gene (1952–), artist, b. Dublin, ed. National College of Art. He has had several solo exhibitions in Ireland, Denmark, Holland and England, has exhibited regularly in the Irish Exhibition of Living Art and is a Carroll's award winner. In 1979 he won first prize in the Claremorris National Art Exhibition and in 1982 he represented Ireland at the 14th International Festival of Painting in Cagnes-sur-Mer in France. He also participated in the Guinness Peat Aviation Awards Exhibition 1982. Other awards include the Independent Artists Large-scale Painting Award 1980 and the *Sunday Tribune* Visual Artist of the Year 1985. Lambert's concern with war and related themes is reflected in many of his paintings. While he regularly uses commonplace sources – such as television programmes – to create an image, the distortion of the figure and the violence of the surface mark-making create an effect which is often both disturbing and demanding of attention.

LANE, Sir Hugh (1875–1915), art dealer, collector and benefactor, b. 9 Nov. 1875. A successful picture dealer in London, he was introduced to Irish literary and artistic circles by his aunt, Lady GREGORY, and became an enthusiast for Irish painting after visiting a joint exhibition by NATHANIEL HONE and JOHN B. YEATS in 1901. Donated a collection of 39 paintings, including some of the finest of the French Impressionists, to the Dublin Municipal Gallery on the understanding that it would be provided with appropriate and permanent premises. Sir Edwin Lutyens designed a gallery intended to span the River Liffey but the city corporation rejected the proposal because it was not the work of an Irish architect. Lane then bequeathed the pictures to the National Gallery in London instead but, after becoming director of the National Gallery of Ireland in 1914, changed his mind again and left the collection to Dublin by a codicil to his will, which he neglected to have witnessed. The paintings accordingly went to London when Lane died in the sinking of the *Lusitania*. In 1959 it was finally agreed that the collection would be divided into two segments, each to alternate between Dublin and London for five years at a time in perpetuity.

LANE, Patrick (1934–), politician and president of IFA, b. Co. Clare, 7 Sept. 1934, ed. Crescent College, Limerick and Cadet School, Curragh, Co. Kildare. Commissioned 1954. He was an active and militant member of the National (later the Irish) Farmers' Association and was jailed for his part in the farmers' rights campaign of the mid-1960s. Lane recognised at an early stage how important EEC membership was for Irish farmers, and during his term as IFA president, 1976–80, was heavily involved in lobbying on their behalf in Brussels. In 1989 he won a European Parliament seat for Fianna Fáil in Munster. He is regarded as a very capable and knowledgeable spokesman for those whose interests he represents. He has served on the boards of the Bank of Ireland and Bord Bainne, and on the EC's Economic and Social Committee 1978–82.

LANE, Thomas Joseph Daniel (1894–1967), urologist, b. Ferozepore, Pakistan, where his father, Colonel D.T. Lane, served with the Indian medical service, ed. Clongowes and TCD, graduating MB in 1916. After a brief period as a general practitioner in Co. Limerick, he worked at the Meath Hospital as pathologist and radiologist before finding his *métier* when appointed to the surgical staff in 1923. Lane was attracted to paediatric surgery and orthopaedics before committing himself to urology on a full-time basis, the first surgeon practising in Ireland to do so. This decision followed a visit to the Mayo Clinic, where he realised the potential of transurethral methods in treating prostatic obstruction. Lane's predominance in this field was recognised and the Meath became a national centre for urology.

He was a founder member of the British Association of Urological Surgeons and contributed to the literature of his subject. Hon. M.Ch. (TCD) and hon. FRCSI. The greatest tribute to his work, however, took the form of bricks and mortar when the Minister for Health opened the new urological unit at the Meath Hospital in 1955.

LARCHET, John Francis (1884–1967), composer, teacher and academic, b. and d. Dublin. Studied under ESPOSITO at the RIAM and at TCD. Musical director Abbey Theatre 1907–34. Professor of Composition and senior vice-president of RIAM 1920–55. Music adviser to army 1923. Established music as a discipline at UCD, where he was professor 1921–58. Hon. D.Mus. (NUI) 1953. Fellow of the RIAM. Commendatore of the Italian Republic 1953.

LARKIN, James, snr (1876–1947), trade unionist and political leader, b. Liverpool to Irish parents, d. 30 Jan. 1947. Went to live with his grandparents in Newry in 1881. Began work in 1885 as a labourer and later a seaman; joined the National Union of Dock Labourers in Belfast in 1907, transferring to Dublin in 1908. In both Belfast and Dublin he rapidly established a reputation as a charismatic leader who was not afraid to use the strike weapon, and was a thorn in the flesh of contemporary Irish employers. His combative

nature involved him in frequent conflicts as well; his association with the dock workers' union ended and he was instrumental in founding the Irish Transport and General Workers' Union in 1908–9. Expelled from the Irish Trades Union Congress in 1909, the union was readmitted in 1911, when his paper, the *Irish Worker*, secured a fast-increasing circulation for its compelling mixture of socialist rhetoric and passionate denunciation of the conditions under which the Dublin working class lived.

In 1912 he was elected to Dublin Corporation. The following year he was a key figure in the Dublin Lock-out, which, although won by the employers, established Larkin in particular as a major figure within the trade union movement nationally. In Aug. 1914 the *Irish Worker* was suppressed and in Oct. he left for an extended visit to the USA, where he engaged in considerable agitational activity and was imprisoned for a brief period in Sing Sing, from which unusual vantage point he denounced the Treaty which brought an end to the War of Independence. He returned to Ireland in 1923 but lost the internal battle for control of the ITGWU which had commenced in his absence. In the same year he formed the Irish Workers' League, which was affiliated to the Communist International, and campaigned electorally against the Labour Party. In June 1924 he founded the Workers' Union of Ireland, of which he was general secretary until his death.

During a period marked by his hostility to the Irish Labour Party (not least because of Labour's intimate association with the ITGWU), he was elected to the Dáil in 1927 as a TD for North Dublin, losing his seat in the 1932 election. He lost his Dublin Corporation seat in the 1933 municipal elections, amid widespread criticism of him and his supporters for their communist sympathies (a number of his journalistic initiatives were intermittently proscribed by government for the same reason). He nevertheless won his Corporation seat back in 1936 and his Dáil seat in 1937 in Dublin North-East, only to lose the latter again in 1938. Rejoining the Labour Party in 1941, he was re-elected to the Dáil in 1943 but, at a time typified by the split between Labour and National Labour, lost his seat in 1944. Although his final years were characterised by a certain eirenicism, it was a late growth, and the divisions of the Irish political and industrial movement in its early period – divisions into which he entered with characteristic vigour and disregard for the consequences – owed more than a little to that unwillingness to compromise which was at once his greatest strength and his most telling weakness as a leader and an organiser.

LARMOR, Sir Joseph (1857–1941), FRS, mathematician and physicist, b. Magherall, Co. Antrim, 11 July 1857, ed. Royal Academical Institution, QUB and St John's College, Cambridge. Professor Queen's College, Galway 1880–85. Lecturer in mathematics Cambridge 1885–1903, Lucasian professor 1903–32. MP for Cambridge University 1911–22. Publications include many papers in mathematics and physics. Also collected editions of works by Stokes, Kelvin, J.J. Thomson, Clerk Maxwell, Fitzgerald, Cavendish.

LAVERTY, Maura (1907–1966), novelist and playwright, b. Rathangan, Co. Kildare, ed. Brigidine Convent, Carlow, d. Dublin. Went to Spain at the age of 17 to work as a governess and within a short time became private secretary to Prince Bibesco, husband of Princess Bibesco. Subsequently worked as a journalist and continued to do so on her return to Dublin in the late 1920s. Her first novel, *Never No More*, was published to considerable acclaim in 1942. It was followed by *Alone We Embark* (1943), *No More than Human* (1944) and *Lift Up Your Gates* (1946), which was adapted for the stage in the 1950s under the title *Liffey Lane*. Other plays from this period include *Tolka Row*, which formed the basis of a successful RTÉ television series during the 1960s, and *The Tree in the Crescent*.

LAVERY, Cecil (1894–1967), lawyer, b. Armagh, ed. Castleknock, UCD and King's Inns, d. 16 Dec. 1967. Called to Bar 1915, Senior Counsel 1927, Fine Gael TD for Dublin County 1935–8, Attorney-General and senator 1948–50, Supreme Court judge 1950–66. Lavery's reputation and income grew steadily over 35 years at the Bar and by the early 1940s he was regarded by his colleagues as the ablest advocate in practice. Some of his judgments have not, however, been free from criticism.

LAVERY, Sir John (1856–1941), artist, b. Belfast, d. Kilkenny, 10 Jan. 1941. His parents died young and he was sent to live with relatives in Glasgow. He studied at the Glasgow School of Art and later in London and Paris. Already established as an independent artist in his mid-twenties, from the late 1880s he consolidated his career as one of the most fashionable artists of his time. He was knighted in 1918 and elected a member of the Royal Academy in 1921. In 1910 he married the American Hazel Martyn, whose exceptional beauty he captured in a portrait which appeared on all Irish banknotes 1928–77 and was used as a watermark on the subsequent series of notes. Official British war artist in World War I. Among his better-known works are *The Tennis Party* (Neue Pinakothek, Munich), *Spring* (Musée de Luxembourg, Paris) and *Polymia* (National Gallery of Italy, Rome). His autobiography, *The Life of a Painter*, was published in 1940.

LAVIN, Mary (1912–1996), writer, b. Massachusetts, ed. UCD, d. 26 Mar. 1996. Short story collections included *Tales from Bective Bridge* (1942), for which she received the James Tait Black memorial prize 1943, *The Becker Wives* (1946), *A Single Lady* (1956), *The Great Wave* (1961), *Collected Stories* (1971), *The Shrine* (1977), *A Family Likeness* (1985). Novels included *The House in Clewe Street* (1945) and *Mary O'Grady* (1950). Won the Katherine Mansfield prize 1961, the Éire Society gold medal, Boston 1974, the Gregory medal of the IAL 1975. Elected Saoi by Aosdána 1992. Essentially a storyteller – preferably of short stories – she holds the reader with a clarity of style and a choice of location and circumstance with which many Irish people can readily identify. The problems faced by her characters, and sometimes overcome, arise from social or family pressures within tightly knit communities constricting the expression of personal freedom. Simple narratives thus turn into lessons of universal relevance on the human condition.

LAWLOR, Hugh Jackson (1860–1938), Church of Ireland cleric and scholar, ed. Dublin, d. 26 Dec. 1938. Ordained deacon 1885, priest 1886. After several years at St Mary's Cathedral, Edinburgh, returned to Ireland in 1898 to take up the position of curate at Bray, Co. Wicklow and Professor of Ecclesiastical History at TCD. By 1924 he was dean of St Patrick's Cathedral, while continuing to hold his professorship. Engaged in the most exacting research and produced a great deal of importance, as well as being editor of the *Irish Church Quarterly*. Of his many publications, perhaps best known are his *Fasti of St Patrick's Cathedral, Dublin* (1930) and *Eusebius*, with J.E.L. OULTON (two vols. 1928), but his work on the early Irish Church in general is still admired. A scholarly liturgist; member of the Prayer Book Revision Committee set up in 1909.

LEASK, Harold Graham (1882–1964), architect, b. Harold's Cross, Dublin, s. of Robert H. Leask, engineer and architect. Studied under his father and with the AAI, later entering the offices of George P. Sheridan. In Sept. 1909 he joined the OPW as assistant surveyor and worked his way up to become inspector of national monuments in Oct. 1923, a position he held until his retirement in 1949. His sophisticated and scholarly appreciation of historical architecture, particularly the medieval, singled him out from his contemporaries. He contributed extensively to historical journals, notably those of the Royal Society of Antiquaries of Ireland, of which he was president 1941–4, and the RIA, of which he became a member in 1930. *Irish Castles and Castellated Houses* (1941) and *Irish Churches and Monastic Buildings* (three vols. 1955–60) remain fundamental to the study of Irish architecture. Honorary degrees of Master of Architecture (NUI) 1942 and LL D (TCD) 1951.

LE BROCQUY, Louis (1916–), artist, b. Dublin, 10 Nov. 1916, ed. St Gerard's School, Bray, Co. Wicklow and TCD. Left family business to become a painter; studied in England and on the Continent but essentially self-taught. Exhibited at RHA from 1937. Arising from a suggestion by his mother, Sybil le Brocquy, the annual Irish Exhibition of Living Art was set up by EVIE HONE, MAINIE JELLETT and others in 1943 to introduce the public to contemporary styles and developing trends in painting and sculpture; Louis le Brocquy was a founder member. MRHA 1949. He has described his own paintings as palimpsests, ideas superimposed on ideas. Their meaning can be elusive but their popularity suggests that they somehow embody the uncertainties of the age. Taught at London's Central School of Arts and Crafts 1947–54 and Royal College of Art 1955–8. Member of the Irish Council of Design 1963–5 and a director of the Kilkenny Design Workshop 1965–77. He has been a director of the Irish Museum of Modern Art since 1989. He received honorary doctorates from TCD (1962) and NUI (1968), is a Chevalier of the Légion d'honneur (1988) and a Saoi of Aosdána.

LEDWIDGE, Francis (1887–1917), poet, b. Slane, Co. Meath, 19 Aug. 1887, son of an evicted tenant farmer. His formal education ended at the age of 12 when he became a labourer but he continued to develop his interest in poetry. Continued to work after gaining recognition as a poet, and eventually became secretary of the Co. Meath farm labourers' union. A nationalist and a member of the Irish National Volunteers, he followed JOHN REDMOND's call to contribute to the war effort in 1914. He survived Gallipoli but was killed in Belgium on 13 July 1917. His first collection, *Songs of the Fields*, was published in 1916 and the *Complete Poems* in 1919. Ledwidge's growth into poetic maturity owed much to the patronage of his neighbour, Edward Plunkett, Lord DUNSANY, himself a poet, playwright and author, who gave Ledwidge access to his library as well as providing sympathetic criticism of his work. Emotionally, a broken-off romance, the experience of war, and the execution of friends and fellow poets after the Easter Rising of 1916 combined to draw out Ledwidge's deepest feelings, which he expressed in religious and mythological forms but most movingly in images drawn from the countryside of the Boyne valley, where he was literally and spiritually most at home.

LEE, Joseph (1942–), historian, b. Tralee, ed. Gormanston, Co. Meath and UCD. Sometime fellow of Peterhouse, Cambridge and visiting professor University of Pittsburgh. Professor of Modern History UCC 1974. His *Ireland 1912–1985* (1989), a major work that was many years in preparation, brought a new tone – stimulating, provocative, highly readable – to the writing of Irish history and quickly became the standard reference on the period. Editor of two volumes of broadcast lectures on historical subjects and frequent contributor on radio and television to the discussion of current political developments.

LEECH, William J. (1881–1968), artist, b. and ed. in Dublin. He trained at the RHA school (where one of his teachers was Walter Osborne) and later in Paris, shortly after PAUL HENRY. In 1903 he went to Concarneau in Brittany, remaining there 15 years and producing some fine early work, such as *The Goose Girl* (National Gallery of Ireland, 'star' of the Post-Impressionist Exhibition, London, 1980).

After 1918 Leech settled in England, working in Hampstead and Surrey until his death. He visited France yearly – *Un Matin*, a major study of an aloe shrub (Dublin's Hugh Lane Municipal Gallery, in Parnell Square where Leech was born), dates from visits in the 1920s to Provence. Usually, however, his subject matter was that which he found around him, typically looking downwards on a table, window sill, garden or public park. These 50 years gave us pictures which one authority has described as 'all tranquil in mood: none express commotion, disturbance or violence'.

The artist's early ties with the RHA, his friendship then with Dermod O'Brien and later with Leo Smith ensured that Ireland received a large share of Leech's work and that gradually he became an important figure in Irish art.

LEMASS, Seán Francis (1899–1971), revolutionary and politician, b. Ballybrack, Co. Dublin, 15 July 1899, son of a well-established Dublin hat manufacturer with Parnellite sympathies, ed. O'Connell School, m. Kathleen Hughes, one s. three d., d. Dublin, 11 May 1971. Joined the Irish Volunteers 1914, fought in the GPO during the Easter Rising (because he was unable to reach his own battalion, under its commandant EAMON DE VALERA, in Bolands' Mills). His renewed activity in the Volunteers led to internment in Ballykinlar during the War of Independence. He opposed the Treaty, served in the Four Courts at the outset of the Civil War, was again interned and upon his release moved gradually away from militant republicanism towards the political wing of the movement,

in which he was soon showing his organisational ability. In Nov. 1924 he was elected TD for Dublin South but in line with republican policy abstained from taking his seat.

He now advocated pragmatic and progressive economic policies in place of what he saw as sterile ideology. De Valera later acknowledged that it was Lemass who took the initiative which resulted in the formation of the Fianna Fáil party in 1926. When FF abandoned abstentionism, Lemass mounted strong attacks in the Dáil on the Cumann na nGaedheal government. His famous remark that FF was 'a slightly constitutional party' represented his serious political views only to the extent that he had little patience with administrative niceties when he saw reforms frustrated by what he considered foot-dragging conservatism on the part of civil servants, political opponents and, not least, members of his own party like SEAN MACENTEE, with whom he would have policy differences which continued well after they entered government in 1932.

De Valera then appointed Lemass Minister for Industry and Commerce (rather than Finance, which he would have preferred). Ably aided by JOHN LEYDON, his inspired choice as secretary of the department, Lemass put in hand a major programme of tariff protection for private industry and state intervention to develop resources beyond the capacity of private enterprise at the time: Bord na Móna, Aer Lingus, Irish Shipping and the Irish Tourist Board were among the state companies he was to set up. Such economic dynamism would have been remarkable anywhere in those years of the Great Depression; in a small, impoverished country it was especially impressive – and might have been more so if de Valera had not looked to protectionist policies as a weapon against Britain in the so-called 'Economic War'.

During World War II he held the crucial post of Minister for Supplies, where he had to ensure that the country had access to sufficient essential foodstuffs, fuel and petrol, and that these were fairly rationed. It was a task suited to his energy but a distraction from possibilities which had opened up just before the world conflict with the end of the land annuities controversy and the hope of a beneficial trade agreement with the UK. Increasingly, he felt that the future of the Irish economy lay in competitiveness, success in a free trade environment rather than protection, although the state would continue to participate as before where the private sector was weak. The post-war years should have been his opportunity to move the country in this direction but the ageing de Valera showed no sign of relinquishing the party leadership, and twice FF lost office to inter-party coalitions before Lemass finally became Taoiseach upon the election of de Valera as President of Ireland in 1959.

By then, however, he had already been able to encourage the economic planning associated with T.K. WHITAKER, secretary of the Department of Finance, which became the keystone of Lemass's policy as Taoiseach. His approach was marked by plans, programmes, projections. Typically, he sought membership of the EEC for Ireland; when that had to be deferred as an incidental consequence of de Gaulle's opposition to British membership, he set out to maximise a relationship with the rival European Free Trade Association and concluded an Anglo-Irish Free Trade Agreement in 1965. In Jan. of that year he travelled to Belfast for the first of two historic meetings with the then Prime Minister of Northern Ireland, TERENCE O'NEILL: another break in the ideological logjam which he had for so long seen as an impediment to Ireland's progress towards prosperity. Other policies initiated by his governments included free secondary education and national wage agreements with the trade unions which foreshadowed the later concept of 'social partners'. He introduced a number of younger TDs to their first experience of government, as junior ministers, although more cautiously than is recalled in folk memory. He retired from office in Nov. 1966.

LENIHAN, Brian (1930–1995), politician, b. Dundalk, Nov. 1930, ed. Marist College, Athlone, UCD and King's Inns, d. Dublin. Barrister. Elected to the Seanad in 1957; elected TD (FF Roscommon) on his third attempt 1961. Appointed parliamentary secretary to the Minister for Lands, then in 1964 moved to the Department of Justice, where he was responsible for introducing a

sizeable amount of reforming legislation. Minister for Education 1968–9, Transport and Power 1969–73. Minister for Foreign Affairs briefly in 1973 and again 1979–81, 1987–9. Minister for Forestry and Fisheries 1977–9, Agriculture Mar.–Nov 1982. He lost his Dáil seat in the 1973 election and spent four years as leader of the Fianna Fáil group in the Seanad.

In 1989 he underwent a successful liver transplant in the USA. The general election of that year took place while he was in hospital and he was the first TD to be declared re-elected. He returned to the Dáil to a standing ovation, a measure of the affection in which he was held on all sides. He was appointed Minister for Defence, a post from which he was removed during the 1990 presidential election, in which he was a losing candidate – the first time any FF seeker of the office had suffered such a defeat. His removal from office came about because he had given differing accounts concerning FF attempts to persuade President HILLERY not to dissolve the Dáil after the collapse of the Fine Gael–Labour coalition in early 1982; asked to resign by Taoiseach CHARLES HAUGHEY, he refused and was dismissed. He retained his seat in the 1992 general election and became the first chair of the new Oireachtas Committee on Foreign Affairs. A recurrence of his illness led to his death on 1 Nov. 1995.

His father, Patrick, was also an FF TD but, uniquely in 20th-century Irish history, was first elected to the Dáil after his son; Lenihan's own son became an FF TD in 1996. Brian Lenihan was a brother of MARY O'ROURKE.

LENNON, Joseph (Joe) (1934–), Gaelic footballer, b. Poyntzpass, Co. Armagh. He won three All-Ireland senior medals with Down, in 1960, 1961 and 1968, when he captained the team which defeated Kerry, and also helped the county to three National League wins, in 1960, 1962 and 1968 (again as captain). He won four Railway Cup medals with Ulster, in 1960, 1964, 1966 and 1968, when he captained the province. With his club, Aghaderg, he won seven Ulster senior football medals between 1959 and 1970. A PE teacher by profession, he wrote a well-received book about fitness for Gaelic footballers.

LEONARD, Hugh (1926–), pseud. of John Keyes Byrne, playwright, b. Dalkey, Co. Dublin, ed. Presentation College, Dún Laoghaire. He shares with BRIAN FRIEL the distinction of being the most successful Irish dramatist since the 1950s. Leonard worked for the Land Commission from 1945 to 1959, discovered the theatre, was script editor for Granada Television and literary editor of the Abbey Theatre. Although he has written scores of stage plays, he has achieved international acclaim through his television scripts and film work. The poignant *Da*, written in 1973 and subsequently filmed, is arguably his masterpiece and enjoys frequent revivals. Television work: *Strumpet City* (1979), *The Irish RM* (1985), *Troubles* (1987) and *Parnell and the Englishwoman* (1988). Film work includes *Herself Surprised* (1977), *Da* (1984) and *Widow's Peak* (1994). He has also written two volumes of autobiography, a memoir – *Rover and Other Cats* (1990) – and a novel, *The Off-shore Island* (1993).

LESLIE, James Blennerhassett (1865–1952), Church of Ireland clergyman and historian, b. Co. Kerry, 28 May 1865, ed. Kilkenny and Dublin, d. 20 Apr. 1952. Rector of Kilsaran (Armagh) 1899–1952. Historians of the Church of Ireland and the wider academic community are indebted to him for the series of diocesan succession lists that he compiled, using sources in many cases subsequently destroyed. Some lists were published (with the encouragement and support of William Tempest of the Dundalgan Press), others remain in typescript in the library of the Representative Church Body. Also contributed to the *Handbook of British Chronology*. Hon. D.Litt. (QUB).

LESTER, Sean (1888–1959), international civil servant, b. Carrickfergus, Co. Antrim, ed. Methodist College, Belfast. Held several jobs, including one with the Belfast and County Down Railway which he had to leave when it was discovered that he was colour-blind, not knowing red from green. Unusually for a Protestant, he joined the Gaelic League in Belfast, attended Irish classes and became a member of the IRB. News editor of the *Freeman's Journal*. In Jan. 1923 he joined the newly created Department of External Affairs, then consisting of two other principal officials and himself. He was appointed Irish representative to the League of Nations at Geneva in 1929, and in 1933 the League sent him to Danzig as High Commissioner for the Free City. The job was partly judicial, partly mediatory but especially diplomatic, and involved reporting any breaches of the status which established it as a Free City after the Treaty of Versailles. Constantly attacked in the German press, Lester showed great courage in protests against the Nazi persecution of the Jews. In 1940 he was appointed acting secretary-general of the League in Geneva. As World War II ground on and as the position of the League itself deteriorated, he found himself increasingly isolated there. When the charter of the United Nations was adopted in 1947, the League was ignored and it was left to Lester to wind it up. His courage and integrity were rewarded by honorary doctorates from the NUI and TCD. He also received the Woodrow Wilson award.

LETTS, Winifred M. (1882–1972), dramatist, novelist and poet, b. Dublin, ed. St Anne's Abbots, Bromley, Kent and Alexandra. She began as a playwright, writing two one-acters for the Abbey, *The Eyes of the Blind* (1907) and *The Challenge* (1909), yet it was not until 1941 that her third play, *Hamilton and Jones*, was mounted by the Gate Theatre. She is best remembered for her dialect poems, which celebrate the lives of the country people of Leinster. They are charming, though by no means outstanding. By far her finest work is *Knockmaroon* (1933), a memoir that is reminiscent of J.M. SYNGE's recollections of Co. Wicklow. She was also the author of several novels and two volumes of hagiography, *The Mighty Army* (1912) and *St Patrick the Travelling Man* (1932). Her poetry was published as *Songs from Leinster* (1913), *Halloween and Poems of the War* (1916), *The Spires of Oxford and Other Poems* (1917) and *More Songs from Leinster* (1926).

LEVENTHAL, Abraham Jacob ('Con') (1896–1979), critic and academic, b. Dublin, ed. Wesley and TCD. He joined the first Zionist Commission immediately after World War I, spent a year in Palestine, where he co-founded the *Palestine Weekly*, and later worked for the *Zionist Review* in London. He returned to Dublin in 1922 and submitted a review of

JAMES JOYCE's *Ulysses* to the *Dublin Magazine*, thereby befriending editor SEUMAS O'SULLIVAN. The review was censored by the printers. Leventhal agitated against all censorship, was closely involved with the short-lived, iconoclastic journal *Tomorrow*, edited by FRANCIS STUART. He greatly admired SAMUEL BECKETT, whom he succeeded as lecturer in French at TCD, and thought him an even greater talent than Joyce. He was a prolific 'man of letters' and loved theatre. On his retirement from TCD he went to live in Paris, where he continued to contribute to Irish and international newspapers.

LEWIS, Clive Staples (C.S.) (1898–1963), writer, b. Belfast, 29 Nov. 1898, ed. Malvern College and Oxford. After serving in World War I, in 1925 he became a fellow of Magdalen College, Oxford, where he spent most of his working life until his appointment to the chair of medieval and renaissance English at Cambridge in 1954. His critical work includes *The Allegory of Love* (1936) and *English Literature in the Sixteenth Century* (1954). Having strayed from Christianity, he rediscovered it in the late 1920s and became a well-known broadcaster and writer on religious matters, with works like *The Screwtape Letters* (1940). He also wrote science fiction and children's books, most notably *The Chronicles of Narnia*, a seven-volume series which has never lost its popularity. Richard Attenborough's film *Shadowlands* (1993) was based on the autobiographical *Surprised by Joy* (1955), which describes Lewis's relationship with American poet Joy Davidman Gresham.

LEYDON, John (1895–1979), public servant, b. Arigna, Co. Roscommon, ed. St Mel's College, Longford and Maynooth. One of Ireland's outstanding civil servants, best remembered in that capacity as secretary of the Department of Supplies during the years of World War II. Previously secretary of the Department of Industry and Commerce since 1932, a position he resumed when the war was over and retained until 1955. Chairman of Aer Lingus and Aer Rianta 1937–49, of Irish Shipping 1941–9, of Aer Línte 1958–61. After retirement from the civil service he became chairman of the National Bank and a director of the Central Bank. First president of the Institute of Public Administration, he was also a member of the executive committee of the Irish Management Institute.

LINDSAY, Patrick (1914–1993), barrister and politician, b. Dublin, 18 Jan. 1914, d. 29 June 1993. Elected to the Dáil in the Mayo constituency in 1954, on his sixth attempt. In 1956 he served as parliamentary secretary at the Departments of Education and the Gaeltacht and was then made Minister for the Gaeltacht, a post he held until the coalition government lost office in 1957. Re-elected that year, he was defeated in the 1961 general election. He was Leas-Cathaoirleach of the Seanad 1961–5 and unsuccessfully contested the Dáil constituency of Dublin North-Central for Fine Gael in 1969 and 1973. After the latter election he was appointed master of the High Court.

He was renowned as an entertaining raconteur and his anecdotal autobiography, *Memoirs*, was published shortly before his death.

LISTON, Eoin ('Bomber') (1957–), Gaelic footballer, b. Ballybunion, Co. Kerry, 17 Oct. 1957. From the Beale club, he won an All-Ireland under-21 medal with Kerry in 1977 and went on to become prominent in the county's subsequent run of success. He played on six victorious All-Ireland senior teams; he was notable in Kerry's four successive wins 1978–81 (although missing the 1980 final due to injury), was on the side defeated by Offaly in 1982, then shared in Kerry's three-in-a-row run 1984–6. Other achievements include two Railway Cup medals with Munster (1981, 1982), four All-Star awards (1980–82 at full-forward, 1984 at centre-half forward) and international Compromise Rules football against Australia.

LOCKE, Josef (1917–), tenor, b. Joseph McLaughlin, Derry, 23 Mar. 1917. Enlisted in the Irish Guards aged 16 before being auditioned and hired by variety star JIMMY O'DEA. Moved to London in 1944 where he quickly established his stage career. His name was too long for many billboards and the Victoria Palace theatre solved the problem by shortening it to the form by which he became famous. With good looks, sexual magnetism and an impressive voice, the 6' 2" redhead was a swashbuckling entertainer. A huge, highly paid star in the UK in the 1940s and 1950s, with songs such as 'I'll Take You Home Again,

Kathleen', 'Hear My Song', 'The Old Bog Road' and 'Blaze Away', he broke all records by playing 19 straight seasons in Europe's busiest holiday town, Blackpool. Came back to Ireland 1958 following tax difficulties in Britain, but eventually agreed a settlement and rejoined the Blackpool cabaret circuit 1968. He finally returned to Ireland in 1971 and married Carmel Dignam. Retired to Co. Kildare, had several comebacks and occasional charity concert appearances.

LOFTUS, Seán Dublin Bay Rockall (1927–), politician, b. Dublin, ed. Coláiste Mhuire, CUS, UCD and King's Inns. After working in England and Scotland for some years, returned home to study law. Called to Bar 1958, lectured on Irish affairs in the USA 1959–61, practised at Bar 1962–7, lecturer in law DIT. Member (later alderman) Dublin City Council for many years, TD (Ind. Dublin North-East) 1981–2, Lord Mayor of Dublin 1995–6. Has long been committed to developing the potential and protecting the environment of Dublin Bay; also campaigned to have Irish ownership of Rockall recognised so that the country might enjoy the benefit of oil or other resources found within North Atlantic territorial waters around the rock; incorporated 'Dublin Bay' and 'Rockall' in his name by deed poll in order to signal his concerns, not least on voting papers at election time.

LOGUE, Michael (1840–1924), cardinal, b. Carrigart, Co. Donegal, 1 Oct. 1840, ed. hedge school, private school in Buncrana and Maynooth, d. Armagh, 19 Nov. 1924. Ordained 1866 and appointed Professor of Dogmatic Theology at Irish College in Paris. Appointed curate of Glenswilly, Co. Donegal 1874. Dean and Professor of Irish and Theology in Maynooth 1876. Bishop of Raphoe 1879, Archbishop of Armagh 1888, Cardinal 1893. Voiced his protests against Charles Stewart Parnell and the O'Shea divorce case. Patron of the Gaelic League.

LONDONDERRY (Charles Stewart Henry Vane-Tempest-Stewart), seventh Marquess of (1878–1949), b. 13 May 1878, ed. Eton and Sandhurst, d. 11 Feb. 1949. Conservative MP for Maidstone 1906–15. Second in command of the Royal Horse Guards from 1915, twice mentioned in dispatches. Londonderry became a privy councillor in Ireland 1918, in Northern Ireland 1921 and in Britain 1925. Knight of the Order of the Garter 1919. UK undersecretary for air 1920–21, NI Minister of Education and leader of the Senate 1921–6. As education minister he formed a rapport with Cardinal PATRICK O'DONNELL which carried some promise of a relaxation of entrenched unionist and nationalist positions in NI but was terminated by the cardinal's untimely death. First commissioner of works 1928–9 and Aug.–Oct. 1931. Secretary of State for Air 1931–5. Lord Privy Seal and leader of the Lords 1935. Chancellor of QUB from 1923, of Durham University from 1931. Lord lieutenant of Co. Durham from 1928, chief commissioner of the Civil Air Guard from 1938. His Majesty's lieutenant for Co. Down. In 1936 and 1937 Londonderry visited Germany, where he was received by leading Nazis. In turn he later received Ribbentrop, the German ambassador, at the family seat of Mount Stewart near Newtownards, Co. Down. In 1996 it was revealed that a copy of Londonderry's tract, *Ourselves and Germany* (1938), which he had signed for Hitler, was among items captured by Russian troops and taken back to Moscow in 1945.

LONGFORD (Edward Pakenham), sixth Earl of (1902–1961), playwright and theatre producer, b. 29 Dec. 1902, ed. Eton and Christ Church, Oxford, m. Christine Trew who became a distinguished playwright, d. Dublin, 4 Feb. 1961. Lord Longford rescued the fledgling Gate Theatre from financial difficulties in 1931 and became a member of the board. The company split in two in 1936, due to disagreements between Longford and the Gate's founders, MICHEÁL MACLIAMMÓIR and HILTON EDWARDS. The latter duo retained title to the company name and Longford established his own company, Longford Productions. Each group occupied the theatre for six months of the year and toured for the remaining six. Longford Productions stimulated a strong amateur drama movement throughout rural Ireland, performing several original plays by Longford himself, including *Yahoo* (1933), based on the life of Jonathan Swift. Lord Longford was largely responsible for saving and restoring the Gate Theatre, which had been condemned by Dublin Corporation in

1956, and Lady Longford continued to run it after his death.

LONGLEY, Edna (1940–), literary critic, b. Cork, ed. TCD, m. MICHAEL LONGLEY. Professor of English QUB. One of Ireland's most outspoken critics, her volumes of criticism include *Louis MacNeice: A Study* (1988), *From Cathleen to Anorexia: The Breakdown of Ireland*, a pamphlet (1990), and *The Living Stream: Literature and Revisionism in Ireland* (1994). She has also edited Edward Thomas's poetry and books on the English countryside, in addition to *The Selected Paul Durcan* (1985), *Across the Roaring Hill: The Protestant Imagination in Modern Ireland*, with GERALD DAWE (1985), *Poetry in the Wars* (1986), *Alice in Wormland: Selected Poems of Dorothy Hewett* (1990) and *Culture in Ireland: Division or Diversity?* (1991).

LONGLEY, Michael (1939–), poet, b. Belfast, ed. Royal Academical Institution and TCD, m. EDNA LONGLEY. A former poetry critic of *The Irish Times*, his collections include *No Continuing City* (1969), *An Exploded View* (1973), *Man Lying on a Wall* (1976) and *The Echo Gate* (1979). He is a former editor of *Causeway: The Arts in Ulster* (1971) and has produced an anthology of children's verse, *Under the Moon, Over the Stars* (1971). Longley worked as a teacher in England and Ireland 1962–9 prior to joining the Arts Council of Northern Ireland, of which he became combined arts director. His eye for detail and ear for the spoken word give his vignettes a clarity which makes for powerful impact when he deals with the horrors of war or terrorist killings. In quieter mood, he catches the flavour of urban flats or terraced housing, finding poetry in the thoughts and memories of ordinary people living ordinary lives.

LOUGHNANE, Gerard (Ger) (1954–), hurler. Playing for the Feakle club and St Patrick's in Dublin, he made his senior county début for Clare in 1972 and starred in the teams which won the National League in 1977 and 1978, having lost the 1976 final in a replay. He won three Railway Cup medals with Munster (1976, 1978, 1981, at right corner-back) and was the first Clareman to win an All-Star award, in 1974, an honour he again achieved in 1977, both times at right-half back. But his greatest achievement was as a manager, steering Clare to the All-Ireland title

of 1995, the county's first championship since 1914.

LOVETT, Ann (1969–1984), b. Granard, Co. Longford. On 31 Jan. 1984 Ann Lovett was found dying of exhaustion and exposure after giving birth to a baby boy in a grotto devoted to the Virgin Mary in her home town. The infant died very shortly after birth. Her life and death were seen by many, especially in the women's movement, as a symbol for the disadvantages under which some Irish women lived. Little has become publicly known about her life or the circumstances surrounding her death and that of her child.

LOWRY, Lord Robert Lynd Erskine (1919–), lawyer, b. Belfast, ed. Royal Academical Institution and Cambridge. Served with the British forces 1940–46, MA 1944. Called to Bar (Northern Ireland) 1947, QC (NI) 1956, counsel to Attorney-General for NI 1948–56. High Court (NI) judge 1964–71, Lord Chief Justice of NI 1971–88, a period that witnessed most of the North's violence of the past quarter-century. Member of Anglo-Irish Law Enforcement Commission 1974, chairman of NI Constitutional Convention 1975.

LUCE, Arthur Aston (1882–1977), philosopher, b. Gloucester, 21 Aug. 1882, ed. England and TCD, d. 28 June 1977. Ordained Church of Ireland priest 1907, deacon 1908. Professor of Moral Theology TCD 1934–49 and Berkeley Professor of Metaphysics 1953–77, Vice-Provost TCD 1946–52. Precentor of St Patrick's Cathedral 1953–77. Many publications, but noted in particular for his work on Bishop George Berkeley, whose biographer and interpreter he was.

LUKE, John (1906–1975), artist, b. Belfast, the son of a fireman, ed. Hillman Street NS, Belfast School of Art and Slade School of Art, London, d. Belfast. Luke was renowned for the exactitude of his work and his tremendous facility for literal description. His formal artistic training began with evening classes in the Belfast School of Art while he was still employed as a riveter in the shipyards. He won a scholarship to the Slade, where he studied with Henry Tonks, and returned to Belfast following some time at the Westminster School of Art. He painted several murals, including those in the dome of the City Hall, Belfast and in the Rosemary Street Masonic Hall. His most famous painting is *The Rehearsal*.

LUNNY, Donal (1947–), multi-instrumentalist, singer, composer and record producer, b. Tullamore, Co. Offaly but raised in Newbridge, Co. Kildare, ed. National College of Art. Particularly noted for his role in establishing the bouzouki as a mainstream instrument in Irish music. Founder member of Planxty 1971 and in 1975 formed the Bothy Band with Matt Molloy, Paddy Keenan, Tommy Peoples, Tríona Ní Dhomhnaill and Micheál Ó Domhnaill; despite its relatively short life the group had an enormous impact on the development of ensemble traditional music. The very popular Moving Hearts, formed in 1981, specialised in new musical directions.

LYNAM, Joss (1924–), mountaineer, b. London, 29 June 1924, ed. Highgate School and TCD. Qualified and practised as a civil engineer, specialising in marine projects. An enthusiastic walker and climber from an early age, he has led nine expeditions to the Himalayas, mostly as leader, ranging from Kashmir in 1946 to Garhwal in 1991, as well as making climbing trips to the Chinese Tien Shan (1995), Greenland, the Andes, the Rockies and east Africa. He has made 22 Alpine visits, as well as climbing extensively in Britain and Ireland. His knowledge of the hills and mountains of Ireland is unrivalled. Chairman of the expeditions commission of UIAA (the world body for mountaineering). President of the Association for Adventure Sports, in which capacity he has been heavily involved in adventure sports training. Since 1983 he has been one of the principal movers behind the development of the Irish system of waymarked trails. He has edited and written a number of walking guides to the country. Irish Life Pensioner of the Year 1991.

LYNCH, Fionán (1889–1966), revolutionary, politician and judge, b. Cahirciveen, Co. Kerry, ed. St Brendan's, Killarney, Rockwell, Blackrock and UCD. He worked as a national teacher in St Michan's in Dublin from 1912 until the Easter Rising, in which he fought with the 1st Battalion of the Dublin Brigade of the Volunteers. He was elected Sinn Féin TD for South Kerry in 1918 and again in 1921. He supported the Anglo-Irish Treaty

and was a brigadier in the Free State army during the Civil War. Minister for Education in the Provisional Government in 1922, for Fisheries 1923–7, Land and Fisheries 1928–32. Thereafter, having been called to the Bar, he was in legal practice for a number of years before becoming a highly regarded Circuit Court judge.

LYNCH, Jack (1917–), politician, b. Cork, 15 Aug. 1917, ed. St Vincent's, North Mon. and King's Inns, m. Maureen O'Connor. Qualified as a barrister while working as a civil servant in Dublin. He was one of Cork's most outstanding athletes, winning one football and five hurling All-Ireland champion-ships. First elected to the Dáil in 1948 (FF Cork City) and held a seat until his retirement in 1981. Parliamentary secretary 1951–4, then joined the cabinet as Minister for Education 1957–9. Minister for Industry and Commerce 1959–65, Finance 1965–6. Elected leader of Fianna Fáil and Taoiseach in 1966 as a compromise candidate following the retirement of SEÁN LEMASS. He became known as the 'reluctant' Taoiseach although he was later to reach heights of popularity unscaled by any contemporary holder of high office (his successor as Taoiseach, LIAM COSGRAVE of Fine Gael, described him as the most popular Irish leader since Daniel O'Connell). He was the longest-serving leader of his party after EAMON DE VALERA.

In the 1969 general election many had believed that FF's 12 years of unbroken rule would come to an end but Lynch led them once again to victory, successfully fending off a challenge from a Labour Party which had edged to the left but, in doing so, had scared off many voters. The fruits of victory turned bitter as conflict between nationalists and unionists in Northern Ireland deepened. The government lost its public cohesion after some militant speeches by cabinet members, notably NEIL BLANEY.

Lynch's approach to the Northern problems was pragmatic and cautious. Incipient crisis in Dublin became real when in 1970 he dramatically fired two of his cabinet ministers, Blaney and CHARLES HAUGHEY, for not subscribing fully to government policy on Northern Ireland (a third minister, KEVIN BOLAND, resigned in protest). Lynch suspected that the dismissed ministers were guilty of involvement in illegal importation of arms to aid Northern nationalists, but charges to that effect were later dismissed in the courts. It was a difficult period for the Taoiseach but the overwhelming majority of his party sided with him and against the former ministers. When Haughey, having been acquitted, tried to goad Lynch into standing down, the party leader took him on openly and brushed aside the challenge. Victory was his but the seeds for future dissent had been planted.

Lynch lost the 1973 general election, but only narrowly and in obviously difficult circumstances. The opposition years which followed were marked by uncertainty and hesitancy, and carried no hint of the landslide FF victory which was to come, again under Lynch's leadership, in the 1977 general election. Within two years the FF tide had rapidly ebbed and the party lost two crucial by-elections in Lynch's native city of Cork in 1979. Late that year he stepped down. To his chagrin, Charles Haughey defeated finance minister GEORGE COLLEY for the succession. In the ensuing years, Jack Lynch was almost airbrushed out of the party's history. He continued to espouse the cause of Haughey's major opponent, DESMOND O'MALLEY, even when the latter was expelled from FF and founded the Progressive Democrats. On retirement from politics he took up a number of company directorships.

LYNCH, Patricia (1900–1972), author, b. Cork, 7 June 1900, ed. various convent schools in Ireland, Britain and Belgium, d. Dublin, 1 Sept. 1972. She published more than 50 books for children and became one of the most respected and popular writers of children's literature in Europe. Her books have been translated into several languages and have won many awards. *The Grey Goose of Kilnevan* was selected as one of the best 100 books published in America in 1941, in all genres, by the Cardinal Hayes Literature Committee. Her best-known books are *The Turf Cutter's Donkey* (1934) and the *Brogeen* series, beginning in 1947. Although her books were written for children, they are also widely read by adults. The autobiographical *Story-teller's Holiday* (1947) is an evocative and amusing reminiscence of childhood.

LYNCH, Patrick (1918–), economist, public servant and academic, b. Dublin, ed. CUS, UCD and Peterhouse, Cambridge. Civil servant Department of Finance 1941; assistant secretary to the inter-party government 1948–51 led by JOHN A. COSTELLO, whom he and ALEXIS FITZGERALD helped persuade to adopt a Keynesian approach in economic policy. Successively lecturer 1952, associate professor 1966 and professor 1975–80 of political economy at UCD, he influenced much economic thinking in both the public and the private sectors from the 1950s to the 1990s. Chairman Aer Lingus 1954–75, board member Provincial Bank of Ireland (from 1966 part of AIB) from 1959. Served on many educational and economic advisory bodies, was treasurer of the RIA 1972–80 and wrote extensively on educational, economic and social questions.

LYND, Robert Wilson (1879–1949), essayist, b. Belfast, d. 6 Oct. 1949. Already a socialist republican as an undergraduate, he became BULMER HOBSON's most effective writer in the *Republic* and a leading light in the Irish community in London. (His wife, Sylvia – later a considerable poet – was one of his pupils in Gaelic League classes.) He was a friend of ROGER CASEMENT and, although strenuously opposed to the Easter Rising, campaigned vigorously for his reprieve. Literary editor of the *Daily News* (later the *News Chronicle*) 1913–47. Produced over 30 volumes, mainly collections of the deceptively light essays which as 'YY' he wrote weekly for the *New Statesman* 1913–45, but also books on Ireland and literature, his twin passions.

LYNN, Kathleen Florence (1874–1955), physician and revolutionary, b. Cong, Co. Mayo, the daughter of a canon of the Church of Ireland, ed. Alexandra and in England and Germany. In 1899 was one of the first women to graduate in medicine from the RUI. Elected house surgeon to the Adelaide, she faced opposition as a woman and her appointment was not ratified. FRCSI 1909. A long-standing commitment to the Women's Suffrage Movement drew her to republican ideals and during the 1913 Lock-out she became a member of the Citizen Army, organising ambulances and first-aid instruction at Liberty Hall. As the Citizen Army's chief medical officer she was arrested on Easter Monday 1916 and held in custody until her deportation to England in June. Released in 1917, she was elected a member of the standing committee of Sinn Féin. Following the round-up of SF leaders in 1918 and having been on the run for some time, she appeared at the SF Convention and then inserted a notice in the press indicating that she had retired to her residence at 9 Belgrave Road, Rathmines. She was arrested but when the Lord Mayor of Dublin made representations on her behalf, 'with a view to having her professional services made available during the influenza epidemic', was once again released. Vice-president of the Irish Women Workers' Union. In 1919, inspired by the work of Inghinidhe na hÉireann and by the harsh reality that 164 out of every 1,000 Dublin infants died each year from preventable diseases, Lynn and a colleague, with combined resources of £70, launched Teach Ultan, a hospital 'for the medical treatment of infants under 1 year of age'. Only women were to be employed at the hospital. It became the front line in the battle against infant mortality and the BCG unit was established there. Lynn was elected to the Dáil as an SF deputy in 1923. In keeping with the party's abstentionist policy, she did not take the seat, but continued to be an active member of Rathmines UDC.

LYONS, Francis Stewart Leland (1923–1983), historian, b. Derry, ed. TCD, d. Dublin. Lecturer in history Hull and TCD. Professor of Modern History University of Kent 1964–74. Provost TCD 1974–81. His biographies of JOHN DILLON (1968) and Parnell (1977) confirmed his reputation as a leading authority on the Irish Parliamentary Party. *Ireland since the Famine* (1971) remains a reliable general survey of the period. Because of the clarity of his writings and his acute feeling for the impact of personality on the course of events, he succeeded more than any other historian of his day in bringing professionally researched Irish history to a wide public.

M

McADOO, Henry Robert (1916–), Church of Ireland archbishop and theologian, b. 10 Jan. 1916, ed. Cork and Dublin. Ordained deacon 1939, priest 1940. Dean of Cork 1952–62. Elected Bishop of Ossory, Ferns and Leighlin 1962. Archbishop of Dublin 1977–85. Hon. FTCD. Retired 1985. Publications (mainly on Anglican theology) include: *The Structure of Caroline Moral Theology* (1949), *The Spirit of Anglicanism* (1965), the Hale lectures delivered at Seabury-Western Theological Seminary, from which he received an honorary doctorate in theology, and several works on Jeremy Taylor, including *The Eucharistic Theology of Jeremy Taylor* (1988) and *First of its Kind: Jeremy Taylor's Life of Christ* (1994). Co-chairman of ARCIC 1, the Anglican–Roman Catholic International Commission set up by the Pope and the Archbishop of Canterbury, whose *Final Report* (1982) addressed itself in particular to those issues on which controversy between the two communions had centred: the Eucharist, the meaning and function of the ordained ministry, and the nature and exercise of authority in the Church.

McALISKEY, Josephine *Bernadette* (1947–), née Devlin, politician and civil rights activist, b. Cookstown, Co. Tyrone, 23 Apr. 1947, ed. St Patrick's Girls' Academy, Dungannon and QUB (psychology). As a prominent member of the People's Democracy movement she took part in all the major Northern Ireland Civil Rights Association marches 1968–9. In 1969 she became the youngest woman ever to be elected to Westminster (Independent Unity, Mid-Ulster), taking her seat on her 22nd birthday; she would hold it until Feb. 1974. In Aug. 1969 she stood at the barricades which had been erected by the people of the Bogside in Derry to prevent police encroachment into their area, and was later sentenced to six months' imprisonment for riotous behaviour. Although seriously injured in a loyalist gun attack in Feb. 1981, she was a central figure in the National H-Block Committee during the hunger strike by republican prisoners that year.

MacALISTER, Robert Alexander Stewart (1870–1950), archaeologist and academic, b. Dublin, ed. Rathmines School, Dublin and Cambridge, d. Cambridge, Apr. 1950. Director of excavations Palestine Exploration Fund 1900–9. Professor of Celtic Archaeology UCD 1909–42. President Royal Society of Antiquaries 1924–8, PRIA 1926–31, chairman National Monuments Advisory Council 1930–43. Promoted a major archaeological survey of Ireland and pioneered many aspects of archaeological investigation himself, especially decipherment of carving and iconography on ancient monuments. A leading interpreter of ogham writing and the scenes depicted on the high crosses, particularly those at Monasterboice, Co. Louth. His extensive published work includes *Ireland in Pre-Celtic Times* (1921), *The Archaeology of Ireland* (1927), *The Secret Language of Ireland* (1937) and *Monasterboice* (1946).

Mac AMHLAIGH, Dónall (1926–1989), novelist and short story writer, b. Galway. Emigrated to England to work as a navvy in 1951. His works are primarily autobiographical. Publications include: *Dialann Deoraí* (1960), *Saol Saighdiúra* (1962), *Diarmaid Ó Dónaill* (1965), *Sweeney agus Scéalta Eile* (1970), *Schnitzer Ó Sé* (1974) and *Beoir Bhaile* (1981). Apart from books, Mac Amhlaigh wrote in English as well as Irish for *The Irish Times*. RTÉ transmitted his award-winning television drama *Saighdiúirí* in 1965, but he remains essentially the most important literary witness to the pain and endurance of mid-century Irish emigrants forced by economic circumstances to find work in post-war Britain.

McANALLY, Ray (1926–1989), actor, b. Buncrana, Co. Donegal, 30 Mar. 1926, ed. St Eunan's College, Letterkenny and Maynooth, d. 15 June 1989. One of Ireland's most gifted and successful actors of the latter half of the century, McAnally was a member of the Abbey Theatre Company 1947–63, appearing in over

150 plays. His major stage credits include *Philadelphia, Here I Come!*, *The Field*, *Da*, *The Cherry Orchard*, *A Doll's House* and *The Hostage* at the Abbey and *Translations* with Field Day Theatre Company. Television appearances include *A Very British Coup*, in which he memorably played an embattled Labour prime minister, John le Carré's *A Perfect Spy*, for which he won a Royal Television Society award, and *Scout*, written by FRANK McGUINNESS. Film appearances include *She Didn't Say No*, *Shake Hands with the Devil*, *The Naked Edge*, *Billy Budd*, *We're No Angels*, *The Mission* and *No Surrender*; he received the *Evening Standard* best actor award for his performances in the latter two.

MacARDLE, Dorothy (1899–1958), historian, b. Dundalk into a well-known brewing family, ed. UCD. English teacher at Alexandra. She was an active member of the Gaelic League and a strong supporter of Sinn Féin. Close to MAUD GONNE MACBRIDE and EAMON DE VALERA, she rejected the Treaty and took the republican side in the Civil War. Her monumental work, *The Irish Republic* (1937), was undertaken at de Valera's specific request. Although partisan, its research is formidable and it remains one of the most important works in 20th-century Irish history. She also wrote *Tragedies of Kerry* (1946), as well as plays and novels. Drama critic of the *Irish Press* in its early days. During the war, she performed outstanding humanitarian work in refugee aid. President Irish Association of Civil Liberties 1951.

McARDLE, John Stephen (1859–1928), surgeon, b. Dundalk, ed. St Mary's College, Dundalk and the Catholic University Medical School, Cecilia Street, Dublin, d. 14 Apr. 1928. Graduated LRCP&SI 1879–80. Appointed to the staff of St Vincent's Hospital in 1882 and took FRCSI in 1884. McArdle was one of the most skilled surgeons of his time. Despite a heavy clinical load, he had many articles published in the *Dublin Journal of Medical Science* and held the chair of surgery at Cecilia Street.

McATEER, Edward (1914–1986), politician, b. Coatbridge, Scotland, where his Donegal father lived before moving back to settle in Derry two years later, ed. CBS, Brow-of-the-Hill, d. Derry, 25 Mar. 1986. Served as a tax officer before becoming an account-ant. He was returned unopposed as Stormont MP for Mid-Derry in 1949 and later for Foyle in 1953. He led the Nationalist Party, which was encouraged by TERENCE O'NEILL's reforms to become the official opposition. The civic disturbances after 1968 brought younger politicians to the fore and McAteer was defeated in Foyle by JOHN HUME. During the 1950s and 1960s he spent much time in London attempting to persuade British politicians and newspapers of the need for political reform in Northern Ireland. By the time the British government was forced to step in, both McAteer and his party had been swept away.

McAUGHTRY, Samuel (Sam) (1923–), writer and senator, b. in the loyalist Tiger's Bay area of Belfast. Left school at 14 and served in the RAF 1940–46, being discharged with the rank of flying officer. He later joined the Northern Ireland civil service, becoming a deputy principal in the Department of Agriculture. A long-time member of the Northern Ireland Labour Party, now supports the campaign to have the British Labour Party contest NI constituencies. He was also chairman of the Peace Train Organisation, which opposed IRA attacks on the Belfast–Dublin train service – the organisation disbanded in 1995. The publication of his first book, *The Sinking of the Kenbane Head*, led to radio and newspaper contributions. He has produced eight books to date. In Feb. 1996 he became a member of the Seanad with the support of the three parties in the ruling FG–Labour–DL government. McAughtry once noted: 'I'm happy to be living in the United Kingdom. I want this to be allied with the fact that I'm happier still to be Irish.'

McAULEY, David (Dave, 'Boy') (1961–), boxer, b. Larne, Co. Antrim, 15 Jan. 1961. With the Larne club, he won the Irish Amateur Senior Championship at flyweight in 1980, he turned professional in 1981 and in Oct. 1986 became British champion, when he beat Joe Kelly of Scotland with a ninth-round KO. He narrowly missed winning the WBA world title in 1987 and 1988 to Fidel Bassa of Colombia, but in June 1989 he defeated the IBF champion Duke McKenzie on points at Wembley. He was the first home-based boxer, either British or Irish, successfully to defend a world title five times and to compete in eight world title bouts. In 1992 he lost the title to Rodolfo Blanco of Colombia in a controversial points decision. He was made an MBE in 1992.

MacBRIDE, John (1865–1916), revolutionary, b. Westport, 7 May 1865. After studying medicine for a short period, he worked with a Dublin firm of wholesale chemists. As a young man he fought on the side of the Boers in South Africa with the rank of major. He settled in Paris and married MAUD GONNE MACBRIDE in 1903; their son was SEÁN MACBRIDE. When he returned to Ireland he helped to organise and train the Irish Volunteers. He was shot on 5 May 1916 for his part in the Easter Rising.

MacBRIDE, Maud Gonne (1865–1953), revolutionary and republican campaigner, b. Aldershot, 4 Feb. 1865, ed. France, d. 27 Apr. 1953. Her father, an army officer of Irish ancestry, brought her to live in Ireland in 1882. Returning to France, she fell in love with Lucien Millevoye, who sparked her interest in nationalist causes, including Irish independence. They had a daughter, Iseult, but eventually parted. Maud continued to campaign for Irish freedom, publishing a news bulletin in Paris as well as lecturing in Britain and America. In Dublin in 1900 she founded Inghinidhe na hÉireann, a women's organisation to combat 'English influence' in literature and music. W.B. YEATS, who had once hoped to marry her, gave her the title role in *Cathleen ni Houlihan*. She became a Roman Catholic and married JOHN MACBRIDE in Paris in 1903, but the marriage collapsed shortly after the birth of their son, SEÁN MACBRIDE. She kept up her nationalist activities, came back to Ireland and was briefly jailed in England in 1918. She devoted herself to the welfare of republican prisoners' families after the Anglo-Irish Treaty, which she opposed. In 1926 she became embroiled in controversy with SEAN O'CASEY over *The Plough and the Stars* and in 1938 she wrote a volume of autobiography.

MacBRIDE, Seán (1904–1988), politician and lawyer, b. 26 Jan. 1904, s. of JOHN MACBRIDE and MAUD GONNE MACBRIDE, ed. France (he retained strong French inflections throughout his life), Mount St Benedict, Gorey, Co. Wexford, UCD and King's Inns,

d. 15 Jan. 1988. In 1921 MacBride accompanied MICHAEL COLLINS to the Treaty negotiations in London as his personal aide. He opposed the Treaty and was very involved with the republican movement throughout the 1920s and 1930s, including a period when he served as chief of staff of the IRA. Called to the Bar in 1937, he defended a number of IRA members in a series of famous cases during the 1940s.

Along with other republicans, disillusioned with Fianna Fáil, he founded the Clann na Poblachta party in 1946. The party enjoyed considerable success – although well below members' expectations – in winning ten seats in the 1948 general election. It was sufficient to end Fianna Fáil's 16 years of unbroken rule. A multi-party coalition was constructed, in which Clann na Poblachta participated, MacBride becoming Minister for External Affairs. During the lifetime of that government, partly because of the 'Mother and Child' scheme introduced by his party colleague and Minister for Health NOEL BROWNE, he and Browne became deeply estranged. The scheme had caused a sharp row with the Catholic hierarchy and elements in the medical profession, and MacBride demanded Browne's resignation: radical on some issues, Seán MacBride was always a conservative on Irish social matters. The row led quickly to the collapse of the coalition government and started the rapid decline of Clann na Poblachta, although MacBride remained a TD until he lost his seat in the 1957 general election, having helped to bring down a second multiparty coalition, in office since 1954.

Later he became involved in many international organisations, including various UN bodies. Chairman of Amnesty International 1973–6 and in that capacity received the Nobel peace prize in 1974. He was later (1977) awarded the Lenin peace prize and (1978) the American medal for justice. He served as UN commissioner for Namibia before that country got its independence. During a period working with the Council of Europe he was one of those responsible for the European Convention on Human Rights. He chaired the UNESCO International Commission for the Study of Communication Problems, whose controversial findings, published in 1980 as

Many Voices, One World, became known as the MacBride Report. In the 1980s he made a number of unsuccessful interventions with the Provisional republican movement in order to secure an IRA ceasefire but in the same years he won some congressional support in the USA for proposals called 'the MacBride Principles' to counter anti-Catholic discrimination in Northern Ireland.

McBRIDE, William James (Willie John) (1940–), international rugby player, b. Toomebridge, Co. Antrim, 6 June 1940. He and Syd Millar are the two greatest players from Ballymena RFC. Between 1962 and 1975 McBride played 63 times for Ireland, 12 as captain, a record until it was surpassed by Mike Gibson. He went on a record five tours with the British Lions: to Australia and New Zealand in 1966 and 1971, and to South Africa three times, in 1962, 1968 and 1974, playing in a record 17 Tests. He thus participated in two of only three series-winning Lions sides in history – New Zealand in 1971 and South Africa in 1974, when he was captain; the Lions were undefeated on that tour and won the Test series 3–0, with the final Test drawn. He was manager of the unsuccessful Lions tour to New Zealand in 1983, captained by Ciaran Fitzgerald, and was coach to the national team for one season, 1983–4.

MacCABE, Alexander (Alasdair MacCába) (1886–1972), businessman, b. near Ballymote, Co. Sligo, 5 June 1886, ed. Summerhill College, Sligo and St Patrick's College, Dublin, d. 31 May 1972. Appointed principal of Drumnagranchy NS, Sligo 1907. Joined the IRB and was elected a member of its supreme council 1914. Elected Sinn Féin TD for Sligo–Mayo in the general election of 1918. He supported the Anglo-Irish Treaty but retired from politics in the early 1920s to resume his teaching career. In 1935 he co-founded the Educational Building Society, of which he was appointed a full-time managing director in 1941. Under his stewardship it became one of the leading societies in Ireland.

McCABE, Eugene (1930–), playwright and fiction writer, b. Glasgow, ed. Castleknock and UCC. He dairy-farmed in Co. Wicklow for ten years after graduation and began writing in 1962. *The King of the Castle* won him

prominence and the Irish Life drama award at the Dublin Theatre Festival 1964. There followed *Breakdown* (1966) and *Swift* (1969). McCabe made the transition from stage to television with *Roma* (1979). His concern for and understanding of the divided peoples of Northern Ireland is shown in the trilogy he wrote for RTÉ, *Cancer* (1976), and in his short novel, *Victims*, derived from the television plays and published the following year; it has been likened to Liam O'Flaherty's *The Informer*. His other dramas are: *Pull Down a Horseman* (1979), about James Connolly, and *Gale Day* (1979), about Patrick Pearse. He has also published three books of short stories and a novel, *Death and Nightingales* (1992). He farms his family's holding in Co. Monaghan.

McCABE, Patrick (1955–), novelist and short story writer, b. Clones, Co. Monaghan. Hennessy award 1979. He started writing novels in the 1980s and published *Carn* in 1989. His finest work is *The Butcher Boy*, which was nominated for the Booker prize and won the *Irish Times*/Aer Lingus literature prize in 1992. Other works include *Music on Clinton Street* (1986) and *The Dead School* (1995). He has also published a book of stories for children: *The Adventures of Shay Mouse, The Mouse from Longford* (1994). He lives and teaches in London.

McCAFFERTY, Nell (1944–), journalist and writer, b. Derry, 28 Mar. 1944, ed. Thorn Hill College, Derry and QUB. Reporter *The Irish Times* 1970–80, columnist *Irish Press* 1980–85, contributing editor *MS* magazine, TV critic *Sunday Tribune*, *Hot Press* columnist and regular broadcaster. Renowned for her feminist and nationalist convictions and not least her sense of humour. Since her seminal 1970s 'In the Eyes of the Law' articles about the small, daily tragedies witnessed in Dublin's District Court, her work has been imbued with a strong commitment to social justice and solidarity with the oppressed. Her books include: *In the Eyes of the Law* (1981), *A Woman to Blame* (1985), *Goodnight Sisters . . .* (1988) and *Peggy Deery* (1989).

McCANN, Donal (1943–), actor, s. of John McCann, ed. Terenure College and Abbey School of Acting, Dublin. Early stage successes included roles in *On Baile's Strand*, *Waiting for Godot* and Hugh Leonard's *The*

Au Pair Man. McCann then worked in television in England for a time and appeared in RTÉ's version of *Strumpet City*. He marked the beginning of the 1980s with one of his most famous performances, that of Frank Hardy in BRIAN FRIEL's *Faith Healer*. Other notable appearances include *Translations* at the Gaiety Theatre and several performances as Captain Boyle in SEAN O'CASEY's *Juno and the Paycock*. One of his greatest critical triumphs to date has been in the central role in SEBASTIAN BARRY's *The Steward of Christendom*, an astonishing tour de force for all who saw it. Among his film work is *Sinful Davey*, *Mackintosh Man* and *The Dead*, all directed by John Huston, *High Spirits*, directed by NEIL JORDAN, Thaddeus O'Sullivan's *December Bride* and Bob Quinn's *Budawanny*.

McCANN, Eamonn Joseph (1943–), journalist and civil rights activist. Expelled from QUB 1965 while a student of psychology because of his political activities. One of the organisers of the civil rights march in Derry on 5 Oct. 1968 which is often viewed as the start of the Troubles. As a Labour candidate he unsuccessfully contested the Foyle seat for Stormont in 1969 and the Westminster Derry constituency in 1970. McCann is now a broadcaster and journalist. In Aug. 1994 he commented on 'the battle of the Bogside': 'I believe that all working-class people should see any uprising against oppression in a positive light. The circumstances of 1969 were chaotic and events moved at great speed. Many now remember this or that detail differently. But in essence it was an uprising against oppression.' Author of *War and an Irish Town*.

McCANN, John (1905–1980), playwright and politician, b. Dublin, ed. Synge Street. Although McCann's works were once dubbed 'soap operas', most were tremendously popular with Abbey Theatre audiences and swelled the company's receipts for two decades. Yet his first and last love was politics: having worked in journalism for several years, he was elected TD in 1939, was Lord Mayor of Dublin 1946–7 but lost his Dáil seat in 1954 at a time when his drama was receiving wide recognition. His satire on marathon Irish courtships, *Twenty Years A-Wooing*, was a huge hit for the Abbey that year. He also wrote a number of radio dramas, in addition to short stories. Among his plays were: *The Dreamer, Blood is Thicker than Water, Give me a Bed of Roses, I Know Where I'm Going, Put a Beggar on Horseback, A Jew called Sammy* and *Early and Often*. Father of DONAL MCCANN.

McCANN, Neil (1924–), businessman, ed. St Mary's College, Dundalk and Castleknock. Chairman Fruit Importers of Ireland, which acquired the international fruit firm Fyffes in 1986. Company later renamed Fyffes plc, with McCann as chairman and chief executive. Already the largest fruit importing and distributing firm in Ireland and a major operator in other markets, Fyffes acquired a majority holding in the Madrid-based Grupo Angel Rey in 1995, which made the Irish multinational the biggest trading company in the fruit and vegetable sector in Spain.

McCARRISON, Sir Robert (1878–1960), medical scientist, b. Portadown, Co. Armagh, ed. Queen's College, Belfast and Dublin's Richmond Hospital, m. Helen Stella Johnston 1906. Graduated MB (RUI) in 1900. Working for the Indian medical service, he carried out important research on endemic goitre and deficiency diseases. He was awarded the Kaisar-i-Hind gold medal for public service but the war interrupted his work. In 1929 he became director of the Nutrition Research Laboratories at Coonor, which under his stewardship became one of the most highly respected of such centres in the world. After retirement in 1935 Major-General McCarrison lived at Oxford. Chairman of the local medical war committee 1939–45, first director of postgraduate medical education for the region 1945–55. To mark his 75th birthday a Festschrift was published, *The Work of Sir Robert McCarrison*.

McCARTAN, Jim and **Dan**, Gaelic footballers. Renowned brothers who were major contributors to Down's All-Ireland victories of 1960 and 1961. Jim captained the Ulster Railway Cup winning team in 1969 and also shared in the victories of 1964 and 1965, while Dan won similar honours in 1964, 1965, 1966 and 1968, as well as another All-Ireland medal in 1968. Jim managed the Down team which won the National League in 1983 and Dan went on to serve as a county selector.

McCARTHY, Charles (1924–1986), trade unionist and academic, b. Cork, 25 Jan.

1924, ed. Presentation College, Cork, UCD and King's Inns, m. Muriel Breslin 1951, d. 8 Sept. 1986. Was an actor with Radio Éireann Repertory before becoming a vocational teacher and then general secretary of the Vocational Teachers' Association. During a career marked by active membership of many bodies, he was a member of the executive committee of the ICTU, and successively vice-president and president of Congress. Subsequently Professor of Industrial Relations at TCD (1979), head of the TCD School of Business Studies and dean of the faculty of economic and social studies. FTCD. He acted frequently as a mediator and consultant on industrial relations to government departments and private enterprises, and served also as chairman of the board of the Abbey Theatre. Publications include *The Distasteful Challenge* (1968) and *Trade Unions in Ireland* (1977). Member RTÉ Authority 1973–6.

McCARTHY, Donal (1908–1980), academic, statistician and public servant, b. Midleton, Co. Cork, ed. Rockwell, UCC and University College London, D.Sc., Ph.D. in statistics, LL D (NUI). Statistics branch Department of Industry and Commerce 1930. Lecturer in mathematics UCC 1931; Professor of Mathematical Physics 1944. Deputy director Central Statistics Office 1949, director 1957. Member of the International Statistics Institute, the UN Statistical Commission (chairman 1960–65), the Planners Conference, the UN Social Development Programme 1967 (chairman) and the Conference of European Statisticians. He was closely associated with two important Irish projects, 'Investment in Education' and 'Science and Irish Economic Development'. Director ESRI 1965. President UCC 1967–78.

McCARTHY, Mick ('Captain Fantastic') (1959–), international footballer, b. Barnsley, 7 Feb. 1959. He played at club level for Barnsley for seven years, when they were promoted from the fourth to the second division, Manchester City, Glasgow Celtic (one Scottish Premier League title and two Scottish Cup medals), Olympic Lyonnais and Millwall, where he became player-manager. From 1984 on he won 56 caps for the Republic of Ireland, playing notable roles in the 1988 European Championship and the

1990 World Cup finals in Italy. In 1996 he was appointed successor to JACK CHARLTON as manager of the Republic of Ireland team.

McCARTHY, Niall St John (1925–1992), lawyer, b. Cork, ed. CBS, Dún Laoghaire, Co. Dublin, Clongowes, UCD and King's Inns. BA 1945. Called to Bar 1946, Senior Counsel 1959. Brilliant advocate and an outstanding and witty public speaker, built up a substantial general practice, mainly in Dublin. Defended CHARLES HAUGHEY in 1970 Arms Trial and represented major oil company in long-running Whiddy Tribunal. Appeared for Attorney-General in significant constitutional case of McGee v. A.-G. (1974) relating to importation of contraceptives, in which the Supreme Court established a constitutional right to marital privacy. Outspoken critic of aspects of Irish legal system; publicly opposed the re-establishment in 1974 of the Special Criminal Court. Chairman of Bar Council 1980–82, first chairman of National Archives Advisory Council in 1986. Said to have become top earner in Law Library when appointed direct from the Bar to the Supreme Court in 1982 following the retirement of JOHN KENNY. On the Supreme Court he quickly gained a reputation for liberal views, which were evident in his judgments in e.g. the NORRIS case (1984) on homosexuality, the 'X' case (1992) on when abortion was permissible, and A.-G. v. Hamilton (1992) on cabinet confidentiality. He and his wife both died in a traffic accident in Spain, 1 Oct. 1992.

McCLELLAND, John Alexander (1870–1920), FRS, academic, b. Coleraine, Co. Derry, ed. Academical Institution, Coleraine, Queen's College, Galway and Cambridge, d. 13 Apr. 1920. McClelland was appointed Professor of Experimental Physics at UCD in 1900, just three years after completing his MA at Cambridge. He received the Boyle medal from the RDS in 1917 in recognition of an outstanding research career, mainly devoted to studying radioactivity and examining the ionisation of gases.

Mac CONGHAIL, Muiris (1941–), television producer, journalist and film-maker, s. of MAURICE MACGONIGAL, ed. Ring, Co. Waterford, Blackrock, Maynooth and King's Inns. Joined RTÉ 1964, editor television current affairs (*Seven Days*) 1967–71, head of radio features and current affairs 1971–3. Left the broadcasting service in 1973 to become assistant secretary in the Department of the Taoiseach (effectively government press secretary). Returned to RTÉ 1975, became Ceannaire (controller of programmes) Radio na Gaeltachta, served twice as controller of programmes RTÉ 1 between 1977 and 1986. Chairman Irish Film Board 1982–7, member of Abbey Theatre board 1986–90. Independent film producer since 1986 with his own company, Scannáin Chéad Snámha/First Run Films. His many documentary films, distinguished by exhaustive research and sensitivity to atmosphere, have included *Oileán Eile/Another Island, Clear Eye and Open Hand* and *The Religious Strain*.

MacCONNAILL, Michael Aloysius (1902–1987), anatomist, b. Ballymena, ed. St Mary's School and QUB (B.Sc. 1922, MB 1925, D.Sc. 1950), m. Eileen Coyle, three s. one d. Influenced by Professor Thomas Walmsley, he devoted his career to anatomy. Following a demonstratorship at QUB, he worked under Professor Elliot Smith in University College London. Senior demonstrator and lecturer at the Department of Anatomy in Sheffield University until his election in 1942 to the chair of anatomy in UCC, from which he retired in 1973. His massive intellect enabled MacConnaill to apply principles of biology, mathematics, physics and chemistry to his investigations in anatomy. His chief interest was the locomotor system; much of his work was done in association with orthopaedic surgeons and constitutes an important contribution to bioengineering. Publications include *An Cholann Bheo* (1949).

McCONNELL, Adams Andrew (1884–1972), neurosurgeon, b. Belfast, ed. Royal Academical Institution and TCD. Graduated MB (1909), FRCSI (1911). Appointed to the staff of Dublin's Richmond Hospital, he devoted himself to neurosurgery, a pioneer in this field. He visited American clinics to study the latest techniques and introduced Dandy's ventriculography to Europe. Founder member of the Society of British Neurological Surgeons in 1926. President of the RCSI 1936–8, Regius Professor of Surgery to DU 1946–56, president of the Royal Academy of Medicine in Ireland 1946–7 and chairman of the board

of governors of St Laurence's Hospital 1943–58.

McCONNELL, Albert Joseph (1903–1993), academic, b. Ballymena, 19 Nov. 1903, ed. Ballymena Academy, TCD and University of Rome. Lecturer in mathematics TCD 1927–30, fellow 1930–52, Professor of Natural Philosophy 1930–57, visiting professor University of Alexandria 1946–7, University of Kuwait 1970. Provost of TCD 1952–74. Member of Council of State 1973. Chairman governing body and member of the council, School of Theoretical Physics, DIAS. MRIA and honorary fellow Oriel College, Oxford. Publications include *Applications of the Absolute Differential Calculus* (1931) and, with A.W. CONWAY, *The Mathematical Papers of Sir William Rowan Hamilton* (vol. 2 1940).

McCONNELL, Monsignor James Robert (1915–), theoretical physicist, b. Dublin, 25 Feb. 1915, ed. O'Connell School, UCD 1932–6 (MA in mathematics), Lateran University, Rome 1936–40 and Royal University of Rome 1940–41 (D.Sc.Mat.). Professor of Mathematical Physics Maynooth 1945–68, dean of science 1957–68. Has written widely on relativity, elementary particle theory, group theory and the philosophy of physics. *Quantum Particle Dynamics* (1958) was published in two editions and translated into Russian. Elected to the RIA 1949, fellow of the British Institute of Physics 1968, member of the Pontifical Academy of Sciences. Received the RDS Boyle medal in 1986.

McCORMACK, Inez, trade unionist. National Union of Public Employees representative. Member of the ICTU executive council 1980–81, 1987–91 and 1993. At the 1983 ICTU conference McCormack successfully proposed that seats be reserved for women on the executive council. One of the signatories of the SEÁN MACBRIDE fair employment principles, she was also chairperson of NIC ICTU in 1984–5.

McCORMACK, John (1884–1945), tenor, b. Athlone, ed. Dublin and Milan, where he studied with Vincenzo Sabatini, d. Dublin. Made his stage début under the assumed name of Giovanni Foli in 1906 in Mascagni's *L'Amico Fritz* at the Teatro Chiabrera in Savona. Made his Covent Garden début in 1907 and sang as Don Ottavio in Mozart's

Don Giovanni the same year – his recording of 'Il Mio Tesoro' is one of the most beautiful ever made. Also appeared with the New York Metropolitan, Boston and Chicago Opera Companies. However, it was as a recitalist, with his unique voice and flamboyant personality, that he won a following of millions. Performing in his early years with Patti, Tetrazzini and Melba, and at the end of his life on radio with Bing Crosby, his career covered a vast span in the history of singing. He also appeared in films, the most notable of which was *Song o' my Heart.* McCormack made numerous recordings; among the songs he popularised are 'The Fairy Tree', composed by his first teacher in Dublin, Vincent O'Brien, 'I Hear You Calling Me', and 'The Old House', specially written by General Sir Frederick O'Connor for his farewell performances. He received honours and awards, including a doctorate of literature from Holy Cross, Massachusetts in 1917 and a doctorate of music from the NUI in 1927. In 1928 he was made a hereditary papal count for his services to charity. His singing at the open-air religious services in Ireland for the centenary of Catholic Emancipation (1929) and for the Eucharistic Congress (1932) epitomised these ceremonies in the memory of thousands who then heard him.

Mc CORMACK, William John (1947–), literary critic and poet (writing under the name Hugh Maxton), b. near Aughrim, Co. Wicklow, ed. TCD. He has lived in Derry and Yorkshire and now resides in Dublin. Currently lectures at Goldsmiths College, University of London. Mc Cormack is held to be Ireland's foremost literary historian and has made important contributions to the appreciation of Anglo-Irish literature. His poetry likewise concerns itself with history, and the artist's struggle for self-creation beneath the weight of past generations. Poetry: *Stones* (1970), *The Noise of the Fields* (1976), *Jubilee for Renegades* (1982), *The Enlightened Cave* and *Inscriptions* (1983), *Snapdragons* and *Passage, with Surviving Poems* (1985) and *At the Protestant Museum* (1986). Biography: *Sheridan Le Fanu and Victorian Ireland* (1980). He has written several volumes of literary history, among the most recent being *The Dublin Paper War of 1786–1788* (1993) and *From Burke to Beckett* (1994).

McCORMICK, F.J. (1889–1947), actor, b. Peter Judge, Skerries, Co. Dublin, d. Apr. 1947. McCormick worked briefly as a civil servant in Dublin and London before joining the Abbey Theatre Company in 1918. He appeared in over 500 productions with the Abbey, was considered one of the greatest actors ever to grace its stage and was particularly noted for his performances in the plays of SEAN O'CASEY. He toured the USA with the company five times and acted in several films, including *Odd Man Out* (1947). He was married to another famous Abbey member, actress Eileen Crowe.

McCORMICK, James Stevenson (1926–), medical practitioner and professor, b. Dublin, 9 May 1926, ed. Avoca School, Leys School and Clare College, Cambridge and St Mary's Hospital. He is Ireland's foremost specialist in community health and, after nearly 20 years' experience as a general practitioner, served as dean of the faculty of health science in TCD 1973–91. Chairman of the Eastern Health Board 1970–71, president of the Irish College of General Practitioners 1986.

McCORMICK, Liam (1916–1996), architect, b. Derry, ed. St Columb's College, Derry and Liverpool School of Architecture. He was architect-planner to Ballymena UDC in 1945–6 and entered practice 1948, the year in which he won the competition for the new church at Ennistymon, Co. Clare, in partnership with F.M. Corr. In the 1960s McCormick came to the fore of contemporary Irish ecclesiastical architecture with a series of churches – most in Ulster – distinguished by their authoritative integration of modern style, traditional craft and an uncommonly impressive spiritual ethos. He received an honorary doctorate from NUU and, for his church at Burt, Co. Donegal, the RIAI triennial gold medal for 1965–7. He served on the councils of the RIAI and the Royal Society of Ulster Architects as well as acting as high sheriff of Derry city in 1970–71.

McCRANN, Maighréad (1963–), violinist, b. Dublin, ed. TCD. Winner of the 1982 RTÉ 'Musician of the Future' competition. Made her soloist début at the Musikverein in Vienna in 1986. In Oct. 1993 appointed concert master of the Austrian Symphony Orchestra. Has played in all the major European cities as a soloist and chamber musician. Member of both the Chamber Orchestra of Europe and Concentus Musicus. Founder member of the chamber music ensemble Contrasts Vienna.

McCREA, Sir William (1904–), FRS, Ph.D., Sc.D., mathematician and astronomer, b. Dublin, 13 Dec. 1904, s. of Richard Hunter McCrea and Margaret McCrea, ed. Chesterfield Grammar School, Cambridge and Göttingen, m. Maria Nicol Core Webster 1933, one s. two d. Lecturer in mathematics Edinburgh 1930–32, reader in mathematics QUB 1936–44. Temporary principal science officer Admiralty 1943–5. Professor of Mathematics Royal Holloway College 1944–66. Research professor Sussex University 1966–72. Visiting professorships and fellowships: Berkeley, Cambridge, Case Institute, Louvain, Vancouver, Istanbul and Otago. Emeritus professor Sussex since 1972. President Royal Astronomical Society 1961–3, Mathematical Association 1973–4. Honorary degrees for contributions to mathematics and relativity: NUI, QUB, Sussex, Dublin and Cordoba. Honorary fellow Royal Holloway College, freeman of the city of London 1988. Publications: *Relativity Physics* (1935), *Analytical Geometry of Three Dimensions* (1942) and *Physics of the Sun and Stars*.

McCULLOUGH, Denis (1883–1968), revolutionary, b. Belfast, ed. CBS. Founded Dungannon Clubs with BULMER HOBSON in 1905 to promote the idea of a republican Ireland and used them to reactivate the moribund IRB, in which he became a member of the supreme council. Shared Hobson's critical opinion of ARTHUR GRIFFITH's policies and left Sinn Féin 1910. After the Easter Rising he was interned in Frongoch, where MICHAEL COLLINS interested him in the project for an insurance organisation to keep Irish investment within Ireland: this was the origin of the New Ireland Assurance Company, with which McCullough would be prominently associated in later years.

McCULLOUGH, Wayne ('The Pocket Rocket') (1970–), boxer, b. Belfast, 7 July 1970. In 1988 he won the National Senior Championship at flyweight, as well as the under-18 and junior titles, and he won the bantamweight title in 1992. He reached the third round in the 1988 Seoul Olympic Games

and in 1990 he took the flyweight gold medal in the Commonwealth Games at Auckland, later that year winning a bronze World Cup medal at Bombay. In the 1992 Barcelona Olympics he won a silver medal at bantamweight, before turning professional in 1993. In 1995 he won the WBC version of the world bantamweight title.

MacCURTAIN, Tomás (1884–1920), nationalist, b. Ballyknockane, Co. Cork, 20 Mar. 1884, ed. Bunfort NS and North Mon., d. 20 Mar. 1920. Worked as a clerk with City of Cork Steam Packet Company. Joined Sinn Féin, the IRB and the Irish Volunteers. Elected for Sinn Féin to Cork Corporation and in Jan. 1920 became the first republican lord mayor of the city. He was shot dead in his home: a coroner's jury blamed the RIC.

MacDERMOT, Frank (1886–1975), politician, b. Coolavin, Co. Sligo, ed. Downside and Queen's College, Oxford, d. London. War service Flanders. Banker New York 1919–27. TD (Ind. Roscommon) 1932. With JAMES DILLON founded National Centre Party to promote a united Ireland within the Commonwealth. After winning 11 seats at the 1933 general election, he merged his party with Cumann na nGaedheal to form the United Ireland Party (later Fine Gael). He quickly became disenchanted with EOIN O'DUFFY's leadership and admiration for fascism. Despite O'Duffy's resignation in 1934, MacDermot himself soon afterwards resigned from FG over what he saw as the party's unprincipled attitude on the Italian invasion of Ethiopia (it represented EAMON DE VALERA's support for sanctions as politically motivated). A Taoiseach's nominee to the Seanad as re-established under the constitution of 1937 (of which he disapproved), he joined MICHAEL TIERNEY in proposing an inquiry into the then popular concept of vocational organisation, supposedly but not in fact reflected in the composition of the second chamber. The resultant commission set up by de Valera was too unwieldy (and possibly so intended) to produce satisfactory findings. MacDermot was correspondent for the London *Sunday Times* in Dublin from 1938, in New York from 1942 and in Paris 1945–50. His *Life of Wolfe Tone* appeared in 1939.

McDERMOTT, John Clarke (1896–1979), lawyer, b. Belfast, ed. Campbell College, Belfast and QUB, d. 13 July 1979. Served in France during World War I. Graduated LL B and called to Irish Bar 1921. Lectured in jurisprudence QUB 1931–5. KC (Northern Ireland) 1936, Unionist MP for QUB at Stormont 1938–41, Minister of Public Security for NI 1940–41. Attorney-General (NI) 1941–4; High Court judge (NI) 1944–7, created life peer on his appointment; Lord of Appeal (NI) 1947–51. Pro-Chancellor QUB 1951–69. Chaired Isle of Man Constitution Committee 1958.

Mac DIARMADA, Seán (1884–1916), revolutionary, b. Kiltyclogher, Co. Leitrim, 28 Feb. 1884. Through his friendship with BULMER HOBSON he joined the Belfast circle of the IRB in 1906, and in 1907 he became a full-time organiser for Sinn Féin. Despite a crippling attack of polio in 1912 he continued to work for the republican movement and was manager of the IRB journal, *Irish Freedom*. He became an influential figure in the Irish Volunteers and in 1915 was co-opted onto the secret military council established by the IRB to plan a rebellion. He fought in the GPO during the Easter Rising and was a member of the Provisional Government of the Irish Republic declared at its outset. He was executed on 12 May 1916.

MacDONAGH, Donagh (1912–1968), district justice, broadcaster, poet and playwright, s. of THOMAS MACDONAGH, b. Dublin, ed. Belvedere and UCD. His most successful play was *Happy as Larry* (1946), which received the best reviews of the decade when it was performed in London. More opera than drama, it has since been produced all over the world, adapted for RTÉ and translated into a dozen languages. In the same vein were *God's Gentry* (1951), a play about tinkers, and *Step-in-the-Hollow* (1957). He also wrote a version of the Deirdre legend: *Lady Spider*. He co-edited *The Oxford Book of Irish Verse* with LENNOX ROBINSON, and his own collections were *Veterans and Other Poems* (1941), *The Hungry Grass* (1947) and *A Warning to Conquerors* (1968); his poems appear in several anthologies. He practised as a barrister 1935–41 and served as a district justice in the Dublin Metropolitan Courts until his death on 1 Jan. 1968.

McDONAGH, Enda (1930–), theologian, b. Bekan, Co. Mayo, ed. Maynooth, Rome and Munich. Ordained Roman Catholic priest for the archdiocese of Tuam 1955. Has written many books on religious topics, among them *Challenges to Theology*, *The Making of Disciples*, *Between Chaos and the New Creation* and a moving collection of meditations, *The Small Hours of Belief*. His theology is at once rooted in a profound sense of place – the Mayo of his childhood, the Maynooth of his student days – and the universal vision of a mind steeped in the poetry of diverse cultures as much as the rigours of his chosen discipline. His emphases on liberation, reconciliation and the realities of the human condition as shaped by historical experience have put him in the first rank of modern theologians. He was Professor of Moral Theology and Canon Law at Maynooth until his retirement in 1995 and has lectured widely in Europe and the USA.

MacDONAGH, Thomas (1878–1916), revolutionary and poet, b. Cloughjordan, Co. Tipperary, 1 Feb. 1878, ed. Rockwell. After teaching for a number of years in Kilkenny and Fermoy, he moved to Dublin in 1908 and helped to establish St Enda's School with PATRICK PEARSE. He graduated MA in English in 1911 and, while working as a lecturer in UCD, edited the *Irish Review* with JOSEPH PLUNKETT and helped to found the Irish Theatre with EDWARD MARTYN. Director of training of the Irish Volunteers 1914, he organised the Howth gun-running operation in July of that year. In 1916 he joined the IRB and became a member of the secret military council which planned the Easter Rising. He was one of the signatories to the Proclamation of the Republic and commanded a battalion at Jacob's factory during Easter Week. He was executed on 3 May 1916.

Published poetry collections include *April and May* (1903), *The Golden Joy* (1906) and *Lyrical Poems* (1913). In 1908 the Abbey Theatre produced his play *When the Dawn is Come*. His doctoral thesis, *Literature in Ireland*, was published posthumously in 1916.

MacDONALD, Walter (1854–1920), theologian, b. Mooncoin, Co. Kilkenny, ed. St Kieran's College, Kilkenny and Maynooth, d. Maynooth. Ordained priest 1876. Professor of Theology Maynooth 1881–1920 and prefect of the Dunboyne Establishment, Maynooth from 1888. Founded the *Irish Theological Quarterly* 1906. A spirited writer, controversial because he was ahead of his time rather than because – as his critics imagined – he was unorthodox. Most of his books on theology were refused an imprimatur although he was never deprived of his chair. His autobiography, *Reminiscences of a Maynooth Professor*, published posthumously in 1925, provides a valuable insight into Irish ecclesiastical attitudes in the early years of the century. A general improvement in the quality of teaching at Maynooth during his time was attributed to his insistence that only scholars of proven merit should be recruited.

MacDONNELL, Antony (1844–1925), public servant, b. Shragh, Co. Mayo, ed. Summerhill College, Sligo and Queen's College, Galway, d. London. Joined Indian civil service, instituted major land reforms and famine relief measures in Bengal. Knighted 1893. Lieutenant-governor Agra and Oudh 1895. Permanent under-secretary (head of the civil service) Ireland 1902–8, as which he played a leading advisory role when the legislation, later known as the Wyndham Act, was being drafted to complete the transfer of land ownership to the former tenants. He was also much involved in the creation of the NUI and QUB from the former Queen's Colleges and UCD (RUI). Favoured a proposal to devolve powers from London to Dublin, which displeased nationalists because it fell short of home rule, and unionists because it seemed to be home rule in embryo. Ennobled in 1908 as Baron MacDonnell of Swinford. Chairman Royal Commission on the Civil Service 1912–14. Opposed imposition of conscription on Ireland.

McDOWELL, Kay, trade unionist, originally from the North, where her family owned a string of off-licence shops. In 1910, when Kay and her brother, Willie, were orphaned, her grandfather assumed parental responsibility and maintained a home for both in Dublin. Educated Holy Faith, Glasnevin, where she was considered an exceptional pupil. She studied commerce at Rosses College and at the age of 20 left for London. In 1921 she returned to Dublin and was introduced to LOUIE BENNETT. The following year McDowell was invited to apply for a position in the Irish Women Workers' Union, the beginning of a lifelong commitment to serve the working women of Ireland.

In 1948 she was a founder member of the People's College, in 1949 a Labour Party delegate to the British Labour Party annual convention and in 1951 seconded to act on the Government Prices Advisory Committee. She was elected general secretary of the IWWU in 1957 and became the first woman to be elected to the administrative council of the Labour Party. In 1959 she joined the executive committee of the ICTU.

McDYER, James (1911–1987), Roman Catholic priest and social reformer, b. Kilraine, Glenties, Co. Donegal, 14 Sept. 1911, ed. St Eunan's College, Letterkenny and Maynooth, d. Glencolumbkille, Co. Donegal, 25 Nov. 1987. After ordination 1937 he spent the war years in London, ministering especially to Irish workers. On his return he served first on Tory Island, Co. Donegal, then in 1951 was appointed curate at Glencolumbkille, with which his name was to become synonymous. The remote area had virtually no modern amenities but under his inspired leadership the community, organised co-operatively, soon acquired piped water, electricity and paved roads. Centres for vegetable processing and craftwork were set up as well as a knitwear factory and a museum of social history. A holiday village of 'Irish Cottages' was built and a fish-processing plant. He became parish priest in 1971. Wrote *The Glencolumbkille Story* (1962) and an autobiography, *Father McDyer of Glencolumbkille* (1982).

McELLIGOTT, James J. (1893–1974), public servant, b. Tralee, ed. UCD (classics and economics). Entered the civil service in 1913, assigned to the Local Government Board. Joined the Irish Volunteers on their formation that year and served in the GPO during the Easter Rising. Deported to England, he was interned in various jails, ending up in Stafford Jail in the next cell to MICHAEL COLLINS. On release in 1917 he became a freelance journalist and editor of the *Statist*. He was invited back to Dublin in 1923 as an assistant secretary in the Department of Finance and in 1927 succeeded JOSEPH BRENNAN as secretary, remaining in this office until 1953. Governor of the Central Bank 1953–60 and subsequently a director.

He played a key role in the formation of the economic policies of the new state. Member of all the important economic and financial commissions of his time, including the Tariff Commission 1926–30 (of which he was chairman) and the Commissions on Banking of 1926 and 1934–8. President of the Institute of Bankers 1956 and first president of the Economic Research Institute (now the ESRI). Received an LL D from the NUI in 1946. Conservative in outlook, he was more in sympathy with the theories of Adam Smith than with those of Keynes and adhered strictly to the principle of curbing public expenditure and taxation, moderated by recognition of the need for major productive developments such as the ESB. His achievements in the Department of Finance include the launching of the first national loan, guiding politicians and civil servants alike through the shoals of the first change of government in 1932, advocating the establishment of a Central Bank and advising the government in the devaluation crisis of 1949. Died suddenly on 23 Jan. 1974.

McELLIGOTT, Thomas Joseph (1888–1961), sergeant RIC, b. Duagh, Listowel, Co. Kerry. As *Pro Patria* an articulate propagandist for the rank and file, agitated for reform of the RIC as an unarmed force and an end to the cadet system; wrote letters to the national press. Organiser in Ireland of the short-lived National Union of Police and Prison Officers; at a conference in London in Mar. 1919 succeeded in having resolution adopted calling for disarming of RIC. Forced to resign under threat of transfer from Trim, Co. Meath to Belmullet, Co. Mayo. In 1920 proposed an all-Ireland police conference to provide a focus for discontent in the ranks, and supplied a list of sergeants and constables prepared to assist a patriotic movement in the RIC. At the invitation of MICHAEL COLLINS, he joined Police Organising Committee under MICHAEL STAINES; resigned, 'for reasons best known to himself', according to Garda commissioner EOIN O'DUFFY. Took the anti-Treaty side in the Civil War and was arrested and interned. Investigator Irish White Cross.

MacENTEE, Sean (1889–1984), politician, b. Belfast, 22 Aug. 1889, ed. St Malachy's College, Belfast and Belfast Municipal College of Technology, m. Margaret Browne, later a UCD lecturer and a sister of Cardinal MICHAEL BROWNE and PÁDRAIG DE BRÚN, d. 9 Jan. 1984. MacEntee's initial political involvement was with JAMES CONNOLLY's Irish Socialist Republican Party. He was condemned to death for his part in the Easter Rising but the sentence was commuted to penal servitude for life and he was released in the general amnesty the following year. He was a member of the First Dáil, having been elected an MP in the 1918 Westminster election. He fought in the War of Independence and in the subsequent Civil War on the anti-Treaty side. In 1926 he was one of the founder members of the new Fianna Fáil party. Having stood unsuccessfully in the 1923 election as a republican, in 1927 he was elected an FF TD in Dublin County and by 1933 had become the poll-topper there. He repeated the feat in the Dublin Townships constituency in 1937, 1938, 1943 and 1944. He represented Dublin South-East 1948–69. On the formation of the first FF government in 1932 he was appointed Minister for Finance, holding the post until 1943, when he became Minister for Local Government and Health. In 1951, when FF returned to office after three years in opposition, he went back to the finance ministry, until the party was ousted in the 1954 election. His last ministerial appointment was as Minister for Health 1957–65. He was a very tough political fighter much feared by opponents. His early radicalism rapidly disappeared and he was one of the most conservative FF ministers, especially on economic and social welfare issues. In 1918 he published a collection of poetry. Father of MÁIRE MHAC AN tSAOI.

MacEOIN, Sean (1910–), DSM, lieutenant-general, b. Cooley, Co. Louth. He joined the defence forces as a cadet in 1930 and was commissioned the following year. Commandant Military College 1957 and in 1960 first graduate of the college to be appointed chief of staff. The following year appointed force commander of the UN troops in the Congo (now Zaïre) and served for 15 months there, commanding a force of over 20,000. UN secretary-general U Thant praised his handling of the situation and he was awarded the Distinguished Service Medal. Returned to Ireland in 1962 and resumed as chief of staff until his retirement in 1971.

McEVOY, Eleanor (1967–), singer-songwriter, b. Dublin, 22 Jan. 1967, ed. TCD, honours degree in music. She began her musical career as a violinist in the National Symphony Orchestra. In 1991 she recorded her first album, *Eleanor McEvoy*, on the Geffen Records label. Shortly afterwards she collaborated with three other Irish female performers to record an enormously successful compilation album, the title track of which was her own composition, 'Only a Woman's Heart'. She has won several major awards from the Irish music press, including *Hot Press* Best Songwriter and Best Solo Performer 1994. She also won the Irish National Entertainment Awards Best New Artist of 1993. Her second album, *What's Following Me?*, was released in 1996.

McFADDEN, Roy (1921–), poet, b. Belfast, ed. QUB. A solicitor, he published his first collection of verse, *Swords and Ploughshares*, in 1943. With Barbara Edwards, he co-edited *Rann* (1948–53), an influential journal of Ulster writing. Like his contemporary ROBERT GREACEN, he published little or nothing in the 1950s and 1960s, but since 1971 he has produced five volumes. His early verse addressed some of the public cultural ambiguities of Northern Ireland; his later work has been more personal in its concerns.

MacGABHAIN, Liam (1908–1979), journalist, b. Valentia Island, Co. Kerry, ed. locally and at St Patrick's College, Dublin. Closely associated with the republican movement, he was briefly editor of *An Phoblacht* 1933 and a frequent contributor in Irish and English to republican publications. He joined the *Irish Press* as one of its first reporters and feature writers in 1932, having worked for some years as an organiser with CATHAL O'SHANNON in the ITGWU. A colourful writer, he was known for his heartfelt if sometimes sentimental reports, and made a great impact with his account of the burial of the Kirkintilloch disaster victims, a number of Irish potato pickers burned to death in a bothy in Scotland. Later worked for the *People* newspaper, Radio Éireann and *The Irish Times*. Won the Benson & Hedges award as the outstanding journalist of 1979.

McGAHERN, John (1934–), novelist and short story writer, b. Dublin, brought up in Cootehall, Co. Roscommon, ed. Presentation College, Carrick-on-Shannon, St Patrick's College, Dublin and UCD. He gained notoriety when his second novel, *The Dark*, was banned in 1965 and its author dismissed from his teaching post in Clontarf, Dublin. Since then McGahern has proved to be the most important Irish novelist writing today, acquiring, among his many accolades, multiple awards from the Arts Council and an honorary D.Litt. from TCD. He has been a visiting professor throughout the USA, was an arts fellow at Newcastle University and has written plays for television and stage. *Amongst Women* was shortlisted for the Booker prize 1990. Other novels: *The Barracks* (1963), *The Dark* (1965), *The Leavetaking* (1974) and *The Pornographer* (1979). Short stories: *Nightlines* (1970), *Getting Through* (1978), *High Ground* (1985) and *Collected Stories* (1992).

MacGARRITTY, Joseph (1874–1940), republican, b. Carrickmore, Co. Tyrone. Emigrating to the USA in 1892, he was one of the most prominent members of the Irish-American support organisation Clan na Gael. Through his financial backing for several nationalist and republican groups, he had considerable influence over affairs in Ireland. He formed the Friends of Irish Freedom with JOHN DEVOY and Judge Daniel Cahalan to provide assistance to Dáil Éireann during the War of Independence. In 1918 he founded an American-based paper, the *Irish Press*, to support the republican cause, and he managed EAMON DE VALERA's tour of the country 1919–20. He was implacably opposed to the Anglo-Irish Treaty and remained a strong supporter of the IRA until his death. A collection of his poetry, *Celtic Moods and Memories*, was published in 1942.

McGARRY, James Gerard (1905–1977), priest, academic and editor, ed. St Jarlath's College, Tuam and Maynooth. Ordained 1930, later DD, briefly teacher of English at St Jarlath's, Professor of Pastoral Theology Maynooth 1939. In 1950 he founded the monthly journal the *Furrow*, which he edited until his death and through which he exercised what was arguably the most beneficial influence of his time on the Roman Catholic Church in Ireland. His judicious selection of topics and contributors prepared his fellow priests and interested laity for the changes brought about by the Second Vatican Council; he provided articles of comment and reflection on conciliar themes which were almost invariably progressive in tone but never offensively assertive. He shunned publicity yet moulded the minds of a generation of thinking Irish Catholics. He also did much to promote the visual image of the Church by his encouragement of young painters, sculptors and architects. He became parish priest of Ballyhaunis, Co. Mayo in 1969 and died nearby in a motor accident eight years later.

MacGILL, Patrick (1891–1963), novelist, b. near Glenties, Co. Donegal, eldest of 11 children of a tenant farmer, d. Massachusetts. His novels, all based on first-hand experience, contain graphic and often harrowing descriptions of the lives of farm labourers in Scotland, navvies in London and infantrymen in the trenches during World War I. The brutal realism of *Children of the Dead End* and *The Rat Pit* helped to raise public awareness of the conditions of child labour. He joined the London Irish Brigade in 1914 and his war experiences are chronicled in *The Great Push* and *The Red Horizon*.

McGILLIGAN, Patrick (1889–1979), lawyer, politician and academic, b. Coleraine, Co. Derry, 12 Apr. 1889, ed. St Columb's College, Derry, Clongowes, UCD and King's Inns, d. Dalkey, Co. Dublin. Called to Bar. Joined Sinn Féin 1910, elected TD (C. na nG., later FG; NUI, later Dublin North-West and Central) 1923–65. Secretary to Irish delegation Imperial Conference 1923. Minister for Industry and Commerce 1924–32, also Minister for External Affairs 1927–32. Persistent in seeking maximum independence for Commonwealth dominions in areas ranging from treaty-making powers to the royal prerogative and the abolition of appeals to the Privy Council; co-author of the Statute of Westminster 1931. Established the ESB in 1927 as the first state-sponsored body in the modern sense of the term, having earlier approved the building of the Shannon Hydroelectric Scheme – a massive undertaking for a relatively poor country but the basis on which much subsequent industrial development took place.

Professor of Constitutional, International and Criminal Law at UCD 1934–59, acting professor 1959–65; a formative influence on a generation of judges. Minister for Finance in the inter-party government 1948–51, as which he concentrated on the improvement of social welfare, export promotion and reordering the budgetary system by separating capital from current spending. In the second inter-party government, 1954–7, he served as Attorney-General.

McGINTY, Thom ('The Diceman') (1952–1995), street performer, b. Strathclyde, d. 20 Feb. 1995. His skills as a mime artist were used as an unorthodox form of advertising and promotion by several businesses in Dublin during the 1980s, and he was given the name 'The Diceman' because of his work for a shop of the same name. His uncanny ability to remain motionless for several hours, his outrageous costumes and his wonderfully expressive face endeared him to thousands of shoppers on Dublin's Grafton Street. He also performed in several European cities, including Moscow, Berlin and Seville. Shortly before his death he was guest of honour at a Hallowe'en party hosted by Ireland's top musicians and performing artists.

Mac GIOLLA, Tomás (1924–), politician, b. Co. Tipperary, 25 Jan. 1924, m. May McLoughlin. Member of Dublin Corporation since 1979. TD Nov. 1982–Nov. 1992. Lord Mayor of Dublin 1993–4. A republican activist, he was interned in the 1950s. He was among those who, after the failure of the 1956–62 border campaign, tried to push Sinn Féin leftward. When SF split in 1970 he headed the official wing of the party, which was rapidly overtaken in numerical strength by the so-called 'Provisionals'. Mac Giolla's section subsequently changed its name to Sinn Féin the Workers' Party and then simply the Workers' Party. Standing down as leader of the Workers' Party in 1988, Mac Giolla was succeeded by PROINSIAS DE ROSSA. The sole TD to remain with the party when its six other deputies departed in early 1992 to form Democratic Left, he lost his seat in the general election the Nov. following.

McGIRL, John Joe, republican and politician, b. Co. Leitrim. Joined the IRA in the early 1940s and was heavily involved in its reorganisation in the immediate post-war period. Arrested in 1946 and imprisoned for

IRA activity. Member of the IRA army council during the border campaign of the 1950s and briefly served as chief of staff in 1958. In the 1957 general election he was elected TD (Sinn Féin) for South Leitrim but he lost his seat in 1961. A central figure in the establishment of Provisional Sinn Féin after the 1970 split in the republican movement and a member of its Ard-chomhairle.

McGLYNN, Sean Patrick (1931–), chemist, b. 8 Mar. 1931, ed. NUI (B.Sc. 1951, M.Sc. 1952) and Florida State University (Ph.D. physical chemistry 1956). Fellowships in chemistry Florida 1956 and University of Washington 1956–7. Assistant professor/professor Louisiana State University, Baton Rouge, Boyd Professor of Chemistry 1968–81 and appointed vice-chancellor for research 1981. Concurrent positions: associate professor Yale 1961; lecturer National Science Foundation 1963 and 1964; biophysics program consultant Michigan State University 1963–5; consultant American Optical Co. and American Instrument Co. 1963 and Bell Telephone Labs 1965; fellow Alfred E. Sloan Foundation 1964; US senior scientist award Alexander von Humboldt Foundation 1979.

McGONAGLE, Stephen, trade unionist and public servant, b. Derry. McGonagle was active in the ITGWU and in 1972 became president of the Northern Ireland committee of the ICTU. Parliamentary commissioner for administration (ombudsman) and commissioner for complaints 1974–9. Chairman 1977–83 of the Police Complaints Board, which was set up to investigate complaints against the RUC; resigned in response to unionist protests following his appointment to Seanad Éireann. He also presided at the initial 1982 inquiry into sexual abuse at the Kincora Boys' Home in Belfast, and was a Labour Party delegate to the New Ireland Forum in 1983.

MacGONIGAL, Maurice (1900–1979), artist and revolutionary, b. Dublin, Jan. 1900, ed. Synge Street, d. Dublin, 31 Jan. 1979. Apprenticed in 1915 to the stained-glass studios of Joshua Clarke, who was married to his aunt, Brigid MacGonigal, and whose son was HARRY CLARKE. Inspired by the Easter Rising, MacGonigal took part in the War of Independence until his internment in Dec.

1920 in Kilmainham and later in Ballykinlar. Winning the RDS Taylor scholarship 1923 allowed him to attend the Metropolitan School of Art full-time. He was much influenced by Dutch landscapes and old masters of the Spanish school which he saw on an extended visit to the Netherlands; Van Gogh's use of colour made a particularly strong impression. Back in Ireland his sense of national identity responded to the scenery of Connemara, which was to feature in many of his most popular paintings. He also produced striking images of men and women against the backdrop of the west, part portraits, part landscapes. He taught painting at the National College of Art, becoming professor in 1961, but resigned in 1969 rather than compromise with the international student revolt of that year in its local form of a sit-in at his class. PRHA 1962–78. Father of MUIRIS MAC CONGHAIL.

McGOVERN, Eilis (1955–), heart surgeon, b. Mount Charles, Co. Donegal, ed. St Louis Convent, Monaghan, UCD and Mater Hospital, m., two d. Awarded gold medal in surgery, MB, B.Ch. (1978) and FRCSI (1982). Gaining operative experience in junior posts, she then trained in cardiothoracic surgery, held a Council of Europe fellowship and completed an advanced one-year fellowship at the Mayo Clinic. Joined the staff of the National Centre for Cardiac Surgery as consultant surgeon and became involved in the National Cardiac Surgical Foundation, set up to augment facilities for cardiac surgery in the public sector. First woman member of the council of the RCSI.

MacGOWRAN, Jack (1918–1973), actor, b. Dublin, ed. Synge Street, d. New York, Jan. 1973. MacGowran worked as an insurance clerk before becoming a professional actor. He performed at the Abbey and Gate Theatres and with the Radio Éireann Repertory Company, and after 1953 in London's West End. He appeared in films directed by David Lean, John Ford and the young Roman Polanski, among others, but is best remembered for his interpretation of the work of SAMUEL BECKETT. He won the British TV Actor of the Year award in 1961 for his portrayal of Vladimir in *Waiting for Godot* and in 1971 became the first non-American to receive the New York Critics'

Actor of the Year award for his performance in *Beginning to End*.

McGRATH, Joseph (1888–1966), revolutionary, politician and businessman, b. Dublin, ed. CBS, James's Street. Accountant with the ITGWU, then with Craig Gardner. Joined the Irish Volunteers and during the Easter Rising saw action in Marrowbone Lane. Imprisoned in Wormwood Scrubs and Brixton. Returned for Dublin in 1918 election and in Sept. 1920 became Minister for Labour. Voted for the Treaty and was Minister for Labour again in the Second Dáil. In the Provisional Government he was Minister for Industry and Commerce and Economic Affairs until Sept. 1922. Director of intelligence in the Civil War. Founder member of Cumann na nGaedheal and Minister for Industry and Commerce until 7 Mar. 1924, when he resigned over the government's handling of the 'Army Mutiny'. Leaving active politics, he was out of work and in financial difficulties when the government appointed him director of labour at the Ardnacrusha site of the Shannon Hydroelectric Scheme in 1925. Under an Act passed in 1930 McGrath, Richard Duggan and Spencer Freeman set up Hospital Trust Ltd to organise sweepstakes in aid of the run-down hospital system. The Sweeps achieved instant and worldwide success. In an increasingly depressed and protectionist global economy, 30 million people were personally interested in the result of every draw. In the early 1950s McGrath revived Waterford Glass and Donegal Carpets. His principal interest was racehorse owning and breeding. His Arctic Prince won the Epsom Derby 1951. Member of the Turf Club 1951, of Racing Board 1945–66 (chairman 1956–62); president Bloodstock Breeding Association of Ireland 1953.

McGRATH, Paul (1959–), international footballer, b. Greenford, Middlesex, 4 Dec. 1959, s. of an Irish mother and Nigerian father. Grew up in Monkstown, Co. Dublin. Signed by Manchester United from St Patrick's Athletic for £30,000 in 1982, he helped United to win the FA Cup in 1985. He moved to Aston Villa in 1989 and in 1994 won a League Cup medal with them. He was first capped for the Republic of Ireland in 1985 and was a prominent and popular figure in Ireland's European Championship and World Cup campaigns. He was FAI Player of the Year in 1990 and 1991 and won the prestigious Players' Player of the Year award in Britain in 1993.

McGRATH, Raymond (1903–1977), architect, painter and designer, b. New South Wales to Irish parents, ed. Fort Street School, Sydney and Sydney University: his illustrated thesis on Chinese architecture was so beautiful that it was preserved in the Australian National Gallery, where it can still be seen. Went to England on a travelling fellowship and after working in several art schools became the first research student of architecture at Cambridge. He was accepted into the most vibrant literary and artistic circles of the day, wrote for the *Architectural Review* and was appointed decoration consultant for the BBC's new Broadcasting House. At Cambridge he had already remodelled Finella, an old house on the Backs, to make it an example of what could be done with modern materials. Artists and architects, including Epstein, Eric Gill and Charlotte Perriand from Le Corbusier's office, came to see it and praise it. His reputation continued to grow as he built houses in the home counties, produced a number of industrial designs and published two books, *Twentieth Century Houses* (1934) and *Glass in Architecture and Decoration* (1937).

Work for architects in England ceased with the outbreak of the war. McGrath transferred to Dublin in 1940, taking a post as senior architect in the Board of Works. In 1948 he became principal architect of the OPW. Although no major buildings were completed in Ireland to his design, not even his impressive project for the Kennedy Memorial Concert Hall, he was responsible for the decor and redesigning of the State Apartments in Dublin Castle and Áras an Uachtaráin as well as Irish embassies in London, Paris, Rome, Washington and Ottawa: work which enabled him to foster the revival of Waterford Glass and Donegal Carpets. He resumed painting when he came to Ireland; his work was shown at the Irish Exhibition of Living Art and later at the RHA, where he became Professor of Architecture. Shortly before his death in Dublin he was elected president of the RHA.

MacGREEVY, Thomas (1893–1967), art critic and curator, b. Tarbert, Co. Kerry,

d. Dublin, 16 Mar. 1967. Officer in Royal Field Artillery, World War I, after which he went to TCD, graduating in history. Lectured in English at University of Paris. Befriended JAMES JOYCE, through whom he secured appointment as critic for an arts journal; Joyce made him his executor. He wrote for English journals also (*Studio*, *Times Literary Supplement*) and lectured at the British National Gallery. Returned to Dublin 1941. Director National Gallery of Ireland 1950–64. Chevalier Légion d'honneur 1948. His writings included works on JACK YEATS, Poussin and pictures in the Irish National Gallery. His collected poems were published posthumously in 1971.

Mac GRIANNA, Seosamh (1901–1990), novelist and short story writer, b. Rannafast in the Donegal Gaeltacht, ed. St Eunan's College, Letterkenny, St Columb's College, Derry and St Patrick's College, Dublin. Qualified as a teacher 1921. Interned as a republican prisoner 1922–4. Translated many books from English to Irish for An Gúm. Like his brother SÉAMUS Ó GRIANNA, with whom he agreed to use the 'Mac' form of their name rather than the 'Ó' to avoid confusion between them, he is considered one of the finest modern Irish writers. Having lived in and around Dublin in the 1940s and 1950s, he returned to Donegal in 1957. He was unable to continue writing due to poor health and spent many years in an institution in Letterkenny, where he died. In recent years there has been a revival of interest in his work. He received belated recognition in 1969 when he was granted the Irish-American Cultural Institute award for his novel *An Druma Mór*, written in the 1930s but hitherto unpublished. Publications include: *Dochartach Duibhlionna agus Scéaltaí Eile* (1925), *An Grádh agus an Ghruaim* (1929), *Eoghan Ruadh Ó Néill* (1931), *Pádraic Ó Conaire agus Aistí Eile* (1936) and an autobiography, *Mo Bhealach Féin* (1940).

McGRORY, Paddy (1923–1994), lawyer, b. Belfast, ed. QUB. Best known as the lawyer who represented the families of the three IRA members killed by the SAS in Gibraltar in 1988. Although a staunch nationalist, McGrory's only direct involvement in politics was during a brief spell working with GERRY FITT in the 1960s. While he was vehemently opposed to the use of the 'supergrass' system and to

non-jury Diplock courts, he was held in high regard by the police. During his career he represented both loyalists and republicans, commenting: 'My life was lived among Belfast working-class people of both religions, so it was enormously hurtful to hear yourself described as if you were a lawyer for one section only. That would make you only half a lawyer.'

McGUCKIAN, Medbh (1950–), née McCaughan, poet and teacher, b. Belfast, ed. Dominican Convent, Fortwilliam Park, Belfast, where she also taught for a number of years, and QUB. She won an Eric Gregory award 1980, a Rooney prize and an Arts Council bursary 1982, an Alice Hunt Bartlett award 1983 and a Cheltenham prize 1989. She has been visiting fellow at Berkeley, California and was the first female writer in residence at QUB 1986–8. Her verse has little in common with that of other Northern Ireland poets, inasmuch as it is private and introspective. Her work to date comprises: *Single Ladies: Sixteen Poems* and *Portrait of Joanna* (1980), *Trio Poetry 2*, with Damian Gorman and Douglas Marshall (1981), *The Flower Master* (1982), *The Greenhouse* (1983), *Venus and the Rain* (1984), *On Ballycastle Beach* (1988), *Two Women, Two Shores*, with Nuala Archer (1989), *Marconi's Cottage* (1991) and *Captain Lavender* (1994). She also edited the anthology *The Big Striped Golfing Umbrella* (1985). Her verse is included in *Contemporary British Poetry* (1982).

McGUIGAN, Finbar Patrick (Barry) (1961–), boxer, b. Clones, Co. Monaghan, 28 Feb. 1961. As an amateur, he won a gold medal at featherweight in the 1978 Commonwealth Games at Toronto, and took the Irish senior bantamweight title the same year. He lost in a third-round bout at the 1980 Moscow Olympics, before turning professional under manager BARNEY EASTWOOD and trainer Eddie Shaw. He won the British featherweight title in 1983, when he was also European champion, and in 1985 he became the WBA featherweight world champion. After a couple of successful defences of the title, he lost it to Steve Cruz in Las Vegas and then retired, later making a short, four-bout comeback.

McGUINNESS, Catherine (1934–), politician and lawyer, b. Belfast, ed. Dunmurry Public Elementary School, Alexandra, TCD and King's Inns. Labour Party activist and parliamentary officer in the 1960s. Called to the Bar 1977, Inner Bar 1989. Independent senator (DU) 1979–87. Circuit Court judge 1993, High Court 1996. Chairperson Forum for Peace and Reconciliation 1994–6.

McGUINNESS, Frank (1953–), playwright, b. Buncrana, Co. Donegal, July 1953, ed. UCD (BA and M.Phil. in medieval studies). Lecturer in English at Maynooth. Probably the most gifted of the post-FRIEL generation of Irish playwrights, subverting and updating Irish and world theatre. His work displays an iconoclastic imagination, a poet's sense of language and a sensitivity to the crisis points at which personal, national and sexual identity intersect.

His first play, *The Factory Girls* (1983), staged at the Peacock Theatre, as were many of his subsequent pieces, featured virtually an all-woman cast and was set in a Donegal shirt factory. His breakthrough work was *Observe the Sons of Ulster Marching Towards the Somme* (1985), which won the *Evening Standard* Play of the Year award in 1986. Bringing us close in sympathy to a culture which has been either denied or misrepresented, the play dramatises the collective fate of an Ulster Protestant regiment fighting in World War I, above all to defend Northern Ireland as an integral part of the United Kingdom.

Innocence, McGuinness's drama of Caravaggio staged at the Gate Theatre in 1986, is a complex meditation on creativity. A Catholic counterpart to the Protestant emphasis of his earlier play, *Carthaginians* (1988) shows three men and three women, along with a cross-dressing member of each camp, gather in a Derry graveyard and struggle with the legacy of Bloody Sunday in their lives. The characters are required to perform their own healing ritual and, like their creator, use jokes, songs and the carnivalesque to address the most sombre of themes.

His later plays include *Mary and Lizzie* (1989), *The Bread Man* (1990), *Someone Who'll Watch Over Me* (1992) and *The Bird Sanctuary* (1994). In addition to original plays, McGuinness has produced versions of European classics, staged in Dublin, London and elsewhere, by Ibsen (*Peer Gynt*, *Rosmersholm*), Chekhov (*Three Sisters*) and Lorca (*Yerma*, *The House of Bernarda Alba*).

McGUINNESS, Gerard (1938–), publisher, b. Dublin, ed. Terenure College, Dublin and London School of Economics. After an early career in advertising, he founded the *Sunday World* in 1972, Ireland's first tabloid newspaper. Based on many marketing surveys aimed at discovering what readers actually wanted, it quickly established itself as one of the great success stories of modern Irish journalism.

McGUINNESS, Martin (1950–), politician, b. Bogside, Derry. He became active in the republican movement at the beginning of the Northern conflict in 1969. In 1971, having already served several terms of imprisonment in both Northern Ireland and the Republic, he became leader of the Provisional IRA in Derry. His status within the republican movement was recognised when he was included in the IRA delegation that met William Whitelaw, Secretary of State for Northern Ireland, and other British officials in July 1972 during the IRA ceasefire. Together with GERRY ADAMS, he was one of the younger group of republicans who ensured that control of the movement was effectively transferred from Dublin-based elements to the North and, although for a time head of the IRA 'Northern Command', he also favoured the developing emphasis on a political strategy. With the increasing involvement of Sinn Féin in Northern politics in the 1980s, his public profile rose significantly. Elected to the NI Assembly 1982–6, which he did not attend in accordance with SF policy. During the IRA ceasefire of 1994–6 he was a participant in discussions with the Irish government as well as with British government officials. Elected to NI Forum, May 1996.

McGUINNESS, Norah (1903–1980), painter, b. Derry, ed. Metropolitan School of Art, Dublin, Chelsea School of Art, London 1924, with André Lhote, Paris 1929–31. Founder member of the Irish Exhibition of Living Art. Honorary member RHA 1957; hon. D.Litt. (TCD) 1973. Exhibited in Derry, Dublin, London, New York, Monaco; is in collections in Dublin, Belfast, Coventry, New York. Having started as an illustrator, from the 1940s on she painted mostly landscapes and still lifes, using oils.

McGUINNESS, Paul (1951–), band manager, b. Rinteln, near Hanover, Germany, son of an RAF officer, ed. by his mother, a Corkwoman, later Clongowes and TCD. The family relocated often during his childhood: England, Malta, England again, Ireland. He joined the Trinity Players and directed two plays while at TCD, as well as editing the college magazine. He began contributing pieces to Dublin newspapers, started a mobile disco in the early 1970s, then moved to London, where he drove a minicab, worked in a book warehouse and became a tour guide in Lourdes. Back in Ireland he worked in the film industry at Ardmore Studios, Bray, Co. Wicklow and made television commercials. He managed the folk-rock group Spud before being approached by U2 in 1978. He has managed them since that time, charting their rise to be one of the world's leading bands of the era.

McGUIRE, Edward (1932–1986), painter, b. Dublin, ed. Slade School of Art, London, also studied art and art history in Florence and Rome. He began to exhibit with the Irish Exhibition of Living Art in the mid-1950s and with the RHA in 1966. In 1976 he won the DOUGLAS HYDE gold medal at the Oireachtas and was elected to the RIA. While living in London he was encouraged to develop a painting career by PATRICK SWIFT, and his early work was much influenced by Lucian Freud. Regarded as one of the finest portrait artists of his generation, his best-known paintings are those of literary figures. He was a meticulous artist, extremely thorough in the preparation of his materials and in his study of colour and anatomical structure. McGuire's portraits are strongly representational and there is a scrupulous attention to detail in the rendering of the face and posture of his subjects. However, his ability deftly to display penetrating insights into the personality of the sitter, and the slightly bizarre, almost surreal setting in which the subjects are sometimes placed, defy any attempt to categorise him as merely a very accomplished academic or literal painter.

McHUGH, Roger Joseph (1908–1987), playwright, critic and academic, b. Dublin, 14 July 1908, ed. UCD. Best known for his studies of Anglo-Irish literature but also worked on a number of books on Irish nationalist history. He edited *Carlow in Ninety-eight* (1949) and *Dublin 1916*, a collection of essays on the Easter Rising (1966). He also wrote a short biography of Henry Grattan (1936). Lecturer in English, UCD 1949, Professor of English 1965–7, Professor of Anglo-Irish Literature 1967–78, filled a number of visiting professorships in the USA. In 1982 his *Short History of Anglo-Irish Literature* was published. He was a member of the Seanad 1954–7.

MacINTYRE, Tom (1933–), playwright and poet, b. Cavan. Much of MacIntyre's work has been performed at the Peacock Theatre and directed by PATRICK MASON. This includes *Jack Be Nimble* (1976), *Find the Lady* (1977), *The Bearded Lady* (1984), *Rise up Lovely Sweeney*, *Dance for your Daddy* and *Snow White*. Actor Tom Hickey has also been an important collaborator, and during the mid-1980s worked with MacIntyre and Mason in exploring an imagistic, physical form of theatre that was most successfully realised in their landmark 1983 production of *The Great Hunger* (adapted from PATRICK KAVANAGH's poem), which subsequently toured to the UK, France, Russia and the USA. MacIntyre's later work includes *Kitty O'Shea* (1990), *Chickadee* (1992) and *Sheep's Milk on the Boil* (1994), of which the last two were directed by Hickey. He has also written a novel, *The Charollais* (1969); short story collections, *Dance the Dance* (1970) and *The Harper's Turn* (1982); and poetry, *Blood Relations* (1972), *I Bailed Out at Ardee* (1987) and *Fleurs-du-lit* (1990).

MACKEN, Edward (Eddie) (1949–), international showjumper, b. Granard, Co. Longford, 20 Oct. 1949. He made his international début in the Nations Cup at the RDS in 1970. Macken narrowly missed major rewards when he was runner-up in the World Championship in 1974 (on Pele) and 1978 (on Boomerang), the former in a jump-off and the latter by 0.25 points, the smallest ever winning margin. He was runner-up (on Kerrygold) in the 1977 European Championship and tied for third place in the 1979 World Cup final. Major achievements include four Hickstead Jumping Derby wins (1976–9), to equal the record, three Hamburg Derby wins, and membership of Ireland's Aga Khan Cup-winning team 1977–9. He represented Ireland at the Olympic Games in 1992 (Barcelona) and 1996 (Atlanta).

MACKEN, Walter (1915–1967), novelist, actor and playwright, b. Co. Galway, 3

May 1915, ed. Patrician Brothers, Galway, d. Co. Galway, 22 Apr. 1967. As a school leaver became an actor in the Galway theatre An Taibhdhearc, for which he also wrote plays in Irish. After some years in London, joined the Abbey Theatre and continued to act there while writing a succession of plays in English, the most popular of which was *Home is the Hero*. Strong characterisation marked his plays and books alike, and his well-constructed evocation of Cromwellian Ireland in the novel *Seek the Fair Land* made an abiding impression on his readers, as did his similar treatment of the Famine era in *The Silent People*.

McKENNA, Daniel (1892–1975), lieutenant-general, b. Draperstown, Co. Derry. Joined the army in Sept. 1922 as a colonel commandant. He served mainly in administrative appointments in his early days. In 1929 he became deputy quartermaster-general and in 1931 director Supply and Transport Corps. He was also a member of the Special Powers Tribunal 1933–4. Director of cavalry 1935–8 then reappointed as deputy quartermaster-general. In 1940 he succeeded Lieutenant-General Michael Brennan as chief of staff. As he was junior in rank to men such as HUGO MACNEILL and MICHAEL COSTELLO, his selection caused some surprise. He proved an inspired choice, however, quickly building the defence forces into an effective, if poorly armed, deterrent against invasion. He retired in 1949.

McKENNA, John (1880–1947), traditional musician, b. Tarmon, Co. Leitrim. The flute is especially associated with the north Connacht region so there was no scarcity of expertise to coach him. In 1911 he, his wife and family emigrated to New York by way of Scotland. Enrolling in the City Fire Department, he remained a patrolman until after his wife's death in 1926. He was in considerable demand as a musician. In addition to solo work he on occasion played in duo with JAMES MORRISON and was a member of the Rosaleen Quartet. His first of many recordings was made in 1921 and the last in 1937. He died in New York, but in 1990 a monument was erected in Tarmon by the Traditional Society named in his honour.

McKENNA, Patricia (1957–), politician, b. Castleshane, Co. Monaghan, ed. St Louis Convent, Monaghan and NCAD. Taught art at St Mary's College, Rathmines, campaigned against the Single European Act, joined the Green Party 1987. MEP (Green, Dublin) 1994: her election, topping the poll in the capital, was a shock to the established parties, whose concern for environmental issues noticeably increased thereafter. As MEP she urged the closure of the Sellafield nuclear plant in Cumbria (which many believed to pose a threat to the health of the people on the east coast of Ireland) and secured a ban on drift-net fishing for the protection of dolphins – to the anger of Irish tuna-fishing interests. During the campaign prior to the 1995 referendum on divorce she took successful proceedings in the High Court to have the spending of public monies on the promotion of one side's viewpoint in a referendum declared unconstitutional. The government in consequence had to cancel its advertising in support of divorce. Ironically, McKenna and her party favoured the government's position on the question at issue.

McKENNA, Siobhán (1923–1986), actress, b. Belfast, 24 May 1923, ed. St Louis Convent, Monaghan and UCG, d. Dublin, 16 Nov. 1986. She first acted at An Taibhdhearc, Galway in Irish and in 1944 joined the Abbey Theatre, Dublin. She went on to perform in Britain, France and the USA as well as in Ireland, in cinema and on television as well as on the stage. Following her London début in 1947, her reputation as one of the outstanding actresses of the day was established. Her most memorable roles were as Pegeen Mike in J.M. SYNGE's *The Playboy of the Western World* and Joan in both GEORGE BERNARD SHAW's *Saint Joan* and Brecht's *St Joan of the Stockyards*, parts especially suited to the intensity of feeling and conviction which always marked her acting. Her one-woman presentation *Here are the Ladies* won much acclaim, particularly for her performance of Molly Bloom's soliloquy from JAMES JOYCE's *Ulysses*. Films included *Dr Zhivago* and *Of Human Bondage*. Among her many awards was an honorary D.Litt. from TCD. Member of the Council of State 1975–86. She was married to the actor Denis O'Dea, who predeceased her in 1978.

MacKENNA, Stephen (1872–1934), translator and scholar, b. Liverpool, ed. locally and Radcliffe College, Leicestershire. He met J.M. SYNGE in Paris in 1896 and they remained firm friends until the latter's death. MacKenna fought on the Greek side in the Graeco-Turkish war of 1897. He was European correspondent for the *New York World* and covered the Russian Revolution, famously interviewing Tolstoy at one time. He returned to Dublin in 1907 to work for the *Freeman's Journal*. His most important contribution to scholarship was his magisterial translation of the *Enneads of Plotinus* in five volumes, a labour to which he devoted more than two decades; it was published 1917–30. Offered a gold medal for his translation by the RIA in 1924, MacKenna, a committed republican, refused to accept it from a society that still called itself 'Royal'. A volume of his *Journals and Letters*, edited by E.R. DODDS, was published in 1936.

McKENNA-LAWLOR, Susan, physicist, ed. UCD. M.Sc., Ph.D. (NUI). Associate Professor of Experimental Physics at Maynooth. Participated in the 'Solar Flares' project of NASA's SKYLAB Mission and later on its Solar Maximum Mission. In 1980 she formed an international team to propose the first Irish instrument to fly on a European Space Agency spacecraft. This was the highly successful EPONA instrument on the Giotto Mission to Halley's Comet, which in 1990 was to record historic data during Earth Fly-by – the first occasion that an interplanetary probe re-encountered the earth. Headed the international team that flew the first Irish experiment on a Soviet spacecraft: the SLED instrument on the Phobos Mission to Mars and its moons. Honours include Irish Person of the Year for scientific achievement, the Tsiolkovsky gold medal for contributions to cosmonautics, membership of the International Academy of Astronautics 1993.

MACKEY, Michael (Mick) (1912–1982), hurler, b. Castleconnell, Co. Limerick, 12 July 1912, d. 13 Sept. 1982. With the Ahane club he won 20 County Senior Championship medals, 15 in hurling and five in football. He first played at senior level for Limerick in 1930, aged 18. In the 1936 Munster final against Tipperary he scored a record five goals and three points, and he captained Limerick to All-Ireland victory that year and in 1940, having previously won an All-Ireland medal with

the successful 1934 side and played in the losing finals of 1933 and 1935. He won eight Railway Cup medals and five successive National League medals 1934–8. He trained the Limerick team which defeated Clare in 1955 in the Munster final, and the Mackey Stand at the Limerick Gaelic Grounds is named in his honour.

McKIERNAN, Catherina (1969–), athlete, b. Cornafean, Co. Cavan, 30 Nov. 1969. She was Irish national senior cross-country champion 1990–94 and for four successive years was second in the World Cross-Country Championships. She won three successive Grand Prix events in Belgium, France and Mallusk in 1991–2, and subsequently won the World Cross-Country Challenge series. She won this event again in 1993, 1994 and 1995, and in 1994 was the first European women's champion. On the track she has not matched that success, but in 1994 ran 31:19.11 for the 3,000 m in winning a European Cup race for Ireland.

McLAUGHLIN, Patrick (1921–), commissioner Garda Síochána, b. Malin, Co. Donegal, ed. St Eunan's College, Letterkenny. Costing clerk. Garda 1943, rose through the ranks. Wide experience, operations and administration. He was a tactful successor to Commissioner EDMUND GARVEY – taking over in 1978 – and guided the force out of stormy waters. Directed the police organisation for the papal visit to Ireland in 1979; personally attended Pope John Paul II at the principal public events. Instituted the annual Garda pilgrimage to Rome on the occasion of the diamond jubilee of the Garda Síochána in 1982. Resigned 1983 with Deputy Commissioner Thomas Joseph Ainsworth as a result of the telephone-tapping affair involving government ministers. Honorary treasurer Multiple Sclerosis Care Centre.

McLAUGHLIN, Thomas A. (1896–1971), engineer, b. Drogheda, ed. UCD, d. Benidorm, 15 July 1971. Assistant lecturer in physics UCD 1914. Qualified as an electrical engineer 1922, going for further training to the Siemens-Schuckert firm in Berlin. Drew up a plan for hydroelectric generation on the River Shannon, secured the support of Siemens and persuaded PATRICK MCGILLIGAN, Minister for Industry and Commerce, to adopt it. Despite commercial opposition, the government decided to proceed with the Shannon Scheme and in 1927 set up the Electricity Supply Board, the first state-sponsored body, to ensure the provision of electricity for industrial and social development; McLaughlin was appointed managing director. His vision became reality with the opening of the Ardnacrusha generating station in 1929. McLaughlin had differences of opinion with governments and fellow directors over the years and eventually retired from the ESB in 1958. His monument remained in the modern economy which could not have been built up without the electric power he made so widely available.

Mac LAVERTY, Bernard (1942–), author and teacher, b. Belfast. After finishing school he worked as a laboratory technician in QUB, where he later took a degree. Much of his work concentrates on the personal experience of individuals caught up in Northern Ireland's political violence. His talent shows particularly well in the depiction of loneliness, but he can also write in a pleasing humorous vein, as in his short story 'Language, Truth and Lockjaw'. *Cal* (1983), which deals with the guilty response of a young man after taking part in the killing of a policeman, and *Lamb* (1980), the story of a Christian Brother working in a reform school who is forced to examine the meaning of his vocation and his faith, were both made into successful films. Other books include *Secrets and Other Stories* (1977), *A Time to Dance and Other Stories* (1982) and *A Man in Search of a Pet* (1978). He has also written a number of plays for television and radio, including *My Dear Palestrina*, broadcast on BBC in 1980.

McLAVERTY, Michael (1907–), author, b. Carrickmacross, Co. Monaghan, spent part of his childhood on Rathlin Island, Co. Antrim, ed. St Malachy's College, Belfast and QUB (B.Sc.). He taught maths in, and was headmaster of, St Thomas's Secondary School, Falls Road, Belfast before retiring in 1972. His main writings are *Call my Brother Back* (1939, reissued 1970), *Lost Fields* (1942), *The Three Brothers* (1948), *The Choice* (1958) and *Collected Short Stories* (1978).

MacLIAMMÓIR, Micheál (1899–1978), actor, author, theatrical designer and artist, b. Kensal Green, London (not in Cork, as he represented throughout his professional career),

25 Oct. 1899, named Alfred Willmore, ed. Board School (possibly in Kilburn), Middlesex Polytechnic and Slade School of Art, London, d. 6 Mar. 1978. Appeared as a child actor in a number of London productions, including some by Beerbohm Tree's company. Became interested in Irish literature, joined the London Gaelic League and attended Irish-language classes. He also developed an enthusiasm for the Abbey Theatre, whose productions he may have seen when the company visited London on tour. Had adopted the name Michael before coming to Ireland in 1917 and eventually Gaelicised 'Michael Willmore' into 'Micheál MacLiammóir'.

He spent some years working as a freelance graphic artist and part-time actor in Dublin and travelling in Europe, acquiring languages and further experience in painting. In 1927 he joined the repertory company of his brother-in-law ANEW MCMASTER, then touring Ireland, and met fellow actor HILTON EDWARDS, with whom he set up a theatre both to stage new plays and to introduce Irish audiences to the classic works of foreign and Irish playwrights. The Gate Theatre opened in the Abbey's Peacock Theatre in 1928, moving to its own premises in the Rotunda Assembly Rooms in 1930. In 1928 MacLiammóir was also heavily involved with LIAM Ó BRIAIN in setting up the Irish-language theatre Taibhdhearc na Gaillimhe, which opened in Galway a few weeks before the Gate in Dublin. MacLiammóir wrote, designed and took the lead part in *Diarmaid agus Gráinne*, the Taibhdhearc's first production, in Aug. By July 1929 he was holding audiences enthralled at the Peacock in the Gate's staging of DENIS JOHNSTON's *The Old Lady Says 'No!'*

Thereafter he was central to the story of the Gate, becoming in the judgment of many the outstanding actor in a city of more than one great actor. He was in the best sense theatrical – cherishing, revelling in, moulding himself to whatever part he had to play, caressing the words in his uniquely resonant baritone voice. He wrote more plays, the best remembered perhaps *Ill Met by Moonlight*; reminiscences, such as *All for Hecuba*; books in Irish; and the brilliant one-man show on Wilde, *The Importance of being Oscar*. He designed sets and costumes, performed in many countries, was elected to the IAL, made a member of the Légion d'honneur and (together with Edwards) a freeman of Dublin.

MacLYSAGHT, Edward Anthony Edgeworth (1887–1986), genealogist and scholar, b. at sea when mother was en route to Australia. Boyhood in Raheen, Co. Clare, ed. Rugby, Oxford and UCC. Worked variously as a farmer, publisher and journalist. Member Irish Convention 1917; senator 1922–5; member governing body UCC 1927–31. Journalist in South Africa 1932–7. Inspector Irish Manuscripts Commission 1939–42. On staff of National Library 1942, genealogical officer and keeper of manuscripts 1949–55. Chairman Irish Manuscripts Commission 1956–73. Publications included two novels, *The Gael*, under name Lysaght (1919), and *Cursaí Thomáis* (1927). His major writings were on genealogical subjects, especially Irish families and surnames, e.g. *Irish Families, Their Names, Arms and Origins* (1957, supplementary vols. 1960, 1964) and *Guide to Irish Surnames* (1964, revised and enlarged editions between 1965 and 1985). As well as editing a number of state and family papers, he wrote an autobiography, reminiscences of WILLIAM O'BRIEN (1852–1928) and an important work of historical research, *Irish Life in the Seventeenth Century* (1939).

MacMAHON, Bryan (1909–), short story writer, playwright and novelist, b. Listowel, Co. Kerry, ed. St Michael's College, Listowel and St Patrick's College, Dublin. National school teacher for 45 years. Co-founded the Listowel Drama Group and Listowel Writers' Week, which has become a forum for new literary talent. His plays include *The Bugle in the Blood*, *The Song of the Anvil*, *The Honey Spike*, *The Death of Biddy Early* and *The Gap of Life*. Among his novels and short story collections are *The Lion Tamer*, *Children of the Rainbow* and *The Tallystick*. His autobiography, *The Master*, published in 1992, was a best-seller for months. LL D (NUI) 1972; American Ireland Fund literary award 1993. President of Irish PEN 1972–3, former committee member IAL, appointee on a number of government commissions. His knowledge of the travelling community is unrivalled among Irish writers and contributes especially to the impact of the most outstanding of his plays, *The Honey Spike*.

MacMAHON, Tony (1939–), musician and producer/director, b. Miltown Malbay, Co. Clare. His father made fiddles, which he also played, along with the concertina, and the household was a gathering place for musicians. Taking up the accordion, MacMahon developed a unique approach, thoroughly traditional but displaying a rare sensitivity, especially in the interpretation of slow airs – a quality he attributes to a long association with SEAMUS ENNIS. Other musicians he has performed with include accordionist Joe Cooley (whom he cites as a major influence), SEÁN Ó RIADA, WILLIE CLANCY, concertina virtuoso Noel Hill and the Tulla Céilí Band. As a producer/director with RTÉ he has initiated pioneering methods in the media presentation of traditional music, in particular the *Long Note* series on radio, and on television *Ag Déanamh Cheoil*, *Bring down the Lamp* and *The Pure Drop*. Despite the obvious popularity of the Irish musical tradition, he has on occasion expressed fears that certain trends could lead to its destruction.

MacMANUS, Francis (1909–1965), novelist, b. Kilkenny, ed. locally, St Patrick's College, Dublin and UCD. A religious man, he taught at Synge Street for 18 years, and his beliefs are reflected in many of the 11 novels he wrote, chiefly in *The Fire in the Dust* (1950), his most important book. He was appointed as director of talks and features with Radio Éireann in 1948 and was largely responsible for setting up the Thomas Davis lectures. His other novels included a trilogy based on the life of the poet Donnchadh Rua Mac Con Mara, as well as *This House was Mine* (1937), *The Wild Garden* (1940), *Flow on Lovely River* (1941), *Watergate* (1942), *The Greatest of These* (1943) and *American Son* (1959). He also published short stories, biographies, history, essays and travel books. He was a member of the IAL and the RTÉ short story prize is named in his memory.

McMASTER, Anew (1894–1962), actor-manager, b. Monaghan, d. Dublin, 24 Aug. 1962. McMaster's name is synonymous with the old touring 'fit-up' companies. He founded his own company in 1925, which for many years presented Shakespeare plays and popular melodramas the length and breadth of Ireland. McMaster directed and managed the company while acting in its productions. Particularly noted for his performances as Shylock, Richard III and Coriolanus, he also appeared as Hamlet in the Shakespeare Memorial Theatre, Stratford-on-Avon 1933.

MacMATHÚNA, Ciarán (1925–), collector and broadcaster, b. Limerick city, ed. Presentation Convent, CBS, Sexton Street and UCD, where he obtained an MA (1949) for a thesis on folk songs in the Irish language. After teaching and a spell with the Irish Place-names Commission, he was appointed a producer/director/scriptwriter with Radio Éireann in 1954. His responsibilities included the recording of Irish traditional music and song, resulting in extensive travel with the mobile recording unit throughout Ireland and Britain. This fieldwork was shared with listeners through long-running radio series such as *Ceolta Tíre*, *A Job of Journeywork* and *Mo Cheol Thú*. The advent of television provided a further dimension to the presentation of the music. He has also worked in the USA and Scandinavia. For many years a member of the Cultural Relations Committee of the Department of Foreign Affairs, he has served as chairman and director of the Merriman International Summer School. In 1990 he was awarded an honorary doctorate by the NUI and in 1994 declared patron of An tOireachtas, the national festival of Gaelic culture. He married well-known traditional singer Dolly McMahon from Co. Galway, 1955; their three children, Cormac, Ciarán Óg and Deirdre, are all accomplished recorded musicians.

MacMATHÚNA, Seán (1936–), short story writer and teacher, b. Tralee, ed. St Brendan's College, Killarney and UCC. He was director of the National Writers' Workshop, Galway in 1985. MacMathúna is one of the few writers who can work with equal success in English and Irish. Short story collections: *Rafla* (1978), *Ding agus Scéalta Eile* (1983), *The Atheist* (1987). He has written several plays, one of which – *The Winter Thief* – was produced at the Abbey Theatre in 1992.

McNAB, Theo (1940–), artist, b. Dublin, ed. National College of Art, Dublin. Professor of Fine Arts at the NCAD since 1988. In his painting work, he uses abstract geometric forms to explore colour and hue. He has travelled extensively and had his work exhibited in several European countries and in Japan, the USA and China. Member of Aosdána.

McNALLY, John (1932–), boxer, b. Belfast. An amateur bantamweight with the local White City club, he became Irish national senior champion in 1952. Later that year he became the first Irish boxer to win an Olympic medal, when he lost to Finland's Pennti Hamalainen in the bantamweight final at the Helsinki Games. That was Ireland's sole success at Helsinki and also the country's first Olympic silver medal.

MacNAMARA, Brinsley (1890–1963), writer, b. John Weldon near Delvin, Co. Westmeath, 6 Sept. 1890, d. Dublin, 4 Feb. 1963. He joined the Abbey Theatre Company as an actor in 1910, and the following year travelled on its first American tour. He returned to Ireland in 1913, having failed to establish himself in New York, and in 1918 his novel *The Valley of the Squinting Windows* was published. It caused an immediate outcry, being a sly and humorous account of the introversion of village life in Ireland. The book was publicly burned in Delvin, and MacNamara's father, the local schoolteacher, was driven from the neighbourhood. Three more novels followed in quick succession, although none achieved the same instant fame. He became registrar of the National Gallery of Ireland in 1922. Thereafter his career as a novelist flagged but he wrote nine plays for the Abbey between 1919 and 1945, of which *Margaret Gillan* (1933) was the best, if not the most popular. He also wrote comedies, such as *The Glorious Uncertainty* (1923) and *Look at the Heffernans!* (1926), both of them formulaic Abbey plays of the period.

McNAMARA, Kevin (1926–1987), archbishop, b. Newmarket-on-Fergus, Co. Clare, 10 June 1926, ed. St Flannan's College, Ennis and Maynooth, d. Dublin, 8 Apr. 1987. Ordained June 1949. Received DD 1951, H.Dip.Ed. UCC. Taught in St Flannan's for two years before returning to Maynooth as assistant to administrative council 1953. A year later he became Professor of Dogmatic Theology. Vice-President of Maynooth 1968 and consultor to Vatican Secretariat of Christian Unity for five years. Bishop of Kerry 1976,

Archbishop of Dublin Jan. 1985. Opponent of artificial contraception, abortion, divorce.

McNAMEE, Eoin (1961–), novelist and poet, b. Kilkeel, Co. Down. His poetry and fiction are regularly published in Irish papers and periodicals. He has written two acclaimed novels, *The Last of Deeds* (1993) and *Resurrection Man* (1994), and a novella, *Love in History* (1993). A volume of poetry, *The Language of Birds*, was published in 1995.

MacNEICE, Louis (1907–1963), poet and broadcaster, b. Belfast, childhood spent mainly in Carrickfergus, Co. Antrim, where his father, later Bishop of Down, Connor and Dromore, was the Church of Ireland rector; ed. Sherbourne, Marlborough and Oxford; m. first Mary Ezra 1929 (divorced 1937); m. second Hedli Anderson 1942. CBE 1958. MacNeice established his reputation as a poet in England in the 1930s, while he was lecturing in classics at Birmingham and London universities. His name was associated with the left-wing writers of that decade, such as W.H. Auden, Stephen Spender and Cecil Day-Lewis, for whom support for the republican cause in Spain was a defining experience. His lyric verse at this stage in his career was notable for its sense of impending doom as Fascism increased its hold on Europe, and for a sensuous, if sometimes melancholic, appreciation of the immediacy of the passing moment. In 1939 *Autumn Journal* was published, a long autobiographical poem set in the aftermath of the Munich crisis. This exhibited MacNeice's receptivity to the social and political atmosphere of a period, and did much to cement his reputation as a brilliant poetic journalist, which in later life tended to dog him somewhat.

As a feature writer and producer at the BBC 1941–61 he developed the radio drama to the point of art, and in *The Dark Tower* (1946) produced a classic of the genre. However, his poetry during this period did not appear to achieve the lyric intensity that had marked some of his best earlier work. In his last three volumes, culminating with the posthumously published *The Burning Perch* (1963), he was reckoned to have recovered his true voice, now given added depth by an awareness of encroaching death and of the desperate condition of the modern world. Although MacNeice made

his reputation in England, where he resided for most of his adult life, he considered himself Irish. The country of his birth surfaced frequently in his writings as an imaginative alternative to the realities of 20th-century existence. His poetry has found an appreciative Irish audience in the last 20 years and is read as providing a point of origin for some of the most significant Northern poetry of the present.

MacNEILL, Eoin (1867–1945), Celtic scholar and founder of the Irish National Volunteers, b. Glenarm, Co. Antrim, 15 May 1867, ed. St Malachy's College, Belfast and RUI, d. Dublin, 15 Oct. 1945. Worked in Dublin as a court clerk. Founding member of the Gaelic League 1893, editor of the League's paper, the *Gaelic Journal*, 1894, *Fáinne an Lae* 1898, *An Claidheamh Soluis* 1899. Founded the Feis Ceoil 1894. Professor of Early (including Medieval) Irish History UCD 1909–41. Headed the council which founded the Volunteers 1913, became chief of staff of the section which broke with the main body in Oct. 1914 over JOHN REDMOND's policy of recruitment for the British army. Countermanded the order for the Easter Rising, given by PATRICK PEARSE on behalf of the IRB group which had planned the insurrection unknown to MacNeill. Arrested after the Rising and sentenced to life imprisonment but released the following year.

Elected to parliament (SF Derry City and NUI) 1918. Minister for Finance in First Dáil 1919; Minister for Industries 1919–21. Supported the Anglo-Irish Treaty of 1921, becoming Minister for Education 1922–5 in the Executive Council of the Irish Free State. Represented the IFS on the Boundary Commission 1924–5, which determined the Northern Ireland boundary, but resigned before it completed its report, which he refused to accept. He was nonetheless criticised for his part in the Commission, resigned his ministry and in 1927 lost his seat. Thereafter he concentrated on his academic interests, founding the Irish Manuscripts Commission 1927 and becoming PRIA 1940–43. His prolific published work dealt largely with early and medieval Irish texts, and also included *Phases of Irish History* (1919) and *Celtic Ireland* (1921).

MacNEILL, Hugo (1900–1963), major-general, b. Howth, Co. Dublin. A member of Fianna Éireann 1913 and Volunteers from 1917. He joined the defence forces in Feb. 1922 as a lieutenant and served in the Eastern/Dublin Command during the Civil War. Reached the rank of major-general by 1924, when he was appointed adjutant-general. In 1926 he led a military mission to the USA which studied in the various staff colleges, and the following year he headed the temporary plans division which was to devise the tactics and strategy for the developing defence forces. Following appointments as assistant chief of staff and commandant Military College, he became GOC 2nd Division in 1941 and GOC Eastern Command from 1946 until his retirement in 1951. He organised the great army revues such as 'The Roll of the Drum' and 'Tramp, Tramp, Tramp' in the Theatre Royal during the Emergency.

MacNEILL, James (1869–1938), Governor-General Irish Free State, b. Glenarm, Co. Antrim, ed. Belvedere, Blackrock and Emmanuel College, Cambridge. Indian civil service 1890–1914. Returned to Ireland, joined Sinn Féin. Member of drafting committee IFS constitution 1922. IFS high commissioner London 1922–8. Governor-General 1928. He bore the brunt of the Fianna Fáil government's determination to undermine the office of governor-general until his removal Nov. 1932.

McPEAKE FAMILY, instrumentalists and singers. Francis McPeake snr was born in Belfast in 1885. His father, a singer and flute player, originated in Co. Derry. He studied under the Galway uilleann piper John Reilly, winning an award at the 1912 Oireachtas, in time attracting the enthusiastic attention of the composer Carl Hardebec. His son Francis jnr commenced learning the pipes in 1929, the family trio being completed by another son, James, playing an antique McFall harp presented by John Francis Biggar. Later the group was augmented by members of a third generation. The McPeake ensemble was unique in that harmonised singing to pipe and harp accompaniment was hitherto virtually unknown. Some commentators suggested that this approach distanced their music from the strict tradition; nonetheless it had great influence on the development of the folk revival in the early 1960s.

McQUAID, John Charles (1895–1973), Roman Catholic Archbishop of Dublin, b. Cootehill, Co. Cavan, 28 July 1895, ed. St Patrick's College, Cavan, Blackrock, Clongowes, UCD and Gregorian University, Rome, d. Loughlinstown Hospital, Co. Dublin, 7 Apr. 1973. He wished to become a missionary and entered the Holy Ghost Fathers at Kimmage Manor in 1913, but following ordination in 1924 he was appointed dean of studies at Blackrock and in 1931 president. In the same year he was elected chairman of the Catholic Headmasters' Association and consulted by Archbishop EDWARD BYRNE on educational matters. He was a strong supporter of the vocationalism advocated by Pius XI in *Quadragesimo Anno*, and EAMON DE VALERA consulted him on Catholic social teaching when he was drawing up the new constitution in 1937. In 1940 McQuaid succeeded Byrne as Archbishop of Dublin. A surprise choice because he was not from the ranks of the secular clergy, it has been suggested that his relationship with de Valera was a factor in his appointment, but it is more likely that he had impressed Monsignor Robinson, the papal nuncio, who recommended him to Rome.

From the start, he proved to be an outstanding diocesan administrator and devoted himself primarily to the social problems of Dublin. In 1941 he founded the Catholic Social Service Conference, which alleviated the harsh conditions of the city poor during the war years and after. In 1942 he formed the Catholic Social Welfare Bureau, which attended to the well-being of emigrants. An impressive record on social issues followed throughout his episcopate. In 1946, much to the annoyance of de Valera, he sympathised with striking national school teachers in their unsuccessful dispute with the Fianna Fáil government. On a wider horizon, he was conscious of the difficulties which the Church in Europe faced in the immediate post-war period and sought to provide assistance in ways he considered appropriate; in 1948 he delivered a radio appeal which raised £20,000 for the Christian Democrats in Italy in their electoral battle with left-wing parties. At the same time he was quick to respond to the growth of suburban Dublin. Between 1940 and 1965 he built 34 new churches and established 26 new parishes. His episcopate saw an increase in the diocesan clergy from 370 to 600 and in the religious from 500 to 800.

A strong believer in denominational education, he was successful in attracting teaching orders of nuns and brothers into his growing diocese and helped to start up numerous primary and secondary schools. From 1944 he rigorously repeated year by year an existing ban on the attendance of Catholics at TCD without the permission of their bishops. He deemed the NUI colleges 'sufficiently safe as to faith and morals' but they fell short of his ideal of a Catholic university. In 1951 he led the bishops in their opposition to the 'Mother and Child' scheme proposed by NOEL BROWNE. Opinions differ as to the significance of his intervention in the affair. However, Browne's subsequent resignation and the fall of the government served to underline the powerful position of Archbishop McQuaid and his fellow bishops.

Throughout this period he exercised strict control over his own clergy and devoted particular attention to their formation at Clonliffe. A selection of his writings, *The Wellsprings of the Faith*, published in 1956 provided a clear exposition of his view of the Church and society. In 1961 he presided over the Patrician Congress in Dublin, which commemorated the death of St Patrick. He attended the Second Vatican Council and during the opening session adopted a conservative stance which showed him to be at variance with the mood for change in the wider Church. In the years that followed he obediently implemented the reforms of the Council but seemed at times to be temperamentally unsuited for this task. His lack of enthusiasm for change was reflected in his order for the removal of modernistic crib figures from the church at Dublin Airport in 1965, and a decidedly lukewarm response to the growing ecumenism of the time. As late as 1967 he reiterated the ban on Catholics attending TCD. (The ban was finally rescinded by the Irish hierarchy in 1970.) Paradoxically, he accompanied these moves with forward-looking changes, such as the training of priests for involvement in the new medium of television and the establishment of a diocesan press office in 1965. In 1968 Bishop Joseph Carroll, the man he favoured to succeed him, was appointed one of his auxiliaries. By that stage the media were increasingly portraying him as a reactionary figure and many of his own clergy were less than happy with his authoritarian style of leadership. When he retired in Jan. 1972 he was succeeded by Archbishop Desmond Ryan. He withdrew to the seclusion of Killiney, Co. Dublin, where, apart from a controversial visit in 1972 to the IRA leader Sean MacStiofain, who was on hunger strike, he remained an aloof figure.

Mac RÉAMOINN, Seán (1921–), broadcaster, writer in Irish and English, b. Birmingham, ed. High School, Clonmel, Coláiste Iognáid, Galway and UCG. Joined Department of External Affairs 1944. Outside broadcasting officer Radio Éireann 1947, as which he and his colleague SEAMUS ENNIS travelled to Irish-speaking areas to record speech and music which otherwise would never have reached more than a local audience and might in some cases have been lost within a generation. Radio Éireann regional officer Cork 1957–9. Provided memorable radio and television coverage of the Second Vatican Council from Rome as a commentator and interviewer: an exercise seen by many as opening the Roman Catholic Church in Ireland to informed scrutiny and discussion. Continued to provide commentary on cultural and religious developments. Member of the RTÉ Authority 1973–6; controller radio programmes 1974–6; head of external affairs RTÉ 1976–86. Writes and lectures widely on subjects ranging from Gaelic literature to developments within the Christian Churches. Associated with Cumann Merriman since its inception.

MacRORY, Joseph (1861–1945), cardinal, b. Ballygawley, Co. Tyrone, 19 Mar. 1861, ed. Glencull, St Patrick's Seminary, Armagh and Maynooth, d. Armagh, 13 Oct. 1945. Ordained 1885 and in the same year founded boys' secondary school, Dungannon Academy. Two years later moved to Birmingham as Professor of Moral Theology and Sacred Scripture at Oscott College. Appointed Professor of Sacred Scripture and Hebrew at Maynooth 1889, vice-president 1912. Established *Theological Quarterly* with others in the college. Moved to Belfast 1915 as Bishop of Down and Connor. Archbishop of Armagh and Primate of All Ireland 1928. Made cardinal the following year. Attended Eucharistic Congress in Dublin 1932 and in Melbourne 1934.

MacSHARRY, Ray (1938–), politician and EU commissioner, b. 29 Apr. 1938, ed. Summerhill College, Sligo. Formerly a haulier and small business executive, he was elected to Sligo Corporation and County Council 1967 and elected TD (FF Sligo–Leitrim) 1969. Minister of State at the Departments of Finance and Public Works 1979. Late that year he nominated CHARLES HAUGHEY for the Fianna Fáil leadership. Minister for Agriculture 1979–81. Tánaiste and Minister for Finance in the short-lived FF administration of 1982.

He resigned from the FF front bench following the telephone-tapping controversy of 1983 although he had no part in the tapping of journalists' phones by the outgoing government. He was elected to the European Parliament in 1984 and for a period was estranged from the party leadership. But on Haughey's return to power he was again appointed Minister for Finance (1987–9), as which he committed himself to bringing order to the public finances and the huge current account budget deficits. He also had a very successful period as EU Commissioner for Agriculture (1989–93), instigating reforms of the Common Agricultural Policy and laying the groundwork for the GATT agreement of 1994.

Mac SIOMÓIN, Tomás (1938–), poet and short story writer, b. Dublin, ed. CBS, Westland Row, Dublin and UCD. Studied in Holland and the USA (Ph.D. in biology, Cornell University 1974). Lecturer in Kevin Street College of Technology, Dublin. Received Arts Council award 1977. Publications include: *Damhna agus Dánta Eile* (1974), *Codarsnaí* (1981), *Cré agus Cláirseach* (1983) and *Scian* (1989). Occasional editor of *Comhar*.

MacSWINEY, Mary (1872–1942), republican, b. London, childhood spent in Cork, ed. Queen's College, Cork. She worked for a number of years as a teacher but was dismissed after her arrest for nationalist activities in 1916. An active member of Sinn Féin, in 1920 she went to Washington to appear before the American commission on conditions in Ireland. After the death of her brother TERENCE MACSWINEY she became TD for Cork. She

was one of the most vehement critics of the Anglo-Irish Treaty and was imprisoned twice for republican activities during the Civil War. She supported EAMON DE VALERA until his decision to enter the Dáil, and continued to reject the legitimacy of the Free State until her death.

MacSWINEY, Terence (1879–1920), revolutionary, b. Cork, ed. North Mon. and RUI, d. London, 24 Oct. 1920. He responded enthusiastically to the Celtic revival movement in the early years of the century, took an active part in setting up the Cork Celtic Literary Society in 1901 and was co-founder with DANIEL CORKERY of the Cork Dramatic Society in 1908. He was one of the central figures in the forming of the Irish Volunteers in Cork in 1913, becoming a full-time organiser in 1915. Elected TD for Mid-Cork in 1918 and succeeded TOMÁS MACCURTAIN as Lord Mayor of Cork in Mar. 1920. In Aug. 1920 he was arrested and sentenced to two years in Brixton Jail. He immediately went on hunger strike and became the focus of much sympathetic international attention but he died after 74 days, despite an attempt by prison doctors to force-feed him. He was a poet and also wrote several plays, including *The Revolutionist, The Holocaust* and *The Warriors of Coole*. A collection of essays, *Principles of Freedom*, was published in New York in 1921.

McVEAGH, Trevor George Brooke (T.G.) (1906–1968), international hockey, tennis, cricket and squash player, b. Athboy, Co. Meath, 16 Sept. 1906, d. Dublin, 5 June 1968. Regarded by many as Ireland's greatest all-round sportsman, he was Irish squash champion 1935–7, and in 1938 won caps for tennis, hockey, squash and cricket. He helped Ireland to three successive hockey Triple Crowns 1937–9, and at tennis played 17 Davis Cup ties for Ireland, twice beating the great Bill Tilden. At cricket his international batting average was 40.88, and he scored a century and held five catches in Ireland's defeat of the West Indies in 1928. He was an excellent billiards player and one of the best game shots in the country.

McWILLIAM, F.E. (1909–), sculptor, ed. Belfast, Slade School of Art, London and Paris. Transference from representational to abstract and experimentation with the breakdown of the human form are central to his work, which often has a surrealist feel to it. RAF (UK and Far East) 1940–45, member of the Slade School staff 1947–68, member of arts panel Arts Council of Great Britain 1962–8. D.Litt. (QUB) 1964, CBE 1966, Oireachtas gold medal. His bronze collection *Women of Belfast* was inspired by the Troubles.

MAGAHY, Laura (1961–), businesswoman, b. Dublin, 24 Apr. 1961, ed. Regina Mundi College, Cork, UCC (BA music, German) and TCD (MBA). On graduation from UCC, taught English in France and Germany, founded a youth theatre company 1984. Chief executive of the Irish Film Centre 1987, directed its conversion from a Friends' Meeting House. In 1991 she joined Temple Bar Properties, the semi-state body charged with overseeing the regeneration of the Temple Bar area of Dublin, and she was appointed managing director of the £100 million project the following year. Development involves building ten new cultural centres, new businesses (135 have opened since 1991) and residential accommodation, and physical improvement of the area. Temple Bar is now the city's third most popular tourist attraction. Board member of the Arts Council 1993, of CIE 1995, of Dublin Bus 1996, member of Devolution Commission. First winner of the Young Business Achiever award 1996.

MAGILL, Sir Ivan Whiteside (1888–1986), anaesthetist, b. Larne, Co. Antrim, ed. Larne Grammar School and QUB, m. Dr Edith Banbridge, d. 4 Dec. 1986. Magill served with the Irish Guards in World War I and on demobilisation adopted the speciality of anaesthetics almost casually. Finding himself obliged to deal with soldiers having constructive operations on the face and jaws, he devised an endotracheal tube and perfected the art of intubation. This not only facilitated plastic surgery immeasurably but was a stimulus to chest surgery. Ironically, Magill's MD thesis on endotracheal anaesthetics was rejected while his wife's was accepted. QUB made amends in 1945, conferring an honorary D.Sc. Knighted in 1960.

MAGINNIS, Kenneth Wiggins (1938–), politician, ed. Royal School, Dungannon and Stranmillis College, Belfast. A former primary school headmaster, he served in the

B Specials and later in the Ulster Defence Regiment 1970–81, becoming a major. Contested the Fermanagh–South Tyrone by-election for the Ulster Unionists in Aug. 1981 but was defeated by Sinn Féin's Owen Carron. Elected in 1983 and has held the seat since then. A member of Dungannon District Council 1981–93, he was elected to the 1982 Assembly and served as chairman of the non-statutory Security and Home Affairs Committee. Resigned his Westminster seat in protest against the Anglo-Irish Agreement of 1985 but was re-elected. A supporter of a strong security policy, he has been the target of a number of assassination attempts. He was unsuccessful in the 1995 Ulster Unionist leadership campaign but has the reputation of being the UUP MP most liked by Northern voters.

MAGUIRE, Brian (1951–), painter, b. Wicklow, ed. Dún Laoghaire School of Art, Co. Dublin 1968–9, National College of Art, Dublin 1969–74. Subsequently taught art at both of these colleges. Chairman of AAI for a term. Awards include Arts Council bursaries 1976, 1981, 1982, 1984. Has produced designs for TEAM Theatre Company and the Silkscreen Workshop and made banners for the ITGWU.

MAGUIRE, Conor Joseph O'Loughlin (1861–1944), general medical practitioner, b. Carraroe, Co. Galway, ed. Queen's College, Galway. Graduated in medicine from the RUI in 1882. Built up a large practice in Claremorris and was for many years coroner for south Mayo; chosen unanimously as first president of the Medical Association of Éire. Maguire's first language was Irish; he was a founder of the Gaelic League and a close friend of DOUGLAS HYDE. He translated William Rooney's song 'The Men of the West' and Shelley's 'The Cloud' into Irish, and helped to compile a volume giving the Irish names for many plants and flowers.

MAGUIRE, Hugh (1927–), violinist, conductor and teacher, b. Dublin, ed. Dublin, London and Paris, where he studied with Georges Enesco. Has led the BBC and London Symphony Orchestras, the Orchestra of the Royal Opera House (Covent Garden) and the Allegri String Quartet, and conducted the National Youth Orchestra of Ireland. Violin professor at the RAM, London and director of strings Britten–Pears School for Advanced Musical Studies. Hon. D.Litt. (NUU) 1986.

MAGUIRE, Liam (1943–1983), trade unionist and campaigner for the disabled, b. 3 Sept. 1943, ed. CBS, Dún Laoghaire, Co. Dublin, d. 16 Sept. 1983. A trainee pilot with Aer Lingus, he suffered serious injuries in a road accident in 1962 and joined the airline's ground staff. In the following 20 years he was an energetic campaigner with his union, the FWUI, and nationally for the rights of the disabled. He succeeded in a number of objectives in this field, notably in securing a commitment from government for a quota of public service jobs to be allocated to people with disabilities. Chairman of the International Year for the Disabled 1981; he also served as chairman of the Irish Wheelchair Association, on the committee of the National Rehabilitation Board and on the executive of the FWUI.

MAGUIRE, Seán (1924–), fiddler, b. Belfast but with a family background in Mullahoran, Co. Cavan. His father, John Maguire, played whistle and piccolo. During a period in Ireland when it was difficult to purchase traditional music on record, the playing of Seán Maguire was arguably more familiar to the public than that of any other musician. He demonstrated astonishing technical ability. His version of 'The Mason's Apron', in particular, became a well-known showcase on the airwaves. It introduced a style, owing much to North American fiddling, which Maguire himself described as 'progressive traditional'.

MAHAFFY, John Pentland (1839–1919), academic, b. Switzerland, 26 Feb. 1839, ed. at home in Donegal and at TCD, d. Dublin. FTCD 1864, Professor of Ancient History TCD 1869–99, provost 1914–19. PRIA 1911–16, knighted 1918. An outstanding scholar in his field. Famous as a sharp-tongued conversationalist and wit, he scorned the Irish-language revival and republican nationalism but at the Irish Convention of 1917, to which he was host, argued in favour of a federal constitution on the Swiss model for Ireland.

MAHER, T.J. (1922–), politician, b. Cashel, Co. Tipperary, ed. CBS, Cashel. Farmer. President IFA 1967–76. President Irish Co-operative Organisation Society 1976–83. MEP (Ind. Munster) 1979–94.

MAHON, Derek (1941–), poet, b. Belfast, 23 Nov. 1941, ed. Royal Academical Institution and TCD. One of Ireland's premier poets. Travelled around North America and France, returned to Ireland in 1967, then moved to London three years later. He has worked as a screenwriter, theatre critic, poetry editor, features editor for *Vogue*, as well as contributing regularly to *The Irish Times*. He has lectured at major European and US universities and received a number of prizes, including the American Ireland Fund literary award, the C.K. Scott-Montcrieff prize for translation, the Eric Gregory award and the DENIS DEVLIN memorial award. Mahon's best work is outstanding. 'A Disused Shed in Co. Wexford' is generally regarded as his greatest achievement to date and has been described by JOHN BANVILLE as the 'most beautiful single poem produced by an Irishman since the death of Yeats', a judgment many would endorse. Recent collections: *The Yaddo Letter* and *Selected Poems* (1992) and *The Hudson Letter* (1995). He has also successfully adapted the work of Molière, de Nerval, Racine and Euripides. Member of Aosdána and FRSL.

MALLIN, Michael (1880–1916), revolutionary, b. Dublin. He joined the British army at a young age and served as a soldier in India for several years. After returning to Dublin he worked as a silk weaver and became active in union affairs. In 1913 he joined the Irish Citizen Army and became its chief of staff. His army experience proved useful and he wrote several articles on military matters for the *Workers' Republic*. During the Easter Rising, he commanded the Citizen Army detail which held the Royal College of Surgeons on St Stephen's Green. He was court-martialled as one of the leaders of the Rising and executed on 8 May 1916.

MALLON, Seamus (1936–), politician, b. 17 Aug. 1936, ed. St Joseph's College of Education, Belfast. He was involved in the civil rights movement in Armagh in the 1960s. After several attempts he won the Westminster seat for the constituency in 1986, and retained it in subsequent elections. Deputy leader SDLP since 1979. Member of the Seanad (Taoiseach's nominee) May–Dec. 1982; consequently excluded from NI Assembly 1982–6 – which SDLP was in fact refusing to attend.

As the party's law and order spokesman he was highly critical of the official handling of the controversial shooting incidents involving the RUC in the early 1980s. A strong and articulate opponent of IRA violence, he has also continued to criticise the operations of the security forces in NI and to urge reform of the police system. Elected to the NI Forum, May 1996, and member of the SDLP delegation to the all-party talks on the future of NI which began in June.

MALONE, Patrick (1910–), commissioner Garda Síochána, b. Riverstown, Dundalk, son of a farmer, ed. CBS, Dundalk. Garda 1931, rose through the ranks. As a chief superintendent Crime Branch he was a witness at the Arms Trial 1970. Garda commissioner 1973–5. A conscientious and self-effacing administrator, he stabilised the Garda Síochána in stressful times for the force. Established the Garda museum and archives 1974.

MANNIX, Daniel (1864–1963), Roman Catholic archbishop, b. Charleville, Co. Cork, 4 Mar. 1864, ed. Mercy Convent, Charleville, St Colman's, Fermoy and Maynooth 1882, d. Melbourne, 6 Nov. 1963. Ordained 1890. Appointed Professor of Mental and Moral Theology at Maynooth 1891, Professor of Theology 1894, President of Maynooth College 1903. Appointed coadjutor in Melbourne Oct. 1912, archbishop 1917. Actively promoted cause of Irish independence. Received freedom of New York 1920. Archbishop for almost 47 years, he established hundreds of parishes and schools, founded Newman College for men and St Mary's Hall for women at Melbourne University.

MARA, Patrick (P.J.) (1942–), government press secretary, subsequently freelance consultant, b. Drumcondra, Dublin, ed. Coláiste Mhuire and St Patrick's College, Dublin. Proprietor Beehive Products, clothing manufacturers, later sold to Penneys. Joined Fianna Fáil 1963, member of its national executive and vice-chairman of its national organisation committee 1981–4. Joined press office 1983. Close ally of CHARLES HAUGHEY before the latter's comeback in politics in the 1970s; supported him during Arms Trial and later accompanied him on a nationwide tour of FF grass-roots cumainn. Mara stood and lost in Dublin Corporation and Seanad elections but

Haughey appointed him to the Seanad twice. Made a cult figure in *Scrap Saturday*, satirical radio programme in early 1990s. Adopted Mussolini's slogan 'Uno duce, una voce' to describe Haughey's status as his 'boss' and leader of FF. Worked with Guinness Peat Aviation 1991–3.

MARCUS, David (1924–), journalist, novelist and literary critic, ed. Presentation Brothers, Cork, UCC and King's Inns, m. ITA DALY. Practised at the Bar for some years before becoming editor of the quarterly *Irish Writing* 1946–54 and of *Poetry Ireland* 1948–54. Worked for 13 years in London, returned to Ireland to be literary editor of the *Irish Press* 1968–85. Compiled several anthologies of Irish short stories but his most important contribution to Irish literature was arguably his daring introduction in 1968 of the weekly 'New Irish Writing' page in the *Irish Press*: the use of a popular newspaper as the launching pad for work of high merit by mainly young fiction writers, often hitherto unpublished, was an undertaking of national importance. His own novels include *To Next Year in Jerusalem* (1954) and his story of the small Jewish community in Cork, *A Land Not Theirs* (1986), set during the War of Independence.

MARKIEVICZ, Constance (1868–1927), revolutionary, b. London, 4 Feb. 1868, née Gore-Booth, ed. privately at family home, Lissadell, Co. Sligo, d. Dublin, 15 July 1927. Studied painting at Slade School of Art, London and in Paris, where she met the Ukrainian-Polish Count Casimir Markievicz, whom she married in 1900 – thus becoming Countess Markievicz, the title by which she was thereafter known. They settled in Dublin 1903 and the countess increasingly involved herself in aspects of the burgeoning nationalism of the day: the Gaelic League, the Abbey Theatre, Sinn Féin and MAUD GONNE MACBRIDE's Inghinidhe na hÉireann. Founded Na Fianna 1909, a boys' movement analogous to the Boy Scouts but with an emphasis on drilling and nationalist attitudes. Active on the workers' side during the 1913 Lock-out in Dublin, when she maintained a soup kitchen in Liberty Hall. Her husband left Ireland but she remained and joined the Citizen Army, serving as second in command at the College of Surgeons during the Easter Rising. She was reprieved (to her chagrin, it was said). Amnestied 1917, elected MP 1918 (SF Dublin St Patrick's): the first woman elected to the British parliament. Minister for Labour in First Dáil, twice imprisoned. Opposed Anglo-Irish Treaty 1921, against which she campaigned at home and abroad. Founder member of Fianna Fáil 1926. Sister of EVA GORE-BOOTH.

MARRINAN, John (Jack) (1933–), Garda representative, b. Lisdoonvarna, Co. Clare, ed. CBS, Ennistymon. Assistant primary teacher before joining Garda Síochána 1953; on the beat was popular with young people and showed early promise in detective ability but was passed over. Studied at TCD (B.Comm., MA). Emerged as leader of the rank-and-file Garda Síochána during the unrest in the force in 1961; one of 11 suspected ringleaders who were dismissed by Commissioner DANIEL COSTIGAN, later reinstated on the intervention of Archbishop JOHN CHARLES MCQUAID. General secretary Representative Body for Gardaí 1962; conservative by nature but had reputation as tough negotiator. Competed successfully for promotion to sergeant but opted to remain in the ranks. Managing editor *Garda Review*.

MARTIN, Emily Winifred (1866–1944), née Dickson, doctor, b. Dungannon, ed. RCSI. Among those who benefited from Russell Gurney's 'Enabling Act' (1876), which allowed entitled bodies to grant qualifications for medical registration 'to all persons without distinction of sex'. Dickson, LRCP&SI (1891), MB (RUI, 1893), was the most distinguished of Dublin's early women doctors and the first woman to take the coveted FRCSI (1893). Her application for a resident post at the Rotunda Hospital was turned down because of her sex but she was appointed gynaecologist to the Richmond Hospital and assistant master of the Coombe. Her appointment as examiner in midwifery and gynaecology at the RCSI caused a mass protest from its students and from those at the Catholic University Medical School but the council pointed out that it had elected a fellow of the college 'in conformity with the obligation imposed on it'. On her marriage in 1898 Dickson Martin retired from practice but during both world wars she returned to medical work.

MARTIN, Mother Mary (1892–1975), founder Medical Missionaries of Mary, b. Dublin, 25 Apr. 1892, ed. Sacred Heart Convent, Leeson Street, Dublin, Holy Child College, Harrogate and finishing school in Bonn, d. Drogheda, 27 Jan. 1975. Worked as voluntary aid nurse in England, France and Malta during World War I. Returned to Dublin in 1918 to train as midwife at National Maternity Hospital. Motivated to set up religious order of women to operate clinics and hospitals after seeing appalling conditions in Nigeria 1921. Matron of Glenstal 1923. Professed as nun 1937 and founded Medical Missionaries of Mary. Received Florence Nightingale medal from International Red Cross 1963. First woman to be awarded honorary fellowship by RCSI (1966). Received freedom of Drogheda June 1966.

MARTIN, Philip (1947–), pianist and composer, b. Dublin, ed. Dublin and London. Awards include the first Frederick Shinn fellowship at the RAM, London, a Gulbenkian fellowship 1976 and the US–UK bicentennial fellowship 1980. Fellow of the RAM 1987. Member of Aosdána. Performs regularly in Ireland, Britain and the USA. Compositions include concertos, orchestral and chamber music and over 150 songs, many of them written for his wife, Penelope Price Jones, with whom he often gives recitals. Has recorded music by Percy Grainger, Gottschalk and Franz Reizenstein, who was one of his teachers.

MARTIN, Thomas *Augustine* (Gus) (1935–1995), academic, b. Ballinamore, Co. Leitrim, ed. Cistercian College, Roscrea and UCD (MA, Ph. D.). Teacher Cistercian College, Roscrea 1958–65; lecturer in English UCD 1965–79; Professor of Anglo-Irish Literature and Drama UCD 1979–95. Director W.B. YEATS International Summer School, Sligo 1978–81. In 1987 founded the Bailey's JAMES JOYCE International Summer School, held annually in Newman House, where Joyce had studied as a UCD undergraduate. Member of the UCD governing body 1969–95 and of the Seanad (Ind. NUI) 1973–81. Gus Martin was an academic activist, determined to advance the cause of whatever aspect of learning he found himself engaged upon. Thus, when a schoolteacher he co-founded the Association of Teachers of English to reform the syllabus and also became a branch chairman of his union, the Association of Secondary Teachers. As Professor of Drama (*inter alia*) he was elected to the board of the Abbey Theatre, becoming its chairman in 1985. He not only admired the work of PATRICK KAVANAGH but personally negotiated the retrieval of the poet's papers from their repository in the USA. Although he wrote important studies of Yeats, JAMES STEPHENS and Joyce, it may be that his enduring monument will be the textbooks he compiled to introduce Irish school pupils to literature in English – including Irish literature – and the programmes he made to the same end for Telefís Scoile, the educational segment of Irish television in its early years.

MARTYN, Edward (1859–1923), playwright, b. Tulira, Co. Galway, 30 Jan. 1859, ed. Beaumont College, Windsor and Oxford, d. Tulira, 5 Dec. 1923. A neighbour of Lady GREGORY and W.B. YEATS, he was, with them and GEORGE MOORE, a founder of the Irish Literary Theatre in 1899. It was here that his play *The Heather Field* was first produced. A great admirer of Ibsen, Martyn was suspicious of the thrust towards peasant drama in the Irish literary revival. His earlier influence in Irish theatre diminished as he represented a strain of continental realism that would not reassert itself until the foundation of the Gate Theatre after his death. A devout Catholic, he was the founder of the Palestrina Choir at the Pro-Cathedral in Dublin, which he endowed. He was also a founder of the Feis Ceoil. Moore has left a memorable record of him in *Hail and Farewell*.

MASON, Patrick (1951–), theatre director, trained at the Central School of Speech and Drama, London. Voice coach for the Abbey Theatre 1972–3. Fellow in drama Manchester University 1973–4, lecturer in theatre studies 1974–7. Resident director Abbey 1977–80, then worked as a freelance director in Ireland, the UK and the USA. Mason has won three Harvey theatre awards, a *Sunday Tribune* award, a *Time Out* theatre award, an Edinburgh Fringe award and an Olivier nomination. A dominant force in Irish theatre, he is currently artistic director of the Abbey.

MASTERSON, Patrick (1936–), academic, b. Dublin, ed. Belvedere, Castleknock,

UCD (MA) and University of Louvain (Ph.D.). President European University Institute, Florence, appointed 1 Jan. 1994 after almost 30 years' service in UCD as an academic and administrator. He began lecturing in the Department of Metaphysics in 1963 after completing his doctorate, and was appointed professor in the arts faculty in 1972. Registrar of the college 1983, president 1986. During his term as president he took a particular interest in encouraging links between graduates and the university. He has published a number of works on philosophical issues, including *Co-existence of God and Man in the Philosophy of St Thomas Aquinas*, *God and Grammar* and *Ethics and Absolutes in the Philosophy of E. Levinas*.

MATHEWS, Aidan Carl (1956–), author, b. Dublin, ed. Gonzaga, UCD and TCD. Taught at Belvedere 1977–9. One of the most incisive, all-round writing talents of his generation, Mathews came to public notice when he won the *Irish Times* poetry award 1974, to be followed in 1976 by the PATRICK KAVANAGH award, a Macaulay fellowship 1978–9, an Academy of American Poets award 1982, and the Ina Coolbrith poetry prize in 1984 for *Minding Ruth*. He was a fellow at Stanford University, California 1980–82. A gifted playwright, he wrote *The Diamond Body*, *Exit-Entrance* – a drama based on the double suicide of the Hungarian author Arthur Koestler and his wife, which won the Listowel drama award 1984 – and *Antigone* (1984). Short stories: *Muesli at Midnight* (1990), the orthographically adventurous *Adventures in a Bathyscope* (1988) and *Lipstick on the Host* (1994); poetry: *Windfalls* (1977) and *Minding Ruth* (1983). He also edited *Immediate Man*, a tribute to the late CEARBHALL Ó DÁLAIGH (1983). He is a producer with RTÉ.

MAUDE, Caitlín (1941–1982), poet, dramatist and critic, b. Casla, Co. Galway, ed. Spidéal and UCG. Held various teaching posts throughout Ireland. While at secondary school, Maude began to write poetry and to distinguish herself as a sean-nós singer. In Dublin she established an Irish club in North Great George's Street and participated in a radio programme on the Irish language with TOMÁS DE BHALDRAITHE. She canvassed for civil rights for the Gaeltacht and opposed Ireland's entry into the Common Market. She took a sympathetic stance towards the hunger strikers in Long Kesh in the early 1980s; her prose works illustrate a republican outlook in the spirit of JAMES CONNOLLY and PATRICK PEARSE. The great concerns of her life were the Irish language, the Gaeltacht and the underprivileged everywhere. Her work, much of which was published posthumously, includes *An Lasair Choille*, with MICHAEL HARTNETT (1961), and *Dánta* (1984).

MAWHINNEY, Brian Stanley (1940–), politician, b. Belfast, ed. Royal Academical Institution, QUB, Universities of Michigan and London (Ph.D.). Chairman of the British Conservative Party since 1995. Elected for Peterborough 1979, in 1986 he became the first Northern Ireland-born MP to be appointed to the Northern Ireland Office, where, as the minister responsible for education, he helped promote the cause of integrated education. In 1990 he was promoted to Minister of State at the NIO, moving to the Department of Health in 1992 before becoming Secretary of State for Transport in 1994. Mawhinney is usually credited with the idea of 'rolling devolution' on which the 1982–6 NI Assembly was based. Often criticised for his abrasive style, he has been a long-time political ally of Prime Minister John Major. He is the joint author of *Conflict and Christianity in Northern Ireland* (1976).

MAXWELL, Constantia (1886–1962), academic and historian, b. Dublin, ed. Scotland, TCD and Bedford College, London University. Her career thereafter was spent entirely in TCD, where she became successively a lecturer in history 1909–39, Professor of Economic History 1939, Lecky Professor of History 1945. She published a number of historical studies, of which the best-known – and still highly regarded – is *Dublin under the Georges* (1936). Other works included *Irish Town and Country under the Georges* (1940) and *The Stranger in Ireland* (1954). Her history of TCD appeared in 1946. She retired in 1951 and died in Kent, Feb. 1962.

MAY, Frederick (1911–1985), composer, pianist and broadcaster, b. Dublin, ed. RIAM, TCD, RCM, London and Vienna, d. Dublin. Teachers included Gordon Jacob, Vaughan Williams and Egon Wellesz. Music director Abbey Theatre for 15 years. Founded Music Association of Ireland 1948. Broadcast and wrote frequently on musical matters. Compositions include *Songs from Prison* for solo voice and orchestra (1958) and the internationally acclaimed String Quartet in C Minor (1936). Stopped composing in the 1950s following the onset of deafness.

MAYNE, Lieutenant-Colonel Robert 'Paddy' Blair (1915–1955), founder of SAS, ed. Regent House, Newtownards, Co. Down and QUB, where he studied law. The 6' 6" Mayne was capped six times for Ireland between 1936 and 1938 and toured with the British Lions in South Africa in 1938. He was also the Northern Ireland amateur heavyweight boxing champion. At the outbreak of World War II he enlisted in the Royal Artillery, transferring to the Royal Ulster Rifles before becoming one of the founder members of the Special Air Service. In north Africa he was involved in attacks on enemy airfields and on one raid was reputed to have personally destroyed 47 planes. In France he parachuted behind enemy lines after D-Day and operated with the Resistance in attacks on German forces. He was awarded his first DSO in 1942, a second in 1943 for service in Sicily, a third after D-Day and a fourth later in 1944. In Dec. 1945 Mayne set out to join an expedition to the Antarctic but a wartime back injury forced him to return home. He became secretary to the Incorporated Law Society of Northern Ireland Apr. 1946. Mayne was killed in a car crash in his home town of Newtownards. His biography, *Rogue Warrior of the SAS*, was written by ROY BRADFORD and Martin Dillon.

MAYNE, Rutherford (1878–1967), pseud. of Samuel Waddell, playwright and actor, b. Japan to Belfast parents, ed. Royal Academical Institution and QUB. An engineer with the Irish Land Commission, he joined the Ulster Literary Theatre in 1904 as an amateur actor, began playwriting and was the chief creative force behind the young company; it staged nine plays of his between 1906 and 1923, mostly in Ulster theatres but also in Dublin and London houses. He left the Literary Theatre in 1930 and wrote two pieces for the Abbey, *Peter* (1930) and *Bridgehead* (1934), which played with success. He retired as land commissioner and went to live in Dalkey. In 1960, at age 82, he was appointed a trustee of the Lyric Players Theatre, Belfast. Plays included: *The Turn of the Road*, *The Drone* – a farce about an inventor, his most popular work – *The Troth*, *The Red Turf* and *Plays of Changing Ireland*.

MEAGHER, Lory (1899–1973), hurler. He won six County Championship titles with his club, Tullaroan, the first when aged 16 and the last aged 35, in 1934. His senior Kilkenny début was in 1926, and he won three All-Ireland medals with the county, in 1932, 1933 and 1935. Considered one of the best and most stylish midfielders of all time and ranking among the legendary figures in the game, he also won two Railway Cup medals with Leinster in 1927 and 1933, and with Kilkenny won his only National League medal in the latter year.

MEEHAN, Ita (1922–), public servant, b. Ballyfin, Co. Laois, ed. Coláiste Mhuire, Tourmakeady, Co. Mayo. Joined the Department of Supplies as an executive officer in 1941 and retired from the Department of Posts and Telegraphs in 1983 as deputy secretary, only the second woman to have reached that grade. In Posts and Telegraphs she was head of the unit responsible for the reorganisation of half of the then civil service into the state-sponsored bodies Telecom and An Post in 1984. Appointed a director of Bord Telecom 1985, chairwoman trustees Telecom Superannuation Fund and in 1986 chairwoman Telecom Éireann Information Systems Ltd. Had a major involvement in the initial planning and implementation of the Accelerated Tele-communications Development Programme. Director and member governing body National College of Industrial Relations 1988. At various times programme secretary and chairwoman of the executive committee of the Social Study Conference.

MEEHAN, Paula (1955–), poet, b. Dublin, ed. Holy Faith Convent, Finglas, Dublin (from which, she is proud to note, she was expelled for being 'a right handful'), TCD, where she was recently a fellow of the English department, and Eastern Washington University. Meehan acquired a taste for street and experimental theatre while at TCD, later transferring her allegiance to poetry. She won Arts Council bursaries in 1987 and 1990. She has yet to be earmarked for greatness, but was shortlisted for the *Irish Times*/Aer Lingus Irish literature prize for poetry in 1991. Her verse reflects very much an upbringing in a poorer area of Dublin's north side, those same grim cityscapes that fed the art of BRENDAN BEHAN and SEAN O'CASEY; at the same time, her 'Berlin Diary', a series of seven sketches, must rank among her most powerful writing. Her collections are: *The Man who was Marked by Winter* (1991), *Return and No Blame* (1984), *Reading the Sky* (1986) and *Pillow Talk* (1994).

MELLOWS, Liam (1892–1922), republican and socialist, b. Manchester, childhood spent in Inch, Co. Wexford. He was sworn into the IRB in 1912 and became a member of the provisional committee of the Irish Volunteers in 1913. Despite being deported to England in 1916, he managed to return to Ireland and lead minor actions by Volunteers in south Galway during the Easter Rising. He escaped to America afterwards but returned to Ireland in 1920 and was appointed director of purchases during the War of Independence. He regarded the Treaty as a betrayal of the Republic and called for the establishment of a revolutionary civilian government to counter the Provisional Government of the IFS. He was arrested at the outbreak of the Civil War, and together with RORY O'CONNOR, Joseph McKelvey and Richard Barrett was executed on 8 Dec. 1922 as a deterrent against further assassinations of public representatives following the killing of Sean Hales TD.

MHAC AN tSAOI, Máire (1922–), poet, b. Dublin, d. of SEAN MACENTEE, spent much of her childhood in Dún Chaoin in the west Kerry Gaeltacht, ed. UCD and Sorbonne, m. CONOR CRUISE O'BRIEN 1962. Scholar in School of Celtic Studies in the DIAS. Qualified as barrister, entered Department of External Affairs, posted to Paris and Madrid. She has won many awards for her poetry. Publications include: *Margadh na Saoire* (1956), *A Heart Full of Thought* (Irish–English translation) (1959), *Codladh an Ghaiscígh* (1973), *An Galar Dubhach* (1980) and *An Cion go dtí Seo* (1987).

MIDDLETON, Colin (1910–1983), painter, b. Belfast, 29 Jan. 1910, ed. Belfast Royal Academy. Followed father into linen damask designing business; did evening classes at College of Art. Early work before World War II divided into expressionist scenes of Belfast and surrealism, partly influenced by Dali. A pivotal figure in Northern Ireland in the 1940s and 1950s. Constantly experimented with technique and style; went through a cubist phase and a period of extreme romanticism. Taught art in Coleraine and Lisburn; exhibited in Dublin, London, America, Canada, the Netherlands. MBE, MRHA.

MIDGLEY, Harry Cassidy (1892–1957), politician, b. Belfast. A shipyard apprentice at the age of 14. Before the outbreak of World War I, in which he fought, Midgley was active in the Independent Labour Party and supported JAMES CONNOLLY. In the 1921 Northern Ireland parliamentary election he stood on an anti-partitionist platform as an Independent Labour candidate. He won a Belfast Council seat in 1925 as an NI Labour Party candidate, and, as party chairman, won the Belfast, Dock seat at Stormont in 1933. By the 1930s Midgley was increasingly pro-Union. His attacks on the role of the Catholic Church in the Spanish civil war led to his loss of the Dock seat in 1938. In 1941 he won the Willowfield seat at Stormont and resigned from the NILP when the party refused to advocate support of the Union – he formed the Commonwealth Labour Party the following year. He became Minister of Public Security in the BROOKE government 1943, resigning in 1945. In 1947 Midgley joined both the Unionist Party and the Orange Order and became Minister of Labour in the NI administration. Appointed Minister of Education in 1950, he held the post until his death.

MILLER, Liam (1924–1987), publisher, b. Mountrath, Co. Laois, ed. UCD, d. Dublin, 17 May 1987. He first worked in London but returned to Dublin in 1951 to found the Dolmen Press, his life's work. Dolmen's productions were distinguished by fine typography and outstanding design. Its most famous title was THOMAS KINSELLA's translation of *The Táin*, illustrated by LOUIS LE BROCQUY (1969). Founder president of the Irish Book Publishers' Association (Clé) 1967.

MILLIGAN, Alice (1866–1953), poet and playwright, b. Omagh, ed. Belfast and King's College, London. An advocate of home rule, she was active in the Gaelic League and later, together with ETHNA CARBERY, edited the Belfast nationalist and literary magazine

the *Shan Van Vocht* 1896–9. She wrote a forgettable novel, *A Royal Democrat* (1892), and some poetry for *United Irishman, Sinn Féin* and other journals. She will be remembered as one of the first 'Celtic Twilight' dramatists: her *The Last Feast of the Fianna* (1900) was one of the first productions given by the Irish Literary Theatre, the forerunner of the Abbey, which staged *The Daughter of Donagh* in 1920. She was a prolific writer; apart from a half-dozen plays, she wrote a biography, *Life of Wolfe Tone* (1898), and books on mythology. *The Poems of Alice Milligan* was published in 1954.

MILLS, Kathleen (1923–1996), camogie player. She played for the Great Southern Railways (later CIE) club in Dublin, and her 15 All-Ireland senior medals with Dublin in 18 finals is unlikely to be surpassed. One of the finals was a replay, so that she was actually on only two losing sides (in 1941 and 1947) in that astonishing run of success, which included an amazing eight in a row 1948–55. She retired in 1963.

MILLS, Michael (1927–), journalist and ombudsman, b. Mountmellick, Co. Laois, ed. Patrician College, Ballyfin, m., four s. four d. Newspaperman with the *Irish Press*, a percipient, independent and widely respected political correspondent who contributed frequently to radio and television programmes. In 1984 he was appointed Ireland's first ombudsman, an institution which Ireland was behind many European countries in adopting due to the Irish preference for remedies of a political nature. Discussion on the creation of the office began in the mid-1960s but the matter was not considered in the Oireachtas until 1975 and the necessary Act not passed until 1980. It was a further four years before the first appointment, by the president, upon resolutions passed by the Dáil and Seanad. Mills's selection ensured recognition of the office as an independent and credible institution on which citizens can rely to secure justice in regard to reasonable complaints against the public service.

MITCHEL, Charles Gerard (1919–1996), actor and broadcaster, b. Dublin, 8 Nov. 1919, ed. Clongowes and TCD. Appeared for ENSA in Northern Ireland 1943–5, with the Gate Theatre in Dublin and on tour 1947–58. Joined RTÉ in 1961 upon the advent of television. As senior newsreader, his assured presentation of bulletins both on television and on radio established him as the voice par excellence of the national service until his retirement in 1984.

MITCHELL, Francis George (Frank) (1912–), FRS, geologist and landscape archaeologist, b. Dublin, 15 Oct. 1912, ed. High School, Dublin and TCD. Held teaching and administrative posts at TCD 1934–65 and was Professor of Quaternary Studies 1965–77. PRIA 1976–9, elected president of An Taisce 1991. Publications include: *Treasures of Irish Art* (1977), *The Shell Guide to Reading the Irish Landscape* (1986), *Archaeology and Environment in Early Dublin* (1987), *Man and Environment in Valentia Island, Co. Kerry* (1989) and *The Way that I Followed* (1990).

MITCHELL, Thomas (1939–), academic, b. Balla, Co. Mayo, ed. UCG and Cornell University, Ithaca, New York. Appointed Provost of TCD in Aug. 1991, the first Roman Catholic to hold the position since 1690. Mitchell, who has built an international reputation as a classical scholar, taught for several years in Swarthmore College in the USA and became Professor of Classics in TCD in 1979. In 1986 he was appointed to the Cornell visiting professorship for distinguished scholars. Publications include *Cicero: The Ascending Years* and *Cicero, Senior Statesman*.

MOLLOY, Bobby (1936–), politician, b. 6 July 1936, ed. Coláiste Iognáid, Galway and UCG. Member of Galway County Council and Corporation 1967–70, Mayor of Galway 1968–9. Elected TD for Galway West 1965. Until 1986 he was a member of Fianna Fáil but early that year he quitted – in a one-sentence letter – to join the Progressive Democrats; his departure was regarded as a body blow to his former colleagues. Parliamentary secretary to the Minister for Education 1969–70, Minister for Local Government 1970–73, Minister for Defence 1977–9. On the accession of CHARLES HAUGHEY to the leadership of FF he was no longer included in the cabinet, but he had the satisfaction of returning to high office as Minister for Energy 1989–92 on the formation of the coalition government involving the PDs and FF. He was one of the negotiators of the programme on which that govern-

ment was based. On two occasions, in 1989 and 1994, he unsuccessfully contested the Connacht–Ulster constituency in elections for the European Parliament.

MOLLOY, Michael J. (1917–1994), playwright, b. Milltown, Co. Galway, 3 Mar. 1917, ed. St Jarlath's College, Tuam. Studies for the priesthood were abandoned because of illness and Molloy lived most of his life on his small farm near Milltown. Many of his plays are historical, set in the rural Ireland of penal times or the 19th century. His first play, *The Old Road*, was produced at the Abbey Theatre in 1943. It was followed by *The Visiting House*, *The King of Friday's Men*, *The Paddy Pedlar*, *The Wood of the Whispering*, *The Will and the Way*, *Daughter from Over the Water* and *Petticoat Loose*.

MOLONY, Helena (1884–1967), revolutionary and trade unionist. By profession an actress and a member of the Abbey Theatre, Molony had joined MAUD GONNE MACBRIDE's Inghinidhe na hÉireann in 1903. In 1908 she became editor of *Bean na hÉireann*, advocating 'complete separatism, the rising cause of feminism, and the interests of Irish women generally'. Arrested in 1910 for protesting during the visit of George V to Dublin, she became, briefly, one of the first political prisoners of her era. After 1913, in tandem with JAMES CONNOLLY, she accepted the task of organising women workers, many of whom had lost their employment in the battle for the right to join the fledgling Irish Women Workers' Union. By 1915 she was a member of Cumann na mBan. In the wake of Easter 1916 she was interned in England, returning to the ranks of the IWWU on her release. She opposed the Treaty and took part in the Civil War. By the 1930s her resistance had found focus in other quarters: she welcomed the Vocational Education Act of 1930 but challenged the corporatist disposition of the Commission on Vocational Organisation and 'stressed the wide platform of social justice' based on the papal encyclicals. In 1936 she was elected president of the Trades Union Congress.

MOLYNEAUX, James Henry (1920–), politician, b. 27 Aug. 1920, ed. Aldergrove School, Co. Antrim. MP (UUP) for South Antrim 1970–83, for Lagan Valley since 1983. He took over the leadership of the Ulster Unionist Party from HARRY WEST in 1979, having been leader of its MPs since 1974 when West lost his seat. During the early 1980s Molyneaux had to fend off the threat that IAN PAISLEY's Democratic Unionist Party would overtake the UUP as the major political voice of Ulster unionism. His adoption of a critical stance vis-à-vis the Conservative government of Margaret Thatcher helped to this end, and in the elections of 1982 (to the Northern Assembly) and 1983 (to Westminster) the UUP re-established its predominant position. The rivalry between the two parties was shelved in 1985 in order to form a united opposition to the Anglo-Irish Agreement, which allowed the government of the Republic a limited say in the affairs of Northern Ireland. The alliance around the slogan 'Ulster Says No' resulted for a time in the boycotting of parliament and local government, but Molyneaux soon began to stress more positive policies, such as the demand for a devolved administration in Northern Ireland. By 1988 he was engaging in 'talks about talks' with the Secretary of State, and by 1992 he was in dialogue with the government in Dublin, despite the continuing claim in the Republic's constitution of a right to jurisdiction over the whole island of Ireland. While he continued to act independently of the Conservatives in Westminster on such issues as the Maastricht Treaty, he gave a guarded welcome to the Downing Street Declaration of Dec. 1993, unlike Paisley, who rejected it root and branch. By now, however, his age was telling against him as speculation grew over the approaching need for the UUP to find a new leader. He continued vigorously to articulate unionist scepticism, the paramilitary ceasefires notwithstanding, in regard to Sinn Féin, the IRA and the Dublin government until his retirement in Sept. 1995, when he was replaced by DAVID TRIMBLE.

MONAGHAN, John Joseph ('Rinty') (1920–1984), boxer, b. Belfast, 21 Aug. 1920, d. Belfast, 3 Mar. 1984. He won his first professional fight at the age of 14, but 12 years passed before his London début, when he knocked out Terry Allen in the first round. In Mar. 1947 he outpointed Dado Marino of Hawaii to win the vacant NBA world flyweight title. His seventh-round KO of Jackie Paterson both retained the title and made him British and Empire champion, and with a sub-

sequent points victory over Maurice Sandeyron (France) he became European champion. In his third defence of the world title, he drew with Allen in 1949, then retired undefeated, suffering from tuberculosis. Monaghan used to celebrate victory by singing 'Danny Boy'; his career record (1935–49) was 66 fights, 51 wins, six draws, nine defeats.

MONAHAN, Philip (1894–1983), public servant, b. Dublin, ed. CBS, Westland Row and North Richmond Street, Dublin. Secondary teacher 1915–23. Joined the Irish Volunteers, was arrested and interned. On release, joined Sinn Féin and was elected Mayor of Drogheda and member of Louth County Council 1920. Supported the Anglo-Irish Treaty. The new Free State government acquired powers to discipline incompetent or neglectful local councils. First to fall was Kerry County Council and Monahan was appointed by the Minister for Local Government to run the county's affairs. In 1924 he was appointed commissioner of Cork Corporation. When in 1929 the government introduced a system derived from the American method of city management, Monahan was uniquely appointed city manager for life. While his stewardship inspired mixed reactions, it has had a significance far beyond the city boundaries: on the Cork model, management spread to Dublin, Dún Laoghaire, Limerick, Waterford and then to all the counties.

MONTAGUE, John (1929–), poet, b. New York, where his Catholic father had fled to exile after the Civil War, spent his childhood on the family home near Garvaghey, Co. Tyrone, ed. St Patrick's College, Armagh, UCD and Yale. Between 1954 and 1972 he travelled in the USA, lecturing and organising poetry workshops. He also worked as a correspondent for *The Irish Times* in Paris 1961–4 and lectured at the University of Vincennes 1969–70 before returning to Ireland. Publications include: *Poisoned Lands* (1961 and 1978), *Death of a Chieftain* (1964), *A Chosen Light* (1967), *The Rough Field* (1972) and *A Slow Dance* (1975). Much of his work deals with exile and a nostalgic longing for home. His memories of Ulster, captured in sharply drawn vignettes of typical men and women of the countryside, lead him sometimes to voice a powerful subliminal awareness of history and myth, the origins of the communities caught up in the tribal warfare of the Northern Troubles. He can also turn to more intimate human emotions. *The Great Cloak* (1978) is concerned with the breakdown of marriage and the fulfilment of a new union. He edited *The Faber Book of Irish Verse* (1974) and until 1988 was a senior lecturer in English in UCC.

MONTEITH, J. *Dermot* (**'Monty'**) (1943–), international cricketer, b. Lisburn, Co. Antrim, 2 June 1943. A left-arm spinner and right-hand batsman, he is regarded as Ireland's finest post-war player. He played for QUB and Lisburn, and at first-class level for Middlesex. In his international career, his 326 wickets for an average of 17.37 is an Irish record not likely to be surpassed. His 209 first-class wickets is also an Irish record, and he took five or more wickets in an international match a record 27 times. He scored 1,712 international runs for an average of 20.62 in 99 innings, including seven 50s. He was capped 76 times and captained Ireland on 37 occasions.

MONTGOMERY, Alan Moore (1912–), journalist, b. England, 18 Mar. 1912, s. of LESLIE MONTGOMERY, ed. privately in Ireland, m. Bertine Phipps, two d. He joined *The Irish Times* as a reporter in 1934 and was appointed chief reporter seven years later, making him the youngest news editor in the country at the time. He introduced a less formal style of newspaper reporting to Irish journalism, especially in the post-war years, when he recruited many young men who had broadened their horizons in the fighting services and encouraged them not just to report day-to-day events but to find and investigate the unusual. Dublin correspondent of *Time* magazine, *Life* and *Sports Illustrated* for more than 20 years, and one of the originators of the *Irish Times* style book, for generations a bible for newspaper reporters. Assistant editor of *The Irish Times* 1959; managing editor of the *Evening Mail* 1960; editor of *The Irish Times* 1961. In 1963 appointed chief information officer for Ireland with the Guinness Group. On retirement in 1977 he joined Murray Consultants, a public relations firm.

MONTGOMERY, David John (1948–), newspaper executive, ed. Bangor Grammar School, Co. Down and QUB. Chief executive of Mirror Group Newspapers since 1992. A freelance journalist for the *Belfast Newsletter* before being offered a place on the *Daily Mirror* training scheme. Sub-editor at the *Daily Mirror* 1973–8 and assistant chief sub-editor until 1980. He held a similar position with the *Sun* before becoming assistant editor with the *Sunday People* in 1982. Assistant editor *News of the World* 1984–5 and editor until 1987. Managing director of News UK and editor of *Today* 1987–91, he has also served as a director on the boards of a number of newspaper and television companies. He has been criticised by business opponents as ruthless and as having an autocratic management style. Derek Jameson, the former *Mirror* editor, recalled that in Manchester Montgomery would 'hover around my office and say: "With great respect, editor, I think you've got the wrong splash, the best story is on page seven." I knew he was destined for the top.'

MONTGOMERY, Leslie Alexander (1873–1961), humorist, b. Downpatrick, Co. Down, ed. Dundalk. Began work as a bank clerk at the age of 16 and remained with the same company until his retirement. He wrote under the pseudonym 'Lynn Doyle'. Although a prolific playwright in the 1920s, Montgomery's fame rests on his Ballygullion stories, the first collection of which appeared in 1918. Told in dialect – a literary form popular at the time but which reads somewhat tediously today – the stories celebrate an imaginary northern Irish district and its people. They are: *Ballygullion* (1918), *Lobster Salad* (1922), *Dear Ducks* (1925), *Me and Mr Murphy* (1930), *Rosabelle* (1933), *The Shake of the Bag* (1939), *A Bowl of Broth* (1945), *Green Oranges* (1947), *Back to Ballygullion* (1953), *New Stories* (1957) and a selection entitled *The Ballygullion Bus* (1957). His was the dubious honour of being the first Irish writer to be appointed to the Censorship Board, in 1936; he resigned the post some months later.

MOODY, Theodore William (1907–1984), historian, b. Belfast, ed. Royal Academical Institution and QUB, d. Dublin, 11 Feb. 1984. Professor of Modern History TCD 1939–77. In 1938 founded the journal *Irish Historical Studies* with ROBIN DUDLEY EDWARDS. Moody favoured the use of modern media as vehicles for bringing history to the people and it was at his instigation that

RTÉ established the Thomas Davis lectures on radio, through which a given historical theme would be examined under a variety of headings by a number of contributors and the result subsequently published as a book. He adapted this approach for a remarkable television series, *The Course of Irish History*. His personal interest was best represented in his biography of Michael Davitt (1981), and at the time of his death he was editing volumes of the *New History of Ireland*. He was a member of the RTÉ Authority dismissed in 1972 for an alleged breach of the order issued under section 31 of the Broadcasting Authority Act. As a Quaker and a Northerner, he was particularly committed to the search for reconciliation between Christians, and he served for a number of years on the executive board of the Irish School of Ecumenics.

MOONEY, Ria (1904–1973), actress and drama producer, b. Dublin, ed. Metropolitan School of Art, Dublin, d. Dublin, Jan. 1973. Having shown early promise as an actress, joined Abbey Theatre 1924; chosen by SEAN O'CASEY to play Rosie Redmond in first production of *The Plough and the Stars* (1926). After tours of England and the USA, directed plays for the Civic Repertory Theatre, New York, but returned to Ireland before World War II. Acted with Gate Theatre until 1944, when she was appointed director of the Gaiety Theatre School of Acting, also in Dublin. Returned to the Abbey as a producer.

MOORE, Brian (1921–), novelist, b. Belfast, ed. St Malachy's College, Belfast. As a young man, Moore served with the ARP and saw the effects of the German blitz on Belfast (which he describes in *The Emperor of Ice Cream*, 1966). He joined the British Ministry of War Transport in 1943 and in that civilian role worked for the UN Refugee Commission. In 1948 he emigrated to Canada, where he sought to establish himself as a writer of fiction.

He won wide acclaim with *Judith Hearne* (1955), the first novel published under his own name, later issued as *The Lonely Passion of Judith Hearne*. Subsequent books confirmed his reputation as one of the most inventive and popular of contemporary English-language novelists. While he has chosen diverse settings for his later works, he has remained significantly involved with the complex fate of being Irish,

and his characters are almost always Irish (at least in background) or Catholic, or both. In 1959 he moved from Canada (where he had taken citizenship) to California. He visits Ireland frequently.

Moore's work from the start has been engaged with the defining crises that determine individual fate (he has been particularly attentive to the problems of female identity). In his early novels these crises develop in the context of highly traditional society in which the claims of family, religion and nation constitute an almost Joycean constriction of human possibility. In his later work, crises of conscience and of faith present themselves in a secularised, desacralised world in which the issue of individual responsibility is explored in a heavily determined social reality. This varies from the overwhelming consumerist abundance of the North American cosmopolis (*Fergus*, 1970) to the oppressive constraints of eastern European communism (*The Colour of Blood*, 1987). Moore's technique is marked by a primary realism which has admitted experiment (in such works as the fantasy *The Great Victorian Collection*, 1975, the elegant fable *Cold Heaven*, 1983, or the historical novel *Black Robe*, 1985) without compromising the essential readability which has made him one of the most immediately enjoyable of present-day writers. Many later books display cinematic influences. *Judith Hearne, Catholics* (1972) and *Black Robe* have been realised in film form.

Awarded Guggenheim fellowship 1959, fiction award of the Governor-General of Canada 1961 and 1975, the W.H. Smith award 1973, the James Tait Black memorial prize 1975, the Royal Society of Literature and the Heinemann awards 1986, and the *Sunday Express* Book of the Year award 1987.

MOORE, Christy (1945–), singer and songwriter, b. Newbridge, Co. Kildare. His parents were Andy Moore and Neans de Paor, whom he cites as a major influence on his career along with DONAL LUNNY, Liam Clancy (of the CLANCY BROTHERS), Luke Kelly (of THE DUBLINERS) and Ewan MacColl. Giving up a career in the bank for that of a singer, his first album, *Prosperous*, proved something of a watershed, leading to the formation of the folk group Planxty with Lunny, Andy Irvine and LIAM O'FLYNN. As singer, guitarist and bodhrán striker he has been much involved in ensemble work (including the innovative group Moving Hearts), but his major contribution to Irish music is rooted in his outstanding ability as a solo performer and songwriter. Much of his composition is concerned with social and political deprivation and environmental issues, yet he has also the knack of producing verses of rare humour. His brother Luka Bloom (Barry Moore) is a singer of international reputation and his sister Eilish a singer of great persuasion and an organiser of folk-related events.

MOORE, George Augustus (1852–1933), writer, b. Ballyglass, Co. Mayo, ed. Oscott College, Birmingham, d. London. He lived in Paris 1873–9, hoping to find a career within the artistic and literary milieu of the newly established Third Republic, but eventually accepted that there was little future for him there. Having settled in London, he somewhat tardily became a popular novelist, especially after the publication of *Esther Waters* (1894). He returned to Ireland in 1901, involved himself in the literary revival of the day and the founding of the Abbey Theatre. In 1911 he went back to London and his best-known work, the autobiography *Hail and Farewell*, was published in three volumes between then and 1914. Later novels included *The Brook Kerith* (1916) and *Heloise and Abelard* (1921), both well regarded at the time. His large output extended also to dialogues, conversations, confessions and, finally, romanticised history. His short stories on Irish themes still merit reading for their authenticity and credibility, but he outlived the literary fashions of Edwardian London and Dublin within which he was most at home, and, although writing to the end, he had long lost his status as a foremost author of the day when he died.

MOORE, H. Kingsmill (1853–1943), educationalist, b. Liverpool, 11 Dec. 1853, ed. Midleton, Co. Cork (where his father was headmaster) and Balliol College, Oxford, d. 1 Dec. 1943. Appointed Cork diocesan inspector of schools 1881 and made a remarkable contribution to the educational work of the Church of Ireland. First principal of the newly constituted Church of Ireland Training College 1884–1927. In close association with Archbishop Plunket he was responsible for placing the college on a secure footing and for housing it in new buildings to replace those inherited from the Kildare Place Society. A prolific writer on educational matters, methodological (in which he was sometimes ahead of his time) and historical, he was invited to appear before several government inquiries, including the crucial Palles Commission on Intermediate Education in 1898.

MOORE, Henry Francis (1887–1954), physician, b. Cappoquin, Co. Waterford, ed. UCD, taking first place and first class honours in his final medical examination in 1912, m. Frances Thomas, one s. A travelling scholarship enabled him to study in Berlin and at the Rockefeller Institute, New York. On his return to Dublin he joined the honorary staff of the Mater Hospital. He was the city's leading clinical scientist at a time when laboratory investigation was introduced, but his vision of establishing a major research centre was frustrated by lack of funds. He held a part-time chair of medicine at UCD and conducted a large practice.

MOORE, Theodore Conyngham Kingsmill (1894–1979), lawyer, b. Dublin, ed. Marlborough College and TCD, d. 21 Jan. 1979. Served with Royal Flying Corps in World War I and later on editorial staff of *The Irish Times*. Called to Bar 1918, Senior Counsel 1935. Elected to Seanad (DU) 1943 and 1944, his nomination papers on the latter occasion being signed wholly by women graduates. High Court judge 1947–51, Supreme Court judge 1951–65. Co-author of a textbook on landlord and tenant law and author of a book on fishing. First chairman of the Broadcasting Complaints Committee (later Commission) 1974–9.

MORAN, David Patrick (1871–1936), journalist and author, b. Co. Waterford, ed. Castleknock, d. Sutton, Co. Dublin. Joined the Gaelic League and Irish Literary Society in London, returned to Ireland in 1898 and went on to found and edit the *Leader*, through which he promoted his vision of an Irish nationalism free from what he considered to be the shallow imitation of English values in vogue among middle-class nationalists. He also attacked W.B. YEATS and the Anglo-Irish literary revival for an artificial Celticism. His appeal to national and Roman Catholic self-confidence attracted a wide audience for a time, boosted by his book *The Philosophy of Irish Ireland* (1905), but was eventually superseded by the more positive and broadly based independence movement associated with the Volunteers, of which Moran was, ironically, a founder member.

MORAN, Frances Elizabeth (1893–1977), lawyer, b. Dublin, ed. Dominican College, Eccles Street, Dublin and in Belgium, King's Inns and TCD (BA 1915, LL B 1918, LL D 1919), d. 7 Oct. 1977. Called to Bar 1924 and to English Bar (Gray's Inn) 1940; in 1941 the first Irish woman to become Senior Counsel. Practised in Dublin, specialising in conveyancing. Reid Professor of Law TCD 1925–30, Professor of Laws 1934–44, first woman professor in TCD and first woman on college board. Lecturer in property law King's Inns 1932–58. Holding two vital legal academic posts, she was a dominant figure in Irish legal education for over a quarter of a century. Attended Nuremberg War Trials as an observer. President of International Federation of University Women 1950–53. FTCD 1968.

MORAN, Kevin (1954–), international footballer and Gaelic footballer, b. Dublin, 29 Apr. 1954. He is the only person to win both All-Ireland senior football medals and FA Cup medals. His All-Ireland medals were won with Dublin (1976, 1977) and the FA Cup medals with Manchester United (1983, 1985). Other clubs included Sporting Gijon in Spain and Blackburn Rovers, whom he helped to promotion to the new English Premier League in 1992. He was first capped for the Republic of Ireland against Sweden in 1980 and played prominent roles in the Republic's campaigns in the 1988 European Championship, the 1990 World Cup in Italy and the build-up to the 1994 World Cup in the USA.

MORGAN, Dermot (1952–), comedian, b. Dublin, 31 Mar. 1952, ed. Oatlands College and UCD. On graduation he taught English in a Dublin secondary school. His first success as a comic came with the creation of the very successful Fr Trendy character for comedy sketches on the RTÉ television series *The Live Mike* 1979–82. Left teaching 1980 and toured the country with the Fr Trendy show. Cowrote *Scrap Saturday*, a hugely popular radio programme of political satire in the early 1990s.

A satirical television quiz show, *Newshounds*, was cancelled by RTÉ prior to the planned broadcast date in 1993. Presented *Guten Morgan* on radio station 98 FM five days a week 1993. Toured Ireland with Black Humour show 1993–4. Played the title role in the popular Channel 4 comedy *Father Ted*, of which two series were screened 1995–6. Jacob's award, National Entertainment Personality award 1991. *Father Ted* won a Bafta award for Best British TV Comedy 1996.

MORRISON, Daniel Gerard (1953–), republican. Became active in the republican movement at an early stage in the Northern Ireland Troubles and was interned for a time in the 1970s. He first came to public prominence in 1981 as director of publicity for Sinn Féin and as spokesman for the hunger strikers in the Maze Prison. The familiar phrase used to describe republican strategy in the Northern conflict, 'an Armalite in one hand and a ballot paper in the other', was coined by him at the 1981 Sinn Féin Ard-fheis. He stood as SF's candidate in the 1984 European election and received 91,476 votes (13.3% of total). In 1992 he was convicted on a charge of false imprisonment.

MORRISON, James (1893–1947), fiddler, teacher and bandleader, b. Drumfin, near Collooney, Co. Sligo. Inherited his music from his mother's family, the Dolans of Lackagh, where his uncle frequently entertained prominent local musicians and gave dancing lessons (his students included the young MICHAEL COLEMAN). Two of Morrison's brothers were established instrumentalists and he himself started serious study of the fiddle at 13. At 17 he was employed by the Gaelic League as a dancing master but he continued with the fiddle, winning the senior competition in the Sligo Feis Ceoil in 1915. That same year he emigrated to Boston to join five of his siblings. He moved to New York, where his talents gained the recognition of a recording session in 1921. This was the start of a recording career lasting 15 years and resulting in some eighty-four 78s. In his latter years there was a deterioration in his health and spirits. He died in the Bronx, but his playing is echoed in the fiddle masters of contemporary Ireland such as Charlie Lennon, Kevin Burke and Frankie Gavin.

MORRISON, Van (George Ivan) (1945–), musician, b. Belfast. Few Irish artists are held in the same esteem. It may be in some part due to his gruff personal style but it is mostly because of his incredible body of work, which has influenced a whole generation of singer-songwriters, including Mike Scott, Liam Ó Maonlaí (of HOTHOUSE FLOWERS) and Jeff Buckley. As a founder member of Them, Morrison helped to kick-start the Irish beat scene of the early 1960s, which saw staid showbands being eclipsed by more exciting and original R & B groups. He left the group in 1966 to embark on his solo career, making his début with the single 'Brown Eyed Girl', which was a US top ten hit. *Astral Weeks* (1968) became a critics' favourite and is now considered a seminal album. During the early 1970s, as Morrison's reputation grew, he appeared in the charts with albums such as *Moondance* (1970), *Tupelo Honey* (1971), *Saint Dominic's Preview* (1972) and *Hard Nose the Highway* (1973).

After the deeply personal *Veedon Fleece*, Morrison took a three-year break from touring, emerging only to guest on the Band's farewell concert film, *The Last Waltz*, and on Rolling Stone Bill Wyman's solo album. He returned in 1977 with *A Period of Transition*, following with *Wavelength* (1978), *Into the Music* (1979), *Common One* (1980), *Beautiful Vision* (1982) and *Inarticulate Speech of the Heart* (1983). His recorded output maintained its high standard right through the 1980s, and he also began to collaborate more with other artists, including Bob Dylan, Tom Jones, THE CHIEFTAINS, Cliff Richard and John Lee Hooker. In 1992 Morrison received an honorary DL from the NUU, the following year he was inducted into the Rock and Roll Hall of Fame and in 1996 he was awarded an OBE.

MORRISSY, Mary (1957–), fiction writer. She won the Hennessy award for short stories in 1984 and her fictions have appeared in various magazines and anthologies. Staff journalist on *The Irish Times* and a regular book reviewer for that paper, as well as for the *Independent on Sunday*. Short stories: *A Lazy Eye* (1993). Her novel, *Mother of Pearl* (1996), charts a young woman's psychologically perilous and emotionally charged hunt for her lost roots; it has been serialised on BBC radio. Morrissy is a superb stylist who has barely reached the foothills of her considerable powers.

MORTON, Mary *May* Elizabeth (1876–1957), poet, b. Co. Limerick, ed. locally and trained as a teacher in Belfast, where she settled in 1900. She was chairperson of the Belfast branch of PEN and a founder of the Young Ulster Society. She held various posts in education in Cos. Tyrone, Down and Armagh and was vice-principal of a girls' school in Coleraine, Co. Derry 1934–7. Her poems were published in many newspapers and periodicals in Britain and Ireland and broadcast on radio. She won the Festival of Britain Northern Ireland award for poetry. Collections: *Dawn and Afterglow* (1936), *Masque in Maytime* (1948) and *Sung to the Spinning Wheel* (1952).

MORTON, William (Billy) (1905–1969), sports promoter, d. Dublin. One of the truly colourful characters of Irish sport, he became renowned as the visionary and indomitable pioneer of major athletics meetings, chiefly in Ireland but also in Britain. His name will always be associated with the Clonliffe Harriers club, and he was Irish national marathon champion in 1936. An optician by profession, he was a sports impresario at heart, and the media persons of his era held that he was the first in Ireland to recognise – and skilfully exploit – the publicity value of the organised press conference. He promoted countless historic athletics meetings in Dublin in the 1950s, the greatest and most famous of them being at Santry Stadium in 1958, when Herb Elliott set a new mile world record and was one of five runners to complete the distance in under four minutes.

MOYNE (Walter Edward Guinness), Lord (1880–1944), politician and traveller, b. Dublin, 20 Mar. 1880, s. of Edward Cecil Guinness, Earl of Iveagh, ed. Eton and Oxford. He combined a lifelong interest in science and travel with service in several Conservative governments. Under-secretary of war 1922–3, financial secretary to Treasury (under Churchill) 1923–4, 1924–5, Minister of Agriculture 1925–9. His travels took him to Asia Minor on an extensive map-making expedition and to New Guinea in search of rare specimens for the London Zoological Society. On 6 Nov.

1944 he was assassinated by the Zionist Stern Gang in Cairo, where he had been serving as Minister of State.

MULCAHY, John (1932–), publisher, ed. Clongowes and TCD. He worked for several years in the financial and investment business before taking over as publisher and editor of the fortnightly current affairs magazine *Hibernia* in 1968. Under his control the magazine became a vehicle for a searching liberal critique of Irish society. He was editor of the *Sunday Tribune* for a short time in the early 1980s, and in 1983 he founded *Phoenix* magazine. Over the years *Phoenix* has subjected Ireland's business, political, media and artistic circles to a great deal of unwanted attention, and has reported their affairs in a satirical, sometimes outrageous fashion.

MULCAHY, Michael (1952–), artist, b. Cork, ed. Clongowes, Crawford Municipal School of Art, Cork and NCAD. After graduating in 1973 he spent two years travelling in north-west Africa. His first solo exhibition was in Wexford in 1981. He had two further extended periods of travelling, in Australia and Papua New Guinea in the mid-1980s, and later in Korea, where he pursued his interest in Buddhism. Mulcahy has always drawn on his experiences of other cultures, but this is particularly true of his 'Do-Gong Series', which formed the basis of two major exhibitions in Dublin in 1994. Unlike his earlier work, which confronts the viewer with a maelstrom of riotously contrasting colours and vigorous brushwork, the paintings from the later series use bold but controlled calligraphy-like strokes to bring the canvas more gently to life, while retaining the same warmth and vibrancy.

MULCAHY, Richard (1886–1971), revolutionary, soldier and politician, b. Waterford, ed. Mount Sion and CBS, Thurles, m. Josephine (Min) Ryan, six children, d. 16 Dec. 1971. Elected MP 1918 and TD at all Dáil elections, apart from 1937 and 1943, until his retirement in 1961, representing first North Dublin and from 1944 Tipperary. Working for the Post Office in Dublin, he enrolled with the IRB in the first decade of the century; he also joined the Irish Volunteers and the Gaelic League. He took part in the Easter Rising at Ashbourne, Co. Meath and was interned at Frongoch. As IRA chief of staff he played a crucial role in the War of Independence. He took the pro-Treaty side in 1921 and during the Civil War was involved with MICHAEL COLLINS in covertly supplying arms to IRA members in Northern Ireland. Commander-in-chief after Collins's death, he vigorously pursued the Free State campaign against anti-Treaty republicans. As Minister for Defence in 1924 he was criticised by a government-appointed inquiry for his handling of the 'Army Mutiny' and resigned his office, but in 1927 he returned to the cabinet as Minister for Local Government.

In 1932 he joined the Army Comrades Association, soon to be known as the Blueshirts, a militant organisation with the stated aim of defending Cumann na nGaedheal meetings from IRA attacks. Its more moderate elements were absorbed into the Fine Gael political party, founded – by Mulcahy among others – in a merger of Cumann na nGaedheal with other groups opposed to Fianna Fáil. Leader of FG 1944–59. He helped to bring about the first inter-party coalition government in 1948, and because of objections to his role in the Civil War stood aside as Taoiseach in favour of JOHN A. COSTELLO. Minister for Education 1948–51 and 1954–7. As with many old Sinn Féin leaders, he was relatively conservative on social and economic issues but was selfless in his dedication to his role in public life.

MULCAHY, Risteárd (1922–), cardiologist, b. Dublin, s. of RICHARD MULCAHY, ed. UCD. Graduating MB, B.Ch., he proceeded MD 1948 and in that year was admitted MRCP, London, while medical registrar at the Hospital of SS John & Elizabeth. On his return to Dublin in 1950 he joined the visiting staff of St Vincent's Hospital, where some years later his interest in coronary heart disease led to his being placed in charge of a newly built coronary care ward. In 1963 he wrote two of the earliest clinical papers linking cholesterol and smoking to heart disease, marking the beginning of a long and influential series of studies into prevention and rehabilitation. Mulcahy was founder president of the Irish Heart Foundation and played a major role in setting up the Kilkenny Health Project, Ireland's community programme for cardiovascular disease prevention. In 1980 he was appointed to a chair of preventive cardiology, located at St Vincent's, which he occupied until 1988. After ostensibly retiring he continued to write, lecture and travel.

MULDOON, Paul (1951–), poet, b. Eglish, near Portadown, Co. Armagh, reared in Co. Tyrone, ed. St Patrick's College, Armagh and QUB, where he was a student of SEAMUS HEANEY. He worked for many years as a radio producer for BBC Northern Ireland before moving to the USA in the late 1980s. He has taught at Columbia and Princeton, where he is at present director of the creative writing programme. His volumes of poetry include *New Weather* (1973), *Mules* (1977), *Why Brownlee Left* (1980), *Quoof* (1983), *Meeting the British* (1987) and *Madoc: A Mystery* (1990). He was editor of *The Faber Book of Irish Verse* (1986). His poetry is slyly allusive and verbally dextrous, using the wit of a cool, worldly observer to invest the work with a sense of detachment. Of those Irish poets born since the end of the war, his critical reputation stands very high.

MULHOLLAND, Carolyn (1944–), artist, b. Lurgan, Co. Armagh, ed. Belfast College of Art. In 1965 she won the prize for sculpture from the Ulster Arts Club, and she had her first solo exhibition there in 1968. She has been awarded a number of Arts Council of Northern Ireland bursaries and travel awards. Sculptural commissions include work for the Church of the Resurrection, Cavehill, Belfast, 1982, New Ireland Assurance, Dublin 1986, the Dublin Sculpture Symposium 1988 and Irish Life, Dublin 1992. Her work is also represented in collections in Europe, South Africa and the USA. She has completed numerous portraits, including busts of R.H. McCandless and Joseph Tomelty. Her figurative sculptures, often made with bronze fibreglass and large in scale, are quite animated and are infused with sufficient energy and tension to create a strong sense of movement.

MULKERNS, Val (1925–), novelist and short story writer, b. Dublin, ed. Dominican College, Eccles Street, Dublin. Civil servant 1945–9, moved to London in 1951. Associate editor of the *Bell* 1952–4. She has contributed short stories to many magazines and anthologies, and her work has been broadcast on RTE radio and abroad. She wrote a weekly column for the *Evening Press* 1968–83 and

has been writer in residence at Mayo County Library, where she edited an anthology, *New Writings from the West* (1988). Short stories: *Antiquities* (1978), *An Idle Woman* (1980) and *A Friend of Don Juan* (1988). Novels: *A Time Outworn* (1951), *A Peacock Cry* (1954), *The Summerhouse* (1984), which won the AIB prize for literature, and *Very Like a Whale* (1986). Widely respected as a lecturer in creative writing, she has conducted classes in Europe, the USA and Canada. She is a distinguished participant in the Arts Council's writers-in-schools project.

MULLEN, Karl Daniel (1926–), international rugby player, b. Courtown Harbour, Co. Wexford, 26 Nov. 1926. He ranks as one of Ireland's greatest captains, leading his country to its only Grand Slam, in 1948, at the age of 21 and to a second Triple Crown the following year, as well as a Five Nations Championship title in 1951. From the Old Belvedere club in Dublin, he won 25 international caps (1947–52), 15 as captain, with ten wins as skipper. Regarded in his day as one of the world's finest hookers, he was rewarded with the captaincy of the first postwar Lions, touring New Zealand and Australia, and played in three of the five Tests. He was a national selector 1961–4.

MULLINS, Brian (1954–), Gaelic footballer, b. Dublin, 27 Sept. 1954. With the St Vincent's club, he won three Dublin County Championship medals and an All-Ireland Club Championship medal (1976). He was a major player in Dublin's All-Ireland victories in 1974, 1976 and 1977, before a car accident in 1980 halted his career. He returned to win another All-Ireland medal in 1983, and played on the losing sides of 1975, 1978, 1979, 1984 and 1985. Other achievements include National League victories (1976, 1978) and captaining Leinster to Railway Cup success. He also played rugby with Blackrock College and Clontarf.

MULROY, James (1899–1986), sergeant Garda Síochána, b. Straide, Co. Mayo, son of a farmer, d. 7 Aug. 1986. Irish Volunteers; joined the new police force, Ballsbridge Depot, 1922. First Garda heavyweight boxing champion. Won the first Walter Scott medal for valour, setting the high standard for the award of the Garda medal; the first unarmed policeman in Ireland to be so decorated. In 1923, at O'Callaghan's Mills, Co. Clare, he and a comrade on public house duty were held up by two armed criminals who demanded their notebooks. Mulroy disarmed one man and was shot at, wounded and beaten unconscious by the second. District Justice Dermot Gleeson described Guard Mulroy's bravery as a 'startling example of what an unarmed policeman can do against an armed coward'.

MUNNELLY, Tom (1944–), collector, b. Dublin. Leaving school at 15, he was employed as a factory worker until 1971, collecting songs on his own initiative. Recognising his impeccable research techniques, BREANDÁN BREATHNACH invited him to collect folk songs in the Department of Education project, later taken over by the Department of Irish Folklore at UCD. Moving to Miltown Malbay, Co. Clare in 1978 to continue fieldwork, he served as chairman and committee member of the WILLIE CLANCY Summer School until 1991. In 1982 he founded the Clare Folklore Society, in 1986 became a member of the Arts Council for two years and in 1987 founded and acted as chairman of the Irish Traditional Music Archive. Perhaps the most noteworthy example from his extensive range of cassettes, recordings and articles is *The Mount Callan Garland*, in that it represents an 18-year working relationship with a single singer and source of folklore, Tom Lenihan (d. 1990) of Miltown Malbay. Munnelly's personal contribution to the UCD folklore department amounts to the largest corpus of folk song ever collected in Ireland.

MURPHY, Denis, fiddler, one of the most celebrated exponents of the Sliabh Luachra fiddle style, along with his sister Julia Clifford. Born in Gneeveguilla, Co. Kerry, in the 1920s both became pupils of PÁDRAIG O'KEEFFE, as well as being musically influenced by their father. Apart from playing the jigs and reels common to many regional traditions, they specialised in the polkas and slides so strongly associated with the Cork/Kerry border. They often showed a specific family style, playing in octaves. In 1935 Julia settled in London and married the accordionist John Clifford, whom she had known since childhood. Denis emigrated to the USA in the

mid-1940s but later returned. In 1953 the Cliffords also returned to live in Newcastle West, Co. Limerick, where they formed the Star of Munster Céilí Band; within five years they were back in Britain, founding the Star of Munster Trio with their flute-playing son Billy.

MURPHY, Dervla (1931–), travel writer, ed. Ursuline Convent, Waterford. Her first book, *Full Tilt: Ireland to India on a Bicycle*, published in 1965, was a best-seller and an Alternative Book Society Choice for that year. Unquestionably Ireland's best travel writer, Murphy finds humour in situations that most of us would regard as uncomfortable, and her writing bursts with a love of humanity in its myriad manifestations. She wrote a study of Northern Ireland, *A Place Apart* (1978), which won the Christopher Ewart-Biggs memorial prize, and a memoir of her childhood, *Wheels within Wheels*. In *Changing the Problem: Post-Forum Reflections* (1984) she again examined Northern Ireland, in terms of its future. Her concern with nuclear weapon proliferation was mirrored in *Race to the Finish* (1981); *Tales from Two Cities* (1987) contained further social comment. Her recent travel books are *Cameroon with Egbert* (1989), *Transylvania and Beyond* (1992) and *The Ukimwi Road* (1993).

MURPHY, Richard (1927–), poet, b. Milford House, Co. Galway, spent his first eight years in Ceylon, ed. at home, public schools in England, Magdalen College, Oxford and Sorbonne. Became variously a reviewer, nightwatchman on the Erriff River, a teacher of English in Crete and writer in residence at Pacific Lutheran University, Washington State. His poems, often narrative in form, offer meditations on historical themes or on landscape, seascape or wildlife keenly observed. Much of his work is about the lives of fishermen in Connemara and on neighbouring islands. His journeys with friends and visitors on a local trawler which he bought serve as a backdrop to *Sailing to an Island* (1955) and *The Last Galway Hooker* (1961).

MURPHY, Séamus (1907–1975), sculptor, b. near Mallow, Co. Cork, 15 July 1907, ed. St Patrick's NS, Cork. Prompted by one of his teachers, DANIEL CORKERY, he left school early to study at the Crawford Municipal School of Art in Cork while working as an apprentice in a stoneyard. Winning the Gibson scholarship in 1931 enabled him to study at the Académie Colorossi. He knew Arthur O'Connor, the American sculptor, while in Paris but his work carries no hint of O'Connor's influence. Back in Cork he concentrated on carving public monuments and figures for church buildings but he also sculpted a number of portrait busts, including those of all the presidents of Ireland in his lifetime. His approach was representational, with an emphasis on strong lines, and he showed a special talent for hinting at the subject's personality. His bust of SEÁN O'FAOLAIN has been particularly admired, as have his bas-reliefs of the seasons, in the Fitzgerald Park, Cork. He was elected associate of the RHA in 1944 and MRHA in 1966. His autobiography, *Stone Mad* (1950), with its stories of the world of stone-carving and the craftsmen he had known, was highly praised – not least by his fellow Corkman SEÁN Ó TUAMA, who wrote of 'a sculptor who set headstones dancing with his carefree lore'.

MURPHY, Suzanne (1941–), soprano, b. Limerick, ed. Bruff Convent, Limerick and the College of Music, Dublin, where her teacher was Veronica Dunne. Made her operatic début with the Irish National Opera in *La Cenerentola* (Rossini) 1974. Joined the Welsh National Opera in 1976 as Constanze (*Die Entführung aus dem Serail*, Mozart) and has since performed over a dozen leading lyric coloratura roles with the company. Made her Vienna Staatsoper début in 1987 as Electra (*Idomeneo*, Mozart). She has performed worldwide and made numerous recordings. Awarded an honorary fellowship from Welsh Polytechnic in 1989.

MURPHY, Tom (1935–), playwright and novelist, b. Tuam, ed. St Patrick's College, Dublin as a metalwork teacher. Served on the board of the Abbey Theatre in the 1970s. Murphy has written 15 full-length plays, two one-acters and a number of adaptations. His plays fall into two categories: those set in and around Galway and written in a vein of closely observed satiric realism, and those which follow characters at the end of their tether through extremes of elation and despair in the symbolic settings of forest, church or psychiatrist's office.

His first full-length play, *A Whistle in the Dark* (1962), is a work of unrivalled verbal ferocity and genuine tragedy in its portrait of the Carney family, Dada and his sons, when they come to visit Michael and his wife in England. As they proceed to wreak havoc, Murphy stages his own attack on the well-made play; polite, formal exchange gives way to shouting, singing, elaborate physical mime, jokes, crosstalk, monologues, repeated words and motifs. Murphy balanced this tragedy with the comedy *A Crucial Week in the Life of a Grocer's Assistant*, where John Joe resists the urge to emigrate as a response to the pressures of family and friends.

Murphy himself moved to London in 1962, where he wrote *The Orphans*, his weakest play, *Famine*, his personal favourite, and *The Morning after Optimism*, his most ambitious. With the opening of the new Abbey Theatre in 1966 and of the Peacock Theatre the following year, there was a stage and company to perform his works and this, combined with the tax-free status accorded to writers, led him to return to Dublin in 1970. In 1975 *The Sanctuary Lamp* brought walkouts and heated debate back to the Abbey in its iconoclastic subversion of the rituals and dogma of the Catholic Church.

In 1983 he returned to the Abbey stage with his masterpiece, *The Gigli Concert*, a harrowing yet deadly funny three-hander playing out all the possibilities of Irishness and Englishness, man and woman, love and loathing, in an operatic context. For two years in the mid-1980s Murphy was writer in association with Galway's Druid Theatre, whose artistic director, GARRY HYNES, staged *Bailegangaire* in 1985 with SIOBHÁN MCKENNA in her final role as Mommo, a senile old woman confined to a bed and telling a never-completed story of her and Ireland's past in the chaotic conditions of the present.

MURPHY, William Martin (1844–1919), businessman and newspaper proprietor, b. Bantry, Co. Cork, 21 Nov. 1844, ed. Belvedere, d. Dublin, 26 June 1919. Took over the family contracting business 1863. Constructed churches, schools and bridges in Ireland, and railways and tramways in Britain and the Gold Coast. Director and then chairman of the Dublin United Tramways Company. In 1905 he restructured Parnell's *Irish Daily Independent* and made it, as the *Irish Independent*, the first halfpenny popular paper in order to break the monopoly of the Parnellite *Freeman's Journal*. Irish Party MP 1885–92. Owner of the *Irish Catholic*, the Imperial Hotel and Clery's department store, Dublin. Refused knighthood from Edward VII 1906. President of the Dublin Chamber of Commerce 1912–13; he revitalised that organisation and in Jan. 1913 gave the most novel and wide-ranging address the Chamber had heard, exhorting employers to 'consider with sympathy the conditions and wages of their employees' and to help remedy the 'insanitary surroundings of the poorer classes'. He had, he said, experienced no labour trouble in 50 years in business.

Later in 1913, when the tramway members of JAMES LARKIN's ITGWU went on strike for higher wages, a lock-out followed that brought riots, baton charges and starvation to 25,000 workers, paralysed the city and united the employers in a strong federation. Despite this victory, Murphy told employers in Jan. 1914 that the outcome did not absolve them from the obligation of seeing that their workers should 'receive a wage which will enable them to live at least in frugal comfort'. He and his *Irish Independent* condemned the 'insane and criminal' Easter Rising. Murphy opposed Partition at the Irish Convention 1917 and in *The Home Rule Act 1914 Exposed* (1917).

MURPHY, William Richard English (1890–1975), DSO, MC, major-general, commissioner DMP and deputy commissioner Garda Síochána, b. Danes Castle, Bannow, Co. Wexford, ed. QUB and UCD (MA), d. 5 Mar. 1975. After service in the National Army (GOC Kerry Command; command adjutant South-Western Command 1923), he was DMP commissioner 1923–5 and restored morale in the force, undermined by the 1913 Lock-out, the Easter Rising and the War of Independence. Deputy Garda commissioner 1925–55. Initiated the Garda Technical Bureau 1934. Organised the Local Security Force in the Emergency 1939–46. Secretary/treasurer Olympic Council of Ireland 1924, president Irish Amateur Boxing Association 1928–39, International Amateur Boxing Council: executive committee 1948, president of honour 1952.

MURRAY, Ann (1949–), mezzo-soprano, b. Dublin. One of the leading singers of her generation. Studied in Dublin, Manchester and London, making her début in 1974 with Scottish Opera in Aldeburgh. Married to tenor Philip Langridge. Has sung at the world's major opera houses, and is equally at home on the concert platform. Particularly admired for her portrayal of the 'trouser' roles such as Cherubino (*The Marriage of Figaro*, Mozart), the Composer (*Ariadne auf Naxos*, Richard Strauss) and Xerxes (Handel). Numerous commercial recordings encompass the operatic, oratorio and recital repertoire.

MURRAY, Charles (1917–), public servant and economist, b. Dublin, ed. Synge Street and London University. Joined civil service as executive officer in the Office of the Revenue Commissioners. Secretary of the Flour and Bread Tribunal, following whose report he was assigned to the Department of Agriculture. As assistant secretary in the Department of the Taoiseach he was the principal collaborator with T.K. WHITAKER in the preparation of *Economic Development* in 1958. This landmark document owed its origin largely to the sense of emergency precipitated by the traumatic experiences of the mid-1950s and by the unprecedented level of emigration revealed by the 1956 census. It led to the establishment of a committee of departmental secretaries, with Murray as co-ordinator, to draw up future development policy, which in turn gave rise to the government's first Programme for Economic Expansion. Murray was transferred to the Department of Finance in 1959 to head a new economic development branch, and in 1969 became secretary of the department. A founder member, first chairman and later president of the Institute of Public Administration. Governor of the Central Bank 1976–81. Hon. LL D (UCD). For a time deputy chairman of Co-operation North.

MURRAY, Ruby (1935–), singer, b. Belfast. Toured Northern Ireland as a child singer and made her first television appearance at the age of 12. In 1954 she travelled to London, where she became the resident singer on BBC television's *Quite Contrary*. Her first record release, 'Heartbeat', made the UK top five in 1954 and 'Softly, Softly' was number one the following year. In early 1955 she had five singles in the top 20. Other Ruby Murray songs include 'Happy Days and Lonely Nights' and 'You are my First Love'. In the mid-1950s she appeared in the film *A Touch of the Sun* with Frankie Howerd and Dennis Price and had her own television show. In the 1960s she toured with her then husband, Bernie Burgess, as a double act. A compilation album, *Ruby Murray's EMI Years*, was released in 1989.

MURRAY, Thomas Cornelius (1873–1959), playwright, b. Macroom, Co. Cork, 17 Jan. 1873, ed. St Patrick's College, Dublin, d. Dublin, 7 Mar. 1959. Taught in schools in Cork before being appointed headmaster of the Inchicore Model Schools, Dublin. He co-founded the Cork Little Theatre with TERENCE MACSWINEY, DANIEL CORKERY and Con O'Leary – the company produced his first play, *Wheel of Fortune*, in 1909. *Birthright*, staged by the Abbey Theatre the following year, established Murray as one of the country's leading playwrights. He wrote about a dozen other plays, notably *Maurice Harte* (1912) and *Autumn Fire* (1924). He also wrote poetry and a novel and contributed to the *Bell*, *New Ireland Review* and *Dublin Magazine*.

N

NAGLE, John C. (1910–1996), public servant, b. Cork, ed. CBC, UCC, UCD, TCD and Cambridge (B.Comm., M.Econ.Sc.). Joined the Department of Finance as administrative officer and was subsequently transferred to the Department of Agriculture, of which he was secretary from 1958 until he retired in 1971. Chairman (part-time) of the finance committee of the Food and Agriculture Committee of the UN and chairman of the EC Committee for the Control of Foot and Mouth Disease. He was the Irish delegate on countless trade missions abroad, representing agricultural interests. After his retirement he was chairman of the NCEA, which later conferred on him the honorary degree of LL D. Author of *Agricultural Trade Policy*.

NALLY, Dermot (1927–), public servant, b. Dublin, ed. Synge Street, UCD (BE Mech.) and London University (MA English language and literature). Worked in the ESB and OPW before becoming an administrative officer in the Department of Local Government in 1952. In 1973 he was appointed assistant secretary in the Department of the Taoiseach and in 1980 secretary to the government, a position he held until his retirement in 1993. At various times chairman of the Top Level Appointments Committee, member of the three-person Civil Service Commission, member of the boards of the Irish Productivity Council, An Foras Forbartha and the Institute of Public Administration. Part-time lecturer in public administration under the auspices of the City of Dublin Vocational Education Committee 1960–70. From 1973 he was the closest official adviser to five Taoisigh on EC and foreign relations generally, on Northern Ireland and on matters coming before government. One of the two Irish officials who negotiated Irish membership of the European Monetary System. On the negotiating team for the Sunningdale Agreement 1973, head of the Irish official delegation that negotiated the Anglo-Irish Agreement 1985 and eight years later the Downing Street Declaration.

NAPIER, Oliver (1935–), politician, b. 11 July 1935, ed. QUB. Solicitor. First political involvement was in New Ulster Movement. Founding member in 1970 of the Alliance Party, which aimed to attract support from both sides of the divided community in Northern Ireland. Leader Alliance Party 1972–84. Represented the party at the Sunningdale conference 1973 and headed the office of Law Reform in the power-sharing Executive 1974. Member of the NI Constitutional Convention 1975–6, Belfast City Council 1977–89 and the NI Assembly 1982–6 but failed in three attempts to secure election for East Belfast to Westminster parliament and in 1979 to European Parliament. His political career can fairly be judged a measure of the limited appeal of Alliance, with its middle-class image and middle-ground stance. Knighted in 1985, chaired the Standing Advisory Commission on Human Rights 1988–92.

NEALON, Ted (1929–), broadcaster and politician, b. Coolrecull, Co. Sligo, Nov. 1929, ed. St Nathy's College, Ballaghaderreen, Co. Roscommon. Journalist. Editor *Sunday Review* before becoming presenter and commentator on current affairs programming RTÉ 1965–75. Head of Government Information Services 1975–7. Elected TD (FG Sligo–Leitrim) 1981. Minister of State at the Department of Agriculture 1981–2 and at the Department of Posts and Telegraphs Feb.–Mar. 1982. Minister of State at the Department of the Taoiseach with special responsibility for Arts and Culture 1982–7 and at the Department of Communications with special responsibility for Broadcasting 1983–7. Editor and compiler of *Nealon's Guide to the Dáil and Seanad*, currently in its eighth edition.

NEESON, Liam (1953–), actor, b. Ballymena. Ireland's most successful film star to date, Neeson began his acting career as a bit-part player with the Lyric Theatre, Belfast in 1976. Leading roles soon followed and he played in many Abbey Theatre productions before director John Boorman spotted him in a performance of *Of Mice and Men*; he cast him – with GABRIEL BYRNE – in *Excalibur* (1981), as Sir Gawain. Neeson has since won acclaim as a very talented character actor, at home in demanding, sensitive parts. He shone as the monk in *The Mission* (1986), appeared in *Suspect* (1987), Clint Eastwood's *The Dead Pool*, in which he played a low-life director of low-rent horror movies (1988), and *The Big Man*, as a boxer (1990), turning in his finest performance to date as Oskar Schindler in Steven Spielberg's *Schindler's List* (1993), which earned him an Oscar nomination. Plays·the leading role in NEIL JORDAN's film *Michael Collins* due for release in late 1996.

NELIGAN, David (1899–1983), chief superintendent Garda Síochána, b. Templeglantine, Co. Limerick, parents both national teachers, d. 4 Oct. 1983. Policeman. Agent for MICHAEL COLLINS in the War of Independence. Colonel National Army, director of intelligence 1922–3. Rejoined DMP, chief superintendent Detective Division; took over as head of Crime Branch, Garda Síochána, on amalgamation of the two police forces in 1925. Suspended from duty 1932, having authorised a collection for detectives dismissed for ill-treating prisoners at Kilrush, Co. Clare. Out of the force, a desk was found for him in the Land Commission. In retirement, reading voraciously, he made himself an expert in medieval French history.

NELSON, Havelock (1917–1996), composer and conductor, b. Cork, d. Belfast, 5 Aug. 1996. Joined BBC Northern Ireland in 1947, working as conductor, accompanist and broadcaster. Founder and director of the Studio Opera Group. Director of the Ulster Singers 1954. Artistic director of Trinidad and Tobago Opera Company 1976. He also conducted with Sadler's Wells Opera and RTÉ and adjudicated at music festivals worldwide. Noted for his choral and vocal arrangements of Irish folk music. Awarded doctorates in music by several universities in Ireland, Great Britain and Trinidad; OBE 1966.

NEWMAN, William Alexander (Alec) (1905–1972), journalist and editor, b. Waterford, ed. Royal Academical Institution and TCD, d. Dublin, 6 Mar. 1972. Newman was a distinguished classics student at TCD and taught at the High School, Dublin 1927–9. He also contributed freelance articles to *The Irish Times* during this period, and in 1930 joined the staff as a leader writer. He became assistant editor to R.M. SMYLLIE in 1934, and on Smyllie's death 20 years later became editor, a position he held until 1961. He then moved to the *Irish Press*, where he worked as leader writer and commentator on current affairs. Newman had an encyclopedic memory and was a regular participant on Radio Éireann's *Information Please*, the BBC's *Round Britain Quiz* and, in the 1960s, RTÉ's newspaper quiz programme, *Information Please*.

Nic DHIARMADA, Bríona (1957–), academic and critic, b. Waterford, raised in Co. Wexford, ed. TCD and UCD. Has written extensively in Irish-language journals on contemporary Irish literature, in particular on the poetry of NUALA NÍ DHOMHNAILL, and in the area of critical theory, with special emphasis on feminist theory. She is an authority on the early years of the language revival in the last century, especially on the influence of women in that movement. Lecturer at UCD and a contributing editor to vol. 4 of the *Field Day Anthology of Irish Writing*. Publications include: *Ceist na Teanga: Dioscúrsa na Gaeilge, An Fhilíocht agus Dioscúrsa na mBan* (1982), *Bláthú an Traidisiún* (1987) and *Léirmheas ar Cé hí sin Amuigh?* (1993).

Nic DHONNACHADHA, Lil (Lilian Duncan) (1891–1984), teacher and Irish-language worker, b. Belfast, 9 Oct. 1891, ed. Alexandra and TCD (one of the ten first women graduates), d. 9 Mar. 1984. Principal of Coláiste Móibhí, the Church of Ireland preparatory college for national teachers, until she retired in 1951. An ardent member of the Gaelic League and of Cumann Gaelach na hEaglaise (The Irish Guild of the Church), and a source of inspiration and encouragement for the latter's regular Irish services at Christ Church Cathedral. She contributed articles to the *Revue Celtique* and *Eriú*. The Irish-language version of the *Book of Common Prayer* (1965) owed much to her work, as did the new translation of the New Testament into Irish (1970).

Nic EOIN, Máirín, academic, biographer and critic. Has written extensively in Irish-language periodicals on the work of modern poets and in particular on the way women have been represented in the texts. Lecturer in Irish department at St Patrick's College, Dublin. Publications include: *An Litríocht Réigiúnach* (1982), *Eoghan Ó Tuairisc: Beatha agus Saothar* (1988) and 'Léiriú na mBan sna Leabhair' from E. Ó hAnluain (ed.), *Leath na Spéire* (1992).

Ní CHUILLEANÁIN, Eiléan (1942–), poet, b. Cork, d. of EILIS DILLON, ed. Ursuline Convent, Cork, UCG and Oxford, m. MACDARA WOODS. One of Ireland's leading poets, with a special affinity for Renaissance verse. She won the *Irish Times* poetry award in 1966 and the PATRICK KAVANAGH award in 1973. Together with Woods, PEARSE HUTCHINSON and LELAND BARDWELL, she founded the literary magazine *Cyphers* in 1975, and is still joint editor. She has lectured in medieval and Renaissance English at TCD since 1966. Her poetry hymns the natural world in strikingly idiosyncratic fashion; there is water, water everywhere, it seems, but myth and magic too, found by Ní Chuilleanáin in unexpected places. Collections: *Acts and Monuments* (1972), *Site of Ambush* (1975), *The Second Voyage* (1977), *Cork*, with artist Brian Lalor (1977), *The Rose-geranium* (1981), *The Magdalene Sermon* (1989) and *The Brazen Serpent* (1994). She has also edited *Irish Women: Image and Achievement* (1985).

Ní DHOMHNAILL, Nuala (1952–), poet, b. England, ed. Lancashire, Ventry, Co. Kerry and UCC. She has lived in Holland and Turkey, where she taught at a university in Ankara 1972–80. She was later a tutor in Irish at Maynooth 1985–8. She is one of the most important poets writing in Irish, a language she describes as being imbued with 'Hag Energy', never having been 'patriarchalised' – thus an ideal vehicle for her verse, which treats of the realities of women in modern Ireland. Ní Dhomhnaill's work has been extensively translated by MICHAEL HARTNETT. Publications include: *An Dealg Droighin* (1981), *Féar Suaithinseach* (1984), *Rogha Dánta*, dual language with trans. by Hartnett (1986), *Pharaoh's Daughter*, trans. by various poets, and *Bunduchas* (1990), *Feis*, ed. with Philip O'Leary (1991), *The Astrakhan Cloak*, English trans. by PAUL MULDOON (1992), *Spíonáin is Róiseanna Compánach don Chaiséad* (1993) and *Jumping off Shadows*, ed. (1995).

Ní DHUIBHNE, Éilís (1954–), writer and academic, b. Dublin, ed. Scoil Bhríde, Scoil Chaitríona and UCD, where she took a Ph.D. in Irish folklore. She has lived most of her life in Ireland, with some sojourns in Scandinavia. Winner of a number of literary prizes and scholarships, she is a keeper at the National Library and lectures on Irish folklore at UCD. Contributor of scholarly articles to *Béaloideas* and *Sinsear*, of poetry to national papers and anthologies; she has furthermore selected material for the folklore section of the fourth volume of the *Field Day Anthology of Irish Writing*. She has published a novel – *The Bray House* (1990) – and short stories: *Blood and Water* (1988) and *Eating Women is Not Recommended* (1991). She is also the author of three books for children: *The Uncommon Cormorant* (1990), *Hugo and the Sunshine Girl* (1991) and *The Hiring Fair* (1993), and editor of *Voices on the Wind: Women Poets of the Celtic Twilight* (1995).

Ní GHLINN, Áine (1955–), poet, broadcaster and teacher, b. Co. Tipperary, ed. UCD. Received Oireachtas na Gaeilge prize in 1985. Publications include *An Chéim Bhriste* (1984) and *Gairdín Pharthais* (1988).

NOLAN, Christopher (1965–), poet and short story writer. Nolan's story is one of the most poignant and courageous to emerge from Ireland in recent times. An accident at birth left him severely brain-damaged and physically disabled, yet with his mother's help he learned to type with a stick strapped to his forehead. Thus was created a volume of poems and short stories, *Dam-burst of Dreams* (1981), that received the highest accolades from critics and public alike for its intelligence and beauty. He followed up this achievement with an unusual yet highly readable autobiography, *Under the Eye of the Clock* (1987).

NOLAN, John James (1887–1952), academic, b. Omagh. Graduated from UCD in 1909 and joined the staff of the university the following year. He succeeded J.A. McCLELLAND as Professor of Experimental Physics in 1920 and became registrar in 1940, holding both posts until his death. Together with his brother P.J. NOLAN, he established the Atmospheric Physics Research Group in UCD, which came to be known internationally as the 'Nolan School'. PRIA 1949–52.

NOLAN, Patrick J. (1894–1984), academic, b. Omagh, ed. UCD (B.Sc. 1914, M.Sc. 1915, Ph.D. 1922, D.Sc. 1930). Boyle medal 1971. Assistant in Department of Experimental Physics UCD 1920, lecturer 1929, Professor of Geophysics 1954–64. Shortly after World War I he spent a period working in the Cavendish Laboratory in Cambridge under Sir J.J. Thompson. When he returned to Dublin he concentrated on atmospheric physics; together with L.W. Pollak he developed the photoelectric nucleus counter, the standard instrument for measuring condensation nuclei (tiny particles present in the atmosphere on which water vapour condenses). With brother J.J. NOLAN he established the Atmospheric Physics Research Group in UCD, which is still thriving.

NOONAN, Michael (1943–), politician, b. Limerick, May 1943, ed. St Patrick's School, Glin, Co. Limerick, St Patrick's College, Dublin and UCD. Secondary teacher. Elected TD (FG Limerick East) 1981. Minister for Justice 1982–6, Industry and Commerce 1986–7, Energy 1987. Minister for Health since 1994.

NORMAN, Conolly (1853–1908), psychiatrist, b. All Saints' Glebe, Newtown Cunningham, Co. Donegal, fifth s. of the Revd Hugh Norman, ed. at home, because of his delicate health, and TCD, m. Mary Emily Kenny 1882, d. 23 Feb. 1908. Graduated LQCPI and LRCSI in 1874. After much experience in county asylums in Monaghan and Castlebar, Norman was appointed resident medical superintendent to the Richmond District Asylum (now St Brendan's Hospital), Ireland's largest mental institution. Here he did what he could to change prevailing punitive attitudes, to brighten and decorate the wards and to provide facilities for games. A member of the Medico-Psychological Association and its president 1894–5, he was joint editor of the *Journal of Mental Science*. He contributed to Tuke's *Dictionary of Psychological Medicine* and Allbutt's *System of Medicine*. Hon. MD (TCD), fellow and vice-president of the RCPI, Norman was one of the best-known psychiatrists of his time.

NORRIS, David (1944–), academic and campaigner for homosexuals' rights, ed. St Andrew's College and High School, Dublin

and TCD. An international authority on the works of JAMES JOYCE, he taught in the Department of English in TCD from 1968. Elected to Seanad Éireann (DU) 1987. He has written widely in scholarly journals and is chairman of the James Joyce Cultural Centre in Dublin. A witty conversationalist, he established a national reputation as a lecturer and broadcaster and also as one of the first and most prominent people openly to declare his homosexuality. He campaigned for the decriminalisation of homosexual acts between consenting adults and successfully challenged Irish legislation, securing a European Court ruling in 1988 that Irish law in this regard was in contravention of the European Convention on Human Rights. As a result the law was changed in 1993 to legalise such acts between consenting adults aged over 17.

NORTON, William (1900–1963), politician, b. Kildare, ed. locally. He came into politics via the trade union movement, after his election at 20 to the national executive of the Post Office Workers' Union, in which he held various executive positions for 37 years. First elected to the Dáil for Kildare in 1926, he became leader of the Labour Party following the 1932 election. Although politically conservative – he succeeded in securing the removal of the term 'Workers' Republic' from the party's constitution after the Catholic hierarchy had criticised it – he also made strenuous efforts to heal the division in the labour movement by encouraging the return of JAMES LARKIN to the parliamentary party after the 1943 election. The ITGWU, and all its associated TDs, disaffiliated to form National Labour, creating a split which lasted until after the formation of the inter-party government in 1948, in which Norton was the first Labour Party leader to be appointed Tánaiste; he was also Minister for Social Welfare. Again Tánaiste in the second inter-party government 1954–7, he held the portfolio of Industry and Commerce, but when the party lost seven seats in the 1957 election it became evident that a change at the top was imminent. He resigned the leadership in 1960, to be succeeded by BRENDAN CORISH. He was still a TD for Kildare at his death; his son, Patrick Norton, lost the ensuing by-election and later joined Fianna Fáil.

O

Ó BEIRN, Séamus (*c.* 1882–1935), dispensary doctor and MOH, b. Tawin, an island off the Co. Galway coast, ed. Queen's College, Galway. Graduated MB (RUI) in 1905 and took the DPH in 1908. When he was appointed medical officer to Clonbur dispensary district, typhus and tuberculosis were still familiar diseases. He gave lectures through Irish on the importance of sanitation, attracting support from PATRICK PEARSE and from the Gaelic League, of which he was a member. Funds from the League enabled him to employ a locum and devote himself to his lectures on anatomy, physiology and hygiene at centres throughout Connemara. He visited cottages and advised on such measures as the installation of concrete floors or outhouses; he also produced a book on the subject of hygiene.

O'BOYLE, Seán (1908–1979), collector and Gaelic scholar, b. Belfast, ed. St Malachy's College, Belfast and QUB. On graduation he took up a position at St Patrick's College, Armagh, where he taught until retirement in 1973. Between 1952 and 1954 he engaged in a survey of the folk music of Ulster in co-operation with Peter Kennedy and SEAMUS ENNIS. This resulted in two major radio series on the BBC Northern Ireland service, *As I Roved Out* and *Music on the Hearth*, which he compiled and presented and which had an impact far beyond the catchment area of the station. Publications include *Cnusacht de Cheoltaí Uladh*, *The Irish Song Tradition* and *Ogham, The Poet's Secret*.

Ó BRÁDAIGH, Ruairí (1932–), republican. He joined the IRA as a student and was active in the border campaign of the 1950s. IRA chief of staff 1958–9 and 1961–2, elected TD (SF Longford–Westmeath) 1957. When the republican movement split in Jan. 1970 he became the first president of Provisional Sinn Féin. In 1973 he was convicted of IRA membership and sentenced to six months' imprisonment. He attended the Feakle talks between the IRA leadership and Protestant churchmen in 1974. Ó Brádaigh lost the leadership of SF to GERRY ADAMS in 1983 and suffered a major defeat in 1986 with the dropping of the party's abstentionist policy. He was leader of a faction which left the party and went on to form Republican Sinn Féin.

Ó BRIAIN, Liam (1888–1974), revolutionary and scholar, b. Dublin, ed. O'Connell School, UCD, Germany and France, d. Dublin, 11 Aug. 1974. Interned for two years for taking part in the Easter Rising and stood unsuccessfully as Sinn Féin candidate for Mid-Armagh in the 1918 election. He served a further two terms of imprisonment, the second for presiding over an illegal republican court during the War of Independence. Professor of Romance Languages UCG 1917–58. He helped to establish the Irish-language theatre Taibhdhearc na Gaillimhe in 1928 and translated several plays from French, Spanish and English into Irish, including Molière's *Le dépit amoureux* (*Grádh Cásmhar*), Diego Fabbri's *Procés à Jésu* (*An Chúis i nAghaidh Íosa*) and J.M. SYNGE's *Deirdre of the Sorrows* (*Déirdre an Bhróin*). He also worked as a broadcaster and served as chairman of An Club Leabhar. In 1951 he was made a Chevalier of the Légion d'honneur.

O'BRIEN, Conor Cruise (1917–), intellectual, writer and politician, b. Dublin, Nov. 1917, ed. Sandford Park, Dublin and TCD, m. first Christine Foster 1939 (dissolved 1962), m. second MÁIRE MHAC AN TSAOI 1962. A brilliant undergraduate career led to a series of appointments in the public service, most notably in the Department of External Affairs, where he was active in the anti-partition campaign in the 1940s. Secondment to the UN during the Congo crisis in 1961 led to his resignation in circumstances involving conflicting international interests. Chancellor of the University of Ghana 1962–5, Albert Schweitzer Professor of Humanities at New York University 1965–9. He returned to Ireland to win a seat for the rejuvenated Labour Party in the 1969 general election.

While serving as Minister for Posts and Telegraphs in the 1973–7 coalition government, he developed an articulate and deepening hostility to militant Irish republicanism. His challenging of traditional nationalist ideology caused considerable dissension within the Labour Party and controversy outside it. In 1977 he lost his seat but was elected to Seanad Éireann for the DU constituency, resigning in 1978 to become editor-in-chief of the *Observer*, where he remained until 1981. He has held visiting professorships and lectureships in a wide range of universities, particularly in the USA, and has been a prolific journalist, most notably for *The Irish Times* and, more recently, for the *Irish Independent*. Pro-Vice Chancellor of the University of Dublin until 1994. In 1996 he joined the United Kingdom Unionist Party to express his support for nonsectarian unionism. He secured a seat in the NI Forum following the elections in May 1996 and was a member of his party's delegation at the all-party talks which began in June. Publications include: *Maria Cross* (1952), *Parnell and his Party* (1957), *To Katanga and Back* (1962), *States of Ireland* (1973), *The Siege* (1986) and his magnum opus on Edmund Burke, *The Great Melody* (1992).

O'BRIEN, Dermot, Gaelic footballer and musician. A centre-half forward, he played on the Louth team which lost the All-Ireland senior football semi-final in 1953. He captained the county in its All-Ireland victory in 1957, when Cork were defeated by two points, Louth's sole such success in modern times, the only two previous wins having been in 1910 and 1912. He went on to become a renowned accordionist and bandleader.

O'BRIEN, Edna (1932–), writer, b. Tuamgraney, Co. Clare, ed. Convent of Mercy, Loughrea, Co. Galway and the Pharmaceutical College, Dublin. Her novels *The Country Girls* (1960), *Girl with Green Eyes* (first published as *The Lonely Girl*, 1962) and *Girls in their Married Bliss* (1964), which formed a trilogy, were controversial when they first appeared. The author's offence in the eyes of the censorious was that she dared to suggest that Irish girls might harbour sexual instincts and desires. She went on to write with equal success on more sophisticated and cosmopolitan themes. Among her other novels are *August is a Wicked Month*

(1965), *Johnny I Hardly Knew You* (1977) and *Returning* (1982). She has also written volumes of short stories, including *The Love Object* (1968) and *A Fanatic Heart* (1985).

O'BRIEN, Flann (1911–1966), pen-name of Brian O'Nolan, who also wrote under the pseudonym Myles na gCopaleen, b. Strabane, Co. Tyrone, 5 Oct. 1911, ed. Blackrock and UCD (graduating in Celtic languages 1932), d. Dublin, 1 Apr. 1966. Carried out linguistics research in Germany before joining the Irish civil service, from which he retired in 1952 due to ill health. His first book, *At Swim-two-birds* (1939), a comic fantasy, incorporates plots within plots, mythological Celtic characters and vignettes of student life in Dublin. Other publications include *The Third Policeman* (written 1940, published 1967), *An Béal Bocht* (1941) – his only book in Irish – and *The Hard Life* (1961), and plays *Faustus Kelly* (1943) and *Thirst*. For over 20 years he wrote a richly imaginative satirical column in *The Irish Times* entitled 'An Cruiskeen Lawn'. *The Dalkey Archive* (1964) was dramatised by HUGH LEONARD as *When the Saints Go Cycling In* and staged at the 1965 Dublin Theatre Festival. O'Brien's talent for undermining the pomposity, hypocrisy and ignorance of persons pretending to a concern for historical and cultural values in mid-century Ireland tended to conceal the quality of his writing. So also did his inability to resist poking affectionate fun at some of his own enthusiasms, not least the literary devices typical of the great sagas in the Irish language. O'Brien's subject matter was so entertaining that the genius at work in his play on words, his experimentation with ideas and his profound commitment to true scholarship was largely overlooked in his lifetime. His status as a major figure of modern Irish literature was acquired posthumously and continues to grow.

O'BRIEN, George (1892–1973), academic, economist and senator, b. Dublin, ed. CUS, UCD and King's Inns, d. Dublin, 31 Dec. 1973. Called to Bar 1913. Made a dramatic impact on the economic thinking of the day with his three-volume *Economic History of Ireland* (1918–21). Professor of the National Economics of Ireland UCD 1926–61, also of Political Economy 1930–61. His analyses of the economic aspects of subjects as diverse as the Protestant reformation and the partition of Ireland won him international respect – not least from John Maynard Keynes. He served on many government committees and was particularly influential on the Banking Commission 1934–8, on which he clashed famously with ALFRED O'RAHILLY. Represented the NUI in the Seanad 1948–65.

O'BRIEN, Kate (1897–1974), writer, b. Co. Limerick, 3 Dec. 1897, ed. Laurel Hill, Limerick and UCD, d. Kent, 13 Aug. 1974. Worked in London as a journalist for the *Manchester Guardian* and in Spain as a governess. Her first literary success was the play *Distinguished Villa*, which had a three-month run in London during 1926. Her first novel, *Without my Cloak* (1931), won both the Hawthornden and James Tait Black memorial prizes. It was followed by *The Ante-room* (1934), *Mary Lavelle* (1936) and *The Land of Spices* (1941), which was banned in Ireland on the strength of a single sentence hinting at homosexual practices. Much of her work concerned the struggle of the individual (individual women especially) to find self-identity notwithstanding the conformity encouraged by social mores, religious norms and the genuine but stifling affection within the family circle. *The Last of Summer* appeared in 1943, and, perhaps her finest novel, *That Lady*, set in 16th-century Spain, was published in 1946. O'Brien was refused entry to Spain for the next 11 years because of its portrayal of Philip II. A dramatisation of the book played on Broadway in 1949. She also produced travel books and biography.

O'BRIEN, Tommy (1905–1988), broadcaster, b. and d. Clonmel. Worked as a journalist in the *Clonmel Nationalist*, of which he eventually became editor. Music – especially opera – was his abiding passion, however, and his collection of records grew to be one of the largest in private hands in Ireland. In 1947 he began to broadcast a weekly radio programme entitled *Your Choice and Mine*, which established him as a national institution. His rich, creamy Tipperary brogue allied to a plain man's enthusiasm brought the world of grand opera to a popular audience.

O'BRIEN, Vincent (1917–), horse trainer, b. Churchtown, Co. Cork, 9 Apr. 1917. Before starting as a trainer in Co. Cork in 1943, he was an amateur jockey, riding his first winner in the same year. Ballydoyle House in Co. Tipperary, where he moved in 1951, ranks among the world's greatest training centres, and he initially had notable success with jumpers. He won all the major National Hunt races, including the Grand Nationals of 1953 (Early Mist), 1954 (Royal Tan) and 1955 (Quare Times), four Cheltenham Gold Cups and the Champion Hurdle, which Hatton's Grace won four times. In flat racing he trained winners of 16 English Classics, a run which included six Epsom Derbys, as well as 27 Irish Classics. Among his most famous horses was Nijinsky. He won three Prix de l'Arc de Triomphe, in 1958 (Ballymoss) and 1977–8 (Alleged). O'Brien's partnership with Lester Piggott is one of racing's legends. Ireland's champion trainer 13 times, and in Britain on the flat in 1966–7 and on jumps 1952–3 and 1954–5. He retired in 1994.

O'BRIEN, William (1852–1928), journalist and politician, b. Mallow, Co. Cork, 2 Oct. 1852, ed. Cloyne Diocesan College and Queen's College, Cork, d. London, 25 Feb. 1928. Edited Parnellite paper *United Ireland* 1881–90, spent time in prison for his virulent opinions. MP (IP Mallow) 1883, launched Plan of Campaign with JOHN DILLON and Timothy Harrington in 1886. Anti-Parnellite at 'split', founded United Irish League and helped reunify the Irish Parliamentary Party. Edited his own paper, the *Irish People*, 1899–1908. Supported the Wyndham Act, thereby quarrelling with Dillon. Formed All for Ireland League 1910, dedicated to nationalist–unionist reconciliation. Retired from politics 1918. Wrote novels and reminiscences.

O'BRIEN, William (1881–1968), trade unionist, b. Ballygurteen near Clonakilty, Co. Cork, 23 Jan. 1881, ed. St Patrick's School, Drumcondra, Dublin, d. Bray, Co. Wicklow, 30 Oct. 1968. Apprenticed as a tailor 1898. TD 1922–3, 1927 and 1937–8; president Trades Union Congress 1913, 1918, 1925 and 1941. One of the pioneers of Irish trade unionism and labour politics, he received his initial political education from his two older brothers, both committed socialists. Joined the Irish Socialist Republican Party in 1898. He helped JAMES LARKIN to establish the ITGWU in 1908–9, although the two would later become bitter enemies. Secretary of the Lock-out committee in 1913. He was deported and interned in England after the Easter Rising and again in 1920; on the second occasion he gained his release after a hunger strike. Full-time official with the ITGWU from 1909 and general secretary for 22 years. A key figure in the split in the Irish labour movement during the 1940s.

Ó BROIN, León (1902–1990), public servant, b. Dublin, ed. CBS, d. 26 Feb. 1990. After school worked in Great Southern Railways, Kingsbridge and in the agriculture department of the First Dáil. Called to the Bar in 1924 and in 1925 became an administrative officer in the Department of Finance as a result of the first examination held for the grade in the Irish Free State. Regional commissioner 1940–45, secretary Department of Posts and Telegraphs 1946–67. Had overall responsibility for Radio Éireann until RTÉ was established in 1961. Friend and colleague of FRANK DUFF, he edited the Legion of Mary journal. Combined a career in charge of the largest government department with a considerable amount of writing, many of his books dealing with the period surrounding the establishment of the state: of special importance as contributions to Irish history were *Dublin Castle and the 1916 Rising* (1966) and *In Great Haste: The Letters of Michael Collins and Kitty Kiernan* (1983; posthumous extended edition ed. Cian Ó hEigeartaigh 1995).

Ó BUACHALLA, Domhnall (1866–1963), Governor-General Irish Free State, b. Maynooth, Co. Kildare. Led Irish Volunteers from Maynooth to Dublin during the Easter Rising. TD 1918. Opposed the Treaty. Founder member of Fianna Fáil. In 1932, at EAMON DE VALERA's instigation, he was appointed governor-general as a figurehead to play down the significance of the office.

O'BYRNE, John (1884–1954), lawyer, b. Co. Wicklow, ed. Patrician College, Tullow, Co. Carlow and UCD (MA 1908), d. 14 Jan. 1954. Served in civil service in London and in Irish Land Commission in Dublin, participated in Sinn Féin movement. Called to the Bar 1911, legal adviser to Irish delegation at Anglo-Irish Treaty negotiations 1921, member of Irish Free State Constitutional Committee 1922, which drafted the IFS con-

stitution, and of Judiciary Committee 1923, which reorganised the court system. Senior Counsel 1924, Attorney-General 1924–6, High Court judge 1926–40, Supreme Court judge 1940. Close friend of W.T. COSGRAVE.

Ó CADHAIN, Máirtín (1906–1970), short story writer, novelist and teacher, b. in Irish-speaking area of Spiddal, Co. Galway, ed. St Patrick's College, Dublin. Qualified as a teacher 1926. In the 1930s he joined the IRA and was dismissed from his job. Interned at the Curragh Camp, Co. Kildare 1940–44. He joined the translation staff of Dáil Éireann in 1949, became a lecturer in modern Irish at TCD 1956 and Professor of Irish 1969. Received the Irish-American Cultural Institute award in 1967 and was the first writer in Irish to become a member of the IAL. Ó Cadhain was an authority on Irish literature and culture and contributed to the German encyclopedia of world literature. He translated from Scottish Gaelic, Welsh and Breton into Irish, as well as from English and French. Considered the most outstanding writer in Irish of his generation, both at home and abroad, he is remembered in particular for his evocation of rural intrigues. His writing style, however, was complex and this served further to limit the already limited readership which he could hope to reach through the medium of his native language. On his death a number of unpublished manuscripts were found, some of them evidence of his perfectionism, which inhibited publication of any text before he was entirely satisfied with it. His novel *Cré na Cille* (1949) was chosen by UNESCO for translation into a number of other European languages. Other publications include: *Idir Shúgradh agus Dáiríre* (1939), *An Braon Broghach* (1948), *Cois Caoláire* (1953), *An tSraith ar Lár* (1967), *An tSraith dhá Tógáil* (1970) and *An tSraith Tógtha* (1977).

O'CALLAGHAN, Julie (1954–), poet, b. Chicago, ed. USA, moved to Dublin 1974, m. DENNIS O'DRISCOLL. Her first collection, *Edible Anecdotes and Other Poems* (1983), was a Poetry Book Society Recommendation. This was followed by *Taking my Pen for a Walk* (1988) and *What's What* (1991). She has also written an atmospheric pen portrait of the TCD library hall entitled 'The Long Room Gallery' (1994). O'Callaghan has not only a sharp eye for her surroundings but an ear so finely attuned to contemporary Dublin speech patterns that she can render them flawlessly and with great wit and feeling. She has also written several collections of poetry for children, including *Bright Lights Blaze Out*, with Alan Bold and Gareth Owen (1986). She is a librarian at TCD.

O'CALLAGHAN, Patrick (Pat) (1905–1991), athlete, b. Kanturk, Co. Cork, 15 Sept. 1905, d. Clonmel, Dec. 1991. He first represented Ireland in 1921, and won the gold medal in the hammer (51.39 m) at the 1928 Amsterdam Olympics (having taken up the sport only the previous year) and again at the Los Angeles Games in 1932 (53.92 m). He set European records in 1931 and 1933, and bettered the world record with 59.56 at Fermoy on 22 Aug. 1937, but this was not recognised since political disagreement meant that the Irish governing body was not affiliated. Other Irish achievements: six hammer titles (1927, 1928, 1930–32, 1935), five shot-put (1930–32, 1934, 1935), four 56 lb weight (1928, 1930–32), three high jump (1930–32) and one discus (1931). A qualified doctor by age 20, he was too young to practise in Ireland so he served in the RAF Medical Corps 1926–8.

Ó CAOIMH, Pádraig (1897–1964), secretary of the GAA, b. Roscommon, ed. CBS, Cork, where he later became a teacher, d. Dublin, 15 May 1964. He joined the Irish Volunteers in 1916 and served as an active service captain with the 1st Cork Brigade. Arrested in Dec. 1920 and sentenced to 15 years' penal servitude, he was in prison in England until his release in 1922. He opposed the Anglo-Irish Treaty of 1921 and fought on the republican side during the Civil War. At the end of hostilities he returned to teaching, before becoming general secretary of the GAA in 1929. He held that office until his death, by which time the Association had become the largest and most powerful sporting organisation in the country. Páirc Uí Chaoimh in Cork is named in his honour.

O'CASEY, Sean (1880–1964), playwright and prose writer, b. Dublin, 30 Mar. 1880, m. actress Eileen Carey 1927, d. 18 Sept. 1964. John Casey, as he was known until his adulthood, was the youngest surviving son of clerk Michael Casey and Susan Archer. Sickly as a child, he was educated mostly at home. The

Church (St Barnabas for Sunday school) and the theatre (amateur dramatics) were two major educative forces, and the oral influence of the Bible and of Shakespeare and Boucicault emerged later in his writing. O'Casey grew up in the grinding poverty and overcrowded tenements of inner-city Dublin in the late 19th century; these furnished the settings of his plays and the conditions he laboured against during a long, active life. He joined a succession of organisations: nationalist at first (the Gaelic League, the IRB), then socialist (the ITGWU with JAMES LARKIN). He became increasingly hostile to the takeover of the socialist movement in Ireland by the middle-class nationalists and was especially critical of JAMES CONNOLLY for throwing in his lot with PATRICK PEARSE in 1916, views which inform his most famous and controversial play, *The Plough and the Stars*.

Having seen OLIVER ST JOHN GOGARTY'S *Blight: The Tragedy of Dublin* at the Abbey Theatre in 1917, O'Casey decided to become a dramatist, resolving that he could do better in portraying the experience of inner-city life. The first three plays he submitted were rejected but not without words of encouragement, from Lady GREGORY in particular. The fourth, *The Shadow of a Gunman*, was accepted without alterations and staged at the Abbey on 12 Apr. 1923. *Juno and the Paycock* followed on 3 Mar. 1924, *The Plough and the Stars* on 28 Feb. 1926.

According to LENNOX ROBINSON these plays saved the Abbey from bankruptcy; this was no less true artistically. They made three innovative contributions to Irish drama: offering characters who spoke a recognisable Dublin idiom, using an urban rather than a pastoral setting, and treating of recent and still vivid moments of historical crisis – the War of Independence (*Shadow*), the Civil War (*Juno*) and the Easter Rising (*Plough*). The last led to protests, for the events were treated not in terms of a nationalist or even Yeatsian heroism but with a revisionist, disillusioned realism. O'Casey's plays put in the foreground the lives of the people on whose behalf these battles were ostensibly fought and registered how little the conditions of their lives were altered for the better. They mixed high with low, classical tragedy with music-hall repartee and song, melodramatic emotional extremes with unflinching satire, and furnished a memorable ensemble of characters (played by such Abbey stalwarts as BARRY FITZGERALD, F.J. McCORMICK and SARA ALLGOOD) who spoke with great verbal resource and wit while barely surviving in material terms.

The Silver Tassie, which took World War I as its subject, was rejected by the Abbey. O'Casey responded by vigorously defending his choice of material and his use of expressionist techniques to represent the horrors of the battlefield. But by this time he was living in London and relations with the Abbey, once broken, were never to be repaired (despite the fact that it belatedly staged *Tassie* in 1953). He continued to write plays for the rest of his life, in the main politically socialist and satirical-visionary comedies (*Purple Dust* and *Red Roses for Me* notable among them). These broke increasingly with the style of his earlier plays and drew on a wide range of music, dancing and stylised visual elements. He suffered from the lack of a working relationship with a living theatre and these plays have yet to receive a fully satisfactory staging.

O'Casey also wrote a series of autobiographical volumes, six in all, from *I Knock at the Door* (1939) to *Sunset and Evening Star* (1954). These give not only a vivid description of his Dickensian childhood but an invaluable close-up account of some of the most important political and cultural movements in the founding of the Irish state. One of his last plays, *The Drums of Father Ned*, was to be staged at the Dublin Theatre Festival in 1958 but was opposed by Archbishop JOHN CHARLES McQUAID, and O'Casey in turn banned all subsequent staging of his plays in Ireland. He lifted the ban shortly before his death, and the three Dublin plays have been in almost continuous production there since. O'Casey's plays have a worldwide reputation, with frequent performances in London, New York and Berlin. He was survived by his widow, who has written several memoirs of her husband, a son, Breon, and daughter, Shivaun, who has directed her father's plays.

Ó CEALLAIGH, Cormac (1912–), experimental physicist, b. Dublin, 29 July 1912, ed. UCD (1930–34), Paris (1934), Cambridge (1935–8) and Bristol (1949–51),

m. Millie Carr, three d. Lecturer UCC 1937–53. Senior professor DIAS 1954–82. Visiting professor Tata Institute, Bombay 1966–7. Publications include numerous papers on cosmic rays and fundamental particles.

Ó CEALLAIGH, Seán T. (Seán T. O'Kelly) (1882–1966), revolutionary, politician and President of Ireland, b. Dublin, 25 Aug. 1882, ed. O'Connell School. As a young man he joined the IRB and the Gaelic League, of whose journal, *An Claidheamh Soluis*, he became manager. Founder member of Sinn Féin 1905. Member Dublin City Council 1906–32; general secretary Gaelic League 1915. He fought in the GPO during the Easter Rising and was later interned. Elected MP (SF Dublin, College Green) 1918. Dáil envoy 1919–22 to Paris Peace Conference, Rome and USA to promote recognition of Irish independence. Opposed Anglo-Irish Treaty 1921, founder member Fianna Fáil 1926. Vice-President Executive Council of the Irish Free State and Minister for Local Government and Public Health 1932–7; Tánaiste and same ministry 1938–41; Tánaiste and Minister for Finance 1941–5. Elected President of Ireland 1945–52, returned unopposed for second term 1952–9.

Ó CONAIRE, Pádraic (1882–1928), novelist and short story writer, b. Galway city, orphaned at an early age, lived with relatives in Rosmuc, Co. Galway, ed. Blackrock, m. Molly MacManus 1903. Entered the civil service in London. His Irish teacher at school had awakened a love for the language and he joined the Gaelic League, where his ambition to write in Irish was fostered. He won the Oireachtas na Gaeilge prize in 1904 and 1908. Ó Conaire's alcoholism, which was to blight the rest of his life, reached a peak in London and in 1914 he left his wife and children to return to Ireland. He earned his living from then on by contributing to journals and newspapers. In his day he was considered the most significant prose writer since the revival, influenced as he was by European writers of the period. Publications include: *Nóra Mharcuis Bhig* (1909), *Deoraidheacht* (1910), *An Chéad Chloch* (1914), *Seacht mBuaidh an Éirighe Amach* (1918), *Síol Éabha* (1922) and *Scothscéalta* (1956).

O'CONNELL, J.J. (**'Ginger'**) (1887–1944), soldier, b. Co. Mayo, ed. Clongowes and UCD. He joined the Irish Volunteers in 1914 after a period of service in the American army. Interned after the Easter Rising, he was assistant to RICHARD MULCAHY during the War of Independence. He supported the Anglo-Irish Treaty, became a general and was deputy chief of staff of the Free State army in 1922. During the Civil War he served as assistant to Mulcahy and EOIN O'DUFFY. He was kidnapped by anti-Treaty forces in June 1922 and held for a time in the Four Courts. Army posts after the war included that of quartermaster-general 1932–4.

O'CONNELL, John (1930–), politician, doctor and publisher *Irish Medical Times*, b. Dublin, Jan. 1930, ed. St Vincent's, Glasnevin, Dublin and RCSI. TD (Labour) 1965–81, elected as an Independent 1981 but took Fianna Fáil whip 1983. TD (FF) 1983–7 and 1989–93; Minister for Health Feb. 1992–Jan. 1993. Ceann Comhairle June 1981–Dec. 1982; senator 1987–9 (Taoiseach's nominee). Labour MEP 1979–81. Alderman Dublin City Council 1974–9, member since 1985. A Labour poll-topper for many years, he retained his popularity when he changed his political allegiance. He resigned from the Dáil in Feb. 1993 on health grounds.

O'CONNELL, Michael (Mick) (1937–), Gaelic footballer, b. Beginish Island, Valentia Harbour, Co. Kerry, 4 Jan. 1937. Regarded as one of the game's most accomplished and stylish players, he was renowned for his spectacular high catching and unerring point-scoring from dead ball positions. He played in nine All-Ireland senior football finals for Kerry, and was on the winning sides of 1959 (when he was captain), 1962, 1969 and 1970. Other achievements include six National Football League medals (1959, 1961, 1963, 1969, 1971–2), a Railway Cup medal (1972) and an All-Star award at midfield (1972). His autobiography, *A Kerry Footballer*, was published in 1974.

O'CONNELL, Thomas J. (1882–1969), politician, trade unionist and teacher, b. Knock, Co. Mayo, ed. St Patrick's College, Dublin, d. Dublin, 22 June 1969. Taught for 15 years; elected general secretary of the Irish National Teachers' Organisation in 1916. TD for County Galway 1922–7, for South Mayo 1927–32. He was Labour Party leader during

the latter period and a member of the Seanad until 1944. Founder member of the Educational Building Society and a director for many years.

O'CONNELL, Timothy (1882–1970), agriculturalist, b. Aghabullogue, Co. Cork, ed. Royal College of Science. A senior member of the technical division of the Department of Agriculture, he was director of agriculture during World War II. He acquired an international reputation as one of the world's leading authorities on the growing and cultivation of wheat. Represented Ireland at the World Wheat Council in Washington from 1947 and was also involved in the technical arrangements for the implementation of the Marshall Plan.

O'CONNOR, Sir Charles Andrew (1854–1928), lawyer, b. Roscommon, ed. St Stanislaus's College, Tullabeg, Co. Offaly and TCD, d. 8 Oct. 1928. Called to the Bar 1878, QC 1894, Solicitor-General for Ireland 1909–11, Attorney-General for Ireland 1911–12, Master of the Rolls in Ireland 1912–24 (knighted on this appointment). Judge of the Supreme Court of the Irish Free State 1924–5, having elected to transfer to the new judicial system.

O'CONNOR, Christopher (Christy), snr (1924–), golfer, b. Knocknacarragh, Co. Galway, 21 Dec. 1924. Between the times of Henry Cotton and Tony Jacklin he was arguably the best player from Ireland and Britain, renowned for his effortless swing. His 24 victories made him the outstanding golfer during the early days of the PGA tour, he headed the Order of Merit twice (1961, 1962) and was second five times (1964–6, 1969–70). He failed to win the British Open but finished seven times in the top five, his best being second in 1965. He was relatively late coming to golf, beginning his professional career in his late twenties and winning his first British title in 1955 at the Penfold Swallow Tournament. Other achievements include the Dunlop Masters (1956, 1959), the PGA Match Play (1957) and the World Seniors (1976, 1977), and he was Irish professional champion ten times (1958, 1960–63, 1965–6, 1971, 1975, 1978). He and HARRY BRADSHAW (1913–90) won Ireland the World Cup in 1958, and he took part in the competition 15 times between 1956 and 1975. He played a record ten Ryder

Cup matches, 1955–73, with 11 wins, 20 defeats and four halves. Uncle of golfer Christy O'Connor jnr.

O'CONNOR, Frank (1903–1966), short story writer, novelist and translator, b. Michael O'Donovan, Cork, ed. St Patrick's NS, Cork, m. first Evelyn Bowen 1939 (divorced 1953), m. second Harriet Rich 1953. MIAL 1932. His national school teacher DANIEL CORKERY fostered his love for the Irish tradition. Fought in the War of Independence. During the Civil War, in which he took the republican side, he was interned in Gormanston Camp. Embarked on a career as a librarian but was swiftly drawn into the circle of writers and critics associated with GEORGE RUSSELL's journal the *Irish Statesman*. He settled in Dublin in 1928, where he enjoyed the friendship of W.B. YEATS.

The publication in 1931 of *Guests of the Nation* and in 1936 of *Bones of Contention* established his reputation as a gifted short story writer, while his novel *The Saint and Mary Kate* (1932), his translations from the Irish and his biography of MICHAEL COLLINS made him one of the most well-known of the post-revival Irish writers. In the 1930s O'Connor served four turbulent years on the board of the Abbey Theatre. During the war years he was for a time poetry editor of SEÁN O'FAOLAIN's periodical, the *Bell*, one of the very few outlets for Irish writing available, where several of his finest stories first saw publication. Like others of his generation, he encountered censorship, the novel *Dutch Interior* (1940) being banned. An outspoken critic of Irish society, O'Connor experienced increasing difficulty in the 1940s in finding the broadcasting and journalistic work that sustained his artistic career.

The autobiographical *An Only Child* (1961) and *My Father's Son* (1968) are classics of the genre. In 1951 O'Connor moved to the USA, where he taught at various universities and produced some of his best work. *The Lonely Voice* (1963), a study of the short story form, remains an influential text. His selection of translations, *Kings, Lords & Commons* (1959), was a valuable contribution to the popularisation of the Gaelic tradition. In his last two years O'Connor gave the lectures at TCD (where he had been awarded an honorary doctorate in 1962) that formed the basis of his pioneering study of Anglo-Irish literature, *The Backward Look* (1967).

O'CONNOR, Joseph (1963–), novelist and journalist, b. Glenageary, Co. Dublin, brother of SINÉAD O'CONNOR, ed. UCD, whence he took his MA in 1986 for *Even the Olives are Bleeding*, a study of the poet CHARLES DONNELLY. He travelled extensively in the USA, Central America and Spain, lived in London for many years, and now divides his time between there and Dublin. O'Connor writes very much with the *vox populi*; his two novels, *Cowboys and Indians* (1991) and *Desperadoes* (1994), volume of short stories, *True Believers*, a collection of his journalism, *The Secret World of the Irish Male* (1994), and a play, *Red Roses and Petrol* (1995), are peopled with young exiles whose experiences are not a million miles removed from those of the author. He has written a weekly column for the *Sunday Tribune*, a monthly column for *Esquire* magazine and has contributed to *The Late Show* on BBC 2. He also introduced and contributed to the anthology *Ireland in Exile* (1993). *Sweet Liberty: Travels in Irish America* appeared in 1996.

O'CONNOR, Pat (1943–), film director, b. Ardmore, Co. Waterford, ed. CBC, Lismore, Co. Waterford and Cork, University of California at Los Angeles and Ryerson Institute, Toronto. Worked at a variety of jobs in Ireland and Britain before moving to North America to study liberal arts in Los Angeles and take a film and video degree in Toronto. Returned to Ireland 1970 and worked with RTÉ 1971–83. *The Ballroom of Romance* (1981), from a WILLIAM TREVOR story, earned him a BAFTA award for best picture and a New York Silver TV award. *Cal* (1984), from the BERNARD MAC LAVERTY novel, was also an award-winner. After *A Month in the Country* (1987) O'Connor moved to Hollywood and directed a number of mediocre films (*Stars and Bars, The January Man* – on the set of which he met his wife, film actress Mary Elizabeth Mastrantonio – and *Fools of Fortune*). Recent ventures include the enormously successful *Circle of Friends* (1995), the adaptation of a MAEVE BINCHY novel, and *Zelda*, the story of F. Scott and Zelda Fitzgerald.

O'CONNOR, Rory (1883–1922), revolutionary, b. Dublin, ed. Clongowes and UCD. Graduated in arts and engineering. He joined the IRB in 1915 on his return from Canada, where he had worked for a number of years. Wounded during the Easter Rising, he was director of engineering of the IRA during the War of Independence. Opposing the Anglo-Irish Treaty, he was one of the leaders of the republican garrison established in the Four Courts in Apr. 1922. On 28 June the army of the Provisional Government attacked the republican positions and O'Connor was captured. He was executed on 8 Dec. 1922 with three other republicans, Richard Barrett, Joseph McKelvey and LIAM MELLOWS, as a deterrent against further assassinations of public representatives after the killing of Sean Hales TD.

O'CONNOR, Sinéad (1966–), singer, b. Glenageary, Co. Dublin, sister of JOSEPH O'CONNOR. She had a deeply troubled childhood, about which she has spoken frankly in public. *The Lion and the Cobra* (1987), her début album, reached both the UK and the US top 40, and the single 'Mandinka' made the British top 20. Her big breakthrough was with 'Nothing Compares 2 U', written by Prince, which reached number one in 17 countries and made O'Connor a household name. Her musical achievements have been overshadowed by controversial gestures such as refusing to allow the American national anthem to be played at one of her US gigs and tearing up a picture of the Pope on television, but her 1994 album, *Universal Mother*, proved that she could still perform with power and passion.

O'CONNOR, Thomas Power (1848–1929), publisher, b. Athlone, 5 Oct. 1848, ed. Athlone and Queen's College, Galway, d. London, 18 Nov. 1929. His first job in journalism was as a reporter for *Saunders Newsletter* in Dublin. He later joined the London *Daily Telegraph*. Nationalist MP from 1880 (for Galway until 1885, thereafter until his death for the Scotland Division, Liverpool). With Liberal Party support, he founded a London evening newspaper, the *Star*, in 1887 which broke fresh ground in journalism with brisk short news items, interviews and lively headlines, but also with articles by leading writers of the day, including GEORGE BERNARD SHAW. It was the breeding ground for many famous journalists, but O'Connor himself, having determined its style and approach to the

news, had to surrender his interest in it after two years because of his lack of business sense. A later venture, the first *Sun* newspaper, collapsed for want of financial backing. The more literary and long-lived *T.P.'s Weekly* followed in 1902. O'Connor was appointed film censor when the post was established in 1917, became a privy councillor in 1924 and was Father of the House of Commons when he died.

O'CONNOR, Ulick (1929–), lawyer, sportsman, writer and playwright, b. Dublin, ed. St Mary's College, Rathmines, UCD, Loyola College, New Orleans and King's Inns. Irish pole vault champion 1947–51, British universities boxing champion 1950. Called to the Bar 1951. His biographies include *Oliver St John Gogarty* (1964) and *Brendan Behan* (1970), on both of whom he has also performed one-man shows, and *Celtic Dawn* (1984), 'a biography of the Irish literary renaissance'. *Biographers and the Art of Biography* (1991) won critical acclaim. His plays include *Execution* (1985) and *A Trinity of Two*. He has written verse plays in the Japanese Noh form and produced several volumes of poetry.

O'CONOR, John (1947–), pianist and teacher, b. Dublin, ed. Belvedere, UCD and Hochschule für Musik, Vienna. Won first prize at the Beethoven (1973) and Bösendorfer (1975) piano competitions. In 1976 he joined the teaching staff of the RIAM, where he is Professor of Piano; appointed director 1994. Has performed worldwide and worked with many leading orchestras. Recordings include the 32 Beethoven sonatas, the Mozart concertos with Sir Charles Mackerras and the Scottish Chamber Orchestra, works by John Field and chamber music with the Cleveland Quartet. In 1988 he founded the GPA Dublin International Piano Competition, of which he is artistic director. Hon. D.Mus. (NUI) 1985.

Ó CRIOMHTHAINN, Tomás (1856–1937), writer, stonemason and fisherman, b. Great Blasket, Co. Kerry, m. 1878 and reared ten children on a stony smallholding. With the revival movement of the late 19th century, scholars sought the purest sources of the language. Robin Flower, the English scholar and translator of Irish, and Norwegian scholar Carl Marstrander were both taught by Ó Criomhthainn. A friend, Brian Ó Ceallaigh of Killarney, encouraged him to write, and when he left Blasket Ó Criomhthainn sent him daily accounts of the island's doings, which Ó Ceallaigh had edited by PÁDRAIG Ó SIOCHFHRADHA. *Allagar na h-Inise* was first published in 1928, followed by the celebrated autobiography *An t-Oileánach* in 1929. This was quickly recognised as one of the greatest achievements of Irish literature. Flower's translation of the text (1934) was not a success, accounting for its neglect by English critics. Towards the end of his life Ó Criomhthainn dictated stories to Flower, who transcribed them as *Seanchas ón Oileáin Thiar* (1956).

Ó DÁLAIGH, Cearbhall (1911–1978), lawyer and President of Ireland, b. Bray, Co. Wicklow, ed. Synge Street, UCD and King's Inns, m. Máirín Nic Dhiarmada, d. 21 Mar. 1978. Graduated 1921 in Celtic studies. Called to Bar 1934, Senior Counsel 1945. Joined *Irish Press* on its foundation 1931, Gaelic editor until 1942. Twice unsuccessful Fianna Fáil candidate in general elections, once defeated by SEÁN MACBRIDE. Attorney-General Apr. 1946–Feb. 1948 (the youngest to hold the post until the appointment of John Rogers 1984) and again Jan. 1951–July 1953. Supreme Court judge 1953, promoted Chief Justice Dec. 1961. In Dec. 1972 appointed Ireland's first judge at the Court of Justice of the European Communities, where his fluency in several European languages proved an asset, and of whose first chamber he was elected president in 1974. On the death in office of ERSKINE CHILDERS in 1974, Ó Dálaigh was unanimously elected President of Ireland, the first person to have been both Chief Justice and head of state. Resigned Oct. 1976 in protest at Minister for Defence PATRICK DONEGAN's public criticism of him for referring the Emergency Powers bill to the Supreme Court. Ó Dálaigh's period of almost 20 years (11 of them as Chief Justice) on the Supreme Court bench was marked by a revolution in Irish constitutional jurisprudence, as the liberal members of the court (among them BRIAN WALSH, SEAMUS HENCHY and F.G.O. BUDD) expanded the concept of judicial review to establish a series of fundamental constitutional and human rights that they held were implicit in the constitution.

O'DEA, James Augustine (Jimmy) (1899–1965), comedian, b. Dublin, d. Dublin, 17 Jan. 1965. Schoolfriend of SEÁN LEMASS. Although he qualified as an optician, from 1927 onward he made the stage his career, becoming the best-loved variety comedian of the mid-century. His most famous persona was that of Biddy Mulligan, 'The Pride of the Coombe', a role created for him by HARRY O'DONOVAN, with whom he set up the O'Dea–O'Donovan Productions partnership, which continued for some 30 years and was responsible for a hugely popular annual pantomime in Dublin featuring O'Dea and MAUREEN POTTER. He also took part in the entertainment programme series *Irish Half-hour*, scripted by O'Donovan and broadcast on BBC radio during World War II.

Ó DIREÁIN, Máirtín (1910–1988), poet, b. Aran Islands. A native Irish speaker, he was involved in the Irish-language movement and acted in Taibhdhearc na Gaillimhe. Entered the Post Office in Galway 1928. Moved to Dublin 1938 and began to write poetry. Worked in Department of Posts and Telegraphs and then Department of Education until his retirement in 1978. Won many prestigious prizes and awards, including the Irish-American Cultural Institute award in 1967; MIAL 1970. Hon. D.Litt. (NUI) 1977, Ossian-Preis from FVS Foundation of Hamburg. *Coinnle Geala* (1942) and *Dánta Aniar* (1943) established him as a major writer, and *Rogha Dánta* (1949) and *Ó Morna agus Dánta Eile* (1957) confirmed his status as one of the most significant Irish voices of his age. *Feamainn Bhealtaine* (1961), his only prose work, contained much valuable biographical material. Ó Direáin's early poetry was remarkable for its nostalgia for Aran, while his later work reflected the alienation he felt from city life.

Other publications include: *Ár Ré Dhearóil* (1962), *Cloch Choirnéil* (1967), *Crainn is Cairde* (1970), *Ceacht an Éin* and *Dánta 1939–79* (1980), *Béasa an Túir* (1984) and *Tacar Dánta*, with Douglas Sealy and TOMÁS MAC SIOMÓIN (1984).

O'DONNELL, Mary (1954–), poet, critic, fiction writer and broadcaster, b. Monaghan, ed. St Louis Convent, Monaghan and Maynooth. She has worked successively as a teacher, translator, library assistant and as drama critic for the *Sunday Tribune*. Her verse secured for her a William Allingham award 1989 and a Listowel Writers' Week award 1990 and she was twice nominated for a Hennessy award. She has published two collections to date: *Reading the Sunflowers in September* (1990) and *Spiderwoman's Third Avenue Rhapsody* (1994). O'Donnell's poetry gives voice to the tensions felt by woman in contemporary society; there is an underlying quest for the sacred that is immanent in the mundane. She has also published an exquisitely wrought novel, *The Light-makers* (1992), in addition to a book of short fiction pieces, *Strong Pagans and Other Stories* (1991).

O'DONNELL, Patrick (1856–1927), conciliator and cardinal, b. Kilraine, Glenties, Co. Donegal, 28 Nov. 1856, ed. national school, Letterkenny and Maynooth, d. 22 Oct. 1927. Ordained 1880, Professor of Theology Maynooth the same year. Bishop of Raphoe 1888, Coadjutor Bishop of Armagh 1922, Archbishop of Armagh 1924, Cardinal 1925. The outstanding intellectual in the Irish hierarchy, he was an adviser to Cardinal LOGUE and, although a convinced nationalist, constantly sought common ground in the controversies of his day. He played a prominent part in healing the divisions of the 1890s in the Irish Parliamentary Party and tried through the unsuccessful Irish Convention of 1917 to resolve the conflicting visions of the country's future then being trenchantly urged. He opposed conscription and, as a native speaker of Irish himself, favoured the language revival, but his commitment to the traditional form of constitutional politics left him somewhat isolated during the War of Independence. More of a realist than many of his fellow bishops, and more concerned to achieve positive benefits for his people than to adopt adversarial attitudes, he preferred to influence policy-making from within the Church–state system as he found it. This was especially evident on educational questions. He served on the Killanin Committee on Primary Education in 1919 even though he disapproved of its tendencies and conclusions, and as cardinal he negotiated an agreement on teacher-training in Northern Ireland with the Minister of Education, Lord LONDONDERRY. O'Donnell's unexpected death at Carlingford, Co. Louth deprived the country and the Roman Catholic Church in Ireland of a greatly needed and practical peacemaker.

O'DONNELL, Peadar (1893–1986), writer and socialist, b. Meenmore, Dungloe, Co. Donegal, 22 Feb. 1893, ed. St Patrick's College, Dublin, d. Dublin, 13 May 1986. He won a scholarship to St Patrick's in 1910, although he first paid a visit to Scotland to see the hardship suffered by Irish migrant farm labourers there. After a period teaching on the Aran Islands he became a full-time organiser for the ITGWU in 1918. Joining the IRA in 1920, he was wounded during the War of Independence. He sided with the anti-Treaty forces during the Civil War and was imprisoned for two years until his escape in 1924. He was elected Sinn Féin TD for Donegal while still in prison, but he never took his seat nor did he seek re-election. He edited the IRA newspaper, *An Phoblacht*, 1926–34, and together with FRANK RYAN recruited volunteers for the International Brigade during the Spanish civil war. Left the IRA in the mid-1930s; in the same period founded the Republican Congress with Ryan and GEORGE GILMORE. He was editor of the highly influential journal the *Bell* from 1946 until its demise in 1954. His novels include *Storm* (1926), *Islanders* (1928), *Adrigoole* (1929), *The Knife* (1930), *On the Edge of the Stream* (1934), *The Big Windows* (1955) and *Proud Island* (1975). He also wrote a play and three autobiographical works, *The Gates Flew Open* (1932), *Salud! An Irishman in Spain* (1937) and *There Will Be Another Day* (1963).

O'DONOGHUE, Martin (1933–), politician, b. May 1933, ed. CBS, Crumlin Road, Dublin, UCD and TCD. Doctor of economics. Economic consultant Department of Education 1962–4, economic consultant Department of Finance 1967–9, economic adviser to Taoiseach JACK LYNCH 1970–73. O'Donoghue was elected to the Dáil in 1977. The main architect of the Fianna Fáil manifesto for that election, in which the party secured a crushing victory, on his first day in Dáil Éireann he became Minister for Economic Planning and Development. The post was discontinued after CHARLES HAUGHEY succeeded Lynch in 1979. In Haughey's second government, in 1982, he was restored to the cabinet as Minister for Education, as which he resigned in Oct. of that year, having refused to guarantee his support for the party leader in the course of a move to unseat him. He lost his Dáil seat in Nov. but was elected to the Seanad, where he served until 1987, by which stage he had drifted out of FF to support the PDs.

O'DONOVAN, Denis Kenry (1909–), physician, b. Limerick, ed. Castleknock and UCD (MB 1934). Availing himself of a travelling scholarship, he took a Ph.D. at McGill University, Montreal. Visiting physician St Vincent's Hospital, Dublin. Holding the chair of medicine at UCD, he exerted a major influence on medical education. For many years chairman of the Medical Research Council of Ireland. Publications include *The Specific Metabolic Principle of the Pituitary*, *An Association between Crooked Fifth Finger and Goitre* and *The Role of the Fifth Digit in Music*.

O'DONOVAN, Gerald (1871–1942), Roman Catholic priest and novelist, of a Cork family but b. in Co. Down, ed. Cork, Galway, Sligo and Maynooth. His father was a builder of piers who travelled much around the country. Ordained priest 1895; appointed to Loughrea, Co. Galway, cathedral town of the diocese of Clonfert, the following year. Here he made a considerable impact. His interest in the arts caused him to invite SARAH PURSER, JACK B. YEATS, MICHAEL HEALY and A.E. Child to work on the decor of Loughrea Cathedral, then nearing completion and destined as a result of his impetus to become the Irish cathedral perhaps most impressively endowed with works of high artistic merit. O'Donovan was also an early supporter of the co-operative movement and together with EDWARD MARTYN represented Connacht in HORACE PLUNKETT's Irish Agricultural Organisation Society. He found himself at odds, however, with the new bishop, Thomas O'Dea, appointed to Clonfert in 1903. He left the priesthood in frustration in 1904, and later the Catholic Church. His attitude was probably represented in his finest novel, the quasi-autobiographical *Father Ralph* (1913), where he wrote of the priest-hero who was embarking on a similar course: 'He would take with him all the religious values that meant so much to him. He was simply choosing life instead of death.' O'Donovan went to England, married, wrote five more novels, worked in the propaganda department of the British government during World War I and later in the publishers Collins.

O'DONOVAN, Harry (1896–1973), drama producer and scriptwriter, b. Dublin. Played in amateur drama and in the touring theatrical productions so popular in Irish small towns in the earlier decades of the 20th century. Formed O'Dea–O'Donovan Productions with JIMMY O'DEA in 1924 to stage variety shows, scripted and produced by O'Donovan, with O'Dea in a range of comic roles thought up by his colleague and performed with hilarious mastery. O'Donovan's best-remembered productions were the Christmas pantomimes which he provided for Dublin audiences over many years, while his best-loved creation for Jimmy O'Dea was a widowed, irrepressible and raucous Dublin stallkeeper:

You may travel from Clare to the County Kildare,
From Drogheda down to Macroom,
But where will you see a fine widda like me,
Biddy Mulligan, the Pride of the Coombe?

He also wrote for radio, mainly for Radio Éireann but also for the BBC, which broadcast an *Irish Half-hour* series scripted by O'Donovan during World War II.

O'DONOVAN, John Purcell (1921–1985), playwright, broadcaster, critic and journalist, b. Dublin, ed. Synge Street. He held various jobs in Dublin and Belfast before becoming a music critic and authority on GEORGE BERNARD SHAW. He wrote successful plays for the Abbey Theatre, which included the celebrated, long-running *The Less We Are Together* (1957) as well as *The Shaws of Synge Street* (1960) and *Copperfaced Jack* (1962). Other plays were *A Change of Mind* (1958) and *Dearly Beloved Roger* (1967). Author of a number of critical studies, including *Shaw and the Charlatan Genius* (1965) and *Bernard Shaw* (1983) a short biography. He later turned to writing for RTÉ television and radio and made many entertaining broadcasts on cultural topics. He hosted 'Dear Sir or Madam', a selection of readers' letters, for many years; it was one of RTÉ radio's longest-running and most popular programmes. He was a founder member of the Society of Irish Playwrights and a senior vice-president of RIAM.

O'DONOVAN, Patricia (1953–), trade unionist, b. Cork, ed. UCC and King's Inns.

Occupies the most senior executive position ever held by a woman in the ICTU, that of assistant general secretary. Called to the Bar in 1975, she worked briefly with the European Commission in Brussels and the Council of Europe, Strasbourg. On her return in 1977 she was appointed EEC officer in ICTU and by 1982 was also its legislative and equality officer. She represented ICTU on the NESC, the National Pensions Board and the Employer–Labour Conference, and in the international arena at the European Trade Union Confederation and the International Labour Conference in Geneva. Her appointment as assistant general secretary has broadened her public role in relation to negotiation with the social partners at the level of national agreements, and within the Congress now she holds overall responsibility for economic policy, for social policy and for European and international affairs. In 1991 President MARY ROBINSON appointed her to the Council of State. ICTU representative on the Central Review Committee (Programme for Economic and Social Progress); has a specific interest in the Social Chapter and in economic and monetary union.

O'DONOVAN ROSSA, Jeremiah (1831–1915), Fenian, b. Rosscarbery, Co. Cork, d. 30 June 1915. He became involved in nationalist political activity in Skibbereen during the 1850s, and in 1856 he accepted IRB founder James Stephens's invitation to join the movement. He managed the Fenian paper, the *Irish People*, from 1863 until his arrest for sedition in 1865. In 1871, after serving a particularly harsh term of imprisonment, he was released with four other Fenians and accompanied them to the USA. Although he remained active in nationalist politics while in America, serious divisions emerged between him and his former comrades and he broke with Clan na Gael in 1880. The oration by PATRICK PEARSE at his funeral established him as an important symbol of continuity in the Irish revolutionary separatist tradition.

O'DOWD, Dan (1903–1989), uilleann piper and pipe maker, b. in the Liberties of Dublin. Initially learned the Highland pipes as a member of the JAMES CONNOLLY Pipe Band. Interned during the War of Independence. Taking up the uilleann pipes in 1926, he received tuition from Dublin pipers Liam

Andrews (b. 1873) and LEO ROWSOME. Throughout his life he dedicated himself to the art of piping and craft of pipe making and he is regarded as the embodiment of a spirit that kept the tradition alive in the capital. A close friend of WILLIE CLANCY, he became an enthusiastic participant at the annual summer school in Miltown Malbay. An example of his slow air playing is included on an anthology of piping issued on the Claddagh label.

O'DRISCOLL, Dennis (1954–), poet and poetry editor, b. Thurles, m. JULIE O'CALLAGHAN. Works in Dublin at the head office of Irish Customs. He has published three collections of poems: *Kist* (1982), *Hidden Extras* (1987) and *Long Story Short* (1993), as well as a long poem about the business world, *The Bottom Line* (1994). SEAMUS HEANEY commented that *Kist* – which won an Arts Council bursary in 1985 – was 'movingly and abundantly' written. O'Driscoll's verse is immediately recognisable, with its characteristic blend of poignancy and wryness, its finger always on the pulse of modern life. His criticism has appeared in the *Southern Review, London Magazine, Agenda, PEN Review, Poetry Review* and in many Irish publications. He also co-edited with PETER FALLON *The First Ten Years: Dublin Arts Festival Poetry* (1979) and is a former editor of *Poetry Ireland Review*.

O'DRISCOLL, Kieran (1920–), obstetrician, b. Kildare, ed. Clongowes and UCD. Graduated MB in 1943, later proceeding MAO and MD and elected FRCOG, FRCPI. After working at the Royal Maternity Hospital, Liverpool in the 1940s, he was assistant master at the National Maternity Hospital, Dublin, consultant gynaecologist to St Laurence's Hospital, then master of the NMH 1963–9. As a result of a critical study of the process of labour and childbirth, and his minute observations of first-time mothers, O'Driscoll introduced a principle incorporated in the title of his book, *Active Management of Labour* (1980), written with Declan Meagher, his successor in the mastership. Their recommendations, initially controversial, are now widely followed.

O'DRISCOLL, Timothy Joseph (1908–), public servant, b. Cork, ed. Presentation College, Cork and TCD. BA, LL D (h.c.). Order of Prince Henry the

Navigator (Portugal), Commander Order of George I (Greece). Departments of Agriculture, Defence, Finance, Industry and Commerce, 1928–48; Irish representative to OEEC (now OECD) 1948–50; assistant secretary Department of Foreign Affairs 1950–51. Chairman and chief executive Irish Export Promotion Board 1951–5; Irish Minister to Netherlands 1955–6; director-general Irish Tourist Board 1956–71. Subsequently consultant on tourism under various UN programmes. At various times member of the board of directors of Aer Lingus, vice-president of the Institute of Public Administration, chairman and president of An Taisce, chairman Algemene Bank Nederland (Ireland).

O'DUFFY, Eoin (1892–1944), general, commissioner Garda Síochána, b. Castleblayney, Co. Monaghan, son of a farmer. Trained as engineer; assistant surveyor Co. Monaghan. Irish Volunteers 1917, staff officer. Elected to Dáil Éireann, Co. Monaghan, 1921; voted for the Treaty. National Army: assistant chief of staff, director of organisation. GOC South-Western Command during Civil War; replaced RICHARD MULCAHY as chief of staff on death of MICHAEL COLLINS; recalled briefly to military service as inspector-general of the defence forces following the 'Army Mutiny' in 1924. Garda commissioner 1922 in succession to MICHAEL STAINES, selected by KEVIN O'HIGGINS. Loyally supported the government in its policy to disarm the police service in Ireland, despite the risks in the Civil War, contributing his great energy and organising genius to this end. But the soldier in his personality reasserted itself in 1926 when Sergeant James Fitzsimmons and Guard Hugh Ward were murdered in a night of widespread attacks on Garda stations. In an emotional response, O'Duffy proposed the rearming of the force.

With EAMONN BROY and W.R.E. MURPHY he was a strong supporter of sports in the Garda Síochána, and was particularly involved with the boxing team. Chief marshal 31st International Eucharistic Congress 1932; the following year, as president of the National Athletic and Cycling Association and encouraged by the organisational triumph of the Congress, he proposed the 1936 Olympic Games for Dublin. He appealed to the idealism of the new young policemen, and in various imaginative ways sought to raise the social status as well as the professional standing of the new police force. But in his public utterances he was often carried away by his enthusiasm. He was removed from office in 1933 in the watershed of Fianna Fáil's victory in two successive general elections.

O'Duffy then became head of the ex-soldiers' benevolent body, the Army Comrades Association, renamed it the National Guard and gave it a political role as a rallying force for opponents of FF. The newly created Fine Gael party appointed O'Duffy as its president 1933 but soon distanced itself from his movement, which was showing a taste for the trappings of Fascism: the wearing of a distinctive uniform, in particular, which caused its members to be popularly known as 'Blueshirts'. The Blueshirts declined but O'Duffy went on to organise and lead an Irish Brigade 1936–8 which fought on the side of General Franco in the Spanish civil war, despite the government's prohibition of Irish involvement in that conflict. O'Duffy returned home to retirement. He died 30 Nov. 1944 and was given a state funeral appropriate to a gazetted general officer of the defence forces.

O'DWYER, Michael (Mick, 'Micko') (1936–), Gaelic footballer and coach, b. Waterville, Co. Kerry, June 1936. From the Waterville club, he first played for Kerry in 1952, was an automatic choice by 1958 and won one Munster and four All-Ireland senior medals with the county. In the victories of 1959 and 1962 he played at left cornerback, and he was at full-forward in 1969 and 1970, having retired for two years between times. Other successes included eight National League medals (1959, 1961, 1963, 1969, 1971–2, 1973–4) and a Railway Cup medal (1972). He retired in 1974, took over as Kerry coach in 1975 and guided the county to eight All-Ireland wins in 15 years (1975, 1978–81, 1984–6), which are said to have made him Gaelic football's most successful coach.

O'FAOLAIN, Julia (1932–), novelist and short story writer, b. London, d. of Eileen and SEÁN O'FAOLAIN, ed. UCD, Rome and Paris. She worked as translator for the Council of Europe 1954 and as a teacher and cook in London 1955–7. Taught French at Reid College, Portland, Oregon; Italian at Portland

State University 1957–61; interpreting in Florence 1962–5. One of Ireland's most outstanding authors, she acquired both success and a certain notoriety with her first volume of short stories, *We Might See Sights!* and with the novel *Godded and Codded* (1970), the erotic adventures of an Irish Catholic girl in Paris, intent on sloughing off a cloistered past. Since then she has published six further novels, including *No Country for Young Men* (1980) – her best work to date – and three more collections of stories, as well as editing *Not in God's Image*, with husband Lauro Martines (1973), and her father's memoir, *Vive Moi!* (1993). She has also translated two books from the Italian.

O'FAOLAIN, Seán (1900–1991), short story writer, novelist, biographer and editor, b. John Whelan, Cork, ed. Presentation Brothers, Cork, UCC and Harvard, m. Eileen Gould 1928. He joined the Irish Volunteers in 1918 and took the republican side in the Civil War. Disillusioned by developments in Ireland, in 1926 he left to take up a fellowship at Harvard, followed by a teaching job in England. He returned to Ireland in 1932 determined to make his way as a writer of fiction. From this period date his three early novels and some of the best of the short stories upon which his reputation as an artist will ultimately depend. He also wrote the first of his historical biographies, a life of Daniel O'Connell entitled *King of the Beggars* (1938). In the 1930s O'Faolain's fiction fell under the interdiction of the draconian literary censorship which operated in independent Ireland following the Censorship of Publications Act of 1929. From 1940 to 1946 he edited the *Bell*, a literary and cultural monthly that opposed censorship and the narrow versions of Catholicism and Irish identity that sustained it.

Other publications included a life of Hugh O'Neill, *The Great O'Neill* (1942), travel writings, a biography of Cardinal Newman and an autobiography (*Vive Moi!*, 1964). O'Faolain continued to write short stories which bear on the ironies and pathos of middle-class life in a provincial capital, on the transient pleasures of love and the compensations of cosmopolitan experience. His most original work, however, was in the short stories of his young manhood in which he explored the tensions between the call of nationalism and the necessity for the artist to achieve individual liberty. Visiting professor at various North American universities. MIAL 1932, awarded American-Irish Foundation literary award, elected Saoi in Aosdána 1986, made freeman of Cork 1987.

Ó FARACHÁIN, Roibeárd (1909–1984), broadcaster, poet and critic, b. Dublin, trained at St Patrick's College, Dublin and UCD. He was a teacher for ten years before joining Radio Éireann, where he held various posts 1939–74: he was controller of radio programmes from 1953 until his retirement, by which time Radio Éireann had long been amalgamated with Telefís Éireann as the combined broadcasting service of RTÉ. He co-founded the Lyric Theatre with AUSTIN CLARKE and was an Abbey director 1940–73. He was a religious poet, whose oeuvre includes *The First Exile* (1944), an epic poem on the life of St Colmcille, arguably his greatest work. Yet he was active on many more literary fronts: as verse-playwright for the Abbey with *Assembly at Druim Ceat* and *Lost Light* (1943); as a critic, with *Towards an Appreciation of Poetry* (1947), *The Course of Irish Verse in English* and *How to Enjoy Poetry* (1948); he published a collection of short stories in Irish, *Fíon gan Mhoirt* (1938) and four books of poetry in English. He also edited *Éire: Bliainiris Ghaedheal, Rogha Saothar Ghaedheal mBeó* (1940) and translated a play by FRANCIS MACMANUS as *Toirneach Luimnighe* (1935).

Ó FIACHÁIN, Eamonn (1925–), sergeant Garda Síochána, b. Dublin, son of a constable in the DMP, ed. St Vincent's CBS. Trained as a fitter. Ballistics expert Garda Technical Bureau. As a young garda on traffic direction duty at the junction of Grafton Street, Nassau Street and Suffolk Street in the mid-century, he epitomised the efficiency of the Dublin city-centre pointsman. Declared a conscientious objection to wearing the uniform helmet as a symbol of the old regime, and was credited with having it withdrawn.

Ó FIAICH, Tomás (1923–1990), historian and cardinal, b. Crossmaglen, Co. Armagh, 23 Nov. 1923, ed. St Patrick's College, Armagh, Maynooth, UCD and Louvain, d. Lourdes, 8 May 1990. Ordained priest 1948. Lecturer in modern history Maynooth 1953, professor 1959, college president 1974.

Archbishop of Armagh 1977, Cardinal 1979. He was a noted authority on the work of the Celtic missionaries in France and Germany during the Dark Ages. Spoke Irish fluently and promoted its revival. Member of the NUI Senate. As its president, he completed the delicate task of making Maynooth a secular university within the state system as well as the national seminary for the priesthood. A harder task again awaited him in Armagh, where he was leader both of the Irish Church as a whole and of the Catholic minority in Northern Ireland, at that time under severe stress because of paramilitary violence and the counter-measures adopted by the security forces. Crossmaglen, his home village close to the border, was the centre of much agitation, and the cardinal's concern for its people – almost all of them Catholic – was interpreted in Britain as fellow-travelling with the IRA. In fact Cardinal Ó Fiaich repeatedly denounced violence but this was noticed less than his protests against the mistreatment of prisoners. In the Republic he was a voice of restraint, qualifying through the Episcopal Conference the more extreme positions adopted by some of the bishops on the abortion and divorce referenda of 1983 and 1986 respectively.

O'FLAHERTY, Kathleen Mary, academic and author, b. Enniscorthy, ed. Ursuline Convent, Waterford, University of Lille and UCC (Ph.D.). Assistant to the President of UCC 1944–53, assistant lecturer in French UCC 1947, lecturer 1954, Professor of French 1970. An authority on Chateaubriand; her published work also includes *The Novel in France* (1945 and 1965), *Voltaire, Myth and Reality* (1945) and *Paul Claudel and 'The Tidings Brought to Mary'* (1948).

O'FLAHERTY, Liam (1896–1984), novelist and short story writer, b. Gort na gCapall on the Aran Island of Inishmore, ed. Rockwell, Blackrock and UCD, m. Margaret Barrington 1926, separated 1932. O'Flaherty came of the small farmer stock in the Aran Gaeltacht whose lives he was to chronicle in some of his most powerful fictions. He seemed destined for the priesthood until he lost his vocation and in 1915 enlisted in the Irish Guards. He saw action at the Somme in northern France and was discharged shell-shocked in 1917. Took the republican side in the Civil War and in 1922

began his writing career. Over the next three decades he produced the short stories, novels, autobiographical works and polemic that made him one of the most compelling writers of the post-revival period. In his last years his work was brought once more to the attention of an Irish readership through his association with the Wolfhound Press in Dublin, which issued in 1976 a collection of previously unpublished and uncollected short stories (*The Pedlar's Revenge*) and reissued the novels *Skerrett* in 1977 and *Famine* in 1979. He was primarily an English-language writer but his fiction was influenced, in the rhythms of its prose and the syntax of its dialogue, by the bilingual reality the author had known in his Aran boyhood. A collection of stories in the Irish language (*Dúil*) was published in 1953.

O'Flaherty's fictional oeuvre comprises three distinct kinds of work. There are his intense explorations of extreme states of feeling in psychological novels that suggest the presiding genius of Dostoevsky; of these, *The Informer* (1925), the basis of a John Ford film, is probably the most fully realised example. Then there are the historical fictions that reckon with the Irish past, the finest being perhaps *Famine* (1937). It is, however, in the short story form that O'Flaherty makes his greatest claim on posterity; in his often brief tales of elemental struggles between man and man, and man and nature, and in his charged, animistic celebrations of animal life, he produced a small body of wholly original writing in which an epic, unsentimental, vital vision of the world finds memorable expression. In Irish fiction there is nothing quite to compare with such stories as 'The Snipe', 'The Landing', 'Going into Exile' and 'The Cow's Death'. Member IAL 1932, Aosdána 1981. Cousin of Stephen O'Flaherty and uncle of Breandán Ó hEithir.

O'FLAHERTY, Stephen (1902–1982), businessman, b. Passage East, Co. Waterford. Worked in England and returned to Ford's in Cork about 1928. After World War II he and his wife formed Motor Distributors Ltd in Dublin, whose first business coup was the assembly and sale of 11 Adler cars imported before the war. In 1949 O'Flaherty broke the hegemony of American and English cars by securing the first franchise for Volkswagen outside Germany. He acquired the British VW franchise and later the UK and Irish rights to distribute Mercedes-Benz. Cousin of LIAM O'FLAHERTY.

O'FLANAGAN, Kevin Patrick (1919–), international rugby player and footballer, b. Dublin, 10 June 1919. One of Ireland's most versatile sportsmen, he and his brother Michael (b. 1922) were both capped at rugby and soccer, and played soccer together for Ireland against England in 1946. Kevin was a scratch golfer, was Irish 100 yards champion (1941) and national long jump champion four times between 1938 and 1943. His soccer career began with Bohemians at 16 and he won seven international caps before World War II. After the war, he signed as an amateur with Arsenal, won three more caps and also played for Brentford, as well as playing rugby for London Irish, winning his sole rugby cap against Australia in 1947. He was medical officer to Ireland's Olympic team three times (1960, 1964 and 1968), was later a member of the Olympic Council of Ireland and in 1976 was elected to the International Olympic Committee. Michael won his one rugby cap against Scotland in 1948, thus sharing in Ireland's only Grand Slam in history to date.

O'FLANAGAN, Michael (1876–1942), Roman Catholic priest and republican, b. Cloonfower, Castlerea, Co. Roscommon, ed. Summerhill College, Sligo and Maynooth, d. Dublin, Aug. 1942. Ordained in 1900. His involvement with politics began in 1915 with a dispute over turf rights in his parish in Cliffoney, Co. Sligo. In 1917 he successfully managed Count Plunkett's campaign in the Roscommon by-election. Although censured by his bishop, he went on to become vice-chairman of Sinn Féin and vice-president of the Gaelic League. He opposed the Treaty and went to the USA to rally support for the republican cause. On his return he helped draw up a social programme for SF. Unlike most of his fellow clerics, he supported the republican side in the Spanish civil war.

O'FLYNN, Liam (1945–), uilleann piper, b. Kill, Co. Kildare. His father played the fiddle and his mother was a cousin of Junior Crehan. Learned the pipes from Garda sergeant Tom Armstrong; later he was taught or influenced by LEO ROWSOME, WILLIE CLANCY and SEAMUS ENNIS, and many would regard him as Ennis's natural successor. His professional career began in the early 1970s when he joined the group Planxty. Involved with SHAUN DAVEY in orchestral works such as *The Brendan Voyage* and *Granuaile*. He has performed widely, contributed to film soundtracks and worked with American composer John Cage.

Ó GAOITHÍN, Mícheál (1904–1974), poet and writer, b. Blasket Islands, Co. Kerry, s. of PEIG SAYERS, whom he helped in the writing of her memoirs. He was known locally as 'An File' (The Poet). Publications include *Is Truagh ná Fanann an Óige* (1953), *Coinnle Corra* (1968) and *Beatha Pheig Sayers* (1970).

O'GRADY, Desmond James Bernard (1935–), poet and educator, b. Limerick, ed. locally, Roscrea and UCD. He grew up in west Clare and the Kerry Gaeltacht. Taught at the Berlitz School, Paris 1954–6 and in Rome 1957–62, while working as European editor for *Transatlantic Review*. In Italy he befriended Ezra Pound, whom he considers a major influence. He also taught in the USA, Iran and Egypt. O'Grady is one of the few contemporary Irish poets who embraces epic, heroic subjects; he draws on Celtic verse and the wealth of his own experience. His many collections and translations include: *Chords and Orchestrations* (1956), *Reilly* (1961), *Separazioni* (1965), *The Dark Edge of Europe* (1967), *Off Licence*, trans., and *The Dying Gaul* (1968), *Hellas* (1971), *Separations* (1973), *Stations* (1976), *The Gododdin*, trans., and *Sing me Creation* (1977), *A Limerick Rake: Versions from the Irish* (1978), *The Headgear of the Tribe* and *His Scaldcrane's Nest* (1979), *Grecian Glances*, trans. (1981), *Alexandrian Notebook 1935–* (1989), *The Seven Arab Odes*, trans. (1990), *Tipperary* (1991), *These Fields in Springtime* (1993) and *Trawling Traditions*, trans. (1994).

Ó GRIANNA, Séamus (1891–1969), short story writer and novelist, pen-name 'Máire', b. Rannafast in the Donegal Gaeltacht. Became a teacher in 1912 and worked in Tyrone, Dublin and Donegal. Organiser for the Minister for Education in the Second Dáil. Republican prisoner 1922–4. Worked in civil service from 1932, translating from French and English into Irish. Ó Grianna is considered one of the best writers of the period, creating the authentic character and life of the people of his native Donegal. Publications include: *Cioth is Dealán* (1926), *Nuair a Bhí Mé Óg* (1942), autobiography *Saoghal Corrach* (1945), *Tarngaireacht Mhiseóige* (1958) and *Oidhche Shamhraidh agus Scéalta Eile* (1968). Brother of SEOSAMH MAC GRIANNA, with whom he agreed to use the 'Ó' form of their name rather than the 'Mac' to avoid confusion between them.

O'HAGAN, Sheila (1933–), poet, b. Dublin, ed. locally, left for London when she was 19. She settled, married and reared three children before taking degrees in art, English literature and theatre. She began writing poetry at Birkbeck College, University of London in 1984 and since then has three times won prizes at Listowel Writers' Week, in addition to the Goldsmith award in 1988, the PATRICK KAVANAGH award in 1991 and a Hennessy award in 1992. Her poetry has appeared in many Irish and international journals and newspapers, in particular in Canada and Australia. She lives in Dalkey, Co. Dublin and Clapham, London, and is a member of the Dublin Writers' Workshop. Collections: *The Peacock's Eye* (1992) and *The Troubled House* (1995).

O'HARA, Maureen (1921–), pseud. of Maureen FitzSimons, actress, b. Dublin, 17 Aug. 1921, ed. Abbey School of Acting, Dublin and London College of Music. She made her American film début in *Jamaica Inn* (1939), co-starred with Charles Laughton in *The Hunchback of Notre Dame* the same year and with Roddy McDowell in *How Green Was My Valley* (1941). In her subsequent career she was largely confined to the role of the 'fiery redhead'. This required her first to dismiss but eventually to succumb to the charms of the leading man. Her best-known films are *Miracle on 34th Street* (1947) and *The Quiet Man* (1952). After an absence of 20 years she returned to film work in 1991 to co-star with John Candy in the comedy *Only the Lonely.*

O'HARE, Daniel (1942–), scientist and academic, b. Dundalk, ed. CBS, Dundalk, UCG and St Andrews (Ph.D.). Research work (aspects of spectroscopy) Michigan State University and University of Southampton. Principal Letterkenny Regional Technical College 1971–4; principal Waterford RTC 1974–7. First director NIHE, Dublin 1977, as

which he undertook considerable expansion of the Institute in both the range of its curricula and its campus facilities. When it became DCU in 1989 he was appointed president.

Ó hÉANAÍ, Seosamh (Joe Heaney) (1920–1984), singer and storyteller, b. Carna, Connemara. One of the finest exponents of the sean-nós tradition, coming from a region famous for singers in this idiom, such as Tom Pháidi Tom, Seán Mac Donncha, Máire Áine Ní Dhonnchadha and Darach Ó Catháin. In 1947 he emigrated to England, where his singing was admired by performers such as Ewan MacColl and Peggy Seeger, with both of whom he later appeared. He returned to Ireland in 1957 but within three years had re-emigrated, this time to the USA. Based in Seattle he travelled nationwide to festivals and concerts, singing at the 1966 Newport Folk Festival. For some years prior to his death he lectured on sean-nós singing at the University of Washington.

O'HEGARTY, Patrick S. (1879–1955), civil servant and writer, b. Carrignavar, Co. Cork, ed. North Mon. Joined the civil service in Cork and subsequently transferred to London, where he worked 1902–13. While there, he was active in many Irish organisations, including the supreme council of the IRB. Transferred back to Cork as postmaster in 1913 but on the outbreak of World War I reassigned to England. In 1918 when the oath of allegiance became obligatory he resigned and set up the Irish Bookshop in Dawson Street, Dublin. Appointed secretary of the Department of Posts and Telegraphs in 1922, he held the position until his retirement in 1944. He was also a prolific writer on matters Irish. Apart from being a regular contributor to the *Irish Book Lover* and *Irish Freedom*, he edited a short-lived journal the *Separatist*, which sought to heal the split caused by the Treaty and the Civil War. Publications include: *John Mitchel: An Appreciation* (1917), *The Indestructible Nation* (1918), *Sinn Féin: An Illumination* and *Ulster: A Brief Statement of Fact* (1919), *The History of Ireland under the Union* (1922) and *The Victory of Sinn Féin* (1924).

O'HEHIR, Micheál (1920–), broadcaster and sports commentator, b. Michael Hehir, Glasnevin, Dublin, 2 June 1920, ed. St Patrick's, Glasnevin, O'Connell School and UCD. An enthusiastic, flamboyant commentator for almost 50 years, he covered a record 99 All-Ireland finals and was the voice of Gaelic games at home and abroad. His commentaries were heard as far away as New Zealand and Kenya, earning him international celebrity status and job offers from some of the world's largest television networks. His first public broadcast was the All-Ireland football semi-final between Monaghan and Galway (14 Aug. 1938), his first All-Ireland hurling final Kilkenny v. Cork (1939). Before television, in the 1940s and 1950s, O'Hehir was the 'eyes and ears' of the nation and became part of its folklore. Creating pictures of the players and detailing their family sports history was a distinctive trait. Credited with making bad matches sound good, he always responded to the excitement of the crowd. Started racing commentating and for many years was BBC commentator at Becher's Brook, Aintree for the Grand National. Sub-editor then racing correspondent with the *Irish Independent*. RTÉ's first head of sports 1961–72, then returned to being a freelance journalist. Commentated for RTÉ and America's NBC television and wrote articles for various newspapers, including a column in the *Sunday Press*. He did some news reporting, covering the visit of President Kennedy to Ireland 1963 and his funeral the following Nov. He has not broadcast since he suffered a stroke in Aug. 1985. M. Molly Owens, five children, two of whom are in journalism: Tony a racing commentator, Pete a sports journalist.

Ó hEIGHEARTAIGH, Seán Sáirséal (1917–1967), publisher, b. Wales but returned to Dublin as a child, ed. St Andrew's College, Dublin and TCD, d. Dublin, 14 June 1967. A career civil servant but his principal accomplishments lay in the area of Irish-language publishing. Founder director of *Comhar* magazine in 1941 and four years later founded Sáirséal agus Dill, the first private sector publishing house specialising in works in Irish. His finest achievement was the first publication of MÁIRTÍN Ó CADHAIN's masterpiece *Cré na Cille* in 1949.

Ó hEITHIR, Breandán (1930–1991), journalist, writer and broadcaster, b. Aran Island of Inishmore, nephew of LIAM O'FLAHERTY, ed. Coláiste Einde, Galway and UCG, d. Oct.

1991. Irish editor *Irish Press* 1957–63, editor Irish magazine *Comhar*. One of the principal journalists on *Féach*, RTÉ, he helped to modernise Irish for television and was for many the 'acceptable face' of the Irish-language movement, doing much to rid it of its tight, conservative and anti-British bias. An astute and often acerbic commentator on Irish life, both in his journalism and in his books. Publications include: *Lig Sinn i gCathú* (1977), *Over the Bar* (1984), *This is Ireland* (1987) and *The Begrudger's Guide to Irish Politics* (1986), and with his son Ruairí he edited *An Aran Reader* (1991).

Ó hEITHIR, Daniel. See under O'Hare.

Ó hEOCHA, Colm (1926–), biochemist and President of UCG, b. Dungarvan, Co. Waterford, 19 Sept. 1926, ed. Coláiste na Rinne, CBS, Dungarvan, Coláiste Iosagáin, Baile Mhuirne, Co. Cork, UCG and University of California. Teaching assistant University of California at Los Angeles 1950–51, research assistant University of California La Jolla 1952–5, research associate University of Minnesota 1961–2. Lecturer UCG 1955, Professor of Biochemistry 1963, president 1974–96. Chairman of the New Ireland Forum 1983–4, appointed chair of the Arts Council 1989.

O'HIGGINS, Kevin (1892–1927), politician, b. Stradbally, Co. Laois, ed. Clongowes, Knockbeg College, Co. Carlow, Maynooth and UCD. While in UCD he joined the Irish Volunteers and in 1918 was arrested in what the British authorities called a 'German plot'. He contested the general election of that year from jail and was elected MP for Queen's County (now Laois). He took his seat in the new Dáil Éireann and was assistant to local government minister W.T. COSGRAVE. He was a strong supporter of the 1921 Treaty and made one of the most impressive arguments for it in the Dáil. In the post-Treaty Provisional Government he was Minister for Economic Affairs and when the first Free State government was formed became Minister for Home Affairs.

He strongly approved of the Free State prosecution of the Civil War, despite the cost. He was a member of the cabinet that agreed the execution of republican prisoners as a deterrent against further assassinations of public representatives following the killing of Sean

Hales TD, a decision in which O'Higgins concurred only with great reluctance: among the executed was RORY O'CONNOR, who had been best man at O'Higgins's wedding a year earlier. His own father was shot dead in his home because of his actions as a minister. O'Higgins was largely responsible for the establishment of the Garda Síochána as an unarmed force. He brought in an Intoxicating Liquor Act in an effort to curb excessive drinking by restricting public house opening times. Irish delegate to the Imperial Conference of 1926; while his idea of a dual monarchy for Ireland got a negative response from unionists, he made a major impact overall.

On 10 July 1927 he was assassinated on his way to church by an IRA group which came across him by accident. As he lay dying, he repeatedly forgave his murderers. An austere and melancholy character, he was one of the most powerful figures in the early governments of the state, much admired, and much hated by his most militant opponents.

O'HIGGINS, Thomas (1916–), politician, lawyer and judge, b. Cork, s. of Dr T.F. O'Higgins and nephew of KEVIN O'HIGGINS, ed. St Mary's College, Rathmines, Dublin, Clongowes, UCD and King's Inns. Called to Bar 1938, Inner Bar 1954. TD (FG Laois–Offaly) 1948–73. Minister for Health 1954–7, as which he established the Voluntary Health Insurance Board, a non-profit state-sponsored body for the provision of private insurance against the costs of medical treatment and hospitalisation. Within Fine Gael in the 1960s he encouraged the progressive thinking of DECLAN COSTELLO and GARRET FITZGERALD. FG candidate at the presidential election 1966, when his modern and pluralist image brought him within 11,000 votes of defeating the incumbent president EAMON DE VALERA in the national poll. He was less successful at the next presidential election (1973), which the Fianna Fáil candidate, ERSKINE CHILDERS, won by a majority of nearly 50,000. Chief Justice 1974–85: he delivered the Supreme Court judgment in the case of McGlinchey v. WREN (1982), in which he laid down that a charge associated with terrorist activity should not per se be assumed to be the allegation of a political offence such as would justify refusal of extradition. Judge of the EU Court of Justice 1985–91.

Ó hUIGINN, Pádraig (1924–), public servant, b. Cork, ed. St Finbarr's College, Cork and University of Edinburgh (M.Sc.), m., four children. Retired in 1993 as secretary of the Department of the Taoiseach, his tenure having been extended by four years. His position and his talent as chairman and conciliator made him one of the most widely recognised civil servants of his time. Earlier posts included managing director An Foras Forbartha, economic affairs officer UN Office, Geneva, chairman NESC and chairman International Financial Services Centre Committee. Played a major part in bringing about consensus among the social partners in the NESC, and was the chief negotiator on behalf of the government in the Programme for National Recovery and the Programme for Economic and Social Progress. On his retirement he was appointed chairman of Bord Fáilte.

O'KEEFFE, Daniel (Dan, 'Danno') (1907–), Gaelic footballer, b. Fermoy, Co. Cork. As Kerry's goalkeeper 1931–49 he became the first player to win seven All-Ireland medals (1931–2, 1937, 1939–41, 1946). His ten All-Ireland appearances was also a long-held record. He won 15 Munster senior football medals, three Railway Cup medals and in 1932 his only National League medal.

O'KEEFFE, John ('Johnno') (1951–), Gaelic footballer, b. 15 Apr. 1951. Captained his club, Austin Stacks, to win the All-Ireland Club Championship of 1977, having previously captained St Brendan's, Killarney to success in the 1969 Hogan Cup. With Kerry he won six All-Ireland senior football medals (1970, 1975 and 1978–81). Other achievements include six National Football League medals (1971–4, 1977 and 1982), five All-Star awards (at midfield 1973, at full-back 1975–6, 1978–9) and four Railway Cup medals. In the early 1990s he trained the Limerick senior football side.

O'KEEFFE, Paddy (1923–), agriculturalist and newspaper editor, b. Fermoy, Co. Cork, ed. CBS, Fermoy, Athenry Agricultural College, Albert College and UCD. B.Ag.Sc., Dr.Ag.Sc. (h.c.). Agricultural adviser Co. Louth; farm development manager St Ita's Hospital Portrane. Editor *Irish Farmers' Journal* (which he took over from Macra na Feirme with Michael Dillon) Nov. 1951–88. Chairman of Agricultural Trust 1993, of FBD (Farm Business Development) Insurance and of Irish Farm Centre. Former chairman Bord na gCapall, former member of RTÉ Authority. Director Lithographic Universal; former director Ceimicí Teo. and Wheat Industries Council; member of Irish Goods Council. Member of the Ward Union, the South County Dublin and the Duhallow Hunts.

O'KEEFFE, Pádraig (1889–1963), fiddler and teacher, b. Glentaune, Co. Kerry. He occupies a legendary role in the traditions of the south-west, forming a link with historic musicians such as Tom Billy and his own uncle Cal O'Callaghan. He succeeded his father as schoolmaster in 1915 but left the position in 1920 to become a travelling fiddle master, devising a means of notation to pass on tunes to the musically illiterate. His students included instrumentalists who were to play a major part in the national and international arenas. The most comprehensive collection of his playing is available on an RTÉ CD produced by the piper and broadcaster Peter Browne and consisting of items originally recorded on acetate discs by SEAMUS ENNIS in 1948 and 1949.

O'KELLY, Kevin (1924–1994), journalist and broadcaster, b. 12 June 1924, ed. CUS, d. suddenly 31 Aug. 1994. Spent his earlier career as a journalist with *Irish Press* newspapers, the Irish News Agency and Radio Éireann. Became a reporter-presenter in RTÉ, covering such major stories of the 1960s as the American space exploration programme, the Second Vatican Council and the early years of the Northern Ireland crisis; member of the original team presenting the radio programmes *The News at One-thirty* and *This Week*. Broadcast the report of an interview with Sean MacStiofain, the supposed chief of staff of the IRA, which resulted in the dismissal of the RTÉ Authority in 1972; holding that it would be a breach of journalistic ethics, he subsequently refused in a case before the Special Criminal Court to identify MacStiofain as his source and was jailed briefly for contempt of court. Became editor of radio news features and later religious affairs correspondent for both radio and television. Retired 1986 but continued to broadcast the highly regarded religious affairs *Addendum* programme from

foreign and home locations. Chairman of the Camphill Communities in Ireland and public relations consultant to the Eastern Health Board at the time of his death.

O'KELLY, Michael J. (Brian) (1915–1982), archaeologist, b. Limerick, ed. Rockwell and UCC as well as partly training as an architect. In 1944 he was appointed curator of the Cork Public Museum, before succeeding SEÁN P. Ó RÍORDÁIN as Professor of Archaeology at UCC in 1946. He was ever reluctant to 'take things on trust' and became a great exponent of 'experimental archaeology'; among his many papers are reports on his experiments in fields as diverse as iron smelting and primitive cookery. His archaeological interests were wide and his publications range from the excavation report on a court tomb at Shanballyedmond, Co. Tipperary to a detailed analysis of the belt shrine from Moylough, Co. Sligo. From 1962 onwards he spent 14 years excavating at Newgrange, Co. Meath, the report on which, *Newgrange: Archaeology, Art and Legend*, appeared in 1982. His masterly *Early Ireland: An Introduction to Irish Prehistory*, prepared for publication by his widow, Claire, was published in 1984.

O'KELLY, Seán T. See under Ó Ceallaigh.

O'KELLY, Seumas (d. 1918), author and journalist, b. Mobhill, Loughrea, Co. Galway, date uncertain, variously given as 1875 and 1881, ed. locally. He began as a reporter in 1903 on the Skibbereen *Southern Star* and soon became editor; he then edited a succession of national papers, lastly *Nationality*, in whose office he died suddenly. He was a republican, a close friend of ARTHUR GRIFFITH and other revolutionary leaders. O'Kelly wrote a vast amount of journalism, drama, fiction and poetry. A number of his plays did well at the Abbey: *The Shuiler's Child* (1909), *The Parnellite* (1911), *Meadowsweet* (1912) and *The Bribe* (1913); another, *Driftwood*, was produced in London in 1913 by Abbey patron Annie Horniman. He wrote two novels, *The Lady of Deerpark* (1917) and *Wet Clay* (1922), but his reputation rests on his superb short stories, of which 'The Weaver's Grave' (1920) is considered to be his masterpiece. It has been successfully adapted for stage and radio.

Ó LAOGHAIRE, Peadar (1839–1920), Roman Catholic priest and writer, b. Macroom,

Co. Cork, ed. at home and in Maynooth. Ordained 1867, he served as a chaplain in several places throughout Cork and as a parish priest in Castlelyons from 1891. He was a supporter of the Land League and became active in the Gaelic League: his novel *Séadna* was serialised in the *Gaelic Journal* 1894–7. He saw the need for reading matter in Irish and began writing short stories, especially for young people, using the speech of the people he had grown up with in west Cork. His output included religious essays, translations, memoirs and the retelling of classical tales. His work has become the model for all modern Irish prose, although its content is sometimes considered confined. Publications include: *Niamh* (1907), autobiography *Mo Sgéal Féin* (1915), *Ag Séideadh agus ag Ithe* (1918) and *Críost Mac Dé* (1925).

O'LEARY, David Anthony (Dave) (1958–), international footballer, b. Stoke Newington, London, 2 May 1958. He moved back to Dublin as a child and played for Shelbourne before signing for Arsenal aged 15. A renowned defender with the club 1975–93, he played a record number of games with them, including 558 in the Football League. He won FA Cup medals in 1979 and 1993, when he came on as a substitute, as well as helping Arsenal to the League titles of 1989 and 1991, before moving to Leeds United in 1993. He played 67 times for the Republic of Ireland 1977–93, having earlier captained the national schoolboy and youth teams. He will be remembered for his winning goal in the 1990 World Cup penalty shoot-out with Romania.

O'LEARY, Jane (1946–), composer, b. Connecticut, ed. Vassar College and Princeton University (doctorate in music composition). Married an Irishman and moved to Ireland in 1972. Former chairwoman Music for Galway. Director of contemporary chamber music group Concorde. Chairwoman Contemporary Music Centre. Member of board of directors of National Concert Hall and of Aosdána. Executive board member of International League of Women Composers. Works include *Islands of Discovery* (1991), *The Petals Fall* (1986–7), and *From the Crest of a Green Wave* (1994), commissioned for the third GPA Dublin International Piano Competition.

O'LEARY, Liam (1910–1992), cineaste, b. Youghal, Co. Cork, 25 Sept. 1910, ed. St

Peter's, Wexford and UCD, d. 14 Dec. 1992. Clerked in the Department of Industry and Commerce. A founder of Ireland's first theatre workshop, the Dublin Little Theatre Guild, 1934. Produced plays for Radio Éireann and for the Abbey Theatre but the cinema was his true *métier*. Co-founder (1936), and for eight years honorary secretary, of the Irish Film Society and directed its film school. Acted in two films, *Stranger at my Door* (1948) and *Men against the Sun* (1952). Moved to London, acquisitions officer of the British National Film Archive 1953–66. Returned to Dublin 1966, film acceptance officer for Telefís Éireann, viewed 40,000 films before his retirement in 1986.

Wrote the first Irish book on cinema, *Invitation to the Film* (1945), as well as *The Silent Cinema* (1965) and the biography *Rex Ingram – Master of the Silent Cinema* (1980). Organised Cinema Ireland exhibition in TCD 1976 to celebrate the country's film heritage. Set up the Liam O'Leary Film Archive 1977, composed mainly of stills, posters, scripts and other printed material, which he later donated to the National Library.

O'LEARY, Michael (1936–), politician, b. 8 May 1936, ed. Presentation College, Cork, UCC and Columbia University. Active in student and labour politics, employed in the ITGWU. Education officer for ICTU and in 1965 elected to the Dáil (Labour Dublin North-Central). Promoted the link between Labour and the unions in the 1960s and urged the party to adopt a more left-wing stance. Proposed the anti-coalition motion at the party's 1968 conference but after the 1969 election joined in the successful attempt to alter this policy. Minister for Labour in the 1973–7 coalition with Fine Gael. In 1977 was narrowly defeated for the Labour leadership by FRANK CLUSKEY. After his election to the European Parliament for the Dublin constituency in 1979 he played little part in Dáil or party activities, but on Cluskey's defeat in the 1981 general election he was selected unanimously to succeed him. He was Tánaiste and Minister for Energy 1981–2. At the 1982 party conference, however, his proposal to qualify the right of the general membership to decide for or against participation in coalition was defeated. Shortly afterwards he resigned as leader and within weeks had joined FG, for whom he won a seat (Dublin South-West) in the subsequent general election. Later he moved to Cork and practised as a barrister on the southern circuit.

O'LEARY, Olivia (1949–), journalist and broadcaster, ed. Convent of Mercy, Carlow and UCD. Reporter with *Carlow Nationalist* 1969–72 and with RTÉ news and features 1972–8, for which she received a Jacob's radio award in 1974. Moved to the *Irish Times* political reporting staff 1978–84, then briefly to the BBC, for which she presented the nightly programme of political analysis, *Newsnight*. In 1986 she resumed broadcasting on RTÉ, becoming a regular interviewer-presenter on leading current affairs television programmes like *Today Tonight* and its successor, *Prime Time*: she won two Jacob's television awards. During these years she also presented the Yorkshire Television documentary series *First Tuesday*. In 1994 she returned to newspaper journalism, writing in-depth political reportage for the *Sunday Tribune*.

O'MAHONY, Eoin (1904–1970), raconteur, lecturer, writer and broadcaster, b. Cork, ed. Presentation College, Cork, Clongowes, UCC, TCD and King's Inns, d. Dublin, 15 Feb. 1970. Auditor in a number of college debating societies, many awards for oratory. Practised as a barrister for some years, dabbled in politics without success. Became a household name as the genealogist-presenter of *Meet the Clans*, a Radio Éireann programme series in the 1950s and 1960s on which he was able to display with infectious enthusiasm his prodigious knowledge of the facts and apocrypha of Irish family history. Lectured in the USA and travelled widely in Europe, maintaining contact with a vast range of persons of distinction. It was a lifestyle appropriate to a genial gentleman scholar and Knight of Malta, the role in which he flourished and for which he was held in much affection. He was known as 'the Pope', for reasons lost in the mists of time: it was not intended, as might be imagined, to suggest that he was given to pontificating, for the hallmark of his talk was enthusiasm, not dogmatic assertion.

O'MAHONY, James (1924–), public servant, b. Upton, Co. Cork, ed. St Finbarr's College, Cork and TCD (BA, B.Comm.), m., one s. two d. Spent entire career in the Department of Agriculture – of which he was secretary 1977–88 – save for a year in the Department of Finance and 1961–4 as economic counsellor in the Irish Embassy, London. President of the International Sugar Council 1965. Member of the four-man team that negotiated Ireland's accession to the EEC in 1973. Irish delegate at high-level meetings of the EC, GATT and OECD and at bilateral trade negotiations with the UK, USA and other countries. Of a retiring nature, he was the quintessential civil servant.

O'MALLEY, Desmond (1939–), politician, b. 2 Feb. 1939, ed. Crescent College, Limerick, UCD and Incorporated Law Society, m. Patricia McAleer, two s. four d. Solicitor. Nephew of DONOGH O'MALLEY and his successor as Fianna Fáil TD for Limerick East. Has held the seat since 1968, first for FF and from Dec. 1986 for the PDs. Parliamentary secretary to Taoiseach JACK LYNCH 1969. Minister for Justice 1970–73, he took a strong line against the IRA, introducing legislation that established a special no-jury court to deal with subversive-style cases. Minister for Industry, Commerce and Energy 1977. In the 1979 contest for Lynch's successor, O'Malley supported GEORGE COLLEY, having developed an antagonistic relationship with CHARLES HAUGHEY. The latter appointed him Minister for Industry, Commerce and Tourism, a post he held until 1981. In the short-lived return to office of FF in 1982 he became Minister for Trade, Commerce and Tourism, from which position he resigned in Oct., having refused to promise Haughey support in one of the several attempts to depose him as party leader.

In 1985 he was expelled from FF for 'conduct unbecoming' because he had not supported the party stance in a vote about contraception, and late that year he was persuaded to form a new party, the Progressive Democrats, of which he became leader. In 1989 Haughey and O'Malley led their parties into a coalition, the first time FF had taken such a step. O'Malley was appointed Minister for Industry and Commerce.

Relations between the two improved greatly but there was renewed tension when ALBERT REYNOLDS took over from Haughey early in 1992. When Reynolds accused O'Malley of being 'deliberately dishonest' during the so-called 'Beef Tribunal', the PDs pulled out of the coalition government, precipitating a general election. FF then formed a new co-alition with Labour. O'Malley retired as party leader in Oct. 1993, to be succeeded by MARY HARNEY. He ran for the European Parliament in the Munster constituency in June 1994 but lost to Pat Cox.

O'MALLEY, Donogh (1921–1968), polit-ician, b. Co. Limerick, ed. Crescent College, Limerick, Clongowes and UCG, d. 10 Mar. 1968. Engineer. Elected Fianna Fáil TD for Limerick East at the 1961 and 1965 general elections. Parliamentary secretary to the Minister for Finance 1961–5. Minister for Health 1965, for Education 1966–8. In the latter post he introduced free secondary schooling, which was arguably the most important development of the century in Irish education and made possible successful careers at home and abroad for thousands of young people over the follow-ing decades. His proposal for a merger between UCD and TCD, however, was defeated – in part by an ad hoc combination of tradition-ally minded academics in the two institutions. His cavalier and zestful attitude to life endeared him to many of his contemporaries, although it alienated senior members of FF and the civil service, who disliked O'Malley's disregard for conventional approaches in the formulation and announcement of policy decisions. Uncle of DESMOND O'MALLEY.

O'MALLEY, Earnán (Ernest) (1898–1957), republican and writer, b. Castlebar, childhood spent in Dublin, ed. UCD, d. Dublin, Mar. 1957. He fought in the Easter Rising and commanded the 2nd Southern Division of the IRA during the War of Independence. Taking the anti-Treaty side in the Civil War, he was arrested after the siege of the Four Courts 1922, escaped and later became the IRA's director of organisation. He was recaptured after a gun-battle in which he was severely wounded, and went on hunger strike in prison. After his release he travelled widely, developing a career as a writer and broadcaster. His accounts of the War of Independence, *On Another Man's Wound*, and the Civil War, *The Singing Flame*, were pub-lished in 1936 and 1978 respectively.

O'MALLEY, Mary (1949–), playwright and poet, b. Galway, ed. UCG. Taught at the University of Lisbon for eight years. In 1990 she published her first collection of poetry, *A Consideration of Silk*, for which she received a Hennessy award and an Arts Council bursary. Long involved with the Cúirt Poetry Festival, she sits on its organising committee and writes its educational programme. She has been active on poetry projects, which resulted in antholo-gies *100 Natural Highs* (1993) and *100 Close Encounters* (1995). Works closely with the Lyric Theatre, Belfast, for which she wrote *Once a Catholic* (1978), *Look Out – Here Comes Trouble* (1979) and *Never Shake Hands with the Devil* (1990), as well as editing *Threshold*, an account of the company's history 1957–86. She has also edited *A Needle's Eye* by John Boyd (1979). *Sweatshop: A Woman's Guide to Self-employment*, non-fiction, was published in 1983. Her most recent poetry is *Where the Rocks Float* (1993).

O'MALLEY, Michael George (1886–1961), surgeon, b. Kilmilkin, Connemara, ed. Rockwell, UCG and UCD, one of the NUI's early medical graduates (1910). Worked at the Mater Hospital, Dublin, the Middlesex Hospital, London and St Peter's Hospital for Stone. Returning to Galway, O'Malley (FRCS, 1914) secured appointments at the Infirmary and the Central Hospital and was elected to the chair of surgery at UCG in 1924. Four of his 13 siblings also entered the medical pro-fession, three practising in London and the fourth, Conor O'Malley (1889–1982), becom-ing an ophthalmologist.

O'MALLEY, Tony (1913–), artist, b. Callan, Co. Kilkenny. O'Malley did not begin to paint until 1948 during recuperation from a long illness. In 1959, after several visits, he settled in St Ives in Cornwall, renowned for its thriving artistic community. He moved back to Callan with his wife, Jane Harris, in 1980 and has lived there since. Although O'Malley's work is inspired by the landscape with which he is familiar, it does not attempt literal descriptions of scenes. He conveys the hidden essence of a place through an abstract rendering of that aspect of the landscape he finds most evocative. He is particularly admired for his skill as a colourist and for the varied exploration of texture on the surface of his paintings. His work forms part of several major private and public collections all over the world. Awards include the *Guardian* art critics' award and the Irish-American Cultural Institute award 1989.

O'MEARA, John (1915–), classical scholar, b. Eyrecourt, Co. Galway, ed. Rockwell, UCD and Oxford. Jesuit novice and scholastic 1933–45. Professor of Latin UCD 1948. A scholar of international reputation, his published work includes a translation of St Brendan's *Navigatio* and a study of Johannes Scottus Eriugena.

Ó MÓRÁIN, Dónall (1923–), promoter of Gaelic cultural revival, b. Kerry, 6 Sept. 1923, ed. St Finian's School, Waterville, Co. Kerry, Coláiste Mhuire, UCD and King's Inns. Called to Bar 1946. Managerial posts in publishing and printing 1946–63. Ceannasaí (chief executive), 1963, of Gael-Linn, the cultural organisation devoted to promoting the use of the Irish language in Irish life and the economic development of the country, especially the Irish-speaking districts. Chairman RTÉ Authority from 1970 to 1972 when the government dismissed its members, holding that they had breached the terms of a directive to refrain from broadcasting material which might promote the aims of organisations committed to the use of violence (RTÉ had carried KEVIN O'KELLY's account of an interview with the supposed chief of staff of the IRA). After a change of government, reappointed chairman of the Authority 1973–6. Continued on board of Gael-Linn; managing director of the weekly newspaper *Anois*, published by the organisation from 1984.

Ó MÓRDHA, Seán (1943–), film documentary-maker, b. Dublin, ed. Coláiste Mhuire and UCD (BA Celtic studies and modern history). Edited RTÉ current affairs programmes *Seven Days* and *Féach* in the early 1970s. Left RTÉ 1985 and has since worked as an independent producer for BBC 2. Made *The Blue Note*, a profile of SEÁN Ó RIADA (1981). Producer, director of *Is There One Who Understands Me – The World of James Joyce* (1982). Directed two films on SAMUEL BECKETT, *Silence to Silence* (1984) and *As the Story was Told* (1987); *Spendthrift of Genius* (1986) on Oscar Wilde; *Cast a Cold Eye* (1989) on W.B. YEATS. Also made literary films about SEAMUS HEANEY, Richard Ellmann, JOHN MCGAHERN and THOMAS KINSELLA, most of which were screened at international festivals in Europe and America. Won an Emmy award (1982) for JOYCE film and a Celtic Film award (1985) for the first Beckett film.

Ó MUIRÍOSA, Máirín (1906–1982), poet, journalist and scholar, b. Dublin, ed. Monaghan and Luxembourg. BA in Celtic studies and MA in Welsh, UCD. Director of An Club Leabhar for over 20 years. Member of the Board for Higher Education and president of Oireachtas na Gaeilge. In 1978 Ó Muiríosa became the first person to write a textbook in Irish on the history of Irish literature. Her other works deal with those involved in the early days of the language revival, and her own poetry won several Oireachtas na Gaeilge prizes. Publications include *Réamhchonrathóirí* (1968), *Gaeil agus Breatnaigh Anallód* (1974) and *Traidisiún Liteartha na nGael* (1978).

Ó MUIRTHILE, Liam (1950–), poet and journalist, b. Co. Cork, ed. Coláiste Críost Rí, Cork and UCC. Received the Irish-American Cultural Institute award in 1984. An early participant in *Innti*, currently works for RTÉ and *The Irish Times*. Publications include *Tine Chnámh* (1984).

Ó MUIRTHUILE, Seán (1881–1941), lieutenant-general, b. Cork. Prominent in the Gaelic League, he became its general secretary in 1920. Member of the IRB from 1912, secretary 1916 following the Rising. Involved in the reorganisation of the Volunteers after 1916. Joined the army on the outbreak of the Civil War. Commandant Kilmainham Jail for a short period, then, after serving as assistant adjutant-general, was appointed quartermaster-general in Jan. 1923. Forced to resign in Mar. 1924 because of the 'Army Mutiny'. Became manager of the Cork office of the Irish Sweepstakes 1931.

O'NEILL, Francis (1849–1936), collector, author and flute player, b. Tralibane, near Bantry, Co. Cork, into a household noted for hospitality to musicians. Learning the flute, he showed an extraordinary ability to memorise tunes (he never learned to read music). At 16 he ran away from home and there followed a period of high adventure, which included being shipwrecked in the Pacific. Settling in the USA, he tried various occupations before enrolling in the Chicago Police Department, of which he was appointed chief in 1905. He worked closely with his colleague James O'Neill, originally from Co. Down, in compiling a vast collection of tunes and airs remembered from childhood or learned from famous Irish musicians in America. He gathered 1,850 of these pieces in *The Music of Ireland*, published in 1903, and a further 1,001 in *The Dance Music of Ireland* (1907), which among traditional musicians became known simply as 'the book'. In 1908 he produced *O'Neill's Irish Music for Piano and Violin*, in 1910 *Irish Folk Music, A Fascinating Study* and in 1916 *Waifs and Strays of Gaelic Melody*, with an enlarged edition in 1922. *Irish Minstrels and Musicians* (1913) is a substantial volume of analysis and commentary, with illustrated biographical sketches of over 300 musicians, collectors and instrument makers. He bequeathed his library and papers to the University of Notre Dame.

O'NEILL, John Joseph ('**Jonjo**') (1952–), jockey, b. Castletownroche, Co. Cork, 13 Apr. 1952. He rode a record 149 winners when he was champion National Hunt jockey in 1977–8. In a career which lasted from 1972 to 1986 he rode 885 winners, three times going past the 100 mark in a season. His major wins were two Cheltenham Champion Hurdles (Sea Pigeon in 1980 and Dawn Run in 1984), two Cheltenham Gold Cups (Alverton in 1979 and Dawn Run in 1986) – a historic double – and two Scottish Champion Hurdles. He fought a brave battle with cancer after his retirement, going on to pursue a successful career as a trainer.

O'NEILL, Martin (1904–1991), footballer, hurler and handballer. He won Leinster senior football medals and an All-Ireland junior hurling medal with Wexford, as well as an All-Ireland junior football medal with Wicklow, in the 1920s and 1930s. He won three Railway Cup medals with Leinster, in 1928, 1929 and 1930, the last as a substitute, and played Tailteann Games football for Ireland against the USA in 1928 and 1932. He twice won (with Luke Sherry) the All-Ireland handball softball doubles title, in 1930 and 1931, and refereed three All-Ireland senior football finals, in 1932, 1933 and the famous New York Polo Grounds game in 1947. First full-time Leinster provincial GAA secretary 1927–70; founder

member of the Leinster Handball Council, secretary 1932–47.

O'NEILL, Sean, Gaelic footballer, b. Co. Down. From the Newry Mitchell's club, he was one of the game's outstanding forwards, scoring 85 goals and over 500 points for Down, and was a major figure in the county's All-Ireland victories of 1960, 1961 and 1968. He won seven Ulster senior football medals and a provincial record of eight Railway Cup medals, in 1960, 1963–6, 1968 and 1970– 71. He won three National Football League medals, in 1960, 1962 and 1968, as well as two All-Star awards, 1971 and 1972. Other honours include a Sigerson Cup medal with QUB, whom he later coached to further wins; subsequently he was coach and adviser to the Ulster team.

O'NEILL, Terence (1914–1990), politician, ed. Eton, d. 13 June 1990. Captain in the Irish Guards. He was elected MP for Bannside in 1946. In 1963, after serving as Minister of Finance for seven years, he succeeded Lord Brookeborough (Sir BASIL BROOKE) as Prime Minister. From the outset of his premiership he stressed the need for economic co-operation with the Republic of Ireland, and also sought to mollify the alienation of the nationalist community from the political system of Northern Ireland. It came as a major surprise, however, when he received the Taoiseach, SEÁN LEMASS, at Stormont in Jan. 1965 – a meeting arranged jointly by O'Neill's private secretary, Jim Malley, and the secretary of the Department of Finance in the Republic, T.K. WHITAKER. While highly significant at the symbolic level, the contact involved no serious policy decisions, but nevertheless caused major dissension within unionist ranks and brought the Revd IAN PAISLEY into prominence as an opponent of concessions to nationalism. Of greater importance in the years immediately following O'Neill's initiative was the growth of the civil rights movement on the one hand and on the other a revival of hardline unionism opposed to his more liberal approach. These factors came to a head in the aftermath of the violent police reaction to a civil rights demonstration in Derry in Oct. 1968. A programme of reforms to combat discrimination resulted in further unionist criticism of the Prime Minister; despite victory in the general election of Feb.

1969 his position soon became untenable and in Apr. he resigned. He subsequently became a peer, with the title Lord O'Neill of the Maine.

O'NOLAN, Brian. See under O'Brien, Flann.

OPIK, E.J. (1893–1985), astronomer, b. Estonia. Worked at Armagh Observatory from 1947 until his retirement at the age of 88. His work ranged from the astronomical aspects of meteors to planetary science to the internal constitutions of the stars and the scientific exploration of space.

O'RAHILLY, Alfred (1884–1969), academic, polymath and churchman, b. Listowel, Co. Kerry, Oct. 1884, ed. Blackrock and UCD (RUI), d. Dublin, 2 Aug. 1969. Entered Jesuits but left the order in 1914 before ordination. Ph.D. (Gregorian) 1919; D.Sc. (NUI) 1940. Professor of Mathematical Physics UCC 1917–43, registrar 1920–43, president 1943–54. Ordained priest 1955, monsignor 1960. Joined Sinn Féin 1916, imprisoned 1921, supported the Treaty. TD (Cork City) 1923–4. Although primarily a mathematician, his expertise ranged from theology to electromagnetism, and his involvement in public affairs from advising the drafters of the constitutions of 1922 and 1937 to membership of the Banking Commission of 1934–8 and the Commission on Vocational Organisation 1939–43.

O'Rahilly was the outstanding controversialist in the Ireland of his day, presenting trenchantly argued – if often idiosyncratic – views on virtually every topic of public debate. His output of articles, both in academic journals and in the popular press (especially the Roman Catholic weekly *Standard*), was prodigious, and he wrote a number of books, from religious tracts to a treatise on money. A consistent theme throughout his life was his commitment to papal social teaching, which he sometimes expressed in terms more polemical than didactic. His enduring memorial is the extramural programme whereby he provided access to university education in social and economic subjects for trade unionists, farmers and others unable to undertake full-time study. He also founded Cork University Press. He retired from UCC shortly after his wife's death and was ordained to the priesthood by his friend of many years' standing, Archbishop JOHN CHARLES MCQUAID.

O'RAHILLY (Michael Joseph Rahilly), The (1875–1916), revolutionary, b. 21 Apr. 1875, Ballylongford, Co. Kerry, ed. Clongowes. Emigrated to America, married and returned to Ireland 1909. Member central executive Gaelic League 1912; founder member Volunteers 1913; guaranteed personally the funds needed for the *Asgard* arms landing at Howth 1914. Supported EOIN MACNEILL's countermand of the order for rebellion Easter 1916 and delivered it to Limerick, but returned to Dublin and took part in the fighting once it broke out, saying, 'If the men I trained to fight are going into action, I must be with them,' or as W.B. YEATS has him tell PATRICK PEARSE and JAMES CONNOLLY in his ballad-poem 'The O'Rahilly':

Because I helped to wind the clock
I come to hear it strike.

He was killed on 28 Apr. 1916 in Moore Street while leading a charge of Volunteers from the GPO, by then in flames.

O'RAHILLY, Thomas Francis (1883–1953), scholar, b. Listowel, Co. Kerry, ed. Blackrock and UCD. He established an early reputation as a precocious scholar of both modern and medieval Irish. Professor of Irish TCD 1919; research professor at UCC 1929–35 and thereafter at UCD. Director School of Celtic Studies, Dublin Institute for Advanced Studies on its foundation in 1940. A figure of great influence, his two principal books were *Irish Dialects, Past and Present* (1932) and *Early Irish History and Mythology* (1946). He also edited anthologies of Irish poetry and was founder editor of the journal *Celtica*.

Ó RAIFEARTAIGH, Tarlach (1905–1984), educationalist, b. Carrickmore, Co. Tyrone, ed. St Patrick's College, Armagh and UCD (MA in modern and early Irish). Lecturer St Patrick's College, Dublin 1925–31. Successively inspector of secondary schools, assistant chief inspector and chief inspector 1932–48. Assistant secretary Department of Education 1948–55 and secretary 1955–68. First chairman of the Higher Education Authority 1968–75. Chairman of the Committee for Higher Education and Research of the Council of Europe 1971–2. Chairman of the Advisory Committee for Cultural

Relations, Department of Foreign Affairs. Council member of the RIA. Commandeur in the Ordre des palmes académiques and Chevalier of the Légion d'honneur. Knight of the Order of St Gregory the Great.

Hon. LL D from: Iona College, New York (1960), NUI (1964) and TCD (1975). Various articles on St Patrick and related subjects in *Irish Historical Studies* (of which he was secretary for 20 years), *Celtica, Irish Ecclesiastical Record, Journal of the Royal Society of Antiquaries of Ireland, Maynooth Review* and *Encyclopaedia Britannica*. General editor of *The Royal Irish Academy*, published on the occasion of the Academy's bicentenary in 1985. 'The Enigma of Saint Patrick' was published in *Seanchas Ardmhacha* (vol. 13, no. 2).

O'REGAN, Brendan (1917–), airport services pioneer, b. Sixmilebridge, Co. Clare, ed. Blackrock. Worked in the family hotel business until 1943, when he was appointed comptroller of sales and catering at Shannon Airport, a position he retained until 1973. Generally credited with the idea of having a duty-free shop at the airport, from which developed the international hotel school at Shannon, advanced in-flight catering, a mail order service and other innovations. Chief executive Shannon Free Airport Authority 1957–9; chairman of the Shannon Free Airport Development Company 1959–78. A visionary who can recall the building of Shannon Airport on what was once a flat, boggy, desolate place, leading to an industrial estate, a new town and a great international airport in an area which has over 100 companies serving world markets. In 1987 first chairman of a consortium of major companies at Shannon formed to promote a Centre for International Co-operation. Chairman Co-operation North 1979–82 and Co-operation Ireland 1982–4; joint president Co-operation North–Co-operation Ireland 1984–5. He received the Paul Harris award 1984 for promoting peace through understanding. Hon. LL D (1978) NUI.

O'REILLY, Anthony Joseph Francis Kevin (Tony, A.J.F.) (1936–), international rugby player and entrepreneur, b. Dublin, ed. Belvedere, UCD, TCD and in the United States; BCL, Ph.D., D.Litt., also qualified as a solicitor. A raconteur, public speaker and world businessman with infinite charisma, he shares with MIKE GIBSON the record for Ireland's longest international rugby career, with 16 seasons 1955–70. He won 29 caps, with a gap of seven years between his penultimate and final appearances, the latter being against England at Twickenham in 1970, when he was recalled to the team at short notice. He learned his rugby at Belvedere, and at club level played for Old Belvedere, Dolphin and Leicester. He toured South Africa in 1955 and Australia and New Zealand in 1959, playing in ten Tests and scoring six international tries, which is a record. He is also the Lions' most capped wing, with nine Tests (he won one cap as a centre), and his 23 tries – which include 17 in 17 matches in New Zealand – is a Lions tour record. O'Reilly was in turn managing director of An Bord Bainne (the Irish Dairy Board), the Irish Sugar Company and H.J. Heinz UK, before becoming president and chief executive worldwide of the Heinz Corporation. Numerous other commercial activities include Fitzwilton, Waterford Wedgwood, Independent Newspapers (of which he is chairman) and global media interests. Chairman of the Ireland Funds of the USA, Canada, Britain, Australia, France, Germany and New Zealand, which have made vast financial contributions to peace projects and to economic and cultural enterprises in Northern Ireland and the Republic.

O'REILLY, Frank (1884–1957), secretary of the Catholic Truth Society of Ireland, b. Drogheda, ed. CBS, Drogheda and Belfast, d. Dublin, 19 Oct. 1957. Official in surveyor's department of the Post Office 1904–18; in 1918 appointed secretary and manager of CTSI in succession to John Rochford. Reorganised the Society, placing it on a sound financial footing and substantially increasing its pamphlet sales. Secretary to the committee that organised the Catholic Emancipation centenary celebrations 1929 and director of organisation for the Eucharistic Congress 1932. In 1937 he was selected by the hierarchy to sit on an official committee to examine a request by the bishops that Catholic broadcasts become a part of the scheduled programming of Radio Éireann – a scheme which eventually foundered due to opposition from EAMON DE VALERA. He managed to continue the publication work of the CTSI during World War II and was involved in organisational work for the Holy Year in 1950.

O'REILLY, John Joseph (John Joe), Gaelic footballer, b. Co. Cavan. After early successes with St Patrick's College and his club, Cornafean, he captained the Cavan team which won All-Ireland Senior Football Championships in 1947 (at the New York Polo Grounds) and 1948, having also played on three losing sides in the final. He won 11 Ulster senior football medals, as Cavan took the title each year except two 1937–49. He won a National Football League medal and four Railway Cup medals, in 1942 and 1943 (when he was the first Cavan captain), 1947 and as captain again in 1950. His brother, Tom O'Reilly, played on the 1947 team and also won Railway Cup medals for Ulster 1943 and 1944.

Ó RIADA, Seán (1931–1971), composer, arranger and musician, b. Cork. Studied music under ALOYS FLEISCHMANN at UCC, in Italy and in France. Musical director to the Abbey Theatre. In 1960 he was commissioned to compose the score for *Mise Éire* (and subsequently its sequel, *Saoirse*), a film documentary directed by George Morrison which traced the story of the foundation of the Irish state. His brilliant use of folk themes caught the imagination of the public at large.

To evening gatherings in his home Ó Riada invited musicians schooled in the traditional ethos, the pipes and whistles of Paddy Moloney, the fiddles of Martin Fay, John Kelly and later Sean Keane, the accordions of EAMON DE BUITLÉAR and Sonny Brogan. Ó Riada himself played bodhrán and eventually harpsichord, with Ronny McShane on bones. The group became known as Ceoltóirí Cualann. As well as presenting his interpretation of Irish dance music and airs, Ó Riada set out to popularise the work of the 17th- and 18th-century Irish harpists/composers. In 1961 he returned to film music with the score for *The Playboy of the Western World*. Ceoltóirí Cualann made few live public appearances but became nationally known through two radio series, *Reachtaireacht an Riadaigh* and *Fleadh Cheoil an Radio* and in 1969 performed at a spectacular concert in the Gaiety Theatre. On being appointed to an academic position in UCC, Ó Riada moved with his family to Cúil Aodha

in the Gaeltacht. Troubled by ill health from the late 1960s, he died in a London hospital.

There is no single pigeon-hole in which Ó Riada's contribution to Irish culture in general, and to music in particular, can be placed. He had undoubted prejudices but also great vision. Above all he was a catalyst, moving a generation to think again, and to remember.

Ó RÍORDÁIN, Seán (1917–1977), poet and journalist, b. Ballyvourney, Co. Cork, ed. North Mon. Worked for Cork Corporation 1936–65. Had poetry published in the magazine *Comhar*, and by the time his first collection, *Eireaball Spideoige* (1952), appeared, he was recognised as a unique and controversial writer. Became one of the major Irish poets of the 20th century despite recurrent ill health. His work included translations into contemporary Irish of early medieval Gaelic religious poetry. He wrote a column for *The Irish Times* 1967–75. Hon. D.Litt. (NUI) 1976. Publications include: *Brosna* (1964), *Rí na nUile*, with Seán Ó Conghaile (1966), *Línte Liombó* (1971) and *Tar éis mo Bháis* (1978).

Ó RÍORDÁIN, Seán P. (1905–1957), archaeologist, b. Co. Cork, d. Dublin, 11 Apr. 1957. National school teacher prior to winning an NUI travelling studentship in 1931 which enabled him to study archaeology in Britain and on the Continent. Joined the Irish Antiques Division, National Museum of Ireland before becoming Professor of Archaeology UCC in 1936, as which he commenced a major series of excavations at Lough Gur, Co. Limerick, involving sites dating from a number of different periods. Professor of Celtic Archaeology UCD 1943–57. Undertook further important excavations at Tara and Newgrange, Co. Meath. Publications included *Antiquities of the Irish Countryside* (1942), *Tara: The Monuments on the Hill* (1954) and *New Grange and the Bend of the Boyne* (posthumously, 1964) with Professor Glyn Daniel of Cambridge.

ORMSBY, Frank (1947–), poet and editor, b. Enniskillen, ed. St Michael's College, Enniskillen and QUB. He has edited the *Honest Ulsterman* since 1969, alone and jointly. Won the Eric Gregory award for poetry 1974. He is a poet with a sharp eye; some find him dour, yet he is always compassionate and never dishonest. Collections: *Ripe for Company* and *Knowing my Place* (1971), *Business as Usual* and *Spirit of Dawn* (1973), *A Store of Candles* (1977), *Being Walked by a Dog* (1978), *A Northern Spring* (1986) and *The Ghost Train* (1995). Regarded as one of Northern Ireland's most important editors, Ormsby has done much to promote Ulster poets.

O'ROURKE, Colm (1957–), Gaelic footballer, b. Co. Meath, 31 Aug. 1957. From the Skryne club, he made his senior début for Meath in 1976 and was a member of the team which won three successive Leinster titles 1986–8. He won All-Ireland medals in 1987 and 1988 and captained the Meath team which lost to Cork in the 1990 final. He won his fifth Leinster medal in 1991, and shared in Meath's championship campaign the same year, including the legendary four games against Dublin, which ended with defeat by Down in the final. Other honours include two National Football League medals and two All-Star awards, in 1982 (at full-forward) and 1991 (at right corner-forward).

O'ROURKE, Mary (1937–), politician, b. 31 May 1937, ed. St Peter's, Athlone, Loreto Convent, Bray, Co. Wicklow, UCD and Maynooth, m. Enda O'Rourke, two s. Former secondary teacher. Member of Athlone UDC 1974–87 and Westmeath County Council 1979–87. Senator 1981–2. Elected a Fianna Fáil TD in Longford–Westmeath Nov. 1982 and at the subsequent two general elections. In the redrawn Westmeath constituency she topped the poll in 1992. Minister for Education 1987–Nov. 1991, then Minister for Health. On ALBERT REYNOLDS's succession as party leader she was dropped from cabinet and appointed Minister of State first at the Department of Industry and Commerce, with responsibility for Trade and Marketing, then at the Department of Enterprise and Employment, with responsibility for Labour Affairs. In Feb. 1992 she had contested the leadership of FF with Reynolds and Michael Woods but won just six votes. When BERTIE AHERN became party leader in late 1994 she was appointed his deputy. Her father, Patrick Lenihan, was also a TD, and she and BRIAN LENIHAN in 1987 became the first brother and sister to serve in the same cabinet.

ORPEN, William (1878–1931), artist, b. Stillorgan, Co. Dublin, 27 Nov. 1878, ed. Metropolitan School of Art, Dublin and Slade

School of Art, London, d. London, 29 Sept. 1931. Successful and fashionable painter, especially of portraits. Elected RHA 1908. Taught in the life class at the Metropolitan School, through which he was to influence SEÁN (JOHN) KEATING, Leo Whelan and SEAN O'SULLIVAN. Close friend of OLIVER ST JOHN GOGARTY, whose portrait he painted in 1911. Served as a war artist in France during and after World War I, where he produced harrowing pictures of the battlefields and ruined towns. His painting of the signing of the Treaty of Versailles was widely reproduced. Knighted 1918; elected RA 1921. Wrote *An Onlooker in France 1917–1919* and *Old Ireland and Myself.*

ORR, William M'Fadden, mathematician. Elected FRS 1909. Professor of Mathematics Royal College of Science until its abolition in 1927; Professor of Pure and Applied Mathematics UCD 1927–33.

Ó SEARCAIGH, Cathal (1956–), poet and broadcaster for RTÉ, b. Donegal Gaeltacht, ed. NIHE, Limerick (French, Russian and Irish) and Maynooth (Celtic studies). Lives on mountain farm in Co. Donegal. Publications include: *Miontraigéide Cathrach* (1975), *Tuirlingt* (1979), *Súile Shuibhne* (1983) and *Suibhne* (1987).

O'SHANNON, Cathal (1889–1969), trade unionist, journalist and socialist, b. Randalstown, Co. Antrim, ed. St Columb's College, Derry, d. Dublin, Oct. 1969. Working as a clerk with a steamship company in Belfast, O'Shannon joined the Gaelic League and became a sworn member of the IRB. He joined the Belfast staff of the ITGWU in 1912 and contributed to JAMES CONNOLLY's *Workers' Republic*, the *Peasant*, *Sinn Féin* and other nationalist papers. He mobilised with 100 volunteers at Coalisland, Co. Tyrone on Easter Sunday 1916 but dispersed following orders from Dublin. A week later he was arrested in Belfast and imprisoned in Reading Jail. On his release in 1917 he became editor of the ITGWU paper, the *Voice of Labour*, and, following its suppression in 1919, of *Labour Watchword*. O'Shannon was arrested again in 1920 while attending an international labour meeting in London. He was imprisoned in Mountjoy Jail, Dublin but released after a 17-day hunger strike. He continued to campaign for independence and was elected Labour TD for Louth–Meath in 1922. Secretary to the Irish Trades Union Congress 1941 and subsequently to the ITGWU-led breakaway Congress of Irish Unions. He was appointed to the Labour Court on its establishment in 1946 and continued to serve until his retirement in 1969. Father of CATHAL (ÓG) O'SHANNON.

O'SHANNON, Cathal (Óg) (1928–), journalist and broadcaster, s. of CATHAL O'SHANNON, ed. Coláiste Mhuire. Reporter *The Irish Times* Dublin and London 1948–63, reporter/presenter BBC current affairs 1964–5, RTÉ current affairs 1965–78. Broadcast work includes the documentary *Even the Olives are Bleeding*, a retrospective on the Irish involvement in the Spanish civil war, and *The Wine Geese*, a series about the wines and vineyards planted or developed by Irish émigrés. He twice won a Jacob's award. He became public affairs director for metallurgical firm Aughinish Alumina in 1978 but continued to broadcast as a freelancer.

O'SHEA, Jack ('Jacko') (1957–), Gaelic footballer, b. Cahirciveen, Co. Kerry, 19 Nov. 1957. After winning three successive All-Ireland under-21 titles with Kerry, he went on to win seven All-Ireland senior medals during the county's great era in the 1970s and 1980s. He was a star midfielder in the successive wins of 1978–81 and 1984–6. Other achievements include two National Football League medals (1982, 1984), four Railway Cup medals (1977–8, 1981–2) and six successive All-Star awards (1980–85). He captained Ireland in the Compromise Rules series against Australia in 1984 and 1986 and played in the 1987 and 1990 series.

O'SHEA, John (1944–), founder and director of GOAL, journalist, b. Limerick, 28 Feb. 1944, ed. CBS, Westport and Monkstown, and UCD, where he studied history and philosophy. On leaving school, worked as a coal clerk with P. Donnelly. Studied at night, started writing 'Sports Mix' column for the *Evening Press* 1965, full-time sports journalist 1967–91. In 1977 he set up the Third World relief and development agency GOAL, using his sports and journalistic contacts to fund-raise. Since its foundation GOAL has spent £40 million on supplies and development programmes in Sudan, Somalia, Tanzania, Rwanda and

throughout the Third World, with over 100 volunteers working in 16 countries. O'Shea holds medals for rugby, Gaelic football, soccer and basketball, and has five international basketball caps. Played rugby with Blackrock for 28 years. Board member of Agency for Personal Service Overseas 1986–91. Member of Irish Aid Advisory Committee 1996. Won People of the Year award 1992, was the subject of a *Late Late Show* tribute programme Mar. 1995.

O'SHEA, Paudie (1955–), Gaelic footballer, b. Dingle, Co. Kerry, 16 May 1955. A Kerry minor footballer 1971–5, he captained St Michael's College, Listowel to their first county college title. He went on to win 13 Munster senior football medals with Kerry, and a record-equalling eight All-Ireland senior football medals 1975, 1978–81, 1984–6. He won four Railway Cup medals with Munster (1976, 1978, 1981–2), four National Football League medals (1974, 1977, 1982, 1984) and five consecutive All-Star awards (1981–2 at right-half back, 1983–5 at right full-back).

Ó SIADHAIL, Mícheál (1947–), linguist, poet and educator, b. Dublin, ed. Clongowes, TCD and Oslo University, where he studied Scandinavian languages and folklore 1969–73. A lecturer in Irish at TCD, he resigned his post to pursue a career as a writer. Ó Siadhail has broadcast extensively on RTÉ, in addition to holding poetry readings for French and Norwegian radio. He is one of Ireland's most distinguished bilingual poets. Collections in Irish: *An Bhliain Bhisigh* (1978) and *Runga* (1980); in English: *Springnight* (1983) and *The Image Wheel* (1985). He also co-wrote *Cumann*, with Arndt Wigger (1982), and published the collection *Hail! Madam Jazz* (1992). He has compiled language textbooks and courses, including *Córas Fuaimeanna na Gaeilge* (1975), *Téarmaí Tógála agus Tís as Inis Meáin*, a lexicon (1978), *Learning Irish: An Introductory Self-tutor* (1980) and *Modern Irish*, a grammar textbook (1989). He is currently linguistics researcher at the DIAS.

Ó SIOCHFHRADHA, Pádraig (1883–1964), novelist and short story writer, penname An Seabhac, b. and ed. Dingle, Co. Kerry. Became organiser for the Irish Volunteers in 1913 and was imprisoned three times. Teacher and organiser for the Gaelic League in Munster.

He worked in the civil service 1920–32. Editor for the Irish-language publisher An Gúm and director of the Educational Company. He wrote textbooks, short stories, plays and new versions of old texts. Senator 1946–54. Two of his books, short story collection *Máirín, An Baile Seo 'Gainne* (1913) and novel *Jimín Mháire Thaidhg* (1921), made him one of the best-loved writers of the century. Edited diaries of Wolfe Tone as *Beatha Theobald Wolfe Tone* (1937) and *An t-Oileánach* by TOMÁS Ó CRIOMHTHAINN.

Ó SÚILEABHÁIN, Muiris (Maurice Sullivan) (1904–1950), writer, b. into the Irish-speaking community of the Great Blasket Island, son of a farmer/fisherman and a fisherman himself. Joined the Garda Síochána in 1927; while stationed at Indreabhán in the Connemara Gaeltacht he wrote his classic autobiography, *Fiche Bliain ag Fás* (1933), a nostalgic account of a way of life on the Blaskets now vanished for ever. Resigned from the guards to take up writing as a career but, having produced the one book that was in him to write, he was obliged to rejoin the force. He died on 25 Jan. 1950 in a drowning accident while bathing.

Ó SÚILLEABHÁIN, Mícheál (1950–), musician, composer and ethnomusicologist, b. Clonmel, m. singer Nóirín Ní Riain. Successfully combines the roles of practical musician and academic. Although immersed in the Irish tradition, has introduced innovative ideas in all aspects of his work – for instance, relating musical concepts drawn from diverse idioms such as jazz, Irish traditional and classical. Joined the music department of UCC 1975 and was instrumental in developing an integrated curriculum involving both traditional and classical music and musicians. Visiting professor Boston College 1990 and founded an archive of Irish traditional music in America; subsequently invited by the Federation of Irish Societies to pursue a similar initiative in Britain. Chairman of both the Irish Traditional Music Archive and Maoin Cheoil an Chláir, the Clare music education centre. In 1994 became first professor of music at UL. A multi-instrumentalist, he is perhaps best known for his piano and keyboard interpretations.

O'SULLIVAN, Denis Jeremiah (1925–), physician, b. Carrigadrohid, Co. Cork, ed. Presentation Secondary School, Cork and UCC. Graduated MB, B.Ch., 1948, admitted MRCP 1954 and elected FRCP 1967, FRCPI 1973. Having held formative training posts in the Manchester Royal Infirmary and the Royal Hospital, Wolverhampton, he was appointed to the chair of medicine in UCC in 1961 and exerted a strong influence on the development of clinical science and medical research in Cork. On retiring from the chair, and from his post as consultant physician to the Regional Hospital, in 1990 he briefly held the position of medical director at the Ibn al Bitar Hospital, Baghdad. Publications include papers on renal disorders and on diabetes mellitus and other endocrine disorders.

O'SULLIVAN, Donal J. (1893–1973), scholar, b. and ed. Liverpool, d. 15 Apr. 1973. His parents were Irish and through their influence his interest in Ireland began early. He became a civil servant, first in London, transferring to Dublin at the earliest opportunity. Clerk of the Senate 1925–36, later wrote the definitive work on the subject, *The Irish Free State and its Senate* (1940). However, his reputation rests on his work as a scholar of traditional Irish music, as which he was outstanding. He edited *The Bunting Collection of Irish Folk Music and Song* (1939). His magnum opus was *Carolan: Life and Times of an Irish Harper* (1958), which established Carolan's central place in the sensibility of contemporary Irish musicians. It influenced SEÁN Ó RIADA and later THE CHIEFTAINS. O'Sullivan's *Songs of the Irish* (1960) and *Irish Folk Music, Song and Dance* (1961) also contributed a scholarly foundation to the revival of traditional music which was such a feature of the 1960s and after. He was director of studies in Irish folk music UCD 1951–62.

O'SULLIVAN, Gearóid (1891–1948), lieutenant-general, b. Skibbereen, Co. Cork. A brilliant academic, he was awarded an honours degree in Celtic studies 1913, a H.Dip.Ed. the following year and an MA in educational science 1915. Enrolled as a Volunteer at the initial meeting in the Rotunda 1913. Member of GPO garrison during Easter Week 1916. Interned in Frongoch. Elected to the supreme council of IRB 1921. Adjutant-general IRA 1920–22. Elected TD for Carlow and Kilkenny in 1921 and again the following year. Appointed adjutant-general of the army 1922; forced to resign as a result of the 'Army Mutiny' 1924 although later vindicated by the Army Enquiry Committee. Became a barrister and was appointed Judge Advocate-General in 1927.

O'SULLIVAN, John Marcus (1881–1948), academic and politician, b. Killarney, ed. St Brendan's College, Killarney, Clongowes, UCD and Heidelberg (Ph.D. 1906). Professor of Modern History UCD 1910. TD (C. na nG. North Kerry) 1924–32. Parliamentary secretary to Minister for Finance 1924–6, Minister for Education 1926–32.

O'SULLIVAN, Marcus (1961–), athlete, b. Cork, 22 Dec. 1961. Possessing a powerful finish, he became EAMONN COGHLAN's successor as the world's finest indoor miler, winning the Wannamaker Mile at the Millrose Games in New York five times between 1986 and 1991 and coming second another five times up to 1995. In Meadowlands in 1989 he set a world 1,500 m indoor record at 3:35.6, and he won the world indoor title at the same distance three times, at Indianapolis in 1987, Budapest in 1989 and Toronto in 1993, coming fourth in 1991. He won the European indoor silver medal at 1,500 m in 1985 but was less successful outdoors, being sixth at the 1986 European Championship and eighth in the 1988 Olympics, the only time he reached the final in four Games 1984–96. He was Irish champion at 1,500 m in 1984 and 800 m champion in 1986, 1989 and 1992, and won the AAA 1,500 m title in 1985. He ran on the 4 x 1 mile team which set an Irish record in 1985 and he set three Irish 800 m records – best 1:45.85 – in 1984–5.

O'SULLIVAN, Maureen (1911–), actress, b. Boyle. Went to Hollywood and starred with JOHN MCCORMACK in *Song o' my Heart* (1930). Best known for playing Jane to Johnny Weismuller's Tarzan in the pre-war film series but she appeared in many other productions, among them *The Barretts of Wimpole Street* (1934) and *Pride and Prejudice* (1940). Mother of the actress Mia Farrow.

O'SULLIVAN, Sean (1905–), Gaelic scholar, also known as Seán Ó Súilleabháin, b. Co. Kerry. Attached to the Folklore Commission 1935–75, he travelled widely in Europe – Sweden in particular – and the USA,

lecturing on Irish folklore and gathering comparative material from many sources. Native Irish speaker. His chief works in Irish were: *Saoghal na bPáistí* (1935), *Diarmuid na Bolgaighe agus a Chóimhursain* (1937), *Láimh-leabhar Béaloideasa* (1938) and *Caitheamh Aimsire ar Thorraimh* (1961). His principal writings in English included *Handbook of Irish Folklore* (1942), *Religious Folktales; The Types of Irish Folktale; Folktales of Ireland* (1967) and *Irish Wake Amusements* (1967), a translation from the author's own 1961 work. He also made valuable contributions to the *Encyclopaedia of Ireland* (1968) and to scholarly journals in Ireland, Britain, Germany, Sweden and the USA.

O'SULLIVAN, Sean (1906–1964), painter, b. Dublin, ed. Synge Street, Metropolitan School of Art, Dublin, Central School of Art, London and Académie Julian, Paris, d. Nenagh, 4 Apr. 1964. MRHA 1931. He carried out a number of portraits of notable figures in Irish politics and the arts. Achieving considerable success at a young age, he had already completed portraits of MAUD GONNE MACBRIDE and Margaret Pearse before painting EAMON DE VALERA in 1931. Other subjects included DOUGLAS HYDE, JAMES JOYCE, W.B. YEATS, JAMES LARKIN and Sir ALFRED CHESTER BEATTY. He also designed a number of commemorative stamps and painted a moving Stations of the Cross for a church in Portarlington, Co. Laois.

O'SULLIVAN, Seumas (1879–1958), poet and editor, b. James Sullivan Starkey, Dublin, ed. locally, m. ESTELLA SOLOMONS. He published poems in the *Irish Homestead*, *United Irishman*, and *Celtic Christmas* in 1902; further verses were collected in *New Songs*, a volume edited by GEORGE RUSSELL. O'Sullivan co-founded the publishing firm Whaley and Company 1904 and one year later published his first book of poetry, *The Twilight People*. His poems were not unlike early work by W.B. YEATS and Russell: semi-magical and spiritual. He was a friend of ARTHUR GRIFFITH, OLIVER ST JOHN GOGARTY, JAMES JOYCE; founded the *Dublin Magazine*, which he edited until his death. In 1939 UCD conferred on him an honorary Litt.D. Poetry includes: *The Earth-lover and Other Verses* (1909), *Mud and Purple* and *Requiem and Other Poems* (1917), *The Lamplighter and Other Poems* (1929), *This* *is the House* (1942), *Dublin Poems* (1946) and *Translations and Transcriptions* (1950).

O'SULLIVAN, Sonia (1969–), athlete, b. Cobh, Co. Cork, 28 Nov. 1969. She became the first Irish woman to break a world track record by winning the indoor 5,000 m in 15:17.28 in 1991. Finishing fourth in the 3,000 m at the 1992 Barcelona Olympic Games, she broke five Irish records from 1,500 m to 5,000 m within 11 days that year. She was disappointingly beaten into fourth place, behind three Chinese athletes, in the 1993 Stuttgart World Championship, but took the silver in the 1,500 m, becoming the first Irish woman to win a medal at a major championship. In 1993 she won four IAAF Grand Prix events, finished overall second and collected $100,000. In successive weeks in July 1994 she set the world record for 2,000 m (5:25.36) and the 3,000 m European record (8:21.64), and then won the European gold medal at 3,000 m. A graduate of Villanova University – for which she won NCAA titles at 3,000 m in 1990–91 and cross-country in 1990 – she was World Student Games champion at 1,500 m and 2,000 m in 1991. During 1995 and the first half of 1996 she was the leading 5,000 m runner in the world and started as warm favourite for the event in the Atlanta Olympics. However, a mystery illness caused her to drop out of the final about two-thirds of the way through the race.

O'TOOLE, Peter (1932–), actor, b. Connemara, 2 Aug. 1932, grew up in Leeds, ed. RADA. Made his amateur stage début at the Leeds Civic Theatre aged 17. Worked at the Bristol Old Vic 1955–8. His first screen appearance was in *Kidnapped* (1960) but he made his mark playing T.E. Lawrence in David Lean's epic *Lawrence of Arabia* (1962), for which he received an Oscar nomination as best actor (one of seven nominations, though he has never won). In 1972 he gave acclaimed performances in *Arms and the Man* and *Waiting for Godot* on the Dublin stage. Went on to appear in a succession of mostly mediocre films. O'Toole, who generally plays caddish figures in a tongue-in-cheek style, has in latter years emerged as one of film's top character actors.

Ó TUAIRISC, Eoghan (Eugene Watters) (1919–1982), poet, novelist, playwright and soldier, b. Ballinasloe, Co. Galway, ed. Garbally Park, St Patrick's College, Dublin and UCD. Served in the army during the war. Taught in Finglas, Co. Dublin but after the success of his first two novels resigned to become a full-time writer 1961. Editor of Gaelic League journal *Feasta* and a member of Aosdána, he won many prizes for his work, including the HYDE memorial award in 1966 and the Oireachtas na Gaeilge prize in 1967 and 1977. He wrote in English and Irish. Publications include: *L'Attaque* (1962), *Lux Aeterna* (1964), *Dé Luain* (1966), *Lá Fhéile Mhíchil* (1967), *An Lomnochtán* (1977), *Aisling Mhic Artáin* (1978), *Fornocht do Chonac* (1981), *Dialann sa Díseart*, poetry with Rita Kelly (1981), and *Religio Poetae agus Aistí Eile* (1987).

Ó TUAMA, Seán (1926–), poet, playwright and critic, b. Cork. Professor of Irish Language and Culture at UCC. Has lectured extensively in French, American and English universities. His anthology *Nuabhéarsaíocht 1939–1949* (1950) was a major influence in gaining recognition for contemporary Irish poetry. Publications include: *An Grá in Amhráin na nDaoine* (1960), *Caoineadh Airt Uí Laoghaire* (1961), *Faoileán na Beatha* (1962), *Moloney agus Drámaí Eile* (1966), *Gunna Cam agus Slabhra Óir* (1967), *Saol fó Thoinn* and *Filí faoi Sceimhle* (1978), *An Duanaire: Poems of the Dispossessed*, with THOMAS KINSELLA (1981), *An Grá i bhFilíocht na nUasal* and *An Bás i dTír na nÓg* (1988).

OULTON, John Ernest Leonard (1881–1957), Church of Ireland theologian, b. 22 Mar. 1881, d. 2 Feb. 1957. After working in Dublin parishes he held several positions in the Divinity School in TCD, becoming Regius Professor of Divinity. He was an influential teacher and his patristic writings gained him a high reputation at home and abroad. His work on St Patrick (in which he expressed his considerable debt to Newport White) possibly reached its widest readership with his chapter in W. Alison Phillips's *History of the Church of Ireland*.

OWEN, Nora (1945–), née O'Mahony, politician, b. Dublin, June 1945, ed. Dominican Convent, Wicklow and UCD. Industrial chemist. TD (FG Dublin North) 1981–7 and since 1989. Fine Gael deputy leader 1993 and Minister for Justice 1994. Grand-niece of MICHAEL COLLINS and sister of Mary Banotti MEP.

P

PAISLEY, Ian Richard Kyle (1926–), clergyman and politician, b. Armagh, 6 Apr. 1926, ed. Ballymena Model School and South Wales Bible College. Throughout his long political career, he has vehemently opposed any weakening of the union between Great Britain and Northern Ireland, or any reduction in unionist political hegemony within the North itself. Before becoming involved in politics in the early 1960s, he established the North's first Free Presbyterian Church. From its pulpit and from the pages of his own daily newspaper, the *Protestant Telegraph*, he preached a fundamentalist and virulently anti-Catholic brand of Protestantism. His sniping at the unionist establishment, whom he accused of betraying Ulster's Protestants by pandering to Catholic demands for civil rights, eventually brought Paisley the political support he required. He won seats both in the NI parliament 1970 and at Westminster 1971, when he set up the Democratic Unionist Party. Since the imposition of direct rule from Westminster in 1972 he has consistently demanded the restoration of a legislative assembly for NI. However, he has always been totally opposed to any internal settlement based on power-sharing with the nationalist minority, and was heavily involved in the 1974 Ulster Workers' Council strike which brought down the power-sharing Executive. His attempt to orchestrate a repetition of this success in 1977 was an embarrassing failure, but in the European Parliament elections of 1979 he was elected with over 170,000 votes. The rivalry between the DUP and the UUP was suspended in 1985 in order to build a united opposition to the Anglo-Irish Agreement. This rapprochement, always uneasy, ended when the UUP decided to support the Conservative government elected in 1992. Elected to the NI Forum in May 1996. Participated in the multi-party talks on the future of NI which began in June of that year.

PALLES, Christopher (1831–1920), lawyer, b. Dublin, ed. Clongowes, TCD, King's Inns and Gray's Inn, London, d. 14 Feb. 1920. BA (1852), LL B and LL D (1860). Called to Bar 1853, QC, Solicitor-General for Ireland Feb. 1872, Attorney-General for Ireland Nov. 1872, unsuccessfully fought election for Liberals in Derry same year. Appointed last Lord Chief Baron of the Court of Exchequer by Gladstone in 1874, 12 hours before the fall of the Liberal government. Member of English Privy Council 1892. Friend of Cardinal Paul Cullen and Archbishop WILLIAM WALSH, advocated greater educational facilities at third level for Catholics. An outstanding lawyer who remained on the bench for over 40 years, retiring at 85 because of ill health.

PANTRIDGE, James Francis, cardiologist, b. near Hillsborough, Co. Down, ed. locally and at QUB. Graduated MB 1939. Serving with the RAMC in the Far East, he won the Military Cross and survived a 'death camp' in Burma. On his return, he proceeded MD and MRCP, engaged in research at Ann Arbor, Michigan and was appointed physician, later cardiologist, to the Royal Victoria Hospital, Belfast. In the early 1950s he prevailed upon T.B. Smiley, a chest surgeon, to operate on patients with mitral valve stenosis, thus initiating cardiac surgery in Northern Ireland. Pantridge also argued for the use of portable defibrillators to treat emergency cases, coronary attack victims who would die before reaching a hospital. The introduction of the first 'cardiac ambulance' in Belfast in 1966 was controversial, particularly as regards its cost-effectiveness. The concept was accepted more readily in American than in British cities, but the portable defibrillator is now a piece of standard medical equipment. The proceedings of an international symposium on pre-hospital coronary care were published as a Festschrift for Pantridge (1987) and his autobiography, *An Unquiet Life*, appeared in 1989.

PARKER, Dame Dehra (1882–1963), the only woman member of a Northern Ireland cabinet, b. Kilrea, Co. Derry, the only child of James Kerr-Fisher, d. 28 Nov. 1963.

She entered politics after the death of her first husband, Robert Spencer Chichester, in 1921 and was Unionist MP for Derry City and County 1921–9, 1932–60. She was appointed parliamentary secretary to the Minister of Education in 1937 and served as Minister of Health 1949–57. Although an able politician, Parker was dismissive of the political grievances of nationalists under the Stormont government.

PARKER, Stewart (1941–1988), playwright, b. Belfast, ed. QUB, d. Nov. 1988. Although he had already published a collection of verse, *The Casualty's Meditation* (1966), Parker first came to prominence at the 1975 Dublin Theatre Festival with *Spokesong*, which was produced in London the following year to considerable acclaim. Further plays included *Catchpenny Twist* (1977), *Nightshade* (1985), *Northern Star* (1985) about the 1798 Protestant rebel Henry Joy McCracken, and *Pentecost*, produced by Field Day in 1987. He wrote several scripts for radio, including *The Kamikaze Ground Staff Reunion Dinner*, and for television. Imagination, parody and music, with the Northern Troubles for backdrop, marked much of his output. Sadly, Parker died in his artistic prime, and the Stewart Parker Trust was instituted in his memory to promote the work of young dramatists in both the north and the south of Ireland.

PARKER, Thomas *John* (1942–), shipbuilder, ed. Belfast College of Technology. Chairman of the Babcock International Group. Joined Harland and Wolff as an apprentice in 1958. He worked on the company's design staff 1963–9 and was general manager of sales and projects 1972–4. He then left to become managing director of Sunderland shipbuilders Austin-Pickersgill. Parker was British Shipbuilders' director of marketing 1977–8, board member for shipbuilding 1978–83, also deputy chief executive 1980–83. He later returned to Harland's and was chairman and chief executive 1983–93. During a time of recession in the British shipbuilding industry and a period of transition brought about by privatisation, Parker remained popular with the workforce and is credited with being largely responsible for the company's survival.

PATERSON, Saidie (1906–1985), trade unionist and peace activist, b. Belfast, 25 Nov. 1906, ed. Woodvale NS, Belfast. Paterson was born and spent all her life at 32 Woodvale Street, off the Shankill Road. By 1918 both her parents were dead – her father, a shipyard blacksmith, died at the age of 27 and her mother, who had remarried, died in childbirth because the family could not afford a doctor. Shortly afterwards Paterson became an apprentice linen weaver at Ewart's linen factory on the Crumlin Road, and while there came under the influence of Ernest Bevin and Bob Getgood of the Amalgamated Transport and General Workers' Union. She organised the women workers of the mill, and after a seven-week strike in 1940 they won a pay increase and holiday pay. Paterson became a full-time official with the union the same year. During the 1970s she worked to promote peace in the North. She chaired Women Together and helped the Peace People to arrange a march of 50,000 women along the Shankill Road in 1976. She was injured when a follow-up march along the Falls Road was stoned, but her commitment to peace and reconciliation remained steadfast. Paterson's life's work was recognised by several awards, including the Joseph Parker Peace Prize and the World Methodist Peace Prize, and she was nominated as one of the world's 50 most distinguished women by the organisers of International Women's Year 1975.

PATERSON, Thomas George Farquhar (1888–1971), local historian and antiquarian, b. Canada, 29 Feb. 1888, d. 6 Apr. 1971. Curator and 'virtually creator' (E. ESTYN EVANS) of Armagh County Museum and a foundation trustee of the Ulster Folk Museum. Contributed regularly to the *Ulster Journal of Archaeology* and *Seanchas Ardmhacha* (journal of the Armagh Diocesan Historical Society), and to the *Preliminary Survey of Ancient Monuments of Northern Ireland*. Compiled 25 typescript volumes of 'Armagh Miscellania', comprising his notes and lectures.

PATTERSON, Glenn (1961–), novelist, b. Belfast, ed. QUB. He won the Rooney prize for *Burning your Own* (1988). He has been writer in residence at the University of East Anglia, UCC and QUB. Other novels: *Fat Lad* (1992), which was shortlisted for the GPA book award, and *Black Night at Big Thunder Mountain* (1995).

PAULIN, Tom (1949–), poet, playwright and academic, b. Leeds, ed. Belfast, University of Hull and Oxford. He has lectured in poetry at Nottingham University, the University of Virginia and Oxford. Within a relatively short period of time Paulin established a reputation as one of Ulster's most powerful poetic voices. He grew up in loyalist Belfast but has consistently refused to take sides in the sectarian conflict, choosing healing above strife. Yet his verse is unashamedly political, sometimes employing dialect. His first collection, *A State of Justice* (1977), won a Somerset Maugham award. There followed: *Personal Column* (1978), *The Strange Museum* (1980), *The Book of Juniper* (1981), *Liberty Tree* (1983), *The Argument at Great Trew* (1985), *Fivemiletown* (1987), *Selected Poems 1972–1990* (1993) and *Walking a Line* (1994), and he has edited two anthologies. Paulin is a well-known critic and an award-winning playwright, has adapted Sophocles and Aeschylus. He is a director of the Field Day Theatre Company, founded by BRIAN FRIEL and STEPHEN REA in 1980.

PEARCE, Colman (1938–), conductor, pianist and composer, b. Dublin. Principal conductor RTÉ Symphony Orchestra 1981–3. Principal guest conductor Bilbao Symphony Orchestra 1984–7. Appointed principal conductor and music director of the Mississippi Symphony Orchestra 1987. A champion of Irish musicians and composers, whose works he has premiered in Ireland and abroad, he has made guest appearances as a conductor worldwide.

PEARSE, Patrick Henry (1879–1916), revolutionary, writer and educationalist, b. Dublin, 10 Nov. 1879, ed. CBS, Westland Row, Dublin, UCD and King's Inns, becoming a barrister but practising only briefly. He is best known for his role as commander-in-chief of the Volunteers during the Easter Rising and President of the Provisional Government of the Irish Republic that it proclaimed. However, prior to his emergence as the dominant figure in the revolutionary separatist movement, he had already made significant contributions to Irish cultural life in the fields of literature and educational theory. He joined the Gaelic League in 1895, becoming editor of its journal, *An Claidheamh Soluis*, in 1903. Although he used its pages to attack the anglicisation of Ireland and to argue

for the revival of Irish as a spoken language, he had an inclusive notion of Irishness and strongly disapproved of the narrow linguistic nationalism of some Gaelic Leaguers. He was also a bitter critic of the existing Irish educational system, seeing it as the antithesis to his own anti-authoritarian approach which took as its goal the development of each child's individual personality and intellect. In 1908, with his brother, WILLIAM PEARSE, he founded St Enda's School (Scoil Éanna), near Rathfarnham, Co. Dublin, in order to put his theories into practice.

The failure of the third Home Rule bill in 1913, and the strong opposition to it from Conservatives and Ulster Unionists, convinced Pearse that Ireland could win independence only through force. He was a founder member of the Volunteers in 1913 and shortly afterwards joined the IRB. The outbreak of World War I left the IRB in effective control of those Volunteers who refused to support the British war effort, and Pearse became a member of the military council planning to lead them in a rebellion. Despite numerous setbacks, the Rising went ahead on Easter Monday 1916. Pearse established his headquarters in the GPO, outside which he read the Proclamation of the Republic. He surrendered on 29 Apr. and was executed on 3 May after a court martial.

Pearse was a prolific polemicist, playwright and poet. His writings include *The Murder Machine*, a treatise on education, and *Suantraidhe agus Goltraidhe* (Songs of Sleep and Sorrow), a collection of poems in Irish. His style was strikingly forceful in its exalted language, whether Irish or English, its intermingling of religious and patriotic sentiment, and its often premonitory tone. He so phrased some of his thoughts that they entered the national consciousness, providing sustenance for genuine love of country and nationalist extremism alike. Thus, long remembered was the dramatic assertion with which he ended his graveside oration on O'DONOVAN ROSSA: 'the fools, the fools, the fools! – they have left us our Fenian dead, and while Ireland holds these graves, Ireland unfree shall never be at peace'. Still deeply moving are his eve-of-execution poems for his brother and his mother, the latter of which begins:

I do not grudge them: Lord, I do not grudge
My two strong sons that I have seen go out
To break their strength and die, they and a few,
In bloody protest for a glorious thing . . .

PEARSE, William (1881–1916), sculptor and revolutionary, b. Dublin, 15 Nov. 1881, ed. CBS, Westland Row, Dublin. He became a fine sculptor, obtaining a distinction in the Metropolitan School of Art, Dublin and studying in Paris. Founded St Enda's School (Scoil Éanna) 1908 with his brother, PATRICK PEARSE. He was also a talented actor and appeared in many productions at the Irish Theatre in Hardwicke Street. A captain in the GPO during the Easter Rising, he was executed on 4 May 1916.

PEARSON, Noel (1942–), theatre and film producer, ed. Belcamp College, Malahide, Co. Dublin. A cost accountant, he switched to the entertainment business and was manager of THE DUBLINERS for 14 years. He founded Tribune Records in 1967 but his first love was theatre and in 1970 he became an impresario, producing many successes (*Cabaret, West Side Story, Jesus Christ Superstar*). In recent years he has taken plays to Broadway, the most notable being *Dancing at Lughnasa* by BRIAN FRIEL in 1992, and in 1994 *An Inspector Calls*, which earned Pearson a Tony award; it toured the USA in 1996. His production company Ferndale Films has had solid triumphs, such as *My Left Foot* (1989) and *The Field* (1991), both directed by JIM SHERIDAN and both nominated for Oscars. His most recent film is *Frankie Starlight* (1996), which features GABRIEL BYRNE.

PENTLAND, John Howard (1855–1919), architect, b. 20 July 1855, ed. TCD (arts and engineering). Entered partnership with his uncle, the talented Victorian architect James Rawson Carroll. He was elected a member of the RIAI 1883 and became a member of the Royal Society of Antiquaries of Ireland 1888. In 1884 he entered the Board of Works as assistant surveyor, senior surveyor 1891, principal surveyor 1900, a position he held until his retirement in 1918. Elected to the RHA in 1894, he became an academician there in 1895. Vice-president of the revived AAI 1896–8 and president 1898–9. Pentland's strength lay less in design – he was responsible for the Triumphal Arch on St Stephen's Green

(1907) and the post office at Blackrock, among others – than in his promotion of new technologies, including reinforced concrete and electric lighting.

PEROLZ, Marie, revolutionary and trade unionist. Member of the Irish Citizen Army and of Cumann na mBan. As a delegate for the Irish Women Workers' Union to the Annual Irish Trades Union Congress and Labour Party conference in 1916, she ensured that all resolutions addressing the concerns of working men were amended to include 'the working women' of the rank and file. Contributed to the formulation of the National Labour Programme 1916, which at her suggestion was expanded to include schemes for 'the medical inspection of school children, maternity centres and similar reforms to promote the physical welfare of the children of the working classes'.

PETERS, Mary Elizabeth (1939–), athlete, b. Halewood, Greater Manchester, 6 July 1939. Placed fourth in 1964 and ninth in 1968, she won the Olympic pentathlon title with a world record 4,801 points (4,841 on the 1984 tables) in the 1972 Munich Games. She had to run a personal best in the 200 m – the final event – and accomplished it, then endured an agonising delay until confirmation that she had ended ten points ahead of Heide Rosendahl. She had won the Commonwealth pentathlon for Northern Ireland in 1970, when she also won the shot. Achievements include winning eight WAAA pentathlons, in 1962–6, 1968, 1970 and 1973; two shots, in 1964 and 1970, outdoors; indoor shot titles in 1964–6, 1970 and 1972. She set British records at shot, 100 m hurdles and six pentathlons. BBC Sports Personality of the Year 1972, awarded an MBE 1973 and CBE 1990. A successful team manager of UK squads, she was a member of the Northern Ireland Sports Council 1973–93 and of the Great Britain Sports Council 1987–93.

PIRRIE, William (1847–1924), shipbuilder, b. Quebec, 24 May 1847, s. of James Pirrie from Co. Down, childhood spent at Conlig in Down, in the house of his grandfather William Pirrie, a Belfast shipping merchant, ed. Royal Academical Institution, d. 7 June 1924. He joined Harland and Wolff as an apprentice in 1862 and rose to partnership in 1874. By 1895 Pirrie was chairman of the company and the world's leading shipbuilder. He was responsible for some of the major design and engineering innovations of the day, including massive liners like the *Olympic*. His politics were influenced by the non-subscribing Presbyterian radical tradition in which he was reared, and he identified with the constructive unionism of Sir HORACE PLUNKETT.

PLANT, George (1904–1942), republican, b. St Johnstown, Fethard, Co. Tipperary, ed. locally. Joined the local branch of Fianna Éireann in 1918 and became a member of the IRA a year later. Took the anti-Treaty side during the Civil War and was a member of the 7th Battalion of the 3rd Tipperary Brigade. Imprisoned in Templemore Jail but escaped and made his way to North America, where he spent a number of years. Returned to Ireland in 1938 and joined the IRA shortly after the appointment of SEÁN RUSSELL as chief of staff. In Feb. 1942 Plant was convicted by a military court of the murder of an alleged informer and was executed.

PLUNKETT, Sir Horace Curzon (1854–1932), agriculturalist, b. Gloucestershire, s. of Lord Dunsany, ed. Eton and Oxford. He left the family estate in Meath 1878 to improve his poor health by ranching in Wyoming. Returned considerably wealthier in 1888 and was dismayed at the sad state of Irish farming. Can claim credit for two major Irish institutions, the agricultural co-operative movement (with Lord Dunraven and Fr Tom Finlay, SJ) and the Department of Agriculture and Technical Instruction (1899), of which he was vice-president. Returned as a Unionist MP for Dublin 1892. In 1904 he published his controversial *Ireland in the New Century*. A man of little tact and less humour, he was attacked for criticising the political parties, the educational system and the Catholic Church. President Theodore Roosevelt frequently acknowledged Plunkett's inspiration and guidance of the American Rural Life Commission. Plunkett's friend GEORGE RUSSELL became a travelling organiser for his Irish Agricultural Organisation Society and later edited the co-op movement's weekly, the *Irish Homestead*, to which JAMES STEPHENS, W.B. YEATS and JAMES JOYCE contributed. Plunkett organised the seminal Recess Committee, was a member of the Congested Districts Board and was

elected chairman of the Irish Convention 1917, the failure of which bitterly disappointed him. He was a nominated member of the new Seanad 1922 but a year later, after his Foxrock house, Kilteragh, was burned down by republicans in the Civil War, Plunkett left the country for good.

PLUNKETT, James (1920–), pseud. of James Plunkett Kelly, novelist, short story writer and playwright, ed. Synge Street and College of Music, Dublin. Clerk with the Dublin Gas Company for seven years and thereafter an official of the Workers' Union of Ireland (at first working under JAMES LARKIN, who was to feature prominently in Plunkett's novels and dramas) until he joined Radio Éireann as an assistant programme head in 1955. By then he had written a number of short stories for the *Bell* under the influence of SEÁN O'FAOLAIN and FRANK O'CONNOR, had had several radio plays broadcast, and had published a well-received collection of stories under the title *The Trusting and the Maimed* (1955). In 1961 he transferred from radio to television, becoming one of the first producers in Telefís Éireann. Among other writings, two fine novels were still to appear, *Strumpet City* (1969) and *Farewell Companions* (1977), which between them provided an affectionate – if often searing – picture of life at many levels in Dublin during the first half of the 20th century. *Strumpet City* was widely translated and was made into a successful television serial by RTÉ.

PLUNKETT, Joseph Mary (1887–1916), republican and poet, b. Dublin, s. of George Noble, Count Plunkett, ed. Belvedere, Stonyhurst and UCD. He returned to Dublin in 1911 after several years living abroad, and helped to launch the *Irish Review* with THOMAS MACDONAGH. In 1914 he joined the Irish Volunteers and the IRB, later becoming one of the first members of the military council which planned the Easter Rising. In 1915 he accompanied ROGER CASEMENT to Berlin on his mission to secure arms from the German government. He was unwavering in his support for an uprising and, although seriously ill, took part in the fighting in the GPO. As a signatory to the Proclamation of the Republic, he was executed on 4 May 1916, having married artist Grace Gifford the night before.

POGUES, The, rock band. Fronted by songwriter Shane MacGowan, the Pogues drifted together in London in 1983 under the name Pogue Mahone (from the Irish for 'Kiss my arse'). They signed to Stiff Records, shortened their name and released *Red Roses for Me*, a manic mix of punk and sentimental ballads which reflected their Anglo-Irish identity. Their second album, *Rum, Sodomy and the Lash*, and the *Poguetry in Motion* EP made the UK charts. The Christmas song 'Fairytale of New York', with Kirsty MacColl, was a hit in 1987, by which time MacGowan's reputedly excessive lifestyle had gained him much notoriety. In 1988 he collapsed on the way to a support slot with Bob Dylan and the rest of the group had to carry on without him. MacGowan finally left in 1991. The band's 1993 album, *Waiting for Herb*, featured Spider Stacy on lead vocals and MacGowan released a solo album, *The Snake*, in 1994.

POTTER, Archibald James (Archie) (1918–1980), musician, b. Belfast, ed. national school, Belfast, Clifton College, Bristol and RCM, London, where he studied composition under Ralph Vaughan Williams. War service in Europe and the Far East. Worked in west Africa before returning to Ireland *c.* 1950, when he joined St Patrick's Cathedral choir. Radio Éireann Carolan prize for composition 1952 and 1953. Mus.D. (TCD) 1953. Professor of Composition RIAM 1955. Arts Council Marten Toonder award 1978. His numerous compositions included opera, ballet, choral and orchestral works, brass band music and scores for radio and television.

POTTER, Maureen (1925–), actress, ed. St Mary's, Fairview, Dublin. Hon. LL D (TCD) and conferred with the freedom of Dublin (1984). Has had a long and distinguished career in the Irish theatre, mainly as a comedienne but also as a straight actress, in roles including Maisie Madigan in *Juno and the Paycock*. Toured abroad before World War II as a singer and dancer with Jack Hylton and his orchestra. First appeared professionally with JIMMY O'DEA in pantomime 1935, thereafter their partnership became a much-loved staple of the Dublin theatrical calendar. She has appeared frequently on television and in cabaret.

POWER, Albert (1883–1945), sculptor, b. Dublin, ed. Metropolitan School of Art, Dublin, d. Dublin, 10 July 1945. He was elected RHA in 1919 and was represented at the exhibitions of Irish art in Paris 1922 and in Brussels 1930. In 1924 he designed the medals for the Tailteann Games, which were revived that year, and was also commissioned to make a statuette of Queen Maeve to commemorate the event. He is best known for his sculpture portraits of famous Irish people, many of which are in public places, including those of PÁDRAIC Ó CONAIRE, Eyre Square, Galway, TOM KETTLE, St Stephen's Green and W.B YEATS, Sandymount Green, Dublin. Other celebrated subjects were MICHAEL COLLINS, HUGH LANE and EAMON DE VALERA.

POWER, Arthur (1891–1984), artist and critic, b. Guernsey, 22 July 1891, raised in Co. Waterford, d. Dublin, 7 May 1984. He lived in Paris for a number of years after World War I and became a close friend of JAMES JOYCE. Although he did not begin to paint until he was in his thirties, he played an important role in encouraging the acceptance of modernism in Ireland. In 1922 Power and PAUL HENRY arranged an exhibition in Dublin, called Modern Pictures, which featured a number of works by artists with whom he was familiar from his time in Paris, including Modigliani and Maillol, whom he knew personally, as well as Cézanne, Matisse and Vlaminck. He was the art critic of *The Irish Times* for several years and also wrote for the *Bell*. While living in France he was a columnist for the *New York Herald*. In 1940 his first book, the autobiographical *From the Old Waterford House*, was published and in 1974 he published *Conversations with James Joyce*.

POWER, John (Jackie) (1916–1996), hurler and Gaelic footballer, b. Annacotty, Co. Limerick, 30 May 1916. From the famous Ahane club, he shares with the brothers John and MICK MACKEY the record of 20 Limerick County Senior Championship medals, 15 in hurling and five in football, and he also played senior football for the county. His career spanned 15 years, during which he won two All-Ireland senior hurling medals (1936, 1940), seven Railway Cup medals with Munster (1940, 1942–6, 1948) and five National Hurling League medals (1934–8). He coached the Limerick team which won the 1973 All-Ireland final.

POWER, Richard (1928–1970), writer, b. Dublin, ed. TCD and Iowa University, d. Bray, Co. Wicklow, 12 Feb. 1970. A civil servant, his reputation rests on two novels: *The Land of Youth* (1966), a study of the arrested sexuality of a young woman on the Aran Islands whose love for a seminarian is doomed to frustration, and the technically more assured *The Hungry Grass* (1969), which traces with great sensitivity the last year in the life of a rural priest.

POWERS, Mary Farl (1948–1992), artist, b. Minnesota, ed. Dún Laoghaire School of Art and National College of Art, Dublin. Director of the Graphic Studio in Dublin, which she joined in 1973 and where she helped to establish the gallery in 1983. She had her first solo exhibition in the Peacock Theatre Gallery in Dublin in 1979 and later had shows in the USA and Mexico. Represented at several International Print Biennales, including Ljubljana, Yugoslavia 1974, Frechen, Germany 1976, Heidelberg, Germany 1980 and Fredrikstad, Norway 1984. She was the subject of retrospective exhibitions in the Graphic Studio 1976 and the Irish Museum of Modern Art, Dublin 1995.

PRAEGER, Robert Lloyd (1865–1953), natural historian, b. Holywood, Co. Down, 25 Aug. 1865, ed. Royal Academical Institution and Queen's College, Belfast, d. Craigavad, Co. Down, 5 May 1953. Although a trained engineer, Praeger was a botanist at heart. He worked with the Belfast water service from 1886 until 1893, when he moved to Dublin to join the staff of the National Library. He retired as librarian in 1923 to pursue his botanical interests full-time. He performed famous surveys of Lambay Island (1905) and Clare Island (1909–22), co-founded and edited the *Irish Naturalist* and wrote prolifically, including *Irish Topographical Botany* (1901) and *The Way that I Went* (1937), which has been reprinted regularly. Elected PRIA 1931.

PRENDERGAST, Kathy (1958–), artist, b. Dublin, 5 Sept. 1958, ed. NCAD and Royal College of Art, London (MA 1986). While still a student, she exhibited in New York, Dublin and at the Paris Biennale in 1982. She won the 1981 Guinness Peat Aviation award for emerging artists and represented Ireland at Rosc '88 in the Hop Store, Dublin.

Prendergast uses a variety of materials and techniques in her sculpture and installation work. She is particularly interested in the mathematical representation of landscape through maps, and a number of works dealing with this theme formed a part of the exhibition which won her the Best Young Artist award at the 1995 Venice Biennale.

PRENDERGAST, Peter (1939–), political adviser and businessman, b. Galway, ed. Clongowes and UCD. Marketing executive with the Irish Sugar Company and then Unilever. He joined Fine Gael in 1969 and twice stood unsuccessfully in Dáil elections. He came to public notice as general secretary of the party under GARRET FITZGERALD 1977–81. On the formation of FitzGerald's short-lived coalition in the latter year he became an adviser to finance minister JOHN BRUTON. Government press secretary 1982–6. Throughout the late 1970s and early 1980s he was one of the key organisational figures in FG as it reached the height of its electoral popularity. His ruthless efficiency provoked hostility in more traditional party activists. Very liberal on social issues, he was one of the strongest influences on FitzGerald. Since leaving public life he has worked in Brussels as director of the EU Consumer Service Agency.

PRICE, Elinor Dorothy (1890–1954), née Stopford, physician, b. Dublin, niece of Alice Stopford Green, ed. St Paul's Girls' School, London, after death of her father, returning to TCD to study medicine 1916. Despite her unionist upbringing, she supported Sinn Féin in the aftermath of the Rising, became a member of Cumann na mBan and later held anti-Treaty opinions. She graduated in 1921 and three years later married District Justice Liam (William George) Price. Appointed to the staff of St Ultan's Hospital and clinical assistant to Baggot Street Hospital, Price became interested in the problem of tuberculosis in children, making this the subject of an MD thesis. She stressed the necessity of tuberculin testing and X-rays in early diagnosis. She studied abroad, corresponded with Walter Pagel, Arvid Wallgren and other authorities and introduced the BCG vaccine to Ireland in 1937, campaigning for a national scheme of inoculation. *Tuberculosis in Childhood* was published in 1942.

PROUD, Malcolm (1952–), harpsi-chordist, organist and teacher, b. Dublin, ed. Dublin, Denmark, RIAM and Waterford Regional Technical College. Organist and choirmaster St Canice's Cathedral in Kilkenny; also one of the organisers of the city's arts festival. Member of the Orchestra of the Age of Enlightenment and of the Baroque Orchestra of Ireland. Has enjoyed international success and made numerous recordings since winning the Edinburgh International Harpsichord Competition 1982.

PURCELL, Deirdre (1945–), writer, b. Dublin, ed. Dublin and Mayo. She worked for a time as a civil servant and came to the attention of the Abbey Theatre when perform-ing in amateur drama. She was recruited for the permanent company and in 1968 became actress in residence at Loyola University, Chicago. Returning to Dublin in 1973, she joined RTÉ and pursued a successful broad-casting career until 1983. She has since worked for the *Sunday Tribune* and other papers and is regarded as one of Ireland's top journalists, winning the coveted Benson & Hedges and Cross awards. Purcell has written five best-selling novels: *A Place of Stones* (1991), *That Childhood Country* (1992), *Falling for a Dancer* (1993), *Francey* (1994) and *Sky* (1995). She has also published the non-fictional *On Lough Derg* (1988) and collaborated with GAY BYRNE on *The Time of my Life: An Autobiography* (1989).

PURCELL, Mary (1906–1991), biog-rapher, b. Carrigeen, Co. Monaghan, ed. Monaghan and Dublin, d. Dublin. National school teacher 1928–58. Wrote many lives, mainly of prominent personalities in the late medieval and early modern Church. Her pro-lific output was based on diligent research, to undertake which she travelled widely in Europe. Publications include: *The Halo on the Sword* (1950), *The Great Captain* (1962), *The World of Monsieur Vincent* (1963) and *The Quiet Companion* (1970), which dealt respectively with Joan of Arc, Gonzalo de Cordoba, Vincent de Paul and Peter Favre. She also wrote a life of MATT TALBOT (1954).

PURCELL, Noel (1900–1985), actor, b. Dublin, 23 Dec. 1900, ed. Synge Street, d. Dublin, 3 Mar. 1985. Toured Ireland and Britain in variety with JIMMY O'DEA and HARRY O'DONOVAN. Played in numerous light entertainment productions in Dublin theatres, especially pantomime, but was also adept in serious roles. He featured in many films, from *Captain Boycott* to *Mutiny on the Bounty*, usually typecast in parts suited to his expressive craggy features and the white beard of his later years. He never hid his nostalgic affection for his native city and in 1984 became a freeman of Dublin.

PURCELL, Sean, Gaelic footballer, b. Co. Galway. He won an All-Ireland colleges medal with St Jarlath's College, Tuam in 1946, and in his career with the Tuam Stars club won ten County Championship titles. He won one All-Ireland senior football medal with Galway, in 1956, and captained the team which lost to Kerry in the 1959 final. Purcell formed a powerful footballing partnership at club and county levels with FRANK STOCKWELL, the pair being known as 'The Terrible Twins'. He won three Railway Cup medals with Connacht, in 1951, 1957 and in 1958, when he was captain. He is widely regarded as one of the game's greatest centre-half forwards ever.

PURSER, Sarah Henrietta (1848–1943), artist and patron of the arts, b. Kingstown (now Dún Laoghaire), Co. Dublin, 22 Mar. 1848, ed. Switzerland, Metropolitan School of Art, Dublin and Paris, d. Dublin, 7 Aug. 1943. She was a fashionable and wealthy portrait painter but her major contribution to the arts was as a promoter of the talents of others. She organised the NATHANIEL HONE/ JOHN B. YEATS exhibition in 1901 that stim-ulated Sir HUGH LANE's interest in Irish art. In 1903 with EDWARD MARTYN she found-ed An Túr Gloine ('The Tower of Glass') in Dublin, a co-operative stained-glass work-shop. MICHAEL HEALY was to base himself there for most of his career and EVIE HONE worked in An Túr for ten years. Purser acquired Mespil House near the Grand Canal in Dublin in 1911 and held regular afternoon salons at which the leading literary and artistic figures of the day met and exchanged views. She founded the Friends of the National Collections in 1924, helped to secure Charlemont House as a home for the Municipal Gallery of Modern Art, and with her cousin Sir John Purser-Griffiths established travelling scholarships in the history of art at UCD and TCD – from which developed the art history departments at both universities. She continued to paint until she was well over 80.

PYE, Patrick (1929–), artist, b. Dublin, ed. National College of Art, Dublin and Jan Van Eyck Academy, Maastricht, Holland. He began working with stained glass in the 1950s and has completed several commissions for churches throughout Ireland, including Glenstal Abbey, Co. Limerick, the Convent of Mercy, Cookstown, Co. Tyrone and the Church of the Resurrection, Cave Hill Road, Belfast. Among the many triptychs he has painted on religious themes are *Woman and Serpent*, a study of the expulsion from Eden, and *An Easter Triptych*, both of which are in private collections. He has also made a quintriptych for Fossa Chapel, Killarney. In both his paintings and his stained-glass work Pye has successfully used a contemporary style to depict ancient sacred narratives. He has likened the function of art to that of the sacraments in that they both open 'doors of perception' which unite the spiritual and temporal worlds.

Q

QUIGLEY, Thomas Ambrose Joseph (Joe) (1919–1993), surgeon Garda Síochána, b. Carna, Co. Galway, both parents national teachers, ed. Garbally Park and UCG, d. 30 Apr. 1993. MB, B.Ch., BAO. Athlete, track events and hurling. Commandant Army Medical Corps. Garda surgeon 1958–84. Recognised stress as an occupational hazard for policemen, exacerbated during the period of rapid change in the 1960s when the first generation of gardaí was replaced by better-educated young men who agitated for improved conditions of service. It was a period also of intense competition for promotion under a new meritocracy introduced by Commissioner DANIEL COSTIGAN. Quigley tested the medical fitness of every member of the new force and personally attended to the casualties of change. A distinguished philatelist and member of the Post Office Philatelic Advisory Committee.

QUIGLEY, Sir William *George* Henry (1929–), public servant, ed. Ballymena Academy and QUB (Ph.D. 1955). Chairman of Ulster Bank Ltd since 1989 and a director of the National Westminster Bank since 1990. Formerly permanent secretary at the Northern Ireland Department of Manpower Services 1974–6, Commerce 1976–9, Finance 1979–82 and Finance and Personnel 1982–8. An advocate of greater economic co-operation between NI and the Republic. Chairman of Belfast's Royal Group of Hospitals after 1991, he announced his resignation in Dec. 1995, three months after attacking government funding of hospitals. In Feb. 1996 George Quigley noted that the previous year had seen clear evidence of the peace process and expressed the wish that the breakdown of the ceasefire could be rapidly repaired.

QUILL, Michael (1905–1966), trade union organiser, b. Kilgarvan, Co. Kerry, ed. Kilgarvan NS. Fought in the War of Independence and the Civil War (anti-Treaty). Emigrated to USA 1926 and worked on the New York subway. In 1934 with John Santo of the Communist Party he founded the Transport Workers' Union. Member of the New York City Council. International vice-president of the Congress of Industrial Organisations. As the Cold War developed, Quill dropped his Communist allies. His greatest battle was his last. He called out the 33,000 New York subway and bus workers on New Year's Day 1966. His 12-day confrontation with Mayor John Lindsay ended with a contract worth $62 million and with Quill's death two weeks later.

QUIN, Charles William Cosslett (1907–1996), Church of Ireland cleric and scholar, b. 27 Feb. 1907. Served in parishes in the dioceses of Kilmore, Glendalough and Cork as well as holding, from 1961, the chair of biblical Greek at TCD. Author of several devotional works and noted for his exceptional contribution to the translation into Irish of liturgical and biblical works. Contributor to *An Bíobla Naomha* (Maynooth 1981).

QUINN, Aidan (1959–), actor, b. Chicago, 8 Mar. 1959, spent most of his childhood in Belfast. Returned to Chicago, where he worked as a roofer. Progressed from amateur theatre to professional roles, making his first screen appearance in *Reckless* (1984). However, his big breakthrough came in 1985 when he played Rosanna Arquette's projectionist boyfriend in *Desperately Seeking Susan*. Subsequent film work included *The Mission* (1986), *The Playboys* (1992), shot in Ireland, and *Legends of the Fall* (1994).

QUINN, Edel (1907–1944), Legion of Mary envoy to east Africa, b. Kanturk, Co. Cork, 14 Sept. 1907, ed. Loreto College, Enniscorthy and at Upton, Cheshire. Trained as a secretary. Joined the Legion in Dublin in 1927 and was appointed praesidium president two years later. She hoped to enter the Poor Clares but developed TB and was unable to pursue this vocation. She was admitted to Newcastle Sanatorium, Co. Wicklow in Feb. 1932 and remained there for 18 months. On leaving, she resumed her work with the

Legion. She went to Wales briefly in 1936 to extend the organisation there and in Oct. was appointed envoy to east Africa. In the years that followed, despite failing health, she established the Legion in Kenya, Uganda, Tanganyika, Nyasaland and Mauritius, setting up 250 praesidia in a little over four years. But in Mar. 1941 she fell seriously ill at Lilongwe, Nyasaland. After a lengthy period of convalescence in South Africa, she returned to her base at Nairobi in Jan. 1943 but died on 12 May 1944 and was buried there.

QUINN, Feargal (1936–), supermarket owner and senator, ed. Newbridge, Co. Kildare and UCD. Opened a supermarket in Dundalk 1960 but went on to concentrate on the Dublin suburbs, where he set up a number of stores over the following decades. Frequently appears on radio and television to comment on business developments, especially in the grocery trade. At the request of the government, served as chairman of An Post 1979–90. Senator (Ind. NUI) since 1993.

QUINN, Ruairí (1946–), politician, b. Dublin, 2 Apr. 1946, ed. Blackrock, UCD (B.Arch.) and School of Ekistics, Athens. TD (Labour) 1977–81 and since 1982; member of the Seanad 1976–7 (filled a vacancy on the Taoiseach's list of nominees) and 1981–2. Minister of State at the Department of the Environment, with special responsibility for Urban Affairs and Housing, 1982–3. Minister for Labour Dec. 1983–Jan. 1987; for the Public Service Feb. 1986–Jan. 1987; for Enterprise and Employment Jan. 1993–Nov. 1994; for Finance since Jan. 1994. Quinn was elected deputy leader of the Labour Party in 1989 and was director of elections during MARY ROBINSON's successful presidential campaign 1990 and the local elections of the same year. Private business: Ruairí Quinn and Associates, architectural and planning consultants. He worked as an architect with Dublin Corporation 1971–3 and was a partner with Burke-Kennedy Doyle & Partners 1973–82.

R

RABBITTE, Pat (1949–), politician, b. Co. Mayo, 18 May 1949, ed. St Colman's College, Claremorris and UCG. Former trade union official ITGWU. Elected TD (Workers' Party, later DL, Dublin South-West) 1989. Minister of State since 1994 to the government and at the Department of Enterprise and Employment.

RACKARD, Nicholas (Nicky) (1922–1990), hurler, b. Killane, Co. Wexford, 28 Apr. 1922. He was the star player, aided by brothers BILLY and BOBBY RACKARD, in the great Wexford teams which won the All-Ireland finals of 1955 and 1956. He was top scorer in hurling in both years, with 91 points in 18 matches and 155 points, respectively. From the Rathnure club, he captained the Wexford team beaten by Tipperary in the 1951 All-Ireland final, and was in the side which lost to Cork in the final of 1954. He won a Railway Cup medal in 1956. Also an accomplished Gaelic footballer, he played on the Leinster side defeated in the 1950 Railway Cup final.

RACKARD, Robert (Bobby) (1927–), hurler, b. Killane, Co. Wexford, 6 Jan. 1927. Brother of NICKY and BILLY RACKARD. Playing with the Rathnure club, he won four Wexford County Championship medals, and he was a senior inter-county player 1945–57. With his brothers, he won two All-Ireland senior medals, in 1955 and 1956, and was on the teams which lost the finals of 1951 and 1954. He also won National Hurling League and Railway Cup medals in 1956.

RACKARD, William (Billy) (1930–), hurler, b. Killane, Co. Wexford. Brother of NICKY and BOBBY RACKARD. He won four County Championship medals with Rathnure, also playing for Faughs in Dublin, and was a senior inter-county player 1950–63. Honours include three All-Ireland medals (1955, 1956, 1960), four Railway Cup medals with Leinster (1954, 1956, 1962, 1964), two National Hurling League medals (1956, 1958) and four Oireachtas medals. He also played inter-county Gaelic football for Wexford.

REA, Stephen (1947–), actor, b. Belfast, ed. QUB. Began his acting career in the late 1960s with the Young Abbey in Dublin. He moved to London in the early 1970s, where he worked for a number of years with the National Theatre; productions included BRIAN FRIEL's *The Freedom of the City*, Dion Boucicault's *The Shaughraun* and J.M. SYNGE's *The Playboy of the Western World*. Rea and Friel co-founded the Field Day Theatre Company in 1980 – its début production, Friel's *Translations*, was a landmark in Irish theatre history and was central to the company's preoccupation with national identity. Rea played lead roles in most of Field Day's subsequent productions, including *The Communication Cord*, *Double Cross*, *Pentecost*, *The Riot Act* and *Making History*; he directed *Three Sisters* and co-directed SEAMUS HEANEY's *The Cure at Troy*. Nominated for an Oscar in 1993 for the film *The Crying Game*, directed by NEIL JORDAN, with whom he had previously made *Angel*.

REDMOND, John Edward (1856–1918), politician and national leader, b. Ballytrent, Co. Wexford, 1 Sept. 1856, son of an MP, ed. Clongowes, TCD and Gray's Inn, London, d. 6 Mar. 1918. Called to English and Irish Bars but did not practise. MP (IP, New Ross, later North Wexford and, from 1891 until his death, Waterford). A fine orator, he not only made a strong impression on the House of Commons in promoting Irish interests but raised substantial sums for the Irish Parliamentary Party on visits to the USA and Australia 1882–4. Remained faithful to Parnell at the time of the 'split' and was chosen as leader when the party reunited in 1900. A long period of Tory rule in Britain followed by an overwhelming victory for the Liberals in the election of 1905 (which relieved them of the need for Irish support) meant that Redmond was unable to exert pressure to obtain his objective of Home Rule, and so he concentrated for a time on pursuing other reforms, such as the Wyndham Act of 1903, which completed the process of transferring land ownership to the people, and the establishment of the NUI in 1908.

When the Liberal majority had been whittled down in successive elections, he was able to force the hand of Prime Minister Asquith. The result was the third Home Rule bill, introduced in 1912 and finally passed on the eve of World War I, subject to amending legislation. While the bill incorporated a temporary partition of Ireland to mollify the Ulster unionists, its creation of an Irish parliament with considerable autonomous powers put an end to the Act of Union and was widely judged by nationalists to be an outstanding achievement. The long wait for Home Rule, however, had brought about a revival of militant separatism, represented by the adherents of Sinn Féin and the IRB within the Volunteers.

If Redmond's greatest virtue was a stubborn loyalty – to Parnell, to Home Rule, to Ireland – his greatest failing was an innocent generosity of spirit which was perilous in politics. When he accepted the government's decision to suspend implementation of the Home Rule Act until after the war, undertook that the Volunteers would defend the country if the British wanted to withdraw their troops for war service, and – in a disastrous speech at Woodenbridge, Co. Wicklow – advised young Irish men to join the British army, Redmond provoked an outraged response from the militants. A minority of the Volunteers left the main movement: under IRB control they were to become the principal body of insurgents in the Easter Rising. Redmond sought leniency from the government for the rebel leaders but was ignored. Their execution was followed by a massive transfer of popular support from the IP to Sinn Féin. A convention proposed by Redmond to bridge the differences of opinion in Ireland met in 1917 but made no impact on the course of events. It was still in session when he died. Brother of WILLIAM REDMOND.

REDMOND, William (1861–1917), politician, b. Ballytrent, Co. Wexford, ed. Clongowes. MP (IP, Wexford 1883, North Fermanagh 1885, East Clare 1891 until his death). Favoured dominion status for Ireland. Joined British army 1914 and was killed in action, France, 7 June 1917. Brother of JOHN REDMOND.

REID, Christina (1942–), playwright, b. Belfast. Her father was a docker with a gambling problem and consequently her mother, by means of part-time work, was increasingly the breadwinner. The family was Ulster Protestant working class and Reid grew up in an environment of contradictory allegiances. She left school aged 15 and was a civil servant until her compulsory resignation upon marriage. She went to night school and later QUB as a mature student. Her first play, *Did you Hear the One about the Irishman . . . ?*, won the Ulster TV drama award in 1980 and went on to tour London and New York. Reid has never looked back. Her plays include: *Tea in a China Shop* (1980), for which she was made writer in residence at the Lyric Theatre, Belfast, *The Belle of Belfast City, Joyriders* and *The Last of a Dyin' Race* (1986), *My Name, Shall I Tell You My Name?* (1987) and *Lords, Dukes and Earls* (1989).

REID, Forrest (1875–1947), novelist, b. Belfast, ed. locally and Cambridge. He lived most of his life in London and was part of a circle that included Lowes Dickinson, E.M. Forster and Walter de la Mare. He also knew Henry James but they had a falling out when Reid dedicated a homophiliac novel to him. He wrote 16 novels in all, in addition to books of criticism, including *W.B. Yeats: A Critical Study* (1915), *Walter de la Mare: A Critical Study* (1929) and *The Milk of Paradise: Some Thoughts on Poetry* (1946). Also wrote two volumes of autobiography, *Apostate* (1926) and *Private Road* (1940), and a translation of poems, *Greek Anthology* (1943). His best-known novels include: *The Kingdom of Twilight* (1904), *The Garden Gods* (1905), *Following Darkness* (1912), *At the Door of the Gate* (1915), *Pirates of the Spring* (1919), *Pender among the Residents* (1922), *Uncle Stephen* (1931), *The Retreat* (1936), *Peter Waring* (1937) and *Young Tom, or Very Mixed Company* (1944), which won the James Tait Black memorial prize.

REID, Nano (1905–1981), artist, b. Drogheda, 1 Mar. 1905, ed. Metropolitan School of Art, Dublin. Much of her early work consisted of illustrations which were heavily influenced by HARRY CLARKE, one of her tutors in art college. After a period of study in France she returned to Ireland in 1930 and had her first one-woman show in Dublin in 1934. During this period she concentrated on landscape painting, although she also produced some portraits. In 1950 she represented Ireland at the Venice Biennale. She exhibited in the Guggenheim International Award Exhibition 1960 and in Twelve Irish Painters, New York 1965. In 1974 she had a retrospective exhibition in Dublin and Belfast. Although the image conveyed in many of Reid's landscape paintings is one of bucolic repose, the brushwork is vigorous and uninhibited. While seemingly little attention is paid to conventions of composition or perspective, the intimacy with which she deals with the subject is always apparent.

REYNOLDS, Albert (1932–), politician and businessman, b. 3 Nov. 1932, ed. Summerhill College, Sligo, m. Kathleen Coen, two s. five d. Prior to entering politics he was involved in dancehall promotion and the pet-food business. He also developed interests in local newspapers and a cinema. His fascination with politics arose in part from the Arms Trial of CHARLES HAUGHEY, which he attended. He became a member of Longford County Council in 1974 and three years later, after a tough battle for the nomination, won a Dáil seat for Fianna Fáil on his first attempt. Like many of the other backbench TDs who arrived on that year's tidal wave for the party, he became a Haughey supporter. When the latter was elected FF leader and Taoiseach, Reynolds was appointed Minister for Posts and Telegraphs, and Transport and Power. He was Minister for Industry and Commerce 1987–8 and for Finance 1988 to Nov. 1991, when he resigned, supporting an abortive attempt to remove Haughey. When Haughey resigned in Feb. 1992 Reynolds obtained the posts of party leader and Taoiseach with clear majorities.

He was an uneasy leader of the FF–PD coalition government, which he had earlier described as 'a temporary little arrangement'. Relations between the government parties further deteriorated in 1992 during the 'Beef Tribunal' – a sworn judicial inquiry into matters which partly arose out of actions taken by Reynolds while Minister for Industry and Commerce. He and coalition partner DES O'MALLEY, leader of the PDs, presented to the Tribunal contradictory and mutually destructive testimony. When Reynolds accused O'Malley of knowingly telling untruths, the PDs quickly withdrew from government and an election ensued. Reynolds, having swept to power on the promise to lead FF to an overall majority, saw his party fare disastrously, losing nine seats; however, securing vastly increased EC funds for the country enabled him to negotiate a new coalition with a greatly revived Labour Party. He was re-elected Taoiseach early in 1993, over a government with the largest Dáil majority in the history of the state.

Since early in his first term as Taoiseach, Reynolds had been deeply involved in efforts to find a basis for an end to IRA violence. He opened up channels of communication to the republican movement through Belfast priests and to loyalist paramilitaries through Protestant clergymen. The Downing Street Declaration was agreed with British Prime Minister John Major in Dec. 1993 and, after much internal agonising, an IRA ceasefire was announced in Aug. 1994. The successful outcome was widely acclaimed, but within the coalition with Labour tensions had begun to emerge. These finally came to breaking point later in 1994 over an extradition case and the appointment of the then Attorney-General as President of the High Court. In a confused and emotional few days, Reynolds suddenly found himself forced to resign. It brought to an end a brief period in power characterised by enormous swings of political fortune and an unconventional but extraordinarily effective initiative that sought to end 25 years of violence in Northern Ireland.

RICHARDS, Shelah (1903–1985), actress and director, b. Dublin, 23 May 1903, d. of lawyer John Richards and Adelaide Roper, ed. Alexandra and Belgian finishing school, m. DENIS JOHNSTON 1928 (separated 1940s), one s. one d., d. 19 Jan. 1985. Acted with the Dublin Drama League then the Abbey Theatre and was soon promoted to leading roles, including that of Nora Clitheroe in the first, riotous production of SEAN O'CASEY's *The Plough and the Stars* (1926). She was to have a lifelong association with the plays of O'Casey, directing the Irish premiere of *Red Roses for Me* 1947 and *The Plough and the Stars* at the Abbey as late as 1970. She played Blanaid in Denis Johnston's *The Moon in the Yellow River* at the Abbey 1932.

During World War II Richards formed a company of her own, presenting plays at the Olympia Theatre, including GEORGE BERNARD SHAW's *Saint Joan* and P.V. CARROLL's *The Strings, my Lord, are False.* She also made occasional appearances at the Gate Theatre. After the war she became ill with TB but soon returned to the stage. In 1962, with the setting up of Telefís Éireann, she trained as a television director; work included episodes of drama series *The Riordans* and several plays. Mother of JENNIFER JOHNSTON.

RING, Christopher Nicholas (Christy) (1920–1979), hurler, b. Cloyne, Co. Cork, 12 Dec. 1920, d. 2 Mar. 1979. He was among the greatest players the game of hurling ever produced, initially winning a County Junior Championship medal with the Cloyne club in 1939, and later winning a record 11 county senior medals with Glen Rovers. He made his senior début with Cork in 1939 and shares with JOHN DOYLE of Tipperary the distinction of winning eight All-Ireland medals, in 1941–4, 1946, 1952–4. He won a record 18 Railway Cup medals with Munster between 1942 and 1963, appearing in 22 finals in all. He also won four National Hurling League medals with Cork (1940–41, 1948, 1953) and was top scorer in the game three times (1959, when he became the only player to average over ten points a game, 1961 and 1962, when he shared the honours with JIMMY DOYLE of Tipperary). Gael-Linn produced a film about his life in 1964 and Val Dorgan wrote his biography in 1981, both works entitled *Christy Ring.*

ROBB, John (1932–), surgeon, political activist and senator. The bomb victims he saw in the course of duty at the Royal Victoria Hospital, Belfast moved him to campaign for a fresh approach to the problems of Northern Ireland. His core suggestion, repeated over a number of years, was that Great Britain and the Republic of Ireland should each rescind its claim to NI, allowing a constitutional convention within the North itself to determine its future status. He formed the New Ireland Movement, later the New Ireland Group, to press for these objectives. Appointed a member of the RTÉ Authority 1973–7 by the Fine Gael–Labour government; member of the Seanad 1982–9, a Taoiseach's nominee

of both CHARLES HAUGHEY and GARRET FITZGERALD.

ROBERTS, Ruaidhrí (1917–1986), trade unionist, b. 1 Jan. 1917, ed. Belvedere and UCD (B.Comm.). Roberts worked with Bord na Móna 1943–5 before becoming secretary of the Irish Trades Union Congress 1945–9. At the time, ITUC represented about two-thirds of trade unionists in Ireland, the rest being affiliated to the Congress of Irish Unions, which had been established by the ITGWU following the split in the Irish labour movement. He became joint secretary of the re-united Irish Congress of Trade Unions in 1959 and general secretary of Congress in 1967.

ROBINS, Joseph (1923–), public servant, b. Moate, Co. Westmeath, ed. Marist College, Athlone and TCD (B.Comm., Ph.D.). Honorary fellowship in the Institute of Hospital Administration. Civil servant in the Department of Health, retiring with the grade of assistant secretary. Head of the development unit at the time of the establishment of the health boards, when the last vestiges of the 19th-century Poor Law system were removed. Member of several official advisory bodies, including being chairman of the Working Party on Training the Handicapped 1975, the Review Body on Adoption Services 1984, the Advisory Group on Health Promotion 1986, the Working Party on Services for the Elderly 1988 and the Expert Group on the Voluntary Sector 1993. National delegate on various EU committees on health. Publications include *The Lost Children, Fools and Mad, From Rejection to Integration* and *Custom House People.* Member of a large number of voluntary bodies in the areas of health and social disadvantage. Won a People of the Year award in 1993.

ROBINSON, Esmé Stuart Lennox (1886–1958), playwright, b. Douglas, Co. Cork, ed. Brandon. On seeing the Abbey Players perform he became interested in drama. His first Abbey play, *The Clancy Name* (1908), was an unqualified success and ran for three months. Robinson was appointed Abbey manager by W.B. YEATS in 1909 but resigned the following year in order to write. In time he found drama less rewarding than he had hoped and in 1915 he joined the Carnegie Trust. But theatre was in the blood and he returned as Abbey manager in 1919; he was a director from 1923 until his death. His dramas were at best intelligent and carefully crafted, and played very well. They include *The Dreamers* (1915), *The Whiteheaded Boy* (1921), *Never the Time and the Place* (1924), *The Big House* (1928), *The Far-off Hills* (1931), *Drama at Inish* (1933) and *Church Street* (1935). He also wrote a novel, short stories, criticism and biography and edited several anthologies of poetry.

ROBINSON, Gerard (1948–), business executive, b. Co. Donegal, 23 Oct. 1948, ed. St Mary's College, Castlehead. He has enjoyed a highly successful business career in the UK. Chief executive of the giant leisure and media company Granada since 1991, he also holds a very large personal stake in the company. His toughness and commercial acumen were clearly demonstrated in Granada's takeover of London Weekend Television in 1994 and in the successful £3.9 billion bid for control of the hotel and catering group Forte in 1995. He is one of the major figures in the UK television market and is chairman of LWT, ITN and BSkyB. Before taking charge of Granada he was managing director of Grand Metropolitan Contract Services 1984–7 and chief executive of Compass Group plc 1987–91.

ROBINSON, John J. (1887–1965), architect, b. Dalkey, Co. Dublin, s. of John Loftus Robinson, MRIAI, RHA, architect of the Town Hall in Dún Laoghaire, ed. Blackrock and Clongowes, d. 30 Jan. 1965. Apprenticed to G.L. O'Connor, he later worked in a number of offices around Dublin. He qualified in London in 1910 and in 1911 entered the offices of Leonard Stokes, noted for his Catholic churches. Robinson returned to Dublin and in 1913 went into partnership with Richard Cyril Keeffe. In the 1920s he was associated with the introduction of a modern style of architecture into Ireland, often combining it successfully with a more traditional form appropriate to his ecclesiastical commissions. The quality of his work over these years is well represented by his involvement in the Gas Company headquarters on D'Olier Street, Dublin (1928). Robinson was appointed architect for the Eucharistic Congress 1932, for which the NUI conferred on him the honorary degree of master of architecture. RIAI president 1938–9, member of the council of RIBA. He was a Knight of Malta and received the papal honour of Knight of the Order of St Gregory.

ROBINSON, Mary (1944–), née Bourke, politician, constitutional lawyer and President of Ireland, b. Co. Mayo, May 1944, both her parents were medical doctors, ed. Hollymount, Mayo, Mount Anville, TCD, King's Inns and Harvard, m. Nicholas Robinson, two s. one d. She was Reid Professor of Law in TCD 1969–75. In her role as a lawyer she has been involved in many constitutional cases in both Ireland and the European courts, in areas such as women's right to serve on juries, access to legal aid, decriminalisation of homosexual activity and equalisation of social welfare payments. As a senator she introduced the first bill to make contraceptives available in the Republic; it gained only minimal support.

Elected to the Seanad (Ind. DU) in 1969, she held her seat until 1989. In 1976 she joined the Labour Party and in 1977 and 1981 unsuccessfully contested Dáil elections in Dublin. She resigned from the party after the 1985 Anglo-Irish Agreement in protest at the exclusion of unionists from the prior negotiations. She was a member of the New Ireland Forum 1983 and of the Oireachtas Joint Committee on Marital Breakdown 1983–5. Founder and director Irish Centre for European Law 1989–90.

When she decided not to run for the Seanad in 1989 it appeared that her political career was at an end. But in 1990 DICK SPRING asked her to accept a Labour party nomination for the presidential election later that year. She agreed, provided she did not have to rejoin the party or run strictly as a Labour candidate. There was much surprise both at the Labour nomination and at her acceptance. Few predicted that she would do other than put up a good showing. In the event she threw herself into the physically punishing nationwide campaign and struck a chord with community groups all over the country. Her election as Ireland's first woman president was widely welcomed, even by many of those who had opposed her.

Robinson has been the most active president in the history of the state, one of her priorities being visits to deprived or disaster-stricken areas of the world. She has also been assiduous in visiting places like Warrington and Manchester to show solidarity with the victims of paramilitary violence. In 1996 she became the first Irish head of state to pay an official visit to Britain, where she was received with appropriate ceremonial by Queen Elizabeth at Buckingham Palace.

ROBINSON, Peter David (1948–), politician, b. Belfast, ed. Annadale Grammar School, Belfast. In 1975 he became DUP general secretary but was unsuccessful in the Convention election when standing in East Belfast. Elected to Castlereagh Council in 1977, he narrowly won the East Belfast seat from WILLIAM CRAIG in the general election of 1979 and was again returned for East Belfast in the 1982 Northern Ireland Assembly election. In a Jan. 1986 by-election he held the East Belfast seat following his, and other Unionist MPs', resignation in protest at the Anglo-Irish Agreement. In Aug. 1986, in another anti-Agreement protest, he was arrested during a loyalist incursion into the Co. Monaghan village of Clontibret and fined £15,000. In Oct. 1987 Robinson temporarily resigned as deputy leader of the DUP following apparent disagreement over the tactics used against the Anglo-Irish Agreement. He has served a number of brief prison sentences for refusal to pay fines arising from anti-Agreement protests.

ROBINSON, Tim (1935–), writer and map-maker, b. Yorkshire, ed. Cambridge. He taught in Istanbul, then worked as an artist in Vienna and London in the 1960s. Moving to the Aran Islands in 1972, he produced maps of the islands in 1975 and 1980, which were followed by maps of the Burren and Connemara. He founded the Folding Landscapes project, dedicated to cartographic and archaeological studies of Connemara, the Burren and the Aran Islands, an enterprise which earned him a conservation award in 1987. Robinson's reputation rests on his *Stones of Aran: Pilgrimage* (1986), a highly individualistic and encyclopedic survey of the coastline of Aranmore. It won the IBA literature medal and a Rooney prize special award in 1987. *Stones of Aran: Labyrinth* (1995), an exploration of the Aranmore hinterland, is the closing part of this monumental exercise. Further work: *Connemara* (1990), *Mementos of Mortality: The Cenotaphs and Funerary Cairns*

of Arainn (1991) and an edition of J.M. SYNGE's *The Aran Islands* (1992).

ROCHA, John (1953–), fashion designer, b. Hong Kong, 23 Aug. 1953, ed. CBS, Hong Kong, Bamstead Hospital, Surrey (psychiatric nursing) and Croydon School of Art, London (HND in fashion design). On seeing his graduation show, a winter collection using Irish wools, the Irish Trade Board invited him to Dublin. Set up business with Eily Doolan 1978, with outlets in Dublin and Cork. Business closed 1982. In 1983 he started Chinatown label with business partner Odette Gleeson (his wife), closed down 1988. Went to Milan, where he produced his own line for Reflections 1988–9. Returned to Ireland, under licence for two labels, Chinatown and John Rocha, for Brown Thomas. Set up a new studio in Dublin 1995, with plans to open his own shop. Known for simple tailored shapes, soft layers and innovative use of fabric, he designs for both women and men. The only Irish-based designer that does catwalks in Paris. British Designer of the Year 1993.

ROCHE, Adi (1955–), anti-nuclear campaigner, b. Clonmel. Worked for Aer Lingus for eight years. Active in the anti-nuclear movement since the 1978 proposal to build a nuclear power station at Carnsore Point, Co. Wexford. Took voluntary redundancy 1986 to work as a full-time volunteer for Irish CND. In 1988 she devised a 'peace education programme' which now covers 50 schools a year. She initiated the Chernobyl Children's Project in 1990 and is its current director. The Project has brought over 1,000 children to Ireland for life-saving operations, rest and recuperation; terminally ill children have gone to the special Paul Newman centre in Co. Kildare. The Project sends regular supplies of medicine, ambulances and general humanitarian aid to hospitals and orphanages in the contaminated zones of Belarus and western Russia. Roche researched and co-produced the first English-language documentary on the effects of the Chernobyl disaster: *Black Wind, White Land* has been screened in more than 30 countries. Her book *Children of Chernobyl* (1996) became an immediate best-seller in Ireland. European Person of the Year 1996.

ROCHE, Billy (1949–), novelist and playwright, b. Wexford. He has been an actor and has toured Britain and Ireland as a musician working the cabaret circuit. Stage plays include *A Handful of Stars*, which won the John Whiting award and the Plays and Players award for the most promising playwright, *Belfry* and *Poor Beast in the Rain*, which won the Thames TV bursary award for the best play of 1990, as well as the George Devine award and the Charrington Fringe award. In 1989 he was writer in residence at the Bush Theatre, London. His characters are sub-O'CASEY – even sub-SYNGE – and come close to rendering to perfection life in small-town Ireland, *Poor Beast in the Rain* in particular, set as it is in a Wexford bookmaker's shop. Roche has also written *Amphibians* (1992), a play for BBC Scotland and the stage play *The Cavalcaders* (1993). He is the author of two novels, *Tumbling Down* and *The Sound of a Lonely Note*.

ROCHE, Kevin (1922–), architect, b. Dublin, s. of Eamonn Roche, TD and manager of Mitchelstown Creameries, ed. Rockwell and UCD. Graduated B.Arch. (1945) and worked for MICHAEL SCOTT in Dublin, Maxwell Fry in London and (as office boy) with the planning office of the UN building in New York. Hired by Eero Saarinen, the eminent corporate architect who died suddenly in 1961, leaving Roche and his colleague John Dinkeloo to inherit the practice. When Dinkeloo died in 1981, Roche kept the name Kevin Roche, John Dinkeloo and Associates. Has produced some of the most visually arresting designs of the 20th century – for instance, the headquarters of General Foods – while always keeping in mind the people who will use the building. Won the Pritzger architectural prize 1982.

ROCHE, Stephen (1959–), cyclist, b. Dublin, 20 Nov. 1959. Having won the Rás Tailteann in 1979, finished 24th in the road race in the 1980 Moscow Olympic Games and won the Paris–Roubaix as an amateur, he turned professional in 1981. He won the Paris–Nice race that year, as well as the Tour de Corsica. His achievements in 1987 – which place him among the top Irish sportspersons of all time – were matched only by the great Eddy Merckx: he won the Tour de France (the first Irishman to do so), the Giro d'Italia, the rainbow jersey as world road champion and the Super Prestige Pernod Trophy for the

Cyclist of the Year. His Tour de France victory was dramatic: he was in second place entering the Alps followed by Spain's Pedro Delgado, who opened up a huge gap when Roche fell, but he countered in an effort which hospitalised him overnight, recovering to keep the yellow jersey into Paris the following day. He also won the World Championship at Villach in Austria, and for his feats became the first sportsperson to be made a freeman of Dublin. In 1983 he had been third in the world professional race and he came third in the 1985 Tour de France, in which he finished 13th in his last season, 1993.

RODGERS, W.R. (1909–1969), poet, b. Belfast, ed. QUB and Presbyterian Theological College, Belfast. Presbyterian minister Loughgall, Co. Armagh 1935–46. Rodgers first came to public attention through broadcasting, when his work was featured on Radio Éireann. Upon publication, the vigour and variety of the language in his early poems (*Awake! and Other Poems*, 1941) was wrongly attributed to the influence of Gerard Manley Hopkins, with whose work Rodgers was in fact unacquainted. He resigned the ministry in 1946 and joined the features department of the BBC in London as a producer and scriptwriter. He made many memorable radio broadcasts on the newly established Third Programme, drawing on his Ulster background and Irish literary themes. His powerful later poems ('The Net', 'Europa and the Bull') celebrate a somewhat guilty escape from puritan morality. Elected to the IAL 1951 and awarded an Irish Arts Council annuity 1968. He died in Los Angeles, 1 Feb. 1969, and is buried in Loughgall.

ROONEY, John J. (1935–), chemist, b. Co. Down, 22 Oct. 1935, ed. Downpatrick High School, Co. Down and QUB (B.Sc. 1957, Ph.D. 1960), m. Angela Keenan, four s. three d. Researched for his Ph.D. with Charles Kemball, was ICI fellow at QUB 1960–62 and Hull 1962–5. He won the Meldola medal of the then Royal Institute of Chemistry 1965. Successively lecturer (1965–8), reader (1968–80) and Professor of Catalytic Chemistry (1980) at QUB. He is a member of the RIA and was the Ciapetta lecturer of the Catalysis Society of North America 1994. Principal research interest: the mechanistic relationship of homogeneous to heterogeneous catalysis. He has carried out a variety of studies of hydrogenation–dehydrogenation, skeletal rearrangements and cyclisation reactions of hydrocarbons. He is generally regarded as a senior international authority on the understanding of catalytic mechanisms.

ROONEY, Michael Henry (1902–1990), journalist, b. Ardglass, Co. Down, ed. local national school, d. 20 Feb. 1990. Became a newsboy for Belfast nationalist daily *Irish News* while still in his teens. Joined the IRA, elected company captain by 500 fellow republican prisoners in Crumlin Road Jail. Returned to the editorial department of the *Irish News* in the early 1920s. Joined the *Irish Independent* in 1931, becoming assistant editor in 1935 and editor in 1961 on the retirement of long-serving editor FRANK J. GEARY, retiring himself in 1968. As editor he substantially modernised the content and image of his newspaper, in particular through expanding the coverage by its own reporters of foreign events and promoting popular understanding of the issues of the day by carrying articles of comment from a variety of viewpoints. A lifelong admirer of EAMON DE VALERA and a friend of SEÁN LEMASS, Rooney was also for 40 years the chief Irish correspondent of the Associated Press of America.

ROS, Amanda M'Kittrick (1860–1939), novelist and poet, b. Ballynahinch, Co. Down. She acquired notoriety as the author of some of the most delightful drivel ever (self-)published. The novel *Irene Iddlesleigh* (1897) was followed by *Delina Delaney* and *Donald Dudley*. Her verse was as altitonantly alliterative in title as her prose, entering the world of letters as *Poems of Puncture* and *Fumes of Formation*. Her admirers formed a London club which met to exchange quotations from her works. The following – taken from *Irene Iddlesleigh* – should illustrate how its members may have passed many an enjoyable hour: 'Every sentence the able and beautiful girl uttered caused Sir John to shift his apparently uncomfortable person nearer and nearer, watching at the same time minutely the divine picture of innocence, until at last, when her reply was ended, he found himself, altogether unconsciously, clasping her to his bosom, whilst the ruby rims which so recently proclaimed accusations and inno-

cence met with unearthly sweetness, chasing every fault over the hills of doubt, until hidden in the hollow of immediate hate.' Her other works appeared posthumously: *Bayonets of Bastard Sheen*, letters (1949), *St Scandalbags* (1954) and *Helen Huddleston* (1969).

ROSEN, Albert (1924–), conductor, b. Vienna. Studied under Hans Swarowsky. Irish début at the Wexford Festival Opera 1965. Principal conductor RTÉ Symphony Orchestra 1968–79 and subsequently its principal guest conductor. Made laureate of the orchestra – now the National Symphony Orchestra – on the occasion of his 70th birthday. Works regularly with the Dublin Grand Opera Society and was director of two opera houses in Prague. Has also held conductorships in Adelaide and Perth with the Australian Broadcasting Corporation and made guest appearances throughout the world.

ROSENSTOCK, Gabriel (1949–), poet, playwright, translator and journalist, b. Kilfinane, Co. Limerick, ed. UCG, where he became associated with the *Innti* group of poets. He was assistant editor of the Irish-language publisher An Gúm until 1981. He is a former chairman of *Poetry Ireland* and has published ten collections of poetry, the latest being *Rogha Rosenstock* (1994), and verse for children. He is also author of 11 volumes of translations into Irish, including work by W.B. YEATS, SEAMUS HEANEY, Georg Trakl, Günter Grass and Peter Huchel. His collections include *An Béar Bán: rainn do pháistí*, lyrics (1978), *Portrait of the Artist as an Abominable Snowman* (1989) and *Cold Moon* (1995). His translations include: *Rina Catóire*, from a novel by Jan Terlouw, *An Béar sa Choill*, a children's story by Ivan Gantschev (1982), *Byzantium* by Yeats, with J.W. Hackett (1991), *Thirty Zen Haiku* (1994). Short stories: *Lacertidae* (1994). Drama: *Amanthar*, plays for radio and TV (1989), and *Cá bhfuil Daidí?*, a children's play (1992).

ROWSOME, Leo (1903–1970), uilleann piper and teacher, b. Dublin. He and his brothers represented the third generation of a piping dynasty which included his grandfather Samuel and father, William. FRANCIS O'NEILL wrote of a visit to William's premises in 1906: 'The spirit of the music was in the performer unmistakably, for while he touched the keys of his regulators airily and in good rhythm, his eyes sparkled with animation and his whole anatomy seemed to vibrate with a buoyancy which found suitable expression in the clear tones of his chanter.' Leo Rowsome took over his father's pipe-making business in 1925, and grew to be one of the most influential figures in traditional music in the 20th century. Successful appearances at the Feis Ceoil resulted in his presidency of the Dublin Pipers' Club, which he was active in revitalising in 1936. He gave many concert appearances in Britain and Ireland and took part in television programmes in the USA. Perhaps his main legacy is through his role as a teacher. He was appointed as a tutor at the Municipal School of Music at the age of 16. A list of former pupils is a litany of many of the finest pipers of the epoch – Paddy Moloney, LIAM O'FLYNN, Peadar Broe, Tommy Reck and DAN O'DOWD. Rowsome's son Leon is a recorded piper, Liam, a fiddler, has also recorded and his daughter, Helena, is a whistle player.

RUSSELL BROTHERS, traditional musicians. The fact that the small community of Doolin on the west coast of Co. Clare has been visited over the years by thousands of music enthusiasts from many countries is largely a tribute to the three Russell brothers of Doonagore: Pakie, a concertina player, Gus, a tin whistle player, and Miko, who played both whistle and flute. Their mother, who grew up in an area where Irish was still generally spoken, sang and played the concertina. Exactly why Doolin became a centre of cosmopolitan musical activity, largely centred on Gus O'Connor's pub, is a question to which none would seem to have an answer. Pakie, a stonemason by trade, was not a man to venture far from home, and the visitors were already in abundance by the time Miko began to engage on music tours abroad, including an appearance at the American bicentennial celebrations. The music of the Russells, who in fact rarely played together, had wide appeal and yet was indigenous to the tradition of their own area. Pakie died in 1977 and Miko was killed in a road accident in 1994.

RUSSELL, George (AE) (1867–1935), author, editor and promoter of co-operative movement, b. Lurgan, Co. Armagh, 10 Apr. 1867, ed. Rathmines School and Metropolitan School of Art, Dublin, where he became a close friend of W.B. YEATS, d. Bournemouth, 17 July 1935. His first book, *Homeward: Songs by the Way*, appeared in 1894 and was followed by a prodigious output of poetry, novels and other works marked by his taste for fantasy. His play *Deirdre* was staged in 1902 by the Irish Literary Society, later to become the Abbey Theatre. There was a strictly practical side to him as well: under the influence of Sir HORACE PLUNKETT he joined the Irish Agricultural Organisation Society and was editor of its journal, the *Irish Homestead*, from 1906 to 1923, when he became editor of the *Irish Statesman* (until 1930). The mystical element in his poetry and painting attracted other artists of the day and the wide range of his interests made his home in Rathgar, Dublin a meeting place for the intellectual discussion of art, literature and theatre as well as economics and practical politics. Although he had been an advocate of Irish independence and favoured the Anglo-Irish Treaty, he became increasingly disillusioned with what he saw as the contraction of cultural values, and in 1933 he returned to England. He was invited to the USA to assist in drawing up Franklin Roosevelt's plans for coping with the agricultural aspects of the Depression, but through illness was unable to make a major contribution.

RUSSELL, Seán (1893–1940), republican, b. Dublin, ed. St Joseph's CBS, Dublin. Fought in the Easter Rising, IRA director of munitions during the War of Independence. He opposed the Anglo-Irish Treaty and remained active in the IRA after the Civil War. He resisted the attempts within the organisation to develop new republican socialist groups like Saor Éire. In the late 1930s, against the wishes of other leading republicans, he sought support for a war against Britain. Became IRA chief of staff in Apr. 1938 and pursued his objective of having selected British targets bombed. He died aboard a U-boat in Aug. 1940 while returning to Ireland from Germany.

RYAN, Brendan (1946–), politician, activist and lecturer, b. Athy, Co. Kildare, Aug. 1946, ed. CBS, Athy, St Patrick's Seminary, Roscommon and UCD (BE). Senator (NUI) 1981–92. Executive committee Cork Simon Community since 1974, honorary president since 1985. President Cork Council of Trade

Unions 1980–81. Ryan has long been a vocal and passionate champion of the poor and oppressed, both in Ireland and abroad. He has been a patron of the Irish Anti-Apartheid Movement and the Irish Nicaragua Support Group and vice-president of Cork CND. He lectures in engineering at the Regional Technical College, Cork.

RYAN, Cornelius (1920–1974), journalist and author, b. Dublin, 5 June 1920, ed. Synge Street, d. New York, Nov. 1974. His exhaustively researched and skilfully written books on World War II have sold over ten million copies. Joining the *Daily Telegraph* as a war correspondent in 1943, he covered the D-Day invasion in 1944 and the subsequent progress of General Patton's Third Army. His account of D-Day, *The Longest Day*, took ten years to prepare and was eventually published in 1959. It was an instant best-seller. *The Last Battle* (1960), on the fall of Berlin, and *A Bridge Too Far* (1974), an account of the disastrous Battle of Arnhem, each sold several million copies.

RYAN, Desmond (1893–1964), author, historian, secretary to PATRICK PEARSE, journalist, b. London, s. of William Patrick Ryan, journalist, ed. St Enda's School, Dublin, d. Dublin. Fought in the GPO during the Easter Rising and became a journalist after his release from internment. Wrote *The Man Called Pearse* (1919), *James Connolly* (1924), *Remembering Sion* (1934), *The Phoenix Flame* (1937) and *The Rising* (1949).

RYAN, Frank (1902–1944), republican socialist, b. near Elton, Co. Limerick, ed. St Colman's College, Fermoy, Co. Cork and UCD. Fought on the republican side in the Civil War and later became a leading figure in the IRA and editor of *An Phoblacht*. Founder member of Saor Éire 1931, a left-wing republican pressure group, and of the Republican Congress with PEADAR O'DONNELL and GEORGE GILMORE. On the outbreak of the Spanish civil war in 1936, he organised a party of over 200 Irish volunteers who fought for the Republic in the International Brigade. Wounded in 1937 at the Battle of Jarama. Following a convalescence in Ireland he returned to Spain but was captured in 1938 and sentenced to death. Following appeals from the Irish government the sentence was commuted to 30 years' imprisonment. He was

released into the custody of the German government a year later and in Aug. 1940 was brought to Berlin, where he met IRA chief of staff SEÁN RUSSELL. Together they were put on board a German submarine bound for Ireland but Russell died suddenly on board and Ryan returned to Berlin. In 1943 his health worsened dramatically and he died in a sanatorium in Dresden the following year.

RYAN, Hugh (1873–1931), chemist, b. near Nenagh, ed. Blackrock, Queen's College, Galway and University of Berlin, d. 27 Mar. 1931. Ryan worked 1897–9 in Berlin as part of Emil Fischer's group, which carried out classical research on sugars. He was appointed Professor of Chemistry in the Catholic University School of Medicine, Dublin 1899. When the NUI was founded in 1908 he became Professor of Chemistry at UCD, a position he held until his death. Ryan, the sole or joint author of over 70 scientific papers, was in his day Ireland's leading organic chemist. He took a deep interest in the application of chemistry to industry and was an internationally renowned peat expert.

RYAN, James (1891–1970), medical doctor and politician, b. Taghmon, Co. Wexford, ed. St Peter's College, Wexford, Ring College, Co. Waterford and UCD. Joined Irish Volunteers, medical officer in GPO during Easter Rising, where he tended the wounded JAMES CONNOLLY, interned Frongoch. TD (SF Wexford) 1918. Opposed Anglo-Irish Treaty 1921. Among the founders of the New Ireland Assurance Company. Founder member Fianna Fáil 1926. Minister for Agriculture 1932–47, for Health and Social Welfare 1947–8 and 1951–4, for Finance 1957–65. As Minister for Finance he gave important support to the thinking of T.K. WHITAKER, who had been appointed secretary of the Department of Finance by the preceding inter-party government in 1956. This led to the first Programme for Economic Expansion (1958), which brought a major upturn in the Irish economy under the governments of SEÁN LEMASS.

RYAN, John (1925–1992), editor, b. Dublin, ed. Clongowes and National College of Art, Dublin, d. 1 May 1992. In his time he was broadcaster, critic, editor, painter, publisher, and proprietor of the Bailey pub and restaurant, Dublin, where Leopold Bloom's Eccles Street hall door was preserved. Ryan was founder editor of *Envoy*, 1949–51, whose poetry editor was VALENTIN IREMONGER. He edited the *Dublin Magazine* 1970–75, was secretary of the JAMES JOYCE Society of Ireland 1970–74 and MIAL. He was the author of two books, one of which – *Remembering How We Stood: Bohemian Dublin at the Mid-century* (1975) – is a memoir of PATRICK KAVANAGH, FLANN O'BRIEN, BRENDAN BEHAN and other notables whom Ryan befriended (and sometimes 'sponsored'); the other is *A Wave of the Sea*, a marine celebration (1981). He also edited *A Bash in the Tunnel: James Joyce by the Irish* (1970).

RYAN, Patrick J. (Paddy) (1882–1964), athlete and hammer-thrower, b. Old Pallas, Co. Limerick. Emigrated to New York. Won the American (AAU) hammer title eight times (1913–17, 1919–21). His record 189' 6" throw on 17 Aug. 1913 stood for 25 years, 40 years in the USA. Ryan won the gold medal in the hammer for the USA at the 1920 Olympic Games in Antwerp, where he also won a medal in the 56 lb weight event. He had won his first Irish championship in 1903 and was successful again after his return to the country in 1919, bringing his haul of Irish titles to 12.

RYAN, Richard (1946–), poet and diplomat, b. Dublin, ed. UCD. A member of the Irish foreign service, he is currently ambassador to South Korea. His published volumes of poetry include *Ledges* (1970) and *Ravenswood* (1973).

RYAN, Thomas Anthony (1936–), businessman, b. 2 Feb. 1936, ed. CBS, Thurles and Northwestern University, Chicago. Worked in Aer Lingus posts at home and abroad and eventually in senior management 1956–75. Founded Guinness Peat Aviation (GPA), an aircraft leasing company, 1975. The business prospered and developed into a major international group, leasing planes to some 100 airlines around the world. It virtually collapsed, however, after the failure of an unfortunately timed flotation in 1992. The American corporation General Electric rescued the ailing firm, effectively by absorbing it, and Ryan became chairman of GE Capital Aviation Services Inc., set up to manage the remaining business of GPA.

In 1995 he joined the board of Ryanair, the independent Irish airline controlled by his sons, becoming non-executive chairman in Jan. 1996. He announced plans for a telemarketing subsidiary which would substantially increase employment in Ryanair and involve an investment of £2.5 million. He also announced a sharp rise in the airline's turnover and pre-tax profits, but was disappointed when the government turned down the company's proposal for a second Dublin airport at Baldonnel. He is a governor of the National Gallery of Ireland and holds honorary doctorates from TCD, NUI and UL.

RYAN, Tom (1929–), artist, b. Co. Limerick, ed. Limerick School of Art and National College of Art, Dublin. He studied painting under JOHN (SEÁN) KEATING in the National College of Art and taught there briefly himself before becoming a full-time painter. MHRA 1971, PRHA 1982–92. He has exhibited widely in solo and group exhibitions throughout Ireland, and has also had one-man shows in Lithuania and the Ukraine. His portraits and figurative paintings are academic in style and are distinguished by the expertise of the modelling and the classical skills in rendering and in the use of colour.

RYAN, William Patrick (1867–1942), journalist, b. Templemore, Co. Tipperary. After establishing himself as a successful journalist in London, he returned to Ireland in 1905 to edit the *Irish Peasant*. A socialist and an advocate of radical land reform, his views were reflected in the columns of the paper and drew the wrath of the clergy – including Cardinal LOGUE – who forced its closure. Ryan revived it first as the *Peasant* and later as the *Irish Nation*. But his secular audience, mostly petit bourgeois nationalists, were no more receptive to his socialism than the clergy had been and by 1910 he had closed the paper and returned to London, where he lived the rest of his life. He never lost his interest in Ireland, however, and remained a sympathetic, if caustic, observer of Irish life and politics. A prolific writer, he published widely in a number of different genres. His work included *The Irish Literary Revival* (1894), *The Pope's Green Island* (1912) and *The Irish Labour Movement* (1919).

S

SAGARRA, Eda (1933–), née O'Shiel, academic and author, ed. Loreto Convents, Bray, Co. Wicklow and Foxrock, Co. Dublin, Farnborough Hill Convent, England, UCD and Universities of Freiburg, Zurich and Vienna (D.Phil. 1958). Lecturer in German literature and history Manchester University 1958. Professor of German and head of the Department of Germanic Studies TCD since 1975; dean of international studies 1979–86, registrar 1981–6. Vice-president RIA 1990. Her numerous highly regarded books in a field rarely explored by Irish scholars include *Tradition and Revolution: German Literature and Society 1830–1890* (1971), *A Social History of Germany 1648–1914* (1977) and *An Introduction to Nineteenth Century Germany* (1980).

SALKELD, Blanaid (1880–1959), poet, b. Chittagong, India (now Pakistan), grew up in Dublin but went to Bombay with her husband in 1901. She returned to Ireland and joined the Abbey Players as Nell Byrne. Author of a number of verse plays but only one – *Scarecrow over the Corn* (1933) – was ever staged. She published several small volumes of poetry, most of which is metrically destitute; moreover, it relies on a rather arcane system of punctuation. Yet some of the verses are extremely beautiful and sensitive, particularly several contained in . . . *the engine is left running* (1937). Her other collections were *Hello Eternity!* (1933), *The Fox's Covert* (1935) and *Experiment in Error* (1955). Her granddaughter Beatrice married BRENDAN BEHAN.

SALMON, George (1819–1904), mathematician and theologian, b. Cork, 25 Sept. 1819, ed. Cork and TCD, d. 22 Jan. 1904. Ordained Church of Ireland deacon 1844, priest 1845. After a highly distinguished undergraduate career as a mathematician, lectured in both mathematics and theology. Wrote extensively on both subjects, his most notable early work being *Conic Sections* (sixth ed. 1879). Regius Professor of Divinity TCD 1866–88, spanning the critical period of disestablishment, where his influence in theological debate

was on the 'Protestant' side. Wrote on religious topics, both devotional and theological. Contributed to *Dictionary of Christian Biography* (1877–87). His *Introduction to the New Testament* (seventh ed. 1894) won general acclaim, and he became known to a yet wider public through *The Infallibility of the Church* (second ed. 1890). Honorary degrees from Oxford, Cambridge, Edinburgh and Christiania (Oslo). Appointed Provost of TCD 1888, died in office.

SANDS, Bobby (1954–1981), republican, b. Rathcoole, Belfast, d. 5 May 1981. In 1972 Sands's family was intimidated by loyalists into leaving its home in Twinbrook in west Belfast and soon afterwards he became active in the IRA. Imprisoned for the second time in 1976, he immediately joined the protest by republican prisoners against the removal of special category status earlier that year. Leader of the IRA prisoners in the H-blocks during the 1980 hunger strike. Started refusing food himself on 1 Mar. 1981 when the protest was resumed following the failure to win concessions from the government. Elected an MP in the 1981 Fermanagh–South Tyrone by-election with a vote of over 30,000. He died on the 66th day of his fast.

SAW DOCTORS, The, rock band. Played gigs in and around their home county of Galway, often being joined on stage by Mike Scott and Anton Thistlewaite of the Waterboys. The single 'I Useta Lover' became a surprise Irish hit, turning the Tuam five-piece into overnight heroes. Although disdained by the serious rock press, the Saw Doctors' popularity grew and they turned their energies to the UK market, playing sell-out concerts the length and breadth of Britain. In late 1994 their independently released 'Small Bit of Love' single reached the British top 30.

SAYERS, Peig (1873–1958), storyteller, b. Dún Chaoin, Co. Kerry, d. Dingle, Co. Kerry, Dec. 1958. She married Pádraig Ó Gaoithín, from the Great Blasket Island, where she lived for more than 40 years. Sayers's memory for folklore and storytelling drew the attention of the Irish Folklore Commission. Her autobiography *Peig* (1936) was dictated by her to her son MÍCHEÁL Ó GAOITHÍN. A second volume, *Beatha Pheig Sayers*, was published posthumously in 1970. She also produced *Machnamh Sheanmhná* in 1939, which appeared in SEAMUS ENNIS's translation as *An Old Woman's Reflections* (1962). In 1953 the entire population of the Great Blasket Island was resettled on the mainland.

SCAIFE, Brendan Kevin Patrick (1928–), academic, b. 19 May 1928. Lecturer in electrical engineering TCD 1961–6, reader 1966–7, associate professor 1967–72, Professor of Microelectronics and Electrical Engineering 1972. Member Institution of Electrical Engineers 1949, Institute of Physics 1961, Institution of Engineers of Ireland 1969, RIA 1973. Boyle medal 1991.

SCANLAN, Patricia (1956–), novelist and poet, b. Dublin, ed. Our Lady of Victories, Ballymun and Dominican Convent, Eccles Street, Dublin. She has worked for Dublin Public Libraries from the time she left school in 1974. Her novels are not so much sex 'n' shopping as romance 'n' shopping, recounting as they do the amorous adventures of young Dublin women with a predilection for men in possession of lots of disposable income. They include: *City Girl* (1990), *Apartment 3B* (1991), *Finishing Touches* (1992), *City Woman* (1993) and *Foreign Affairs* (1994). Scanlan has also published poetry: *Three-dimensional Sin* (1988), the daring – if perhaps typographically challenged – *Yell Ow* (1988) and *Selected Poems* (1993).

SCANLON, James (1952–), artist, b. Brosna, Co. Kerry, 18 Oct. 1952, ed. Cork and studied mime before attending the Crawford Municipal School of Art 1974–8. His film *The Cage* won a British award in 1982. In the late 1970s he set up a stained-glass studio in Cork with MAUD COTTER, where they etched, did metalwork and learned the technique of making stained glass. Scanlon showed his first small panels at the Triskel in Cork in 1983 and in 1984 was commissioned to make four stained-glass windows for Woodfield Hotel, Limerick. Further commissions confirmed his imaginative understanding of the relationship between stained glass and architecture. With Cotter he exhibited in London in 1986: this led to com-

missions in Britain and Japan and invitations to exhibit in New York and Cracow. Instead of leading, Scanlon layers glass sheets, etching and aciding and sometimes painting them, favouring strong colours. At Sneem, Co. Kerry, in *The Pyramids*, a sculptural architectural project, he has incorporated glass in quasi-beehive huts, standing by water. More recently he has turned to computer technology for a window in the Crawford Gallery in Cork.

SCANLON, John O. (1937–), academic, ed. St Mary's College, Dundalk (BE, ME, D.Sc.) and University of Leeds (Ph.D.). Research engineer Philips Research 1959–63. Professor of Electrical and Electronic Engineering University of Leeds 1963–73, Professor of Electronic and Electrical Engineering UCD 1973. Publications include *Tunnel Diode Circuits* (1968) and *Circuit Theory* (two vols. 1973); he is also editor of the *International Journal of Circuit Theory and Applications*. He has been secretary and president of the RIA and is a director of Telecom Éireann.

SCHRÖDINGER, Erwin (1887–1961), theoretical physicist, b. Vienna, 12 Aug. 1887, d. Vienna, 4 Jan. 1961. Schrödinger was perhaps the most distinguished scientist working in Ireland in the 20th century, although his greatest achievements lay behind him when he arrived in 1940 to become professor at the Dublin Institute for Advanced Studies. He had previously held posts in various European cities, including Stuttgart, Breslau, Zurich, Berlin and Oxford. His early work was classical but carried the seeds of a lifelong interest in statistical mechanics. Prince Louis de Broglie had suggested that matter had characteristic waves associated with it and Schrödinger developed from this the wave equation which bears his name and which even today is part of the daily working equipment of the physicist. After the more abstract probability interpretation (which developed into the 'Copenhagen interpretation'), Schrödinger, like Einstein, withdrew – somewhat disillusioned – from the quantum mechanics area and, again like Einstein, devoted most of the rest of his life to the search for the Unified Field Theory. He retained an interest in statistical mechanics, however, as well as venturing into biology with his book *What is Life?* (1946). He retired from his senior professorship at the DIAS in

1956 and returned to Vienna, where he was nominated unsuccessfully for the presidency of the city. In 1933 he had shared with Paul Dirac the Nobel prize for physics, and he received many honorary degrees and awards, including the rare honour of foreign membership of the Royal Society of London. For a number of years he was an Irish citizen.

SCOTT, Francis Leslie (1928–), chemist, b. Co. Cork, 3 July 1928, ed. UCC. Lecturer organic chemistry UCC 1951–3, Lilly fellow University of California at Los Angeles 1953–5, lecturer organic chemistry 1955–7. Project leader/group leader Pennwalt Chemical Corporation, Rochester, New York, 1957–60. Professor and head of UCC chemistry department 1960–73. Visiting professor UCLA, director chemical research, pharmaceutical division, Pennwalt, since 1973. Senior fellow OECD Switzerland 1964/Poland 1965. Member RIA and American Chemical Society.

SCOTT, Michael (1905–1989), architect, b. Drogheda, d. Jan. 1989. The leading figure in the introduction of modern architecture to Ireland. Apprenticed himself with the Dublin firm of Jones and Kelly 1923–6, worked briefly with Charles C. Dunlop and the OPW, then commenced his own practice in 1928. In 1931 he entered partnership with Norman Good. After a series of impressive modern works, including projects in the increasingly important field of hospital architecture, Scott came to the fore in 1937 with the design of his own house, Geragh, in Sandycove, Co. Dublin, and his appointment as architect to the Irish Pavilion at the World's Fair of 1939, to be held in New York. The pavilion combined modern functionalism with traditional symbolism – a shamrock-shaped plan and the dominating figure of 'Mother Éire' – and set a new standard for Irish architecture. After the war, Scott quickly rose to a pre-eminent position, notably with his designs for the capital's new bus station, Busáras (1944–51), for which he was awarded the RIAI triennial gold medal for 1953–5. Major public commissions followed, including the Abbey Theatre (1951–66). Scott expanded his practice in 1958–9 by taking into partnership his assistants, two of the country's finest rising architects, RONALD TALLON and ROBIN WALKER, to create Michael Scott & Partners.

This firm was to dominate Ireland in the 1960s, though by this time Scott himself was playing a less significant role. He was a generous patron of the arts and the moving force behind the establishment in 1967 of Rosc, Ireland's international art exhibition. Scott retired in 1975, the year in which the RIBA awarded him its royal gold medal, and continued to promote the arts until his death. He received honorary doctorates from the Royal College of Arts (1969), TCD (1970) and QUB. Recent scholarship has emphasised the contribution of Scott's assistants to his early work, but the authority and consistency with which he shaped modern Irish architecture could have been achieved only through the control of a man certain of his vision.

SCOTT, Michael Peter (1959–), folklorist, b. Dublin, ed. St Aidan's. Antiquarian bookseller and collector of Irish folklore. He has published some of the fruits of his exhaustive research in *Irish Folk and Fairy Tales* (three vols. 1982–3), *The Children of Lir* (1983), *Hall's Ireland* (two vols. 1984) and *Celtic Odyssey: Tales from the Land of Erin* (trans. *Voyage of Maeldún*, three vols. 1985).

SCOTT, Patrick (1921–), artist, b. Kilbrittain, Co. Cork, 24 Jan. 1921, ed. Monkstown Park, St Columba's and UCD. He had his first one-man show in Dublin in 1944, but continued to work as an architect from the time of his graduation from UCD in 1945 until he became a full-time artist in 1960. He has been a very successful painter and his work is represented in several important collections, including the Museum of Modern Art in New York and the Joseph J. Hirsborn Museum in Washington, but he is equally well known as a designer of tapestries, employing primary colours in abstract geometric designs. He represented Ireland at the XXX Biennale in Venice in 1960 and in Rosc '88.

SCOTT, William (1913–1989), artist, b. Greenock, Scotland, 11 Feb. 1913, to Irish-Scottish parents, the family returning 1924 to his father's home town, Enniskillen, ed. Belfast College of Art (1928) and Royal Academy, London (1931), first training as a sculptor and subsequently turning to painting. He moved to England in 1941 to teach at the Bath Academy of Art and held his first solo show in London in 1942, volunteering for active service the same year. In 1946 he returned to the Bath Academy to teach for ten years, joining the London Group and in 1950 showing in the Irish Exhibition of Living Art in Dublin. His almost abstract still lifes of this period were painted from frying pans and saucepans hung on the rough whitewashed walls of his studio, and grouped initially with fish or fruit. Gradually the objects moved half off the canvas, or receded into it, as Scott became interested in the 'half-said', the inexpressible.

During the 1950s he visited New York, meeting abstract impressionists Pollock, de Kooning, Rothko and Kline, as a result of which his own canvases became larger. The primitive paintings in the Lascaux caves in France led him to reduce colour and image again, and with palette knife and brush to lay more emphasis on textural marks. In 1958 he was given a retrospective at the Venice Biennale and commissioned to paint a 45-foot mural for Altnagelvin Hospital, Derry. A mural commission for RTÉ followed (1966–7).

He had a major retrospective at the Tate Gallery, London 1972 and in 1980 was represented in Rosc in Dublin.

SCOTT, William Alphonsus (1871–1921), architect, b. Dublin, 1 Sept. 1871, eldest s. of noted architect Anthony Scott (1845–1919). William Scott studied in the Metropolitan School of Art, Dublin and in his father's office in Drogheda. In partnership with his father he gained his first success in the competition for the Town Hall in Enniskillen (1897–9). After three years in the architects' department of London County Council, he returned to Dublin in 1902 to establish his own practice. Beginning most notably with his church at Spiddal, Co. Galway, Scott rapidly established a substantial practice with a style inspired by the English architect C.F.A. Voysey, relying on an artistic and eclectic yet essentially sympathetic reformulation of medieval prototypes, often with a distinctly Irish character. His O'Growney Memorial in the graveyard of Maynooth College (1905) represents his more antiquarian manner, while his St Mary's Diocesan College, Galway, of 1911–12 (altered), noted for its progressive style and construction, indicates a more personal response to the holy grail of a national style. He was Professor of Architecture in UCD from 1911

until his death. Scott's work combines a progressive appreciation of abstract ornament, which continues from C.R. Mackintosh to art deco, with a sympathy for materials which has its roots firmly in the arts and crafts movement. Works representing this special balance of contrasting values include the garden village at Sheestown, Co. Kilkenny (1907), the Town Hall, Cavan (1908–10), the gateway and lodge at Spiddal (1910), his work at Lough Derg (1910) and W.B. YEATS's Thoor Ballylee in Galway (c. 1917–20).

SEMPLE, Thomas (Tom) (1879–1943), hurler and long puck exponent, b. Thurles, 12 Apr. 1879, d. 11 Apr. 1943. He won three All-Ireland Senior Hurling Championships: in 1900 (with the Two-Mile-Boris Selection), in 1906 (with the Thurles Selection) and in 1908, again with Thurles, being captain on the last two occasions. In 1906 he won the Long Puck Championship of Ireland, when with a 'lift and hit' he drove a nine-ounce ball 96 yards. The GAA's Semple Stadium in Thurles is named after him.

SEYMOUR, St John Drelincourt (1880–1950), Church of Ireland clergyman and historian, b. 15 Apr. 1880, d. 25 May 1950. Ordained deacon 1903, priest 1904. Archdeacon of Cashel and Emly. Publications include the succession list of the clergy of Cashel and Emly (1908) and work on the records (many since destroyed) of the Cromwellian period in Ireland. His major academic achievement was *The Puritans in Ireland* (1921), 'the only systematic study based on the records destroyed in 1922'.

SHACKLETON, Ernest Henry (1874–1922), Antarctic explorer, b. Kilkea, Co. Kildare, 15 Feb. 1874, s. of Dr Henry Shackleton and Henrietta Gavan. Family moved to London and in 1890 Shackleton began a career in the merchant navy. Joined Robert Scott on 1901 expedition to Antarctica, on which he fell ill. Stood unsuccessfully for parliamentary seat as Liberal Unionist in 1906. Returned to Antarctica to lead 1907 *Nimrod* expedition and came within 100 miles of South Pole, but displeased Scott by making use of his previous Antarctic base.

Celebrated and knighted on his return, Shackleton organised a further expedition in 1914. His ship *Endurance* became trapped in Antarctic ice and in Oct. 1915 was crushed and destroyed, 1,000 miles from the whaling base at South Georgia. He led his 27-man crew in small boats to Elephant Island, and from there with five companions (including fellow countrymen THOMAS CREAN and M. McCarthy) sailed 800 miles in a small boat through the fearsome Weddell Sea and reached South Georgia. After three attempts he succeeded in rescuing his men from Elephant Island on 30 Aug. 1916, ending what was perhaps the greatest Antarctic exploit.

In 1918–19 Shackleton held a post in the north Russian expeditionary force. He set off in 1921 on his fourth Antarctic journey but died on South Georgia on 4 Jan. 1922, a controversial figure but a man of extraordinary courage and resource.

SHANAHAN, Joseph (1871–1943), missionary bishop, b. Glankeen, Borrisoleigh, Co. Tipperary, ed. Templederry NS, Co. Tipperary. Studied at the Holy Ghost seminary near Paris and at Rockwell, where a senior seminary for the Irish province was being launched. In Apr. 1900 he was ordained to the priesthood and appointed dean of the boarding school at Rockwell. In 1902 he was posted to southern Nigeria and within three years was appointed head of the mission. Confronted by a serious shortage of personnel, he concentrated on training native lay catechists and evangelising the people through the children educated in the mission schools. The success of these efforts may be gauged from the fact that with under 2,000 Catholics in southern Nigeria at the time of his arrival, by 1934 there were 118,085 baptised Catholics and 91,876 catechumens. When the mission was raised to vicariate status Shanahan was ordained bishop at Maynooth in 1920. He founded the Missionary Sisters of the Holy Rosary 1924 and was closely associated with the founding of St Patrick's Missionary Society and the Medical Missionaries of Mary. Overwork, coupled with long treks throughout his vast mission, forced him to resign due to ill health in 1931. He returned to Ireland and retired to Blackrock College. Chaplain to the Carmelite Sisters in Nairobi 1938. He died 25 Dec. 1943 and was buried in the Holy Ghost Cemetery there. In recognition of his exceptional contribution to the Nigerian mission his remains were transferred to Onitsha, Nigeria, Jan. 1956.

SHATTER, Alan (1951–), politician, b. Dublin, Feb. 1951, ed. High School, Dublin, TCD and University of Amsterdam. Solicitor. TD (FG Dublin South) since 1981. Demoted from front bench for opposing party leadership of JOHN BRUTON 1994. Introduced the Judicial Separation bill 1989 and the Adoption bill 1991, the only private member's bills enacted by the Oireachtas in more than 30 years.

SHAW, Bob (1931–1996), science fiction writer, b. Belfast. A graduate mechanical engineer who had also worked in industrial public relations and journalism, he began contributing short stories to British SF magazines in 1954. Shaw's background in engineering served his fiction well: his plots are plausible and rooted in 'hard' science, placing him comfortably in the league of American greats such as Isaac Asimov and Robert Heinlein, and British writers of the calibre of Arthur C. Clarke. His novels, which were published initially in the USA, include *Night Walk* (1967), *The Two-timers* (1968), *Shadow of Heaven* and *The Palace of Eternity* (1969), *One Million Tomorrows* (1970), *Ground Zero Man* (1971) and *Other Days, Other Eyes* (1972). *Orbitsville* (1975), *Orbitsville Departure* (1983) and *Orbitsville Judgement* (1990) form a trilogy whose scenario – an ambitious space building project as a means of relieving an overpopulated earth – is not unlike that of Larry Niven's acclaimed *Ringworld*. Short stories: *Tomorrow Lies in Ambush* (1973). His last book was the manual *How to Write Science Fiction* (1993).

SHAW, George Bernard (1856–1950), playwright and polemicist, b. Dublin, 26 July 1856, ed. Central Model Schools and Wesley, s. of George Carr Shaw, a failed businessman and alcoholic, and Lucinda Elizabeth Gurley, a musician whose entanglement with her teacher Vandeleur Lee provided young 'Sonny' with the first of many surrogate fathers. He left school at 15, working in an estate agent's office and collecting rents among Dublin's poor, an experience which convinced him of the city's hopelessness. In 1876 he emigrated to London, where he embarked on a drastic programme of self-education and self-discipline, honing his skills as an orator and controversialist.

Between 1879 and 1883, he wrote five unsuccessful novels, of which *Cashel Byron's*

Profession was the best: its strategy of taking a single profession (in this case prizefighting) as a metaphor for society would serve Shaw well in future years. The reading of Marx's *Das Kapital* in the British Museum during this period 'made a man of me', and he became an active member of the Fabian Society in 1884. His first real fame, however, was as a music critic, a position from which he crusaded for Wagner. Close study of Henrik Ibsen led to a career as a dramatist, beginning with a 'social problem play', *Widowers' Houses* (1892), and to a post as drama critic for the *Saturday Review* in 1895.

In 1893 his play on prostitution, *Mrs Warren's Profession*, was refused a licence by the Lord Chamberlain. Undaunted, he wrote many more dramas, including *Arms and the Man* (1894), *You Never Can Tell* (1896) and *Man and Superman* (1903), but it was only after *John Bull's Other Island* (1904), a hilarious study of Anglo-Irish relations, that his abilities as a playwright were recognised. King Edward VII broke his chair laughing at the production, to which the British Prime Minister brought cabinet colleagues in search of wisdom on 'the Irish Question'.

In 1898 Shaw married the heiress Charlotte Payne-Townshend; in 1906 the couple, who remained childless, settled in Ayot St Lawrence, Hertfordshire, where they spent the remainder of their days. From there, Shaw produced a steady flow of plays, among them *The Doctor's Dilemma* (1906), *Androcles and the Lion* (1911), *Pygmalion* (1912 – later filmed as the musical *My Fair Lady*), *Heartbreak House* (1916) and *Back to Methuselah* (1921). He was awarded the Nobel prize for *Saint Joan* (1923), arguably his greatest play. It took the Maid of Orleans, recently canonised by the Roman Catholic Church, and suggested that, by listening to her inner voices and bypassing the authority of priest and bishop, she was one of Europe's first Protestant mystics. At a time when the new Irish state was beginning to adopt a Catholic self-image, it subversively implied a link between Protestant self-election and national self-determination.

Shaw was widely hailed as the leading dramatist of his time, with more than 700 performances of his plays by the Court Theatre over a three-year period. During World War I he supported dissident pacifists, as well as opposing British repression in Ireland. His voluminous prefaces to his plays became famous in their own right for their paradox and wit. In addition, he wrote noted works such as *The Quintessence of Ibsenism* (1891), *The Perfect Wagnerite* (1898), *The Intelligent Woman's Guide to Socialism and Capitalism* (1928) and *The Black Girl in Search of God* (1932).

Age did not slow Shaw. He visited Russia, and continued to write and pontificate until his death. He left some of his vast fortune to support the National Gallery of Ireland, in which he had first learned to love art and esteem artists.

SHEEHAN, Canon Patrick Augustine (1852–1913), novelist and poet, b. Mallow, Co. Cork, ed. Fermoy, Co. Cork and Maynooth. He was a curate in Plymouth and Exeter, then back in Cork in Cobh and Mallow. Parish priest in Doneraile 1895, canon 1903, he served the parish until his death. He wrote poetry but is best known as the author of *Glenanaar* (1905) and a succession of other novels which are still read with enthusiasm. In his day he enjoyed a wide readership both in Ireland and abroad. His first books were *Geoffrey Austin, Student* (1895) and its sequel, *The Triumph of Failure* (1898); *My New Curate* ran first in the *American Ecclesiastical Review* and appeared as a novel in 1900. There followed many more, including *Luke Delmege* (1901), *Lisheen* (1907), *The Blindness of Dr Gray* (1909), *The Queen's Fillet* (1911) and *The Graves at Kilmorna* (1915). He also wrote *The Literary Life and Other Essays*, published in 1921; a volume of his poems appeared the same year.

SHEEHY, Michael (Mikey) (1954–), Gaelic footballer, b. Co. Kerry, 28 July 1954. One of five Kerry footballers to share the record of eight All-Ireland senior medals in 1975, 1978–81, 1984–6, he was also on the teams defeated in the finals of 1976 and 1982. He won seven All-Star awards, all at right full-forward, in 1976, 1978–9, 1981–2, 1984 and 1986. Earlier in his career he won two All-Ireland Under-21 Championship medals with Kerry, in 1973 and 1975, and an All-Ireland Club Championship medal with Austin Stacks in 1977.

SHEEHY SKEFFINGTON, Francis (1878–1916), socialist and writer, b. Bailieborough, Co. Cavan, ed. locally and UCD,

m. Hanna Sheehy 1903. MA (RUI). Registrar of UCD 1902–4, he resigned after a dispute with the college president over the appointment of women academics. He was a committed feminist and helped his wife, whose surname he took in addition to his own, to found the Irish Women's Franchise League in 1908. He also edited the suffrage paper the *Irish Citizen*. In 1908 his biography of Michael Davitt was published. He was active in the labour movement and became vice-chairman of the Irish Citizen Army in 1913. He edited the *Nationalist* with THOMAS KETTLE and undertook a tour of the USA in 1915 supported by Clan na Gael. However, he was a convinced pacifist and, although he had many friends among the leadership of the revolutionary republican movement, was opposed to the use of violence for political ends. During the Easter Rising he was arrested by a British patrol while trying to prevent looting and summarily executed.

SHEEHY SKEFFINGTON, Owen (1909–1970), academic and politician, b. Dublin, ed. Sandford Park, Dublin and TCD, s. of Hanna and FRANCIS SHEEHY SKEFFINGTON, d. June 1970. After graduating he spent some time in France, where he met his future wife, Andrée Denis. They were married in 1935. On his return to Ireland he taught in the French department at TCD. Represented TCD in the Senate 1954–61, 1965–70, having already established himself as a courageously independent voice in matters of public controversy. A liberal, a socialist and a humanist, Sheehy Skeffington was one of the minority who championed enlightenment values and democratic pluralism in the traditionalist-Catholic Ireland of his day.

SHEPPARD, Oliver (1865–1941), sculptor, b. Cookstown, Co. Tyrone, 10 Apr. 1865, ed. Metropolitan School of Art, Dublin and South Kensington Art School 1889–91, d. Dublin, 14 Sept. 1941. After a short period in Paris he taught in Leicester and Nottingham in the 1890s. Instructor in modelling Metropolitan School of Art 1902. Professor of Sculpture RHA. He exhibited regularly at the RHA and the RA for most of his life. His *Death of Cúchulain* now stands in the GPO as a memorial to the Easter Rising, although the work had been carried out some years before the rebellion.

SHERIDAN, Jim (1949–), playwright, director, screenwriter and actor, b. Dublin, ed. St Laurence O'Toole's and O'Connell School, Dublin and UCD. He began with children's theatre, moved to England and in 1981 to New York, where he was manager for seven years of the Irish Arts Center in Manhattan. His first film, *My Left Foot*, on the life of CHRISTY BROWN, was nominated for five Oscars in 1989 – Daniel Day-Lewis and BRENDA FRICKER each winning – and established Sheridan's reputation. *The Field* (1990) followed, then the multi-Oscar-nominated *In the Name of the Father* (1993), which won the Golden Bear award at the 1994 Berlin Film Festival. He also wrote the script for *Into the West* (1992). His radio play *The Risen People* was staged in the Gaiety, Dublin in 1994. Sheridan has also written *The Fighting McGuigan* (1985), a biography of the champion boxer BARRY McGUIGAN.

SHERIDAN, John D. (1903–1980), writer, b. Glasgow, ed. O'Connell School and St Patrick's College, Dublin and UCD, d. Dublin, 1 May 1980. He was a national school teacher in Dublin and later worked as a publisher with the Educational Company of Ireland. For many years he was a humorous and enormously popular columnist on the *Irish Independent*. Some of his columns were collected in book form; he also produced novels, poetry and essays. Sheridan's voice was that of the introverted, provincial Ireland of the 1940s and 1950s. His writing was competent, witty, bland and rather harmless. In the last 15 years of his life he was also distinguished as a public controversialist, being strongly opposed to liberal changes in Church and state.

SHERIDAN, Margaret Burke (1889–1958), soprano, b. Castlebar, ed. Dominican Convent, Eccles Street, Dublin, RAM, London, and in Rome under the noted teacher Alfredo Martino, d. Dublin. In 1918 she made her operatic début in Rome as Mimi (*La Bohème*, Puccini). She made her Covent Garden début the following year, again as Mimi, and appeared in the first London performance of Mascagni's *Iris*. First heard by Puccini in 1919, when she performed his Cio-Cio-San (*Madama Butterfly*) in Milan. The title role of Catalani's *La Wally* in 1922 was the first of many performances at La Scala, where she also sang Candida in the world premiere of Respighi's *Belfagor* in 1923. Coached personally by Puccini in 1923 for the title role of *Manon Lescaut*, which was to become perhaps her most successful part. Numerous recordings include the first ever complete recording of *Madama Butterfly* (1930). She worked with such eminent conductors as Toscanini – who dubbed her 'the Empress of Ireland' – Barbirolli and Bellezza, and with singers such as Beniamino Gigli, Renato Zanelli and Aureliano Pertile. Final operatic role was as Verdi's Desdemona (*Otello*) at Covent Garden in 1940. At the outbreak of World War II she returned to Ireland, where she spent the rest of her life.

SHORTT, John Purser (1894–1966), Church of Ireland cleric and hymnologist, b. 14 Sept. 1894, d. 28 Sept. 1966. Ordained deacon 1918, priest 1919. He served most of his ministry in Dublin, and through his encyclopedic knowledge of hymnology made a major contribution to the compilation and publication of the 1960 edition of the (Irish) *Church Hymnal*.

SIMMONS, James Stewart Alexander (1933–), poet, playwright, editor and critic, b. Derry, ed. Foyle College, Derry, Campbell College, Belfast and Leeds University. He left Ireland 1949 and travelled extensively before returning in 1956. He was a schoolteacher in Lisburn, Co. Antrim in 1958, during which time he wrote and performed songs on the radio. He lectured in Nigeria 1963–6, returned to Belfast in 1967 and has taught at NUU since 1968. He founded and edited the magazine the *Honest Ulsterman* 1968–70 and was literary editor of the *Linen Hall Review* and *Fortnight*. His many publications include poetry: *Ballad of a Marriage* (1966), *Songs for Derry* (1969), *No Ties* (1970), *Energy to Burn* (1971), *No Land is Waste, Dr Eliot* (1973), *Memorials of a Tour in Yorkshire* (1975), *Constantly Singing* (1980), *From the Irish* (1985) and more. Plays include: *An Exercise in Dying* (1970), *The Death of Herakles* (1975), *Doily McCartney's Africa* (1981), *Elegies* and *Mainstream* (1995). He also wrote a biography, *Sean O'Casey* (1983), and edited poetry. He received the Cholmondeley award in 1977.

SIMMS, George Otto (1910–1991), Church of Ireland archbishop, b. 4 July 1910,

ed. Cheltenham and TCD (double moderatorship in classics/ancient history and political science), m. Mercy Gwynn 1941, three s. two d., d. 15 Nov. 1991. Ordained deacon 1935, priest 1936, bishop 1952. Having served his first (and only) curacy at St Bartholomew's, Dublin, he was appointed chaplain of Lincoln Theological College in 1938. Dean of residence (C. of I. chaplain) TCD 1939–52, combining the position with that of chaplain secretary, in effect principal, of the Church of Ireland Training College, Dublin. He was elected successively Bishop of Cork, Cloyne and Ross (1952), Archbishop of Dublin (1956) and Archbishop of Armagh (1969).

Awarded his Ph.D. in 1950 for work on the Book of Kells, the great illuminated manuscript with which his name came to be closely associated. Lectured regularly and widely on the subject and wrote about it in scholarly yet popular form, being awarded a Reading Association of Ireland prize for *Exploring the Book of Kells* (1988).

Chairman of the Liturgical Advisory Committee, whose work culminated in the *Alternative Prayer Book* (1984). An intensely practical person, he also chaired an Advisory Committee on Administration (1957), many of whose wide-ranging recommendations were later implemented. Through his ministry he exercised enormous influence and moral authority, and his achievements in ecumenical work were very real. The rapport he established with leaders of other Churches, and especially with Cardinals WILLIAM CONWAY and TOMÁS Ó FIAICH, played no small part in bringing into being the Inter-Church Conference, whose regular meetings of representatives of the Roman Catholic and other Churches were unique to Ireland at the time.

SIMONDS-GOODING, Maria (1939–), artist, b. Quetta, India, has lived in Co. Kerry since 1947, ed. National College of Art, Le Centre de Peinture, Brussels and Bath Academy of Art. She has exhibited regularly in the RHA and in Oireachtas exhibitions. She won a Carroll's award at the Irish Exhibition of Living Art in 1970 and an Oireachtas landscape award in 1986. She has had several solo exhibitions in Ireland and has also had shows in New York, London, New Mexico and the Hague. A retrospective exhibition of her paintings, graphics and etchings was held in Cork in 1985. Simonds-Gooding often uses oil paint on plaster, a versatile technique which allows her to emphasise the distinctive features of a landscape by creating low relief with the plaster or carving into the surface of the painting. These expressionist paintings examine the distinguishing marks left by man as he reshapes the landscape in his search for security, sustenance and community.

SINCLAIR, Elizabeth (Betty) (1910–1981), trade unionist and communist, b. Belfast, ed. St Mary's Church of Ireland School. Sinclair worked in Ewart's mill as a reeler. In 1932 she joined both the Revolutionary Workers' Group and the Flax and Other Textile Workers' Union (later part of the Transport and General Workers' Union), representing the latter on Belfast Trades Council. In Oct. 1932 she was influential in the strike of outdoor relief workers. From Sept. 1933 she attended a course of political education in Moscow, arriving back just before the Belfast riots of July 1935. In late 1940 she was imprisoned for two months after the Communist Party of Ireland's newspaper published an article by the IRA. On her release she became a full-time worker for the party. In the 1945 Stormont election she polled over 4,000 votes in the Cromac ward of Belfast. Secretary to the Belfast Trades Council 1947–75, she was elected chairperson of the Northern Ireland Civil Rights Association in 1968 but resigned in Mar. 1969 in opposition to what she believed were the organisation's increasingly extremist and dangerous demands. In the late 1970s she lived in Prague for three years. Sinclair died as the result of a fire in her flat. She was described by her biographer, Hazel Morrissey, as 'the only woman in a man's world'.

SIRR, Peter (1960–), poet and editor, b. Waterford, moved to Dublin in 1969, ed. TCD. He spent some years in Holland and Italy and now lives in Dublin, where he is director of the Irish Writers' Centre and one of the editors of *Graph*. He won the PATRICK KAVANAGH award in 1982 and the poetry prize at the Listowel Writers' Week in 1983. His verse is intelligent, keen and witty, and is characterised by its ingenious tropes and original imagery. For example, here is Sirr on clouds: 'Who'd have thought the gods so woolly?' His collections are *Marginal Zones* (1984), *Talk,* *Talk* (1987), *Ways of Falling* (1991) and *The Ledger of Fruitful Exchange* (1995).

SLATTERY, John Fergus ('Slatts') (1949–), international rugby player, b. Dún Laoghaire, Co. Dublin, 12 Feb. 1949. Ireland's most capped flanker, he made 61 international appearances between 1970 and 1984, 17 times as captain (five victories), and scored three international tries. He captained Ireland on two overseas tours, to Australia in 1979 and to South Africa in 1981. His first 28 caps were consecutive but he then missed seven matches through injury; after he returned to the team, against Scotland in 1977, he went on to win the next 33 in succession. Ireland's third most capped player, in his later career he formed a formidable international back row with John O'Driscoll and his Blackrock College clubmate Willie Duggan. With them, he shared in the Triple Crown win in 1982, Ireland's first since 1949. He toured New Zealand with the 1971 series-winning Lions, but did not make the Test team. However, he played in all four Tests for the undefeated Lions in South Africa in 1974, when he had a late try disallowed in the final Test, which ended in a 13-all draw.

SMITH, Con (1931–1972), businessman, b. Cavan, ed. Terenure College, Dublin and UCD. Developed family business in Cavan and in 1950s sold reconditioned Ferguson tractors imported from England. By 1964 he had about 25 garages in the Smith Group and obtained the Renault franchise, assembling cars in Wexford. Spreading the group's interest into construction, property, finance and department stores, in 1969 he essayed a merger with Vincent Brittain, who had the British Leyland franchise. The partnership was short-lived but Smith emerged in 1970 with a Stock Exchange listing. A merger with W. and H.M. Goulding, the fertiliser firm, would have made Smith managing director and Sir Basil Goulding chairman. The documents were at the point of being signed when the Staines air disaster of 1972 deprived the country of the cream of its business talent, including Con Smith, who was 41 when he died.

SMITH, Michelle (1969–), international swimmer, b. Rathcoole, Co. Dublin, 16 Dec. 1969. She made Irish sporting history at the Centenary Olympic Games in Atlanta when she became the first woman competitor from Ireland to win an Olympic medal. She won successive gold medals in the women's 400 m individual medley, the 400 m freestyle and the 200 m individual medley. She went on to take the bronze medal in the 200 m butterfly. This was the best Olympic performance by any Irish athlete, surpassing the gold medal won by PAT O'CALLAGHAN at the Olympics of 1928 and 1932. In the previous year – 1995 – she had won three gold medals at the World Cup in Hong Kong, setting new standards in her events, and had also done well in the European Championship in Vienna. Smith, who is a fluent Irish speaker, studied communciations at the University of Houston, Texas, specialising in radio and TV, but is now a full-time swimmer.

SMITH, Rosemary (1937–), rally driver, b. Dublin, 7 Aug. 1937. During the 1960s she was the leading woman rally driver in the world, winning the ladies' awards in all the top international rallies, including the London–Sydney, the RAC and the Monte Carlo. In 1965 she was the outright winner of the Tulip Rally and was also chosen as a Texaco Sportstar of the Year.

SMITHSON, Annie Mary Patricia (1873–1948), novelist, b. Sandymount, Dublin, ed. Dublin and Liverpool. She trained as a nurse and midwife, was a district nurse 1929–42 and secretary and organiser of the Irish Nurses' Organisation; edited the *Irish Nursing and Hospital World* in the 1930s. She was active as a nurse in the Civil War, in which she took the republican side. Smithson wrote more than 20 'romantic' novels, the titles of which, if they were published for the first time today, would appear embossed in gold. They were best-sellers and are still being reprinted and read avidly, almost 50 years after her death. They include *By Strange Paths* (1919), *Carmen Cavanagh* (1925), *For God and Ireland* (1931), *The Marriage of Nurse Harding* (1935), *Wicklow Heather* (1938), *By Shadowed Ways* (1942), *Margaret of Fair Hill* (1951) and *The Walk of a Queen* (1959). She also edited nurse Lina Kearns's wartime memoir, *In Times of Peril* (1921). Her autobiography, *Myself and Others*, was published in 1944.

SMURFIT, Michael W.J. (1936–), businessman, ed. St Mary's College, Rathmines,

Dublin and Clongowes. After management training in the USA, joined the corrugated box-making firm founded by his father, Jefferson Smurfit. Director and chief executive since 1977 and director of a number of other companies within the group. Through his initiative and drive Smurfit developed a small family business into a major multinational in packaging, print and financial services, with branches, holdings, subsidiaries or associated companies in the USA, Latin America and a number of European countries. His group's purchase of the French packaging conglomerate Cellulose du Pin for £684m in 1994 was the biggest foreign acquisition in Irish corporate history. Smurfit's thereby became not only the largest firm in Ireland but one of the largest in the paper industry worldwide. At the government's request, Michael Smurfit served as chairman of the Interim Telecommunications Board (later Telecom Éireann) 1979–91. He was also chairman of the Racing Board 1985–90, is a fellow of the International Academy of Management and holds honorary doctorates from TCD, NUI and the Universities of Missouri and Scranton. He is honorary consul of Ireland in Monaco.

SMYLLIE, Robert Maire (1894–1954), journalist and editor, b. Glasgow, eldest s. of Robert Smyllie, a Scottish journalist, and an Irish mother, his family moving to Sligo towards the end of the 19th century, ed. at the local model school, Sligo Grammar School and TCD (1912), d. 11 Sept. 1954. Being on a continental tour, on the outbreak of World War I he was interned as an enemy civilian alien in Ruhleben, near Berlin, a sojourn which he always claimed completed his education. After the Armistice, because of lack of funds he could not continue his education at TCD, but John E. Healy, then editor of *The Irish Times*, engaged him to cover the Versailles Treaty talks. Legend has it that Smyllie got his first scoop interviewing Lloyd George, an exclusive story that was subsequently picked up by other newspapers worldwide. On his return to Ireland he became an editorial assistant in the newspaper, concentrating on European affairs. He was made assistant editor to the austere Healy and contributed many new ideas, including 'An Irishman's Diary', a daily column which he first wrote in 1927 and which has been running ever since. He became editor in 1934. Whereas Healy had been cold towards the Free State's attitude to Britain, Smyllie clearly saw a new wind blowing in the country. He believed in the Commonwealth and in Ireland's future as a member of it, but approached the question from an Irish rather than a British angle.

Under his editorship *The Irish Times* became a truly liberal newspaper, uncommitted and unconnected to any political party. He made full use of his editorial freedom, negotiating the tripwires laid for him by a sometimes anxious commercial board of owners, who continued to represent the old Protestant Ascendancy. In World War II those same skills stood him in good stead against a restrictive and often foolish censorship imposed by the government.

Smyllie was a familiar and approachable figure in the literary and bohemian Dublin of the 1930s, 1940s and early 1950s. He had a keen eye for up-and-coming journalists, and his wartime decision to give Brian O'Nolan (FLANN O'BRIEN) a thrice-weekly column not only boosted the newspaper's circulation but allowed a literary genius regular access to an audience. Smyllie's own column, light and chatty, appeared weekly under the pseudonym 'Nichevo'.

SOLOMONS, Bethel (1885–1965), obstetrician, b. Dublin, ed. St Andrew's College, Dublin and TCD. Played rugby for his university and was capped ten times for Ireland. The selectors of one of those Irish teams were rebuked by a critic who spoke of 'fourteen Protestants and a Jew', a remark which Solomons, whom it amused, repeated in his autobiography, *One Doctor in his Time* (1956). Graduating MB in 1907, he was master of the Rotunda 1926–33. A cryptogram in *Finnegans Wake* – 'in the bethel of Solyman's I accouched their rotundaties' – posed little difficulty for Irish readers.

A tall, handsome man who affected a broad-brimmed hat and flowing tie, Solomons was a recognisable figure in the street. He was gynaecologist to Mercer's Hospital, and author of *Handbook of Gynaecology* (1919) and *Obstetric Diagnosis and Treatment in General Practice* (1925). His mastership earned for him a truly international reputation. A further honour was the presidency of the RCPI 1946–8, where his portrait by his sister ESTELLA SOLOMONS now hangs.

SOLOMONS, Estella (1882–1968), painter, b. Dublin, ed. finishing school in Germany, RHA school under Walter Osborne and the Metropolitan School of Art, Dublin, m. SEUMAS O'SULLIVAN. In 1903 she visited Paris, taking classes at Colorossi's; continued her studies in London under ORPEN. Much influenced by visit to Amsterdam to see Rembrandt tercentenary exhibition in 1906. She moved away from the subdued Impressionist manner of early landscapes to light contrast in portraits. Honorary RHA member. Joined Cumann na mBan and was active behind the scenes during the Easter Rising. In the subsequent years her studio became a haven for those on the run.

SOMERVILLE, Edith Anna Oenone (1858–1949), writer, b. 2 May 1858 in Corfu, where her father was stationed on military service, d. Drishane, Skibbereen, Co. Cork, 8 Oct. 1949, ed. Alexandra. Lived most of her life at the family home in Drishane. Her partnership with her cousin Violet Martin under the names Somerville and Ross established them as witty and satirical observers of Irish life, in a series of novels such as *The Real Charlotte* (1894) and *Some Experiences of an Irish RM* (1899). Following Martin's death in 1915 Somerville continued to write under their joint names. *Irish Memories* (1917) and *The Big House at Inver* (1925) represent her best work from this period.

SOUTER, Camille (1929–), artist, b. Betty Pamela Holmes, Northampton, raised in Ireland. After leaving school she studied nursing. She began to paint while recuperating from TB. During the 1950s she spent a lot of time travelling and painting in Italy and in Ireland, especially Achill Island, and had a number of exhibitions in Dublin. Her work has been represented in the Irish Exhibition of Living Art 1957, Twelve Irish Painters, New York 1965 and Oireachtas art exhibitions. One of her few one-woman shows was the retrospective exhibition in the Douglas Hyde Gallery, Dublin in 1980. The subtle use of colour and of light in Souter's expressionist paintings combine to create a shifting surface pattern, giving the impression of a landscape almost continually subject to changes in light, tone and clarity.

SOUTH, Seán (1929–1957), republican, b. Limerick, ed. locally. He was one of three IRA activists killed during raids on various targets in Northern Ireland at New Year 1957. An Irish-language enthusiast and a prolific writer on a number of subjects, he also edited and published his own magazine, *An Gath*. Although the New Year's Eve attack on Brookeborough RUC barracks, in which both South and his comrade Fergal O'Hanlon died, was a débâcle, both volunteers achieved prominent positions in republican martyrology. South became the subject of several ballads and there was a huge attendance at his funeral on 4 Jan. 1957.

SPENCE, Augustus Andrew (**Gusty**) (1933–), loyalist, b. Belfast. An early member of the modern UVF, Gusty Spence served with the Royal Ulster Rifles in West Germany and Cyprus. He was sentenced to 20 years' imprisonment for the murder of a Catholic barman on the Shankill Road in 1966 – a crime which he denied committing. While on parole in 1972 he was kidnapped by other members of the UVF in an attempt to draw attention to his case – he was recaptured four months later. In 1977, while still in the Maze Prison, he issued a statement attacking the use of violence and supporting reconciliation, and in the following year he resigned as UVF commander in the prison. Since his release in Dec. 1984 Spence has been active in community politics and he is currently a leading member of the Progressive Unionist Party. He remains arguably the most widely respected individual within loyalist circles.

SPENDER, Sir Wilfrid Bliss (1876–1960), UVF commander and public servant, b. Plymouth, ed. Winchester and the Staff College, Camberley. Spender resigned from the army general staff in 1913 as a result of the Ulster crisis. Served as a UVF officer 1913–14, then returned to the general staff and was awarded the DSO and MC in 1918. Commanded the UVF in 1919 and established the B Specials in 1920. First secretary to the Northern Ireland cabinet 1921–5, permanent secretary to the Minister of Finance and head of the NI civil service 1925–44. He described the devolved NI administration as a 'factory of grievances'.

SPILLANE, Patrick (**Pat**) (1955–), Gaelic footballer, b. Co. Kerry, 1 Dec. 1955. The elder brother of Mike and Tom Spillane, also Kerry players of note, he won eight All-Ireland senior football medals, in 1975, 1978–81, 1984–6, and was in the Kerry teams defeated in the All-Ireland finals of 1976 and 1982. Other honours include four National Football League medals (1974, 1977, 1982, 1984), four Railway Cup medals with Munster (1977, 1978–9, 1981) and eight All-Star awards, the highest in either football or hurling: in 1976 (at left full-forward) and in 1978–81, 1984–6 (at left-half forward). He is generally regarded as one of the game's truly great players.

SPRING, Daniel (1910–1988), politician, b. Tralee, July 1910, ed. Strand Street NS, Tralee, d. Tralee, 6 Sept. 1988. Long before his death Spring had become a Labour Party legend, famed for holding onto his seat regardless of the party's fortunes. TD for Kerry North 1943–81, elected on 11 consecutive occasions. He joined the ITGWU in 1934 and became a prominent organiser throughout Munster. As a politician, Spring was on the conservative wing of the Labour Party. He was one of the breakaway group that formed the National Labour Party during the 1940s in response to the return of JAMES LARKIN to the official Labour Party, although he also acted as mediator between the two sides before their eventual rapprochement in the early 1950s. Spring was parliamentary secretary to the Minister for Local Government 1956–7. He won two All-Ireland football medals with Kerry. Father of DICK SPRING.

SPRING, Dick (1950–), politician, b. Tralee, 29 Aug. 1950, s. of Dan Spring, ed. Cistercian College, Roscrea, TCD and King's Inns, m. Kristi Hutcheson, 11 June 1977, two s. one d. He was appointed a junior minister in the 1981–2 coalition government on his first day as a Dáil deputy, having succeeded his father in the Kerry North constituency. His first foray into politics was in the 1979 local elections in Kerry, in which he was helped not only by his family tradition but by his sporting prowess: he played both Gaelic football and hurling for the county in the 1970s and won three rugby caps for Ireland in 1979. In the wake of MICHAEL O'LEARY's unexpected resignation from the leadership of the Labour Party in 1982, Spring easily defeated BARRY DESMOND and MICHAEL D. HIGGINS in a contest for the position. He inherited a party that was severely demoralised and subject to organisational fissures. Tánaiste 1982–7, he was Minister for the Environment 1982–3 and for Energy 1983–7. During this period he was closely involved in the workings of the New Ireland Forum 1984–5 and in the negotiations leading to the Anglo-Irish Agreement 1985.

He was also asserting his control over the party, particularly by ensuring the defeat of the entryist militant tendency, and securing a narrow but decisive victory over the strong anti-coalition groups in the party at annual conference. His credentials were strengthened when, in 1987, he led his party out of government on budgetary issues. His choice of MARY ROBINSON as a candidate for the presidential election in 1990 rapidly came to be seen as inspired: her subsequent victory enhanced both his personal status and that of the party as a whole. In the 1992 election, when – not least by dint of careful candidate management and an impressive display of party unity – Labour doubled its total to 33 Dáil seats, he negotiated successfully with all other parties before finally concluding a coalition agreement with Fianna Fáil which saw him Tánaiste for the second time. Since that date he has also been Minister for Foreign Affairs. In late 1994 Labour split with FF in a row about the presidency of the High Court and entered coalition with Fine Gael and Democratic Left.

Spring is an able parliamentary performer and astute tactician, and his politics – more liberal and left-inclined than those of his father – matched the mood of the early 1990s almost exactly. In his second phase in government he instituted a *cabinet* system which, although criticised by opposition politicians, had the effect of ensuring a Labour input into all government departments; his cabinet and sub-cabinet appointments, additionally, gave strategic prominence to younger deputies, to women and to the left wing of the party. He has been especially active in his role as head of the Irish delegation to the Anglo-Irish Inter-Governmental Conference. His relations with his British counterpart, the Northern Ireland secretary, Sir Patrick Mayhew, have sometimes seemed abrasive but despite such serious setbacks as the collapse of the IRA ceasefire in Feb. 1996 and the volte-face by the NI authorities over the Orange–nationalist confrontation at Drumcree in the following July the two have manifestly sought common ground in the ongoing peace process. In July 1996 Spring became ex officio president of the EU Council of Ministers upon the commencement of the Irish EU presidency for the latter six months of the year.

STACK, Austin (1879–1929), revolutionary, b. Ballymullen, Tralee, 7 Dec. 1879, ed. CBS, Tralee, d. 27 Apr. 1929. He was involved in the attempted landing of arms by Sir ROGER CASEMENT for use in the Easter Rising and was arrested, but released in June 1917. In the 1918 general election he became TD for Kerry and he served as Minister for Home Affairs Aug. 1921–Jan. 1922. He took part in the truce negotiations in London in 1921 and later fought against the Treaty in the Civil War. Captured in Apr. 1923, he led a hunger strike for 41 days in Kilmainham Jail, an ordeal from which he never fully recovered.

STAINES, Michael Joseph (1885–1955), commissioner Garda Síochána, b. Newport, Co. Mayo, d. 26 Oct. 1955. Gaelic League, Sinn Féin, Irish Volunteers. Staff officer in GPO during Easter Rising: one of JAMES CONNOLLY's stretcher-bearers. Camp commandant Frongoch. IRB member. Alderman Dublin Corporation. MP (St Michan's, Dublin 1918); present at first meeting of Dáil Éireann 1919. Headed Police Organising Committee, appointed commissioner Civic Guard (Garda Síochána) Mar. 1922. He relied heavily on the professional advice of former RIC officers, especially District Inspector Patrick Walsh, who was appointed deputy commissioner by the Provisional Government. Established depots at RDS, Ballsbridge, Dublin and Artillery Barracks, Kildare. In Kildare anti-Treaty supporters of RORY O'CONNOR within the Civic Guard served Staines with an ultimatum demanding the expulsion of Walsh and other former Constabulary officers. He paraded the entire force, close on 1,500 young untrained men, and with conspicuous moral courage called out the names of the ringleaders, who shouted him down. Staines resigned as 'the only honourable course'. On leaving office in Sept. 1922 he issued the first operations instructions to the Civic Guard, in which he defined the role of police in the new Ireland: 'The Garda Síochána will succeed not by force of arms or numbers, but on their moral authority as servants of the people.' He was appointed to the Seanad by W.T. COSGRAVE 1923 and went into business as a manufacturer's agent.

STANFORD, Charles Villiers (1852–1924), composer, conductor, teacher and organist, b. Dublin, ed. Dublin, London, Cambridge, Leipzig and Berlin. Started composing at an early age. Appointed organist at TCD 1873. Both his First Symphony and *The Resurrection*, a large work for soloists, choir and orchestra, date from 1875. He wrote his *Festival Overture* in 1877, as well as the first of ten operas, *The Veiled Prophet of Khorassan*, which received its premiere in Hanover. He became the first Professor of Composition and Orchestral Playing at the Royal College of Music in London at its opening in 1883, and Professor of Music at Cambridge in 1887, both of which posts he held until his death and through which he could be said to have exercised more influence than anyone else on composition teaching in England at this time. Conductor of the London Bach Choir 1885–1902 and of the Leeds Triennial Festival 1901–10. His interest in Irish folk music is reflected in pieces such as the five *Irish Rhapsodies* and his *Irish Concertino*. He composed seven symphonies, *The Revenge* and other cantatas, a requiem and much church music. Awards and honours included honorary doctorates of music from Oxford (1883) and Cambridge (1888), and he was knighted in 1902. His ashes are buried in Westminster Abbey, next to those of Purcell.

STANFORD, William Bedell (1910–1984), academic and politician, b. Belfast, ed. Bishop Foy School, Waterford and TCD. FTCD 1934; Regius Professor of Greek TCD 1940–80; Pro-Chancellor DU 1974–82; Chancellor 1982–4. Senator (Ind. DU) 1948–69. Opponent of view prevailing among Protestants in the early decades of the Irish state that they should concentrate on their commercial or professional activities and eschew political involvement. Visiting professor and lecturer to a number of North American universities. Member RIA and General Synod, Church of Ireland. Chairman DIAS 1972–80. Many contributions to academic journals as well as Irish newspapers, sundry books on the Greek classics, edited the *Odyssey* of Homer (two vols. 1947–8), wrote (with R.B. McDowell) a life of J.P. MAHAFFY (1971).

STAPLETON, Frank (1956–), international footballer, b. Dublin, 10 July 1956. The captain of the Republic of Ireland team which performed well at the 1988 European Championship in Stuttgart, he was also in the national squad which competed in the World Cup finals for the first time, in Italy in 1990. First capped against Turkey in 1976, he won 71 caps (30 as captain) and scored an Irish record 20 international goals. Signed for Arsenal in 1972 and began his League career the next year. He won an FA Cup medal in 1979, scoring the second goal in the 3–2 win over Manchester United, and was on Arsenal's defeated FA Cup final teams in 1978 and 1980. Joined Manchester United in 1980 and won two more FA Cup medals, in 1983 and 1985. His other clubs include Ajax Amsterdam, Derby County, Le Havre and Blackburn Rovers.

STARKIE, Enid (1899–1970), academic, b. Killiney, Co. Dublin, ed. Alexandra, RIAM, Oxford and Sorbonne. She lectured at Exeter University and at Oxford, where she was a fellow in 1935 and reader in French literature 1946. She was honoured by the Sorbonne and the French Academy, and made Chevalier of the Légion d'honneur for her magnificent critical and biographical works, which include: *Les sources du lyrisme dans la poésie d'Emile Verhaeren* (1927), *Baudelaire* (1933), *Arthur Rimbaud in Abyssinia* (1937), *Arthur Rimbaud* (1938), *Pétrus Borel in Algérie* (1950), *André Gide* (1953), *Pétrus Borel, The Lycanthrope: His Life and Times* (1954), *From Gautier to Eliot: The Influence of France on English Literature, 1851–1939* (1960), *Flaubert: The Making of the Master* (1967), *Flaubert the Master: A Critical and Biographical Study, 1856–1880* (1971). Edited *Les fleurs du mal* by Charles Baudelaire (1942), and edited jointly with Will Moore and Rhoda Sutherland *The French Mind: Studies in Honour of Gustave Rudler* (1952). She also published a memoir, *A Lady's Child* (1941).

STELFOX, Arthur Wilson (1883–1972), entomologist, b. Belfast, 15 Dec. 1883, ed.

Campbell College, Belfast, d. Co. Down, 19 May 1972. Despite having no university degree, Stelfox achieved international standing, and his first publication appeared in 1904. He was an authority on wasps, sawflies and bees, and later worked on the parasitic hymenoptera. He refused two offers of honorary degrees but accepted membership of the RIA in 1912.

STELFOX, Dawson (1958–), architect, mountaineer, the first Irish person to climb Mount Everest, b. Belfast, 24 Mar. 1958, ed. Royal Academical Institution and QUB (B.Sc.Arch., Dip.Arch.), m. Margaret Magennis, two children. RIBA, MRIAI. Climbed extensively in Himalayas, European and New Zealand Alps, South America, Alaska and Iran. A mountain guide, one of three in Ireland, qualified to lead and instruct on mountains anywhere in the world. His supreme achievement, however, has been the conquest of Everest. The Irish team left Dublin 17 Mar. 1993 to climb the North Ridge. Stelfox, the leader, was the only one to reach the summit, on 27 May, day 72 of the three-month expedition. The final ascent took him 12.5 hours. A conservation architect, he works for Consarc Conservation. Chairman of the Mountaineering Council of Ireland 1992–5 and of the Irish Himalayan Trust, created Sept 1993. Member of Historic Buildings Council, Sports Council of Ireland 1990–96. Awarded honorary doctorate from QUB and an MBE for services to mountaineering 1994.

STEPHENS, James (1880/82–1950), writer, b. Dublin, date disputed, but variously given as 9 Feb. 1880 or 2 Feb. 1882. Stephens himself claimed the latter date, thus sharing a birth date with JAMES JOYCE, who, in typically superstitious fashion, particularly valued Stephens because of this supposed coincidence. From 1896 to 1912 he worked as a solicitor's clerk. The latter year was his *annus mirabilis*. Although friendly with many of the leading literary and political figures of the day – including ARTHUR GRIFFITH, GEORGE RUSSELL, GEORGE MOORE, W.B. YEATS and Lady GREGORY – he himself had written little. Now, however, two wholly original novels were published in a single year. *The Charwoman's Daughter* and *The Crock of Gold* have established themselves as central texts in modern Irish literature by their unique blend of real-

ism, fantasy, knockabout comedy and verbal dexterity. He lived in Paris 1912–15, returning to Dublin to take up the position of registrar of the National Gallery of Ireland. He was a key eyewitness to the events of the Easter Rising, and *The Insurrection in Dublin*, written within weeks of the rebellion and published later in the same year, is one of the most valuable contemporary accounts. In 1924 he moved to London, from where he regularly travelled on lecture tours to the USA. In 1927 he first met Joyce, who later proposed that Stephens might finish *Finnegans Wake* in the event of his being unable to do so. The proposed title for this putative collaboration was *JJ & S*, a pun on John Jameson & Sons. From 1937 onwards Stephens broadcast on literary matters on the BBC and became enormously popular with his audience. This unique, quirky man died in London on 26 Dec. 1950.

STEVENSON, Walter Clegg (1877–1931), radiotherapist, b. Calcutta, ed. High School, Dublin and TCD. Graduated MB 1900, proceeding MD 1902. Served in Boer War and World War I with RAMC, having meanwhile been surgeon and radiologist to Dr Steevens's Hospital. In collaboration with John Joly, FRS, in 1904 Stevenson initiated the use of radium for treatment of malignant diseases in Ireland. They introduced the 'Dublin Method' of applying radon in sealed needles and developed the Radium Institute in the premises of the RDS. Unaware of the dangers involved, Stevenson sustained radium burns to his hands. He died from pneumonia.

STEWART, Louis (1944–), jazz guitarist, b. Waterford, 5 Jan. 1944, ed. Synge Street and College of Technology, Kevin Street, Dublin. A self-taught musician. Won a scholarship to Boston's prestigious Berklee School of Music 1969, but decided instead to stay in London playing with the Tubby Hayes quartet and big band, which he had joined in 1968. Played with the Benny Goodman Orchestra 1967–71, touring Europe three times; Ronnie Scott's quartet and quintet 1974–9, playing in Scott's Soho club, touring Europe and Australia; George Shearing Trio since 1980. In recent years has worked mostly in Germany, Norway, Spain and the UK, but always based in Dublin and performing around the city whenever home. Commissioned by the Arts Council, wrote a jazz suite, *Joycenotes* (1982), first performed at the Cork International Jazz Festival. Recorded many albums/CDs, alone and with groups such as the Robert Farnon Orchestra, George Shearing Trio and 4 Sure. Albums include *Louis the First* (1975), *Springtime* (1990), *Here's to Life* (1993) and *Paper Moon* (1996). Won the press prize at Montreux Jazz Festival 1968 and in 1969 the Grand Prix as best soloist, the festival's top award. Best soloist at the Nordring Radio Festival 1980.

STOCKWELL, Frank (Frankie), Gaelic footballer. His earlier career was with Louth but he went on to form a renowned Galway partnership with SEAN PURCELL, building up a great reputation with both opponents and supporters. He scored two goals 15 points (the highest score in a 60-minute final) in Galway's All-Ireland win of 1956, and also played on the team defeated in the 1959 final. Other honours include a National Football League medal (1957), two Railway Cup medals with Connacht (1957–8) and four Connacht senior football medals (1954, 1957, 1958, 1960) with the Tuam Stars club.

STOKER, Abraham (Bram) (1847–1912), author, b. Fairview, Dublin, 8 Nov. 1847, ed. TCD, d. 20 Apr. 1912. Civil servant and theatre critic (unpaid) for the *Evening Mail*. Idolised the actor Henry Irving, who played in Dublin 1876. Became Irving's manager 1878–1905 and manager of the Lyceum Theatre, London. Wrote a number of novels, of which the only one to attain an enduring readership was *Dracula* (1897), based on a vampire story by Dublin novelist Sheridan Le Fanu: it was to be translated into many languages and several times filmed. Also produced *Personal Reminiscences of Henry Irving* (two vols. 1906).

STOKES, Adrian (1887–1927), pathologist, b. Lausanne, presumably during his parents' furlough from India, where his father was a civil servant, ed. TCD. Graduated MB in 1910 and took the FRCSI in 1912. Postgraduate study followed at St Mary's Hospital, London and the Rockefeller Institute in New York. He served as a pathologist in World War I and, bringing a motor bicycle and sidecar with him to France, provided the British Expeditionary Force's first mobile laboratory. Appointed Professor of Bacteriology at TCD in 1919, Stokes moved to a chair at Guy's Hospital, London in 1922. Because of his research experience with spirochaetal jaundice, he was invited to join the Rockefeller Foundation's West Africa Yellow Fever Commission in 1927. He found no support for Hideyo Noguchi's contention that the disease was caused by leptospira; the evidence supported a virus as the cause. The Rockefeller team managed to transmit the fever to rhesus monkeys, thus facilitating its study. But Stokes fell victim to the disease, the virus entering through abrasions on his hands, and he died in Lagos in Sept. 1927.

STOKES, Niall (1951–), magazine publisher and broadcaster, b. Dublin, ed. Synge Street and UCD. He started work as a freelance journalist with *The Irish Times* and the *Irish Independent*. He set up and edited *Book Out*, a Dublin-based magazine, 1972–3, then edited *Scene* magazine 1976–7. He is the publisher of *Hot Press*, Ireland's top-selling pop music magazine, which he founded in 1977. Received an award from the Irish Family Planning Association for the magazine's pioneer work in sexual education. Played guitar with the group Brothers, who recorded the album *Torch* in 1990. Stokes has achieved much for Irish singers and musicians as a publisher and a promoter of Irish interests. Partly responsible for bringing U2 to the attention of the international media, he has since written two books on the band: *The U2 File: A Hot Press U2 History, 1978–1985* (1985) and *U2: Three Chords and the Truth* (1990). Appointed chairman IRTC 1993.

STRONG, Eithne (1923–), poet and short story writer, b. Glensharrold, Co. Limerick, ed. locally, through Irish, and in TCD. She became a dedicated worker for the Gaelic revival in 1942 and published her first book of Irish verse, *An Gor*. Yet it was not until 1961 that her second collection appeared, this time in English. Her poetic endeavour, she says, is to be 'witness to unchangingness as well as change'. She is much in demand as a lecturer and a giver of workshops in Ireland and abroad, tasks she successfully combines with a teaching occupation and freelance journalism. Her poetry in English includes: *Songs of Living* (1961), *Sarah, in Passing* (1974), *Patterns* (1981), *Flesh: The Greatest Sin*, a long poem (1982), *My Darling Neighbour* (1985),

Let Live (1990) and *Spatial Nosing: New and Selected Poems* (1993). Her collections in Irish are: *An Gor* (1942), *Cairt Oibre* (1980), *Fuil agus Fallaí* (1983), *An Sagart Pinc* and *Aoife faoi Ghlas* (1990). Novels: *Degrees of Kindred* (1979) and *The Love Riddle* (1993).

STUART, Francis (1902–), novelist, b. Australia of Ulster Protestant family which returned to Ireland, he spent his childhood outside Derry, ed. Rugby. Stuart fought on the Irish side in the War of Independence 1920–21. He married and separated from Iseult Gonne, daughter of MAUD GONNE MACBRIDE. Later converted to Catholicism. He went to Berlin as a university lecturer in 1939 and stayed in Germany throughout World War II, being interned by the Allies for a year as a result of broadcasts he made in English. These activities also placed him 'outside the diplomatic protection of his own government', in the view of the Department of External Affairs in Dublin, and he lived in Germany, Paris and London until he was allowed to return to Ireland in 1959. His work is deeply rooted in the tradition of Irish republicanism but is dominated by the concept of the individual who finds himself at odds with the society within which he lives: the dilemma of the artist and perhaps also a dilemma which Stuart himself experienced in the post-war years. He also wrote poetry (*We Have Kept the Faith*, 1923) before opting for the novel as his favoured mode of expression, and had two plays produced at the Abbey Theatre. Novels include *The White Hare* (1936), *Redemption* (1949), *The Flowering Cross* (1950) and the autobiographical *Black List, Section H* (1971).

SULLIVAN, Alexander Martin (1871–1959), lawyer, b. Dublin, s. of A.M. Sullivan, KC, MP and editor of the *Nation*, ed. Ushaw, Belvedere and TCD, d. 9 Jan. 1959. Called to Irish Bar 1892, to English Bar 1899, KC 1908. After some time in journalism in New York and Dublin, he practised on Munster circuit, becoming in 1912 King's Serjeant-at-Law, the last to hold the title. In 1916 he was persuaded by Chief Baron PALLES to defend Sir ROGER CASEMENT, being instructed by GEORGE GAVAN DUFFY. Opposed to Sinn Féin movement, he prosecuted for the Crown after 1916 and survived an assassination attempt after his appointment as a temporary High Court judge. He moved to England in 1922 on the establishment of the Irish Free State. In 1949 Sullivan retired and settled in Dublin, but he returned to England in 1958. Always a controversial figure, he gave the impression of being embittered by the success of Sinn Féin, but for which he would probably have been a prominent member of the establishment in a Home Rule Ireland.

SULLIVAN, John (1861–1933), Jesuit priest, b. Dublin, 19 May 1861, s. of Sir Edward Sullivan, Lord Chancellor of Ireland, ed. Portora, TCD and Lincoln's Inn, London. Called to English Bar 1888. Although raised within the Church of Ireland, he was deeply influenced by the zeal of his Catholic mother and in 1896 converted to Catholicism. In 1900 he entered the Society of Jesus and in 1907 was ordained to the priesthood at Milltown Park, Co. Dublin. He was then appointed to the teaching staff at Clongowes, where he spent much of the rest of his life. During this period he gained a reputation in the surrounding area as a healer of the sick. Rector of the retreat house at Rathfarnham Castle, Co. Dublin 1919–24. He spent his final years at Clongowes and died at St Vincent's Nursing Home, Dublin 19 Feb. 1933. In the years that followed, devotion became particularly strong to him among the sick, who put great store by his relics. In the 1930s and 1940s there were several reports from people who believed they had been cured due to his intercession. The cause for his canonisation was opened in 1947. In 1960 his remains were exhumed at Clongowes and transferred to a shrine in the church of St Francis Xavier, Dublin.

SUTHERLAND, Peter (1946–), EC commissioner and former Attorney-General, ed. Gonzaga, UCD and King's Inns. Called to Bar 1969, Senior Counsel 1980. Attorney-General 1981–2 and 1982–4 in Fine Gael–Labour coalition governments. On his advice the Taoiseach, GARRET FITZGERALD, rejected the proposed wording for a constitutional prohibition of abortion on the grounds, *inter alia*, that it could actually lead to the legalisation of abortion. The Dáil voted against the Taoiseach and the wording was put to the people in a referendum, carried and inserted in the constitution; nine years later the Supreme Court decided that it permitted abortion in certain circumstances. Sutherland went on to be the Irish member of the EC Commission 1985–9, as which he was responsible for competition policy, a difficult assignment requiring a critical approach towards a variety of mutually protective arrangements, such as those traditionally entered into between airlines. He was widely praised for his success in carrying out this brief and at the end of his term returned to Ireland to become AIB chairman as well as director of a number of other companies. In June 1993 he accepted an invitation to become director-general of GATT at a time when deadlock appeared to have been reached in a dispute between the EU and the USA over trading policy. The achievement of a comprehensive agreement within six months was largely credited to Sutherland's skill in devising an acceptable compromise on a diversity of conflicting interests.

SWANZY, Mary (1882–1978), artist, b. Dublin, 15 Apr. 1882, ed. Metropolitan School of Art, Dublin, d. London. She went to Paris in 1906 and studied under Delacluse. The impression which Paris made on her is evident in the cubist and fauvist styles of some of her later work. On her return to Dublin she worked as an illustrator and portraitist, and had solo shows in 1913 and 1919. She travelled extensively during the 1920s and completed a number of paintings of tropical landscapes while living in Hawaii and Somoa. These were later exhibited in California, and she also had exhibitions in Paris and London. During World War II she was represented in a group show in London which included works by Braque, Henry Moore and Chagall. A retrospective exhibition of her work was held in the Hugh Lane Municipal Gallery, Dublin in 1968.

SWEENEY, Joseph, major-general, b. Burtonport, Co. Donegal. Member of the GPO garrison during the Easter Rising. Elected for West Donegal 1918; youngest member of the First Dáil. OC 1st Northern Division 1921. He joined the army in Feb. 1922 as commandant-general and was appointed GOC Donegal Command 1923. Acting chief of staff for a short period during the 'Army Mutiny' 1924. He was GOC Western and Curragh Commands, then appointed adjutant-general in 1928. After a short period

as quartermaster-general he was made chief of staff in 1929. In 1931 he resigned and became GOC Curragh Command. GOC Western Command in Jan. 1940, he retired from the defence forces in Dec. of that year.

SWEENEY, Michael (1888–1964), Oblate priest, b. Carrigart, Co. Donegal, 18 Apr. 1888, ed. Belcamp College, Co. Dublin, further study for the priesthood at Liège, Belgium. Ordained 1913. After an 18-month spell at Leith, Scotland, he was assigned to the Oblate Mission House, Inchicore, Dublin. Chosen as preacher for the Irish National Pilgrimage to Lourdes in 1924, the experience inspired him to build a replica of the Lourdes grotto at Inchicore. He was appointed superior at the Mission House in 1925 and by 1928 had initiated the building of what was to become known as the 'Irish Lourdes'. Opened by Archbishop EDWARD BYRNE in May 1930, the Inchicore grotto became a focal point for Marian devotion in Dublin and by 1932 had attracted an estimated two million visitors. In 1931 Fr Sweeney launched the *Lourdes Messenger*, which did much to spread the reputation of his grotto and to make it Knock's rival for much of the decade. He was also closely involved in organising pilgrimages to Lourdes.

SWEETMAN, Gerard (1908–1970), politician, b. 20 June 1908, ed. Downside and TCD. Solicitor. Unsuccessfully contested the 1932 election for Cumann na nGaedheal in Carlow–Kildare, failing again in 1943, after which he was elected to the Seanad. He was finally elected to the Dáil in 1948 and in all subsequent general elections until his death. He was prominent in Fine Gael throughout the 1950s and 1960s, was seen by many (not all of them sympathetic) as its key organisational figure, and was close to successive party leaders. During the 1948–51 coalition he was chief whip, and in its 1954–7 successor was appointed Minister for Finance after PATRICK McGILLIGAN had turned down the post. In that office Sweetman introduced a series of deflationary budgets at a time when the economy was already in recession. He was unsympathetic to the more liberal and social democratic wing of the party emerging in the mid-1960s. He was killed in a car crash, 28 Jan. 1970.

SWIFT, Patrick (1927–1983), artist, b. Dublin, ed. National College of Art, Dublin. Although he also studied art in London and Paris, he was largely self-taught. He spent several years in London during the 1950s, and in 1958 became a founder member of the Art Centre of Digwell. He wrote extensively on the subject of art and was involved in the production of several artistic publications, including the *Bell* and *X – A Quarterly Review of Art and Literature*, which he edited. While in England, he was a friend of Lucian Freud, whose influence is apparent in the painstaking observation and intimate description of his figurative painting of this period. Recognised as an excellent portrait artist, he painted a number of literary figures, including PATRICK KAVANAGH. However, he rarely exhibited. Despite the representational nature of his figurative work it has an expressionist element, and this is more strongly developed in the landscapes he painted while living in Portugal during the 1960s and 1970s. A retrospective of his work was held in the Irish Museum of Modern Art, Dublin in 1992.

SWINBURN, Walter Robert John (1961–), jockey, b. Oxford, 7 Aug. 1961. He was regarded as a boy wonder when he won the 1981 Derby on the renowned Shergar, and by the summer of 1995 he had ridden eight English and nine Irish Classics winners. The son of the top Irish jockey Wally Swinburn, he began his apprenticeship with Frenchie Nicholson in 1977 and rode his first winner at Kempton Park in 1978. He was retained by Michael Stoute as first jockey in 1983 and in that year won the Prix de l'Arc de Triomphe on All Along, as well as three major races in North America, ending with the Washington International. The next year he rode 99 winners in Britain, and in 1990 he reached his first century, with 111. He won his third Epsom Derby in 1995 on Lammtarra, his final burst breaking the 62-year-old record time for the race.

SYNGE, John Lighton (1897–1996), Sc.D., FRS, mathematical physicist, b. Dublin, 23 Mar. 1897, s. of Edward and Ellen Synge (née Price), ed. St Andrew's College, Dublin and TCD, m. Elisabeth Allen, three d. Lecturer in mathematics TCD. Assistant Professor of Mathematics Toronto 1920–25. Fellow and Professor of Natural Philosophy TCD 1925–30. Professor of Applied Mathematics Toronto 1930–43. Professor of Mathematics at Ohio State University 1943–6, at the Carnegie Institute 1946–8. Senior professor DIAS from 1948 to 1972, when he was made emeritus professor. Many visiting professorships, medals and honorary degrees. Publications include, on mathematics: *The Mathematical Papers of Sir William Rowan Hamilton: Geometrical Optics* (with A.W. CONWAY), *Principles of Mechanics*, with B.A. Griffith, *Tensor Calculus: Science: Sense and Nonsense* and *Geometrical Mechanics and de Broglie Waves*; on relativity: *The Special Theory*, *The Relativistic Gas – Kandelman's Krim*, *The Hypercircle in Mathematical Physics*, *Relativity: The General Theory* and *Talking about Relativity*.

SYNGE, John Millington (1871–1909), playwright and director of the Abbey Theatre, b. Rathfarnham, Co. Dublin, 16 Apr. 1871, youngest s. of barrister John Hatch Synge and Kathleen Traill, childhood mainly in Wicklow, ed. TCD and RIAM. Synge's plays were crucial to the establishment of an Irish theatre, focusing on themes of national and sexual identity and drawing on the syntax and sounds of Gaelic to fashion a flexible Irish dramatic speech in English. Raised in an evangelical family, Synge trained initially to be a musician (the violin) but, after a period of study on the Continent, realised he had neither the temperament nor the genius to excel as a performer/composer. In 1896, while living in Paris, he was advised by W.B. YEATS to go to the Aran Islands for his source material as a writer; Yeats knew that Synge had studied Irish at Trinity (along with Hebrew). Between 1898 and 1902 Synge made five annual month-long visits to the islands. His prose account of the experience, *The Aran Islands* (1907), combined a scrupulous recording of the folk narratives he heard there with a faithful account of the daily life of the islanders.

In 1902 he offered Yeats and Lady GREGORY two one-act plays for their new theatre movement, *Riders to the Sea* and *In the Shadow of the Glen*. The first was a moving tragedy of the struggle between an old woman, Maurya, and the sea for the lives of her sons; the second dramatised the mock death and resurrection of an old man determined to catch his young wife in the act of adultery. Synge rewrote this traditional tale to grant a greater measure of independence and verbal freedom to the wife and to introduce the figure and perspective of the Tramp, a wanderer of the roads. Both plays were condemned for excessive morbidity and, in the case of *Shadow of the Glen*, provoked heated discussion in ARTHUR GRIFFITH's *United Irishman* on the subject of unhappy marriages in Ireland. His next play, *The Tinkers' Wedding*, concluded with the priest who has reneged on his promise to wed the tinkers being tied up in a sack, and was never staged during Synge's lifetime. When the Abbey Theatre opened in Dec. 1904, Synge responded with his three-act play *The Well of the Saints*. This ironic parable of a blind couple given the dubious gift of sight by the Saint before choosing to return to their former state did not draw big audiences but has had a great impact and influence on subsequent Irish playwrights such as SAMUEL BECKETT and TOM MURPHY. In 1905 the Abbey became a limited company, with Synge as one of its three directors, the most involved in the production of plays and the day-to-day running of the company.

His full-length masterpiece, *The Playboy of the Western World*, opened on 26 Jan. 1907, with WILLIE FAY as Christy Mahon and Pegeen Mike played by Synge's fiancée, MOLLY ALLGOOD, for whom he had written the part. This tale of an acclaimed father-slayer provoked riots and debate from the start. The play is political in its vivid portrait of a people struggling to emerge from externally imposed authority, in its ambivalent linking of violence and poetic myth-making, and in Pegeen's piercing recognition that she has failed to endorse Christy Mahon's revolutionary transformation into 'the only playboy of the western world'.

Synge had undergone a series of illnesses and operations throughout his short life, and died of Hodgkin's disease on 24 Mar. 1909. His final play, *Deirdre of the Sorrows*, was presented posthumously at the Abbey in 1910, with Molly Allgood in the title role. Through its account of Deirdre's relationship with the ageing King Conchubar, Synge found an enduring dramatic form for his doomed love affair with the young actress.

T

TAAFFE, Patrick (Pat) (1930–1992) jockey, b. Rathcoole, Co. Dublin, 12 Mar. 1930, d. Dublin, 7 July 1992. The second son of Tom Taaffe, trainer of the 1958 Grand National winner, Mr What, he was an amateur from 1945, riding his first winner in 1947. He turned professional in 1950 and won two Grand National winners – Quare Times in 1955 and Gay Trip in 1970. He won the Irish Grand National a record six times (between 1954 and 1966), and the Cheltenham Gold Cup four times, including three wins on the mighty Arkle (1964–6). He was Irish National Hunt champion six times; other wins on Arkle include the Hennessy Gold Cup twice, the Leopardstown Chase twice, the 1964 Irish Grand National and the Whitbread Gold Cup. His son Tom (b. 1963) was a leading jumps jockey, who won the 1987 Irish Grand National on Brittany Boy, and became a trainer in 1994.

TALBOT, Matt (1856–1925), labourer, b. Aldborough Court, Dublin, 2 May 1856, received little formal education apart from a year at age 11 at CBS, North Richmond Street, Dublin. Casual labourer for some time until he found permanent employment with the firm of T. & C. Martin, North Wall. Developed a serious alcohol problem in his teens but took the pledge in 1884 and began a life of prayer, fasting and self-mortification until his sudden death in Granby Lane, 7 June 1925. Had few intimates during his lifetime but in a matter of years a cult of devotion grew up around him. In 1931 Archbishop EDWARD BYRNE initiated an inquiry into his life and thus paved the way for the formal introduction in 1937 of the cause for his canonisation. His remains were moved in 1972 to a tomb at the Church of Our Lady of Lourdes, Sean Mac Dermott Street, Dublin.

TALLON, Ronald (1927–), architect, ed. Coláiste Mhuire and UCD. Graduated in architecture in 1950 and took a post with the OPW, leaving in 1956 to join the practice of MICHAEL SCOTT. There, alongside ROBIN WALKER, he helped to keep the firm at the forefront of Irish architecture from the 1960s. His first major success was the RTÉ Television Building, which displayed a remarkably sophisticated appreciation of the corporate modernism of Mies van der Rohe. This secured Tallon's position in Irish architecture and gained him the first of two successive awards of the RIAI triennial gold medal – a unique distinction – for 1959–61, his second award being for the equally impressive GEC factory in Dundalk. Tallon's later projects represent a continuous refinement of his early interest, the range of his work being demonstrated by his designs for the UCG master-plan (*c*. 1969), the Bank of Ireland head office in Baggot Street (1972) and his house in Foxrock – for which he was awarded the RIAI medal for housing 1971–3.

TAYLOR, Alice (1938–), writer, b. 28 Feb. 1938 near Newmarket, Co. Cork, where she grew up on the family farm. In 1988 *To School through the Fields* was published, the first of a number of autobiographical memoirs recalling her childhood years. Charming, nostalgic and artlessly written, it was a phenomenal best-seller in Ireland, breaking all previous records. Subsequent books, in a similar vein, have included *Quench the Lamp* (1990), *Secrets of the Oak* (1991) and *The Village* (1992).

TAYLOR, Dennis James (1949–), snooker player, b. Coalisland, Co. Tyrone, 19 Jan. 1949. He won one of the game's greatest matches when he defeated Steve Davis in the 1985 World Professional Championship at Sheffield, achieving his 18–17 victory on the black in the last frame, watched by 18.5 million TV viewers. He turned professional in 1971, has won the Irish Snooker Championship six times (1980–82, 1985–7), the 1984 Rothmans Grand Prix and the 1987 Benson & Hedges Masters. With ALEX HIGGINS and Eugene Hughes he shared in Ireland's three World Cup wins 1985–7.

TAYLOR, John David (1937–), politician, b. Armagh, ed. QUB. Northern Ireland's longest-serving politician, active since the

1960s. He became MP for South Tyrone at Stormont in 1965. Seen as being on the right wing of the party, he was critical of TERENCE O'NEILL's leadership. Parliamentary secretary at NI Home Affairs, he was appointed to the NI cabinet in 1970 while in the same department. In 1972 he was severely injured in an Official IRA assassination attempt. He represented Fermanagh–South Tyrone in the 1973–4 NI Assembly and was a strong opponent of the Sunningdale package. In Jan. 1974 the success of his motion calling on the Ulster Unionist Council to reject the Council of Ireland led to the resignation of party leader BRIAN FAULKNER and helped undermine the Sunningdale deal. A Unionist representative at the NI Convention in 1975 and member of the 1982–6 Assembly for North Down, MEP 1979–89, MP for Strangford since 1983 and a member of Castlereagh Council since 1989. In 1995 he was runner-up to DAVID TRIMBLE in the UUP leadership contest and was subsequently appointed deputy leader.

TAYLOR, Mervyn (1931–), politician, b. Dublin, Dec. 1931, ed. Zion School and Wesley, Dublin and TCD. Solicitor. Elected TD (Labour Dublin South-West) 1981. Labour chief whip 1981–8. Government assistant chief whip 1981–2, 1982–7. Minister for Equality and Law Reform 1993–4 and since 1994. In 1995 he had charge of the government proposal to remove from the constitution the prohibition of divorce legislation, steering the relevant bills through the Dáil and Seanad and winning the subsequent referendum by the narrow margin of 0.5 per cent. In the course of the campaign, he survived criticism from opponents of the measure directed at his Jewish faith, and a Supreme Court ruling that public monies could not properly be spent in promoting the government's opinion on a referendum proposal.

THERAPY?, rock band. Formed in Belfast in 1989, made two mini-albums on the independent Wiiija label, *Babyteeth* and *Pleasure Death*, which led to their being signed to A&M Records. Reached the UK top 40 with their first full-length album, *Nurse*, and the single 'Teethgrinder'. They soon began to introduce poppier elements into their hardcore mix, making the top ten with 'Screamager', and also entering the charts with 'Face the

Strange', 'Opal Mantra' and 'Going Nowhere'. In 1994 the *Troublegum* LP sold over half a million copies.

THIN LIZZY, rock band. After a short spell in Dublin rock band Skid Row, Phil Lynott, an Irishman of Brazilian extraction, formed Thin Lizzy in 1969 with guitarist Eric Bell, drummer Brian Downey and keyboard player Eric Wricksen. The band signed to Decca and reached the top ten in 1972 with a rocked-up version of the Irish ballad 'Whiskey in the Jar'. Gary Moore (also ex-Skid Row) joined for a short while but it was the definitive line-up of Lynott, Downey, Scott Gorham and Brian Robertson that brought the band to international fame. They had chart success with albums like *Jailbreak* (1976), *Bad Reputation* (1977), *Live and Dangerous* (1978) and *Black Rose* (1979), and their biggest hits include 'The Boys are Back in Town', 'Don't Believe a Word', 'Dancing in the Moonlight' and 'Waiting for an Alibi'. In 1980 the band made number one with the single 'Chinatown' and in the same year Lynott reached the charts with his own album, *Solo in Soho*, and the singles 'Dear Miss Lonely Hearts' and 'King's Call'. Lizzy's final studio album, *Thunder and Lightning*, reached number four in 1983 and the band played its last gig at Nuremberg in Sept. of that year. In 1986 Lynott died of liver failure brought on by drug abuse. His legacy to Irish rock is inestimable, and every Jan. in Dublin the Irish music fraternity celebrates his birthday with a tribute concert.

THOMPSON, Samuel (Sam) (1916–1965), playwright, b. Belfast. Thompson was a painter at Harland and Wolff, the inspiration for much of his work. He wrote documentary scripts on the Belfast shipyard for the BBC, and his first and best-known play, *Over the Bridge*, centred on sectarianism there in the 1930s. Extremely controversial at the time, *Over the Bridge* was accepted for performance in 1958 but was not staged until two years later. In 1960 artistic director James Ellis resigned when the board of the Group Theatre demanded substantial changes to the script. The play was subsequently switched to another venue and was well received. Thompson's other works included the stage play *The Evangelist*, reputed to be an attack on IAN

PAISLEY, and *Cemented with Love* for television. He stood for the Northern Ireland Labour Party in South Down in the Westminster election of 1964. At the time of his death, NILP colleague Sam Napier said of Thompson: 'No man was more determined or more outspoken in his condemnation of bigotry on either side in Ulster; no man understood better its origins and its hateful consequences.'

THOMSOM, Sir William Willis Dalziel (1885–1950), physician and teacher, b. Anahilt, Co. Down, ed. Campbell College and Queen's College, Belfast, m. Josephine Barron 1914. BA (RUI) 1907, MB (QUB) 1910, postgraduate study in Dublin, London and continental clinics. Practised in Belfast, then held staff appointments at the Mater Hospital and the Royal Victoria respectively. In the army during World War I, he worked with Sir Almroth Wright at Wimereux investigating sepsis, nephritis and trench foot. The team included Dr Alexander Fleming, who remained a friend. Thomsom was awarded the MD with gold medal in 1916. Appointed to the chair of medicine at QUB in 1924. He was president of the NI branch of the BMA 1932, Irish Medical Schools Graduates' Association 1936 and Ulster Medical Society 1939. Publications include *A Clinical Study of Primary Carcinoma of the Bronchi* (1933) and bronchial cancer was the subject of his Lumleian Lecture before the Royal College of Physicians, of which he was a fellow. Deputy lieutenant for the city of Belfast and president of the Association of Physicians of Great Britain and Ireland 1949, he was knighted in 1950.

THORNLEY, David Andrew Taylor (1935–1978), politician, academic and broadcaster, b. Surrey, 31 July 1935, ed. St Paul's, London and TCD (MA, Ph.D.). University lecturer TCD 1959, FTCD, Associate Professor of Political Science TCD 1968. RTÉ broadcaster on political affairs 1966–9. Elected to the Dáil for the Labour Party in 1969 along with other well-known intellectuals such as CONOR CRUISE O'BRIEN, JUSTIN KEATING and NOEL BROWNE, all of whom helped give the party a modern, progressive image. During the 1973–7 coalition with Fine Gael, however, Thornley – who was passed over for ministerial office – grew increasingly disaffected with the Labour leadership, particularly in

relation to policy on Northern Ireland. His electoral defeat in 1977, with Keating and O'Brien, ended a colourful era in Labour Party history.

TIERNEY, Michael (1894–1975), academic and politician, b. Ballymacward, Co. Galway, 30 Sept. 1894, ed. Garbally Park and UCD, m. Eibhlín MacNeill, five s. two d., d. Dublin, 10 May 1975. Won a travelling studentship at UCD and studied classics in the Sorbonne, Athens and Berlin. Lectured in classics at UCD from 1915, Professor of Greek 1923–47, president 1947–64. TD (C. na nG., Mayo North, later NUI) 1925–32, senator 1938–44. Favoured some aspects of the 'corporate state' ideas popular in the late 1930s but quickly became disenchanted with both EOIN O'DUFFY's extremism and W.T. COSGRAVE's conservatism as bases from which to challenge EAMON DE VALERA and Fianna Fáil. As President of UCD he battled ceaselessly for funds and state support in his determination to rebuild it on a site appropriate to its status as the largest university institution in the country. His monument is the extensive modern campus at Belfield, near Stillorgan, Co. Dublin. He wrote many learned papers on classical subjects and edited important studies of John Henry Newman and Daniel O'Connell. His biography of his father-in-law, *Eoin MacNeill: Scholar and Man of Action 1867–1945*, appeared in 1980.

TINNEY, Hugh (1958–), pianist, b. Dublin, ed. Gonzaga and TCD. In 1976 won RTÉ's first 'Musician of the Future' competition. Subsequently won first prize at the Pozzoli and other international competitions and was a prizewinner at 1987 Leeds Piano Competition. Has performed throughout Europe, USA, South America and the Far East. CD recordings include *Harmonies poétiques et religieuses* by Liszt, with whose music – as well as that of Chopin – he has a particular affinity.

TISDALL, Robert Morton Newburgh (Bob) (1907–), athlete, b. Nuwara Eliya, Ceylon (now Sri Lanka), 16 May 1907, to an Anglo-Irish family and raised in Nenagh. He had run only six 400 m hurdles when he won the gold medal in the event at the 1932 Olympic Games in a world record time of 51.7 seconds, which was not recognised under the rules of the time because he had hit a hurdle. Earlier, while at Shrewsbury, he won the Public Schools 440 yards, and at Cambridge he won a record four events – 440 yards and 120 yards hurdles, long jump and shot – in the annual match against Oxford in 1932. He set South African and Canadian records in the 220 yards low hurdles in 1929, a year later setting Greek records in the same event. While at Cambridge in Mar. 1932, he decided to try for a place in the Irish Olympic squad and after he ran 54.2 (a record) for the Irish Championship 440 yards hurdles in June that summer, the authorities agreed to let him run in his new event at the Los Angeles Olympics, where he also came eighth in the decathlon. He eventually settled in Queensland, Australia.

TITLEY, Alan (1947–), novelist, playwright and scholar, b. Cork, ed. Coláiste Críost Rí, Cork, St Patrick's College, Dublin and UCD. Taught in west Africa, then head of Irish department in St Patrick's. Titley has won many awards for his work, notably the Oireachtas na Gaeilge prize for fiction 1977 and the Irish-American Cultural Institute award 1988. He wrote the definitive text on the modern Irish novel, *An t-Úrscéal Gaeilge* (1993). A highly acclaimed production of his play *Tagann Godot* was staged at the Peacock Theatre. Publications include: *Máirtín Ó Cadhain* (1975), *Méirscrí na Treibhe* (1978), *Stiall Fhial Feola* (1980) and *Eiriceachtaí agus Scéalta Eile* (1987).

TÓIBÍN, Colm (1955–), author and journalist, b. Enniscorthy, ed. CBS, Enniscorthy, St Peter's College, Wexford and UCD. Taught in Barcelona and UCD English department. Features editor *In Dublin* 1981; editor *Magill* 1983. Novels include *The South* (winner of the *Irish Times*/Aer Lingus Irish literature prize) and *The Heather Blazing*. He has also written perceptively on people and places in books such as *Walking along the Border* (republished as *Bad Blood*), *Homage to Barcelona* and *The Sign of the Cross: Travels in Catholic Europe*.

TOUHEY, Patsy (1865–1923), uilleann piper and vaudeville artist, one of the most significant figures in the 'golden age' of Irish traditional music in the USA, b. Cahertinna, near Loughrea, Co. Galway, son of a professional piper, his family emigrating to the States when he was three. Touhey, employed in the timber trade, met the well-known piper John Egan and formed a musical partnership, touring many cities with 'Jerry Cohan's Irish Hibernia'. This started a full-time professional involvement with show business, not only as a piper (of which he was one of the finest ever) but as a comedian and comic actor. In 1893 he performed at the Chicago World's Fair, for which Donegal piper Turlough McSweeney also travelled over. Touhey supported the Gaelic League in the USA and appeared at the Feis Ceoil in Carnegie Hall in 1902. One of the first Irish musicians to record, he issued cylinders himself and in 1919 recorded three 78s on the Victor label. *The Piping of Patsy Touhey* (Pat Mitchell and Jackie Small) is a comprehensive analysis of his technique and, most importantly, is accompanied by a cassette of recordings remastered from the collection of Tom Busby of New York.

TRAYNOR, Oscar (1886–1963), politician, b. Dublin, 21 Mar. 1886, ed. CBS, St Mary's Place, Dublin. Woodcarver and compositor by profession. Joined Irish Volunteers, took part in Easter Rising and was interned. Brigadier of Dublin Brigade, Old IRA, led attack on Custom House, 25 May 1921. TD (FF North Dublin) 1925–7 and 1932–61. Minister for Posts and Telegraphs 1936–9; for Defence 1939–48, 1951–4; for Justice 1957–61. President FAI 1948–63.

TREACY, John (1957–), athlete, b. Villierstown, Co. Waterford, 4 June 1957. Having been third in the junior events in 1974 and 1975, he won two World Cross-Country Championships, in Glasgow 1978 and in Limerick 1979. He set Irish track records at 3,000 m (7:45.22, 1980), 5,000 m (13:16.81, 1984), 10,000 m (27:55.80, 1989) and 20,000 m (61:10.1, 1987). He was European junior silver medallist at 5,000 m in 1979, was fourth in the 1978 European Championship and seventh at the 1980 Moscow Olympics. But his best performance was in the marathon at the 1984 Los Angeles Olympics, when he won the silver medal in 2:09.56. Other achievements include coming first in the 1992 Los Angeles marathon and the 1993 Dublin marathon, third in the 1988 Boston marathon (at 2:09.15, his fastest) and the New York marathon of the same year, and second in the Tokyo marathon in 1990. He is one of four Irishmen to have competed in four Olympic

Games, holds an MBA degree from Providence University, USA, and is the first sportsman to be given the freedom of the city of Waterford.

TREACY, Seán (1923–), politician, b. Clonmel, 22 Sept. 1923, ed. St Mary's CBS, Clonmel, Clonmel Technical Institute and UCC (Dip.Soc.Econ.Sci.). Labour TD 1961–85, Independent since 1985; MEP 1981–4. Member Tipperary South Riding County Council and alderman Clonmel Borough Corporation 1955–73; Mayor of Clonmel 1957–8 and 1961–2. Chairman Civil Service and Local Appointments Commission and member Council of State 1973–7 and since 1987. Treacy has been Ceann Comhairle of Dáil Éireann since Mar. 1987, having previously held the post during the 1973–7 coalition. He was Labour spokesman on Education 1961–5, Industry and Commerce 1965–9 and Local Government 1969–73.

TREVOR, William (1928–), penname of William Trevor Cox, author, b. Mitchelstown, Co. Cork, 30 Aug. 1928, the son of a bank official, childhood mainly in Youghal, ed. St Columba's and TCD. He developed an intimate feeling for the people of the countryside and small towns of Ireland, who provided material for a number of his writings while helping to sharpen the observation he brought to bear on more cosmopolitan themes. He has won the Hawthornden prize and (twice) the Whitbread prize for fiction. Novels include *The Old Boys* and *Fools of Fortune*, and *The Ballroom of Romance* is the best known of his short story collections. In 1993 a volume of autobiography, *Excursions in the Real World*, was published.

TRIMBLE, William David (1944–), politician, ed. QUB. Leader of the Ulster Unionist Party. Trimble is a barrister and was a lecturer at QUB 1968–90. Elected to the Northern Ireland Convention in 1975 as a Vanguard Unionist member for South Belfast, he became deputy leader of the party after the split over WILLIAM CRAIG's support for the idea of a voluntary coalition. He joined the UUP in 1978 and subsequently became the party's honorary secretary before winning the Upper Bann by-election in 1990. Involved in the controversial 'siege of Drumcree' in July 1995, Trimble was elected UUP leader in Sept. of the same year. Viewed as being on the right wing of the party, Trimble appeared to be adding a new vitality to the image of Ulster unionism, confirmed by the endorsement of the UUP as the dominant unionist party at the Forum elections in May 1996. His opposition to the role proposed for Senator George Mitchell as chairman of the multiparty talks which followed at Stormont in June, however, was considered outside unionist ranks to be merely disruptive. His return to Drumcree the next month, and his virulent support there for the Orange marchers in their confrontation with the RUC, confirmed for many the impression of his overall political attitude as uncompromisingly hardline.

TULLY, James (1915–), politician and trade unionist, b. Carlanstown, Kells, Co. Meath, 18 Sept. 1915, ed. Carlanstown NS and St Patrick's Classical School, Navan. TD (Labour Meath) 1954–7 and 1961–81, Minister for Local Government in the 1973–7 Fine Gael–Labour coalition. His 1974 Electoral (Amendment) Act for revising constituency boundaries provoked a storm in the Dáil, where Fianna Fáil deputies accused him of gerrymandering. Tully's period as minister was also marked by an extensive public housing programme. He was general secretary for the Federation of Rural Workers 1954–71, having previously worked as organiser 1946–54, and he served in the army 1941–6.

TURNER, Martyn (1948–), cartoonist, b. Wanstead, Essex, 24 June 1948, ed. Bancroft's School, Woodford Green and QUB. He settled in Ireland after graduating, becoming co-editor of *Fortnight* 1972–6, during which time he won a *Hibernia* press award. Political cartoonist *The Irish Times* since 1976, in which role he has become a national figure. He has captured the likenesses of most leading figures in Irish public life with a nice balance of acid and affection – most memorably CHARLES HAUGHEY – and has been a bleak observer of the futility of the Northern Ireland Troubles. Commentator of the Year at the Irish Media Awards 1995, the only cartoonist ever to achieve this honour. Political cartoonist *Sunday Express* 1996. He has published 11 books and edited three others.

TWOMEY, Maurice (1896–1978), republican, b. Clondulane, Fermoy, Co. Cork, ed. CBS. He joined the Irish Volunteers in

1914, and was staff commandant of the 1st Southern Division of the IRA during the War of Independence. Opposing the Treaty, he took part in the Civil War until his arrest in Apr. 1923. He remained active in the IRA after his release in 1924 and became chief of staff in 1927. Although he remained a determined abstentionist, he supported Fianna Fáil against the Blueshirts during the tense years of the early 1930s. However, when FF outlawed the IRA in 1936 Twomey was arrested and imprisoned. He opposed the IRA's bombing campaign of 1939–40.

TYNAN, Katharine (1861–1931), poet, novelist, essayist and journalist, b. Clondalkin, Co. Dublin, ed. Drogheda. Penned by Ireland's most prolific writer ever, the Tynan canon comprises 18 books of poetry, two anthologies, 105 novels, 12 collections of short stories, two plays, seven books of devotions, 12 collections of memoirs, criticism and essays, yet has been largely overlooked by critics and biographers alike. She was at one time the most promising young poet of the literary revival, and her salon in Clondalkin was visited often by the young W.B. YEATS and GEORGE RUSSELL, with whom she enjoyed lifelong friendships. It is likely that she helped steer Yeats towards his explorations of Celtic themes. He proposed to her but she married instead a barrister, H.A. Hinkson, and went to London, where she became a prominent journalist, returning to Ireland when her husband was made a resident magistrate in Mayo in 1914. He died in 1919 and Tynan was forced to write a prodigious amount in order to support herself and her children. She travelled widely in Europe between the wars as a journalist, reporting on the countries she visited. Her reminiscences are contained in four volumes: *Twenty-five Years* (1913), *The Middle Years* (1916), *The Years of Shadow* (1919) and *The Wandering Years* (1922).

TYRRELL, Charles (1950–), artist, b. Trim, Co. Meath, ed. National College of Art, Dublin. He took part in the Irish Exhibition of Living Art 1972–82 and won a Carroll's award in 1974. He has also exhibited in EVA, Limerick 1978 and 1982, at the 1981 Cagnes-sur-Mer International Festival, France and the 1982 Paris Biennale. He had his first solo exhibition in the Project Arts Centre, Dublin in 1974, and since then has exhibited regularly with the Taylor Gallery, Dublin. He taught in Dún Laoghaire School of Art, Co. Dublin 1977–81, and in 1984 moved to the Beara peninsula in west Cork. Tyrrell's early minimalist canvases were painted on a large scale and the apparently random style was strongly reminiscent of 1950s American abstract expression. The geometric elements which have been introduced in recent years have given the work a more studied appearance while retaining the richness in tone and colour of the earlier work.

TYRIE, Andrew (**Andy**) (1940–), leader of the Ulster Defence Association, b. Belfast. Described by *The Sunday Times* as 'a bespectacled, Zapata-moustachioed, wise-cracking, non-smoking, milk-drinking man whose appearance and manner belie his reputation'. As UDA leader 1973–88, Tyrie managed to hold together a disparate organisation which was involved in legitimate community activity on one hand while, on the other, continuing a paramilitary campaign. In 1981 he said the UDA might have to 'terrorise terrorists' in the Republic. Having led the organisation through the successful 1974 loyalist stoppage and the débâcle of the 1977 strike, Tyrie was reluctant to support a similar tactic in the wake of the Anglo-Irish Agreement. In the late 1980s, however, a younger, more hardline, loyalist leadership began to emerge and in Mar. 1988, shortly after a bomb was found under his car, Tyrie resigned as UDA chairman.

U

U2, rock band. In 1976 Larry Mullen jnr pinned an ad on the board at Mount Temple Comprehensive School in Dublin which was answered by Paul Hewson, brothers Dave and Dick Evans and Adam Clayton, who formed a group called first Feedback, then the Hype. When Dick Evans left to join THE VIRGIN PRUNES, Hewson changed his name to Bono, Dave Evans was nicknamed the Edge, and they became U2. After winning a talent contest, the group auditioned for CBS Records and PAUL MCGUINNESS became their manager. Their first EP, *U2-3*, was an Irish bestseller and is now a collector's item, and in 1980 U2 signed to Island Records. Their début album, *Boy*, produced by Steve Lillywhite, encapsulated the band's anthemic style. The next, *October*, made number 11 in Britain, but it was their third album, *War*, that cracked the US charts, reaching number 12. As their live reputation grew, U2 released *Under a Blood Red Sky*, a concert album which captured their almost evangelical stage power. In 1987 *The Joshua Tree* topped both the British and the American charts, confirming their position as the biggest rock band in the world. The singles 'With or Without You' and 'I Still Haven't Found What I'm Looking For' also made number one in the USA.

Double album *Rattle and Hum* and its accompanying film (1988) received mixed reviews, and the band were accused of becoming 'too Americanised'. After a break, U2 returned in 1991 with a radically changed sound, which looked more towards eastern Europe. *Achtung Baby* mixed elements of German techno with a renewed sense of melody, and the self-righteousness was replaced by self-effacement. The album became their best seller to date, and spawned such hits as 'The Fly', 'Mysterious Ways' and 'Even Better than the Real Thing'. Their re-emergence was consolidated by the massive 'Zoo TV' and 'Zooropa' tours, multimedia extravaganzas that broke new ground in live rock presentation. U2 remain one of the world's most successful rock bands.

UNDERTONES, **The**, rock band. Northern Ireland's finest punk-pop group had a string of British hits in the late 1970s and early 1980s with such singles as 'Jimmy Jimmy', 'Here Comes the Summer', 'My Perfect Cousin' and 'It's Going to Happen'. Fronted by the warbling voice of Feargal Sharkey, the Undertones avoided the political comment of other Northern bands like Stiff Little Fingers, choosing instead to celebrate the explosion of youth culture which crossed all barriers and which was best summed up by their début single, 'Teenage Kicks'. Sharkey went solo in 1984 and had a number one hit with 'A Good Heart', composed by Maria McKee, while brothers Damien and John O'Neill formed That Petrol Emotion.

USSHER, **Perceval** *Arland* (1899–1980), writer, b. London, 9 Sept. 1899, ed. Abbott's Home School, Derbyshire, TCD and St John's College, Cambridge, d. Dublin, 24 Dec. 1980. His family home was in Co. Waterford, to which he returned from Cambridge. He learned Irish to a high degree of proficiency and became a translator and belletrist. Ussher rendered the first translation of Brian Merriman's *The Midnight Court* (1926), setting a standard for all who followed. Other works included *The Face and Mind of Ireland* (1949), a mixture of history and national character analysis, and *Three Great Irishmen* (1952), dealing with GEORGE BERNARD SHAW, W.B. YEATS and JAMES JOYCE.

V

VICTORY, Gerard (1921–1995), composer and music administrator, b. Dublin, 24 Dec. 1921, ed. Belvedere, UCD and TCD, d. 14 Mar. 1995. Director of music RTÉ from 1967 until his retirement in 1982. Public appointments included membership of the RTÉ Authority and presidency of the UNESCO International Rostrum of Composers. He wrote prolifically, including orchestral, chamber and instrumental music, pieces for solo voice and for choir, as well as six operas. His works have been performed worldwide and his commercial recordings include *String Quartet* (1963), *Jonathan Swift* (1971) and the requiem cantata *Ultima Rerum* (composed 1984). Mus.D. (TCD) 1973, Order of Merit of the German Federal Republic 1975 and Ordre des arts et des lettres, France 1975.

VIRGIN PRUNES, The, rock band. With a line-up that included Bono's friend Gavin Friday and the Edge's brother Dick Evans, the Virgin Prunes were U2's spiritual opposites, the dark damnation to U2's fiery redemption. Their avant-garde approach to rock was inspired by the Dadaists and the surrealists of the early century, and their stage shows were shocking, subversive and wickedly satirical. While U2 enjoyed mainstream rock success, the Prunes pushed the boundaries of taste and tolerance, overturning preconceptions and thwarting complacency at every turn. They proved too weird for conservative rock tastes and commercial success was never on the cards. Friday went on to carve out a solo career as a Berlin cabaret-style singer, mixing elements of Bowie, Brecht and Brel on his Island albums *Each Man Kills the Thing he Loves* and *Adam 'n' Eve*. In 1993 he collaborated with Bono to write songs for the soundtrack of JIM SHERIDAN's film *In the Name of the Father*.

WADDELL, Helen (1889–1965), medievalist, b. Tokyo, daughter of an Ulster Presbyterian minister, ed. Victoria College, Belfast, QUB and Somerville College, Oxford, d. Mar. 1965. Her study of the troubadours, *The Wandering Scholars* (1927), was probably her most important work of scholarship but she will be best remembered for *Peter Abelard* (1933), her highly popular account of the tragic love affair of Abélard and Héloïse. Her other books ranged from *Medieval Latin Lyrics* (1929) to *The Desert Fathers* (1936).

WADE, Jonathan (1941–1973), artist, b. Dublin. He was raised in the Liberties area of Dublin and left school at 13. After working at a variety of jobs, including woodcarving, he attended evening classes at the National College of Art. He lived in London for a short time in the early 1960s but returned to live in Dublin in 1964, settled in Clondalkin and taught art in the area. He had his first solo exhibition in 1966 and had a number of further shows in the Davis Gallery in Dublin. Some of Wade's work is in the collection of the Hugh Lane Municipal Gallery of Modern Art. His partly abstract explorations of the modern urban landscape are often painted with a cool, smooth metallic finish, and the overall image is one of restriction and entanglement. Wade was killed in a car crash in Dublin.

WALKER, Alexander (1930–), journalist, b. Portadown, Co. Armagh, ed. Portadown Grammar School and QUB. Lecturer in political philosophy and comparative government at the University of Michigan 1952–4. As a journalist Walker worked for the *Birmingham Gazette* 1954–6, was leader writer and film critic for the *Birmingham Post* 1956–9, columnist for *Vogue* magazine 1974–86. He has made frequent radio and television broadcasts. A member of the British Screen Advisory Council 1977–92 and of the board of governors of the British Film Institute since 1989. Named Critic of the Year in the British Press Awards in 1970 and 1974 and commended in 1985. In 1981 he was made a Chevalier of the Ordre des arts et des lettres. His numerous publications include the authorised biography of Peter Sellers (1981) and works on Joan Crawford, Bette Davis, Rex Harrison, Elizabeth Taylor, Woody Allen and Stanley Kubrick. Walker lists one of his recreations as persecuting smokers.

WALKER, Robin (1924–1991), architect, ed. St Columba's and UCD. Walker was one of the triumvirate of architects who, under the banner of Michael Scott & Partners, brought to Ireland a modern style of international repute. In 1947, the final year of his architecture course, he studied with MICHAEL SCOTT and the following year he worked under Le Corbusier in Paris, contributing to the Unité d'habitation at Marseilles. After three years with MacGillivray & Sons in southern Rhodesia, he returned to Scott's employment 1952–6. He spent two years studying at the Illinois Institute of Technology, the centre for dissemination of the International Style of Mies van der Rohe, and worked part-time with Miesian masters Skidmore, Owings and Merril in Chicago. In 1958 he was admitted to partnership in Scott's firm and contributed an intriguing and highly personal balance of Corbusian and Miesian manners to the practice, a perspective epitomised in his restaurant building in UCD – for which he was awarded the RIAI triennial gold medal 1968–70 – and in his earlier and comparable Weekend House at Summercove, Cork – which won him the triennial medal for housing 1965–7. Vice-president of the RIAI 1966–7, president 1968–9. Retiring from Scott Tallon Walker in 1982, he subsequently served on An Bord Pleanála for seven years.

WALKER, William (1870–1918), trade unionist. A carpenter at Harland and Wolff, Walker was Belfast district secretary of the Amalgamated Society of Carpenters and Joiners 1900–11. Elected assistant secretary of Belfast Trades Council, to which he was a delegate after 1892, he became its most prominent figure. Member of the Irish Trades Union Congress executive council 1902–4, Congress president 1904. Became a member of the executive committee of the British Labour Party and stood in the North Belfast by-election of 1905 as a Labour candidate. His unnecessary endorsement of demands made by the Belfast Protestant Association arguably cost him this election. He failed to win the seat in two further elections in the following years and was also defeated as a Labour candidate in Edinburgh. In 1911 he clashed with JAMES CONNOLLY on the issue of whether the Irish labour movement should be completely independent of that in Britain. In 1912 he left his job as an official of the woodworkers' union and became an official in the government's national insurance scheme.

WALL, Mervyn Eugene Welply (1908–), novelist and playwright, b. Dublin, ed. Belvedere, Bonn and NUI. MIAL. Travelled widely in Europe and was a civil servant for 14 years. Worked for Radio Éireann 1948–57, leaving to become secretary of the Arts Council. He wrote a number of novels, best known of which was *The Unfortunate Fursey* (1946) and its sequel, comic satires about a medieval Irish monk. The first was adapted as a musical comedy in 1964, the second as a play. His published works include some successful short stories, a book for children, three plays and a history of the famous Sandycove bathing place, under the delightful title of *Forty Foot Gentlemen Only* (1962). *The Complete Fursey* was published in 1985.

WALSH, Brian (1918–), lawyer, b. Dublin, ed. Ring College, Co. Waterford, Belvedere, UCD and King's Inns. BA 1939, MA 1940. Called to Bar 1941, Senior Counsel 1954, High Court judge 1959–61, Supreme Court judge 1961–90, surprisingly passed over for the vacancy of Chief Justice in 1972, since 1980 a judge of the European Court of Justice. Lecturer in French at Maynooth 1940–50, in social legislation and industrial law UCD 1945–56 and in Roman law and civil law at Pontifical University, Maynooth 1947–58. First president of Law Reform Commission 1975–85. Chairman or member of four government commissions/committees (on workmen's compensation, itinerancy and court procedure); chairman of three Electoral Commissions (1977, 1980, 1983). Leader of Irish delegation to 1974 Anglo-Irish Law Enforcement Commission, set up by Irish and British governments to investigate extradition laws following 1973 Sunningdale Agreement. Prolific writer in Irish, US and continental law journals. Even more than his former judicial colleagues CEARBHALL Ó DÁLAIGH, SEAMUS HENCHY and F.G.O. BUDD, Walsh has been associated with the remarkable growth in constitutional jurisprudence for which the Supreme Court has been responsible in the past 35 years, and was rarely overruled, seldom a dissentient and hardly ever a minority in that court. Probably the two most important judgments he delivered were in the McGee case (1974), on the right to marital privacy, which showed the potential social impact of judicial reviews, and the CROTTY case (1987), which obliged the government to hold a referendum on the Single European Act. In one of his last and most controversial decisions, the Finucane case (1990), Walsh held that the protection of a citizen's personal rights justified the refusal to extradite a Maze escaper who faced a risk of assault by prison or police officers if returned to Northern Ireland. Despite apparent efforts later by the THOMAS O'HIGGINS and THOMAS FINLAY courts to modify the effects of some Walsh decisions, the edifice of constitutional jurisprudence he was instrumental in erecting is likely to remain intact.

WALSH, Edward (1939–), academic, b. Co. Cork, ed. UCC and Iowa State University. Began his career as an engineer in Britain and the USA before taking up academic posts at Iowa State University and Virginia Polytechnic Institute and State University. Appointed director of the NIHE, Limerick upon its establishment in 1970. Guided and presided over its expansion. When it became LU in 1989 he was named its president. Many publications in technical journals as well as textbooks (*Energy Conversion* and *Advanced Energy Conversion*). A trenchant and often controversial critic of Irish attitudes to science, commerce and education.

WALSH, Maurice (1879–1964), author, b. near Listowel, Co. Kerry, ed. St Michael's College, Listowel, d. Dublin, 18 Feb. 1964. Entered the civil service and spent 20 years working in Scotland as an excise officer but returned to Ireland in 1922 following the establishment of the Free State. While it was only at this point that he began to write seriously, once started he was a prolific author. His best-known novel is probably *Blackcock's Feather* (1932) but his most famous work is 'The Quiet Man', a short story from the collection *Green Rushes* (1935), which was made into the celebrated John Ford film of the same name.

WALSH, Michael ('Ducksie'), handballer, b. Butt's Green, Co. Kilkenny. Between 1982 and 1989 he won USA titles at underage levels from 15 to 23, won All-Ireland minor softball singles and doubles titles 1982–4 and minor hardball singles and doubles in 1984, as well as an All-Ireland junior softball doubles in 1983. His nine successive All-Ireland senior softball singles championships 1985–93 was a record, surpassing the eight-in-a-row wins of Paddy Perry in the 1930s. He also won the hardball singles in 1987 and the softball doubles titles in 1985, 1987, 1988 and 1991.

WALSH, Thomas (1914–1988), agricultural scientist, b. Piercetown, Co. Wexford, ed. UCD (B.Agric.Sc. 1937, LL D h.c. 1970) and TCD (Sc.D. h.c. 1980). MRIA 1955. On graduation joined ICI, later worked as an agricultural instructor in north Tipperary. Lecturer in soil science UCD 1938–45. Inspector in Department of Agriculture 1945–58 dealing with soils and grassland research. First director of the Agricultural Research Institute, appointed by the government 1958. First director of ACOT, set up in 1980 to provide training and education services in agriculture. Retired from the public service in 1983. Participated in numerous scientific, educational and voluntary organisations. In the national context he was founder member and president of the Agricultural Science Association and of the Fertiliser Association of Ireland. Chairman of the NCEA and of the State Agencies Development Co-operation Organisation. He was a member of the Commission on Higher Education and chairman of the Garda Training Review Body. His membership of boards and councils of other Irish bodies included the ESRI, the Institute of Public Administration, the Nuclear Energy Board, the Statistical and Social Inquiry Society of Ireland, Thomond College, Limerick, the School of Ecumenics, the Commission for Justice and Peace, the Irish Agricultural Organisation Society.

In the international sphere he was chairman of various committees of the FAO, a member of the American Institute of Biological Sciences

and of the British Society of Soil Sciences. Visiting professor at Madrid University. He received the Boyle medal from the RDS and in 1979 was awarded the freedom of Wexford.

WALSH, Thomas J. (1911–1988), founder and artistic director of Wexford Festival Opera, b. and d. Wexford. Founded the festival in 1951 and was its artistic director for 16 years, during which time it achieved international recognition. Combined his life in opera with the practice of medicine. Wrote books on opera in Monte Carlo and in Second Empire France, as well as in Dublin. Awarded an MA and two doctorates by TCD.

WALSH, William (1841–1921), Roman Catholic Archbishop of Dublin, b. Dublin, 30 Jan. 1841, ed. St Laurence O'Toole Seminary, Catholic University and Maynooth. Appointed Professor of Dogmatic and Moral Theology at Maynooth 1867, vice-president 1878 and president 1881. In 1885 he was appointed to the archdiocese of Dublin, a position which he held until his death. A strong supporter of Catholic education, he was appointed first Chancellor of the NUI. He was one of the leading nationalists in the Irish hierarchy, endorsing various land agitations of the 1880s. Supported Parnell until the split and later JOHN REDMOND and JOHN DILLON. In the latter years of his life he was broadly sympathetic to Sinn Féin and vehemently opposed to partition. A man of wide learning and subtle intellect, he wrote for many newspapers and journals on subjects as varied as scriptural exegesis, Gregorian music, education policy and bimetallism – advocating the use of both gold and silver standards for currency – on which he was a leading international authority.

WALSH, William (1939–), Roman Catholic bishop, ed. Corville NS, Roscrea, St Flannan's College, Ennis, Maynooth, Lateran University, Rome and UCG. Ordained 1959. St Flannan's staff 1963–88; curate, subsequently administrator, Ennis 1988–94. Bishop of Killaloe 1994. Had been priest-director of the Killaloe Catholic Marriage Advisory Council and upon his appointment as bishop spoke of the need for the Church to reach out to people in second relationships following marriage breakdown. Writing in the Maynooth journal the *Furrow* some months later, he decried unwarranted criticism of the media, welcomed diversity of opinion within the Church and said that 'compulsory celibacy must remain on the agenda for debate'. Later in 1995 he endorsed Bishop BRENDAN COMISKEY's view that the celibacy question should be open to discussion; like his colleague, he received a Vatican reprimand as a result. The realism and charity of his opinions on the contemporary Church, expressed on radio and television as well as in print, won enthusiastic approval from Catholics worried about the abandonment of their religion by many – especially among the young – who were alienated by traditional clerical authoritarianism.

WALSHE, Joseph (1886–1956), civil servant, b. Killenaule, Co. Tipperary, 2 Oct. 1886, entered Jesuits 1903, graduated MA in French at UCD. As a scholastic in Clongowes he had among his pupils the future Archbishop of Dublin JOHN CHARLES MCQUAID, as well as the future diplomats DANIEL BINCHY and Sean Murphy. Left the Jesuits before ordination and was recruited as a competent linguist by SEÁN T. Ó CEALLAIGH in 1919 to serve in the Paris office of Sinn Féin. Supported the Anglo-Irish Treaty, became acting secretary, later secretary, Department of External Affairs until 1946. Largely responsible for building up the diplomatic service of the IFS under successive ministers DESMOND FITZGERALD and PATRICK MCGILLIGAN.

Exercised a major influence on the foreign policy of the governments of W.T. COSGRAVE and EAMON DE VALERA, with each of whom he enjoyed a good rapport. Ambassador to the Holy See 1946–54, as which his influence continued with de Valera and the inter-party governments of JOHN A. COSTELLO during the early years of the Cold War. Promoted close links, based on historical relationships, between Ireland and the Vatican while taking a realistic and sometimes very critical view of senior Vatican officialdom. Offered Pope Pius XII asylum in Ireland in the event of accession to power by the Communist Party in Italy, to work against which he secured the support of his minister, SEÁN MACBRIDE. Died on holiday in Cairo, 6 Feb. 1956.

WALTON, Ernest Thomas Sinton (1903–1995), scientist, b. Dungarvan, Co. Waterford, ed. Methodist College, Belfast and other schools, followed by TCD (BA 1926, M.Sc. 1928, MA 1934) and Cambridge (Ph.D. 1931), d. Belfast, June 1995. In 1932, working in Ernest Rutherford's group in Cambridge, he and John Cockcroft achieved the first transmutation of atomic nuclei by artificially accelerated particles, an exercise popularly described as 'splitting the atom'. The instrument they invented for this purpose, the Cockcroft–Walton accelerator, is still widely used in nuclear physics. They were awarded the Nobel prize in 1951 for this work. Earlier, Walton had done calculations on the acceleration of particles in circular orbits. This led to the betatron, developed later by Wideroe and Kerst. He also wrote on microwaves and hydro-dynamics. He remained in Cambridge as Clerk Maxwell scholar until 1934. Returning to TCD, he became a fellow and in 1946 was appointed Erasmus Smith Professor of Natural and Experimental Philosophy. Apart from his teaching, he was active as secretary of the RIA and a member of many committees, and in work for the Royal City of Dublin Hospital. He retired from his chair in 1974 but continued to take a keen interest in the physics department of Trinity College.

WARREN, Michael (1950–), sculptor, b. Gorey, Co. Wexford, ed. Bath Academy of Art, TCD and Accademia di Brera, Milan. He returned to live in Ireland in 1975 and now lives near Gorey. He has had exhibitions in several European countries and in the USA. Major public commissions in Ireland include sculptures for RTÉ, Trinity College, the Irish Museum of Modern Art and the Civic Offices on Wood Quay, Dublin. He has also made site-specific sculptures for the city of Jedda, Saudi Arabia, the Olympic Sculpture Park, Seoul, Korea and the Utsukushi-ga-hara Open Air Museum in Japan, for which he won a major award in 1989. In 1991 he won the Medalla al Merito Artistico in Madrid. The simplicity of form and density of Warren's abstract timber sculptures appear to underline the bulk and imposing solidity of the material's origin in nature. However, the gentle curving of the wood and the ever-upward sweep of the line creates a light, almost ethereal, quality which seems to transcend this earthiness.

WATERS, George T. (1932–), engineer and broadcaster, ed. St Muredach's College,

Ballina, UCD and TCD (doctorate for work on high-definition television). Joined Radio Éireann 1956, worked on the technical preparations for the television service launched in 1961, held a succession of senior posts before becoming director of engineering 1968, as which he expanded and improved the transmission networks for both radio and television, introduced colour television and planned the transmission system for the second television channel. Director-general RTÉ 1978–85. Director of the technical department of the European Broadcasting Union, Brussels (later transferred to Geneva) since 1986. President International Academy of Broadcasting, Montreux since 1994.

WATSON, John (1946–), racing driver, b. Belfast, 4 May 1946. Having started racing in 1963, he had a long Formula One career 1973–85, when his record was five wins and 169 points from 152 starts. He joined McLaren in 1979, replacing James Hunt. His best year was 1982, when he won the US and Belgian Grands Prix, coming second in the championship, five points behind Keke Rosberg of Finland. When McLaren dropped him in favour of Alain Prost, he took up sports car and endurance racing. His best year in the World Sports Car Championship was 1987, when he had three wins and was placed equal second overall. He was awarded the MBE.

WATTS, William Arthur (1930–), academic, b. 26 May 1930, ed. St Andrew's College, Dublin and TCD. Lecturer in botany University of Hull 1953–5, TCD 1955–65; Professor of Botany TCD 1965–80; personal chair of Quaternary Ecology 1980–81; Provost of TCD 1981–91. Adjunct Professor of Geology University of Minnesota 1975–83; member DIAS since 1981. PRIA and governor of the National Gallery of Ireland 1982–5, chair of the Federated Dublin Voluntary Hospitals since 1983 and chair of An Taisce.

WEBB, David Allardice (1912–), academic, b. Dublin, 12 Aug. 1912, ed. Charterhouse, TCD and Cambridge. FTCD 1949, Professor of Botany TCD 1950. Fellow Linnean Society of London, MRIA. Publications include *An Irish Flora* (1943, fifth ed. 1967) and *Flora Europea* (1964), of which he was joint editor/part author. Boyle medallist.

WEJCHERT, Alexandra (1920–1995), sculptor, b. Cracow, Poland, ed. Academy of Fine Arts and Faculty of Architecture, Warsaw University. She studied in Italy 1957–9 before returning to Warsaw to work as both an architect and an artist. She took up painting full-time in 1963 and moved to Ireland in 1965. She won the Carroll's award at the Irish Exhibition of Living Art in 1968 and participated in several other exhibitions in Ireland and abroad. Her work can be found in several important collections, including those of the Hugh Lane Municipal Gallery of Modern Art, Dublin, the Museo Commune di Roma and the Peter Stuyvesant Foundation, Amsterdam. Major sculptural commissions for Irish Life, the Bank of Ireland and several universities. She used a variety of materials, often combing wood or perspex with metal to achieve the relief or sense of movement she required.

WELD, Dermot Charles Kenneth (1948–), horse trainer, b. Tandridge, Surrey, 29 Feb. 1948. He was Irish champion amateur jockey in 1969, 1971 and 1972 and in that last year took out a trainer's licence. Earlier he had been an assistant trainer to his father, Charlie Weld, and to Tommy Smith in Australia. He is established as a most prolific trainer of flat winners from his base at the Curragh. Wins include the Irish and English Oaks in 1981 (Blue Wind), five other Irish Classics and the 1988 Irish Grand National. In 1991 he trained 120 winners on the flat and 30 over jumps, and his Vintage Crop won the Irish St Leger in 1993 and 1994. Between those races, Vintage Crop, ridden by MICHAEL KINANE, became the first European-trained horse to win the Melbourne Cup in Australia.

WEST, Henry William (Harry) (1917–), politician. MP for Enniskillen at Stormont 1954–72. Parliamentary secretary at the Northern Ireland Ministry of Agriculture 1958, NI Minister of Agriculture 1960–66 and 1971–2. Westminster MP for Fermanagh–South Tyrone Feb.–Oct. 1974. West represented Fermanagh–South Tyrone in the 1973–4 Assembly, where he led the anti-power-sharing Unionists, and in Jan. 1974 succeeded BRIAN FAULKNER as leader of the Ulster Unionist Party. He reluctantly backed the Ulster Workers' Council strike in May of that year. Elected to the NI Convention in 1975, he continued to oppose power-sharing at cabinet level. In June 1979 he resigned as party leader following his failure to win a seat in the European parliamentary elections. In the Apr. 1981 Fermanagh–South Tyrone by-election he was defeated by IRA hunger striker BOBBY SANDS.

WHELAN, Bill (1950–), songwriter, composer and record producer, b. Limerick, 22 May 1950, ed. Crescent College, Limerick, UCD and King's Inns. Composed the music for the hugely successful *Riverdance* show (1994). Whelan wrote film theme music for *Bloomfield* 1970. Continued songwriting and performing while studying law. Keyboards player in Planxty 1979–81 and Stacc, co-wrote Planxty's 1981 Eurovision Song Contest centrepiece, *Timedance*. Composer in residence at Abbey Theatre's W.B. YEATS International Theatre Festival 1989–94. Major compositions include: *The Ó Riada Suite* (1987), commemorating the film music of SEÁN Ó RIADA; *The Seville Suite* (1992), first performed at La Maestranza, Seville and recorded on CD; *The Spirit of Mayo* (1993); film scores for *Lamb* (1984) and *Some Mother's Son* (1996). Worked with U2, VAN MORRISON, Kate Bush and PAUL BRADY, produced albums for Andy Irvine and Stockton's Wing. He has also worked extensively in theatre, his orchestrations for *HMS Pinafore* winning a Laurence Olivier nomination. Presented RTÉ/Channel 4 *An Eye on the Music* (1991). Helped design a music technology degree course, TCD.

WHELAN, Ronnie (1961–), international footballer, b. Dublin, 25 Sept. 1961. Joining Liverpool from Home Farm, he won virtually all soccer's major awards with the club, including six League Championships (1981–6), two FA Cup medals (1986, 1989, the latter as captain), a European Cup medal (1984), five Charity shields and three League Cups. Capped for Ireland at youth, under-21 and senior levels, he played an important part in the build-up to the Republic's first participation in the World Cup finals, in Italy 1990. He was also a major figure in the 1988 European Championship at Stuttgart, scoring a memorable goal against Russia.

WHITAKER, Thomas Kenneth (1916–), public servant and economist, b. Rostrevor,

Co. Down, ed. CBS, Drogheda. M.Sc.Econ. by private study from London University, having previously obtained a BA in mathematics, economics and Celtic studies. Awarded first place in each of four civil service examinations: clerical officer in 1934 (Civil Service Commission), executive officer in 1935 (Department of Education), assistant inspector of taxes in 1937 and administrative officer in 1938 (Department of Finance). Made assistant principal in 1943 and principal in 1947. This rapid promotion continued and he was appointed secretary of the Department of Finance at the exceptionally young age of 39, contravening the hitherto sacrosanct principle of seniority.

His appointment took place at a time of unprecedented gloom and depression in the country. Economic growth was non-existent, inflation apparently insoluble, unemployment rife, living standards low and emigration at a figure not far below the birth rate. Whitaker believed that free trade, with increased competition and the end of protectionism, would become inevitable and that jobs would have to be created by a shift from agriculture to industry and services. He formed a team of officials within the department and together they produced a detailed study of the economy, culminating in a plan recommending policies for improvement. The plan was accepted by the government and the policies therein transformed into a White Paper entitled *Programme for Economic Expansion*, published in Nov. 1958. Some days afterwards the plan prepared by Whitaker was published under his name as *Economic Development* – an unprecedented step since civil servants' proposals to ministers are not published – and subsequently became known as the grey book. The programme was widely accepted as a landmark in Irish economic history in that it not only set out a comprehensive statement of policies and objectives for a number of years ahead, but explicitly admitted that self-sufficiency had failed and a change in policy was required.

Together with Jim Malley, private secretary to the Northern Ireland Prime Minister, Whitaker organised and attended the historic meeting at Stormont between SEÁN LEMASS and TERENCE O'NEILL in Jan. 1965. He retired from the Department of Finance in 1969.

He was governor of the Central Bank 1969–76 and was a senator, appointed by two successive Taoisigh, 1977–82. Other appointments included chairman National Industrial and Economic Council 1963–7, president ESRI 1974–87, chairman council of DIAS 1980, PRIA 1985–7, joint chairman Anglo-Irish Encounter 1983, chairman Bord na Gaeilge 1975–8, chairman Agency for Personal Service Overseas 1974–8, chairman Committee of Enquiry into the Penal System 1983–5, chairman Salmon Research Trust of Ireland 1981, member Broadcasting Review Committee 1973–4, director Córas Tráchtála Teo. 1951–6, council member Statistical and Social Inquiry Society of Ireland. Whitaker's honours include D.Econ.Sc. (NUI) 1952, LL D (TCD) 1976, LL D (QUB) 1980, D.Sc. (NUU) 1984, life fellow Irish Management Institute, Commandeur of the Légion d'honneur 1976, fellow of the International Academy of Management. He has been Chancellor of the NUI since 1976. Publications include *Financing by Credit Creation* (1946), *Interests* (1983) and various articles on financial and social topics.

WHITE, Jack (1920–1980), journalist, author and broadcaster, b. Cork, 30 Mar. 1920, ed. Midleton College, Co. Cork and TCD, d. suddenly while representing RTÉ at a meeting in Stuttgart, 13 Apr. 1980. Journalist with *The Irish Times* 1942, London editor 1946–52, features editor and special features writer 1951–61. Chaired the Radio Éireann weekly discussion programme *Round Table on World Affairs* from 1953. Upon the launch of television in 1961 he joined the broadcasting service (later RTÉ) as head of public affairs programming, later becoming assistant controller of television programmes, controller 1974–7, head of broadcasting resources 1977–80. As a writer he was a perceptive observer of human nature, dissecting the values of the Dublin business and academic communities in his novels, *One for the Road* (1956), *The Hard Man* (1958) and *The Devil you Know* (1962). The Abbey Theatre staged his only published play, *The Last Eleven* (1967), which centred on the declining population of a Protestant parish and won the Irish Life Drama Award; its televised version won an international UNDA/WACC prize for religious programmes. He went on to trace the experience of Protestants in independent Ireland in his only historical work, *Minority Report* (1975).

WHITE, James (1913–), administrator and lecturer in the arts, b. Dublin, ed. Belvedere, m., three s. two d. Left school at the age of 16 to take a job with John Player Tobacco Co. and remained there until 1960, when he was appointed curator of the Dublin Municipal Gallery. The years between had been marked by an intense interest in painting, with several visits to galleries abroad. In this period he was appointed art critic to the *Irish Press* and was also a part-time lecturer at both Dublin universities – UCD and TCD. In 1964, its centenary year, he was appointed director of the National Gallery of Ireland. His arrival in the post coincided not only with increased government funding but with the accrual of monies from the estate of GEORGE BERNARD SHAW, some of which had been left to the NGI. These permitted the extension of the building and also the purchase of major old master paintings. White's personal enthusiasm, manner and organisational ability transformed and popularised the National Gallery. Annual attendances increased from 93,000 in 1969 to 926,000 in 1980, the year he retired. Honours accorded include LL D from the NUI (1970); Chevalier of the Légion d'honneur 1974; Order of Merit, government of Italy, 1977; Commander of the Order of Merit, government of the Federal Republic of Germany, 1983. His list of publications is long and wide-ranging, including monographs, catalogues and a survey book, *The National Gallery of Ireland*.

WHITESIDE, Norman (1965–), international footballer, b. Belfast, 5 May 1965. He won two FA Cup medals with Manchester United, in 1983 and in 1985, when he scored the winning goal, before joining Everton. On 17 June 1982 he became the youngest player – at 17 years and 42 days – to take part in the World Cup finals, when he lined out for Northern Ireland against Yugoslavia. He played in four of his country's five matches then, and in Northern Ireland's three matches in the 1986 World Cup in Mexico. Serious injury cut short his career and he retired in 1990.

WHITLA, Sir William (1851–1933), physician, b. Co. Monaghan, ed. Queen's

College, Belfast, having completed an apprenticeship to a pharmacist. He graduated LRCP&S (Edinburgh, 1877), MD (Queen's University of Ireland, 1877). After serving as RMO at the Royal Victoria Hospital, Belfast, he entered family practice and was an overnight success. The best-selling *Elements of Pharmacy, Materia Medica and Therapeutics* (1882) added to his reputation. In those days most doctors compounded their own medicines; this book gave instructions on the necessary pestle and mortar and measuring glasses. Appointed to the staff of the Royal Victoria Hospital, he was a popular teacher and Professor of Pharmacology. His *Dictionary of Medical Treatment* (1891) was another runaway success and he also wrote a two-volume *Manual of Practice and Theory of Medicine* (1908). An imaginative educationalist, he was a Pro-Chancellor of QUB and represented it in parliament. His awards included many honorary degrees and a knighthood.

WHITNEY, Patrick J. (1894–1942), founder of St Patrick's Foreign Missionary Society (Kiltegan Fathers), b. Breenletter, Co. Roscommon, 7 July 1894, ed. Dereenargon NS and St Mel's College, Longford. He entered Maynooth in 1913 to study for the priesthood for the diocese of Ardagh, but following ordination in 1920 volunteered to serve in southern Nigeria under Bishop JOSEPH SHANAHAN. Fr Whitney arrived in Nigeria Dec. 1920 and was assigned to the Emekuku Mission, but in 1924 he was sent back to Ireland to raise funds for the newly founded Holy Rosary Sisters and their convent at Killeshandra, Co. Cavan. With the additional aim of ensuring a steady supply of priests from Ireland for mission work in Nigeria, Whitney planned to establish a new society of secular priests. He sought approval from Rome in 1929 and in 1932 founded St Patrick's Foreign Missionary Society. From its base at Kiltegan, Co. Wicklow, the new society grew steadily from an initial membership of three priests to 172 in 1959. Fr Whitney presided over its earliest years as superior-general and in 1938 was appointed first prefect apostolic of Ogoja in eastern Nigeria. However, his health was failing and he returned to Ireland in 1939. He died 17 July 1942 and was buried in Kilronan, then reinterred at St Patrick's, Kiltegan in 1965.

WHYTE, John Henry (1928–1990), academic, b. Malaya into an Ulster family associated particularly with Loughbrickland, Co. Down, ed. Ampleforth and Oriel College, Oxford, d. suddenly in the USA. Teacher Ampleforth 1953–8. Lecturer in history Makerere University College, Uganda 1958–61, in politics UCD 1961–6, in political science QUB 1966. Professor of Irish Politics QUB 1982, Professor of Politics UCD 1983. Member executive New Ulster Movement 1970–73, committed to promoting reforms to eliminate sectarian discrimination in Northern Ireland. Research fellow Center for International Affairs, Harvard 1973–4; MRIA 1977; fellow in residence Netherlands Institute for Advanced Studies 1979–80. Numerous publications, including *The Independent Irish Party 1850–9* (1958) and *Church and State in Modern Ireland* (1971, second ed. 1984) – the latter being the first, and still highly regarded, authoritative study of a major aspect of modern Irish history.

WILLIAMS, Elizabeth (Betty) (1943–) With MAIREAD CORRIGAN and Ciaran McKeown was one of the founders of the Peace People after the deaths of the three Maguire children. Joint recipient of the Nobel peace prize with Corrigan in 1976. Disputes ensued over how the money from the award should be used, as well as over policy. Williams resigned from the executive of the Peace People in 1980. She divorced and in 1982 left with her daughter for the USA, where she married oil man Jim Perkins. She has been quoted as saying, 'I didn't walk away from Ulster, I ran.' Has since been involved in peace efforts in Sri Lanka, Africa and Asia and lectures on peace and politics in Houston, Texas.

WILLIAMS, T. Desmond (1921–1987), historian, b. Dublin, ed. privately, King's Inns and Peterhouse, Cambridge, d. Dublin, 18 Jan. 1987. Called to the Bar. Fluent in several languages, especially German. At the request of the British Foreign Office, assisted in editing the documents on German foreign policy which fell into the Allies' hands after World War II. Professor of Modern History UCD 1949–83. An outstanding teacher of history who, together with ROBIN DUDLEY EDWARDS and AUBREY GWYNN, revitalised the history department of the UCD arts faculty. Edited, or co-edited with Edwards and Kevin B. Nowlan, a number of books on Irish history (including *The Great Famine*, 1956, and *Ireland in the War Years and After, 1939–51*, 1969) but his primary interest was in Europe of the 19th and 20th centuries, the processes of international diplomacy and political decision-making.

WILLIS, Frederick Andrew Graves (1913–1984), Church of Ireland priest and journalist, b. Dublin, 14 Sept. 1913, ed. High School, Dublin and TCD. Ordained deacon 1937 for the parish of St Nicholas, Wallasey, Chester, and was rector of Urglin, Co. Carlow 1962–83. Contributor to *Encyclopaedia Britannica* and Church of Ireland correspondent of the *Church Times*. As editor of the *Church of Ireland Gazette* 1959–77 he exercised considerable influence on public opinion in the Church and beyond, his editorials not infrequently being quoted by the national press.

WILSON, Gordon (1927–1995), peacemaker and senator, b. Manorhamilton, Co. Leitrim, d. Enniskillen, June 1995. Ran his own drapery business in Enniskillen. He was with his daughter, Marie, a 20-year-old nurse, when she was killed in the IRA bombing at the war memorial in the town on Remembrance Sunday, Nov. 1987. The simple and dignified way in which he described her dying words and his Christian forbearance in the face of tragedy were so moving that he became the embodiment of the desire for peace shared throughout Ireland, north and south. In 1993 the Taoiseach, ALBERT REYNOLDS, nominated him to be a member of the Seanad, a position which he accepted in the hope that it would be a contribution to bridge-building between the different Irish traditions. On his personal initiative he undertook meetings with republican and loyalist paramilitaries in an effort, unsuccessful at the time, to convince both that they should cease their campaigns of violence. In 1994 the Taoiseach appointed him a delegate to the Forum for Peace and Reconciliation.

WILSON, Henry Hughes (1864–1922), British field marshal, b. Currygrane, Co. Longford, 5 May 1864, ed. Marlborough. Gained army commission via Longford Militia. Served in Burma, South Africa and England, becoming commandant of the Staff College

1907–10 and director of military operations 1910–14. Closely involved with Conservative and Unionist politicians, he supported EDWARD CARSON's anti-Home Rule campaign and those army circles resisting military action against the UVF 1913–14. Held various wartime military and liaison posts in France 1914–17 but returned to Britain somewhat out of favour, only to gain regard of Prime Minister Lloyd George and become member of the new Allied Supreme War Council and in Feb. 1918 to replace General William Robertson as Chief of the Imperial General Staff. Appointed field marshal and knighted in 1919, he advocated severe measures against Irish insurgents 1919–21 and opposed any breaking of the Union, but did criticise government's conduct of affairs. On his retirement in 1922 became MP for North Down. On 22 June he was shot dead outside his London home by two Irish veterans of World War I with Irish militant connections.

WILSON, James (1922–), composer and teacher, b. London. Came to Ireland in his twenties and made his home in Dublin. Positions he has held include Professor of Composition RIAM, secretary to the Association of Irish Composers, director of Irish Music Rights Organisation and consulting director of the Performing Rights Society. Member of Aosdána. His compositions include numerous chamber works, two symphonies, concertos for various instruments – including *Menorah* for viola and orchestra – choral music, many song cycles and solo instrumental pieces, a ballet, *Arachne*, and scores for plays. He has written several operas, a medium in which he is particularly happy, including *The Hunting of the Snark* (1965), *Twelfth Night*, first performed at the Wexford Festival in 1969, *Letters to Theo*, a tribute to Van Gogh performed in Dublin on stage and then on television 1984, and *A Passionate Man*, about Jonathan Swift, premiered in Dublin in 1995.

WINDLE, Sir Bertram (1858–1929), FRS, academic, b. Mayfield Vicarage, Staffordshire, 8 May 1858, d. Toronto, 14 Feb. 1929. Although he had a strict Protestant upbringing, Windle was an agnostic by the time he left TCD in 1882, where he had achieved first place in his MB examination. He spent the next 22 years in Birmingham, eventually becoming dean of the medical faculty of Birmingham University. During this period he also became a convert to both Catholicism and Irish nationalism. President of Queen's College, Cork from 1904, he was active in the formation in 1908 of the NUI. Ten years later he lobbied strongly for the establishment of an independent Munster university in Cork. The plan received support from the London government but was aborted in 1919 following Sinn Féin's sweeping electoral success. Windle left Ireland for Canada shortly afterwards and spent the next ten years lecturing throughout North America. He wrote prolifically on science, theology, philosophy and anthropology; he even produced a study of Thomas Hardy's Wessex. He was made a Knight of St Gregory by the Pope in 1909 and knighted three years later.

WOGAN, Michael Terence (Terry) (1938–), broadcaster, b. Limerick, ed. Crescent College, Limerick. Bank clerk until 1960, when he joined Radio Éireann as an announcer. He transferred to television shortly after the 1961 launch of Telefís Éireann, becoming first a newsreader, then host of a quiz show called *Jackpot*. By the mid-1960s he was already working for BBC radio and he moved to England permanently in 1969. His highly popular easy-to-listen-to programmes included the BBC Radio 2 *Breakfast Show*, which copper-fastened his popularity with the British audience. He undertook a number of other programmes, among them the BBC television quiz *Blankety Blank* (from 1977) and *Wogan*, a thrice-weekly television chat show (1985). He later reverted to radio, for which his talent seemed better suited.

WOOD, Charles (1866–1926), composer, teacher and academic, b. Armagh, ed. RCM, London and Cambridge (BA, Mus.D. 1894), d. Cambridge. Appointed to teaching staff of RCM 1888; subsequently became a member of its board of professors. Member of the Associated Board. Appointed lecturer in harmony at Cambridge 1897 and professor 1924. Hon. LL D (Leeds University) 1904. As a composer he is most noted for his choral compositions, which include his setting of St Mark's Passion.

WOOD, Ernest Mountenay (1909– 1991), lawyer, b. Dublin, s. of Albert Wood, KC, prominent British labour lawyer, ed. Aravon School, Bray, Co. Wicklow, Durham, TCD and King's Inns, d. 25 Apr. 1991. Called to Bar 1932, Senior Counsel 1947. Endowed with a resonant baritone voice, he inherited the oratorical skills of his father, who had been known by his colleagues as the Thunderer. Expert in bankruptcy law but became more celebrated for many successful appearances in major defamation actions and notable criminal cases (including the abortive first Arms Trial in 1970). His skilful cross-examinations of public figures and his flamboyant addresses to juries frequently drew crowded galleries, evoking the admiration of colleagues at the Bar.

WOODS, Macdara (1942–), poet and editor, b. Dublin, m. EILÉAN NÍ CHUILLEANÁIN. His maiden voyage into print was with a rather showy poem called 'Decimal D. Sec. Drinks in a Bar in Marrakesh' (1970), followed by his first collection, entitled *Early Morning Matins* (1972). In 1977 he and his sister Orla translated, together with the author, *The King of the Dead and Other Libyan Tales* by Redwan Abushwesha. His collections to date are: *Stopping the Lights in Ranelagh* (1987), *Mix Moon* (1988), *The Hanged Man was not Surrendering* (1990), *Notes from the Countries of Blood-red Flowers* (1994) and *Selected Poems* (1996), and he edited *The Kilkenny Anthology* (1991). An outspoken and highly individualistic voice, he has gained a considerable reputation as a reader of his own poetry and made a number of reading tours of the USA. He is joint editor of the literary magazine *Cyphers* and a member of Aosdána.

WOODS, Stanley (1903–1993), motorcyclist, b. Dublin, Nov. 1903, d. Downpatrick, Co. Down. Woods was the outstanding motorcycling champion of the 1920s and 1930s, the golden era of the sport in Britain. He set a record of ten TT victories in the Isle of Man, which was eventually passed by Mike Hailwood. His first win was in 1923 on a Cotton in the Junior TT, he won the Junior on Nortons in 1932 and 1933, the Lightweight 250 cc and Senior on a Moto Guzzi in 1935, and the Junior again on a Velocette in 1938 and 1939. He was placed in eight Senior TT races, finished 21 races and recorded 11 fastest laps, as well as winning 22 Continental Grand Prix titles. He also excelled at speedway, hill climbs and trials. In 1957, 18 years after retirement, he set a TT course record of 86 m.p.h. in a jubilee celebration, and at the age of 87 he lapped the Isle of Man course at over 80 m.p.h.

WREN, Laurence (1922–), commissioner Garda Síochána, b. Abbeyfeale, Co. Limerick, ed. St Ita's College, Abbeyfeale. Joined the force straight from school 1943 and rose through the ranks. An officer with wide operational, administrative experience, a clear incisive mind and a reputation for straight dealing. In charge of the operation to rescue Dutch industrialist Tiede Herrema, held captive at Monasterevin, Co. Kildare 1975. Garda commissioner 1983–7. Led a Garda Pilgrimage for Peace in Ireland to the Marian Shrine at Lourdes 1984. President North Dublin Conference St Vincent de Paul Society.

WRIGHT, Arthur Dickson (1897–1976), surgeon, b. Dublin, ed. Hillhead School, Glasgow and Medical School of St Mary's Hospital, Paddington, London. His studies were interrupted by World War I and he was a flight commander with the RAF on his return to St Mary's. Graduated in 1922 and soon obtained the FRCS and MS, London. Joining the colonial medical service, Dickson Wright worked in Singapore and at the age of 26 was appointed Professor of Surgery. Back in London in the 1930s he was elected to the staff at St Mary's, where his capacity for work ensured an enormous practice. One of the last of the general surgeons, he could with equal facility remove a brain tumour, set a fracture or deal with a coarctation of the aorta. Hon. FRCSI (1963).

WRIXON, Gerard (1940–), scientist, b. Cork, ed. CBC, Cork, UCC (BE), California Institute of Technology (M.Sc.) and University of California, Berkeley (Ph.D.). Bell Research Laboratories 1969–74, lecturer in engineering UCC 1974–82, director National Microelectronics Research Centre UCC since 1980, Professor of Microelectronics since 1982. Wrixon has been at the forefront of Irish science and technology for over a decade. Under his direction the NMRC, which he established, has developed into a leading international electronics research centre. Chairman of EOLAS 1988–93. Wrixon has also been chairman of the Triskel Arts Centre, Cork

since 1987 and Arts Council nominee to the board of the Cork Opera House.

WYMES, Michael John (1907–1989), commissioner Garda Síochána, b. Drogheda, son of an RIC constable, d. 19 Dec. 1989. Joined as a guard 1928 and rose through the ranks. As detective-superintendent Central Detective Unit, Dublin Castle he investigated the Shanahan's Stamp Auctions fraud involving Paul Singer and others 1959. Assistant commissioner Dublin Metropolitan Area. Garda commissioner 1968–73. In an unprecedented move by the government, he had been nominated as commissioner months before predecessor PATRICK CARROLL was due to retire. At the head of the force during the period when the now powerful Representative Bodies, enabled by the machinery for Conciliation and Arbitration to act over the commissioner's head, presented their case to the (Judge Conroy) Commission on Remuneration and Conditions of Service in the Garda Síochána 1970. Representations by previous Garda commissioners, notably EOIN O'DUFFY and DANIEL COSTIGAN, for a commission on conditions of service in the force had been ignored. Wymes played a low-key role in the proceedings of the Conroy Commission.

WYSE-POWER, Nancy (1889–1963), revolutionary and public servant, b. Dublin, ed. UCD (BA, MA, Celtic studies). Born into a family actively involved in the demands for national independence; her mother, Jennie, was a vice-president of Cumann na mBan when MAUD GONNE MACBRIDE was president, was a strong supporter of the Gaelic League and worked closely with ARTHUR GRIFFITH in the organisation of Sinn Féin. During the Easter Rising Nancy Wyse-Power was one of the messengers sent by PATRICK PEARSE to various provincial commanders to countermand EOIN MACNEILL's orders, and on her return made her way to the GPO, then under siege, to report back to Pearse. In turn, she became one of the two honorary secretaries of Cumann na mBan under the presidency of Countess MARKIEVICZ. When the Dáil was established she was sent on its behalf to Berlin in 1921 to establish a propaganda centre for Irish freedom. (She had previously studied at Bonn University.) She joined the civil service when the Irish Free State was established and retired in 1954 with the rank of principal officer, being one of the first women to reach that rank. Wyse-Power maintained a deep interest in the rights of women and was critical of the discrimination they encountered in the civil service, her efforts hastening the removal of the inequalities against which she railed.

Y

YATES, Ivan (1959–), politician, b. Dublin, Oct. 1959, ed. St Columba's and Gurteen Agricultural College, Co. Tipperary. Farmer and businessman. TD (FG Wexford) since 1981. Formulated FG policy on Trade and Tourism 1990–92 and on Agriculture 1992–3. Spokesperson on Finance 1993. Appointed Minister for Agriculture 1994.

YEATS, Jack Butler (1871–1957), artist and writer, b. London, 29 Aug. 1871, ed. Sligo and London. Christened John Butler, he adopted the signature 'Jack B. Yeats' to distinguish himself from his artist father, JOHN BUTLER YEATS, who signed himself 'J.B. Yeats' or 'JBY'. The greater part of his childhood was spent in Sligo with grandparents. Like his brother W.B. YEATS, he was to use Sligo as the source of imagery for much of his mature work.

Yeats joined his family in London in 1887, attending briefly the South Kensington, Chiswick and Westminster Schools of Art until 1894. His first pen-and-ink illustrations were published in the *Vegetarian* in 1888, and over the next nine years he worked for many comic journals. He also illustrated books. First exhibiting in the RHA in 1895, he was elected an associate of the Academy in 1915 and a member in 1916. In 1897 he and his wife, graphic artist Mary Cottenham Yeats, went to live in Devon. He began to work consistently in watercolour and, from 1898, concentrated on Irish subjects. His first oils date from that time but he did not paint seriously in oil until 1906, and about 1910 abandoned watercolour for the medium. The same year, he left England to live in Greystones, Co. Wicklow. He resumed his cartoon work, now solely for *Punch*, using the pseudonym 'W. Bird' (the cartoons were published 1910–48). In 1912 he produced *Life in the West of Ireland*, a collection of pen-and-ink drawings in the black-and-white tradition, with some reproductions of his early oil paintings.

Between 1917 and 1925 – having moved to Dublin, where he would spend the rest of his life – Yeats painted landscape and incidents in and around the city. His narrative style developed during the early 1920s to become a thoroughly personal manner 1925–7, where the outline gradually disappeared and forms dissolved into dancing colour often squeezed directly from the tube, to be shaped with a knife or thumb, leaving areas of canvas barely stained. Paintings of the late 1920s are richly coloured and romantic, of Dublin and Sligo subjects. During the 1930s, when he did much of his serious writing, the few paintings veer towards fantasy. In the 1940s and 1950s, his most prolific phase, he reached a highly imaginative and visionary plane.

He was the author of several plays and novels, among them *Sailing, Sailing Swiftly* (1933) and *Ah Well* (1942), whose themes and imagery parallel the vivid and personal symbolism of his still figurative paintings. His fascination with words led to friendships with writers like John Masefield, J.M. SYNGE and SAMUEL BECKETT rather than with artists, with whom he rarely associated – though he exhibited with the London Allied Artists, the Society of Dublin Painters and in all major group exhibitions in Ireland and abroad, and he corresponded with Sickert and Kokoschka. He received many public honours during his lifetime, being acknowledged as the greatest Irish artist of the first half of the 20th century and a strong influence on his contemporaries. Retrospectives of his work were mounted in London (1942, 1948), Dublin (1945) and the USA (1951–2). He died in Dublin on 28 Mar. 1957 and is buried at Mount Jerome Cemetery.

YEATS, John Butler (1839–1922), artist and essayist, b. Tullyish, Co. Down, 16 Mar. 1839, ed. Isle of Man and TCD, d. New York, 2 Feb. 1922. Called to Bar 1866 but decided to be a painter instead. Studied in London and lived variously there and in Dublin, where his joint exhibition with NATHANIEL HONE, organised by SARAH PURSER in 1901, resulted in commissions to paint portraits of people prominent in the Irish intellectual establishment. Emigrated to New York in 1908, where he wrote for *Harper's Weekly* and other journals. Father of WILLIAM and JACK BUTLER YEATS.

YEATS, William Butler (1865–1939), b. George's Villa, Sandymount, Dublin, 13 June 1865, the eldest child of JOHN BUTLER YEATS and Susan Pollexfen, daughter of a Sligo shipping family. In 1867 John Yeats moved the family to London and took up portrait painting (another son was painter JACK B. YEATS), but he was never to make a decent income from his art. Susan Yeats and her children hated the city and savoured their summer visits to Sligo on the Pollexfen steamers. Yeats enrolled at the Godolphin School, Hammersmith 1877, and from 1881 attended High School, Harcourt Street, Dublin – the family having been forced back to Ireland through poverty. He failed to gain entrance to TCD and joined the Metropolitan School of Art in 1884. There he met GEORGE RUSSELL, with whom he founded the Dublin Hermetic Society a year later.

He was now launched among the companions who were to inspire his artistic enterprise and support him for decades to come: the poet KATHARINE TYNAN, the old Fenian John O'Leary and DOUGLAS HYDE. His first work, *The Isle of Statues*, was published in 1885, and the following year the poetic play *Mosada*, which dramatised the clash of paganism and Christianity, a theme that was to achieve major orchestration in *The Wanderings of Oisin* (1889). The family returned to London in 1887, where the poet was again miserable. He began to attend seances and in 1888 joined Madame Blavatsky's Theosophical Society, eventually becoming an initiate in the Order of the Golden Dawn 1894, a force which was to dominate his spiritual life for the rest of the century. Despite his unhappiness, Yeats was extremely productive during these London years.

Among his works of this period are *Fairy and Folk Tales of the Irish Peasantry* (1888), *Representative Irish Tales* and *John Sherman and Dhoya* (1891), *The Countess Kathleen and Various Legends* (1892), *The Celtic Twilight* (1893), *The Land of Heart's Desire* (1894), *The Secret Rose* (1897) and the crowning achievement of his early poetry, *The Wind among the Reeds* (1899). In 1889 he met MAUD GONNE (MACBRIDE), who was to inspire in him perhaps the greatest body of love poetry written in modern times. She refused his repeated offers of marriage, granting instead 'spiritual' love and lifelong friendship. Her marriage to Major JOHN MACBRIDE in 1903 shook Yeats psychologically while adding depth and realism to his love poetry.

On 8 May 1899 his play *The Countess Cathleen* was produced at the Antient Concert Rooms, Dublin. From that moment Yeats immersed himself in 'theatre business, management of men' with a zest that was to bring him his own theatre – the Abbey – and provoke a new pugnacious realism in the theme and language of his poetry. His revolutionary play *Cathleen ni Houlihan* (1902), in which Maud Gonne played the title role, placed his work at the controversial centre of Irish life. From that point on there were few public issues that did not spur the poet into vehement utterance – the *Playboy* riots, the LANE Pictures, the 1913 Lock-out, the Easter Rising, the Civil War, the founding of the new state.

The group of writers who worked with him in the theatre movement, Lady GREGORY and J.M. SYNGE in particular, made the Abbey Theatre a vital centre of creative imagination. With the gadfly presence of GEORGE MOORE in Dublin and the emergence of the young JAMES JOYCE – who announced himself with an attack on the movement in *The Day of the Rabblement* (1901) – the Irish literary revival was under way.

The Abbey opened with *On Baile's Strand* (1904), the first of Yeats's plays to feature the Celtic hero Cuchulainn, who haunted his imagination in drama and poetry till his final year, when he wrote a memorable play, *The Death of Cuchulainn*, and the lyric 'Cuchulainn Comforted'. His next three volumes of poetry, *In the Seven Woods* (1903), *The Green Helmet* (1908) and *Responsibilities* (1914), are in sharp contrast to the Celtic Twilight lyricism of the early work: they are concrete in idiom, combative in tone, emphatically of the quotidian world.

In 1907 he visited northern Italy with Lady Gregory and found parallels between Renaissance magnanimity and the patronage and the ambience of her home at Coole Park, where he spent his summers. His reading of Castiglione increased his belief in the need for the 'passionate, serving' aristocratic spirit to promote the survival of beauty in a fallen age.

In the year of the Easter Rising, 1916, Yeats produced his second Cuchulainn play – inspired by the Japanese Noh tradition – in London. He bought a Norman tower-house near Coole and named it Thoor Ballylee. After his marriage to Georgie Hyde-Lees in 1917 it became their summer home, and it figures prominently in *The Wild Swans at Coole* (1917), *Michael Robartes and the Dancer* (1921), *The Tower* (1928) and *The Winding Stair* (1933).

In 1922 Yeats was made a senator of the Irish Free State and in 1923 received the Nobel prize for literature. For health reasons he travelled widely in southern Europe – Sicily, Majorca, the Riviera, visiting Ezra Pound at Rapallo, reading Gentile and absorbing some of the ideology of Mussolini's Italy. To the end he wrote for the theatre: in the year before he died his verse play *Purgatory* provoked a controversy almost as fierce as that which had attended *The Countess Cathleen*. With the death of Lady Gregory in 1932, Yeats settled in Dublin's southern suburbs with his wife and two children. In his last years he became increasingly engrossed in Indian mysticism, translating *The Ten Principal Upanishads* (1937) with the help of a Hindu mystic. At the end of 1938 he visited Roquebrune in the south of France, where he died on 28 Jan. 1939. His remains were brought back to Sligo and interred under the epitaph he had himself composed:

Cast a cold eye
On life, on death.
Horseman, pass by!

YOUNG, Sydney (1857–1937), academic, b. Farnworth, Lancashire, 29 Dec. 1857, ed. Owens College, Manchester and University of London (B.Sc. 1880, Ph.D. 1883). By the time he came to Dublin in 1904, Young was regarded as the world's leading authority on distillation. One of his early research findings was the demonstration that ice sublimes (vaporises without first melting into a liquid) when heated at very low pressure. Appointed lecturer in chemistry at Bristol University in 1882, over the next five years he and Professor William Ramsay wrote more than 30 papers on the relationship between temperature and vapour pressure in different substances and with their critical constants. Succeeding Ramsay as professor in 1887, Young initiated a systematic study of the behaviour of mixed liquids, using glass purification columns he made himself. He perfected techniques that were to find widespread industrial application. His first book, *Practical Distillation*, was published in 1903. On becoming Professor of Chemistry at TCD his output of original research declined somewhat, although he wrote *Stoichiometry* (1908) and *Distillation Principle and Processes* (1922), and contributed several articles to Thorpe's *Dictionary of Applied Chemistry*.

PRIA 1921–6. Retired from TCD 1928 and returned to England. Fellow of the Institute of Chemistry 1888, founder fellow of the Institute of Physics 1893 and president of the chemical section of the British Association 1904.